D0931216

Salmon P. Chase

Chase in his early thirties (about 1840) as an antislavery attorney and Liberty party leader. Courtesy of the Ohio Historical Society.

Salmon P. Chase
A Life in Politics

Frederick J. Blue

The Kent State University Press
Kent, Ohio, and London, England

© 1987 by The Kent State University Press, Kent, Ohio 44242
All rights reserved
Library of Congress Catalog Card Number 86-27664
ISBN 0-87338-340-0
Manufactured in the United States of America

The paper in this book meets the guidelines for permanence and durability of the Committee on Production Guidelines for Book Longevity of the Council on Library Resources.

Library of Congress Cataloging-in-Publication Data

Blue, Frederick J.
    Salmon P. Chase: a life in politics.

    Bibliography: p.
    Includes index.
    1. Chase, Salmon P. (Salmon Portland), 1808–1873.
2. United States—Politics and government—1849–1877.
3. Legislators—United States—Biography. 4. Judges—United
States—Biography. 5. United States. Congress. Senate—
Biography. 6. Ohio—Governors—Biography.
I. Title.
E415.C4B58   1987   973.7′092′4 [B]   86-27664
ISBN 0-87338-340-0 (alk. paper)

British Library Cataloging-in-Publication data are available

For Karen and Eric

Contents

Illustrations

Preface

In June 1868, Salmon P. Chase noted pessimistically that he did
not expect to be nominated for president at the coming Democratic convention. Said Chase, "The talk about me will come to
nothing. The Democracy is not democratic enough yet."[1] The chief
justice was correct in his assessment and for the fourth time in sixteen years a major party bypassed him as its standard-bearer. Chase
knew after three previous disappointments that his position on
rights for blacks—in 1868 it was his advocacy of black suffrage—
was too advanced for his nomination. Throughout his public career
he had been in the vanguard of the movement for racial justice, first
taking up the cause of the fugitive slave as a young Cincinnati attorney in the late 1830s. Through the 1840s and early 1850s he labored
in the Liberty and Free-Soil movements until emerging into greater
national prominence as a founder of the Republican party. Three
unsuccessful tries for that party's nomination revealed him to be too
pronounced an advocate of racial equality to be acceptable. Thus
when the Democrats rejected him in 1868, Chase was prepared for
the outcome.

There were other flaws in Chase's ongoing search for the presidency. Most especially he was regarded by many as an overly ambitious politician willing to stop at nothing to advance his own goals.
Beginning with his controversial election to the Senate in 1849, and
continuing with his use of the governorship of Ohio as a stepping-
stone to the presidency, Chase alienated countless politicians in his

relentless drive for a nomination. Carl Schurz noted in 1860 that he had never met a man more "possessed by the desire to be President even to the extent of honestly believing that he owed it to the country and the country owed it to him."[2]

Chase changed parties at several key times during his career, a strategy that laid him open to further charges of political expediency. Yet political parties were to him not ends in themselves but rather a means to his own personal and ideological goals. His ambition could engender both loyalty and distrust among many. At the same time his concern for others included a deep commitment to his family as well as to black Americans. He revealed the sometimes conflicting tendencies toward political expediency and opportunism on the one hand and stern commitment to principle on the other. Critics refused to recognize that his ambition was not merely for self-gratification and personal advancement but more the result of a desire to implement a program of reform, especially his lifelong goal of black rights.

A life of contradictions, his was also one of accomplishment including the significant achievements of planning the financial direction of the Union war effort and of leading the Supreme Court during the difficult years of Reconstruction.

Salmon P. Chase is perhaps the only major political personality of the Civil War era for whom no modern biography exists. Not since Albert Bushnell Hart's turn-of-the-century study has a historian grappled with Chase's long, diverse, and historically significant life.[3] In part, this lack of scholarship has been due to the diversity in Chase's career. He was an antislavery lawyer, Free-Soil senator, Republican governor, secretary of the Treasury, and chief justice. It may also be due to the overwhelming quantity of Chase's letters and diaries and his horrendous penmanship.

Historians have not served Salmon Chase well. Many who have written about him have stressed the view of many of his contemporaries who believed him to be little more than a selfish, grasping politician. Typical of this interpretation are Thomas and Marva Belden who, in their study of Chase and his overly ambitious daughter Kate during the Civil War years, painted a picture which added an unjustified twist—that of corruption—to the charge of self-seeking politician. Much more revealing is the statement Abraham Lincoln is alleged to have made at the time he appointed Chase chief justice: "Chase is about one and a half times bigger than any other man I ever knew."[4] Although open to various interpretations, the president's comment in all probability was meant as a genuine compliment—one which surely exposes further the inaccuracy of the Beldens' view.

In a similar way Chase has not been given credit for his competent handling of the Treasury in the face of the virtually insurmountable financial burdens of total war. Traditional accounts of his tenure as chief justice have frequently seen him presiding over a passive Supreme Court thoroughly intimidated by revengeful Republican politicians in Congress.[5]

Not all historians have been so harsh in their evaluation of Chase's role in mid-nineteenth-century politics. Eric Foner recognizes the importance of Chase's constitutional view of the federal government's responsibility for slavery and William Gienapp adds much to our knowledge of Chase's relationship with the Know-Nothing movement as he struggled to help create the most effective antislavery party. Similarly David Donald provides a proper appreciation of Chase's difficulties and significant accomplishments as Treasury secretary. David Hughes and Stanley I. Kutler have shown that the Supreme Court under Chase was far from passive and timid in the face of congressional reconstruction.[6] No one since Albert Bushnell Hart in 1899, however, has attempted to look at Chase's whole life in light of the man's obvious failings and significant achievements.

In its simplest terms this book is about a life in politics. I have tried to present a balanced account of Chase's political and private life and endeavored to look at him through the eyes of the nineteenth century. With the death of three wives and four of his six children by the early 1850s, Chase attempted to isolate his private life of pain and tragedy into a separate sphere and pursue his public life all the more vigorously. Yet clearly his family life remained central and had an important impact on his public role. I have left the detailed accounts of Supreme Court decisions while Chase was chief justice to legal historians. Similarly, those looking for a complete account of the workings of the Civil War Treasury Department must look to other sources. Chase was a wholly political person—a politician first and a Treasury secretary and chief justice second. Thus I have felt it important to keep these aspects of his career relatively brief and emphasize instead his political interests and concerns. This description of Chase's long career in public life provides a window into the larger political scene of the mid-nineteenth century and some insight into Chase's complex life as well as the critical events of his era. The description leads to interpretation of Chase's central role in the key issues of his times: abolition, sectional politics, emancipation, and suffrage, all closely tied to an insatiable ambition for political power. For Chase, power was more a means than an end. It was the means to policy implementation, especially on the central question of race.

Much new evidence has become available to historians since Hart wrote, both in Chase materials and those of related political figures. Modern biographies of virtually all of Chase's important contemporaries are now available and have shed considerable light on Chase's activities. In addition, the questions historians ask in political biographies have changed significantly in recent years. This fact in itself would warrant a modern study of Chase. Prominent historians of nineteenth-century America have consistently noted the need for a biography of Chase. The most important sources for such a biography are the large Chase collections at the Library of Congress, the Historical Society of Pennsylvania, and the Ohio Historical Society. In addition, many Chase letters and parts of his diary have been published. The letters of Chase's contemporaries, the records of the Treasury Department in the National Archives, newspapers, and numerous secondary sources have provided a wealth of material.

This book has been made possible because of the valuable assistance of a number of people. I am indebted especially to Professor Dominic J. Capeci of Southwest Missouri State University, who read early drafts of each of the chapters and offered valuable suggestions on revisions, and to Professor Jerome Mushkat of the University of Akron, who read the last half of the manuscript. Both reminded me of the problems of analysis that I had not dealt with sufficiently or had avoided entirely. Professor James P. Ronda of Youngstown State University was helpful and supportive in suggesting many important substantive and stylistic revisions of the manuscript. Vernon L. Volpe of Texas A&M University read the chapters dealing with Chase's Liberty party career and offered constructive and appropriate criticisms. Several other colleagues at Youngstown State University have also been extremely helpful. Hugh G. Earnhart read and recommended necessary changes in the Civil War chapters and Larry E. Esterly, the material on the Supreme Court. Agnes M. Smith was especially helpful in suggesting stylistic changes. Several students have assisted in the research since the project's beginning in 1978. They include Mark Mitcheson, Amy Kyte, David Whitacre, Timothy Fraelich, Robert Fabian, and Thomas Kirker. Susan C. Fogaras spent many hours typing the early drafts and Margaret Carl the final copy; Ruth Hertwig did much of the proofreading.

Special thanks go to the Library of Congress, the National Archives, the Historical Society of Pennsylvania, the Ohio Historical Society, and the Cincinnati Historical Society for the help given me in locating and using Chase materials. I owe special gratitude for the generous help afforded me by Youngstown State University in granting me a faculty improvement leave and research grants. Hildegard Schnuttgen, who heads the Interlibrary Loan Department at Maag Library, Youngstown State University, was most helpful in obtaining numerous sources. Finally, I am indebted to my wife, Judy, for her encouragement and patience as well as for her many hours of assistance on this project.

1

Portrait of an Ambitious Young Man

As the Civil War raged over the battlefields of the Confederacy during the winter of 1863–64, Salmon Portland Chase took time from his busy schedule as secretary of the Treasury to write a long series of autobiographical letters. They were written to be used by his house guest and friend John T. Trowbridge as a campaign biography should the secretary decide to pursue his challenge to Abraham Lincoln for the Republican presidential nomination the following spring. The letters reveal much of what we know about the young Salmon Chase and the environment in which he grew up.[1] They tell of an able and ambitious young man who climbed from an obscure New Hampshire boyhood to a position of national prominence, who was proud of his humble beginnings, yet eager to rise above them.

The story of Salmon P. Chase and his immediate family began on the New Hampshire frontier in 1763 when a struggling young Massachusetts farmer named Dudley Chase moved with his wife, Alice, and seven children to the Connecticut River Valley where they helped to found the town of Cornish. Before the year was over an eighth child, Ithamar, was born.[2] Forty-five years later on January 13, 1808, Ithamar's wife, Janet Ralston Chase, gave birth to Salmon Portland in the same small New Hampshire community. Originally from England in the mid-seventeenth century, the Chase family had become well established in Cornish before Salmon's birth.

Ithamar Chase never enjoyed wealth or prominence. In 1789 he married Janet, the daughter of a Scottish immigrant from nearby Keene, and they settled down to raise a large family and farm the rock-strewn New England soil. Ten of their eleven children survived infancy to share the chores, hardships, and closeness so common among early nineteenth-century rural families. Salmon later recalled his father as "a good man and well informed," who "kept me pretty straight" yet "ruled by kind words and kind looks." Moral suasion rather than corporal punishment was the method of discipline practiced by both parents, and Chase's memories of his early childhood days were pleasant. He remembered "a sleigh-ride with my father up the Connecticut River and the joys of the sleighbells and how pleasant it seemed . . . and how important I felt at the tavern table for the first time in my life." He also recalled that his father was elected regularly by the townspeople of Cornish to the New Hampshire legislature where he became a friend of Daniel Webster. We can only speculate on what effect Ithamar's Federalist politics and his role in state and local affairs had on young Salmon, but Ithamar clearly made a positive impression because Chase described his father with pride as "Justice of the peace with Honorable before his name and Esquire after it."[3]

Ithamar Chase did not confine himself to farming; with his wife's inheritance he invested in a glass factory in Keene. The aftermath of the War of 1812 brought economic difficulties, however, as British glass entered the American market forcing the indebted factory to close. In 1816, Ithamar moved his family from Cornish to Keene and for about a year supplemented a meager income by operating the tavern Janet had also inherited. When Ithamar died unexpectedly in 1817, the family found itself close to poverty with its former stability and tranquility gone. As Chase later noted, when his mother finally settled all debts, "she was comparatively poor, and we children had to depend somewhat on ourselves."[4]

The loss of his father shocked the nine-year-old Salmon. He later remembered his dying father: "He could not speak to us and we stood mute and sobbing. Soon all was over. . . . The light was gone from our home."[5] Yet the Chase family, faced with financial disaster, weathered the crisis and even seemed to thrive on adversity in the years ahead. Despite the hardships, Salmon's education proceeded uninterrupted for the next three years. This was because his mother "sacrificed and stinted herself" for his schooling, which included a private tutor and district schools in Keene and in Windsor, Vermont. By the time he was twelve Chase had learned the rudiments of Latin and Greek. At the ungraded schools he read some old Federalist newspapers and got his "first notions of political parties." During this stage of his childhood development he showed a strong desire to learn and excel, and his success in his schoolwork gave him a strong feeling of accomplishment. Although he could describe himself as a "diligent scholar," Salmon also got into his share of neighborhood scrapes. Economic adversity, compounded by the loss of his father, seemed only to reinforce the typical early nineteenth-century New England education and boyhood Chase experienced. His mother, a simple and pious woman, looked after the spiritual and moral well-being of her son as best she could and taught him the "lessons of thrift and economy; lessons which she rigidly practiced to have her children well educated."[6]

Janet Chase must have been relieved when Salmon's uncle Philander offered to care for the boy if she would send him west. Philander Chase, a priest in the Episcopal church, had recently been chosen bishop of Ohio and had begun organizing parishes there. Knowing that his brother's widow with ten children struggled to make ends meet, and perhaps hoping that Salmon might show an interest in the ministry, Bishop Chase sent the invitation and thus opened a world of new and exciting experiences for his twelve-year-old nephew.[7]

In the spring of 1820 Chase began the long journey to Ohio, a region just past the frontier stage. He traveled with his older brother Alexander as far as Cleveland via stagecoach and Lake Erie steamer. While waiting for several days in Cleveland with a friend of the bishop's he amused himself by canoeing the Cuyahoga River, "taking passengers to and from the Cleveland or eastern side."[8] The young boy made the four-day trip from Cleveland to his uncle's home at Worthington, a tiny rural community in central Ohio, on foot and horseback.

Life on an Ohio farm brought mixed reactions. "Out of school I did chores; took the grain to the mill and brought back meal or flour; milked the cows; drove them to and from pasture; took wool to the carding factory over on the Scioto . . . helped plant and sow in the late spring." He also attended an academy directed by his cousin where he worked hard and continued the kind of classical education he had begun in New Hampshire. In addition to studying Latin he "read some history," and church government; but for the most part "I was simply a farmer's boy doing all kinds of farmer's boy's work." He enjoyed very little of his two-year stay in Worthington. "There were some pleasant rambles, some pleasant incidents, some pleasant associates, but the disagreeable largely predominated. I used to count the days and I wished I could get home, or go somewhere else and get a living by work."[9]

Perhaps part of the reason for Chase's unhappiness was that his uncle was not an easy person to live with. In fact he could be "quite tyrannical" and "often very harsh and severe." Despite the boy's hard work, he seemed never to be able to satisfy the crusty bishop. Philander maintained a strong moral discipline while he preached and practiced life as a grim battleground between the forces of darkness and light. He expected his nephew to show his piety through repentance and conversion. Such pressures surely caused at least some anxiety in the teenage boy. Nevertheless, Chase was influenced in a positive way by his uncle, who could be "exceedingly kind and a delightful companion." Salmon chose not to become a clergyman, but the bishop forged him into "a zealous champion of the Episcopacy." He read books given him by his uncle designed to "convince me that this was the only true church," and he tried unsuccessfully to persuade a companion of the errors of the Methodist church. Under Philander's guidance Chase was confirmed in the Episcopal church while at Worthington. Religion was still not a major part of his life, however, for he admitted that while in church he "did more sleeping than anything else."[10] But Chase's religious nature continued to evolve, and it became a source of strength in later years.

After two years another important change came for Chase with his uncle's decision to assume the presidency of the struggling young Cincinnati College. Financially speaking, Bishop Chase had little choice but to try to increase his meager income elsewhere, "for the Episcopal revenue was scanty" and his salary barely paid his postage bills. Chase would thus have an early opportunity to live in the community which eight years later he would make his permanent home. A commercial town of about twelve thousand residents in 1822, Cincinnati was fast recovering from the effects of the depression of 1819. Soon to replace Pittsburgh as the leading frontier city of the area, its strength and future potential lay in its strategic location on the Ohio River and in the improvements in transportation occurring almost daily.[11] In this new setting Salmon would have little opportunity to become familiar with the town because his arduous farm chores left him little leisure time, and at age fourteen he enrolled as a freshman in his uncle's institution.

Academic standards at Cincinnati College were by Chase's own admission not rigorous, and the young scholar managed to finish the first two years of the curriculum in a year's time. "It was not a study loving set of boys," and Chase explained later that "we made very little progress worth calling such, in our studies." Not surprisingly, there was a good deal of time for mischief, although as a rule Chase refused to join in the fun. "I had little or nothing to do with these sports. . . . When I had time I gave it to reading—either under the bishop's direction or at my own will." Even as a youth he found it difficult to relax and enjoy himself with his peers. His self-righteousness and solemn nature, which would plague him all his life, surely did not endear him to his fellow students at Cincinnati College.[12]

It was with little regret that Chase saw his year at Cincinnati come to a close when the bishop gave up the post as president of the college. Determined to establish a seminary in Ohio for the education of Episcopal ministers, Philander decided to travel to England in 1823 in search of funding. The bishop's efforts helped lead to the establishment of Kenyon College in Gambier, Ohio, the following year. Salmon thus found himself on the move again. He accompanied his uncle as far as Kingston, New York, and then set out on his own for New Hampshire with the three or four dollars the bishop could afford to give him. "I went by steamboat to Albany and thence walked on foot across the Green Mountains." Thus at the age of fifteen Chase returned home after a three-year absence "to the welcoming embraces of my mother and my sisters."[13]

Although determined to pursue his college education at nearby Dartmouth, Chase was unwilling to be a financial burden to his mother. He knew he must earn some money and also engage in further study before he could be admitted. When the adjoining town of Roxbury sought a teacher, Chase eagerly agreed to try his skills, but it was not a happy experience. Hired at a salary of eight dollars a month plus room and board, he immediately got himself into trouble. When provoked by one of the older students, "I gave him a pretty severe blow with the ferule on his head," he recorded. He was unfortunately exhibiting some of the harsh methods of discipline that his uncle had used with him. School officials in Roxbury soon asked Chase to resign because of complaints from the student's parents, and the teenage schoolmaster "walked home rather crestfallen." Not to be deterred, he began attending Royalton Academy in Vermont to prepare for Dartmouth. There he worked hard to make up for his academic deficiencies, knowing that his studies at Cincinnati might not qualify him even as a freshman. A winter and spring of study enabled him to join the junior class at the college in the fall of 1824.[14]

Chase was a member of a class of thirty-six at Dartmouth, where students took a prescribed curriculum designed to provide moral guidance and to discipline the mind. Included were courses in Latin, Greek, mathematics, chemistry, history, rhetoric, and moral philosophy. The carefully regimented life of a Dartmouth student involved set times for rising (5:00 A.M.), prayers, study, church, recreation, and sleep. Keeping or playing cards or dice was punishable by a five dollar fine. Faculty made weekly visits to students' rooms to hear them recite and "to inform themselves concerning each one's moral and literary character." The classical, theological emphasis was in keeping with Chase's previous experiences and training. Although he did not greatly exert himself, he graduated eighth in his class in 1826 after two years of study, a sufficiently strong showing to admit him into Phi Beta Kappa. To help support himself while in college, he taught during the two-month winter recess at a nearby district school. Apparently he had learned something from his first experience, for he later recalled: "My success as a teacher was not marked; but there was no serious complaint . . . [and] I felt that I had really accomplished something for myself."[15] His success was further evidenced when the faculty at Dartmouth chose him to deliver one of the orations at commencement.

College life had been for Chase a significant period of learning and growing as he prepared to enter the adult world. On the one hand, he read widely, but he would soon look back with regret that he had not exerted himself more actively in his studies. He told a friend a year after his graduation that he had spent "so much of my time in reading novels and other light works" that he especially felt "the want of a more thorough knowledge of the history of my own country." He lamented, "Life seems to have been wasted, tho there are few young persons of my age who have been placed in more favorable situations for acquiring knowledge both of men and books than I have been." Reflecting how he had "idly flung away two of the best years of my life when in college," he would soon resolve to "turn over a new leaf." One suspects that Chase was too hard on himself in such criticisms. His disciplined childhood had led him to set high goals, but at this point he remained uncertain about a career. At Dartmouth, he was not an outstanding scholar and missed the guidance his uncle had given him in Ohio, having no one "to point out to me the necessity of earnest study with practical aims."[16]

Life at Dartmouth was important in other respects if not in the acquisition of scholarly habits. In the spring of 1826, a religious revival swept through the school leaving a profound mark on Chase. With his rather staid Episcopalian background he had been taught not "to believe much in the efficacy of such things," but he was clearly impressed by the experience and noted the sobering effect it had on the student body. Chase was moved to greater diligence in his own religious pursuits, and he became convinced of the need for repentance. His faith, already great under his uncle's guidance, was strengthened because of the revival; he noted that the "spirit of God continues to proceed in Hanover." He told a friend in Keene, "It has pleased God in his infinite mercy to bring me . . . to the foot of the cross and to find acceptance through the blood of His dear Son."[17]

Graduation from college at the age of eighteen forced Chase into a career decision. He never considered the Episcopal ministry that Philander Chase so desired for him. Although his profound religious feelings were intensified by the experience at Dartmouth, he apparently took seriously the warning of his older brother against becoming "one of that band of hypocritical Reverends whose pride, lust of power and dominion . . . are the disgrace of the Christian church." Instead, advised Alexander Chase, "If you feel an ambition to be extensively useful to your species . . . and be known and distinguished as a *Man* both at home and abroad, if you wish for wealth, become an honest, conscientious and moral lawyer." During his stay at Dartmouth, Chase had gradually come to the realization that law was the career he desired, but he knew that until he could establish himself financially the law would have to wait. In the meantime, although he had little desire to teach, he would try to establish a school to "acquire the means" to pursue legal studies. Chase reasoned that rural New Hampshire was no place to get started toward such a goal and hence decided to go south. He soon secured the necessary letters of introduction and hurried to Washington, seeking "employment and relief from my embarrassments," realizing that such a location might also be the best place to study law and perhaps to learn the fundamentals of practical politics.[18]

When Chase arrived in the District of Columbia in December 1826, he rented a small and rather unpleasant room; then, he took an advertisement in the *National Intelligencer* announcing the opening of a "Select Classical School," pledging "to promote both the moral and intellectual improvement of those who may be confided to his care." Washington, a city of about fifteen thousand, had an inadequate public school system, and only the children of the poorest families attended its "pauper schools." There were several private academies to which only the fairly wealthy could afford to send their children.[19] Few were willing to entrust their sons and daughters to the little-known youth from New Hampshire, and Chase was deeply discouraged when only one student enrolled in his program. Undaunted, he sought out his uncle, Senator Dudley Chase of Vermont, in search of a government clerkship, hoping "while performing its duties to pursue the study of a profession." The senator's response was one which, as Chase put it, "is not likely to be forgotten. 'Salmon,' said he, 'I once obtained an office for a nephew of mine, and he was ruined by it. I then determined never to ask one for another. I will give you fifty cents to buy a spade with, but I will not help to get you a clerkship.' " Chase recorded no further reaction to his uncle's words, but the rejection did nothing to discourage him from his goal of a legal and political career. He in fact maintained friendly relations with his uncle during his years in Washington and wholeheartedly endorsed the senator's conservative political outlook.[20]

Happily, help was not far off, for Chase soon received a call from A. R. Plumley, a teacher who conducted a classical school in Washington. Unable to manage his school's growth, Plumley offered to divide his student body by giving Chase the twelve boys then in his charge and retaining the girls. Chase wrote that he was quick to accept the offer "with delighted gratitude, and a few days later entered on my duties as teacher." Among his students were the sons of several prominent Washingtonians, including those of Henry Clay and William Wirt.[21]

Despite the new setting, Chase found teaching little more to his liking in Washington than he had in New Hampshire. Again he was not always able to control his temper. One prominent citizen withdrew his son from the school following a whipping Chase administered, and there were other similar incidents of harsh discipline. He readily admitted, "I was poor but sensitive; a young teacher needing to be taught and guided myself."[22] Although he had "as respectable a school as I could wish" and his students were "far more docile and obedient than an equal of brats in the district school in New England would be," he clearly was not happy in his work. He detested the "drudgery and thanklessness of schoolkeeping" but self-righteously consoled himself that it was "good to have borne the yoke in one's youth" and to have done "good to our fellow men." Chase had nothing good to say about the teachers he met in Washington either. "A more miserable group could not be found," and after three years in the city he rather proudly noted that he knew "but one." He could not bring himself to associate with such a "degraded caste."[23] Chase kept himself fully occupied as the number of students in his school rose to a high of twenty-four. He felt that his Dartmouth education had "not properly prepared" him for teaching, and he was "obliged to read a good deal to keep ahead of my scholars." Despite this challenge, he looked to the day when he would "be released from" teaching entirely.[24]

In addition to providing him a modest income, his Select Classical School benefited Chase more directly, for among his pupils were the sons of Attorney General William Wirt, a contact which gave him the necessary start in his long-desired pursuit of a legal career. Within a short time Wirt agreed to guide the young teacher in his legal reading, and a close relationship soon developed. The two had long discussions about Washington politics and about Chase's future law career. From the start, Chase had the "highest respect" for Wirt, and before long Chase's "attachment to him was that of a son to a father."[25] Wirt gave Chase the regard and affection that the autocratic bishop and the heartless senator had not provided, and he became Chase's role model.

How hard the attorney general actually pushed his young protégé remains unclear. On the one hand, Chase planned to spend as much as six hours a day in his reading and after a year in Washington noted that he "had but few idle moments" because of his study. In adopting his brother's advice of several years earlier, he resolved "to become an honest, conscientious and moral lawyer." If Chase read extensively to prepare himself, he also admitted that he read rather "superficially," for as he put it, "my object was rather to finish a certain number of books before I applied for admission to the bar than to acquire legal knowledge." Even more revealing, the kind-hearted Wirt never examined Chase on his progress. "Only once did he ever put a question to me about my studies. He asked me once while I was reading Blackstone if I understood him. I answered confidently yes."[26] In effect, Chase prepared to be a lawyer on his own, for despite his close relationship with Wirt, the attorney general gave him no legal guidance.

As Chase recalled years later, "Very seldom . . . has any candidate for admission to the bar presented himself with a slenderer stock of learning." Although a diligent student, he studied under Wirt for only a little more than two years and answered the questions put to him by the committee only moderately well. The examining committee was satisfied, however, and waived the requirement that three years of study were necessary for admission to the bar. Chief Justice William Cranch, who headed the panel, knew Wirt well and was no doubt influenced by this fact. Chase was also well known to Cranch: "I had been in the habit of going up and playing chess with him and he always beat me." Chase's plea to the panel that he had already made arrangements to go west immediately and begin practice further convinced the panel to waive the three year rule.[27]

In addition to reading law and teaching, Chase spent a great deal of time socially in the company of the Wirt family and especially with two of the attorney general's daughters, Elizabeth and Catherine. He was such a regular visitor that the Wirt residence became a second home to him. He frequently attended services at St. John's Church with the Wirt daughters and spent several evenings a week with them attending concerts or lectures or in their home where the sisters "demanded my attention to the song and the piano." He grew fond of Elizabeth and wrote to his sister, "I know of none to whom I should be more likely to surrender heart and hand." Yet as much as he might contemplate a marriage proposal, his uncertain future stopped him. In 1829, he confided to a friend, "If I were more advanced in the world—even one short year it might be. But ignorant as I am of my future destinies . . . I feel it would be unjust to her to attempt to win her affections."[28]

It was thus a sad day for Chase when the Wirt family left Washington and returned to Baltimore in the spring of 1829. Andrew Jackson's victory over John Quincy Adams ended Wirt's tenure as attorney general and led him to close his Washington home and return to private practice. The void Chase felt in the absence of that family was great. Shortly after the election he wrote a sentimental poem called "The Sisters," which concluded with a note of gloom foretelling the departure of the two young women from Washington and from his life:

> And so must these bright creatures pass from earth
> Leaving behind, to tell that they have been,
> Naught but the memory of their loveliness,
> Like fragrance lingering still around the spot,
> Where late the rose was blooming!

The departure of the Wirt family marked the end of an era for Chase. At a public sale of some of the Wirt furniture he wandered aimlessly through the empty rooms reminiscing about what he had lost. The family "had constituted almost the whole of my society. . . . I could hope for no equivalent substitute." Although he visited them in Baltimore later that year and corresponded with the elder Wirts on occasion, he would never recapture those Washington days.[29]

The impact on Chase was far more than that of one family leaving Washington. The coming to power of the Jacksonian Democrats represented to him all that was wrong with society, an unwelcome intrusion of the lower classes on his previously secure world. Yet their victory did not surprise him. He recognized the lack of popular appeal of the reserved John Quincy Adams and described him as "stiff as a crowbar" after he met the president at a reception. Prior to the election of 1828 he had referred to the coming vote as the most important since the adoption of the Constitution. The results confirmed his worst fears: "The recent election of an ignoramus, rash, violent military chief" was a serious omen "of approaching convulsions." The famous Jackson inaugural reception represented to Chase an office-seeking mob, which he could only abhor: "They swarmed in every room. They pried in every corner. . . . For me I would prefer to fall with the fallen than rise with the rising." [30]

In contrast to Adams, "General Jackson is not a man of mind," but "he excells his predecessor in the art of winning golden opinions from all sorts of men." After observing Jackson and the men around him, especially the "contemptible intriguer," Martin Van Buren, Chase lamented that "the day has passed . . . in this country when a man will be rated according to his intellectual strength, extensive experience [and] moral excellence." "A more savage spirit breathes" in the Jackson administration, he said; for a new "purse proud, vulgar" crowd had replaced the "pure and gentle and refined and cultivated circle" of political leaders like the Wirts. [31]

Although the old order was passing, Chase did not despair completely. With a law career as his goal, he found as his model the eloquent Daniel Webster whom he heard argue several cases before the Supreme Court. Chase found "his language rich and copious, his manner dignified and impressive; . . . his sentiments high and often sublime." If Webster's skills were attainable now, "day and night would testify of my toils." As he reached his twenty-first birthday, he lamented how much time he had wasted. "Yet even now there is time. . . . Future scenes of triumph may yet be mine." And such triumphs would not be confined to the practice of law because, like his models Wirt and Webster, he looked confidently to the day when he could accumulate enough savings "to render me independent of the world and then to run a political career." [32]

Along with ambition and a desire for personal recognition, Chase displayed some early if hesitant interest in serving society through reform. As he explained to a friend, "I confess I desire to be distinguished but I desire more to be useful." In addition to attending several lectures on temperance, he showed his first interest in the antislavery movement. While at Dartmouth, he had indicated no awareness of the one black student among the undergraduates. He certainly knew of the approximately four thousand blacks in Washington, about half of whom were slaves, among the city's fifteen thousand residents. Yet he expressed no reaction to the increased discrimination against the free black population of the city in 1827 in the form of heavier fines for disturbing the peace and a stricter curfew. In contrast, on one occasion he did help a Quaker prepare a petition to Congress calling for the gradual abolition of slavery in the

District. Although his part in the petition drive did not amount to any real commitment to or involvement in the movement against slavery, he had nevertheless lent his name to an unpopular cause. He would later suggest that this modest effort had been "my first anti-slavery work." [33]

Chase's three-year stay in Washington laid the groundwork for a lifetime of activity as a lawyer, reformer, and politician. He began to develop many of the personal habits and characteristics which would prevail in the years ahead. He became a prolific letter writer and started a diary, pursuits which would both simplify and complicate the biographer's task. Many of the qualities of his political personality emerged during the Washington years: his elitism, pomposity, and certainty of opinion along with that degree of smugness which later opponents would find so disconcerting. In his desire for fame and usefulness Chase explained that if he had to choose between the two he would not "hesitate a moment in my choice of the latter." [34]

In light of his overriding ambition in the years ahead it would appear that Chase had already acquired a talent for self-deception— a characteristic which would also remain with him for a lifetime. Lacking humor and charm and being somewhat ponderous, the tall, gangly, yet handsome Chase nevertheless enjoyed good company with those he considered his equal. A conscientious and diligent worker, he was determined to follow the example of his mentor, William Wirt. As he prepared to leave Washington he expressed despair over "making any figure in the world" and felt that his future was "wrapt in obscurity." [35] Such self-doubt was more than compensated for, however, by his determination to make his mark in law and politics. Cincinnati would be the place where the twenty-two-year-old Chase would begin these efforts.

2

Family, Friends, and Fugitives

During his last year in Washington Chase decided to establish his legal practice in Cincinnati. He considered several alternatives and was especially desirous of following the Wirt family to Baltimore, but state law required three years of residency before he could practice in Maryland's civil courts. He would thus be confined "during that time entirely to the criminal court." He might have considered practicing in Maryland in any case if after a year or two the rule could have been suspended, but Wirt was unable to assist him in this regard. Chase considered various other possibilities and even thought briefly of a trip south for a look at New Orleans as a possible residence.[1] Before that time arrived he had set his mind on Cincinnati.

Several factors led Chase to this decision, most importantly his boyhood experiences. Although he had not enjoyed the year spent at Cincinnati College in 1822, his disenchantment had been with conditions at the college and with his uncle's harsh personality rather than with the city. Cincinnati offered exactly the kind of challenge and opportunity he sought. Senator Jacob Burnet of Ohio advised that although the bar was crowded, the city "offers to you stronger inducements than any other place in the West." Indeed, the opportunities there appeared unlimited. No longer a frontier crossroads, Cincinnati was the largest city west of the Appalachians and all-important in the growing east-west as well as north-south trade. Chase's trek in March 1830 from Washington, including a jolting stagecoach ride to Wheeling where he boarded a steamboat for Cincinnati, did suggest the need for transportation improvements; nevertheless, as Chase explained to a friend before departing Washington, "I would rather be *first* in Cincinnati than first in Baltimore, twenty years hence."[2] His initial reactions confirmed his expectations. He sensed that he "must pass thru a long period of probation" before achieving fame, although he was unimpressed with the lawyers he met in Cincinnati; they were "far from being a very talented or highly educated body of men." Taking into account the increasing trade and commerce of the city, he concluded: "Here then is the future scene of my professional labours and here, if anywhere, must I build my reputation."[3]

Chase retained his favorable opinion of Cincinnati during his first several years there. In 1831, he spoke with Alexis de Tocqueville and Gustave Beaumont explaining Cincinnati's rapid growth. He told the French observers of the city's many natural advantages, "of the rich country around it, of the ease with which it could be approached." He found "the moral and intellectual advantages" of the area even greater, for its churches and schools and "its exemption from the curse of slavery" added more to the prosperity of the city than any physical circumstances. Although Cincinnati lacked the cultural refinements of the East, Chase explained that "time . . . will cure this." He had "no doubt that in a few years the society of our city will be unsurpassed."[4]

While he struggled to establish a law practice, Chase was active in intellectual, cultural, and reform efforts. Within six months of his arrival in Cincinnati he had proposed the establishment of a lyceum, presenting "an imperfect outline of its plan." He was a member of the committee to draft a constitution for the organization and used his influence through personal contacts and newspaper articles to publicize it. In the *Cincinnati American,* he invited participation by "all mechanics, manufacturers, merchants, and professional men who may be willing to contribute or desirous to acquire useful knowledge." By January 1831, there were 120 members, many of whom volunteered to offer courses or deliver individual lectures.[5]

Chase was also an active participant, delivering four lectures, two of which were published in the *North American Review,* perhaps the most prestigious national literary journal of that day. Most significant was his lecture "Life and Character of Henry Brougham," in which he praised the British lawyer, politician, and reformer whom he sought to emulate. As a young attorney, Henry Brougham had been elected to Parliament and had sponsored significant reform bills, including antislavery proposals. He had introduced legislation to eliminate the illegal slave trade as well as to better the condition and treatment of slaves in British colonies. He belonged, in Chase's words, to "the party of the friends of freedom." In a letter to Brougham, Chase described himself as "a young member of that profession of which your Lordship is so illustrious an ornament."[6]

Chase's incipient interest in temperance developed into a major concern after his move to Cincinnati. Shocked by the proliferation of taverns and the intemperate behavior of many citizens, he joined the Young Men's Temperance Society and supported the society's unremitting efforts to work until "the monster Intemperance has been driven from among us." He also admitted that participation in the movement might advance his career, for it connected him "with a very large proportion of the worth and respectability of the land." In later years he joined the effort to limit and control Cincinnati's taverns, and while serving a brief term on the city council in 1840 he opposed the licensing of any additional drinking establishments or "coffee houses." Only partially successful in promoting temperance he came to recognize that his position, although popular with temperance people, alienated others: "I don't know what the effect may be on me personally, but I believe I have done right."[7]

Chase's interest in the temperance crusade sprang in part from his religious convictions. For him it was also a means of preserving the traditional ideas and institutions which he believed were so in jeopardy in the bustling community around him. This was the same kind of challenge he had seen represented in Washington by the coming to power of the Jacksonians. As a prelude to his much more active and significant role in the antislavery movement, the temperance movement also gave him valuable experience in a reform organization.

In addition to the temperance crusade, Chase was active in church work, both within his own St. Paul's Episcopal Church and in nondenominational efforts. He helped to organize the Young Men's Bible Association of Cincinnati, which like its parent organization, the American Bible Society, sought to distribute the Scriptures to the general public. Chase served as the president of the local group for ten years beginning in 1834. He also was a member of the American Sunday School Union, which published books for Sunday school use, and he was superintendent of the Sunday school at St. Paul's.[8]

He was constant in his personal religious exercises and at the same time quick to berate himself for even the slightest evidence of laxity in the practice of his faith. He read from the Bible and offered prayers of thanks and supplication each morning before breakfast. A diary entry in 1834 suggests how Chase spent the Sabbath:

> After breakfast I returned to my room and read, but with little attention, a chapter of Romans. I then offered my thanksgivings for past mercies, and supplications for needed aids and blessings, to the great All-Giver. . . . An accidental reference had determined me to read the book of Deuteronomy, and I occupied the hours till church time reading the first chapters. I was much affected by what I read, and, I hope instructed. . . . At length I went to church . . . afterwards, I fell into the common fault of dwelling chiefly upon the defects of the sermon without adverting at all to the instructive thoughts thrown out in it.[9]

Whenever he devoted any part of Sunday to business or politics, Chase was quick to admit his error and seek God's forgiveness. After a serious illness in early 1833, from which he feared he might not recover, he resolved "to try to do more for God than I had before done; to live a more godly life, and to be more instant in prayer, and more abundant in good works."[10] Only through faith in God and the performance of good works did Chase believe he could find salvation. He would later apply his faith with equal diligence to his work within the antislavery movement.

During his first three years in Cincinnati Chase found that there was limited business available for a young struggling lawyer. For the first six months after his move he worked as a student in the office of attorney Nathaniel Wright. In June 1830, at the age of twenty-two, he was admitted to the Ohio bar, since his boyhood residence in the state could be used to meet the state residency requirement. In September he was able to open his own office by renting the first floor of a new brick building on Third Street for six dollars a month. He also used the rear area as his living quarters by dividing the office with a board partition. After two weeks in his office he had only two clients and had received only four dollars in fees. After a month he confessed, "I have earned about fifteen dollars, and *perhaps shall be paid."* [11]

With substantial debts still unsettled, "prospects were gloomy enough for several months," and he managed to make ends meet only with the help of "a generous friend." He used some of his meager income to repay his mother for the assistance she had given when he was at Dartmouth. His hope was to be able to pay all of his debts within three years: "If this be my lot, I shall, at the age of twenty-five, be established in my profession, out of debt with a fair income, and able, and I trust willing to aid others as I have myself felt the need of aid." [12]

Chase continued to struggle alone until the spring of 1832 when he formed a partnership with Edward King of Chillicothe and a local attorney, Timothy Walker. Chase argued a few cases in court but for the most part left that to the more experienced King and Walker, while he attended to matters in the office. The three divided the proceeds of the business equally with Chase acting as the cashier and bookkeeper. He did gain enough courtroom experience to overcome some initial nervousness before the bench, and, after six months with King and Walker, Chase joined in a new partnership with Daniel Caswell. [13]

The chief advantage of this new arrangement was that Caswell was the solicitor of the Cincinnati branch of the Bank of the United States, which Chase, after paying a substantial sum to his partner, was able to share in equally. Eighteen months later, when Caswell moved to Indiana, Chase bought out his interest and continued in the potentially lucrative position as the bank's solicitor. In 1834, he also became solicitor for the new Lafayette Bank, and the combined business of the two accounts allowed him to end his indebtedness. [14] After four years of practice he had thus achieved his initial goal and was secure in his profession. He was also so busy that his literary pursuits, especially his connection with the lyceum, had to be abandoned.

Ambition drove Chase to long hours of legal, religious, and reform activities in the early 1830s. A typical day might begin at half past four and involve devotions and Bible reading and work on a speech before breakfast at seven. By eight he would be at his desk meeting clients, preparing for court at nine and for conferences with bank officials later in the morning. An hour in the middle of the day for dinner might be followed by legal research and writing and more meetings with clients until six. He would conclude the day with further study and devotions from eight to ten. He resolved in his diary that he would "try to excel in all things," yet "not be mortified" if someone else exceeded his accomplishments. Clearly, he did not intend to let that happen very frequently. He wanted so much to make a name for himself that he even considered changing the name his parents had given him to fit more closely the goals he sought. In 1830 he explained in a letter to his friend Charles Cleveland, only half-jokingly, that he had been thinking about changing his "awkward *fishy*" first name and that he might seek the consent of his brothers to change the spelling of his last name "so as to disconnect us *from the world* a little more than we are." He asked his friend how "Spencer De Cheyce or Spencer Payne Cheyce" struck him.[15] Cleveland's reaction is not recorded!

The youthful attorney sought to add to his growing legal reputation, and in 1832 he started the seemingly thankless task of collecting and publishing all of the laws of Ohio from the time of territorial organization in 1788. Those laws, which had never been brought together, were scattered among four volumes of adopted laws, three of territorial statutes, and thirty-one books of state laws. Chase hoped that the project would provide a valuable service to the state's attorneys and courts and that it would also give him additional income and visibility. The three volumes of *Statutes of Ohio,* published in three consecutive years beginning in 1833, brought him the recognition and praise he desired. Chancellor James Kent of New York called them "a great work," which "does credit to your enterprise, industry and accuracy," while Supreme Court Justice Joseph Story was equally lavish in his praise. To this compilation, which had required three years of painstaking effort, Chase added numerous notes and references to produce what soon became the standard source. Twenty years later Chase would immodestly but accurately claim that his *Statutes of Ohio* had "ever since been used by the Bench and Bar as undoubted authority for reference in all cases."[16]

The work did not, however, bring him the anticipated financial rewards. An edition of a thousand copies was printed. The state agreed to purchase one hundred and fifty—fewer than Chase had been led to believe it would buy—and fire destroyed several hundred copies of the second volume. In all he received only about a thousand dollars for the monumental task, but more important for

Chase's future than money, the legal profession of Ohio had been made aware of the name of Salmon Chase.[17]

The *Statutes of Ohio* included more than a collection of laws; Chase prefaced the first volume with a forty-page "Preliminary Sketch of the History of Ohio," the only history of the region then available. He provided a readable and lively account, which began with the coming of white settlers to the area. Not surprisingly, it reflected the bias of most Americans of that day against the Indian people. Chase wrote that during the War for Independence settlers in the East had been "harassed by the murderous invasions of the savages" from Ohio, and that a decade later the first white settlers in Ohio were "disposed to deal justly with their savage neighbors." In most other respects Chase's history remains useful today. Only occasionally did he interject his own biases, although in the atmosphere of growing North-South conflict over slavery, he was strong in his praise of the ban on the institution provided by the Northwest Ordinance of 1787, with the result that "the soil of Ohio bears up none but freemen." He noted that free blacks did not enjoy equality, being denied both the right to vote and the opportunity for a public education; nonetheless, his emphasis remained on the evils of slavery which federal law had, he believed, so fortunately excluded from Ohio. With the nullification struggle between President Jackson and South Carolina only recently resolved, Chase explained that he hoped through his writing "to inculcate national ideas and sentiments and to enlist state pride in the support and maintenance of the national union and the national constitution."[18] Despite his basic antagonism to Jacksonian Democracy, he strongly supported the president in his confrontation with John C. Calhoun. Since nullification represented an indirect defense of slavery, not surprisingly Chase found it more objectionable than Jackson's defense of the Union.

Chase was not always consistent in his views of Ohio and its politics. In his "Preliminary Sketch" he lauded the "freedom, independence and strength" of the state and attributed these in part to the fact that "every man may vote; every man is eligible to any office." On the other hand, he told Tocqueville and Beaumont that the result of universal suffrage in Cincinnati was the election of some unqualified officials. They secured office, he said, "by flattering everybody, a thing which men of character will never do; by mixing with the mob; by basely flattering its emotions; by drinking to-

gether." Only in New England were the people "sufficiently enlight-
ened" in his opinion to choose the most qualified candidates. The
evils resulting from the ascendancy of the Jacksonians in Washington had apparently made inroads in Ohio politics as well. Only
by maintaining a property qualification for voting and officeholding could the Jacksonians be kept from power.[19] Chase's conservative, elitist tendencies remained as strong as they had ever been,
although with an increasing eye toward public opinion, he would
soon express a more politically popular philosophy.

By late 1835, Chase's practice had increased to the point where he
needed a junior partner. In his first two partnerships, his colleagues
had contributed both trial experience and added business, but in the
year since Daniel Caswell's departure Chase had discovered that he
needed help in day-to-day office work, especially as the volume of his
business as solicitor for the two banks increased. Thus he took in
Samuel Eels, "a young gentleman of great promise and one of the
finest orators I ever listened to." The arrangement under which
Chase received two-thirds of the firm's proceeds and Eels the remaining third lasted until 1838. At that point he was joined by Flamen
Ball who had studied law in Chase's office. Ball remained associated
with Chase for the rest of his life and became especially important
as business and politics increasingly required Chase to spend time
either in Columbus or Washington. Ball did the office work, and
the two corresponded regularly on business matters until Chase's
death.[20] Not the most stable of persons and later in life afflicted with
alcoholism, Ball nonetheless kept Chase's Cincinnati practice
running smoothly.

Several other partners joined the firm for brief periods in the
1840s and 1850s, and law students frequently worked in the office.
Chase took a genuine interest in these young men, several of whom
became loyal political supporters in later years.[21] His tolerance of
Ball's struggle with alcoholism as well as his support and encouragement for those young men who read law in his office are indications
of Chase's willingness to take on responsibility for the future and his
desire to be needed by those who would be important in that future.

Opinions differ on Chase's ability as a lawyer. Financially the firm
did moderately well, and by 1845 it was earning close to ten thousand dollars annually.[22] This success allowed Chase to invest in real
estate in the Cincinnati area and elsewhere. His connection with

the Bank of the United States and with the Lafayette Bank bolstered the firm's earnings substantially, although in 1841 the relationship with the estate of the former was severed because the firm's fees were considered excessive. Chase became an expert in banking as well as in commercial and land law, and he was considered by supporters and opponents alike to be an able attorney who prepared and presented his cases well. His training in Washington under William Wirt had been inadequate at best, but he had read widely since that time and had learned quickly from experience on the job. His work on the *Statutes of Ohio* had earned him a measure of respect as had his hard work, determination, and willingness to learn from past mistakes.

The integrity of his law firm was well established. For example, in 1835, he turned down some potentially lucrative business with one of the wealthiest men in Cincinnati, Nicholas Longworth, because Chase believed there was a potential conflict of interest between Longworth's vast real estate interests and his own connection with the Bank of the United States. Unquestionably an upstanding attorney, Chase was meticulous if he was not eloquent. But law for him was always a means, not an end. As he turned more to antislavery and political interests in the 1840s, his practice provided an income which allowed him to pursue other goals with even greater dedication. If these other interests had not taken precedence, Chase's prominence in the legal profession, as well as his personal wealth resulting from it, probably would have grown even more dramatically.[23]

As Chase's law practice developed in the 1830s, he was able to settle his debts and look ahead to marriage and raising a family. He had been unwilling to consider marriage while his future seemed so uncertain in Washington, despite his interest in Elizabeth Wirt. Shortly after his arrival in Ohio he heard of her impending marriage to a naval lieutenant. With obvious regret he observed that "had happier stars shown upon me I would have disputed the prize with them of the Navy." Lacking financial security, he had been unwilling to try "to win her affections." Yet the tall and handsome Chase had never been hesitant with women, and after his move to Cincinnati he sought out their company at every opportunity. The daughter of the wealthy Nicholas Longworth first attracted his attention. A union with one of the most influential families of the city would have given him entry to the upper level of society and the advantage the ambitious attorney sought. Apparently, Cassilly Longworth gave him little encouragement and a serious romance never blossomed.[24]

While visiting Miss Longworth in late 1831 Chase first met Catherine Jane Garniss, who was several years younger than he. It was not love at first sight, and, he admitted, "her appearance did not please me." He thought "her features large and her face plain," and he had the impression that "the Garniss family were pretenders to style and were ambitious to lead the fashions here." Unconsciously, he was perhaps projecting his own attitudes with that description. The relationship developed slowly and for some time they regarded each other merely as good friends. Catherine first thought of Chase as "uncouth" and as having "an unmanageable mouth." Yet she confidently expected to be able to "polish him up a little." As friendship turned to courtship, a deep and lasting love resulted. Chase wrote, "How vastly did I underrate her! What genuine delicacy and depth of feeling, what devotedness and self-sacrifice." The Garniss family might lack the prominence of the Longworths, but Chase soon began to show both respect and affection for them as well. Following the ceremony, performed by Rev. Lyman Beecher on March 4, 1834, the young couple lived at the Garniss home; all evidence suggests that it was a happy arrangement for everyone.[25]

Chase's contentment increased as he shared himself fully with Kitty. A highly intelligent young woman, she gave Chase her complete support as his business grew. At the time they were married he was finishing the *Statutes of Ohio* and had recently added the Lafayette Bank's business to his connection with the Cincinnati branch of the national bank. Kitty encouraged his legal pursuits and understood and shared his desire for advancement and prominence. The birth of their child, Catherine Amelia, in November 1835 increased their happiness as they looked to the future together.[26]

Complications developed following the baby's birth and the mother became delirious with fever, but she soon seemed well enough for Chase to plan a trip to Philadelphia on bank business. When he explained to Kitty that he would not be compensated for the trip and that he feared leaving her during her recovery, she urged him to go anyway, for "you will get reputation by it." Shortly after Chase's departure, Kitty's condition worsened. The Garnisses called in one doctor after another. All, except the original physician,

Chase's brother-in-law, Isaac Colby, recommended the usual practice of bloodletting to rid the patient of infection. The treatment was repeated for several days, a period during which Kitty's demeanor remained "sweet and gentle." She died on December 1, only twenty months after her wedding.[27]

Chase learned of the tragedy en route home when messages reached him at his hotel in Wheeling, Virginia. It was to him the cruelest of blows: "My whole soul was occupied by the idea of reaching home, and receiving the welcome embrace of my dear wife." Arriving in Cincinnati via steamboat after midnight, he hurried to the Garniss home, "hoping even against hope" that the message had been in error. Instead, "the black crape at the door announced that death was within." For a time that night he wandered aimlessly through the city unable to face the reality of his loss. The "silent streets" provided little consolation to the grieving husband as he sorrowfully reviewed the recent days and recalled the happy months he had spent with Kitty. Guilt built within him, and he blamed himself for his absence from her bedside during her illness. He agonized that "had I been at home she would have recovered, but I was far from her." When he finally returned and viewed her body, he could only lament that "the sweet smile, the glance of affection, the expression, the mind was gone. Nothing was left but clay."[28]

The sense of loss took months to heal. Chase visited his wife's grave almost daily in the weeks ahead and appeared lost in grief. For a time he seemed unable to continue without Kitty: "It is heavy work now with me. I have no longer a wife at home interested in all that I do, and gratified by all my success. I am no longer stimulated by a wish to please one whom I love far better than myself." He felt personally responsible for his wife's death because he believed that the disease itself had not killed her. Rather it had been "the injudicious treatment" of bloodletting, which he would have ordered stopped had he been at home.[29]

Other factors increased his sense of guilt as he struggled through the early months of 1836. He especially blamed himself for not having made a more concerted effort to urge Kitty's religious conversion. A few conversations and "faint prayers" instead of "kind and earnest persuasion" had not been enough and now he could not even be sure "that she had died in the faith." He lamented that because of his lack of persistence his wife had not joined the church.

If only he had been more assiduous in his religious practices, she might have accepted his faith as her own.[30]

Chase's grief and guilt were compounded by the problems of raising his daughter. As a caring and loving father he was totally devoted to the child but seemed not always to know how best to cope with his situation as a single parent. The child undoubtedly reminded him of his wife and what life could have been for them had she lived. After Kitty's death, he continued to live with the Garnisses, who took much of the responsibility for raising his daughter, although he came into conflict with his wife's mother over the child's care. In one instance, he resisted her employment of one of the physicians who had attended his wife. He eventually agreed to Mrs. Garniss's choice of doctors, reminding himself "that she is the mother of my dear departed wife, and in every way entitled to respect and deference from me." But tensions escalated until Chase urged his sister Helen to come to Cincinnati from Lockport, New York to be his housekeeper and raise his daughter in the rural home he had purchased outside of Cincinnati.[31]

During his period of mourning for his wife, Chase was reminded of his mother and her wise advice to him. He remembered "her lessons of thrift and economy; lessons which she rigidly practiced from an earnest desire to have her children well educated." He only wished that she and his wife had not been taken from him so soon; he had had so little opportunity to show his love for them.[32] These memories combined with his guilt and grief would be an agonizing and ongoing pressure. Only time and increased involvement in legal and antislavery pursuits would help to ease and eventually displace his pain.

Four years after the death of his first wife, Chase married eighteen-year-old Eliza Ann Smith of Cincinnati. Diaries and letters reveal virtually nothing of their relationship prior to the wedding in September 1839, but subsequent evidence suggests that it was a close and loving union. Although Eliza lacked Kitty's social standing and education, she shared her husband's strong religious faith. Chase rejoiced, "We are in a common dependence on the Savior and in a common hope of immortal life."[33]

They had been married barely three months when tragedy struck again. Chase's four-year-old daughter, Catherine Amelia, died when a scarlet fever epidemic raged through the city. Chase deeply grieved her passing, lamenting that no words could "describe the desolation of my heart."[34] The death of the child broke his only remaining physical tie with his first wife.

The birth of a daughter, Catherine Jane, in August 1840, strengthened his relationship with Eliza. Two more daughters were born in 1842 and 1843, respectively, but the first lived only three months and the second a little more than a year. Chase did not grieve excessively over these deaths, perhaps becoming hardened to what was an all too common occurrence in nineteenth-century America. Nor was his sorrow over the death of Eliza in September 1845 as intense as that he had felt over Catherine's death ten years earlier. The long months of Eliza's illness better prepared him to accept her passing; he noted the winter before her death that her consumption "seems to make slow but certain progress and the hope of a favorable event has become exceedingly faint." On her death he poured out his grief to his friend Charles Cleveland, quoting Naomi's anguish: "The Lord hath dealt very bitterly with me." He continued, "I feel as if my heart was broken. I write weeping. I cannot restrain my tears." But he did not experience the guilt that he had following Kitty's death, and he concluded to Cleveland that "all is not dark. The cloud is fringed with light. She died trusting in Jesus."[35]

In eleven years, Chase lost two wives and three daughters, and in the autumn of 1845 the five-year-old Kate was his only surviving offspring. So many personal tragedies led him increasingly to substitute work for family. Although he remained a devoted father, he entrusted Kate's care to his sister. Not surprisingly, Chase also began to develop a fatalistic attitude. Six years later as his third wife lay near death he would urge the eleven-year-old Kate to lead a more religious life and counsel her that "you may die soon and cannot in any event live very many years." He concluded, "How short then is this life! And how earnest ought to be our preparations for another!"[36]

As Chase became more financially secure, he also assumed more responsibility and leadership for numerous brothers and sisters who were scattered in various parts of the country. Although never extremely close to any of his brothers or sisters, he felt a responsibility to provide support and guidance when possible. In 1834, he became the guardian of his younger sister Helen and soon received a request from a young man who sought permission to marry her.[37]

Chase maintained frequent contact with two of his brothers, Alexander and Edward. The latter, a Lockport, New York lawyer, had business contacts with Chase and was dependent on him for financial advice, while Alexander, the older brother with whom he had traveled to Ohio in 1820, sent frequent requests for money and other assistance.

His most trying family relationship was with his younger brother William. As early as 1832, when William was a student at Colby College in Maine, Chase received complaints about his behavior from college officials, but it was only after William had read law and moved to Saint Louis that he became a burden. A steady stream of accounts reached Chase's desk about William's indebtedness, his gambling and drinking, and his neglect of his wife and children. Chase at first tried encouragement and then threatened to sever financial support unless William agreed to "attend no wine parties and give none and associate with no person of a dissipated or vicious character" and "to have no intercourse with gamblers." When all else failed he even arranged to have William come to live in Cincinnati, hoping that a change of setting would alter his habits. When the wayward brother returned to Saint Louis and to a dissipated life, Chase was forced to abandon responsibility for him. Following William's death in 1852, Chase periodically sent small sums of money to the destitute widow.[38] Throughout his life, Chase, although never wealthy, did what he could to aid various unfortunate relatives and friends. Although the assistance frequently included a stern lecture, Chase willingly assumed responsibility when his status or financial resources could prove helpful.

The evolution of family leadership was accompanied by a gradual change in Chase's attitude toward slavery and race relations. Before coming to Cincinnati Chase had shown an early but passing interest in abolition in the District of Columbia. In his lyceum lecture and subsequent article of 1831, he had expressed admiration for Henry Brougham's role as an English abolitionist. He also had given tentative support to the colonization movement, which sought to persuade free blacks to return to Africa. Twenty-two hundred blacks lived in Cincinnati the year before Chase moved there in 1830, constituting about 10 percent of the population. Living in a ghetto known as Little Africa where their poverty was extreme, blacks had been victimized by a serious race riot in 1829. At that time city officials were threatening to enforce a long neglected Ohio statute requiring blacks to post $500 bonds on entering the state to guarantee their "good behavior." When a white mob pillaged the black neighborhood and the police made no move to stop the destruction, almost half of the blacks made the agonizing decision to move to Canada.[39]

Tense race relations continued after Chase's arrival, and his initial reaction was to endorse the colonization concept. He believed that the two races could not live together in peace and that blacks must leave to avoid further violence. In 1834, he addressed the Young Men's Colonization Society of Hamilton County and supported African colonization as "a sure and powerful mode of extending Civilization and Christianity to that great, but as yet barbarous, continent." He later joined the local colonizationist group and attended a meeting of the state society in Columbus.[40] With his elitist New England background, he believed that blacks were inferior to whites and argued condescendingly that it was in the best interest of blacks to return to Africa. Membership in the Colonization Society as well as temperance and religious organizations appealed to Chase both because he sincerely believed in the causes they represented and because of the improved status, prestige, and publicity that might be accorded him as a result of his participation.

In the early 1830s, his conservative political and social outlook led Chase to associate with business and professional leaders of the city in their efforts to rid Cincinnati of its black population. Chief among such associates were Nicholas Longworth and the president of the Lafayette Bank, Josiah Lawrence. By this time most abolitionists in Ohio and elsewhere had long since rejected the colonization movement, concluding that it was a device of slaveholders and their sympathizers for strengthening the peculiar institution. But Chase remained a colonizationist and showed little sympathy for the abolitionist position. In fact, his diary and correspondence reveal that during his first six years in Ohio he was far more concerned with such organizations as the American Sunday School Union and the Young Men's Temperance Society and with such personal problems as the mounting debts of his brother William than he was with slavery and race relations.

Chase's attitude and priorities changed abruptly in 1836; surely his early associations indicated none of the intensity with which he was about to join the antislavery crusade. Part of the transformation was due to his brother-in-law, Isaac Colby, a leading abolitionist in Cincinnati. Dr. Colby, who had attended Chase's wife, Kitty, during her fatal illness, introduced Chase to many antislavery leaders in the city. These contacts no doubt helped him to fill the void left by his wife's death in December 1835. Still, Chase expressed no special interest or sympathy for antislavery activities until the summer of 1836 when an anti-abolition mob began to harass James G. Birney, editor of the city's recently established abolitionist newspaper, the *Philanthropist.* Cincinnati, with its extensive commercial ties with the South and its many recent emigrants from Kentucky and Virginia, was not a city in which it was any safer for an abolitionist to write or speak than it was for blacks to live. Business leaders and average citizens alike sympathized strongly with the South and slavery and were unwilling to tolerate any view which threatened their southern friends or their ties with them. Thus when Birney began publishing his paper in January 1836, trouble was inevitable.[41]

Violence first erupted July 12, when the office of Birney's printer was broken into and his press destroyed. A mass meeting on July 23 heard such leading citizens as Longworth and Lawrence declare that the group planned to destroy the *Philanthropist* "peaceably if it could, forcibly if it must." Birney explained in the next issue of the *Philanthropist* that he and his supporters had no choice but to continue publication: "We are not more the advocate of freedom for the slave than we are of liberty for those who are yet free." The anti-abolitionist group needed no further urging than this defiance, and on the night of July 30 a mob again broke into the printing office, tore the press apart, and threw it into the Ohio River. The angry crowd then sought out Birney, but, failing to find him, in frustration began four hours of systematic looting of black neighborhoods. Only when Mayor Samuel Davies pleaded, "We have done enough for one night" did the destruction cease.[42]

It was in this setting that Chase first became involved. His sister, Abigail Colby, fearing for her own safety took refuge from the mob in Chase's home. Like so many others of his background and position, Chase had not been sufficiently moved by slavery itself or by the plight of free blacks in his own city to take action. But the challenge to freedom of the press and the threat to Birney's personal safety as well as that of his own family finally brought a response. Personally "opposed at this time to the views of abolitionists," Chase would defend their right to express those views. He concluded that "the Slave Power" was "the great enemy of freedom of speech, freedom of the press and freedom of the person." Following the lead of John Quincy Adams, Chase was more concerned with protecting civil liberties for whites than he was with establishing civil rights for blacks. He thus joined with the editor of the *Cincinnati Gazette,* Charles Hammond, in calling for a public meeting to oppose mob action. On July 31 he and Hammond arrived at the appointed time with resolutions of protest which Chase had written to find that their opponents were already present and in control of the gathering. Instead of supporting Birney and his right to publish, the resolutions adopted approved what the mob had done the night before by claiming that the abolitionists had caused the conflict.[43]

In the meantime, Birney had been persuaded by his friends to stay out of the city until calm was restored. Later the same evening the mob went to the Franklin House, where Birney had at first moved his family, "determined to enter and make search for Mr. Birney." Summoning all his courage, the tall, young, broad-shouldered Chase stood in the doorway and defiantly refused admission to anyone. Chase's own account states: "One of them asked who I was? I gave them my name." One of the ringleaders warned Chase that he would pay for his actions. Chase's record continues, "I told him I could be found at any time." As tensions mounted Chase's imposing physical presence and bold challenge had the desired effect: "The mob did not choose to attack me in my position." Finally, assurances from Mayor Davies that Birney was not inside induced the crowd to disperse. The young lawyer's courageous act immediately labeled him as one of Birney's supporters in the minds of most, but Chase did not yet consider himself "technically an abolitionist."[44]

In defying the mob, Chase had also challenged the leaders of the Cincinnati business community, the Longworths and the Lawrences, who represented the majority's opposition to antislavery agitation. Thus an act of great boldness radicalized Chase in a dramatic way. In a letter published in the *Gazette* some days later, Chase explained that a statement attributed to him—that he would give ten thousand dollars to support an abolition press—was false, but he "would give ten thousand dollars, sooner than see the abolition press put down by a mob." He added that although he opposed many actions of the abolitionists, "I regard all the consequences of their publications as evils comparatively light" when compared with the "mob spirit." Chase's later recollections, as recorded in his autobiographical sketch, imply that the incident placed him on the verge of joining the antislavery men: "I became a decided opponent of slavery and the Slave Power and if any chose to call me an abolitionist on this account, I was at no trouble to disclaim the name."[45] Although differing with many abolitionists as to the best means to end slavery, he had nonetheless accepted their goal that it must be overthrown.

Chase stepped up his antislavery involvement by acting as one of the attorneys for the owners of the *Philanthropist* in the suits brought against members of the mob for damages done to the press and its office. Chase accepted the cases reluctantly, for "I had just begun to acquire a pretty good practice for a young man and among the gentlemen to be sued were several of my personal friends." He feared that these friends might come to regard him as a personal enemy. Always willing to attribute his actions to the highest motives and to exaggerate their significance, he explained his willingness "to surrender every professional prospect when the condition of retaining them is a departure from principle." Secure in his profession by this time, Chase could more easily afford to lose potential business than he could have a few years earlier. There is no evidence to suggest, however, that the suits hurt his practice in any way. Chase took part in two cases tried in 1838, the first of which resulted in only a fifty dollar judgment against the accused mob leaders, despite Chase's eloquent defense of the abolitionists and freedom of the press. The second suit, involving Achilles Pugh, Birney's printer, resulted in a hung jury, although the following year Pugh received damages of fifteen hundred dollars.[46] More importantly, Chase's role in these cases led to even more active involvement in several highly publicized fugitive slave trials—involvement which would bring him national recognition and thrust him into antislavery politics.

Chase had his first opportunity to assist a fugitive in a case brought to his attention by his friend James Birney. A light-skinned mulatto named Matilda had been hired as a maid by Mrs. Birney in 1836 on the assumption that she was white. When Matilda was arrested by city officials in 1837, it was revealed that she was the slave and daughter of Larkin Lawrence of Missouri, who had stopped in Cincinnati the year before en route to Saint Louis. While the boat was tied to the dock she slipped away into the city, hid first in the black community, and, when it appeared safe, sought employment in the Birney household. She was arrested as a fugitive under the federal act of 1793. Because of Ohio's location, slaveowners such as Lawrence frequently passed through the state when traveling westward by land or water. Cincinnati especially had become a major trading center for southerners and virtually all Ohio River traffic stopped there. The city therefore assumed a central place in the issue of whether slaveowners could visit or travel through regions where slavery was illegal and still enjoy legal protection of their slave property. Chase would have the opportunity to challenge the rights of comity in his claim that the ban on slavery in Ohio took precedence.[47]

Following Matilda's arrest, Birney retained Chase and his partner Samuel Eels in her defense, believing that the case would be stronger if a lawyer who was not an avowed abolitionist argued for her freedom. Chase "readily consented to do what I could to protect her" and obtained a writ of habeas corpus from Judge D. K. Este of the Court of Common Pleas. With under twenty-four hours to prepare his case, Chase was tentative and not entirely effective in his argument. He failed to emphasize that Matilda and her master were clearly in transit from one state to another when they stopped in Cincinnati. Instead of stressing that she had not fled to Ohio and thus should not be considered a fugitive—an argument he would develop effectively in later cases—he chose the more difficult approach of challenging the fugitive slave law. He argued that only a federal officer could enforce the national law and that the actions of state officials and state courts were thus void. The law was unconstitutional, said Chase, but in any case not applicable in Ohio because the Northwest Ordinance of 1787 had made slavery illegal there. He also seized the opportunity to suggest that slavery was a violation of the natural right to human liberty, a right "proclaimed by our fathers in the Declaration of Independence." Said Chase, "All men are born 'equally free.' " Judge Este surprised few when he ruled that Matilda was legally a slave and must be returned to her owner. The day after the judge's decision, the unfortunate woman was placed on a boat for New Orleans where she was sold at public auction.[48]

During his defense Chase made only passing reference to the transit-sojourn argument, which might have been used more effectively in convincing Judge Este. This line of defense was based in part on an English precedent established in the case of *Somerset* v. *Stewart* in 1772. He reminded the court that the right to hold a slave "can have no existence beyond the territorial limits of the state which sanctions it except in other states whose positive law recognizes and protects it." Chase might have received a more favorable ruling had he emphasized more forcefully that since the Northwest Ordinance forbad slavery in Ohio, Matilda ought to be free. She had after all been brought to Ohio by her owner.[49]

Chase had an opportunity to present this argument more effectively when Birney was indicted for violating the Ohio law of 1804 against harboring a slave. The prosecution was conducted by some of the same men who had encouraged the mob against Birney and his press in 1836, so determined were they to silence him. Despite Chase's able defense, Judge Este found Birney guilty and fined him fifty dollars. Determined not to let the matter rest and at the same time to receive a wider hearing for their position, Chase and Birney appealed the conviction to the state supreme court where the case was heard in January 1838.[50]

In the appeal Chase effectively argued that Birney could not have harbored "a person being the property of another person" because no such property relationship could exist in a state where slavery was illegal. Again Chase declared that the fugitive law could not be applied to Matilda because she had not escaped from one state and fled to another. "At the time she left the individual who claimed to be her master, she was within the territorial limits of Ohio, by the consent of that individual." Once brought to Ohio by Lawrence, Matilda ceased to be a slave and could go where she wanted. Taking employment in Birney's household "was in no just sense of the term an escape"; instead, "it was the first exercise of that freedom, which the constitution of Ohio had conferred upon her." On the question of granting comity to masters in transit, Chase argued that "plain common sense, fortified by every principle of sound construction" prevented it. Thus since Matilda was not a slave in Ohio, Birney could not have committed an offense. The court reversed Birney's conviction, but it did so on the grounds that he could not have known Matilda was a slave when he hired her and on the technicality that the indictment failed to charge Birney with knowingly assisting a fugitive. Chase's constitutional arguments were ignored.[51]

Despite the immediate victory for Birney, Chase was naturally disappointed that the court had failed to rule on his constitutional arguments. The court did order Chase's opinion printed and circulated. Chase believed that it was "desirous to have the argument brought to the notice of the profession."[52] In the course of two years Chase had dramatically altered his beliefs and had drawn considerable attention to himself by his actions in behalf of Birney and Matilda. By the end of the decade Chase's reform efforts had shifted from temperance and colonization to antislavery and the plight of fugitives and those who assisted them.

Chase had come to Cincinnati in 1830 as an inexperienced and somewhat impressionable young attorney. The early death of his father followed by an unhappy period under his uncle's guardianship had left him without roots or family ties. Reflecting later on his college days, Chase lamented, "I had no friend to advise me," despite "the vast importance to a boy of a wise and practical adviser. I had lost my father. I was separated from my mother."[53] His outlook brightened in Washington, D.C., but his association with the Wirt family was cut short. It is thus understandable that during the first half decade of his professional life Chase concentrated on establishing his legal practice and gravitated toward associations that reinforced his preconceived notions of moral behavior.

His wife's illness and death in late 1835 threw him into closer contact with Colby from whom he developed an appreciation of abolitionist views. Then the mob attack on Birney and his press, along with the possible threat to his sister's safety, moved Chase to active involvement—first for his friends and family and then for the fugitive slave.

Chase's involvement in the antislavery movement took on religious overtones as he became convinced of the sin of slaveholding. Not ready to accept immediate abolition as a goal in the way that Birney and Colby had, Chase nevertheless became involved in the fugitive issue with a religious zeal. His concern soon became all-consuming, and with a strong support system of antislavery friends of all varieties of opinion, he gradually assumed a leadership role.

The changes in Chase that occurred in this period reflect the maturation of the professional and of the individual. His interest in the issue of the constitutionality of slavery evolved as he gained stature in the legal profession and as he attained a measure of professional and financial security. As he matured he also began to turn away from self-aggrandizement toward concern for the welfare of others—his wives, his daughters, his brothers and sisters, young lawyers in his office, clients, fugitives, and even free blacks—all of whom he sought to help as teacher and counselor. It is tempting to speculate that one of the factors causing Chase's conversion to antislavery activism was his desire to become a father figure for those he felt he could help. Perhaps he hoped to provide the kind of assistance and guidance he had missed as a boy. He no longer posed as the young aristocrat or thought of changing his name. Although he would never abandon his personal goals of prestige and power, he nonetheless matured into a complex person with a commitment to others as well as to himself.

The evolution of Chase's thinking from a conservative colonizationist to an active antislavery advocate was by no means unique. Two of Chase's eastern contemporaries and future associates, William H. Seward and Charles Sumner, had similar experiences. Seward, seven years Chase's senior, was admitted to the New York bar in 1822 and rose quickly in Whig politics to be elected governor in 1838. He, like Chase, showed his first concern with slave-related issues in the 1830s and soon became involved in fugitive slave cases. Sumner, three years younger than Chase, was admitted to the Massachusetts bar in 1834 and moved gradually toward reform interests in the early 1840s. Both Seward and Sumner came to their interest in antislavery reform from conservative backgrounds similar to Chase's and both took up the cause with a zeal equal to his.[54]

It would be four years before Chase would again have the opportunity to defend another fugitive slave and those accused of assisting in the escape. In the meantime he began his involvement in antislavery politics, and his thinking on the federal government's responsibility for slavery as well as on the role of the free states evolved into a more defined philosophy. In the cases of the early 1840s, Chase argued that although slavery was legal in some states, the federal government must divorce itself entirely from any responsibility to defend and protect the institution. Nor were the free states under any obligation to assist owners in retrieving escaped slaves within their borders. Chase in effect assumed the position that he would urge on the Republican party in the late 1850s—that Congress could not constitutionally recognize or sanction slavery anywhere within its jurisdiction. This was also the position argued by Supreme Court Justice John McLean in his dissent in the Dred Scott decision of 1857.[55] Chase would be instrumental in convincing the Republican party to adopt such a position on slavery in federal territories, although he was never able to persuade the party to adopt that argument concerning the capture of fugitive slaves in northern states. Not technically an abolitionist because he did not believe that the federal government could interfere with slavery where it was legal in the South, Chase had no trouble working with those who, like Birney, were abolitionists.

Following the Matilda and Birney cases, Chase's reputation as an attorney concerned with the plight of alleged fugitives spread and his involvement in such cases increased. In 1841 he argued again in the Hamilton County court in behalf of Mary Towns, a Kentucky slave who had come to Cincinnati ten years earlier and had lived quietly there as a free person. She was then seized by her former master and tried as a fugitive. Chase secured a writ of habeas corpus from Judge Nathaniel C. Read, who three years earlier had opposed him as an attorney in the Matilda and Birney cases. Of the several arguments Chase presented in behalf of Mary Towns the most telling was that the slaveowner's affidavit did not "state that she had escaped from his service in Kentucky *into the State of Ohio.*" Thus she could not be considered a fugitive slave. Judge Read concurred, and in freeing her explained that in Ohio "liberty is the rule, involuntary servitude the exception." Chase's efforts were making enforcement of the fugitive slave act in Ohio increasingly difficult.[56]

The case which would consume much of Chase's time for five years beginning in 1842 and help him to systematize his thinking on the fugitive issue involved an elderly white man named John Van Zandt who lived on a small farm just north of Cincinnati. On the night of April 22, 1842, nine slaves escaped into Ohio from Kentucky, apparently without assistance. Van Zandt found them on the road, "and moved by sympathy, undertook to convey them, in his wagon, to Lebanon or Springfield." Some fifteen miles north of the city, they were overtaken by "some ruffians," who, suspecting them to be fugitives, seized all but one and forced them back across the river into Kentucky. The captors were soon rewarded $450 for their efforts by the owner but were also indicted for kidnapping. As Chase recalled, "the prosecuting attorney . . . evinced little zeal" and the accused were freed, "more by public sentiment than by the jury, who rendered the verdict of acquittal." The owner of the slaves, Wharton Jones, then filed suit in federal court against Van Zandt, charging him with violating the Fugitive Slave Act of 1793 by harboring escaped slaves. Chase was called in to defend Van Zandt in the trial to be held before Supreme Court Justice McLean at Cincinnati in July. He "very willingly undertook the cause."[57]

In a three hour argument before Judge McLean, Chase emphasized that to be convicted of harboring and concealing a slave "there must be proof of actual notice, to the person charged" that he was protecting a fugitive from slavery. This was the technical ground that had been established in the Matilda case. The judge ruled against Chase's position, however, and agreed with the prosecution that Van Zandt knew the nine blacks were slaves. The jury thus had little choice but to find Van Zandt guilty. McLean did approve Chase's request for an appeal so that the issue could be decided by the full United States Supreme Court. Moreover, in charging the jury, McLean adopted Chase's argument that a slave brought voluntarily into a free state was not recoverable under the fugitive slave law.[58] The slaves in the Van Zandt case, however, were fugitives and thus Van Zandt was liable under the law.

It was four years before the case was finally scheduled, and even then the Supreme Court agreed only to receive written briefs rather than to hear arguments. Chase and William H. Seward presented the defense of Van Zandt, while Senator James T. Morehead of Kentucky appeared for Jones. Chase's argument was a thorough discussion of the harboring and concealing clauses of the Fugitive Slave Act of 1793 and more importantly of the act's constitutionality. Although the court had ruled in 1842 in *Prigg* v. *Pennsylvania* that the law was constitutional, he contended that the federal government had no responsibility for slavery. The institution, said Chase, could exist only where state law protected it, whereas "the Government of the United States has nothing whatever to do" with it. Since the Congress in 1787 had banned slavery in the Northwest Territory, a bondsman automatically became free when setting foot in Ohio: "The very moment a slave passes beyond the jurisdiction of the State in which he is held as such, he ceases to be a slave." Chase concluded that "no claim to persons as property can be maintained, under any clause of the Constitution, or any law of the United States."[59] Slavery was thus purely a state institution, while freedom was national.

It came as no surprise to Chase or Seward when the court ruled against them and their client on all counts and upheld the lower court decision. Chase and Seward gave their services to Van Zandt without compensation, and the poor old man died before the plaintiff could collect. As Chase explained, Van Zandt "has long gone where the Supreme Judge of all certainly holds humanity no crime." Chase did have his lengthy argument printed in a pamphlet and sent to every member of Congress, and Seward's arguments were printed in the *New York Tribune*.[60] Both men had known that a favorable verdict was probably not obtainable and they believed the case had been decided even before the court received the arguments. But more important was Chase's hope that "the discussion will not be without a salutary effect upon the professional mind of the country." He received such a favorable response from his antislavery friends that he foresaw "the approaching deliverance from the despotism of the slave power." He could hope that "even though my poor old client be sacrificed, the great cause of humanity will be a gainer by it."[61]

Chase was involved in two other fugitive slave cases of significance in the mid-1840s. As in the earlier situations he was not able to claim victory nor was he able to see more than a limited amount of progress toward greater justice. In February 1845, Jane Garrison and her five-year-old son Harrison were claimed by the owner's son and a slave agent. They had fled from Kentucky and stayed with Francis Parish, a Sandusky attorney, before continuing their journey to Canada. Parish was charged with harboring the pair in his home and with aiding their escape to Canada. Despite Chase's defense, the jury found Parish guilty and fined him one thousand dollars, even though the only evidence against him was the testimony of the owner's son and the slave agent. To Chase the fact that "such a verdict upon such evidence could ever have been rendered" reflected the mood of the times. He felt only "mortification" at how little his assistance had helped the defendant. He consoled himself with the belief that his assistance had "contributed something toward the preparation of a better state of opinion and feeling concerning the whole subject of slavery."[62]

In January 1845, a slave named Samuel Watson escaped from a steamboat tied up on the Ohio River at Cincinnati. He was soon seized and charged as a fugitive under the act of 1793. Chase agreed to defend Watson's claim to freedom on the grounds that he had not escaped from a slave state into free territory. Instead, since the ship "was made fast to the Ohio shore," he was already free because he had been brought voluntarily by the owner's agent into Ohio. Judge Read, now of the Ohio supreme court, ruled that a steamer on the Ohio River was within slave, not free, territory and hence Watson was a fugitive. Although ruling against Watson's freedom, the judge did agree that if he had escaped from his owner while actually on Ohio soil he would have been a free man: "The Constitution of the United States only recognizes the right of recapture of a fugitive held to service in one state *escaping into another. . . .* If there has been no such escape, the master has no right of recaption."[63] Although the judge was accepting the argument that Chase had tried for years to establish, it was little comfort to Watson who was returned to slavery. Nevertheless, an Ohio supreme court judge had ruled that if an owner voluntarily brought a slave into free territory, that slave must be freed. Chase had thus been instrumental in moving the courts of Ohio to a stronger stand protecting slaves. Except when using the Ohio River and its banks, the rights of masters in transit had become extremely vulnerable and those of the slave much more viable.

Chase's defense of Watson and other slaves led to his recognition by the black community of Cincinnati in May 1845 for his "zealous and disinterested advocacy of the rights and privileges of all classes of your fellow citizens, irrespective of clime, color or condition." As a token of their appreciation they presented Chase with a silver pitcher. In accepting this honor, Chase explained that his concern was not for blacks as a "separate and distinct class" but for the civil rights of all. He then attacked the discrimination faced by free blacks in Ohio and most of the North, including the denial of a public education, of the right to testify in court against whites, and of the right to vote, calling the situation "wrong in principle, and demoralizing in tendency." Most especially he charged that "the exclusion of the colored people as a body from the elective franchise [is] incompatible with true democratic principles."[64] Such an endorsement of suffrage and other rights for blacks separated Chase even further from most of white society and placed him in closer alliance with the black community and with many white abolitionists. At this same time, he was labeled by some Kentucky opponents as the "Attorney General for Runaway Negroes." Although it was not meant as a compliment, Chase soon was using the title with pride, for "I never refused my help to any person black or white; and I liked the office nonetheless because there were neither fees nor salary connected with it."[65]

Chase also became involved in a less controversial humanitarian effort in behalf of the black community of Cincinnati. In a concern unrelated to political controversies he was instrumental in bringing about the establishment of the Cincinnati Orphan Asylum for Colored Children. In 1844, an appeal had been issued by concerned black citizens for white support of temporary as well as prolonged care for homeless or abandoned black children. Several in the community responded, including Nicholas Longworth, who loaned a large home for their needs. Chase donated legal assistance in drawing up a charter for the asylum. In 1845, he was able to secure a special act of the Ohio legislature incorporating the asylum as required by state law. He maintained interest in and support for the institution for the remainder of his life.[66]

In the course of fifteen years in Cincinnati from 1830 to 1845, Chase progressed from a struggling young attorney to a position of prominence in legal and antislavery circles. In matters of civil rights and slavery, he had moved, at first tentatively and then enthusiastically, from apathy in the early 1830s to an active interest in the plight of fugitives. By 1845 he was looked to by both white and black Cincinnatians as the most important attorney in that field. Antislavery for Chase became an all-important dimension of his concern for others and his desire to improve the quality of life for those around him. His political views underwent a similar transition during these years.

3

Liberty Advocate

As Chase gradually established himself in law and reform and turned to antislavery concerns, he inevitably became involved in politics. He left Washington in 1830 predicting dire results from the leveling tendencies of Andrew Jackson and his Democratic party. In Cincinnati, he joined the National Republican party and became active in local politics. In 1831, he was chosen as a delegate to the party convention which nominated Henry Clay. Chase's support for Clay was lukewarm because he much preferred William Wirt. When Wirt accepted the nomination of the Anti Masons, Chase endorsed him, not because he agreed with the third-party movement but "because of my personal affection for him and my active confidence in his public and private virtues and . . . good abilities." Wirt, he felt, was "more likely to conciliate all sections" and restore harmony than was Clay. But because of Wirt's poor chances, Chase voted for a general ticket of electors pledged to the candidate who might win a majority of the electoral college. His main concern was the defeat of Andrew Jackson, for "if he should be reelected all is lost." He believed that his own section would be ruined, and he felt that business and property values had already begun to sink in anticipation of Jackson's reelection.[1]

Four additional years of Andrew Jackson convinced Chase even more of the need for a Whig president. During Jackson's second term Chase became an active organizer of the new anti-Jackson pro-Bank party, formed in Cincinnati in January 1834. Chase was part of the young professional-small business alliance which took the lead in organizing the party on the ward level. He supported Supreme Court Justice and Whig nominee John McLean for president rather than William Henry Harrison, the candidate of many older, more established leaders of the Ohio Whig party. Chase urged McLean to press his own candidacy against Harrison's because the "Whigs can not with consistency support a man for the Presidency on the sole ground of military service." Yet when McLean withdrew from the race in August 1835, Chase agreed to back Harrison "as against Mr. Van Buren of whom I know little and for whom I had no sympathy."[2] Thus at the same time Chase publicly defied the crowd at Franklin House, his political ties remained as conservative as ever.

The next four years brought a gradual shift for Chase. As he developed close ties with Birney, he committed himself to the fugitive slave cause in the Matilda case in 1837. That same year Birney wrote to him as a full antislavery confidant, urging that he stir up opposition to the annexation of Texas.[3] But he was not ready to move with many of his antislavery friends to support Birney and the Liberty party against Harrison in 1840. He retained his Whig ties despite the stormy events of 1836 and 1837 and remained active in the local party organization, still believing that it offered him the best opportunity for a future in politics.

He was not alone, for such men as Samuel Lewis agreed with him that the party could be moved toward a more active antislavery stance. Because the local party continued to have a faction of younger men eager to prevent defections to the new Liberty party, Chase was not ostracized. His Whig background and his competency as a rising young lawyer and politician made him welcome among other party leaders who disagreed with his views on slavery. In March 1840, the first ward Whigs chose Chase, Lewis, and Alexander Ewing as candidates for the city council on a "Log Cabin" ticket pledged to Harrison. The Whigs swept the city elections in April with their first ward candidates outdistancing Democratic opponents by more than two to one. In the presidential contest that followed Chase even prepared resolutions in defense of Harrison against Democratic "slanders" for a public meeting.[4]

Despite this endorsement, Harrison's record on slave-related issues clearly disturbed Chase. As governor of Indiana Territory almost forty years earlier, Harrison had asked Congress for a suspension of the prohibition on slavery there. As a member of the House of Representatives in 1819 he had voted against the Talmadge Amendment limiting slavery in Missouri. Most seriously, in 1835, he had argued that slavery was a southern evil which should not be agitated in the North. But in 1840 when Chase's antislavery friend Gamaliel Bailey attacked Harrison's record and endorsed Birney's candidacy in the *Philanthropist,* Chase agreed, at Harrison's urging, to try to convince Bailey to retract his criticisms.[5] Both believed that the small Liberty vote would hurt Whigs more than it would Democrats.

Clearly, Chase was in a dilemma as the election approached. He felt that Harrison was motivated by a "sincere and elevated patriotism" and was capable of leading "ably and faithfully." Yet, he felt only despair over the complete subservience of both parties toward the South on the "*vital* question of slavery." Still unwilling to take part in a "premature" third-party movement, he clung to a promising future with the Whigs and prospects of victory.[6] In Chase's eyes the Liberty party in 1840 was so tiny and without influence that any other course was unrealistic.

As Harrison prepared to assume the presidency in early 1841, Chase still believed that the Whig party could become antislavery. He publicly urged Harrison to support abolition in the District of Columbia and made several recommendations for presidential appointments. He also urged the president-elect to take no position on slavery in the District rather than to accept the view that Congress could not abolish slavery there without the consent of its inhabitants. Such a stand, Chase advised, would only produce "a schism which may be attended with fatal consequences."[7]

In his inaugural address, Harrison ignored Chase's advice and expressed his opposition to any congressional interference with slavery even in the area outside the slave states. A month later Harrison died and Virginia slaveholder John Tyler became president. This triggered Chase's decision to abandon the Whigs and join his antislavery friends in the Liberty party. The factors which had originally made him a Whig now seemed unimportant. Having already come to favor the independent treasury concept of the Democrats, he found that few issues remained to maintain his Whig loyalties. Much later in life Chase claimed that his support of the Whig party had never been wholehearted. He wrote: "I was not a life-long Whig, but a sort of independent Whig with Democratic ideas, from 1830 to 1841. Sometimes I voted for a Democrat, but more generally for Whigs." From 1841 on, however, slavery loomed paramount to him. He explained later to Charles Sumner that he had supported Harrison "because I imagined that his administration would be less proslavery than Mr. Van Buren's." When he realized his mistake he "was ready to concur in an independent movement." Another racial disturbance directed against the black community of Cincinnati in the summer of 1841, aided and abetted by some of Chase's wealthy Whig friends, further convinced him that his decision had been correct.[8]

Chase's decision to leave the Whig party was agonizingly painful, reached only after much deliberation and with considerable misgivings; in leaving the well-established and smoothly functioning Whigs whom he had helped to organize in Cincinnati, he joined an inexperienced one-year-old party. A small group of antislavery leaders, including Gamaliel Bailey, editor of the *Philanthropist,* and former Senator Thomas Morris, had preceded him in advocating and organizing this third party in Ohio. Bailey, editor since Birney moved to New York in 1837, had, after early opposition to an independent nomination, supported Birney's candidacy even though not in full agreement with him. Although Birney argued that the federal government must abolish slavery everywhere, Bailey shared the position which Chase had since assumed: the need for a complete divorce of the federal government from any responsibility for slavery. He felt that there was no constitutional power to abolish slavery where it already existed.[9] Morris, who had been rejected for reelection to the United States Senate by the Ohio Democratic caucus in 1838, had stepped up his antislavery attacks to the point that he was unwelcome in his old party. Other than Bailey's editorials in support of Birney late in the campaign, and small Liberty meetings in Cincinnati, and in the Western Reserve, there had been no organized statewide third-party effort in 1840. As Chase explained later, "It was more a moral and religious movement. . . . There was no regular political organization." Birney, in fact, received only 903 votes in Ohio out of nearly 275,000 cast.[10]

After the presidential election, state and local antislavery societies became the vehicles for forming a permanent third party, which Chase would join before the end of 1841. A small convention in

January of that year led by Bailey and Morris recommended independent nominations in future state elections instead of the old policy of merely questioning Whigs and Democrats on slave-related issues and voting for the least objectionable candidate or abstaining if neither was acceptable. This recommendation established the Liberty party in Ohio, although supporters were few and potential party leaders still clung to the two-party system. Chase sought reelection to the city council in April 1841 as a Whig but along with many other incumbents was swept out of office by Democrats. His attendance at a Hamilton County Liberty meeting in May was the first sign of personal change. By request, he briefly addressed the meeting of some three hundred.[11]

Chase's hesitancy was still evident during the summer, for, although he appeared ready to leave the Whigs for the third party, he sought the influence which went with a major party. In a final effort to remain a Whig and persuade the party to his beliefs, he sought the party's nomination for state senator. The Whigs of Hamilton County overwhelmingly rejected him at their August convention because of his antislavery position, notifying him that "there was no place in the Whig party for him or his principles." No further reason existed to resist Bailey's appeal to join the third party.[12]

Chase became so discouraged with the prospects for change within the existing two-party system that the Liberty party, despite its weakness and lack of popular appeal, became for him the only option. In noting the emotionally charged atmosphere in Cincinnati which had produced three disturbances against abolitionists and blacks in the past five years, Chase reflected that there was still a surprising "amount of genuine antislavery feelings." Although party leaders denounced the third-party appeal, he had become persuaded that "no mode will be so effectual in bringing the whole question of slavery before the people as Antislavery political action." Rather than a world dominated by greedy Jacksonians and self-righteous Whigs, he now saw one of struggle and oppression. He admitted that the Liberty movement would be unpopular in the beginning. But "it will go on and gain friends constantly."[13]

Chase was firm in his belief that Birney was wrong in his advocacy of immediate abolition by federal action. In Chase's view slavery could be sanctioned exclusively by state law and, where legal, could not be abolished by the central government. The national govern-

ment must quarantine itself "from all connection with and all responsibility for slavery." Such a separation must include abolition in
the nation's capital, repeal of the fugitive slave law, and confinement
of slavery to the existing slave states. That last point became increasingly central to his philosophy later in the 1840s, for with the acquisition of Texas and the Mexican War territories, the problem of the
extension of slavery became more critical. This separation, in
Chase's view, should be the antislavery party's goal. Having reached
this conclusion by the fall of 1841, he was ready to share the leadership which had heretofore been borne by Bailey and Morris in the
nascent Liberty organization. He had finally "become satisfied of the
necessity of political organization" and agreed with Bailey to call a
convention of "the Friends of Constitutional Liberty" to meet in
Columbus in December 1841.[14]

Chase played an enthusiastic and prominent role in this first official statewide Liberty party convention in Ohio and in the campaign
for governor which followed in 1842. In his address, which the two
hundred delegates unanimously adopted as their platform, he presented a political program similar to what Bailey had been
advocating—the divorce of the federal government from slavery. The
meeting represented a small beginning to what Chase confidently
believed would grow into a significant political movement: "In a
little while multitudes will come out of their hiding places and join
the advancing host of Liberty."[15]

Recognizing the seemingly insurmountable odds against a tiny
third party, Chase began a concerted effort to convince antislavery
leaders within Whig and Democratic ranks to join the movement.
He concentrated his greatest efforts on Joshua R. Giddings, Whig
congressman from Ohio's Western Reserve. Giddings had played a
prominent role in the House of Representatives opposing the proposed annexation of Texas. He had also joined with John Quincy
Adams to overcome the House's gag rule, which prevented debate on
antislavery petitions. To persuade Giddings to leave his secure Whig
position to join the new party would be a major accomplishment and
might bring others to the party as well. Thus the Columbus meeting
had barely adjourned when Chase sought his support: "We all look
to you. You can give to the nomination we have made great prospects
of ultimate success, if you concur in it." He also tried to convince
the congressman that the Whig party was on the verge of breaking

up under President Tyler's leadership, arguing that "if we must be in a minority why not be in a minority of our own rather than in a minority of men who despise us." He professed total satisfaction with his own decision to bolt, for he believed "that the expedient and the right in this case are one." Chase, who had had little influence to sacrifice when he left the Whigs, recognized that such was not the case with Giddings.[16]

Giddings showed little interest in chancing his political future on the untried Liberty organization. Chase admitted that he did "not wonder at your hesitation," for "there are so many circumstances calculated to discourage the hope" of third-party success. Still the party did have a chance of winning a balance of power in the legislature and perhaps eventually in Congress, so Chase persisted. In the 1842 election the Liberty vote for governor was six times greater than Birney's Ohio vote had been two years earlier.[17] Should the party continue to grow at this pace, Chase confidently believed that Giddings and other antislavery Whigs would recognize the wisdom of his arguments.

Long before the 1842 campaign in Ohio, Chase had turned his attention to the presidential election of 1844. At the Liberty party's national convention in May 1841, eastern leaders had offered Birney and Thomas Morris the party's nomination for president and vice-president. This group, led by such idealists as William Goodell, Gerrit Smith, Joshua Leavitt, and Henry B. Stanton, agreed with Birney that direct abolition ought to be the party's goal and feared the inroads of those who agreed with Chase's call for separating slavery from the federal government. To prevent a watering down of their abolitionist beliefs, they had moved quickly to nominate Birney. Thus Chase faced a fait accompli when he joined the party in 1841. He nevertheless began a major effort to move the members toward his more moderate stance and to replace the colorless Birney with a more formidable candidate capable of bringing new support to the party. More especially he sought to persuade prominent antislavery Whigs who enjoyed wider appeal, such as John Quincy Adams and William H. Seward, to lead the third party.[18]

When Birney delayed accepting the Liberty nomination of May 1841 until the new year, Chase pursued more attractive candidates than Birney and Morris. The eastern Liberty faction naturally resisted his moves. Joshua Leavitt dismissed his proposal to call another nominating convention and refused to consider Chase's proposal to drop "abolitionist" from the party platform. Undaunted, Chase urged the Ohio Liberty convention of December 1841 to consider Seward and Adams as possible presidential candidates. The delegates also recommended that a national convention be held in Cleveland or Pittsburgh to fill "any vacancy which may occur in the nomination of president and vice president." The following month, Chase wrote to Birney noting that the delegates had indicated their "utmost confidence" in him, but expressing the hope that he would step aside as a candidate "to anyone whose name might be deemed more useful to the cause."[19]

Realizing the desire of Ohio Liberty leaders to find another candidate, Birney moved quickly to accept his party's nomination. In explaining his action to Chase, he questioned how any Liberty man could consider "going out of our ranks for candidates," or think Whigs or Democrats could "be abolitionists." Neither Seward nor Adams had endorsed abolitionism and the latter had shown a lack of devotion to the cause of "human rights."[20]

Undaunted, Chase stepped up his drive to find a more appealing candidate and to urge modification of the strong abolitionist plank. Adams and Seward remained his top choices because of the "great additional strength" that would accrue to the party. He reminded Lewis Tappan, one of his few eastern allies, that if the party insisted on Birney as its candidate "it will . . . become extinct." He admitted to Giddings that few would support someone "as little known as Mr. Birney and who has seen so little of public service." From his own experience in Cincinnati Chase knew that a strong abolitionist plank such as that adopted by the easterners would have little appeal in Ohio. It had been a mistake, he said, to insist on "absolute, unconditional and immediate emancipation throughout all the States." Since Congress had no power to abolish slavery, the Liberty party must not make such a doctrine a political question. "Let the Slaveholders keep, if they will, their slaves under their state laws, but let them know that slavery cannot be extended one inch beyond state limits."[21] Only with such a moderate antislavery position was there any hope of attracting Whigs or Democrats to the party and securing a more prominent candidate, he argued.

In the fall of 1842, Chase appealed directly to Adams as a man of "commanding talents, mature wisdom and ample attainments" whose nomination by the Liberty party would "produce a tremendous effect" throughout the country. When neither Adams nor Seward gave any encouragement, Chase, Lewis Tappan, and Bailey turned their attention to William Jay of New York, a prominent antislavery Whig and son of the first chief justice. Chase's hope was that both Birney and Morris would resign their nominations and leave it up to a national Liberty convention. Both factions had agreed to assemble in Buffalo in August 1843 to try to arouse antislavery support for the 1844 campaign. Bailey wrote to Birney bluntly urging him to let the convention decide on the nominees because "I have doubts as to your being the most eligible candidate." Despite their efforts, Chase, Tappan, and Bailey were frustrated when Jay indicated his continued Whig loyalties because he did not believe that "an abolition candidate could get one electoral vote." [22] After a full year of activity the Chase faction went to Buffalo without a candidate and prepared to acquiesce in the Birney nomination.

Despite their inability to find an alternative to Birney's candidacy, Chase and the Ohio delegation revealed their influence by easily persuading the delegates to accept their antislavery position. Chase drafted the platform resolutions, which omitted any endorsement of immediate abolition. Instead, the Chase philosophy was adopted calling for "the absolute and unqualified divorce of the General Government from Slavery," which was "strictly local" and whose "existence and continuance rest on no other support than State legislation and not on any authority of Congress." The platform also contained a strong denunciation of the Fugitive Slave Act of 1793. The convention adopted over Chase's opposition, a plank calling the fugitive slave clause of the Constitution "null and void." [23] He could not endorse an argument that implied resistance to law and he did his best to de-emphasize that part of the platform during the campaign. Chase could still claim victory on his basic antislavery position. The balance of power was clearly shifting in favor of the Chase faction.

Chase also included in the platform a specific welcome to "our colored fellow citizens to fraternity with us" and a call for "the restoration of equality of rights, among men, in every State where the party exists." The platform thus gave indirect support to black suffrage, a concept which most Liberty men were ready to endorse. One of the reasons Chase had desired that Morris be removed from the ticket was the candidate's reservations on that issue—reservations which were softened during the campaign due to pressure from party members.[24] Thus the concern Chase had shown for Cincinnati's black population was revealed again in his plea in behalf of all northern blacks in the platform. His was a strong enough commitment to run the risk of alienating some voters.

Chase's goal of selecting candidates with a broader appeal in order to unite antislavery voters of all parties remained unattainable for 1844. As he explained to Tappan, "We must make the best of it." Birney, he said, was an honest and good man, devoted to the cause and clearly preferable to any candidates the Whigs or Democrats might nominate.[25] Chase and other Ohio Liberty leaders traveled throughout the state to campaign loyally and enthusiastically for the Liberty ticket in the fall; yet they were not surprised when the party received less than 3 percent of the vote in Ohio, a percentage roughly comparable to that of other nonslave states. The results only confirmed their belief that a more prominent candidate was necessary, and they were now more determined than ever to achieve a broader coalition of antislavery support from all parties. Bailey pointed out that Birney "has no personal claim upon our future support," and Chase began to talk of changing the party name to True Democrat as a way to bolster support.[26] Chase soon began planning for a mass convention to meet in Cincinnati in June 1845 as a first step in creating sentiment for a broader antislavery movement.

Chase and Samuel Lewis were the most prominent Ohioans on the arrangements committee which issued the call for the Southern and Western Liberty Convention. Their hope was to include anyone willing "to use all constitutional means to effect the extinction of slavery," whether Whig or Democrat. Despite the large and enthusiastic attendance of two thousand, including Birney, few outsiders participated. Typical was the response of William H. Seward who failed to attend because of personal duties.[27] Chase was eager to avoid any mention of candidates for 1848 at the Cincinnati convention, and, following his urging, a resolution was adopted to defer Liberty nominations until at least 1847.[28]

It was Chase rather than Birney who played the key role at the convention. The idea for the meeting had been his and his increasing influence meant that his views prevailed. Although by no means in total control of the Liberty movement in Ohio, which remained highly diverse and decentralized, Chase had clearly become the most influential figure by 1845. He was chosen chairman of the committee which prepared the address to publicize the delegates' position. Drafting such statements was becoming a familiar role for Chase, and others in the movement were growing accustomed to depending on him to express their views, summarize their thinking, and appeal to potential voters. Platform writing also became an invaluable tool for increasing Chase's influence and winning supporters to his own philosophy.

The address of the Southern and Western Liberty Convention reflected Chase's and the coalitionists' views of the Constitution and slavery and their hopes for a more broadly based movement. It argued that the Constitution was, in effect, an antislavery document. Although it recognized that the national government was not authorized "to act upon the slavery already existing in the States" and that certain clauses in the Constitution referred to slaves, Chase's address argued that nowhere did the Constitution refer to slavery as "a national institution, to be upheld by national law. On the contrary, every clause which ever has been or can be construed as referring to slavery, treats it as the creature of State law and dependent wholly upon State law for its existence and continuance." Because the Constitution had been violated repeatedly, the government must be rescued "from the control of slaveholders." That rescue must include a prohibition on slaveholding in the District of Columbia, in federal territories, and in all other places "of exclusive national jurisdiction." Nor could the federal government be permitted to assist in the recapture of fugitives.[29] Surprisingly, the platform omitted mention of rights for northern blacks, despite the advanced ground that the Liberty party had taken in its 1844 platform. Perhaps Chase, in his desire for a coalition with the more moderate antislavery Whigs and Democrats, feared antagonizing potential supporters and decided not to call attention to a divisive issue. Such political expediency occasionally tempered his antislavery idealism.

Chase was unsuccessful in getting all he hoped for to encourage a more broadly based coalition. Here Birney and others moderated what they considered to be too open an overture for Democratic coalition and the committee removed those parts thought objectionable. Thus the address recognized that the delegates could not support any party which rejected their position on slavery. Chase's efforts to include in the platform along with the Liberty party name the phrase "or as we prefer to style it the True Democracy of the United States" was rejected by the convention whose members did not share his desire to appeal more directly to the Democrats. In the meantime, the Liberty party remained the only vehicle by which to oppose slavery effectively; and all antislavery Whigs and Democrats were urged to give their support to it, because "the Liberty party of 1845 is in truth the Liberty party of 1776 revived."[30]

Chase reflected the thinking of many antislavery men who still hoped that southerners might recognize the immorality of slavery. He and Bailey had invited slave state residents, several of whom were present from Kentucky and Virginia. He had deliberately called the meeting the Southern and Western Liberty Convention and was constantly on guard against those who would transform hostility against slavery into hatred of the slaveholder himself. The address included a carefully worded overture to both nonslaveholders and slaveholders of the South. To the latter, he appealed to conscience, "for you know that the system of slaveholding is wrong." Promising no outside interference with slavery, he urged southerners to remove it "from each State by State authority."[31]

One of the chief obstacles to Chase's desired coalition was removed in August 1845 when Birney suffered a paralytic stroke following a fall from a horse. Although he gradually recovered, he could never again make a speech and thus never again be a presidential candidate. Birney did remain active behind the scenes and strong in his opposition to Chase's hopes for a coalition.[32] Although Chase no longer had to fear a Birney candidacy, Birney's strong resistance to his own plans for the Liberty party continued. The accident seemed to have as great an impact on Chase as the death of his second wife, Eliza, did the following month. By 1845, he was so totally absorbed in his struggle to dominate the Liberty party that he had relegated his personal life to a totally separate sphere. The devastation he had felt ten years earlier at Catherine's death had almost drained him of his capacity to grieve further over personal tragedy. Only by subordinating his family concerns to his public career could he endure his private losses. The struggle over slavery had become his overriding priority.

Chase and the coalitionists found that the issue of the annexation of Texas and the accompanying threat of war with Mexico increased the likelihood of cooperation with antislavery members of other parties. The Liberty convention which nominated Birney in 1843 had met before the annexation dispute resulted in the proposed treaty with Texas in 1844 and the joint resolution of annexation the following year. The platform had thus been silent on the issue, although Liberty voters clearly were opposed to annexation if slavery were sanctioned there. In 1844, Chase, Bailey, and Lewis led the Ohio Liberty party to pronounce annexation of Texas acceptable only if slavery were abolished. In his address to the Southern and Western Liberty Convention of June 1845, Chase deplored the passage of the joint resolution of annexation and invited those opposed to the extension of slavery into any territory to join the Liberty party in its opposition.[33]

The war against Mexico was a more complex issue for Liberty party members, most of whom agreed with Chase that "the question of slavery seemed paramount . . . to the question of the war." Chase was opposed to Texas's claim to the Rio Grande border as a "bold pretension" by which the slaveholders "extended their own dominion." Neither the national nor the Ohio Liberty conventions of 1847 opposed the war except to challenge the addition of any slave territory resulting from it. In general, Liberty men were too expansionist-minded to oppose accession of new territories, but also quite eager to capitalize on the slave-territory issue. In August 1846, when David Wilmot, antislavery Democrat from Pennsylvania, introduced his proviso banning slavery in any territory acquired from Mexico, Chase quickly recognized the potential importance of the concept to his hopes of bringing antislavery elements of all parties together. He told Gerrit Smith that with the proviso, "we will be soon ready for an aggressive movement in mass."[34]

In his advocacy of the Wilmot Proviso as a means of uniting the opponents of slavery, Chase had to ignore the racist implications of the amendment as advocated by northern Democrats. They typically wanted slavery kept out of the territories to protect the land for free white settlers only. Wilmot himself indicated his disdain for blacks by explaining that the proviso's purpose was to "preserve for free white labor a fair country." He suggested that the phrase "white man's Proviso" was an accurate description of the measure, for it should exclude not only slaves but free blacks as well. At this point, Chase preferred to overlook racist views he could not endorse. Later as a United States senator he would strenuously resist all efforts to exclude blacks from eligibility for land in federal territories. He clearly agreed with Bailey in his attacks on the "expediency and appeal to race" of many northern Democrats.[35] Yet he said nothing publicly at this time which might jeopardize a coalition.

For a time Chase urged the establishment of a new antislavery league which could transcend party lines. Made up of all opponents of slavery regardless of party affiliation, such an organization would "in the best manner and in the shortest time accomplish the work of overthrowing slavery." He told Giddings that since both Whig and Democratic parties included southerners and would allow "no anti-slavery article into their creed," they could not be relied on for "inflexible and uncompromising hostilities to slavery." He thus began sounding out such influential antislavery leaders as Giddings and Senator John P. Hale of New Hampshire who might back or even "issue a call for a national convention to form a national anti-slavery league." Chase also gave his support to the efforts to establish a national antislavery newspaper in Washington under Bailey's editorship. The *National Era,* with strong financial backing from Lewis Tappan, began publication in January 1847 and soon had a circulation of eleven thousand. Important to Chase was Bailey's use of his press to advocate a new antislavery organization—such as his league—to pursue the coalition concept.[36]

When few others expressed interest in a league, Chase sought a prominent Whig or Democrat to accept a Liberty nomination for 1848 instead. Such a nomination might facilitate a broader coalition and avoid sacrificing his own and his party's antislavery principles. Among those whom Chase and others sought as potential candidates were one Democrat and three Whigs. With his hope of redirecting the Democratic party toward a containment-of-slavery position, he first considered former Governor Silas Wright of New York. As an advocate of the Wilmot Proviso and a member of the Van Buren wing of the Democratic party, Wright's appeal would be such that Liberty members would "give him their cordial support."[37] Wright's death in August 1847 meant that Chase would have to look elsewhere.

When on February 11, 1847, Thomas Corwin, senator from Ohio, delivered his memorable speech denouncing the Mexican War and emphasizing what he felt were President Polk's unconstitutional actions in initiating the war on Mexican soil, antislavery Whigs and

Liberty coalitionists alike assumed they had found a potential candidate for the presidency. They soon realized, however, that they had misread his views. In September the senator attacked the Liberty party for its failure to aid Clay in 1844 and further alienated coalitionists by rejecting their insistence on keeping slavery out of the territories. Chase noted with disappointment that Corwin's September speech had "pleased the proslavery people, hereabouts, more than his censure of the war offended them." Corwin could be dropped from the list of potential antislavery candidates unless "he comes to a better mind" on the proviso.[38]

Chase and other Liberty members also sought to convince Supreme Court Justice John McLean to consider a third-party nomination, but the wily McLean refused to be pinned down on slave-related issues because he still hoped for a nomination from the Whig party. Chase had doubts about McLean's acceptability because of his recent ruling in the Van Zandt case and his vague stand on territorial slavery. With McLean remaining aloof, Chase considered other candidates, but the judge's name would surface again after the Whigs nominated Zachary Taylor. Another prominent Whig whom Chase sought as a Liberty candidate was William H. Seward. The New Yorker had earlier resisted Chase's overtures to consider the 1844 Liberty nomination and immediately after Clay's defeat continued to insist that there was "no real cause to distrust the resolve of freedom of the Whig party." Chase refused to give up the idea, however, and in early 1847 described Seward "as one of the very first public men of our country."[39] With the Whig party unwilling to recognize Seward's ability, Chase turned his attention to the candidacy of John P. Hale.

Hale was a former Democratic congressman from New Hampshire who had bolted the party in 1845 over slave-related issues and had won election to the United States Senate the following winter with the support of a broad antislavery coalition. Because no prominent Democrat or Whig seemed interested in a Liberty nomination, support for Hale gained momentum. Although he was not officially associated with the Liberty party, his presence in the Senate gave him the stature lacked by all the Liberty leaders. Hale was not at first receptive to being chosen, but in July 1847, he met with Liberty leaders in Boston and concluded that "if all his friends wished him to accept the nomination and it were tendered to him, he would accept it."[40] Accordingly, the movement among Liberty members to draft Hale grew quickly as they looked forward to an October nominating convention.

Chase's response was somewhat mixed; he recognized that Hale's appeal would be strong among antislavery Democrats and Whigs, but he very much hoped to delay any nomination until the following spring. He told Sumner that "with the developments of the winter recommending it we could form a powerful party of Independents in the Spring." Chase, in fact, worked to have the convention postponed, but the Liberty party's National Central Committee, dominated by the eastern faction, voted eight to three to set the October date. The committee's majority hoped that an early convention would preclude the coalition Chase sought.[41]

Before the Liberty delegates assembled in Buffalo, a movement had developed to give Chase the nomination for vice president on a Hale ticket. Apparently Chase never seriously considered accepting such a nomination despite the efforts of Tappan and Henry B. Stanton to persuade him. Others closer to Chase urged him not to consider it, for, as Bailey advised, it would impair "your ability for future usefulness." Chase agreed, in part because of his opposition to any nominations in the fall of 1847. He knew also that by declining his own nomination he might work more effectively to promote the broad coalition he hoped would develop in 1848. Further, he accepted Bailey's reasoning that a nomination at this early stage would not help to forward his own career. He explained that "a more available man" should be found because "I am comparatively young and unknown and my services to the cause have been slight in comparison with many others."[42] He thus determined to work at the October Liberty convention to delay nominations until northern sentiment for an inclusive antislavery coalition could be developed.

The Liberty party convention in Buffalo in October brought mixed results for Chase. On hand was the eastern faction, now calling itself the Liberty League and including Birney among its leaders. It had met earlier and had nominated the wealthy New York philanthropist Gerrit Smith on a platform arguing that the Constitution made slavery illegal everywhere. The Liberty Leaguers attempted at Buffalo to get their position and candidate approved; in both instances Chase was instrumental in blocking their plans. Rather than labeling slavery unconstitutional everywhere, the platform called for abolition in the District of Columbia, the repeal of the Fugitive Slave Act of 1793, opposition to "the introduction of slavery in any territory," and support for the laws designed "to withdraw the support of the government from slavery." The platform also reflected Chase's concern for the rights of free blacks with the argument that state laws "designed to oppress and degrade particular classes of individuals are indefensible."[43] Chase played a major role in drafting the platform and could rejoice that it was so moderate in tone as to promote a later coalition; the adoption of the Liberty League's position would have had the reverse effect.

Having achieved his platform goals, Chase failed to get the nomination postponed until the following spring. Most of the delegates, caught up in the enthusiasm for Hale, could see no logic in delay. Undaunted by this setback, Chase added his significant influence to that of Stanton, Leavitt, and Tappan in urging Hale's nomination. Only the Liberty League opposed Hale, desiring a total abolitionist and someone who was not so recent a convert to the cause. Their candidate, Gerrit Smith, was swamped by Hale in the delegate vote of 103 to 44.[44] Chase could thus rate the convention an overall success. Unable to postpone the nomination, he nonetheless secured a platform and a candidate that fit perfectly into his strategy.

Much to Chase's liking, Hale responded hesitantly to his nomination, waiting two months before writing a reluctant and provisional acceptance. Chase predicted that Hale would "not stand in the way" as a candidate if a broader anti-extension coalition could be formed. In fact, Chase developed so much influence over Hale that the candidate said he would gladly step aside and "enroll myself among the humblest privates" in a new movement.[45] Chase appeared completely triumphant; his party had both a candidate and a platform that would respond readily to subsequent coalition efforts.

Events in New York and Massachusetts added to Chase's optimism during the fall of 1847. In New York, the Van Buren or Barnburner faction of the Democratic party reacted to its loss of control of the state organization and the rejection of their Wilmot Proviso plank by the rival Hunker faction by pledging their support of the proviso and their refusal to support any Democratic nominee for president who did not agree. In Massachusetts, Van Buren Democrats led by Marcus Morton also found efforts to have their party endorse the proviso blocked at the state convention.[46]

The frustration of these anti-extensionists added to the unrest among other northern Democrats as the time for nominations for the 1848 election approached.

Whigs in Massachusetts were even more divided and gave Chase further cause for hope. Young politicians, calling themselves Conscience Whigs and led by Charles Francis Adams, Charles Sumner, and Henry Wilson, were at odds with the older leaders, labeled the Cotton Whigs, who represented Boston textile manufacturers. Like their Democratic counterparts, the Conscience men lost in their efforts to win a state party endorsement of the Wilmot Proviso in the fall of 1847. As a result, Sumner told Chase, many felt that they had attended their last political meeting as Whigs. Chase, although optimistic over these events, remained cautious, reminding Sumner that "the friends of freedom may be tricked out of the fruits of their labors" by politicians attempting to keep "both parties together upon their old platforms."[47] To prevent this, Chase planned to press ahead with his own efforts to bring antislavery men together from all three parties.

With the New York Democratic factionalism in mind, Chase attended the Ohio Democratic party's convention in Columbus in January 1848. When the convention rejected the antislavery plank and endorsed Lewis Cass for president, Chase took solace in the hope that some individual Ohio Democrats, disgusted with the Polk administration, would follow the Barnburner lead in rejecting their party's position. He believed even more strongly that if, as expected, the national Democratic and Whig conventions refused to endorse the proviso and chose compromise candidates, "a National Convention of the opponents of Slavery encroachment" must be called. At such a meeting, said Chase, the result would be "to merge the Liberty Party in an independent movement" with its own nominees.[48]

In early 1848, the candidate that Chase hoped to see replace Hale was Judge John McLean, "the most reliable man, on the slavery question, now prominent in either party." McLean, still hoping for a Whig nomination, refused an outright endorsement of the Wilmot Proviso despite Chase's urging that he take a stronger antislavery stand, but Chase remained optimistic. He told Sumner, "if the Whigs will not nominate him all will be well. He is emphatically right on the Free Territory Question, nearer right than any so prominent man of the old parties." Eastern Liberty leaders, including

Leavitt and Stanton, warned Chase against being seduced into supporting such men as McLean on "quasi antislavery grounds."[49]

Undaunted, Chase proceeded with his plans for an antislavery coalition based on the Wilmot Proviso. He recognized that the proviso provided a common ground on which Liberty moderates could join with nonabolitionists of the regular parties, and he endorsed Giddings's advice to "say nothing about abolition." In May, Chase announced plans for an Ohio Free Territory convention to be held in Columbus on June 21, shortly after the Democratic and Whig presidential nominating conventions had met. The meeting would be in conjunction with similar meetings led by Barnburners in New York and Conscience Whigs in Massachusetts. Anticipating the probable results of the national conventions, Chase planned the Ohio meeting to protest their nominations and platforms. Overlooking no detail, he carefully arranged the mass Free Territory convention to coincide with the Ohio Liberty gathering. Thus the Liberty men and antislavery people of the major parties would mingle and form a "spontaneous" alliance—a useful step toward the broader coalition he sought.[50]

Chase's skillfully planned strategy worked exactly as he desired. Hopeful that the Liberty party had served its usefulness, he was nonetheless careful not to offend those members whose support would be vital in a larger coalition. He secured a resolution that the Liberty members would cooperate with a forthcoming coalition convention then being planned for Buffalo. Over a thousand delegates attended the Free Territory convention. With Giddings attending the Conscience Whig gathering in Worcester, Massachusetts, Chase had no formidable rival for leadership of the Ohio coalition movement. He drafted the convention's address, which restated his now familiar position calling for the divorce of the federal government from slavery with new emphasis on the Wilmot Proviso. The address praised the "honest and independent" conduct of the Barnburners in New York and expressed full confidence in Judge McLean. It repudiated the recent nominations of Cass and Zachary Taylor and concluded by recommending a Free-Soil convention to meet in Buffalo in August. Before adjourning, the two meetings symbolically combined and the groups agreed to merge. Not surprisingly, the platform and address adopted later at the Buffalo meeting would be strikingly similar to that of the Columbus conclave, for Chase was the author of both.[51]

The following day, June 22, the Barnburner convention met in Utica to protest the Cass nomination, and the repudiation of the Wilmot Proviso. Several days later a Conscience Whig gathering in Worcester did the same for the Taylor nomination and platform. Both endorsed and made plans to send delegates to the national third-party gathering at Buffalo. Chase had carefully coordinated plans for the Buffalo convention with Barnburner and Conscience Whig leaders before the state gatherings. Although Liberty purists feared and protested against a desertion of their principles and candidates, their voices were lost in the excitement and clamor for a broader movement based on the Wilmot Proviso. Still to be decided were the difficult questions of candidates and the exact wording of a coalition platform, but by the end of June, Chase could relate enthusiastically to Sumner that everything was ready for a union of those dedicated to "Freedom, Free Territories and Free Labor."[52]

4

Free-Soil Politico

I n the summer of 1848, Chase helped bring to fruition an antislavery political coalition, although many obstacles still impeded
the kind of union he desired. Most serious was the selection of a
candidate to lead the new third-party ticket. The Ohio and Massachusetts June conventions had deliberately avoided nominations, but
the Barnburners at their Utica meeting had chosen Martin Van
Buren and insisted on his candidacy as a requirement for their participation in the coalition movement. Chase knew that Van Buren's
extreme partisanship as a Democratic leader and his highly questionable record on slave related issues made him an undesirable candidate for Conscience Whigs and Liberty men. Chase found him
acceptable because of his vote-getting ability and his own Democratic leanings; but more typical was Liberty editor Austin Willey's
view of Van Buren as "an old politician of the most servile stamp."
At sixty-five Van Buren was sincere in his desire to remain in retirement rather than lead a movement with so little chance of success,
but the young Barnburners would accept no substitute.[1] Chase realized that reconciling these differences would be difficult.

An easier task for Chase was to persuade John P. Hale to withdraw
as the Liberty candidate and let the Buffalo convention make the
final choice. Hale had quickly agreed to accept the decision of the
Buffalo meeting, noting that if a "union of all the opponents of
slavery" could be formed he was "not only ready but anxious to
withdraw." On July 13, Bailey's *National Era* reported publicly what

Chase and Hale had already concluded in private. Liberty men, such as Lewis Tappan, might urge Hale to hold firm as a candidate and not give in to "expediency," but there was little the Liberty national committee could do.[2] Chase could only hope that if Van Buren were chosen at Buffalo, most Liberty men would support him.

An equally difficult task for Chase was to attract Conscience Whigs to a party headed by the former president. Although they were not enthusiastic about Hale, most would have preferred him to the Jacksonian stalwart. They actually hoped John McLean would be chosen, a preference reinforced by the Whig nomination of Zachary Taylor. Chase believed that the judge would not "accept an Independent Nomination, having suffered his name to go before the Whig Convention." At the same time Chase realized that Giddings and Sumner were increasingly willing to accept Van Buren. New York Liberty leader Henry B. Stanton suggested to Chase that "if Judge McLean would consent to run on the ticket with Mr. Van Buren now," the Barnburners would support him for president in 1852.[3]

By late June, Chase had concluded that a Van Buren nomination would have the greatest appeal and was essential for Barnburner participation. He hoped to persuade McLean to seek the presidential nomination and yet be prepared to accept second place on the ticket. He explained to the judge that because of the Barnburner nomination at Utica it was better "for the cause and for yourself that you should be nominated for the Vice-Presidency with Mr. Van Buren." McLean responded that he would not "assent to be placed on the ticket with Mr. Van Buren." The judge noted further, "I am ready to make any sacrifice, which does not involve principle." Generally given to political expediency McLean could not bring himself to accept second place on a ticket headed by his old nemesis. Chase thus had to try to reconcile the conflicting claims of the supporters of Hale, Van Buren, and McLean and hope for a ticket that would conciliate if not please everyone. Convinced that Van Buren was the best choice, he optimistically told his wife that "the day of the deliverance of our country from the thralldom of the slave power is advancing nigh."[4] Chase's Democratic leanings and hopes for a coalition with the Democrats help explain why he sought a Van Buren nomination. In addition, his affection for candidates with national reputations and vote-getting potential made the former president the most attractive of those available.

The Buffalo convention brought to a close the eight-year history of the Liberty party and gave birth to the Free-Soil party. For Chase it marked the culmination of many months of effort to bring together a broad coalition of antislavery advocates. A camp-meeting atmosphere surrounded the twenty thousand assembled in a huge tent at a city park on August 9. Along with the enthusiasm and lofty idealism of many participants were spokesmen for each of the three major factions. Charles Francis Adams reminisced years later that no convention ever surpassed this one "for plain downright honesty of purpose to effect high ends without a whisper of bargain and sale."[5] Yet political maneuvering and bargaining contributed to the outcome. Chase, along with several Barnburner leaders, engineered the platform and candidates that all elements could accept.

The major decisions were made by the more than four hundred delegates who met privately at the Universalist church, while the mass meeting, presided over by Adams, listened to impassioned speeches in the park. The night before the delegates met, a much smaller group of Liberty and Barnburner leaders agreed on a compromise. Chase, Leavitt, and Stanton arranged to have Preston King, a leading Barnburner with whom they agreed on platform issues, propose a series of strong antislavery resolutions which they knew Liberty delegates would find acceptable. For his part, Chase promised Liberty assistance in nominating Van Buren in return for Barnburner support of the King proposals. Chase later explained his strategy as chairman of the delegates' meeting: "Knowing Mr. Preston King's sentiment I took the liberty of calling upon him for a speech, and at its conclusion moved that . . . his speech should be considered as the platform recommended by the meeting." Chase's motion was approved unanimously. During this private meeting Chase was at his best, using his considerable influence and forcefulness in debate to win the support of skeptical delegates. Not especially effective as an orator, he was persuasive with smaller groups of his fellow politicians. Here his suggestions for strategy were consistently sound, and his ability to compromise so that opposing factions could reach a consensus appeared logical and statesmanlike. As he explained later, his motion "seemed to allay all jealousies on the part of the New York Democrats."[6]

Chase more than most appeared willing to recognize the need for reconciliation among the delegates. They accepted the proposal of

Van Buren supporter Benjamin F. Butler that nominations made at earlier conventions should not be binding. That decision gave the appearance of an open convention. With Chase, Leavitt, and Stanton willing to persuade Liberty delegates to support Van Buren, Barnburner leaders knew that there was little danger Hale or McLean would be chosen.[7]

Before the delegates selected their candidates, a committee on resolutions headed by Butler submitted the platform. Chase took most of the responsibility for drafting it, using his own and King's ideas. Together they prepared a series of planks designed to appeal to every possible faction except the abolitionists. Included were proposals dealing with internal improvements, tariffs, and land policy. On slave-related issues Chase designed the planks largely to satisfy Liberty men. The platform endorsed the Wilmot Proviso and referred to the Northwest Ordinance of 1787 to prove that it was national policy *"not to extend, nationalize or encourage,* but to limit, localize and discourage Slavery." Equally important, the platform called for abolition in the District of Columbia with the Chase doctrine that "it is the duty of the Federal Government to relieve itself from all responsibility for the existence of slavery wherever that government possesses constitutional power to legislate on that subject."[8] Advisably, Chase omitted mention of the fugitive slave issue. Nor did he include a demand for equal rights for blacks in the North, recognizing that Barnburner sensitivity and party unity dictated silence on both issues. He thus permitted the Free-Soilers to become the first antislavery party which evaded the divisive issue of black equality. Surprisingly, Liberty men did not argue these points; most, in fact, were highly satisfied with the finished product.[9] As the chief architect of the platform, Chase realized that any other approach would alienate many more voters than it would please.

In the choice of candidates Chase again played a dominant and controversial role. The first man mentioned was Judge McLean, and immediately Chase withdrew his name. It was charged later that he had acted without the judge's authorization, but a week before the convention McLean had told Chase, "I ought not to be brought before the convention as a candidate for the presidency." Chase later wrote McLean that he could have been nominated had he permitted it, but "your views on this subject" had been "so decidedly stated" that Chase was compelled to act as instructed. Chase and McLean knew that no such nomination was possible, and, given the judge's vacillation before the convention and Chase's prior commitment to Van Buren, Chase probably acted in good faith when he removed McLean's name.[10]

With the judge no longer a factor, Chase's bargain with the Barnburners was quickly completed. Most delegates assumed that nothing had been prearranged, but enough Liberty men had responded to Chase's earlier urging to back Van Buren that his victory was assured. On an informal ballot Van Buren received 244 votes to Hale's 183, with a scattering for Giddings and Adams. Many Conscience Whigs also supported Van Buren because, as Adams explained, with McLean out of the running, "There was no alternative." Stanton summed up the Chase faction's thinking when he later rationalized to Hale that his defeat had been accepted to achieve "a thorough Liberty platform." When the vote was announced, Leavitt conceded Hale's defeat and moved that the convention make Van Buren's nomination unanimous. In a voice choked with emotion, Leavitt said, "The Liberty party is not dead, but translated." Samuel Lewis seconded the motion and it was carried amid great uproar.[11] With only a few insiders aware of what had happened behind the scenes, Salmon Chase and his allies had engineered a significant victory for coalition politics.

The arrangement was completed with the nomination of a Conscience Whig for vice president. Again Chase played a decisive role and perhaps might have received the nomination himself had he sought it. Most understood that a westerner would be chosen, but when Ohio delegates proposed Charles Francis Adams he was quickly nominated by acclamation. Chase later explained why he had not pressed his own claims: "I had been extremely active in getting up this Convention and I was unwilling to have it said that I was influenced by personal considerations." He added with false modesty that his "name was too little known to be properly placed on the same ticket with one distinguished as that of Mr. Van Buren."[12] His reluctance to seek a nomination may also have been predicated on the belief that the party had little chance of victory and that a place on the ticket would do little to advance his career. He also realized the desire of many to pay tribute to the memory of John Quincy Adams and understood the political wisdom of adding a Conscience Whig with the politically powerful name of Adams to the ticket.

When the mass meeting was told of the Van Buren–Adams nominations, pandemonium erupted. As cheer followed cheer, the throng shouted its support for "Van Buren and Free Soil." [13] The idealism of the Liberty party was very much present in the new Free-Soil party, although Chase and others had provided the necessary compromise and political accommodation to give the movement a broader appeal. He believed the new party would present a more meaningful political challenge to the slave interests which dominated the two-party system.

Chase campaigned actively after the Buffalo convention and sought to convince the voters of Ohio that Van Buren was a sincere opponent of slavery. His task was made more difficult by the candidate's continued evasiveness. Shortly after the convention Chase urged Van Buren to endorse the platform, reminding him that many were suggesting that he "will not plant himself upon it." Chase expressed special concern over Van Buren's reluctance to endorse abolition in the District of Columbia. Nonetheless, following a campaign swing through the Western Reserve, Chase optimistically told the candidate that Whigs and Liberty men there were rallying to his support and that he would carry the area by thirteen thousand votes. Because his own speeches were well attended and enthusiastically received, Chase confidently arranged a week's campaign trip through Ohio for Van Buren's son John. [14]

Late in August, John P. Hale, true to his pledge, officially withdrew as the Liberty candidate and urged his followers to a "hearty, energetic and unanimous support of Messrs. Van Buren and Adams." [15] Having firmly committed themselves to Van Buren, Chase, Bailey, and Hale were eager to convince others that the Buffalo delegates had chosen wisely. The three had left their Liberty colleagues little choice in accepting a Van Buren nomination in return for a watered-down Liberty platform. Chase, Bailey, and Hale clearly believed in the value of coalition politics for the antislavery cause, although many in the Liberty movement questioned the wisdom of their approach.

Despite the efforts of Chase and others, the new party had too many obstacles to overcome to make a truly impressive showing in the elections of 1848. Voters remained unconvinced that Van Buren and the Barnburners were sincere in their newly acquired antislavery stance. Northern Whig and Democratic leaders convinced many of their partisans that the containment of slavery was possible with Taylor or Cass as president. Many, especially politicians who feared the loss of position, were unwilling to take a chance with a new and untried party. With less than three months to organize, the new party could not compete with the better-established and better-financed political machinery of the Democrats and Whigs. The *National Era* might claim that northerners were turning to the cause by the thousands, but few of the more realistic shared this view. Surely Chase was disappointed but probably not surprised when Van Buren won only 35,354 votes in Ohio, just 10 percent of the total and a proportion only slightly higher than his support in the national vote. Eight northern states gave the Free-Soil ticket a higher percentage of the vote than Ohio did. As Chase explained to Sumner, "Here in Ohio we did not do near so well as we expected—not near so well as we should have done had the vote been taken immediately after the Buffalo convention."[16]

Chase had thrown himself wholeheartedly into the campaign of 1848 and could rightly claim much of the credit for the party's limited success. Not surprisingly, he had continued to relegate his private life to a totally subordinate place as he had done ever since the death of his first wife in 1835. Although he had married for a third time in 1846, the death of three children and two wives had made for a private life of pain and tragedy. Consequently, he pursued his public career in the Free-Soil movement more vigorously than ever and found there the personal success and acclaim so lacking in the private sphere. At this point he might have run for public office either as the vice presidential nominee with Van Buren or as the third-party candidate for governor of Ohio. Clearly such nominations would have brought him little advantage in apparently hopeless campaigns, but he also realized that he lacked the personal appeal and rhetorical skill needed for public office. Hence, at this early stage in his career, he sought high station instead by operating as a manager and organizer, a behind-the-scenes "compromiser" who also turned his private tragedies into deep, uncompromising concerns for the oppressed.

Despite the party's disappointing showing in 1848 there was cause for optimism among Free-Soil leaders. They had elected twelve members to the House of Representatives, including Giddings and Joseph Root from Ohio's Western Reserve. Rather than nominating its own candidate for governor of Ohio—a nomination Chase could easily have secured for himself—the party had supported the Whig candidate, Seabury Ford, who won a narrow victory on a Wilmot Proviso platform. Ford, under heavy pressure from Chase and other Free-Soilers in return for third-party support, refused to endorse Taylor. Significant to Chase's own future, the Free-Soilers had won enough seats in the Ohio legislature to prevent either Democrats or Whigs from gaining a controlling majority. Because the election of a United States senator would be determined by the legislature, the third-party voice would likely be heard.[17] Chase recognized that if he could work out a coalition with a major party, he might become that senator.

Chase did not have to wait long before both the possible rewards and the problems of coalition politics became obvious. Soon after the election of 1848, the newly elected Ohio legislature faced a number of complex issues generating from the inability of either major party to gain an absolute majority. The election of a senator and the possible repeal of some or all of Ohio's discriminatory black laws were at stake. To influence either decision, the Free-Soilers would have to join with a major party, but the eleven third-party members in the legislature were sharply divided on the issue of coalition.[18] The larger faction, with its Western Reserve Whig background, favored joining the Whigs to elect Giddings to the Senate. The other faction supported a Chase election through cooperation with the Democrats. Revision of the black laws might be possible in either case; thus, the personal ambitions of the two candidates proved critical.

The situation was complicated by the fact that in early 1848 the Whigs had pushed through the legislature an apportionment bill designed to insure their control of subsequent legislatures. In an obvious gerrymander, they devised the law so as to divide Chase's Hamilton County into two districts to increase the chances of a Whig victory in this normally Democratic area. Democrats questioned the law's constitutionality and refused to honor it in the election of 1848. The result was that each newly created district sent two sets of representatives to Columbus.[19]

Because Free-Soilers held the balance of power, they could determine the outcome and elect either Giddings or Chase to the Senate. In the bargaining which followed, Giddings tried to maintain Free-Soil unity and independence and was much less willing to use the party to gain his own election than was his rival. Chase persuaded two Free-Soilers in the Ohio assembly—Norton Townshend, a former Liberty party colleague, and John F. Morse—to vote with the Democrats on the Hamilton County issue. Even though all of the other Free-Soilers favored the Whigs and would eventually vote with them, the support of Townshend and Morse assured the Democrats control of the legislature. If party lines held, Chase's election to the Senate was also assured.[20]

Chase's active participation in the bargaining exposed him to charges of personal ambition. Unlike Giddings, who remained in Washington with Congress in session and left his chances up to his friends in the legislature, Chase appeared in Columbus at strategic times and took advantage of his many Democratic contacts there. He did little to hide his ambition and, when he was away from Columbus, maintained an almost daily correspondence with supporters there. He claimed he was the logical choice because he understood "the history, principles and practical workings of the Free Soil movement as thoroughly as most men." In Columbus, he conferred with Townshend and Morse and urged their support, although he claimed he "would rather never be elected to any office whatever than that a single honest man should be injured by supporting me." Chase's Democratic leanings had been evolving for several years and by 1849 he believed that the best hope for the containment of slavery lay in Free-Soil union with the Democrats. The situation in the legislature gave him that opportunity. Whig critics charged that during the negotiations he favored the Democrats "to an almost dangerous extent." When the third party met in convention in Columbus in December 1848, Chase took control and wrote the platform which endorsed many Democratic positions on economic issues not related to slavery. This naturally pleased the Democrats and made them more willing to support him for senator.[21]

Throughout the drawn-out struggle in Columbus, Chase maintained a cordial, albeit slightly strained, correspondence with Giddings. The congressman would have mixed feelings about leaving the House where his influence was substantial, but, Giddings thought, "the moral effect of my election would be great."[22] Precisely because Giddings was already a member of Congress and would have to give up his seat to become a senator, Chase reasoned his own election was more logical. Otherwise, Chase would "insist on your being preferred to me." Although Chase claimed to be "no opponent" of Giddings, he believed that Whigs would want a "less ultra man," whereas Democrats could easily support himself.[23]

The idealistic Giddings could not easily understand the opportunistic Chase and thus reflected the dismay of many Free-Soilers over Chase's ambitions. Despite the greater logic of electing Chase, who had been Ohio's Free-Soil organizer, his actions and those of his supporters made him vulnerable to charges of political expediency. He professed to be interested only in free soil, hypocritically writing to Morse, "Everything, but sacrifice of principle for the cause, and nothing for men except as instruments of the cause." He would willingly "forego every hope of personal distinction if I could secure the adoption of the great principles of Right, Justice and Humanity." Yet to critics, Chase and his supporters had "abandoned the principles" of the Buffalo platform "for their own aggrandizement."[24] Whatever logic there might be in electing Chase was negated by the divisiveness it created.

Throughout the long bargaining in the legislature, Chase was preoccupied with his chances and alternated between despair and confidence. On February 19, he wrote to his wife, "More delay, more disappointment, foreshadowing I fear the final defeat of my hopes." A decision was finally reached in late February when, after two months of bitter debate and bargaining, the legislature elected Chase on the fourth ballot. Giddings, despite his own disappointment, admitted that the result "would probably promote the cause more than my own elevation." In congratulating the winner, he made it clear, however, that he did not intend to sanction Chase's Democratic leanings because he felt the party must maintain an independent direction.[25] It would not be so easy to calm the angry emotions of other Free-Soilers.

For their part in the coalition the Democrats were rewarded handsomely in those areas that most concerned them. The loss of the Senate seat was more than balanced in their eyes by the election of two Democratic judges to the state supreme court and the potential to control state economic policy in the months ahead. Chase showed his gratitude to his supporters by giving an elaborate victory banquet at the American Hotel. Democrats attended in large numbers and were reported "highly delighted" at both the celebration and the completed bargain.[26]

Whatever their divisions might be, the Free-Soilers of Democratic and Whig leanings could agree with Chase on the need to modify if not repeal the state's black laws. Ohio's discriminatory code was among the harshest in the North and even those third-party men with little interest in the rights of blacks would accept some change. Among the worst of the provisions was an 1807 law requiring blacks to post a five hundred dollar bond before entering the state as security against pauperism. Blacks could not testify against whites; they could not vote or hold public office. The common school system included no provision for black children. During the campaign of 1848, the Ohio Free-Soil platform, at Chase's urging, had called for the repeal of these laws. At the same time, it noted that the party opposed a large, permanent black population "for our state."[27]

Ohio's Free-Soilers did carry out their pledge in the 1849 legislative session, with Chase playing a leading role. He drafted the bill which Morse introduced in the assembly repealing many racist laws, although amendments in the senate weakened the bill so blacks were still denied the right to sit on juries or secure poorhouse relief. Under the new law blacks could enter Ohio without restriction, they could testify against whites, and they were to be provided separate schools.[28] They still could not vote or hold office; this and the denial of integrated schools showed that racism prevailed and that the Free-Soil commitment to equality was far from complete. Not only would many Democrats have balked at going any further, Free-Soilers themselves were not united on the desirability of total repeal. Chase nonetheless felt he had accomplished much, for "I could in no other way do so much good." Repeal, he claimed, was more important to him "than any political elevation whatever; and is worth more to us as a party than the election of any man to any office." Sincerely motivated by the plight of black children in Ohio who had been denied a public education, he was especially elated over the school bill. As his friend Edward S. Hamlin noted, repeal "will be an earthquake shock to the slavery propagandists in Washington City."[29]

Chase was not as unselfish in his support of the repeal of the black laws as he professed to be. He urged Hamlin to "get as many votes pledged to . . . the repeal of the Black laws as possible." But, he admitted, "I should dislike to make this vote on one question of right, contingent absolutely upon other men's votes on another question of right." The amended bills passed both houses with large majorities, although many Democrats agreed only because of party pressure to carry out the bargain. As the *Cleveland True Democrat* noted, Democrats had favored the bill, not because of principle but "by contract."[30] Free-Soil agitation had won significant reform, but only because of political maneuvering, not because of any change of heart by the white majority. Chase, nonetheless, had used the bargaining position of the third party successfully to open a drive for racial justice as well as for his personal ambition.

The bargain completed in the legislature in February 1849, brought Chase the immediate reward of political office and reform of the black laws, but also much partisan abuse and some personal soul-searching over his controversial role in the outcome. The Whigs, the immediate losers, were naturally vehement in their attacks on the new senator. Said the *Ohio State Journal*, "Every act of his was subsidiary to his own ambition. He talked of the interests of Free Soil, he *meant* His Own. He harangued on the benefits of electing a Free Soil Senator—he intended that none but himself should be that Senator." For his part Chase claimed to be satisfied that the Democrats were moving to the Free-Soil position through the coalition but also admitted that "in the counsel I gave last winter I was not uninfluenced by personal considerations." To his wife he confessed, "I sometimes doubt whether I am in the path of duty while even seeming to labor for political position." He revealed his personal misgivings by observing: "How much better is a quiet spirit . . . than the restless anxiety of ambition."[31] What he recognized philosophically he seemed unable to practice.

Free-Soilers outside of Ohio, such as Charles Sumner, admitted that they were confused on seeing party members split between Giddings and Chase; but most, including Sumner, Stanton, and Hale agreed that with Giddings already in Congress the choice of Chase was best for the movement. Sumner told Chase, "We have him already, and now we have you." Yet few could look on his course in early 1849 as a completely honorable one. Two great Free-Soil goals had been achieved in the modification of Ohio's black laws and the election of a senator. Probably some kind of bargain was inevitable, but Chase's self-righteousness and overeagerness for the office helped to divide the third party. To many, he had confused his own ambition with the good of the anti-extension movement. In the process he had laid himself and other Free-Soilers open to charges that the party was simply a temporary means for political gain to be given up at the most expedient time. Yet Chase provided his own best defense when he argued, "I neither modified nor compromised in any way, my political principles."[32] True, he had achieved his personal goal of election to political office, but he viewed that office primarily as a means of achieving the higher goal of affecting public policy on the issue of race relations.

Chase was unable in 1849 to establish a permanent coalition with Ohio Democrats which he felt could advance antislavery interests. Given the Whig background of the majority of Ohio Free-Soilers, most were more interested in unity within the third party than in union with the Democrats. At a Western Reserve convention of Free-Soilers in May 1849, the delegates endorsed "the great principle of Human Freedom" and avoided divisive questions. Giddings and Townshend called for a restoration of the mutual confidence of all Free-Soilers, and those present agreed to a national convention in July for the same purpose. Chase's absence from the May meeting indicated that such unity would be difficult to achieve.[33]

Chase did attend the July gathering in Cleveland which Giddings arranged to commemorate the passage of the Northwest Ordinance. The delegates heard addresses by Giddings, John Van Buren, and Chase and then reaffirmed the principles adopted in Buffalo a year earlier. Temporarily, unity prevailed, but Giddings's hope of preserving Free-Soil independence could not be achieved. With Barnburner-Hunker reunion moving toward reality in New York, the most prominent wing of the Free-Soil party was leading the way toward coalition, and Chase was eager for Ohio to be included. Professing to believe that "the National Democratic party is in the process of regeneration," Chase saw no need for an independent third-party movement. He insisted on calling the party the Free Democracy and stated privately, "I am a Democrat and I feel earnestly solicitous for the success of the Democratic organization and the triumph of its principles."[34]

Chase was unable before the election to work out unification because Ohio Democrats rejected his demand that they endorse the Wilmot Proviso. Coalitions were formed in some districts, but the Free-Soilers elected ten independent members to the legislature. They retained the balance of power in the legislature that they had won in 1848 and could thus be regarded as a permanent part of the

Ohio political structure. The results were far from pleasing to Chase or Giddings. The latter told Sumner that Chase's campaign methods "came near ruining us in this State."[35] The results of a year's Free-Soil agitation in Ohio did not bode well for the future of the party as an independent movement. Chase's policies had helped divide a formerly united and enthusiastic party. His personal ambitions and Democratic leanings had led many Free-Soilers into a highly unsatisfactory and unstable coalition with Ohio Democrats. Others had resisted coalition, leaving the party in a state of confusion. Although Giddings and others had prevented a complete loss of third-party identity, it remained to be seen whether his or Chase's approach would prevail in Washington where a small band of Free-Soilers gathered to do battle with the major parties on slave related issues.

Part of Chase's adjustment to his new life in Washington as senator involved the long months of separation from his family. Following the death of his second wife in 1845, he had been wed a third time about a year later to Sarah Belle Dunlop Ludlow, a member of a prominent Cincinnati family.[36] The couple's first years together were happy ones and included the birth in September 1847 of a daughter Janet (Nettie) Ralston, who was named after Chase's mother. A second daughter, Josephine Ludlow, born in 1849, died within a year, bringing to four the number of young daughters Chase had lost in fifteen years. Only Kate and Nettie would survive their father. Chase had hoped to bring his wife and infant daughter to Washington to live while Congress was in session and expected to be able to board in the capital and maintain a home in Cincinnati for $8,000 a year—a sum which despite Chase's other debts, was within range of a senator's salary. His hope to be with his family did not materialize, however, for Belle soon developed tuberculosis and after a short stay in Washington spent most of her remaining days before her death in early 1852 attempting to recuperate at a sanitarium in New Jersey or at home in Cincinnati.[37] During the long periods of separation Chase wrote to her almost daily describing his work in Washington and expressing constant concern over her declining health.

Family sickness and tragedy would haunt Chase during his first years in Washington. Stoically and philosophically he received the news in 1850 of the loss of his daughter Josephine due to a heart ailment, consoling his wife that "she is spared a life of sickness and suffering" and "is safe in the bosom of her God and Savior." With

Belle also dying, Chase grieved to Sumner, "What a vale of misery this world is. . . . Death has pursued me incessantly ever since I was twenty-five." Still his faith sustained him, as he told Belle shortly before her death: "It is hard to yield hope, and we need not yield it, for 'all is in God's power." When she told him of her fear that she would not recover, he responded poignantly, "My heart sinks within me." Still he took solace in the fact that she was spiritually prepared for death as she drew "nearer and nearer" to Jesus; God, he consoled her, "will not suffer those who trust in Him through Christ to be utterly cast down."[38]

Despite such feelings, Chase had never developed the close personal relationship with either Belle or his second wife Eliza that he had had with his first wife. The tragedy of Catherine's death in 1835, compounded by the death of so many of his children since then, had produced a private life of such pain and misery that he had been driven to pursue his public life even more vigorously. He found the support and nurture in work that many found in their families. Always seeking to avoid the personal hurt brought by Catherine's tragic death, he had learned in his subsequent marriages to avoid such close attachments.

Nonetheless, his tragic losses made him all the more concerned over the welfare of his two surviving daughters. To Kate, who was ten in 1850, he wrote a constant stream of tender letters while she attended Miss Henrietta B. Haines's school for girls in New York, urging her to do her best in her studies and to maintain her faith in God. He eagerly praised every sign of improvement in her school work, yet was quick to advise her to think of others first because "a selfish girl can never be a happy girl." He urged her to "strive to improve in every respect," for "you cannot know a father's anxiety for a child without a mother." With a fatherly concern he was quick to point out her shortcomings: "I was not so well pleased with your last letter as with the one before it. You did not take quite so much pains in forming your letters. They were too small and pinched, looking as if they were cold and shrunken." This from a man whose penmanship approached illegibility! On another occasion he noted with disappointment that Kate ranked only eighth in her class, and he expressed special concern for her poor performance in French. He encouraged her to "put on your thinking cap" and "qualify yourself for a place in Society."[39]

Throughout the rest of his life, Chase was ever solicitous of his daughters' welfare and maintained as close a relationship as frequent separations permitted. Weekly letters and regular visits when school was not in session resulted in Kate and her father being highly supportive of and dependent on each other while the younger Nettie received an equal share of his attention. Chase worried especially about any sign of sickness; on one occasion when Kate had been indisposed, he wrote: "You can hardly realize my anxiety about your health." [40]

Other family and personal financial matters diverted Chase's attention from the pressing issues in Congress. His ne'er-do-well brother William defaulted on a substantial loan in 1849 for which Chase was the cosigner, adding to the anguish and financial hardship he had already experienced over his youngest brother's problems. William's death in late 1852 eased a major source of embarrassment for the Ohio senator. Despite the difficulties William caused, Chase never gave up his concern and hope of reform. He was relieved to learn that William died "in the full faith of a saving atonement." [41]

Chase owned several rental properties in Cincinnati, the income from which, although substantial, fell far short of covering the debts he had accumulated in meeting such family obligations as Kate's education and Belle's medical expenses. In late 1849 these debts had reached a staggering $35,000. Because "debt presses me hard," he sold several of his holdings in Cincinnati, as well as several plots he owned in Lockport, New York. He reluctantly turned down his friend Hamlin's appeal for financial help in establishing a newspaper and explained that election to the Senate "has greatly abridged my income, and my debt, almost intolerably burdensome" before, had become even heavier since. Although family and financial concerns weighed heavily upon him, he would never "allow private grief to withdraw me from my public duties." [42] In 1850 Congress was engaged in a momentous debate on sectional issues, and Chase fully intended to resist any surrender of antislavery principle.

In their desire for compromise, most Whig and Democratic leaders in Congress showed only contempt for Chase and his small bloc of Free-Soilers. Third-party members received the least desirable committee assignments. Few ended up on committees which addressed sectional issues, and most were denied a voice in patronage distribution. Chase expected to be invited to the Democratic caucus because he had been elected "exclusively by Democratic and free democratic votes." Hoping eventually to effect a coalition with Democrats, he unrealistically expected them to allow him immediately to share the influence which was denied to other third-party members in Congress. Many northern senators had been prepared to recognize him as a Democrat in good standing and to reward him accordingly, but southerners objected, so his only appointment was to the Committee on Revolutionary Claims. For a time Chase considered refusing this insignificant assignment and voicing his protest, but he decided instead to endure the discrimination in silence.[43]

Senator Andrew Butler of South Carolina also led a calculated effort to discredit him by claiming that Chase had urged the Democratic party to separate from its proslavery wing and become more northern oriented. Butler also charged that Chase had written the resolution urging noncompliance with the fugitive slave clause of the Constitution for the Buffalo Liberty convention of 1843. Chase immediately denied urging a sectional Democratic party and reminded Butler that he had opposed the Liberty plank dealing with fugitive slaves.[44] Chase would find himself increasingly isolated as the Thirty-first Congress sought a compromise of sectional differences.

The small band of Free-Soilers in Congress were thus drawn together as they found themselves ostracized by Democrats and Whigs. In the House, where twelve Free-Soilers held the balance of power, they created turmoil by their refusal to support either the Whig or Democratic candidate for Speaker, both of whom they felt would be subservient to southern interests. By voting instead for David Wilmot, they succeeded only in delaying a decision and adding further to the disdain with which other congressmen regarded them. In the Senate, Chase's only Free-Soil colleague was John P. Hale. Although William H. Seward could be counted on for support on most issues, he was "too much of a politician" and too ready "to give his support to the Taylor platform of non-action." Chase regarded Hale as "a first-rate guerrilist" but found neither man "willing to adopt and carry out a systematic plan of operations against the slave power." He did not develop a close bond with either Seward or Hale, especially since neither shared his interest in coalition with the Democratic party. Chase lamented that if there were more men who held the same relationship with the Democrats as he did, "the days of doughfacery would be numbered."[45]

Chase as a Free-Soil senator from Ohio, about 1850. Courtesy of the Cincinnati Historical Society.

During his six years as a senator, Chase was only able to develop a close friendship and working relationship with Charles Sumner. Chase corresponded regularly with him during the compromise debates and rejoiced in 1851 when a Democratic-Free Soil coalition in the Massachusetts legislature elected Sumner senator. Chase said, "Now I feel as if I had a brother—colleague—one with whom I shall sympathize and be able fully to act."[46] Not only did Sumner share Chase's interest in a Democratic coalition but the two men were alike in temperament. Both were somewhat elitist and found it difficult to relate easily to their less inhibited and less refined colleagues in Congress. Sumner in fact was the only public figure with whom Chase ever developed a close personal relationship. While this failure to make intimate friendships was no doubt related to the Ohioan's own ambition as well as to his aloofness, it surely was also the result of the deep hurt he had felt with the tragic loss of so many of his immediate family. Work rather than close friendship was for Chase the great escape—the great soother of wounds.

Before Sumner's arrival Chase found what company he could among his fellow Free-Soilers already in Congress. The third-party outcasts were driven together for political and social reasons since they were typically dismissed as extremists and fanatics by the complacent Washington society. Because Chase and many other third-party members opposed the use of alcohol, they were prevented from much social intercourse with those who were not Free-Soilers. On one occasion Chase complained that during Senate debates members were not all "as sober as they should be." Gamaliel Bailey's home and Giddings's boardinghouse became retreats where Free-Soilers gathered regularly to discuss their problems and plans. There Chase and the others mapped their strategy for the congressional debates of 1850.[47]

The introduction of Henry Clay's compromise proposals in January 1850 initiated a nine-month debate on sectional issues in which Chase would play a prominent although not decisive role. The most important features of the Clay package provided for the admission of California as a free state, the organization of Utah and New Mexico territories without reference to the status of slavery, the abolition of the slave trade in the District of Columbia, the assumption of the Texas debt by the United States in return for New Mexico receiving the land claimed by both, and a new and more stringent fugitive slave law. Before it was over most members of Congress had spoken, but the Free-Soil position was largely rejected as the voices of compromise triumphed. Nevertheless, Chase was vehement and at times eloquent in his attack on what he believed to be a victory for slavery—"sentiment for the North, substance for the South." He reminded southern senators that no "menace of disunion" on their part could divert the antislavery men from their determination.[48]

Clay's proposals were by no means the only alternatives available to Congress. A week earlier Zachary Taylor had submitted a message on California and New Mexico which Chase and his Free-Soil colleagues found more to their liking than the Clay recommendations. The president urged the admission of California as soon as a state constitution was submitted. For New Mexico he also expressed doubt as to whether territorial organization was appropriate and suggested that it too should draw up a state constitution for congressional approval. It was a virtual certainty that when California and New Mexico acted they would propose free state constitutions and slavery would be barred. Nor would southerners find the Utah area any more conducive to their interests, for most assumed it was unsuited for slavery. Although in total agreement with the president on California, Chase and other Free-Soilers were unwilling to endorse the president's proposals for New Mexico as a realistic possibility and instead continued to push for the Wilmot Proviso to be applied to the remaining Mexican War territories. Chase told Sumner shortly after the president's message that "no matter how the territorial issue may be decided," the proviso could pass both House and Senate. In ensuing debates he continued to prefer that course over what he labeled the "Taylor Platform of non-action." Congress should act on the territorial issue rather than waiting for New Mexico to act.[49] Nonetheless, he had found the proposals of the slaveholding president surprisingly close to his own.

Chase's major effort to resist the Clay compromise proposals came in a two-day speech delivered in late March. As he prepared his address, "Union and Freedom without Compromise," he told Sumner: "Never in my life did I so painfully feel my incompetency as now." Despite his self-consciousness and his wish that "someone occupied my place more able to satisfy" his supporters, Chase appealed effectively to "the Friends of Freedom" by reminding the

Senate that the original policy of the government was slavery restriction and that Congress could not establish or maintain slavery in the territories.[50]

Although no match for the famed orator Daniel Webster, Chase presented an impressive physical appearance and argued his case forcefully. Tall, erect, handsome, and dignified, he was, in the words of Carl Schurz, "a picture of intelligence, strength, courage, and dignity." Winning few to his point of view, he nonetheless incisively answered Webster's contention that nature had already excluded slavery from the territories. Chase argued, "So long as a powerful and active political interest is concerned in the extension of slavery into new Territories, it is vain to look for its exclusion from them except by positive Law." Precedent for such action he said had been established with the Northwest Ordinance of 1787, which, he noted pointedly, had been supported by several southern states. The speech was well received in antislavery circles with Bailey's *National Era* leading the praise. Chase felt that the effort fell "far short" of what he had hoped to accomplish and that it was "infinitely below my own standards." But he had designed the speech "for the masses" and hoped it would "render a permanent service to the cause." To this end he secured Sumner's aid in getting it published for a wide circulation.[51]

Chase was also active in the efforts to block Senator Henry S. Foote's tactic of joining Clay's compromise proposals in a single omnibus measure. The Ohio senator favored voting on each bill separately, hoping in this way to block at least some of the more objectionable features. Later in the debate Chase countered a Jefferson Davis amendment guaranteeing territorial slavery in New Mexico with one which provided "that nothing herein contained shall be construed as authorizing or permitting the introduction of slavery or the holding of persons as property within said territory." His proposal was rejected by a vote of 36 to 21. Although defeated in his efforts to insert the Wilmot Proviso principle, Chase continued to offer amendments designed for that end. The unexpected death of Zachary Taylor on July 9, was another blow to Free-Soil hopes because by that time they realized that despite their earlier feelings the president was their best hope for protecting their anti-extension principles. Bailey's *National Era* now praised Taylor for attempting to maintain freedom in California and New Mexico, while Chase lamented to his wife that "a reversal of Gen. Taylor's territorial policy" was expected under Millard Fillmore.[52]

Before the end of July the strategy of a single proposal, the omnibus bill, had failed. Stephen A. Douglas then emerged as the leader of the compromise forces and, over strenuous opposition, engineered the passage of the parts of the proposal as separate bills. In meetings with his Free-Soil colleagues at Bailey's home, Chase proposed the strategy which they pursued in Congress to prevent passage. He led the effort in Senate debates to win approval of the Free-Soil position on each issue. He naturally supported the admission of the free state of California as well as the granting of the disputed territory to New Mexico rather than Texas. The real issue, said Chase, was whether there should be more slave or free territory. He strongly opposed the assumption of the Texas debt, which he labeled the "Texas Surrender Bill," a measure that exposed Fillmore's "Whig policy of evasion."[53]

Like other antislavery advocates he reserved his severest criticism for the fugitive slave bill, which greatly strengthened southerners in their efforts to retrieve escaped slaves. Chase returned to the arguments he had used so forcefully as a Cincinnati lawyer in defense of accused fugitives. Since the federal government had no responsibility for slavery, no legislation requiring a federal or free state role in assisting slaveowners in the return of fugitives could be constitutional. Once a slave entered a free area he could not be forced back into slavery. Chase also argued that the section providing for a federal role in enforcing the fugitive slave law in the territories was unconstitutional, for it would be tantamount to sanctioning slavery in such areas. He proposed several amendments dealing with these issues, including one to require a trial by jury for alleged fugitives. All of these were overwhelmingly rejected.[54]

To Chase and other Free-Soilers the compromise bills which were passed and signed in August and September 1850 represented a major surrender to the interests of the Slave Power. He told his Senate colleagues that the fugitive slave law would "produce more agitation than any other which has ever been adopted by Congress." In the next sessions of Congress Chase constantly sought ways to reintroduce the question of fugitive slaves. In February 1851, he presented eight petitions from Pennsylvania citizens asking for the new law's immediate repeal. The fact that northerners from a state other than Ohio would seek his assistance indicated that Free-Soilers throughout the North considered Chase as their spokesman on the fugitive issue. All repeal efforts were scorned by the Senate despite Chase's description of the law as unconstitutional "either from defect of power to enact it or because its provisions are in conflict with the guarantee of liberty contained in the Constitution."[55]

Although Chase's most important contributions in the Senate were as an antislavery advocate, he by no means confined himself to those issues. His work reflected his diligence and commitment to his Ohio constituents and to causes he felt important. He worked successfully to secure funds for construction of a customs house in Cincinnati. He also urged and won support for a Marine hospital in Cincinnati and a canal around the Portland Falls on the Ohio River which proved beneficial to commerce. In 1852, he introduced a bill to cede to Ohio the remaining two hundred thousand acres of public lands in the state, noting that precedent had already been set in land grants to other states. The bill passed the Senate but failed in the House. Later during his term he was a strong advocate of the homestead principle. He noted, "I regard the public lands" as "the estate of the people and Congress merely as a trustee."[56]

Throughout his Senate term he remained uncompromisingly committed to the needs and concerns of the oppressed. In several bills before Congress he opposed efforts to discriminate against immigrants and boldly argued that anyone declaring his intention to become a citizen should receive the equal land benefits as citizens. Giving them the same benefits "would Americanize them, by generosity and justice," for they should "divest themselves as speedily as possible of their foreign character."[57] That proposal was soundly defeated in the Senate. Chase also opposed southern efforts to exclude blacks from eligibility for federal land. Noting that blacks were striving to improve their position despite discrimination, Chase maintained that to exclude them from land benefits was "inhuman and unjust."[58] The extensive debate on homestead proved premature because southerners, fearful of encouraging territorial settlement by nonslaveholding northerners, blocked the bill in the Senate.

Although Chase defended the interests of black Americans, both free and slave, and fought discrimination against them, he did not believe that the two races could live together "except under the constraint of force, such as that of slavery." During the compromise debates he explained to Frederick Douglass that he "looked forward to the separation of the races" because the two were "adapted to different latitudes and countries." Suggesting that the West Indies or northern South America might be colonized by blacks from the United States, Chase stressed in a Senate debate that colonization must be voluntary, for compulsory expatriation was "incompatible with justice." All groups should be dealt with "upon the simple principles of right, of justice, of humanity." When Douglass responded that the future of black Americans was in the United States, Chase maintained that separation was in everyone's best interests. In 1853, when the Senate considered an appropriation to encourage exploration for possible colonization in Africa, Chase supported the bill, saying it would permit blacks to seek "happier homes in other lands."[59] Chase thus differed with those abolitionists who dismissed colonization as a southern device designed to strengthen slavery.[60] His paternalistic views were indicative of the limitations of many antislavery northerners on racial equality. Unable to envisage an integrated society, Chase suggested that blacks were best suited for a different environment. Yet while they did live together, Chase remained a leading opponent of discrimination.

The Ohio senator also supported other groups that faced unjust treatment. He endorsed the crusade of the Massachusetts reformer Dorothea Dix in behalf of the insane by promoting the bill which provided land grants for national hospitals for a group regarded and treated by most Americans as little more than criminals. He pointed out in defense of Dix's efforts: "Her clients are the poor, the friendless and the wretched. . . . For these she has labored; among these she would dispense blessings and consolations."[61] In another legislative effort he described a naval discipline bill as overly "harsh and severe" and degrading because it included the use of the ball and chain and the requirement that a sailor caught stealing must wear a badge marked "Thief."[62] His interest in reform and his concern for oppressed people, perhaps conditioned by his personal loss of so many loved ones, was in marked contrast to the calloused views of many Americans of the period, including many of his fellow senators.

On the national level Chase found it impossible to pursue coalition and eventual union with the Democratic party and maintain his antislavery principles. With southern Democrats unwilling to accept him and with the compromise spirit dominant through much of his six year term, Chase saw no alternative to maintenance of the third party. On the state level, on the other hand, where northern Democrats could be more easily persuaded to adopt moderate antislavery positions, coalition seemed a realistic goal. In Maine, for example, Chase supported third-party cooperation in the election of Democrat Hannibal Hamlin to the Senate. A failure of Free-Soilers to endorse Hamlin would be "to lose the opportunity of rendering so signal a service to the cause of freedom."⁶³

Coalition must be accomplished carefully to avoid surrendering the third-party organization simply to regain status in the Democratic party. This Chase feared, was what had occurred in New York during the summer and fall of 1849 when Barnburners and Hunkers reunited for the state election. During negotiations, Chase advised Benjamin Butler, his Barnburner ally at the Buffalo convention, that a reunion must be based on principle and must include the Buffalo platform. This stipulation would leave out "the entire body of the old Liberty men and nearly all the Progressive Whigs who united with us last fall mainly on the Anti Slavery grounds."⁶⁴ By September the two groups had joined without reference to anti-extension, and Chase complained that the Barnburners "had gone too far, in their anxiety to secure united support of a single ticket." He agreed with Sumner that although the Barnburners desired to maintain principle, "they are politicians, and do as politicians do."⁶⁵ As much as Chase sought a similar reunion in Ohio and nationally, he could not surrender to the compromise spirit.

Despite his unhappiness over events in New York, Chase soon faced charges that he was guilty of some of the same tactics in Ohio in 1850. His efforts to maintain the Democratic coalition appeared to be at the expense of antislavery principles. At the state Democratic convention in January 1850, the delegates refused to endorse the Wilmot Proviso. Although disappointed, Chase hoped the Free Democrats could unite behind the Democratic candidate for governor, Reuben Wood. The Free-Soilers in the legislature refused to join in a legislative coalition even though Chase failed to "see anything in our present relations so different" from those of a year earlier.⁶⁶ Led by the Giddings faction, the third party selected an old Liberty party leader, the Rev. Edward Smith, for governor and strongly condemned the compromise just completed in Washington. Chase persisted in his hopes for coalition and announced he would remain neutral in the gubernatorial election. Few were surprised when after a listless campaign Smith's showing was only about one-third of the party's total two years earlier. Chase had fulfilled Charles Francis Adams's prediction that he would "press for amalgamation of the party with the democracy" so hard as "to throw overboard all the doubters of the Whig side."[67] These developments revealed marked limitations in Chase's political leadership, for not only had he isolated himself from most other Free-Soilers in Ohio, he had also weakened the very coalition he had sought to strengthen.

Chase defended his position in the 1850 state elections by arguing that continued cooperation with Ohio Democrats might result in Giddings's election to the Senate. Despite its poor showing statewide, the third party won enough seats in the legislature to retain the balance of power which had enabled Chase's election two years earlier. He told Giddings that although Democrats would find him "a hard dose" because of his "decided Whig position in times past," they might prefer him "rather than see a regular Whig elected."[68] Chase knew that if Giddings could be persuaded to seek Democratic support, the major obstacle in the way of Chase's desired coalition would be removed. But Giddings was unwilling to make the necessary overtures and sacrifice his political independence.

Chase nevertheless pursued his efforts behind the scenes to use the Senate election to maintain the coalition. So determined was he that, with Giddings eliminated, he urged his supporters to allow the Democrats to name one of their own provided that "he is as good a free soiler as I am a democrat." In return he would expect the election of "an equitable proportion of Free Democrats to other offices." Instead, after a long deadlock the third-party men agreed to support an anti-extension Whig, Judge Benjamin Wade. Over Chase's opposition, Wade received a Free-Soil endorsement because of his vehement opposition to the fugitive slave law. Wade's election to the Senate was a personal defeat for Chase and a definite setback to his hopes for a third-party union with the Democratic party.[69] Still he felt that Wade would not be "derelict to the Antislavery faith" and believed the future dictated that "our Party must be a Democratic Party in *name and fact*."[70]

Despite Chase's best efforts, the Free-Soil party of Ohio remained independent in 1851, and, under Giddings's leadership, the party prepared for an active campaign for the governorship. Chase attended the Western Reserve Free-Soil convention at Ravenna in June. Although he said he had a "glorious time," he noted that "the resolutions were not quite fundamental enough in their democratic character to suit me." Only a platform endorsing the Democratic position on economic issues would have satisfied him. Even before the party nominated Samuel Lewis for governor, Chase indicated privately to Giddings that he would ally himself with the Ohio Democrats and support Governor Reuben Wood for reelection. According to Chase, there was "no old line democracy in the country occupying so advanced a position as the Democracy of Ohio." His official announcement came in a public letter in late August. It pointed to Wood's strong antislavery stance and claimed the Democratic party throughout the North was moving in the same direction. By his support of Wood Chase indicated that his own political future was more secure as a Democrat, "whenever it involve[d] no sacrifice of principles," than as a Free-Soiler. Anticipating the abuse that was sure to be showered on him by his former colleagues, Chase expressed his "regret that I cannot expect the concurrence of all the devoted friends of freedom and progress with whom I have been accustomed to act." [71]

Chase did not have long to wait for the cries of disbelief. Hamilton County Free-Soilers announced that they would no longer "recognize him as our representative," while Birney accused him of placing party over principle. Bailey gallantly defended him in the *National Era* and indicated that his support for Wood was a far cry from support of the national Democratic party. But for the most part Chase found himself isolated and without supporters. He reacted defensively and argued that he had not relented at all in his "opposition to slavery." He charged that his detractors gave him "not a word of confidence, not a word of respect" for "ten years of devoted service to the cause of human liberty." To Giddings Chase admitted that a prime factor in his decision was a desire to keep the confidence of the party which had elected him to the Senate. He could argue that joining the Democrats was the best way to spread the "right view of slavery," but he also knew it was the only way to win reelection to the Senate.[72] He had not, however, joined the national Democratic party; his support was limited to Ohio Democrats and to the 1851 gubernatorial election—a commitment which was by no means irrevocable. Although the state party appeared to him sound on slave-related issues, national Democrats would soon convince him otherwise.

As hard as Chase labored to unite Ohio Free-Soilers with the Democratic party, there was little he could do to convince the national party to take a firm antislavery stance. Chase wanted the "Pro Slave Resolution" of past platforms dropped, but he soon realized that party leaders "were not prepared to surrender the supposed advantages of their slaveholding alliance."[73] Having joined with Ohio Democrats in 1851, Chase was in a dilemma and could only hope that, despite the endorsement of the compromise by a national party, harmony among Free Democrats and Democrats might be preserved in Ohio. Although unable to support Franklin Pierce, Chase urged others to "remain faithful to our democratic principles and positions."[74] He had staked so much on his coalition plans, not the least of which were his hopes to retain his Senate seat, that the national party's actions placed him in an almost untenable position.

Following Pierce's nomination on a platform pledged to resist "agitation of the slavery question," Chase had no alternative but to return to the third party and help it secure a respectable vote. He urged his former Barnburner allies, including Martin Van Buren, to oppose the surrender of the antislavery principles that had been so strong four years earlier. In a lengthy letter to Benjamin Butler which was published in the *National Era,* Chase explained his inability to support "the nominees of the Compromise Democracy." The Democratic convention had left him no other "honorable course" than independent action. If he could regain some of his former influence in the third party, he might move the party toward Democratic coalition after the national campaign was over. What he hoped for from the third party in 1852 was "an Independent Democratic Rally, thoroughly democratic in name and fact." On the other hand, "a *mere free soil* rally will simply elect Pierce."[75]

The prospects for the Free Democratic party in 1852 were indeed gloomy in Chase's eyes. With Van Buren and Butler refusing to heed his appeal, the Barnburner desertion was apparently complete. There was no obvious candidate to lead the party. John P. Hale was most frequently mentioned, although a few urged Chase to run. Neither was eager to lead a ticket with so little chance of an impressive showing. Each man seemed more intent on retaining his seat in the Senate and feared that an active role in the third party might preclude that possibility. Interest in Chase was in fact confined to a relatively few, and many Ohioans were prepared to veto him because of his earlier desertion. Charles Francis Adams summed up this attitude by explaining that "the feeling as it respects Mr. Chase is so bitter in Ohio that it will make his nomination impossible." Chase explained his reluctance to Hamlin and his desire "to be out of the scrape for many reasons," including the feelings against him in Cleveland and Cincinnati. In the same letter he asked Hamlin if there were much chance of his reelection to the Senate: "What . . . are the sentiments of the Democrats toward me?" A nomination by the Free Democrats would "place me in a false position in reference to my democratic friends in Ohio." [76]

Like most Free Democrats, Chase favored John P. Hale for the nomination. He urged Hale to run and pledged his active support. The party assembled in Pittsburgh in August with two thousand in attendance, only about one-tenth the number at Buffalo four years earlier. With the Barnburners absent, the meeting was dominated by leaders from Massachusetts and Ohio. In a calculated decision, Chase was not among them, explaining his absence by noting that the Senate was still in session. Hale was quickly nominated, with George W. Julian of Indiana for vice president. The Chase faction, led by Townshend and others identified with Democratic coalition, had helped block the nomination of Samuel Lewis for the second spot, feeling that only a man of more moderate persuasion could serve their purposes. The platform was also to Chase's liking as the delegates reaffirmed their commitment to his position by calling for "no more slave States, no slave Territory, no nationalized Slavery" and by demanding "the total separation of the General Government from slavery." The Compromise of 1850 and especially the fugitive slave law came in for vehement attack in a platform with which Chase could find little to quarrel. [77]

Yet Chase showed no enthusiasm for the convention results. The Pittsburgh resolutions and nominations, he said, produced little interest in Washington. He would support the party only "because it is more democratic than the Old Line." But, he confided to Hamlin, "I shall not sink my individuality in this organization, which it seems to me must be temporary. I propose rather to maintain my position as an Independent Democrat." Angered by the attacks of many Ohio Free Democrats, Chase seemed incapable of comprehending why anyone could question his past inconsistent course. He complained to Hamlin about those who "maligned" him at Pittsburgh and told Sumner that the "conspiracy" against him would hurt the Hale-Julian ticket. Although he had not wanted the nomination, he had expected to be welcomed back by a forgiving party. Chase did campaign actively for Hale, and for Giddings's reelection to the House, and his efforts helped him to overcome the antagonism felt by Ohio antislavery leaders. Many would never completely trust him again, however, and party unity in his home state seemed as elusive as ever.[78]

The election of Franklin Pierce in 1852 by an overwhelming margin left the Whig party gravely weakened. Although Hale and the Free Democrats had won only a little more than half of Van Buren's total in 1848, the results might conceivably allow the third party to take advantage of Whig misfortunes and gain support accordingly. The results also complicated Chase's future strategy. Union with the victorious Democratic party now seemed remote, and pressure would mount to bring Whigs and Free Democrats together in a coalition of the kind Chase had consistently resisted. Equally disheartening, his seat in the Senate was clearly in jeopardy. He now admitted that an independent party organization was necessary, one which would welcome "progressive Whigs" into its ranks as well as Democrats.[79]

Hopeful of appealing to discouraged Whigs, the Free Democratic party of Ohio assembled in January 1853 to nominate a candidate for governor. The members gathered in a spirit of great enthusiasm and, with success apparently imminent, past differences were almost forgotten. Samuel Lewis agreed to run again and resolutions were adopted commending both Giddings and Chase. The platform, which Chase helped to draft, endorsed temperance and black suffrage.[80] The delegates fully realized that if they could maintain party unity they could take full advantage of Whig disarray and become the second party of the state. Much of the Free Democratic campaign appeal was the result of Lewis's strong advocacy of a prohibition law, patterned after that of Maine. As one Free Democrat reminded Chase, "The great excitement here is about the *Maine Law.*" Yet despite their common feeling on that issue, many obstacles prevented a complete union of Whigs and Free Democrats. Most

Whigs were not yet ready to surrender their old party ties. Equally important, the Chase faction was unenthusiastic over the proposed union, and the idea proceeded no further.[81]

Chase thus found himself in a dilemma. He knew it would be fruitless to try to negotiate a coalition with the firmly entrenched Democrats who would see no need to give up anything of their platform. He reasoned that his best hope lay in winning over individual Democrats and Whigs to the third-party point of view, rather than fusion with either party. He explained to Hamlin that he was "satisfied that an Independent Democracy, thoroughly organized and appealing alike to liberal Whigs and liberal Democrats to unite in action . . . could do our work best."[82] With political realities in mind and his chances for reelection to the Senate all but gone, Chase was beginning to see that cooperation with the Whigs was more promising than ever before. Given the rapidly changing structure of Ohio politics by 1853, he ceased switching parties and trying to change the Democratic party and sought instead to persuade Whigs and Democrats to join the Free Democrats.

The election results in 1853 confirmed the wisdom of that approach. Lewis carried six counties and received fifty thousand votes, only slightly fewer than Chase had predicted. Although the Democrats won easily, the third party received 18 percent of the total and the Whigs only 30 percent. The Free Democrats were in a good position to overtake the Whigs and become the second party of Ohio. But the Democratic sweep had denied the third party its balance of power in the legislature and with it any chance that Chase might retain his seat in the Senate. He had wanted to return to Washington "to redeem the state" from its connections with slavery, but he saw the impossibility of reforming even Ohio Democrats when they endorsed the compromise in early 1854. His disappointment was nonetheless great when the legislature chose George E. Pugh, a former law student of his, to replace him.[83] Chase now had one more reason to seek Whig cooperation in the antislavery movement. In congratulating his successor, he urged "that your action as a Senator would be directed . . . as I fear it will not be, to the discouragement, limitation, and repression of slavery." His chief regret in leaving the Senate was that "my place is not to be filled by a man willing to maintain the rights, interest, and honor of Freemen against

a domineering oligarchy."[84] Yet before his term in the Senate officially ended, Chase played a significant role in launching a more
effective political organization with which to resist slavery—an organization which was destined to join the two-party system and one in
which Chase would attain great prominence.

5

From Columbus
to Washington

I n the fall of 1854, Chase wrote to Charles Sumner, "I am now
without without a party." Earlier that year he had been deeply
involved in the Kansas-Nebraska controversy. In January 1854, Stephen A. Douglas moved to organize the territory. Douglas's complex
motives included the desire to promote the construction of a transcontinental railroad and the development and settlement of western
territories. Equally important, he hoped to find a compromise solution on territorial slavery which might please both northern and
southern moderate Democrats and unite and reinvigorate his divided
party.[1] Chase, who had based so much of his senatorial career on
resisting compromise on slave-related issues, immediately led the opposition to Douglas's efforts. To Chase the Illinois senator was intent
on giving the South what it demanded, which ultimately included
repeal of the ban on territorial slavery north of the 36°30′ line in the
Missouri Compromise of 1820. When the Pierce administration endorsed the bill, Chase concluded that Douglas had "out southernized
the South; and has dragged the timid and irresolute administration
along with him."[2]

Chase's role in the controversy began with his seemingly routine
request on January 24, 1854 to delay Senate discussion of the
Kansas-Nebraska bill for a week. His famous indictment of the
Douglas bill, "The Appeal of the Independent Democrats in Congress to the People of the United States," was completed on January 19 and published several days later in the *National Era*. It was

based on a preliminary draft by Giddings, which Chase revised extensively. Gerrit Smith and Sumner made suggestions for minor changes, but Chase assumed primary responsibility for the document.[3] By attacking the bill as a southern effort to protect slavery in the territories, Chase and Giddings hoped to convince the North of a Slave Power conspiracy to expand slavery despite the ban north of 36°30'. The Slave Power argument would, they hoped, undermine Democratic unity and perhaps encourage organization of a new antislavery party.

The "Appeal" was one of the most effective pieces of political propaganda ever produced. The Kansas-Nebraska bill was, said Chase in moralistic tones, part of "an atrocious plot to exclude" both immigrants and citizens "from a vast unoccupied region" and "convert it into a dreary region of despotism, inhabited by masters and slaves." In the past Chase had attacked the Missouri Compromise as he had all compromises with slavery. But now he recognized the potential of interpreting that act as "a sacred pledge," the removal of which "involves the repeal of ancient law and the violation of a solemn compact." He denied Douglas's assertion that the act of 1820 had been superseded by the Compromise of 1850. The latter, which sanctioned territorial popular sovereignty, applied only to Mexican War territories, whereas the Missouri law dealt directly with Kansas and Nebraska. In fact the New Mexico–Utah territorial legislation of 1850 specifically declared that the prohibition on slavery in the Missouri law would not be affected. "For more than thirty years," said Chase, the Missouri Compromise "has been universally regarded and acted upon as inviolable American law."[4]

In early February, Chase moved to amend the Kansas-Nebraska bill to eliminate the Douglas claim that the Compromise of 1850 had replaced the Missouri Compromise. In his most powerful Senate speech, called "Maintain Plighted Faith," Chase sought to prevent acceptance of the idea that popular sovereignty would decide the slavery question and that Congress could not intervene. He again blamed Douglas for surrendering to the "insatiate demands" of southerners "for more slave territory and more slave States." Carl Schurz, who regarded Chase as "one of the statliest figures in the Senate," described the address as "clear and strong in argument, vigorous and determined in tone, elevated in sentiment." Schurz concluded that the speech "commands respect and inspires confidence." Predictably, opponents disagreed, and Douglas labeled Chase and Sumner "abolition confederates in slander." The "Appeal" was widely accepted in the North, but in the South it helped to unite previously apathetic southerners in support of the Douglas bill.[5]

The response to the "Appeal" and to Chase's Senate speeches was greater than he could have anticipated because he had not foreseen "the profound attention or the immense audience" his words would attract. Chase noted that he had received "compliments from all sides in abundance" and was overjoyed that he had "worthily upheld the honor of our noble State." A supporter praised him for having furnished "*the* argument on the main question." Even the normally hostile *Ohio State Journal* admitted that Chase rather than Douglas had had the better of the argument.[6] With the leadership of the Democratic-controlled Congress and President Pierce determined to win passage, the odds against Chase were heavy, but the encouragement from many northerners led him to continue the fight against the bill.

He attempted, with a series of amendments, to make the bill "less obnoxious," although he did not plan to vote for the legislation in any form. One amendment would have specifically granted the people of the territory the right to "prohibit the existence of slavery therein"—this would amend Douglas's wording which allowed them only "to regulate their domestic institutions." Another would have made one, rather than two, territories out of the region in order to limit the area affected by the repeal of the Missouri prohibition. With Douglas in firm control not only of Senate Democrats but of many southern Whigs as well, the amendments were overwhelmingly defeated as was the effort backed by Chase to guarantee suffrage to immigrants in the territory who were not yet citizens.[7] To discredit the Chase amendments, Douglas and his allies injected into the debate the old charge that Chase had been elected to the Senate "by a corrupt bargain." Such accusations made Chase more determined in his opposition, but it had been clear from the start that the Senate would pass the measure and deal the antislavery forces a major setback. In a final speech when the bill was returned from the House in May, Chase reviewed his arguments and exhorted "Freemen and lovers of freedom to stand upon their guard and prepare for the worst events." When President Pierce signed the bill on May 30, Chase and his compatriots could not realize how successfully they had prepared for a northern reaction. Within three months, so much political change had occurred that Chase could call the "Appeal" "the *most valuable* of my works."[8]

Immediately following passage of the Douglas bill, Chase began organizing an anti-Nebraska political movement. He felt that northerners of all parties might be mobilized to resist what he claimed was a proslavery bill. Organized resistance might also develop into a new coalition party of antislavery northerners. Factions of both major parties would surely be interested. Whigs, unhappy over their party's disastrous showing in the 1852 election and its ineffectiveness in preventing passage of the Douglas bill would join; they were "now where the old Democrats were four years ago, opposed to a Proslavery National Administration." Chase explained: "As we cooperated with the old Democrats then, we ought to cooperate with the Whigs now." Northern Democrats might be interested in a new party because the Pierce administration had "prostrated the old democratic organization by its insistence on the Nebraska bill."[9]

Chase felt that the Free Democratic organization might provide the basis for "organizing a genuine Democracy." Not at first committed to a new party because it might be dominated by his Whig opponents, he hoped that any fusion movement would retain Democratic in its name. Chase soon recognized, however, that only a new organization could "unite all the Independent Democrats, the Liberal Whigs and the Liberals among the old Democrats." According to Henry Wilson, the morning after the passage of the Kansas-Nebraska bill, thirty northern congressmen of all three parties met somewhat spontaneously to discuss such a possibility; they were convinced that only in a new party "lay any reasonable hope of successful resistance to the continued aggressions of the arrogant and triumphant Slave Power."[10] No concrete decisions were reached at this preliminary gathering because no one, including Chase, was prepared at this early date to take the initiative.

Several fusion meetings of anti-Nebraska people took place in Columbus even before the bill became law. Many Ohio Whigs were clearly interested in developing a new party because the Whig organization had suffered a series of shattering defeats, both statewide and nationally. The editor of the *Ohio State Journal,* backed by Chase and Giddings, planned a convention for July 13, 1854 at Columbus. Chase had tried to give direction to the Ohio movement from Washington and had proposed a call for the Columbus meeting using language similar to that in his "Appeal." But more moderate politicians toned down his wording in the official call and prevented any further thought of using Democratic in the name of any new organization which might result. A struggle was already developing between the more advanced antislavery leaders, such as Chase, and more moderate Whigs who hoped only for a temporary union for the fall election.

About a thousand delegates gathered on July 13 and pledged to make the repeal of the Missouri Compromise section of the Kansas-Nebraska Act "inoperative and void." Stronger antislavery planks were rejected, however, and Chase expressed disappointment in the outcome. In his view the convention "took rather low ground," although he determined to "make the best of what was done." As in the past, he was more willing to resist slavery than many who opposed his leadership and feared upsetting the sectional truce. Convention delegates chose candidates for state offices, although they gave no formal name to the new fusion movement.[11]

The new organization had immediate success at the polls in the fall, with Democrats paying the price for the unpopular Kansas-Nebraska Act. All of the fusionist candidates for Congress in Ohio defeated their Democratic opponents, proving beyond doubt the political potential of the movement. Not all was unity, however. Two distinct factions had appeared, greatly complicating Chase's goal of unifying antislavery elements in a new party while promoting his own political future. By the end of 1854 his plan included running for governor of Ohio the following year. The faction he led, made up primarily of Free Democrats, endorsed a strong antislavery position; the Whig–Know-Nothing faction proved much more conservative on sectional issues and unreceptive to Chase's candidacy.[12]

The Know-Nothing movement had grown in significance with declining Whig fortunes. By 1854, it posed a major threat to Chase's plans. Anti-Catholic and protemperance in its appeal, it had appeared first in Ohio in 1853, when Archbishop John Purcell of Cincinnati antagonized many by objecting to the taxation of Catholics for the support of public schools. Rioting against Irish and German Catholics occurred in the fall of 1853 after Archbishop Gaetano Bedini, papal nuncio, made an inflammatory appearance in the city. The Ohio Know-Nothing movement was concentrated in the southern part of the state, although it had an impact on Cleveland as well. Its goals remained somewhat obscure but included opposition to immigrant voting and officeholding. Nationally, the nativists dared not take a strong antislavery stance for fear of alienating the influential southern elements, which demanded that emphasis be left on an anti-foreign, anti-Catholic appeal. The swelling Ohio movement, led by Congressman Lewis Campbell, also opposed a strong antislavery stance, but understood that the only way to displace the pro-immigrant Democratic party lay in cooperation with the Chase people.[13] The two Ohio groups viewed each other with anticipation and suspicion, thus adding to the chaos of the political situation in Ohio in late 1854.

Chase kept the door open to Know-Nothing support while surrendering none of his opposition to slavery. This, he found, was a difficult task. He acknowledged that the Know-Nothing movement might "make the election of a man of my position impossible." As he told Oran Follett, the conservative editor of the *Ohio State Journal*, "My political principles have been based upon conviction and I cannot lightly wave or modify any of them." Noting that both Giddings and Senator Benjamin Wade had urged him to seek the governorship, he nonetheless suggested that "the reasons against being a candidate rather overbalance the reasons for being one." The governorship, he feared, would mean "the loss of professional business and the neglect of private affairs."[14]

If Chase had mixed emotions about his candidacy, many in the Know-Nothing movement thoroughly distrusted his motives. Recalling the 1849 Senate race, many assumed that personal ambition consumed him. Feeling that "Chase would hardly be the man for that post," Cleveland editor Joseph Medill urged Follett to help him "check the movement of the Chase clique" and "its miserable personal ambitions." Jacob Brinkerhoff, the favorite of many Know-Nothings for the nomination, opposed the "rule or ruin" attitude of many Chase supporters and feared that the governorship was merely "a stepping stone" to "Mr. C. being a candidate for the Presidency."[15]

Cooperation appeared unlikely as neither faction was ready to make the initial move. Chase explained his position carefully, noting that if Know-Nothings would not support men of his organization he would assume "an antagonistic position"; if necessary "the People's

movement . . . must go on without the Know-Nothing cooperation."[16] Yet Chase worked for compromise. To pacify the nativists, he
admitted that "in the action of some foreigners there has been something justly censurable and calculated to provoke . . . hostility," although "secret political organizations" were not the answer. He
urged one of his antislavery supporters to "abate something of your
tone against the Kns," for what "is objectionable in their organization will be most likely to cure itself." Aware that his supporters
would insist that he head a coalition ticket, Chase adroitly told Follett that, although he did not seek the governorship, he would accept
the nomination if accompanied by a platform consistent with his
views. When Follett complained that Chase's friends were making
his nomination a requirement for their participation, the senator
responded that the Know-Nothings were even more uncompromising.[17] Throughout the spring of 1855, neither side appeared willing
to budge.

Chase also tried to satisfy the antislavery Whigs by explaining his
controversial role in the 1849 Senate election. Although he had
abandoned the Whigs in order to secure Democratic support, he
insisted to Follett, "There was nothing . . . of which I am ashamed."
Yet he acknowledged that many Whigs would insist on nominating
"another man."[18] In the end, Whigs endorsed Chase's candidacy
more willingly than did the Know-Nothings.

As the July 1855 fusion or People's convention approached, Chase
and his supporters grew more confident. Said one supporter: "the
influence against us is waning." The Know-Nothings appeared "intimidated" and acquiescent and were struggling with factionalism as
one group threatened to bolt and nominate its own slate.[19] Chase
charged that their gubernatorial candidate, Brinkerhoff, was unacceptable because he did not "represent the pure element of opposition to Slavery extension and slavery domination." Chase explained
to Campbell that cooperation with the Know-Nothings did not mean
fusion. Fusion would make Chase "responsible for their doctrines";
cooperation for "the freedom of the territories" was as far as he
would go.[20] Chase and his followers felt confident that antislavery
sentiment in Ohio was stronger than nativism. Although the two
movements did have some common goals, the antislavery tradition
was older and appealed to a stronger fear—that of southern power
in Congress.

Chase's chief strategist, James M. Ashley, urged Chase to play down cooperation with the conservative faction of the Know-nothing movement which called itself the American party. He also encouraged Chase to make his opposition to nativism public "before Seward or any other leading men come out" against the Know-Nothings. Chase agreed with Ashley that anti-extension had a stronger appeal than nativism and that as a result the Know-Nothings would eventually have to bend to his position. Nonetheless, he feared antagonizing them with a public statement of opposition at this time. While hopeful that Know-Nothingism would "gracefully give itself up and die" he realized that he could not win the governorship in 1855 without their support. To Governor James Grimes of Iowa he predicted, "Should I be nominated I shall certainly be elected," and he expected to win by a majority of between twenty-five and fifty thousand votes. By June, Chase had concluded that election to the governorship of Ohio as the anti-Nebraska candidate could provide a springboard to the presidency. There existed, he said, "a strong sentiment" in his favor in the West and "a respectable backing" of him in the East. That belief was based more on impression than on hard political evidence, and Chase would have to overcome deep-seated opposition to his gubernatorial candidacy among Whigs in Ohio and in nearby states as well.[21]

The July 13 fusion convention at the Town Street Methodist Church in Columbus went exactly as Chase expected. With surprisingly little opposition a strong antislavery platform was adopted, promising that "we will resist the spread of slavery under whatever shape or color" and pledging to repeal the Kansas-Nebraska Act. The platform said nothing of nativist principles. Campbell and Follett persuaded Brinkerhoff to step aside and accept Chase's nomination in return for the remainder of the ticket going to Know-Nothings. After his nomination, Chase addressed the meeting, endorsed the platform, and pledged "to work with all men who are willing to unite with me for the defense of freedom." The results could properly be called a victory for neither side because with so many nativists on the ticket, the new party clearly had a significant Know-Nothing foundation.[22] Nonetheless, the convention formally launched the Republican party in Ohio as well as Chase's drive for the White House.

To no one's surprise the campaign of 1855 was bitter. Chase predicted that the Democratic press would do "all it can to identify me with the Kns . . . and to arouse the prejudices of the Old Whigs growing out of my democratic antecedents." And in fact the Democratic *Ohio Statesman* of Columbus charged that Chase and his followers had forgotten their differences with the American party even though Know-Nothingism was "still sworn to put down the Catholic Church and to degrade the alien born." The *Statesman* also labeled Chase a Garrisonian abolitionist, and, quoting a Chase letter of 1845 to the black community of Cincinnati, it emphasized, "CHASE IN FAVOR OF NEGRO VOTERS! CHASE IN FAVOR OF NIGGER CHILDREN ATTENDING THE SAME PUBLIC SCHOOLS WITH WHITE." Throughout the campaign, the Democratic press attempted to exploit the racial prejudice of Ohio voters by attacking Chase's views and his role in the partial repeal of the black laws.[23]

In sharp contrast, the Republican press enthusiastically supported Chase. The *National Era* and the *Ohio Columbian* praised his candidacy and endorsed the role he had played in the Senate. Bailey noted the wisdom of Chase's party in ignoring nativism and stressing slave related issues. Some of the more conservative Know-Nothing or formerly Whig papers had more difficulty accepting Chase's candidacy. The *Cincinnati Gazette* considered his nomination "one we hoped would be averted" because few "have so many bitter prejudices to contend with." By the close of the campaign, however, the *Gazette* noted that "Chase more clearly approaches our views of state policy" than the Democratic candidate, incumbent William Medill. Similarly the *Ohio State Journal* spent more time attacking Chase's opponents than supporting him. Yet it did argue that Chase's "stand on the Nebraska outrage challenged the hearty concurrence of every true friend of freedom."[24]

The *Gazette* feared rightly that Know-Nothings in southern Ohio, especially in Cincinnati, would not endorse Chase. Although the leader of the Know-Nothings in Ohio, Thomas Spooner, urged nativists to support Chase for fear of being charged with "bad faith," many opposed his candidacy. The *Gallipolis Journal* endorsed the candidate of a breakaway faction of Know-Nothings which nominated an eighty-year-old former governor, Allen Trimble. Though small, the Trimble movement represented a serious threat to Chase's chances, for it could be expected to attract only potential Republican voters.

The Democrats, given new hope by the Trimble movement, tried to ignore the Nebraska issue and instead stressed the danger of nativism as represented by both of their opponents.[25]

Chase, accepting the advice of Lewis Campbell, kept his doubts about the Know-Nothings to himself and urged supporters to emphasize the slave expansion issue. Throughout the campaign, he parried Democratic attacks on his past record, attacks led by the *Cincinnati Enquirer,* the *Ohio Statesman,* and Governor Medill. In a Cincinnati speech, Chase again denied being a part of a corrupt bargain in his 1849 Senate election. Further, he refuted charges that he was an abolitionist or a disunionist. He noted that Garrison and southern nullifiers regarded the Union "lightly"; but he shared "fellowship" with neither.[26]

In all, Chase spoke in forty-nine of Ohio's eighty-eight counties, although he was only moderately effective as an orator. Carl Schurz remembered that he "looked as you would wish a statesman to look." He was "tall, broadshouldered, and proudly erect, his features strong and regular and his forehead broad, high and clear." Yet contemporaries also noted that his platform manner was awkward. Jacob Schuckers felt that his voice was "somewhat thick, and his manner lacked in grace," but he added that Chase was "a skillful and successful advocate." As a stump speaker, he was, said another supporter, "most untiring and energetic." His speeches were characterized by "calmness and self-possession, by . . . strong and clear statement of his case." Another contemporary, Rutherford B. Hayes, felt Chase's style was "unimpassioned and spiritless." Said the future president: "He appeared embarrassed and awkward, and lisped slightly."[27] Opinions varied, but the evidence suggests that Chase's oratorical skills were limited.

Chase's margin of victory in the October 1855 gubernatorial election was slender. With Trimble receiving nearly 25,000 votes, Chase defeated Governor Medill by fewer than 16,000 of the more than 300,000 votes cast. Chase ran strongest in northern Ohio, where antislavery sentiment was greatest but finished a poor third in his own Hamilton County, with less than 20 percent of the vote.[28] In Hamilton County Know-Nothings, Germans, and conservative business interests opposed him. Too strong a nativist emphasis had cost him some German support, but if he had ignored Know-Nothing interests completely, he might have sacrificed even more votes. He

recognized that he had "lost on both sides—on the American because not a member of the order and on the naturalized because
connected with the Kns on the ticket." Nonetheless, strong support
from Know-Nothing leaders like Campbell and Spooner helped provide the victory margin. When Campbell claimed credit, Chase readily admitted that he had done the "most service."[29]

The governor-elect and his supporters realized that the victory,
narrow as it had been, put Chase in a strong position should the new
party prove able to organize nationally and participate in the presidential election of 1856. The Republican movement had not done
well elsewhere in 1855, primarily because of the surprising strength
of the Know-Nothings. The Kansas issue had not proven sufficiently
appealing to northern voters to establish the Republicans as a formidable force in national politics. To some, ethnic, religious, and temperance issues provoked greater response. Much depended on events
in Congress and in Kansas as to whether Republicans could organize
and present a meaningful challenge to the Democrats.

Realizing that he could be nominated for the presidency in 1856
if the Republican party did get organized, Chase made every effort to
improve his and the party's stance in the months ahead. He readily
accepted suggestions from several sources that campaign biographies
be published. During the summer of 1855, he traveled in the East
and conferred with Republican leaders in several key states. Governor Kinsley Bingham of Michigan told Chase, "It would please me
best to see your name inscribed as the leader" of the party ticket, a
sentiment that was reaffirmed by James W. Grimes of Iowa.[30]

Although Democrats lamented that Chase's election would advance sectionalism and fuel "the undermining fires of disunion,"
Chase was optimistic. He told Gideon Welles, "Ohio may be put
down as entirely safe in 1856 if we can have a candidate who will be
acceptable to the parties which were harmonized this year." Chase,
of course, viewed himself as that candidate and wrote to Bingham, "I
have as much if not more of the right kind of strength than any other
of the gentlemen named." He was referring to such other contenders
as Seward and McLean. His hope was "to be selected as the expo-
nent of the Anti-Nebraska sentiment."[31]

As a presidential hopeful, Governor Chase kept national issues in
the forefront. He devoted a major part of his inaugural address to
slave related issues. He presented a long recounting of the political

Chase in the late 1850s when he was governor of Ohio. National Archives, 111-BA-688.

history of Kansas, reminding his listeners of his "Appeal" message and his efforts to prevent the passage of the Kansas-Nebraska bill. Rejecting Douglas's popular sovereignty, he argued, "The prohibition of slavery is a necessary prerequisite to a real sovereignty of the people." He explained that Ohio exemplified the benefits of a territory free of slavery and urged Ohioans to defend the rights guaranteed in the Northwest Ordinance. For Chase the importance of the slavery issue transcended "all other political questions."[32]

Chase's message to the state legislature did not go unnoticed outside of Ohio as Horace Greeley's *New York Tribune* noted that "Governor Chase comes boldly out at an opportune moment, and shows himself ready to resist the encroachments of slavery." The *National Era* called the address a "State paper of the first order." During the legislative session which followed, the Republican controlled legislature responded to the governor's urging with a series of strong antislavery resolutions on Kansas as well as one calling for the repeal of the fugitive slave act.[33]

Governor Chase also continued his efforts in behalf of fugitive slaves, though somewhat hampered as a public official to act as aggressively as he had as a Cincinnati attorney. In a number of cases Chase attempted to secure release for fugitives captured in Ohio. Two weeks after his inauguration, a slave family named Garner escaped from Kentucky to Cincinnati where a federal marshal captured them. They were held initially under Ohio law until ordered returned to slavery. By the time Chase learned of the decision, which he regarded as a violation of Ohio's sovereignty, the Garners had already been sent back to Kentucky. Chase petitioned Kentucky Governor Charles Morehead for the Garners' return to Ohio for trial, only to learn that they had already been removed deeper into the South.[34] Failing to appreciate that Chase could not prevent an already accomplished deed, eastern abolitionists criticized his actions. Theodore Parker accused him of "backing down," whereas Gerrit Smith questioned Chase's commitment to antislavery. Bailey defended him in the *National Era*. Years later Chase revealed his frustrations over the limits of his gubernatorial authority, complaining that he had "no more power . . . than any private citizen."[35]

Fugitive slave issues remained prominent and potentially explosive in Ohio throughout the 1850s largely because of the state's proximity to the slave states of Kentucky and Virginia. Under the act of 1850, which Chase had fought so diligently in the Senate, enforcement authority was greatly increased. Governor Chase was thus caught in a dilemma between his respect for federal authority, his belief that the law was unconstitutional, and his desire to help fugitives. His less-than-satisfactory solution was to steer a middle course by defending the rights of the accused while avoiding a confrontation with the central government.

Among the several fugitive slave cases Chase faced during his administration, the one involving John Price best reveals the governor's strategy.[36] Price had been seized in Oberlin and then rescued by an angry mob, thirty-seven of whom were indicted for violating the fugitive slave act. After two of the mob were tried and convicted, the matter was brought to the Ohio Supreme Court where the issue became the constitutionality of the federal law. At an emotional mass meeting in Cleveland protesting the convictions, Governor Chase spoke against violence and the fugitive slave act. Federal authority must not be resisted, he said, even though the act was "a symbol of the supremacy of the Slave States." He urged compliance with whatever decision the state court reached and the use of the ballot box to end the proslavery domination of the federal government. Eventually that court voted three to two to uphold the law; in a compromise the cases against the rescuers were finally dropped as were the counter-suits against those accused of kidnapping Price.[37] The governor had thus helped to avoid a confrontation while maintaining his role as an antislavery advocate.

Chase also made strenuous efforts to keep his Kansas feelings before the public by acting in behalf of Ohioans and other northerners living in Kansas. He corresponded regularly with several free state residents of the territory, one of whom wrote of the slave power plan "to hire several thousand men to come to Kansas" to assure the organization of a proslavery government. Others told of proslavery mobs from Missouri and of threats and property damage. They signed petitions asking for Chase's assistance in securing the "enforcement of their constitutional rights." Chase wrote to Governor Grimes of Iowa that "prompt and efficient succor" must be given to "our outraged brethren."[38] Following the appeal of several Ohioans who were imprisoned in Kansas by the proslavery government, Chase wrote to Kansas Governor John W. Geary and demanded their release, noting that "partisans of the slavery side" went unpunished. Chase's efforts to help the free-state settlers "throw off the galling and oppressive laws of the Missouri invaders" received much attention in the Republican press. Chase also offered advice to free-state leaders in Lawrence and Leavenworth on how to win approval of the antislavery Topeka constitution. He could only have been pleased when free-state Governor Charles Robinson told him that he was "regarded as *the* Champion of our cause" and that his actions would "not soon be forgotten." [39]

Chase instinctively defended his friend Sumner when Preston Brooks caned him in May 1856, following the senator's "Crime Against Kansas" speech. With great compassion, Chase urged Sumner not to return to his Senate seat until he was fully recovered. Like other Republicans, however, Chase also recognized the political value of the attack, for it would do more to show "the true character of the men that slavery makes than ten thousand speeches." In subsequent months he made frequent mention of this fact. [40]

While he kept the focus on national affairs, Chase also proved highly adept in state issues. The governor of Ohio had no veto power and was thus deprived of any direct role in the legislative process. In fact, Chase had written in his "Preliminary Sketch of the History of Ohio" in 1834 that the governor "is a name almost without meaning." Moreover, Chase lacked popular appeal because of his appearance of aloofness and his attitude of moral superiority. Even Jacob W. Schuckers, his contemporary and overly laudatory biographer, described him as "habitually grave and reserved in demeanor; he did not often laugh, and had but a small appreciation of humor; he sometimes told a story, but rarely without spoiling it." Although Chase had little charisma, he was an effective chief executive. In his inaugural address he called for a wide variety of legislation, indicating that he did not intend a passive administration. Included were proposals for improved educational and penal systems, better care for the physically and mentally handicapped, and women's rights. He also asked for reform in the militia system, reduced taxes, and an expanded state banking system. [41] Chase could do little to initiate such ideas, but he did encourage those in the legislature who shared his views.

Many of his proposals remained in the discussion stage during his governorship. His recommendations to the State Teachers Association and the legislature urged improvement in teacher training through the establishment of normal schools and the requirement of universal school attendance and standards of instruction. Reforms in these areas were not accomplished until after the Civil War. [42]

Chase did manage, however, to promote some changes in penal policy. Shortly before the election, he had been chosen president of the Ohio Prison and Reform Association, an organization which sought the rehabilitation of convicted criminals. As governor, he questioned the practice of capital punishment as a deterrent to crime. He called for the expansion and improvement of prison facilities and could report some progress before the end of his tenure, including the establishment of a reform farm to allow young offenders an alternative to the regular prison system.[43]

Like many other antislavery advocates, Chase did not confine his reform interests to the plight of the slave. He was also a spokesman for many other disadvantaged groups in society. Those who knew Chase well recognized a personal warmth and genuine compassion beneath the cold exterior. His imperious manner could not, for example, hide his humanitarian concern for the mentally ill. Because of the lack of facilities for the criminally insane, Chase on several occasions suspended sentences of convicted prisoners. He consistently sought more funds from the legislature to finance existing asylums for the insane, but because of the state's financial plight his efforts met only limited success. Before he left office four asylums had been established, although Chase admitted that many more patients remained without proper care.[44]

The governor also supported the women's rights movement. Petitions to the legislature had brought little change in the unequal status of women before Chase's inauguration, but following his proposals, the legislature in 1857 prohibited a husband from selling his wife's personal property without her consent and granted to wives whose husbands had deserted them the right to make contracts for their own and their children's labor.[45]

Chase also initiated important economic proposals, some of which the legislature enacted. Banking issues continued to be a source of significant partisan division as they had been since the 1820s. For the most part the Republican majority continued the Whig approach of favoring an expansion of banking facilities and paper currency to satisfy credit-hungry business interests. Democrats remained divided between hard money advocates, who opposed all banks, and the more moderate, who favored a limited banking system subject to strict state regulation. In 1845, the Whigs had had their way with the passage of an expanded banking system which was further augmented by a free banking law in 1851. The volatile banking issue had remained largely hidden during the gubernatorial campaign of

1855, although Republicans had talked of the need for better banking facilities. As a Free-Soiler Chase had stood closer to the antibank views of those Democrats with whom he had sought coalition; he thus faced a dilemma when the new Republican party endorsed the free banking views of the Whigs. As governor, Chase moved closer to his Republican colleagues and endorsed their banking proposals as well as a more flexible currency system. He offered a free banking proposal to the legislature, but the measure that was enacted was subject to a popular referendum and was defeated by the voters in 1856.[46] Chase's experience as governor would provide valuable training for his later tenure as secretary of the Treasury.

Chase also dexterously handled the patronage at his disposal, fielding hundreds of requests from those who considered themselves deserving Republicans. Because his party contained antislavery, Whig, and Know-Nothing elements, he had to be especially careful to alienate as few as possible. For example, he rewarded his friend George Hoadly with an appointment to the state supreme court, but on other occasions he had to disappoint loyal followers who sought appointments.[47] There is little evidence to suggest that Chase was able to build a personal machine which might have helped him in his drive for national office, although he did manage to keep most of his fellow partisans content by his appointment policies, an accomplishment which would do him no harm when Republicans met to choose their presidential nominee.

One group that Chase was especially eager to keep content and loyal to himself and to the Republican party was the German Americans who had supported him in the past. This proved especially difficult in Ohio because of the continuing appeal of nativism and temperance, but Chase, through some adroit politics, was at least partially successful. When Cincinnati German leader Stephen Molitor told Chase that failure to reappoint the city's incumbent German collector "would certainly create the cry of persecution on account of birthplace," Chase made certain that the man kept his appointment. When the Republican-controlled Ohio senate pushed through a temperance measure, Molitor warned Chase that "the republican movement among Germans [would] be an utter failure" if the measure became law. Molitor's protest to the governor was important because Chase used his influence with Republicans to persuade the House to kill the bill. Chase also successfully tempered a proposed constitutional amendment requiring a lapse of three years after citizenship before a naturalized American could vote. In the end the proposal was rejected, and German leaders like Molitor and W. F. Hassaurek remained solidly in the Republican camp.[48]

In an attempt to keep the Know-Nothing element in his administration happy as well, the governor reluctantly did not lobby against two Republican-sponsored measures designed to please nativists. One gave church members control over church property; the other, "an act to preserve the purity of elections," was designed to eliminate alleged illegal immigrant voting by tightening residency requirements.[49]

Although Know-Nothing support had been necessary to secure Chase's election to the governorship, many felt that continued association with them could prove a liability in the eyes of Republicans outside Ohio. The most prominent of Chase's friends urging him to repudiate his Know-Nothing association were Bailey and Ashley. Ashley had in fact opposed a coalition for the gubernatorial race and after the election pressured Chase with the prediction that "all will be lost to freedom in the contest of 56." Bailey feared that the Know-Nothings, who were "men trying to serve two masters," would betray him. Chase, he said, should emphasize his antagonism to Know-Nothing doctrines in a "conspicuous and unmistakable" way.[50] The governor, unwilling to alienate the nativists too soon, refrained from denouncing Americanism in his inaugural address and legislative communications. His strategy was to stay on friendly terms with individual Know-Nothings and hope that the movement would die a natural death. In the long run, Chase's approach proved correct.

Those with Know-Nothing leanings had little interest in a Chase presidential candidacy, whether they remained in the third party or joined the Republicans. Lieutenant Governor Thomas Ford sought to persuade Justice McLean to be a candidate and prevent "fanatics" like Chase from capturing the Republican party. Senator Henry Wilson warned Chase that "Ford, Campbell and others of your state are too willing to sacrifice freedom" to strengthen their party.[51] Chase's Republican colleagues feared that nativists in Ohio and elsewhere cared more for their party organization than they did about the efforts to contain slavery. Chase, they felt, should have nothing to do with such an approach.

Part of Chase's strategy for establishing himself as the front runner was to help organize a preliminary meeting of Republicans before a nominating convention was held. His supporters agreed to this at a strategy meeting in Toledo in the fall of 1855 attended by Chase, Ashley, Hamlin, and others. A correspondence committee then contacted the chairmen of state Republican committees and other party leaders around the country. Largely through the efforts of Ashley and Bailey a meeting was called at Pittsburgh on February 22, 1856 for the official purpose "of perfecting a national organization" and planning for the nominating convention. Despite the misgivings of his friend Bailey, Chase still hoped to bring as many northern Know-Nothings, now labeled North Americans, into the Republican movement as possible. At his urging, Thomas Spooner agreed to try to precipitate a bolt of this faction from the American party at their convention in Philadelphia by calling for the party's merger with Republicans. Chase and Ashley hoped the Pittsburgh organizing convention would unite the various anti-Nebraska groups with the North Americans and in the process advertise the governor's candidacy for president.[52]

The Pittsburgh convention officially inaugurated the Republican party nationally. Representatives from twenty-four states elected Francis P. Blair president and heard key addresses by Giddings and Horace Greeley. Chase did not attend, preferring to remain in the background while Ashley and other supporters who dominated the Ohio delegation urged his candidacy. Some of those supporters returned with enthusiastic accounts. One told him that had the meeting been a nominating convention Chase would have been chosen "by two to one." The platform called for an antislavery stance similar to the one Chase had helped write in Buffalo in 1848. It also promised to "resist by every constitutional means the existence of Slavery" in all territories. When the Philadelphia convention of the American party nominated Millard Fillmore on a conservative platform which failed to attack slavery, approximately sixty northern delegates, including Spooner and Ford, seceded. The possibility that these North Americans might later unite with the Republicans now appeared more likely, and Chase believed that he would be the beneficiary. As he told his friend Charles Cleveland: "My own efforts to secure a union of all freemen for the sake of freedom have been unremitting and will probably be successful in this State at least."[53]

There were, however, signs both before and after Pittsburgh that indicated a Chase nomination could not easily be secured. One Ohio delegate told him of significant support for McLean. Bailey wrote that some among conservative Ohioans pledged themselves against Chase's candidacy because he had sought "the Governorship as a stepping stone to the Presidency." Ashley added that some New Yorkers discredited Chase as an abolitionist, and that party conservatives everywhere stressed the need for a candidate who would appeal to a broad cross section of northern voters. Chase could not even count on the support of Bailey and Giddings. Bailey wrote to Chase just before the Pittsburgh convention that he felt Seward was "the strongest candidate," and his *National Era* maintained a strict neutrality. Giddings, then a candidate for Speaker of the House, suggested that he too would remain neutral, lest "Seward's friends" support another candidate for Speaker.[54] Seward's strength would naturally be greater among eastern delegates, but Chase knew that some midwesterners would also back the New Yorker.

Chase nonetheless remained optimistic as the nominating convention scheduled for mid-June in Philadelphia approached. Ashley overconfidently told Chase to expect the majority of votes from New York, Pennsylvania, and the West. Governor Grimes told him that there were "too many old chronic prejudices" against Seward "to allow him to make a respectable poll." Chase wrote to Cleveland that "the majority in Ohio desire my nomination and election." Furthermore, he said, "I am less objectionable" to opponents of the administration than anyone else. He also reminded Sumner that "a year ago you expressed a preference for me."[55]

Yet from Sumner, Bailey, and others Chase learned of a stronger movement than those for Seward or McLean or himself. As so many antebellum parties had done before, the Republicans of 1856 would find it most expedient to choose a candidate who had not been prominent politically and who could conciliate the various factions. Such a man was John C. Frémont, the frontier explorer and persecuted military hero of California. Not identified with any wing of the party, Frémont had no clear-cut position on slavery or economic issues. Murat Halstead, the Cincinnati journalist, suggested that Frémont was everybody's second choice and thus acceptable to all. In lamenting the Frémont movement, Bailey wrote to Chase, "You and Seward are thrust aside" solely for having done "so much service" and having aroused "so much antagonism." Bailey still hoped the convention would reject Frémont, "an amiable honorable gentleman with a gift for exploration and adventure," but one who had little knowledge of politics or "the value and aims of our movement."[56]

Since early in 1856, a powerful group of eastern Republicans, including Blair, Weed, Henry Wilson, and Nathaniel Banks, had emerged as the controlling element in the party by virtue of their experience and influence on the national committee. They, like Chase, recognized the need for cooperation with the North Americans but believed that only a man of more moderate antislavery views than Chase could successfully bring about that unity. Although it was not well known, Frémont agreed with many nativist beliefs. In the eyes of the eastern Republican group, he was therefore a more attractive and available candidate than either Chase or Seward.[57]

Chase remained hopeful of nomination because large numbers of Michigan and Wisconsin delegates reportedly would support him. But he realized he would not have a united Ohio delegation at the convention. Chase expected the Republican state convention to endorse him; instead, it expressed no preference and chose six uninstructed at-large delegates. Many district delegates also failed to support him. Chase remained in the battle, however, and instructed Hamlin to "take all fair measures you can to strengthen our side" at the convention. It still appeared to him "that if the unbiased wishes of the people could prevail," he would be nominated.[58]

The Philadelphia convention of June 1856 brought Chase the first of several disappointments. With such easterners as Blair and Weed in control, the Frémont movement was too strong to stop; Seward's supporters withdrew his name before the nominating began. The Ohio delegation divided its support with about half of the seventy delegates supporting Chase and the remainder divided between McLean and Frémont. With support from less than one-third of the necessary number to win the nomination, Chase's followers decided to withdraw his name too. Chase had given his backers a letter to read if that happened. He made no effort to commit his supporters to either Frémont or McLean, nor did he seek political leverage in the platform with his withdrawal. Whether or not he could have achieved a stronger antislavery platform with that stand is unclear, but his failure to bargain was a measure of Chase's lack of political skill. In his letter the governor noted that the success of the cause "is infinitely dearer to me than any personal advancement." Nothing, he said should "stand in the way of that complete union necessary to end the domination of slavery propagandism." Although McLean's supporters persisted, the convention quickly chose Frémont on an informal ballot.[59]

The platform was one that the Chase people endorsed, for it recognized the power of Congress to prohibit slavery in the territories. In Chase's words, it recognized "all that is most important for us" because "it included denationalization of slavery entire." Perhaps this represented an effort to save face; Chase could not have been pleased with a platform which failed to mention the fugitive slave law or the status of slavery in the District of Columbia. Chase quickly sent his congratulations to Frémont and, promising "cordial and earnest" support, actively campaigned for him in Ohio. But he later complained to Sumner that the party had "committed an act of positive injustice" in failing to nominate men who represented "the great real issue" of the day.[60] Clearly the moderate elements in the Republican party had dealt Chase a stunning setback.

Several factors account for Chase's failure in 1856. Party leaders wanted someone in the middle between its conservative and antislavery extremes, an individual who had not been directly involved in the key sectional issues of the day. By early 1856, they had determined that Frémont best fit their needs. Weed and Henry Wilson had been among those Republicans present at the North American convention, which met in New York several days before the Philadelphia gathering. In New York, moderate Republicans had completed their arrangement for the withdrawal of the convention's nominee, Nathaniel Banks, and the subsequent North American endorsement of Frémont.[61] Despite his own efforts and those of Ashley, Chase had not been able to overcome the desire of many Republicans for a moderate.

Another factor was that Chase could not count on a united Ohio delegation. His record as an antislavery advocate and expedient politician left him with too many enemies. He was also hampered by a failure to establish a smoothly functioning political machine. By nature both egotistical and overly optimistic, Chase accepted the unrealistic claims of supporters that a nomination could easily be his. He thus failed to build up the network of supporters necessary to win delegate backing. Chase's attitude suggested that he deserved the nomination without a struggle because of his past services to the party. Naively, he never recognized that others in the party followed different rules. Both Chase and Ashley had traveled in the East during the summer of 1855 establishing contacts, but few others actively worked for his nomination. Even in Ohio there was too little effort put into organizing a Chase movement for president. After several anti-Chase Ohio delegates were chosen for the Philadelphia convention, the governor unhappily noted that "our friends were not overpowered but out-generaled, [failing] to act with the skill and decision which was required." The problem was even more serious at Philadelphia where Chase's few friends were no match for their more experienced opponents. In the end, as Hiram Barney told Chase, "You have had nobody really and actually at work for you."[62]

Defeat for Chase brought the governor face to face with the issue of reelection in 1857. Ashley pointed out the disadvantages of a second campaign and worried lest a defeat in the October election would give "great trouble" to those who desired his nomination "as the Republican Candidate for President in 1860." Chase denied that 1860 was a factor in his decision, emphasizing that "the sake of our cause" would determine whether he sought reelection. As late as two weeks before the nominating convention he wrote Congressman John Sherman, "Nothing is farther from my wish than a renomination." To accept it would mean the surrender of "all my purposes and plans." On the other hand, if he wanted to control the Republican machinery in Ohio, few other roads were open to him in 1857. Democrats and Republicans questioned his high-minded explanation to run only because of "our cause."[63]

One major factor in Chase's decision to seek reelection was the revelation in June 1857 of a major scandal. State Treasurer William H. Gibson was forced to reveal a shortage of more than half a million dollars. Although the defalcation was primarily the responsibility of Gibson's predecessor, Democrat John G. Breslin, Gibson concealed the matter for more than a year and a half. Chase reluctantly forced Gibson's resignation in order to save his administration further embarrassment. Democrats made the most of the situation by charging the administration and Gibson with corruption and malfeasance, a charge difficult to substantiate when Democrat Breslin fled to Canada to avoid an indictment for embezzlement.[64] Yet for Chase to turn down renomination might give the impression of complicity in the coverup. Hence he sought reelection to exonerate his reputation, hoping to survive the crisis and perhaps even strengthen his chances for 1860.[65]

Since both parties were involved in the controversy, neither could gain much political capital from it. As a result, the campaign revolved around sectional and economic issues instead. The Democrats, led by their nominee Henry B. Payne of Cleveland, contended that Chase had neglected Ohio by emphasizing distant Kansas problems. The *Ohio Statesman* charged anew that Chase, "an undisguised abolitionist," believed "in the right of Congress to abolish slavery in the states and territories." The recent Dred Scott decision rendered these charges ineffectual; instead, Chase immediately attacked the Supreme Court and the Buchanan administration for transforming the territories "into one great slave pen" and making "Slavery National and Freedom Sectional." Republicans knew a hard fight awaited them but determined that they could beat the "Douglas, Nebraska, Dred Scott ticket headed by Payne."[66]

Economic troubles, initiated by the Panic of 1857, gave the Democrats another issue to use against the party in power. Promising to establish a state independent treasury to protect public funds from bank failures, the Democrats campaigned strenuously against the Republican Chase-backed referendum to create additional banks. The overwhelming rejection of the banking proposal for the second consecutive year indicated that the voters agreed with the Democrats on the need to remove state money from corporation control. Chase then proposed that future banking laws could escape the referendum requirement of the state constitution if they were disguised as amendments to the free banking act of 1851. With the election of a Democratic legislature in 1857, however, no further efforts were made to expand banking facilities while Chase was governor.[67] Chase would later, as secretary of the Treasury, recognize the benefits of centralized control over the burgeoning numbers of state banks in the nation.

In the two years following Chase's election as governor, the Know-Nothing movement declined dramatically. In 1855, Chase had been the only Republican on a fusion ticket dominated by nativists. By 1857, all but one of those candidates had been dropped and replaced by Republicans; most significantly, Thomas Ford was replaced against his will by Martin Welker, a German, for the office of lieutenant governor. The 1857 elections would represent the last effort of a separate Know-Nothing party in Ohio. Republicans gave only minimal recognition to the third party in their campaign, concentrating instead on the Democrats.[68]

With the Know-Nothing candidate Philadelph Van Trump attracting 9,200 votes, Chase's plurality over Payne was a mere 1,500 votes out of more than 325,000 cast. Democratic strength resulted in the party gaining control of both legislative houses. Even in the predominantly Republican Western Reserve, Chase's majority was sharply reduced from the 1855 figure. Chase accurately attributed the closeness of the vote to "the concealment by our Treasurer of his predecessor's defalcation and the anti-bank clamor in consequence of the money panic." To the economic factors he added that "the cry of negro equality, amalgamation and the like" turned "the ignorant" against his party.[69]

Having traveled more than thirty-seven hundred miles and spoken in forty-three counties, the governor could attribute his victory largely to his own strenuous campaign effort. Although Chase reasoned that his political appeal was responsible, he failed to recognize that his lack of personal appeal may instead have reduced his margin. His overbearing pompous and ponderous manner failed to win him many friends among voters or politicians, but his championing of unpopular issues was as much the problem as was his personality. Certainly the narrowness of his victory would not deter him from another effort to win the presidential nomination. Shortly after the election, he found that "many are beginning to talk about the election of 1860" and "are again urging my name." Some even insisted that he could generate "more strength than any other man."[70]

Chase thus began his second gubernatorial term with his eyes squarely on the White House. As in his first term, he subordinated state issues to national ones. His relations with the Democratic-controlled legislature proved more difficult than during his first term when the Republicans had the majority. Over the governor's strong objections the Democratic lawmakers repealed the acts of the previous legislature that had been designed to prevent enforcement of the fugitive slave law, including one outlawing the use of Ohio jails to hold accused runaways. The legislature even considered but did not pass a measure to prevent the immigration into Ohio of free blacks. To the governor, such efforts only proved that southerners and their doughfaced allies in the North were determined that slavery should spread even into the free states.[71] More likely it was an indication of the highly partisan nature of Ohio politics in the 1850s as well as of the explosiveness of racial issues. Such questions allowed Chase to keep the focus of his governorship on problems dividing North and South.

In his second inaugural address, delivered to an unfriendly legislature in January 1858, Chase again emphasized the controversy raging in Kansas. The governor explained that although "the majority of Kansans had had no voice in framing the (proslavery) Lecompton constitution," President Buchanan had urged Congress to accept it. Chase asked the legislature to give its "emphatic expression" of opposition to that move because Ohioans "are opposed to this interposition of the Federal Government in behalf of Slavery."[72] The issue was further complicated for Chase and his party when Senator Douglas broke with the president. The constitution was not to be submitted to a popular vote in Kansas, and that violated the senator's cherished principle of popular sovereignty. Some Republicans hoped that an alliance could be worked out with Douglas. Even Giddings, who had for so long been opposed to any association with Democrats, thought it should be considered.[73]

Chase refused cooperation with the man who had sponsored the Kansas-Nebraska bill in 1854. Fearful of rivalry with the Illinois senator should the two groups unite, Chase felt his party was strong enough to proceed independently. Chase concurred with Sumner that Douglas was insincere. They thought it would be "impossible for us to trust him until after a very sufficient probation." Chase's inflated self-image allowed him to question the motives of a rival without understanding that his own motives could be challenged. Douglas had done no more than insist on popular sovereignty, the principle Republicans had opposed ever since their formation as an anti-extension party. When Seward hinted that Republicans might now endorse the Douglas doctrine, Chase resisted because in his view popular sovereignty would sanction "the enslavement of man by his fellow man." The willingness to sacrifice principle sought votes "by means which will make success worse than worthless," he charged. He was certain that the "great masses" of the party agreed with him "in determination to maintain Republican principles without compromise."[74] Eager to prevent any possible Douglas-

Republican cooperation, Chase traveled to Illinois during the senator's contest for reelection with Abraham Lincoln in 1858 to campaign for his Republican colleague.

Chase had one other contact with Lincoln before the election of 1860. In 1859, Ohio Republicans adopted a platform calling for the "repeal of the atrocious Fugitive Slave law." Lincoln, following his defeat by Douglas and during his efforts to maintain leadership of his state party, urged Chase not to insist on such a plank at the Republican national convention of 1860. Should it be adopted, he said, "the cause of Republicanism is hopeless in Illinois." Chase responded in defense of Ohio's Republican party that the law of 1850 was "harsh and severe and almost absolutely useless as a practical measure of reclamation." In addition, he argued, it was unconstitutional. After Lincoln reminded Chase of the fugitive slave clause in the Constitution, their correspondence went no further.[75] Clearly the two men were far from agreement on Republican strategy and ideology.

As the election year of 1860 approached, John Brown's raid at Harpers Ferry further inflamed sectional differences and placed Republicans like Chase in a delicate position. In 1856, he had shown some interest in Brown's activities and, after the abolitionist visited him in Columbus, Chase recommended him "to the confidence and regard of all who desire to see Kansas a free state."[76] The following year Brown asked Chase for financial aid for *"secret service and no questions asked."* Earlier Chase had given him twenty-five dollars for use in Kansas. The governor's response to the news of Harpers Ferry was mixed. On the one hand he admitted that the raid might have "deluge[d] the land with blood" and made "void the fairest hopes of mankind!" Yet he could not help but recognize Brown's "unselfish desire to set free the oppressed." He admired his "bravery—the humanity towards his prisoners which defeated his purposes!" In his 1860 message to the legislature he condemned all attempts to initiate slave insurrections because they might lead to "the calamities of civil, as well as servile war." But in response to Virginia Governor Henry A. Wise's warning against the formation of expeditions in Ohio to rescue Brown, Chase vehemently turned the issue around. He could not, he said, permit similar "armed bodies" from Virginia to enter Ohio to pursue fugitive slaves.[77] Although Chase and other Republicans could not defend Brown publicly, they were in no mood to permit their own state sovereignty to be violated by slave catchers. It was in such an atmosphere that Chase pursued his party's presidential nomination.

Chase's drive for the Republican nomination of 1860 was his most serious and concerted effort of the four attempts he made. His dominance in Ohio politics and his prominence among national Republicans made him a logical and leading contender as early as 1857. His reelection as governor that year in the face of many obstacles proved his vote-getting ability and convinced him and many of his supporters that his strength was increasing.[78]

His support among Republicans appeared to be increasing despite Seward's strength and better organization. Giddings told Chase that the "radical Republicans are rapidly concentrating on you." New York supporters James A. Briggs and Hiram Barney even suggested that Seward did not have sufficient support to win his home state. Ashley found Horace Greeley "*warmly* against Seward and at present favorable to you."[79] George Julian reported from Indiana that Chase's chances were improving there while similar optimistic predictions came from James Grimes in Iowa and Charles Robinson in Kansas. Only occasionally did he receive negative reports through 1859, as when Charles Cleveland noted that Seward men in the East were arguing that "Chase is young enough to wait."[80] Such omens were clearly in the minority, and Chase preferred to ignore them.

The two-year campaign for the presidency in fact revealed that Chase had learned little from his failure in 1856. The obstacles were the same: the candidate's advanced antislavery position at a time when the party sought moderation and his reputation as an expedient politician driven by personal ambition. Nothing he said or did changed that image, and his managers were unable to devise an organization as effective as those of his competitors. Chase was never good at organizational politics; nor was he willing to sacrifice his antislavery position to please the moderates who dominated the party.

Refusing to recognize the seriousness of his organizational problem, Chase did little to correct it other than urge his followers to intensify their efforts. He confidently named a long list of senators and representatives whose support he felt sure of, including Wade, Sumner, Wilson, and Giddings, but he then urged Barney "to adopt some earnest line of action" to secure greater support in the East:

"Find out who concurs with us and get them to act in concert." To Briggs he lamented: "You do not say whether there has been an organization in New York nor what it has done." He wanted "an exact notice of strength" there and elsewhere but then failed to follow up his query.[81]

James M. Ashley remained Chase's most active and effective proponent throughout the preconvention campaigning. Elected to Congress in 1858, Ashley worked in Ohio and throughout the North to persuade Republicans to endorse Chase's antislavery philosophy. In New York in early 1858, he talked to Greeley and others and reported to Chase that the governor's backers there were not working hard enough: "We must have some *active* reliable men in NY" to preserve the cause. Chase's inability to raise sufficient funds prevented Ashley from traveling to Washington to "learn more perfectly how matters stand." In 1859, Ashley sought support in Minnesota and Wisconsin. Wherever he went he realistically reported to Chase the need for a powerful organization and newspaper support to stop Seward, whose friends were making "the most desperate effort" to win the nomination. Ashley alone, however, could not change enough minds, and Chase's chances did not improve.[82] Chase's inability to inspire others to work for him or support him financially was an indication of his ineffectiveness as a leader; his support was unfortunately more rhetorical and self-fulfilling than real.

Although Chase held fast to his antislavery views, Ashley and others convinced him of the need to modify his opposition to protective tariffs. Several years earlier, while attempting to work out an alliance with Democrats, he had endorsed that party's advocacy of low tariffs. Now as a member of a party which included strong protectionists, especially in the iron-producing areas of Pennsylvania, this position hurt his chances. As one supporter told him, Pennsylvania "can be secured only by a platform and candidate pledged to the principle of protection." Seward, a high tariff advocate, was clearly cutting into potential support there.[83] For Chase, protectionism was not a high priority issue, and he was easily persuaded to modify his position to enhance his chances as a candidate. Although "unrestricted commercial intercourse" was the ideal, he recognized that "to afford the greatest possible incidental benefits to industry" tariffs were necessary for the forseeable future. He published a clarification of his position in leading eastern newspapers, explaining that he favored rate discriminations that promoted the "interests of labor."[84] On the tariff issue Chase was clearly concerned with pleasing the greatest numbers of Republican delegates to the Chicago convention.

There were other signs of trouble ahead for Chase even before the spring of 1860. One ominous report came from Carl Schurz, an early supporter who had recently settled in Wisconsin and was chairman of the state's Republican delegation to the Chicago convention. In early 1860, he visited Chase in Columbus with the discouraging opinion that if the party chose an "advanced antislavery man," it would be Seward. Perhaps even more disturbing to Chase was the knowledge that he could not count on the editorial support of Gamaliel Bailey in the *National Era.* Although the editor professed his private preference for Chase, he insisted that his paper remain neutral as it had in 1856. Not wanting to divide Republicans by taking sides before the convention, Bailey even suggested privately that "the field be left free to Mr. Seward." Despite his unhappiness with Bailey's neutrality, Chase was quick to come to the editor's aid when his health began to fail and his financial situation deteriorated. Before Bailey's death in mid-1859, Chase helped to initiate a drive to persuade antislavery allies to make loans to cover Bailey's five thousand dollar indebtedness. Chase continued this drive to aid Bailey's widow even after the *National Era* ceased publication.[85]

Chase's preconvention strategy included his election to the United States Senate by the Ohio legislature in early 1860, a step which he felt would strengthen his hand among the Chicago delegates. He campaigned vigorously for the election of a Republican legislature in 1859 and for the Republican gubernatorial candidate, William Dennison. When both goals were achieved, Chase's chances for a Senate election appeared secure, although conservative Republicans who supported Thomas Corwin for the Senate and who opposed Chase's presidential ambitions might join Democrats to postpone action until after the presidential election. When the legislature agreed to make its decision in February 1860, the Republican caucus easily nominated Chase over Corwin. In the legislative vote, Chase defeated Democrat George Pugh, who had replaced him in the Senate in 1855, by a vote of 76 to 53. Chase's election to the Senate was a valuable step. One supporter indicated that it would serve "as a rebuke to Senator Douglas and his Kansas-Nebraska Act." And, as Congressman John A. Bingham noted, it was the best way "to strengthen [Chase] for the Presidency." Chase agreed and in a letter to Sumner said that his chances "to infuse [the presidency] with the spirit of liberty, justice and equity" had improved. As chief executive he would "add dignity to national character and permanence to national institutions."[86]

Chase's next step was to secure the endorsement of the Republican state convention meeting in Columbus on March 1. Although only four of the state's forty-six delegates would be chosen at that time, a party endorsement would encourage a united Ohio delegation at Chicago. By a vote of 375 to 73 the delegates resolved that Chase was their first choice for the nomination. Chase appeared overjoyed with what he called an "altogether spontaneous" vote, suggesting that he had done nothing to influence the outcome. He said, "It was pure people's work."[87]

Although he must have recognized the folly of such a claim, Chase never mustered the political savvy necessary for a successful national campaign. Only four at-large delegates were actually pledged to Chase, and the remaining forty-two would be chosen at district meetings where opposition was expected to be formidable. Chase did not pay enough attention to Ashley's advice to cultivate his Ohio supporters and ignored the opportunity to address a meeting of young Ohio Republicans in late February. He was also unwilling to appease those, like McLean, who remembered his controversial role as a Free-Soiler. He never appointed a full-time manager to coordinate his campaign, preferring to direct his efforts personally or through the press and his various lieutenants. As a result he was no match for his better organized rivals in Chicago.[88]

As the convention approached, Chase's early advantage all but disappeared. Giddings reported after a western tour that Michigan, Wisconsin, and Iowa were leaning toward Seward, leaving little of the supposedly safe West in Chase's camp. Ashley wrote from Washington that he expected little support from Maryland and Pennsylvania delegations. By April, some of Chase's most enthusiastic supporters were discouraged over Seward's progress; Charles Cleveland bluntly told Chase to "give all thoughts of a nomination by the Chicago convention to the winds." Chase admitted to his friend James S. Pike that indications were that "the choice of Ohio will not be confirmed by the Republican preferences of other States."[89]

It was gradually becoming apparent that Lincoln might emerge as an alternative candidate should Seward's drive—and Chase's—falter. Lincoln indicated tentative support for Chase and told a friend that he had "a very kind side for him." Lincoln said that "because he gave us his sympathy in 1858 when scarcely any other distinguished man did," he wished "to do no ungenerous thing" to him. Although Lincoln was at first considered little more than a favorite son, by mid-April delegates were beginning to look at him as an acceptable alternative candidate.[90]

Chase was not willing, however, to surrender without a fight. He wrote to supporters in various areas urging them to step up their activities. He encouraged his friend Richard C. Parsons in Washington to talk to undecided congressmen to learn "if they have any misapprehensions and so correct them if they have." He also asked Parsons if he should come to Washington to seek support directly. Despite his fear of "seeming to seek votes" and of giving his opponents reason to argue that he was there "to look after my chances," Chase made the trip in late April. There he found Seward the most popular candidate, but the issue was far from decided. Still concerned that the Ohio delegation was not united behind him, he found that the trip confirmed what he had feared for some time— many from Ohio and elsewhere were urging the candidacy of Benjamin Wade.[91]

Interest in Wade as a compromise candidate had been building for several months, especially among such anti-Chase Ohioans as Robert F. Paine of Cleveland and Ben Eggleston of Cincinnati. They felt that Wade's Whig background, his protectionist views, and moderate antislavery stance would make him popular elsewhere. Even James Briggs, Chase's New York advocate, promised to support Wade if Chase's candidacy floundered. Many hoped that after first ballot support of Chase, the Ohio delegation would swing to Wade and move other delegations the same way. Chase had urged his rival to withdraw following the Ohio Republican convention in early March, "satisfied" with the overwhelming endorsement the convention had given him. Wade's reply was polite but noncommittal. Chase called on Wade in Washington but again failed to get the senator to withdraw.[92]

In an attempt to unite the Ohio delegation at the convention, Chase gave instructions to Giddings and others loyal to him in the delegation to support the unit rule, which would require the delegates to vote unanimously for the majority's choice. Should he not be the choice of the majority, he told Giddings, he would be "quite content that they shall withdraw my name." But Chase's supporters, fearing that Wade would benefit from the rule, rejected the proposal to cast a unanimous vote for Chase for two ballots and on any succeeding ballots for the Ohioan who had the strongest support elsewhere. Instead, each delegate was left to vote for his personal preference on all ballots. So determined were they "to defeat the Wade movement at all hazards," they denied Chase the united delegation that he so desperately needed.[93] Divisiveness among Ohio politicians threatened to deprive the state of significant influence at the convention. The Chase and Wade factions appeared so intent on denying the other any advantage that each was willing to sacrifice its own favorite.

The first ballot revealed how weak Chase's chances actually were. He received only 34 of the 46 Ohio votes; but even more discouraging, there were only 15 additional Chase votes compared to Seward's 173½ and Lincoln's 102. On the second and third ballots, Chase's total declined further as Lincoln's steadily increased. When they realized that Lincoln was within 2½ votes of victory, four Ohio delegates, including three pledged to Chase, changed their votes to assure Lincoln's nomination. One of them later explained to Chase that giving Lincoln the necessary votes "leaves you right with the 'incoming administration.' " Chase said that Lincoln was "the only one of the prominent candidates" who had not sought to undermine his Ohio support; Chase and his supporters clearly preferred Lincoln to the other alternative candidates.[94]

A controversy immediately developed over the reasons for Chase's defeat and the role Wade and his supporters had played. Chase's delegates erred in rejecting their candidate's advice on the unit rule and in overestimating Wade's chances to win the nomination, because all indications suggested that Lincoln rather than Wade would benefit if Seward faltered. Chase was convinced that the lack of unity in the Ohio delegation cost him the nomination, and he was quick to put the blame on Wade. He felt that the action of the Ohio convention in his favor meant that the state's delegates at Chicago were "bound by the clearest obligations to do all that they could" to secure his nomination. In congratulating Lincoln, Chase could not help but contrast the loyalty of the Illinois and New York delegations to their candidates with the Ohio delegation's failure to show "the same generous spirit" despite "the clearly expressed preference of their own State convention." Chase's supporters agreed and had encouraged him in such an assessment. His brother Edward observed that Wade's candidacy had the effect of "drawing off many in other states who would have been for you." Another supporter told him that "had Ohio done her duty as her loyal Republican masses expected their delegates to do, you could have been easily nominated." Chase was thus convinced that the treachery of Wade and his supporters had been decisive; his correspondence for the next weeks reflects this bitterness. Some seven months later he told Wade, "you have done me I think some wrong," a charge his rival angrily denied.[95] Chase's bitterness and disappointment, however, blinded him to some much more fundamental flaws in his candidacy.

The lack of planning and direction which had characterized Chase's pre-convention activities continued to plague him at Chicago. Some of his key followers, such as Briggs, were not even present despite the candidate's urging that "emergencies like the present" justified his leaving his other obligations to attend. Chase failed to designate any one to coordinate his convention campaign despite the presence of Ashley and Giddings. Many of his supporters showed little initiative or enthusiasm in the absence of leadership. As one observer indicated, "There are lots of good feelings afloat here for you, but there is no set of men in earnest for you." New York supporters Barney, David Dudley Field, and George C. Opdyke, all of whom had worked for Chase, at the last minute felt themselves "under necessity to effect combinations on Lincoln to defeat Seward." A desire to go with an apparent winner thus took precedence over support of Chase.[96] Nor was there any indication that Chase made any promises of cabinet places to influence delegates as Lincoln's managers had. Throughout the campaign Chase was unable to inspire others beyond mere rhetorical interest. Many were concerned more with blocking Chase's rivals than in forwarding his candidacy. He had designated no one to initiate the necessary collective bargaining with other state delegations. Chase, in fact, had few truly influential Republicans actively supporting him.

Chase's candidacy was flawed in other respects as well. His courageous stands on sectional issues alienated moderate and conservative Republicans. Although incorrectly labeled an abolitionist by his opponents, he was more willing to advocate the antislavery cause than most Republicans. He explained to John Sherman in 1858, "My best years have been devoted, in no wild or fanatical spirit I hope, to the advancement of the antislavery cause." Unfortunately for him, too many Republicans viewed him as one who did have a "wild or fanatical spirit." Despite the yeoman's work he had performed in helping to build the Republican party of Ohio, Chase had not won the loyalty of the majority. His cold and aloof personality kept people at arm's length as did his morally righteous attitude. His role in politics before becoming a Republican had left too many enemies; one Ohio supporter observed: "The old Whigs of this State are eternally hostile to you." Republicans of all persuasions reacted negatively to his single-minded desire to be president and his rather transparent efforts to mask his political ambitions.[97]

Having fallen short in 1856, he repeated some of the same errors in his drive for the nomination in 1860. Both times he naively, and perhaps egotistically, believed that he would be chosen without a struggle. Ashley commented years later that Chase failed to understand his opponents "and might be associated" with "the chief conspirators and be entirely ignorant of their movements or their plots."[98] Thus although Chase was highly capable of identifying political issues, he was inept at winning nominations and elections and in controlling his party. Rarely willing to do what was necessary in his own behalf, he never understood why so many Americans failed to recognize his abilities. In many ways Chase was qualified for the presidency, although he lacked the political savvy necessary to be a successful chief executive. Moreover, the combination of his inability to adapt himself to the rough game of politics and his advanced position on racial issues prevented him from achieving his goal.

Chase did not let his bitterness over the loss of the nomination stop him from an active campaign for Lincoln. Although he was well aware of the possibility of a key cabinet position in a Lincoln administration, his enthusiasm for the candidate was sincere. As he told Briggs in July: "Mr. Lincoln has my hearty and cordial support and his administration will have it likewise." In addition to numerous speeches at Ohio rallies, Chase campaigned in Kentucky and New York. He was especially vehement in his attacks on his old nemesis Douglas and stressed the Republican commitment to the containment of slavery. At the same time he promised Kentuckians that

Lincoln's election would bring no federal interference with slavery because his party opposed "hostile aggression upon the constitutional rights of any State." Despite Chase's disappointments, Lincoln's victory in November made possible what he had been seeking for so long. In congratulating the president-elect, Chase exclaimed, "The object of my wishes and labors for nineteen years is accomplished in the overthrow of the Slave Power." The way was now clear "for the establishment of the policy of Freedom."[99]

Chase thus failed in his goal of a presidential nomination and election because of an unusual combination of antislavery principle, self-interest, and poor politics. A staunch opponent of the proslavery elements of the South, he was unacceptable to those northerners not willing to challenge slavery. At the same time his political ambition intensified the opposition even more and thus helped prevent him from achieving his goals. But Lincoln's victory gave Chase the opportunity to forward his beliefs. Having established a friendly and supportive relationship with the new president, he hoped and expected to play an active role in Lincoln's administration.

6

The Politics
of Finance

S oon after the election of Abraham Lincoln, Chase received inquiries concerning his availability for a cabinet post. Several
factors explain his appeal to the president-elect. As an antislavery
leader, Chase represented those most eager to challenge the peculiar
institution and separate the federal government from any responsibility for it. Some feared Lincoln's position might be too moderate
unless the antislavery wing of the party and Chase, its most prominent member, were included. Said Giddings: "It is important that
Lincoln's administration should take radical grounds." Because of
Chase's brief connection with the Democratic party and his leanings
to Democratic economic positions, his appointment would also help
balance the greater number of appointments which would go to
former Whigs. Further, Chase had ingratiated himself to Lincoln by
going to Illinois to campaign for Lincoln's election to the Senate in
1858; Chase, Lincoln acknowledged, had been "one of the very few
distinguished men" who had helped in his campaign against Douglas.[1] At the Chicago convention several Chase delegates had switched
to Lincoln at a critical time. Chase had accepted his defeat gracefully
and campaigned vigorously for the Republican ticket. Relations between the two men had always been cordial and, despite their ideological differences, Lincoln could expect that Chase would be a loyal
and able administrator.

Chase had mixed reactions to the early speculation about a cabinet appointment. Having just been elected to the Senate he explained

his preference for a legislative rather than an administrative position and noted his duty to his "brother Republicans of Ohio" to serve as elected. Further, he noted, "I have no political objects or aspirations beyond" the Senate. With the Slave Power overthrown and "the denationalization of Slavery . . . sure to follow," he could make more of a contribution in the Senate than in an administrative post. He consistently told those who urged him to seek a cabinet place: "I have no personal interest whatever in the matter." His disclaimers notwithstanding, few believed that his ambitions were limited to another term in the Senate. Most assumed that while appearing politically proper, Chase would eagerly accept a policymaking position which might enhance his political future as well as his ability to influence key decisions. With typical understatement, Chase explained that if a post were offered it would force him to consider "the question of duty." He would accept only if "my obligation to the cause and its friends require it of me."[2]

Part of any consideration of Chase as a cabinet member was the role to be played by other leading Republicans, especially William H. Seward. Many of Chase's supporters hoped that their man might receive the top position as secretary of State. Although Joshua Leavitt assumed that post would be Seward's because "his age entitles him to his choice," others believed that "the post of 'Premier' can be secured" if Chase would authorize them to work in his behalf. Seward's New York ally, Thurlow Weed, had already conferred with Lincoln in Springfield. Chase received an invitation on December 31, 1860, and traveled to Springfield less than a week later. The two-day meeting at the Lincoln home was both awkward and revealing. The president-elect was a gracious host, displaying both friendship and respect, calling on Chase at his hotel and taking him to church. Lincoln was forced to explain that he "had felt bound" to offer Seward the State Department position because he was "the generally recognized leader of the Republican party." The president-elect also noted that had Seward declined, Chase would have been offered the position. Now, however, he wanted Chase to be secretary of the Treasury.[3]

Lincoln's offer was conditional. He asked if Chase would "accept the appointment of Secretary of the Treasury," before the president-elect was "exactly prepared to make that offer." This odd proposal resulted from Pennsylvania Republican opposition to Chase's past support of free trade. Many from that state were pushing Simon Cameron, to whom Lincoln had promised the War or Treasury Department. Cameron was not highly regarded by Republicans outside of Pennsylvania, but he had delivered key votes to Lincoln at the Chicago convention. In return, Lincoln's manager, David Davis, had promised he would urge the president to include Cameron in his cabinet. Lincoln had little desire to appoint him but felt it necessary in order to maintain party harmony in Pennsylvania. With only a conditional offer, Chase replied gravely and sanctimoniously that he did not wish "and was not prepared to say that I would accept that place offered." Although he suggested that he would probably accept the Treasury post if the president-elect offered it to him, he was reluctant to commit himself to giving up his Senate seat. The first of many meetings between the two men thus ended inconclusively, and Chase returned to Columbus with the cabinet question unresolved.[4]

Interest in Chase for the Treasury position was not due to any great expertise in financial matters on his part. Little in his background would suggest that he was experienced or even especially knowledgeable in this area. The same was true of Seward in foreign affairs. Rather, political considerations were the major determining factors, and Lincoln had to decide how best to balance the support for the two men. That Seward and Chase suspected each other's ambitions and desire to win Lincoln's favor is evident in the maneuverings of their partisans. Weed urged Lincoln not to include Chase among his department secretaries, and Chase expressed his fear of a Seward-dominated cabinet. Shortly after his visit to Springfield, Chase reminded Lincoln that one of the reasons he had been nominated was that many Republicans feared the questionable influences surrounding Seward. Chase implied that "the cause of freedom" could best be served by his own appointment to the Treasury. At the same time, he urged friends to visit Lincoln to argue that only with Chase's appointment to the Treasury could the "proper financial and economic policy" be "properly represented in the Cabinet." He gave no indication of what those policies might be; nor had he begun to formulate the strategy he would follow. A few days later an anti-Seward delegation, headed by Hiram Barney and New York merchant and future mayor George C. Opdyke, went to Springfield after stopping briefly in Columbus to confer with Chase. Lincoln indicated to them that no further appointments would be announced until he reached Washington in early March.[5]

Lincoln's delay in naming Chase was not caused by any desire to exclude him, but rather by the need to satisfy each of the conflicting factions. Part of his dilemma was where to place Cameron. In his view Chase's "ability, firmness and purity of character" qualified him best for the Treasury, but there was a need to satisfy the Republicans of Pennsylvania as well. A Chase appointment would also appease many of Seward's political opponents in New York who were angered by his appointment as secretary of state. During the long delay, rumors spread that Chase might reject an offer of the Treasury, preferring to serve in the Senate; this caused many of his friends to renew their efforts to convince him to accept. Sumner wrote that Chase's acceptance was "our only hope." Still Chase wavered, telling Giddings as late as February 1 that there was "no prospect that I shall go in the Cabinet," for "it is against my wish."[6] Few believed that Chase would actually reject the Treasury post if offered. Most assumed instead that he merely wanted Lincoln to say more forcefully that he needed him; this in turn might give him a freer hand in running the Treasury and in influencing other decisions.

Nothing had been decided when Lincoln stopped in Albany for a conference with Weed on his way to Washington in late February. Weed pressed his arguments against a Chase appointment and even arranged to have Lincoln stay at Willard's Hotel in Washington before the inaugural; there it was hoped that Chase's partisans could be kept away. Weed feared that as the head of the Treasury Chase would control valuable New York patronage, especially the lucrative and influential customs house. At his stop in Philadelphia Lincoln was besieged by Cameron advocates who feared that if Chase were named Treasury secretary, he might not commit himself to the new Morrill protective tariff.[7]

Lincoln finally determined to resist the extreme pressure and hold to his original inclinations. He would satisfy the Cameron faction by naming the Pennsylvanian to the War Department post, but Chase would get the Treasury position. On March 4, Chase took his seat in the Senate, and the following day the Republican-controlled body received the president's cabinet nominations. Chase went immediately to see Lincoln and, still playing coy, "expressed my disinclination to accept" the appointment. The president pointed out that a rejection would be embarrassing and that the administration was in extreme need of his services. With that Chase agreed "to take charge of the finances of the country under circumstances most unpropitious and forbidding."[8] He thus impressed on the president that he was doing him a favor to take on the arduous task and would naturally expect Lincoln's gratitude and full support in return.

Lincoln's cabinet, which was quickly confirmed by the Senate, was a diverse group. In addition to Seward and Chase, the ablest members, Cameron and Caleb Smith were included because of promises made to key delegations at the Chicago convention. Smith, the chairman of the Indiana delegation, became secretary of the interior in return for swinging his state to Lincoln at Chicago. Lincoln had hoped to include a southerner from a seceded state but had to be content with two border state representatives, Edward Bates and Montgomery Blair. Bates, a conservative former Whig from Missouri who had opposed any agitation on slavery before being selected, was named attorney general. Blair, the postmaster general and soon to become one of Chase's chief antagonists, was a successful Maryland attorney from an influential family. Gideon Welles, a former Democrat from Connecticut, added geographical and political balance to the cabinet as secretary of the navy.[9] Lincoln chose his department heads more to represent the major ideological and political factions of the party and to make good on promises given to secure his nomination than to provide unity and expertise. Although they were able men, because of their diversity they would rarely be able to agree on important policy decisions. Chase, in fact, would be constantly at odds with several during the difficult years ahead.

During the long period between Lincoln's election and inauguration, speculation had run rampant not only on the makeup of the new president's cabinet, but also on the more immediate critical question of possible compromise to reconcile the South. Moderates of both parties, within and outside Congress, made several efforts between November and March to find a solution which might prevent southern states from seceding. As a leading Republican and possible cabinet member, Chase was never reluctant to express his view. He reacted strongly to any suggestion that Republicans were forcing the South to leave the Union. When his sister-in-law, Mrs. Randall Hunt of New Orleans, appealed to him to help "drive back this flood of disunion" forced on the South "by the Sewardites and

Lincoln's cabinet as depicted by Francis B. Carpenter in his painting "The First Reading of the Emancipation Proclamation." Chase is standing second from left. National Geographic Society Photographer. Courtesy U.S. Capitol Historical Society.

others," Chase responded that the South could gain little by secession. It must recognize that the extension of slavery was no longer a possibility either within or outside of the Union. The president had an obligation to prevent disunion and enforce "the laws of the Union . . . against rebellion." Yet he would recommend compensation to the owners of slaves for lost fugitives as the best solution for both North and South, "infinitely better for all—than disunion."[10]

At the same time Chase believed strongly that Republicans in general and Lincoln specifically must make no concessions to the South before the inauguration. Fearing that Secretary of State-designate Seward might be inclined to compromise too much, Chase advised him in January that southerners must "be plainly told that the Republicans have no proposition to make at present." Only after assuming power would they "be ready to offer an adjustment fair and beneficial to all sections of the country." He warned Lincoln that "the disruption of the Republican party" might follow premature compromise, and he urged the president-elect to pressure Republican leaders in Congress to accept no compromise. "Inauguration first—adjustment afterwards" was the only safe policy. Chase was not alone in this stance; other prominent Republicans, including Sumner and Thaddeus Stevens, expressed similar views. Thus Chase and others reinforced Lincoln's determination to oppose any move to accept the extension of slavery or any other concession before the inauguration.[11]

Congress considered several compromise proposals, most especially that of Senator John J. Crittenden of Kentucky which would have allowed extension by continuing the Missouri Compromise line to the Pacific. Other aspects of the Crittenden Compromise included a constitutional guarantee against congressional interference with slavery and more rigid enforcement of the fugitive slave law. Chase was clearly relieved when Republicans in the Senate rejected the idea at Lincoln's insistence and the plan collapsed. But Chase was somewhat embarrassed when Ohio Governor William Dennison appointed him, without consulting him, to be a delegate to the Washington Peace Conference. Chase wanted to reject the position because he expected no support in resisting "the surrender of our principles," but feared that refusing to participate would "make bad worse." Although the Ohio delegation was made up entirely of Republicans, Chase feared he was the only one "not prepared to go for the Border State Compromise." As he told Lincoln, he strongly believed in "inauguration first—adjustment afterwards."[12] The conference, which met from February 4 to 27, 1861, had been called by the Virginia legislature at the urging of Governor John Letcher and was chaired by former President John Tyler. Attended by several other prominent Republicans, including Charles Sumner, David Wilmot, and William P. Fessenden of Maine, it was boycotted by most antislavery Republicans and received no encouragement from Lincoln. Any chance it might have had for success was weakened before it began by the absence of delegates from five northern states and eight from the South.[13]

Chase took the lead among those resisting compromise; instead, he sought support for a constitutional convention to convene after Lincoln was officially president. In so doing, he knew he had the president-elect's support in refusing any proposal before the inauguration. Chase chaired a meeting of those delegates opposed to any action and spoke twenty-eight times during the convention proceedings. In a major speech he told the delegates that the North would not allow slavery in the territories "where we are responsible for it," but would not "interfere with it at all within State limits." He would also agree to compensation of owners whose slaves had escaped to the North, for "the cost to the national treasury would be as nothing in comparison with the evils of discord and strife." In rejecting the constitutional convention concept, the delegates agreed instead to submit to Congress a plan resembling the abortive Crittenden Compromise—one which Chase argued made "large concessions to the slave interests."[14] He was relieved but not surprised when the plan found few supporters in the Senate and was overwhelmingly rejected two days before Lincoln's inaugural. When the new president took office all compromise efforts had failed, and the country awaited his proposals. Chase warned the Washington delegates that should the South reject Lincoln's proposals and secede the result would be "War! Civil War!"[15]

Lincoln delivered his inaugural address with a spirit of firmness and conciliation. The government, he said, could not recognize secession; nor had it any intention "to interfere with the institution of slavery in the States where it exists." The immediate question was that of federal property in those states which had already seceded and formed the Confederacy, especially Forts Sumter in South Carolina and Pickens in Florida. At the first cabinet meeting, he asked for written opinions: "Assuming it to be possible to now provision Fort Sumter, under all the circumstances is it wise to attempt it?" Negative responses came from Seward, Cameron, Bates, Wells, and Smith; only Chase and Blair were in favor. Blair's response was unconditional, whereas Chase hedged when he argued that if reinforcement brought war and "an immediate necessity for the enlistment of armies and the expenditure of millions," he could not advise it. But he believed that consequence was "highly improbable" and endorsed sending supplies.[16]

When Lincoln again raised the issue of the forts in late March, Chase no longer hesitated; he supported "maintaining Fort Pickens" and "provisioning Fort Sumter." Northern sentiment had shifted dramatically in the intervening weeks and opposition to evacuation was now strong. Chase received numerous letters urging that reinforcements be sent to Fort Sumter. Said one angry correspondent: "If Fort Sumter is evacuated, the new administration is done forever, the Republican party is done."[17] Chase agreed: Sumter should be reinforced; "if war be the result," it might best begin over resistance to

Lincoln's efforts "to sustain troops of the Union stationed . . . in a fort of the Union." Chase had earlier favored letting the South "try its experiment in separation," but the taking of Fort Sumter on April 13 by the Confederacy and the secession of Virginia four days later, left no alternative, said Chase, but "enforcing the laws of the Union by its whole power and through its whole extent." Both during and after the Sumter crisis Chase received a number of letters from southerners telling of their determination to sustain secession—a determination which only seemed to reinforce Chase's belief that the Union must be maintained.[18]

As the president and his cabinet faced the secession crisis, Chase began to deal with the complexities of administering a large and cumbersome department. The problems that Chase inherited on taking office on March 7 were enormous. Among the most difficult and time-consuming was that of making the Treasury Department function smoothly and efficiently on a day-to-day basis, especially in light of the antiquated bureaucratic machinery he inherited from his predecessors. To this effort he poured his entire energies; an early biographer observed that his commitment to his work was such "that he was seen only in going to and coming from the place of his official labors," the imposing Treasury building with its extension under construction on Fifteenth Street next to the White House. Fewer than four hundred clerks administered the department and managed the financial business of the government in March 1861. Included within the Treasury Department were several bureau chiefs with sizeable staffs of their own. Among them were the commissioner of customs, responsible for tariff revenues; the auditors, who oversaw the accounts of the many executive departments; the comptrollers, who were in charge of keeping government accounts; the treasurer, who held the money of the government; and the solicitor, who directed civil suits initiated by the government. In addition, several smaller offices were included under the secretary's responsibility, such as Marine hospitals and the United States Coast Survey.[19]

To head these and other divisions, Chase made a series of highly competent appointments. George Harrington was made assistant secretary; a man with vast financial experience, he supervised the department during Chase's several absences from the capital and provided Chase day-to-day advice. Elisha Whittlesey was appointed comptroller, a position he had held as a Whig under Zachary Taylor.

Francis E. Spinner became treasurer of the United States. George S. Boutwell became the first commissioner of internal revenue in 1862. John J. Cisco retained his post as assistant treasurer at New York, a post with vast patronage influence. Hugh McCulloch directed the national banking system as comptroller of the currency after its establishment in 1863. Chase accepted President Lincoln's request to appoint "my old friend" Nathan Sargent, a long time Lincoln supporter and former Whig journalist, as commissioner of customs.[20] Chase preferred to formulate policy rather than to administer it himself or become involved in day-to-day details. He was thus dependent on his able subordinates, especially Harrington, to implement important decisions.

The size of the department grew enormously during Chase's tenure as new divisions were created and existing ones expanded to deal with war-time taxes, the new national banking system, the issuance of vast numbers of government bonds and treasury notes, and the control of trade and confiscation of property within the Confederacy. Before Chase left office, the number of people carrying out the department's work in Washington and in customs house positions throughout the nation had increased five times over the number of Treasury employees in the previous administration. Although many of the appointments were patronage positions awarded on the basis of the secretary's personal preference and judgment, Chase and Harrington also used an examination system to recognize merit and efficiency; in the process they disqualified many potential officeholders.[21] Overseeing this growing bureaucracy, Chase kept a firm and efficient control.

The secretary of the Treasury had at his disposal a huge patronage empire and the power to satisfy or disappoint thousands who considered themselves worthy and deserving Republicans. Chase could thus please or anger countless politicians in Congress and state government by honoring or rejecting their recommendations. He could also strengthen himself politically by placing his own partisans in influential positions. His basic philosophy was "to give the preference to political friends" in appointments except where "peculiar fitness and talents" made appointment of a political opponent "a public duty." On occasion, he decided that appointment to a particular office should not be determined by party considerations, as when he appointed one Democrat among the six new inspectors of steamboats. In other instances he was able to keep potentially discontented Republicans happy; he appointed his former Ohio Know-Nothing rival turned ally, Thomas Spooner of Cincinnati, to a minor customs position after having earlier denied him a more lucrative and influential position. On still another occasion, he pointedly rejected the request for a collector's post from one whom he accused of trying to promote a "purely personal end." More frequently he had to turn down requests for reasons beyond his control, as when a Senate committee refused to confirm a collector's appointment because it was in the port of a Confederate state.[22]

For more routine appointments Chase often refused to interfere with the heads of the various branches of the Treasury, believing his role should be limited "simply to approval or disapproval" of their recommendations. Nonetheless, he found the task an arduous and time-consuming one and often spent entire days at his desk deciding on whom to recommend for such minor yet potentially significant posts as collectors and assessors.[23] Because these places could be highly lucrative, there were usually many applicants for each office, and Chase knew that for every friend he made, he could make many more enemies.

The requests for government jobs from both friends and those unknown to Chase began as soon as Lincoln was elected and long before Chase's appointment. In the first week after the election, Chase received at least twenty-five requests for patronage positions. One such applicant recognized that his request was "perhaps premature," but he wanted to beat the rush since there would be "a contest for every office of any importance." Following Chase's elevation to the cabinet, he was literally deluged with letters, most frequently requesting appointment as collector in one of the many customs houses. Such requests came from friends, such as New York abolitionist Henry B. Stanton, as well as from total strangers.[24]

Frequently the requests sought the secretary's assistance in securing an appointment in another branch or department of the government. On hearing of the death of Supreme Court Justice John McLean, Noah H. Swayne of Ohio wrote to Chase the same day urging him to use his influence with Lincoln to expedite his elevation to the Court. Several old friends sought his help in securing diplomatic appointments. Chase used his influence to secure the selection of Cassius M. Clay as minister to Russia and the appointment of his old friend Charles Cleveland to the consulate at Cardiff. He also helped secure military appointments and promotions, as when he persuaded Secretary of War Edwin M. Stanton to promote his friend James A. Garfield to brigadier general. On the other hand, he failed to seek the promotion of Colonel John M. Chivington of the Colorado militia.[25]

Normally Chase's role in the appointment process was rather routine, but on occasion he found himself in a major dispute over patronage. The administration was barely three weeks old when Chase complained to Secretary Seward that Ohio was not receiving its fair proportion of diplomatic positions. By his calculations, Ohio had provided one-eighth of the Republican vote in 1860 and thus deserved an equal "share of diplomatic appointments." Of the 269 foreign posts available, he noted that Ohio had so far received only 13 of its deserved portion of 33.[26] He also complained to Seward and to the president when the nomination of his brother Edward for federal marshal of the western district of New York appeared in jeopardy. He reminded Lincoln that Seward could only hurt himself "if he persists in denying the only favor he *can* show me." Seward later relented and agreed to the appointment, but the differences between the two secretaries were only beginning to surface.[27]

The following month Chase tried to retain John Cisco as assistant secretary at New York rather than appointing the candidate that the Seward-Weed faction wanted placed in the lucrative office. He protested to the president that "Mr. Seward *ought not* to ask you to overrule my deliberate judgment as to what is best for the Department and your administration." Seward also complained about Chase's interference in New York patronage. Temporarily, peace was preserved through the intervention of Chase's close friend Hiram Barney, who reminded the Treasury secretary that "patriotism demands much sacrifice of personal feeling." The incident represented only the opening gun in a long-running battle between the two cabinet members over Treasury appointments in the most important port of the Union. On occasion, the two men could cooperate on patronage matters as when, "through the friendly aid of Governor Seward," Chase's friend James Monroe was chosen for the consulate at Rio de Janeiro.[28] Such cordiality would indeed be rare during the next three years.

The feud with Seward over Cisco's appointment was not the only patronage dispute which enlivened Chase's tenure in the Treasury Department. Always protective of his right to make appointments within his department, Chase jealously resisted interference not only from other department heads but also from members of Congress and from the president. When conflict arose he reacted defensively if Lincoln failed to back him and on occasion even threatened to resign over apparently minor incidents. In July 1862, Senator Benjamin Wade protested Chase's selection of George B. Senter as a tax collector in Cleveland because he had been "my bitterest and most unfair and unscrupulous antagonist" in the senator's efforts to win reelection. Chase responded heatedly by reminding Wade that despite his controversial role in denying Chase the presidential nomination in 1860, Chase had not tried to block his reelection to the Senate in 1862. He then lectured Wade on how support of "our common cause" rather than "personal claims" would determine his appointment policies.[29] When the Senate failed to confirm the appointment of a collector of internal revenue in Connecticut, the overly sensitive Chase protested to Lincoln that "the rights of senators or representatives to control appointments" must not be allowed, and he threatened to resign if the president did not back him. In the interest of senatorial courtesy, Lincoln denied Chase's appeal, but the secretary refrained from submitting his resignation.[30] Inherent in many of the patronage disputes with Seward, Wade, and others was the belief of his rivals that Chase was using the great number of offices at his disposal to advance his own political cause. Those rivals practiced the same patronage policies wherever possible, but few leaders had as much opportunity to build support through appointments as did the secretary of the Treasury. A small army of Treasury officials scattered throughout strategic parts of the Union loyal to Chase might effectively campaign for him if he decided to challenge Lincoln in 1864.

Chase was frequently accused by his political rivals of using his Treasury patronage to build up a personal machine. Historians have further claimed that his ambitions worked constantly against Lincoln's overall war efforts.[31] The evidence does not prove such charges. The president was a strong war leader, but he was cast in the Whig model of limited executive leadership in relation to Congress and even to his cabinet on non-war-related issues. He had a tendency to give such men as Chase wide discretion in carrying out their duties. Given Lincoln's attitude, Chase's Treasury appointments do not smack of disloyalty to the president. Chase essentially ran his department politically well within the scope of Republican party theory. While some of his appointments were intended for self-advancement, other cabinet members followed the same practice. Given his political leanings and hopes, it was natural that he would appoint men he trusted to carry out his policies and to show their gratitude to him for their jobs. His difficulty came when he appointed men, as in New York City, who cut across the Sewardite connection. Chase cannot be accused of building a patronage machine with evil intent; rather, his actions were an accepted part of the political process and became accentuated more in hindsight than in contemporary standards of conduct. He was not disloyal to Lincoln but consistent with current practices, especially in light of the one-term tradition of the presidency in the mid-nineteenth century.

Throughout his tenure as Treasury secretary Chase was periodically provoked to offer his resignation when he did not get his way on patronage issues. For example, he had chosen Victor Smith, a Cincinnati newspaperman, abolitionist, and supporter, as a collector of customs and special agent of the Treasury in the Puget Sound district. When Smith became involved in land speculation in Washington Territory, Lincoln decided to remove him from office. To avoid offending Chase, Lincoln offered "to try to find some other place" for Smith. But the secretary took the matter personally and complained bitterly that he had not been consulted prior to the removal. Chase noted indignantly that he could not carry out his duties if such decisions were made "not only without my concurrence, but without my knowledge." He concluded stiffly that if the president could not understand his position, "I will unhesitatingly relieve you from all embarrassment . . . by tendering you my resignation." The two men finally agreed to set aside their differences when Lincoln appointed a man recommended by Chase as Smith's replacement. Lincoln filed Chase's offer to resign with the curt notation, "First offer of resignation."[32] The secretary's efforts to get his way included an initial show of reluctance to accept his cabinet appointment followed by periodic threats to resign if the president did not give him a free hand on patronage. He was only partially successful in these disputes; Lincoln at times compromised to avoid confrontations over minor appointments. But the president became increasingly impatient and unwilling to humor his Treasury secretary as relations between the two men deteriorated over more significant matters.

Financial conditions left Chase only limited time for patronage decisions. He inherited a situation of crisis proportions as secession was followed by war. Conditions in the last years of the Buchanan administration had already converted a Treasury surplus into a sizeable deficit. The Panic of 1857 had resulted in sharply reduced federal income with the government running a deficit each year since. By March 1861, the debt had reached $75 million of which $18 million had been incurred since the secession of South Carolina in December 1860. The tariff of 1857, designed to satisfy southerners, had reduced the major source of national income, although revenues from the new Morrill tariff had not yet been collected. So deep was the distrust of the Buchanan administration and so badly had confidence in public credit failed during the last months that Secretary of Treasury John A. Dix had only been able to obtain loans at the excessive rates of 10 to 12 percent. The purchase of government bonds had been declining for some time. To make matters worse, a momentary recession after Lincoln's election followed the cancellation of loan obligations by southerners as well as their suspension of many of their normal purchases in northern states.[33]

Nor was there any quick solution available for raising necessary government revenues to cope with the situation. Revenue based primarily on tariffs and public land sales could not easily be expanded. Other federal taxes were negligible and would take time to increase through legislation, especially with Congress in a hesitant mood. Federal income had fallen to about one-quarter of expenditures, and the lack of a national bank made placing loans difficult. The Independent Treasury Act of 1846 had further hindered government operations because it denied the government the ability to draw interest on its own deposits. It also intensified cash flow problems because, under its terms, the administration had to pay its bills in hard money. The banking business of the nation was transacted by approximately sixteen hundred state banks, each going in separate directions, issuing some seven thousand different kinds of bank notes, many of them unsound.[34] A financial genius would have found the situation difficult; Chase's lack of experience made his task almost insurmountable.

The administration's response to the economic situation was based on its assumption that the war would be brief and that Congress and the public were averse to major new taxes. Until Congress convened in special session on July 4, 1861, Chase used existing authority to provide makeshift sources of revenue, primarily through loans. With Union generals forecasting a quick victory, Chase, like most other officials expected the war to last no longer than a year. His proposals to Congress reflected that expectation; he sought only traditional means of financing. Chase estimated that the first fiscal year of the administration would require revenues of $320 million, four times the amount raised in the previous year, the increase necessary to finance the military effort. Of this sum, he proposed to raise only one-fourth through the orthodox methods of taxes, tariffs, and the sale of land, for "he has read history to little purpose who does not know that heavy taxes will excite discontent." Thus he failed to recommend a comprehensive taxation program which might have eased the difficulties as the war lengthened. Of the $80 million for non-military needs, $57 million could be expected from tariffs, $3 million from land sales, and $20 million from new internal or direct taxes. In addition to a proposed tax of 3 percent on incomes over eight hundred dollars, Chase requested a "direct tax" to be apportioned among the states. He urged that the rates of the Morrill tariff be adjusted upward with new levies on such items as sugar, tea, coffee, and spices.[35]

During the summer of 1861, Congress responded by enacting most of Chase's tax and tariff proposals, partly due to the sobering news of the rout of Union forces at Bull Run on July 22 and the subsequent realization that victory on the battlefield might not be so easily attained. In August Congress also passed the first Confiscation Act, which authorized the president to seize any property used in promoting insurrection, a measure which was expected to provide an easy way of combining revenue with punishment. Yet by the end of the year, little had been realized from this act; only $2 million had been paid to the Treasury from direct taxation, and the income tax could not be collected until 1863. This hit-and-miss method of raising revenues, designed for a simpler age, was to be augmented through loans which Chase hoped to negotiate.[36]

Congressional acts of July and August 1861, authorized Chase to borrow $250 million for military needs, and in this area the secretary's difficulties began to multiply. Because of the fiscal ineptness of the Buchanan administration, bankers had responded coolly to government needs in the previous year and the debt had continued to mount. Chase asked for eight times the amount obtained in the recent efforts. Congress authorized the secretary to sell bonds payable in twenty years at 7 percent interest. He could also issue two types of Treasury notes. One bore interest of 7.3 percent and matured in three years. A second bore no interest but was repayable in specie upon presentation at the subtreasuries. Chase hoped that this paper, soon labeled "demand notes," would function as a primitive type of national currency.

Armed with this authorization, Chase traveled to New York in August for conferences with bankers of that city, and to Boston and Philadelphia to seek their assistance in selling the bonds. With a distrust of bankers based on his long association with Democratic financial policies, Chase hoped to secure from them short-term loans at low rates of interest rather than the long-term high interest rates bankers preferred. Although Chase sought a broad popular subscription to government bonds, he knew that bankers could most effectively be the agents for handling national loans. Thus negotiations between the two would be difficult. In order to open talks on a friendly basis, Hiram Barney had suggested that a meeting in New York "would secure more sympathy and cooperation and perfect confidence on their part." In conferences held in Assistant Treasurer Cisco's home and in several Wall Street banks, Chase proposed three $50 million loans, the first to be made immediately and the second and third to follow at sixty-day intervals. The bankers would make these advances in exchange for 7.3 percent Treasury notes which would be sold to the public, thus replenishing the coin to be lent to the government.[37]

A major problem in this arrangement developed because the banks assumed that the loans would be handled like an ordinary loan to an individual or corporation; that is, the money would be credited to the Treasury on the banks' books, while the Treasury would make its payments to its creditors by check. This arrangement would allow the bankers to retain their needed gold reserves. Chase unwisely and stubbornly insisted that what the government borrowed be delivered to him in gold. He based his position on the Independent Treasury Act of 1846, a hard money measure whose philosophy he endorsed. The act required the government to pay out and receive only coin, which had to be kept in subtreasuries. Chase took this stand despite the recently passed legislation permitting him to deposit money borrowed "in such solvent specie-paying banks as he may select." Friends had warned him that the loan could not be raised unless the specie clause was eliminated. Elbridge C. Spaulding of New York, an influential member of the House Ways and Means Committee, testified that the purpose of Congress had been to allow Chase to use the banks as government depositories. The secretary feared that he would soon have to accept bank notes for government obligations and thus rejected the intent of Congress.[38]

After a week of negotiations Chase forced the bankers to acquiesce to his terms in return for government business; he thus gravely weakened their specie position. Chase later explained, "I was obliged to be very firm." If the bankers refused his terms, he would "go back to Washington and issue notes for circulation; for gentlemen, the war must go on until this rebellion is put down, if we have to put out paper until it takes a thousand dollars to buy a breakfast."[39] Although frequently willing to compromise on financial issues, Chase's inflexible insistence that the banks transfer their gold deposits in buying government bonds further aggravated an already difficult situation.

All went well at first, despite Chase's refusal to use the banks as government depositories, and the first two $50 million loans were made. With war expenses multiplying, the money was spent as rapidly as it was received. Continued success in the loan policy depended on confidence in the government, which in turn was based on victories on the battlefield. By December, that confidence had been shaken and the banks were forced to suspend specie payments. Several factors were responsible in addition to the faltering war effort, including the publication of the annual report of the secretary of the Treasury on December 10, 1861.

Bankers and others had hoped for a comprehensive plan designed to ease the financial crisis, but they were to be disappointed. Especially they had expected a broad tax program to help finance the war; instead, Chase indicated that borrowing would continue to be the main source of revenue. He appeared much more optimistic than conditions warranted and said little about the government's difficulties in paying its bills. He did call for rigid economy and confiscation of Confederate property, but taxes would be relied on only for ordinary expenses, although he recommended some minor new assessments. For political reasons, Chase was reluctant to propose any significant new taxes, and he shared with Lincoln an aversion to all but the most necessary levies. Many agreed with Ohio Senator John Sherman's conclusion that the "financial condition of the government was more alarming than at any other period during the war," but Chase had little new to propose. The secretary instead gave priority to traditional methods of finance; in so doing he had the support of the president, who, with his traditional Whig belief in a limited executive, preferred to leave fiscal policy to his finance minister and to Congress.[40]

Chase placed the greatest reliance on further borrowing to meet war expenses. Consistent in his belief that the Confederacy would be defeated within six months, he was convinced that the sale of government bonds, Treasury notes, and demand notes circulating as currency would suffice. He did admit that tariff revenues had been disappointing and that the need for a 500,000 man army rather than the 250,000 originally planned had put additional pressures on the Treasury. But he believed a stepped-up loan program building on that already begun would still meet the need. In recent months "the people subscribed freely to the loan," and close to $200 million had been realized, "without resorting to the foreign market." With the war costing $2 million a day, much greater dependence would have to be placed on borrowing. Chase therefore emphasized a scheme to reorganize the banking system so as to compel the banks to buy large quantities of government bonds. With that exception, Chase left most of the initiative to Congress. Thus the disappointment among those who had looked for a more encompassing plan was real, and as James G. Blaine noted, the report produced intense "discouragement in financial circles." Still, Chase had many defenders. Alphonso Taft of Cincinnati reassured him that it was "undoubtedly the report of the year" and "meets the great occasion perfectly."[41] Chase's leadership was in accord with northern expectations of a short war.

The secretary had been authorized by Congress to seek loans abroad and had in fact begun a concerted effort to comply, but a major crisis with Great Britain, coming at the time of his annual report, made such loans unlikely and added to the bleak financial outlook. Rather than send an official representative of the Treasury

Chase as secretary of the Treasury, 1861. Courtesy of Chase Manhattan Archives.

abroad to negotiate loans, Chase had accepted the offer of his New York banker friend, August Belmont, to represent him unofficially. If Belmont failed, "No harm would have been done because nobody would know of the failure," and bad publicity would be avoided. After a month of conversations with British, French, and German bankers, Belmont reported that the times "are not at all propitious" for a loan. He found that those nations preferred neutrality, and that, barring major Union victories on the battlefield and a repeal of the unpopular Morrill tariff, the United States should expect little aid.[42]

Any further chance of a loan was lost after the Trent Affair in November when Confederate diplomats James M. Mason and John Slidell were forced from the British mail packet *Trent* by a Union warship. Although many in the North applauded, the British regarded the action not only as a violation of neutral rights, but a challenge to their national honor; for a time war seemed a possibility. In late December, a crisis was avoided when the Lincoln administration, backed strongly by Chase in cabinet deliberations, made it clear that the American captain Charles Wilkes had acted without government authorization. But as far as Chase's financial policies were concerned the damage had been done. The Trent Affair destroyed any chance that American bonds might be sold in England. As Belmont told Chase, "Not a dozen battles lost could have damaged our good cause as much as the ill-judged, and overzealous act of Capt. Wilkes." Subsequent efforts to negotiate European loans in 1862 and 1863 by New York bankers William Aspinwall and John M. Forbes and former Treasury Secretary Robert J. Walker brought only limited results; for the most part, Chase continued to rely on domestic sources for borrowing.[43]

American bankers found it more and more difficult to maintain specie payments as 1861 drew to a close. Having subscribed to $100 million in government securities by mid-December, they had depleted reserves to such a dangerously low level that they could not pay for the additional $50 million in coin. Assistant Secretary Cisco alerted Chase on December 16 that a meeting of New York bankers was imminent and that those determined "to force a suspension of specie payments . . . will probably succeed." With the secretary still refusing to relax his insistence on payments for bonds in coin, the bankers announced that suspension would take effect on December 30. Although the bankers blamed Chase for their decision, the high costs of war meant that there was simply not enough specie to keep reserves sufficiently high. Surely a more vigorous taxation policy would have partially alleviated the crisis, but it could not have yielded revenue soon enough to meet the military expenses of 1862.[44] The financial crisis had been accelerated by the flagging confidence of the public in the war effort; throughout the fall many had rushed to subtreasuries and presented demand notes for redemption in coin. Chase and congressional leaders were faced with the reality that their emergency actions of the summer had proven inadequate to cope with a war of such dimensions. New methods would be necessary to prevent a financial collapse.

When Congress convened in late December, matters were still unresolved. Debate in the House Ways and Means Committee centered on a bill to authorize Chase to issue $100 million worth of Treasury notes bearing no interest. These could be issued in denominations as small as five dollars and were to be "lawful money, and a legal tender in payment of all debts, public and private." In addition, the $50 million of demand notes approved during the summer were to be included as legal tender. As originally drafted, the bill that was referred to a subcommittee chaired by Elbridge G. Spaulding of Buffalo tied the legal tender proposal with that for a banking association whose member banks could issue national currency on the security of government bonds. Such had been Chase's recommendation in his annual report.[45] Spaulding soon concluded, however, that the two parts of the proposal would have to be separated. The complicated bank bill could not pass Congress for several months because of state bank opposition. This was a delay which he felt "would be fatal to the Union cause" because money had to be raised quickly. With House approval, the two parts were separated, with the banking reform deferred for more thorough study and the legal tender issue receiving immediate attention.[46]

Although eager to strike at state banks and their currencies through a national system which would facilitate the sale of national bonds, Chase was much slower to admit the need for federal paper money as legal tender. Always a hard money advocate, he had argued in his inaugural address as governor of Ohio in 1856 that "the best practicable currency" was coin. As late as his December 1861 report, he argued that the issues of legal tenders might entail "possible disasters" which "far outweigh the probable benefits" of the currency proposal.[47]

The secretary received constant and conflicting advice on the legal tender concept. To Nicholas Trist the idea was not only a "monstrous violation of the Constitution" but it would create unnecessary confusion in the business community without any advantage to the government. The *New York Tribune* viewed it as a "bankers' scheme" designed to destroy government credit. At first Chase tried to forestall the need for such action, but any hope of securing banker adherence to specie payments to prevent paper currency collapsed at a

January 11 meeting in his office with key congressmen and bankers. John A. Stevens, president of the Bank of Commerce of New York, explained that despite his support of hard money and his belief in "the evils of irredeemable paper money," there was now no alternative. Chase's close friend and supporter, Mayor George C. Opdyke of New York City, argued that the proposal had become "indispensable to the maintenance of the credit and honor of the government." Without it the government would soon have "difficulty in obtaining supplies for the army at any price." Both Stevens and Opdyke agreed that the emergency could be met only by combining the legal tender proposal with "liberal and prompt taxation."[48]

As the House committee continued its deliberations through January, Chase was finally convinced that the legal tender measure was required in order to avoid financial collapse. The committee was no more willing than Chase to consider drastic tax increases. Led by Spaulding, Samuel Hooper of Boston, and Thaddeus Stevens, the committee endorsed the bill and on January 22 sent it to Chase for his comments and minor alterations. It was then submitted to the full House where Spaulding defended it as a necessity "to save our Government and preserve our Nationality."[49] Rumors that Chase had withheld his approval for a time threatened the bill's passage; some concluded that the secretary sought the advantage of the measure without assuming responsibility for it. The bill's backers used two letters of endorsement Chase had written to Stevens and Spaulding to prove the secretary's advocacy of the measure. To Stevens he explained his "great aversion to making anything but coin a legal tender in payment of debts," but war expenditures and the suspension of specie payments by the banks had made it "indispensably necessary that we should resort to the issue of United States notes." He warned Spaulding that "the Treasury is nearly empty"; without the bill the banks "will refuse to receive the United States notes." With assurances of Chase's support, the House approved the measure on February 4 by a vote of 93 to 53.[50]

In Senate Finance Committee debates opening on February 7, sharp divisions again appeared. John Sherman led the supporters and chairman William P. Fessenden of Maine the opponents. Chase had urged Fessenden's support but was forced to rely instead on Sherman's leadership to secure passage. Building on the House debates, Sherman defended the bill as absolutely necessary as a temporary war measure and cited Chase's endorsement. Others reminded the Senate that the Confederacy had already resorted to issuing paper money. The bill passed the Senate on February 13 in a slightly amended form by a 30 to 7 margin. Two weeks later the two bodies resolved their differences and approved the bill; Lincoln signed it the same day.[51]

Subsequent legislation in July authorized an additional $150 million and a third measure for the same amount in early 1863. In the course of a year, the Treasury was authorized to issue $450 million in United States notes, quickly labeled "greenbacks" because of their distinctive color. Although resistance diminished in the later Congressional debates, it was clear that only military emergency had forced hard money advocates to abandon their longstanding opposition. Chase later suggested that pressure from members of the House Ways and Means Committee had convinced him to yield: "There was no help for it. It was a political necessity if nothing else, but it was a war necessity also." Some evidence suggests that Lincoln also used his influence to persuade Chase of the need for as well as the constitutionality of the legal tender bill.[52]

Initial response to the bill was mixed. Opdyke wrote from New York that the measure "is gaining friends in this city every hour," with bankers and merchants recognizing its value. Greeley's *Tribune,* an early opponent of the plan, now endorsed it and praised Chase's efforts in coping with "a difficult job in a difficult time." James Shepherd Pike, on the other hand, argued that the legal tender bill was the "one rotten spot" which promised to spread and lead to ruin. The act had both positive and negative effects on the wartime economy. Although the measure provided much of the currency necessary to finance the war, Congress specifically forbade the use of fiat money for paying tariff duties and interest on the public debt. This in turn caused the greenbacks to depreciate, adding to inflation and driving some coins out of circulation.[53]

Chase had agreed to the legal tender concept only on the condition that additional loans and taxes be authorized along with a uniform banking system to sustain the market for federal bonds. Although delaying banking legislation, Congress was much quicker to respond to the first aspect of Chase's request with a new loan law authorizing $500 million in additional bonds. Unlike the original securities of July 1861 which were irredeemable for twenty years and bore an interest of 7 percent, the new bonds carried an interest rate of 6 percent, were redeemable after five years, and matured in twenty.⁵⁴ These "five-twenty" bonds were part of the legal tender bill which became law in February.

In March, debate opened on a tax proposal which the secretary had left to the initiative of Congress. Included were extensive new tariff duties on a large number of items, greatly reducing the free list; it also established a new agency to direct the collection of internal taxes. The bill, which became law in July, meant the assumption of a tax collection function formerly belonging to the states, a radical assertion of federal powers which the states were powerless to resist during the wartime emergency.⁵⁵ The bill represented a major shift in national priorities and drastically challenged traditional ideas of lim- ited central government. Finding buyers for the bonds and realizing the expected revenue from the tax measures would be slower and more difficult, however, than Chase had anticipated.

Chase was able to overcome much of the difficulty in the sale of bonds by appointing Philadelphia banker Jay Cooke as special agent in charge of the five-twenties. The secretary's close relationship with the Cooke family dated back to his governorship when Jay's brother Henry was editor of the *Ohio State Journal* in Columbus. Aware of the services that the paper might render him politically, the governor was seen with the editor frequently before the war, and Cooke's newspaper backed him strongly for the presidential nomination in 1860. At the time he entered the cabinet, Chase had not yet met Jay Cooke, although he was fully aware of the banker's prominence in financial circles. Shortly after assuming the Treasury post, Chase asked Cooke to be assistant treasurer in charge of the subtreasury in Philadelphia, an office he hoped to make into "a true financial de- partment," rather than "a nice political machine." Cooke declined the appointment because it would require him to give up his own banking enterprise. The idea of a small salaried post held little at- traction, for it had already occurred to Cooke that he could be of more service and advance his own business as an agent for the sale of government bonds.⁵⁶

In July 1861, Cooke told Chase that he was about to open a Washington office of his firm under the direction of his brother Henry, "with a view of making our services valuable to yourself." If Chase would give the firm "the management of the loans to be issued by the government" and permit "a fair commission on them," subject to his supervision, "we are ready to throw ourselves into the matter heartily." Chase agreed to appoint Jay Cooke a "Subscription Agent for the National Loan," a position which, although not the monopoly the Cookes sought, might be a step in that direction. Earlier Jay Cooke had accompanied Chase on his trip to New York and assisted in negotiating a $50 million loan with bankers there. Now Cooke set to work to find purchasers of government bonds, especially small subscribers. He reported to Chase in September that "a continual stream" of "clergy, draymen, merchants" had passed through his office to subscribe to the war effort. Many left "with tears in their eyes, so overjoyed [were they] at the patriotic scene."[57]

Cooke was at first only one of several subscription agents, and for a time the government still had trouble marketing sufficient bonds. As the sale of the new five-twenties languished during the summer of 1862, Chase determined to improve the situation by making Cooke a special agent of the Treasury in charge of all bond sales. The presence of Cooke's Washington office on Fifteenth Street, opposite the Treasury Building, had facilitated the Cooke brothers' access to Chase; Henry especially came and went almost at will. Chase's connection with the family strengthened and he became a depositor in their Washington bank. In September Henry told his brother, "The Governor needs you now more than ever before." Chase appointed Cooke the sole subscription agent for the distribution of United States bonds. Chase agreed that the government would pay Cooke a commission of one-fourth of one percent of the value of the bond sales, out of which he was to pay the commissions of local agents and all advertising expenses, retaining one-eighth of one percent for his own compensation.[58]

Without question Jay Cooke succeeded in selling government bonds where previous efforts had fallen disappointingly short. Through newspaper advertisements, appeals to the patriotism of workers to put their savings into bonds, and door-to-door solicitation, the five-twenties were marketed successfully. Although men of wealth and bankers were the chief subscribers, many lower- and middle-income northerners also participated, the number estimated by Cooke at more than half a million. By the end of 1863, Chase could report to Congress that nearly $400 million worth of bonds, in small and large denominations, had been sold "among all classes of our countrymen." Said the secretary proudly, "The history of the world may be searched in vain for a case of popular financial support to a national government." By mid-1864, Cooke had announced bond sales of more than $510 million.[59]

Such a large volume of business generated an extraordinary income for Jay Cooke. Although Chase rejected Cooke's appeal for a higher commission and in mid-1863 even reduced it slightly, the banker managed to earn $220,000 in two years as the "financier of the Civil War." Chase was clearly uncomfortable with the Treasury so dependent on a private citizen. In explaining to Cooke why his commission had to be reduced, Chase noted that his "duty to the country" forbade him from paying "rates which will not be approved by all right-minded men." He concluded, "The people trust me and I feel their trust as a great obligation constantly."[60]

Criticism of the arrangement with Cooke arose from several sources, and Chase was naturally sensitive to it. Some of the opposition came from bankers who were jealous of Cooke's special relationship with the government. New York bankers, led by Chase-appointee Assistant Treasurer John Cisco, protested that the arrangement gave unfair advantage to Philadelphia bankers. The Democratic *New York World* asked what had induced Chase to give Cooke "a monopoly of the five-twenty funding business instead of doing the business by accredited assistant treasurers in the different cities." The paper also implied that Cooke was realizing inordinately large profits through the arrangement. On several occasions, members of Congress suggested an investigation into the connection between the Treasury and Cooke.[61]

Chase and Cooke vigorously defended the legitimacy and ethics of the arrangement as well as the tremendous benefit to the government which could not be realized by any other means. To Cisco, Chase justified Cooke's commission by saying: "I want faithful intelligent and useful service & am not unwilling to reasonable pay." To Speaker of the House Schyler Colfax, Chase noted Cooke's services in organizing a system of twenty-five hundred subagents to conduct the sale of bonds in "almost every town of the loyal states and among all classes of the population." As congressional criticism mounted in late 1863, the secretary explained to President Lincoln that neither of the Cooke brothers had received from him "any favor which they have not earned by strenuous and untiring labors for the public interest." Since much of the criticism was merely political or rival banker jealousy, the president saw no reason to intervene as long as Cooke continued to produce the desired results. Jay Cooke and Chase argued that the limited agencies of the Treasury Department could not have organized the vast distribution and advertising system that the Cookes had developed. Henry Cooke assured his brother that gwell the Governor fears nothing from complaining part "as long as we serve the ies and is willing to take the responsibility of putting it all into our hands." Chase made it clear in his report to Congress in December 1863 that the system had been so successful that he planned to continue with it. During the next year, however, political events would force Chase to reassess his relationship with Cooke.[62]

Chase was also careful not to let his personal business and friendship with the Cookes become entangled in public issues lest his critics have more reason to attack the official relationship. Chase and his daughters Kate and Nettie had become close personal friends with the families of Henry and Jay Cooke. On their visits to Philadelphia, the young women frequently stayed with the Jay Cookes, who were generous in their hospitality and gifts. In late 1861, Jay sent a horse-drawn carriage to Washington for Kate's use, a gift which Chase received for his daughter reluctantly because, he noted, a public official "must accept no presents beyond which the ordinary intercourse of society prompts and allows from friend to friend." The secretary did not, however, hesitate to borrow from Cooke and use his services as a personal investment adviser. In February 1862, he requested a $2,000 loan, and as Kate developed more expensive habits, he found himself calling on Jay frequently for assistance.[63] Ironically Chase seemed better able to manage the nation's finances than he could his daughter's.

Cooke also acted as Chase's investment broker. As the secretary explained, "My public duties for the past thirteen years have left me no time for attention to my private affairs," and expenses and neglect had reduced his property to less than half of its original value. Cooke's investments on Chase's behalf were usually in corporations with which Cooke had no personal involvement, although when he organized the Washington and Georgetown Railroad Company in 1862, Chase became a stockholder in it.[64]

As congressional and banker critics maintained their close watch over the relationship, Chase worriedly urged Cooke to keep their private and public dealings entirely separate. Correspondence, Chase insisted, must not mix the two, for public matters remained on file for open reference. He even urged Cooke to begin all letters on Treasury business to him with "Sir," whereas correspondence on private matters could be addressed "dear Governor or dear friend." Chase's sensitivity to charges that he might profit personally because of the Treasury's relationship with Cooke led him on one occasion to return a check for $4,200 representing profit from shares in the Philadelphia and Erie Railroad purchased for him by Cooke. Chase had not yet made payment for the stock when Cooke sold it. Fearing criticism that he had received advantage from the rise or fall of market prices, Chase concluded that the need for a correct public image made it "essential for me to *be* right as well as to *seem* right and to *seem* right as well as *be* right." Cooke found it difficult to comprehend Chase's reasoning, but he nevertheless honored the request.[65] The relationship between Chase and Jay Cooke was mutually profitable as well as beneficial to the government's economic position, and the evidence suggests all transactions were legal. Chase gave Cooke a privileged position, and the banker in turn produced positive returns for himself and the government. But however honest, the relationship raised questions of ethics, especially in light of Cooke's role in the controversies surrounding Chase's banking policies.

Chase had earlier opposed establishing a national bank with the kind of central authority held by the Second Bank of the United States, but he had since come to realize that such a system could provide control over currency and facilitate the sale of bonds. Since the Second Bank's charter had expired in 1836, the states had had sole control over banking and the issue of currency. Some sixteen hundred banks were providing notes with varying degrees of state control in a bewildering variety of denominations, often counterfeited, and frequently with insufficient security behind them. To Chase, there was an obvious need for a uniform stable currency, since the existing confusion prevented "the successful prosecution of the war."[66] So long as insecure currency existed, any plan for an adequate national currency was doomed. The state banks had also failed to fulfill Chase's expectations for the sale of bonds once the initial patriotic enthusiasm for the war had waned. Chase's willingness to consider a national banking system shows the impact the national emergency had on his prewar economic philosophy of a limited role for the federal government. Having already reversed himself by endorsing a national currency and at least limited increases in federal taxes, he was now led by the pressures of war to recognize the potential benefits of federal control over state banking.

The secretary first raised the issue of major banking reform by calling for a system of national banking associations in his report to Congress in December 1861. The controversial proposal was originally part of the legal tender bill in early 1862, but Chase's supporters in the House, led by Samuel Hooper of Massachusetts, agreed to postpone consideration of it until greater support could be mobilized. Defenders of the state banks feared that those institutions might be swallowed up in a national system, and their opposition meant that passage in early 1862 was unlikely. Yet when the legal tender experiment failed to solve the crisis and the government's financial plight worsened during 1862, Chase renewed his proposal at the end of the year. This time, with the war effort going poorly, Congress appeared ready to listen. Significantly, Jay Cooke endorsed the concept having hesitated earlier for fear of offending the state bankers who were providing many of the loans he was advertising.[67]

Under Chase's proposal, banks joining the system would be furnished circulating uniform notes in the amount of 90 percent of the United States bonds they purchased. The bonds would be held by the Treasury to insure conversion of the notes into coin. A steady market demand for government bonds would thus be facilitated. Chase hoped that the notes would replace the irregular depreciated varieties of state currencies and form a true national currency. Based on the system of free banking in New York state, the plan would meet many objections by requiring that bank notes be secured by deposits of United States bonds as well as meet a specie reserve requirement. As Henry Cooke remarked to his brother, the proposal would bring "uniformity in the currency," as well as create "a large and permanent market for government securities." Lincoln gave the proposal an additional boost in his December 1862 annual message by noting that it promised "certain results" in meeting the financial crisis. He also included in his message Chase's summary of his longer report to Congress. For the president, endorsement of a national banking system required less of a change in economic philosophy than it did for Chase, because as a former Whig, Lincoln had supported efforts to reestablish a national bank after its charter had expired. With the urgency of the war providing added incentive, the president was more willing to intervene in behalf of Chase's plan than he had been on most other economic matters.[68] But the many conflicting and confusing proposals then pending in Congress meant a protracted debate before Chase secured his legislation.

As the third session of the Thirty-seventh Congress began debate, Chase sought support for his plan among members as well as among friends who might influence Congress. He asked Assistant Treasurer Cisco to secure endorsements from bankers. He also urged such editors as Joseph Medill of the *Chicago Tribune* and Horace Greeley of the *New York Tribune* to support it, noting that without the plan "there may be success, but I don't see it." Recognizing the reluctance of Chairman Thaddeus Stevens of the House Ways and Means Committee to go beyond additional borrowing and taxation to sustain the war effort, Chase argued that "the funds necessary for the pay of the army and the prosecution of the war" depended on its approval. Hooper introduced Chase's bill in the House in early January, but Stevens effectively bottled it up in committee so that the bill appeared dead. Not even a letter from Lincoln endorsing the bank plan could force committee action. Both Stevens and Elbridge Spaulding defended the state banks, preferring an increase in legal tender notes to threats aimed at existing state banks.[69] Frustrated by the plan's stagnation in the House, Chase determined by mid-January that action must originate in the Senate.

The senator that Chase chose to guide his proposal was fellow-Ohioan John Sherman. Sherman had led the assault against state bank notes and introduced a bill authorizing a 2 percent tax on them. With Chairman of the Finance Committee William P. Fessenden opposed, Sherman seemed a logical choice to direct the administration's efforts. Not personally close to Sherman, Chase asked Henry Cooke, in the latter's words to "use my influence with him," to persuade the senator to delay the tax on state notes in order to accomplish immediate banking reform. On January 26, Sherman introduced a bill similar to the one Lincoln had urged.[70] The next two weeks saw an intense effort by Chase, the Cookes, Sherman, and the president to push the bill through the upper house.

A series of four letters written anonymously by Sherman and published in the pro-administration *New York Times,* argued that existing state currency must eventually be replaced with a currency which the national banks would furnish. The complex Sherman bill limited the amount of currency the national banks could issue and included other restraints upon banks that agreed to join the national system. Such modifications were worked out by Henry Cooke in consultation with the senator and the secretary. According to Cooke, his family "went to work with the newspapers" and persuaded friendly editors to support the bill. He also circulated a pamphlet, "How to Organize a National Bank under Secretary Chase's Bill." Sherman's speech on February 10 argued that the plan would provide a uniform currency which would be difficult to counterfeit and would contribute toward American unity and nationalism. Because of these efforts, the bill passed by a vote of 23 to 21 on February 12. Henry Cooke exuberantly told his brother, "The Governor appreciates our efforts and knows . . . the value and efficiency of our services." In acknowledging the importance of Cooke's efforts, Chase reminded him that appreciation "must be your sole reward." Chase also knew that the bill could not have passed the upper house without Lincoln's active lobbying among senators who had originally opposed the measure. The president sent one of his private secretaries, William O. Stoddard, to try to persuade two senators, both of whom switched their votes to the affirmative; at the same time, Fessenden reluctantly agreed to support the bill only because of the efforts of Chase and Lincoln.[71]

With Senate action complete, Thaddeus Stevens was forced to allow full House debate. Again appeals to nationalism by Chase and others had their effect, especially in satisfying New Yorkers Spaulding and Reuben Fenton who reversed their opposition. The former no longer viewed the plan as a threat to state banks and conceded its benefits for the future. With a close vote expected, Chase prevailed on Lincoln to urge wavering Illinois congressmen to support it "on your account." After two days of floor debate, during which Chase remained at the Capitol to lobby, the House approved the bill 78 to 64. The secretary immediately informed the president: "It needs your approval only." A conference committee led by Sherman and Hooper in close consultation with Chase worked out the differences, and Lincoln signed the National Banking Act on February 25.[72]

The execution of the act was put under a comptroller of the currency who would supervise the organization of the banking associations. The amount of notes which could be issued under the law was limited to $300 million and the taxation of state notes was delayed—concessions which Chase was forced to accept to placate the friends of state banks. The opposition had been worn down not only by such concessions, but by the logic of replacing a chaotic state system in light of the national financial crisis spawned by the war. Many in Congress accepted a measure they had long opposed because Chase, Lincoln, and others had convinced them it was a necessity. Putting it into effect and making it work effectively would prove almost as difficult as enacting it had been. Nevertheless, wartime necessity had again added to the trend fostered by the administration toward centralization and a weakening of state authority.

Chase chose Hugh McCulloch, an Indiana banker, as comptroller. McCulloch was a surprising choice because he had initially been hostile to the banking plan and had only recently admitted its potential. His major task was to persuade the state banks of the value of conversion to a national charter, and at first he had only modest success. By the end of 1863, only sixty-six banks had applied for charters, although several of the powerful Cooke banks were among the first to join. Progress among New York bankers was especially discouraging because of that city's traditional dominance of the country's money markets. Cooke made a special effort in New York by giving a dinner for all of the editors of the city. Horace Greeley gave the program editorial support, but Chase's friend, Mayor Opdyke, tried in vain to organize national banks. Chase urged Governor Andrew Curtin of Pennsylvania to make it easier for state banks there to join the national system.[73]

Many banks which did join initially were relatively small western ones under Cooke's influence, whereas bankers in major eastern cities remained hostile to the new arrangement. With the taxing of state currencies omitted, the banking act represented little more than permission for national banks to compete with state banks. At first Chase was optimistic about the results, telling Assistant Secretary George Harrington in November that progress was good and that "it will be an easy matter" to bring all banks under it. Yet many banks continued to resist in part because they felt that Chase did not make it sufficiently attractive to join. For example, he required banks to give up their original names and be designated by numbers in the national system. Only later did the secretary admit that the benefits of the plan would be realized in the future rather than immediately. By the end of the year, he reported to Congress on the need for "proper measures" to accelerate the conversion of state into national banks.[74]

Several amendments to the 1863 law were enacted in the next year. These changes met some of the objections, and the number of state banks joining the national system increased. A protracted debate in the spring of 1864 led to the adoption on June 3 of an amended banking bill designed to facilitate the conversion of state banks into members of the national system. The bill, which passed with larger majorities than that of 1863, included changes that were largely technical and made some concessions to state banks. Banks joining the system were now permitted to retain their names, a compromise of major psychological significance. Further conferences among the Cookes, Sherman, Lincoln, and Chase led to the retention of the limitation on national bank notes to $300 million because of their fear of depreciated currency and inflation. National banks were made subject to a federal tax of about one percent on their circulating notes. In these discussions, Lincoln returned to the more limited role he had played on other economic issues. He recognized that, unlike the original bank bill, this proposal had the necessary congressional support without his intervention. Thus he did no lobbying, although he indicated to the cabinet his endorsement of the changes.[75]

Despite Chase's pleas, the measure still did not tax state currencies. He had worked hard for such a tax because he felt that as long as state currencies could not be regulated he could not effectively control the financial aspects of the war; like a ship's navigator, he was "without a chart among forces of winds and currents" which he could not "measure or manage." Although more banks joined the national system after the 1864 law, it was not until March 1865, nine months after Chase had left the Treasury, that Congress finally enacted the punitive 10 percent surcharge on state bank notes that he had sought. Most state banks then finally recognized the futility of resistance and began to convert to the national system. During 1865 alone more than a thousand new national banks were organized, bringing the total to 1,601.[76] Only at the end of the war did Congress finally complete the banking system Chase had called for in 1861—a system which, with all its imperfections, survived until the formation of the Federal Reserve System in 1913.

Before Chase left the Treasury he faced another financial crisis brought on by unfavorable military conditions combined with the continuing presence of state currencies and the depreciation of the legal tender issues. By the end of 1862, the value of a legal tender dollar had fallen to seventy-five cents, a situation which worsened through 1863 and early 1864. The fact that goods purchased outside the country had to be paid for in gold led to increased speculation in the precious metal and abuses of the system. By the spring of 1864, Chase had become so concerned over the depreciation of paper money that with authorization from Congress, he began to sell Treasury gold to hold down the gold premium. Realizing he could not produce the permanent results necessary, he pushed harder but unsuccessfully for the prohibition of state bank notes. Congress finally intervened to limit gold operations to the legitimate needs of commerce. The ratio of paper to gold had reached two to one when, on June 17, 1864, Congress passed the gold bill, forbidding speculative trading in gold. The measure proved unsuccessful and the price of gold soared. Within fifteen days, Congress was forced to repeal the act. With Chase's resignation on June 30, the price rose further before it finally stabilized by September.[77]

Chase believed this crisis could have been avoided if Congress had agreed to tax state currencies and had possessed the courage and wisdom to increase other federal taxes. Through his last months in office the embattled secretary called for an increase in the income and other taxes, until they "provide for at least one-half of our whole expenses." Having earlier resisted suggestions of major increases, he recognized by 1863 that no other solution existed. The financial need became more important than possible political repercussions that unpopular taxes might bring. Taxes, Chase said, must be accompanied by a reduction of "our vast expenditures of which I think 25 to 33 percent might be avoided." Throughout the war he desperately tried to keep military appropriations to a minimum, complaining that whereas he had "tried to do much with little," the military leaders' policy had been "to do little with much."[78]

Chase reminded Senate Finance Committee Chairman Fessenden that "a tax of ten or even twenty percent on all incomes" was better than "the rapid accumulation of National Debt" and "the rapid deterioration of the National credit." With fall elections approaching, Congress resisted Chase's requests for increased taxes and a reduction in legal tenders. Finally, on Chase's last day in office, Congress did agree to increase the income tax from 3 to 5 percent on incomes up to $5,000, reducing the exemption from $800 to $600. A 7^1/2 percent rate would be charged on incomes between $5,000 and $10,000, and those over $10,000 would pay 10 percent. Tariffs were also increased sharply.[79] Still, income taxes produced only a small proportion of the needed revenue to finance the war because political considerations in Congress prevented a heavier reliance on them.

Chase's official duties as secretary of the Treasury were not limited to financing the war. Also involved was the complex problem of regulating trade between Union-controlled areas and the Confederacy. The issue was more complicated than simply preventing trade with the enemy; it also involved the desire of border states to keep old trade patterns open and the necessity of keeping such areas loyal. Trade in parts of the Confederacy under Union control, as in New Orleans and parts of Virginia, Tennessee, and the Sea Islands of South Carolina, also was a Treasury responsibility. The Union need for Confederate products, especially cotton, meant that such exchange had to be carefully regulated to prevent excessive benefit to Confederates and excessive profits for speculators and others seeking special advantage. The Union blockade of the Confederate coast created difficulties and some shortages in ports such as Norfolk which came under Union control early in the war. As northern armies advanced into the Confederacy, Chase's responsibilities for all trade questions increased. Inevitably, trade restrictions and licensing became mired in a bureaucracy of regulations, and Treasury agents assigned to regulate the trade were subject to open invitations to corruption. Rooting out dishonest agents and developing a coherent policy which kept private citizens as well as army and naval officials happy, and which produced an efficient system of control, were beyond the limited resources and capabilities of the Treasury.

Nowhere were the difficulties of trade regulation greater than in the border states, especially western Virginia, Kentucky, and Missouri. As Chase explained to his agent in Wheeling, trade had to be prohibited "between points notoriously disloyal . . . without depriv-

ing loyal citizens of their rightful privileges." For the most part, this
meant that the agent must not grant any licenses for trade into Confederate states, for an act of Congress of July 1861, had prohibited
"all intercourse between loyal and rebel states." Chase could see no
way to permit any trade except within loyal areas. One problem with
such a strict rule was that many Union sympathizers in these areas
might be driven to the Confederate side because of their dependence
on southern trade. The Treasury was flooded with requests for exemptions from the rule, and Chase could only explain that the policy
was "not intended for the injury of loyal citizens." [80] The restrictions
were especially burdensome to merchants in Saint Louis, Cincinnati,
Louisville, and other river ports dependent on southern commerce.
The Treasury received appeals, petitions, and visits from delegations;
all had to be told that such trade would not serve "the successful
prosecution of the war." Not surprisingly, widespread smuggling
and dissatisfaction resulted.[81]

With Union armies advancing south and control of the Mississippi River secured by early 1864, limitations on trade in Missouri
and Kentucky were lifted. The results were controversial at best, for
almost immediately Chase's agents reported that the Confederates
were the beneficiaries of the more relaxed standards. One agent reported that "large quantities of Powder, Shot and Ball" had been
shipped into southern Kentucky and would soon be in "the hands of
Guerillas and other improper persons in Tennessee and elsewhere."
The rebels, said another, "will be supplied with everything they desire" under the new policy.[82] No satisfactory solution was ever found
by Chase or his successors.

Chase and his special agents on occasion came into conflict with
military and naval leaders both in the field and in Washington.
Chase defended his trusted agent William P. Mellen against complaints by General Henry W. Halleck that his enforcement of commercial regulations in the Mississippi Valley was hampering troop
movement. Usually such problems were worked out, and Mellen's
efforts to license legitimate trade typically had the backing of Halleck, Grant, and other generals in the area.[83]

In contrast, Chase was in constant conflict with Secretary of Navy
Gideon Welles over what Welles regarded as the Treasury's too leni-
ent policies. The differences represented an ongoing feud which
eventually had political ramifications. With the Virginia coast in-

cluded in the Union blockade, the citizens of the Union-controlled port of Norfolk sought relief from what Chase and General John A. Dix believed were starvation conditions. Welles, on the other hand, believed that Norfolk was a hotbed of rebellion and feared that any relaxation of restrictions would only help the Confederacy. To Chase's plea in the cabinet to modify the blockade there, Welles responded with contempt that his policy was to do all he could "to make rebellion unpopular." General Dix complained to Chase that Admiral Stephen P. Lee, under Welles's instructions, was refusing permits to ships seeking to bring relief to a people "who are starving with hunger and cold." Welles believed that Chase's leniency was due to "matters of trade and Treasury patronage carrying with them political influence," for "the prize is great. Civilians, quasi military men etc., are interested."[84]

Despite Welles's repeated protests that no blockade at all was preferable to one in which benefits were available only to a favored few, Lincoln agreed to a partial lifting of the blockade in Norfolk in December 1862. The president often sided with Chase on such disputes involving trade within the Confederacy, because he, like his finance minister, believed that commerce could be a means of regaining the loyalty of disaffected areas. The conflict between Chase and Welles extended into 1863 with Welles protesting in vain the granting of clearance to revenue vessels by the Customs House over which the Navy had no control. Welles continued to believe that "some strange permits for trade" were being signed by Dix with Chase's authorization.[85]

The dispute between the two secretaries was not confined to trade in Norfolk. When a Treasury agent sought the Navy Department's approval to grant permission to two private citizens to cut ship-timber in North Carolina, Welles responded haughtily that such permission would be acquiescence in "a species of robbing for the private benefit of speculating favorites who have contrived to get a permit to commit waste." Not only did Chase feel that Welles had misunderstood the purpose of the permits, but he complained that Welles's letter "reads much like a lecture." Perhaps attempting to give Welles a means of graceful retreat, Chase added that he was sure that the navy secretary "neither read nor dictated it."[86]

More serious was the dispute occasioned by the navy's seizure in early 1864 off the North Carolina coast, of two suspicious vessels, the *Princeton* and the *Ann Hamilton,* carrying privately owned goods as well as Confederate currency and cargo. They were operating under Treasury permits conferring broad trading privileges which Welles felt were unwarranted. He therefore demanded an explanation of the clearances and implied that the Treasury's method of granting permits encouraged graft and favoritism. Chase responded heatedly that the two vessels had met all of the requirements for permits. Refusing to censure the naval commanders who had stopped the ships, Welles instead commended them, for, as he lectured Chase, commerce "should be general and not restricted to a few favorites." Finally, at a cabinet meeting Chase was forced to admit that he had not looked beyond the military permit to discover that the ships were carrying contraband. According to Welles, Chase "tried to pass it off as a joke but his jokes are always clumsy; he is destitute of wit." In his eyes, Chase lacked "the courage and candor to admit his errors." Welles clearly enjoyed catching the self-righteous Chase in a mistake and then watching him squirm to try to remove himself from responsibility. Although there was little evidence to prove dishonesty, neither was there any indication that the Treasury made any greater effort to enforce its regulations during Chase's remaining months in office. Commenting later upon Chase's resignation from the Treasury, Welles said he hoped that "we shall get rid of his trade regulations, trading agents and other mischievious machinery."[87]

Beginning in July 1861, Congress enacted a series of trade laws which authorized the secretary of the Treasury to control the exchange with seceded states to serve the Union cause. The initial law was amended on several occasions to deal with abuses that became evident and in general to enlarge Chase's discretionary authority and his power to suppress unauthorized traffic. Chase explained his object was to make the "restrictions as moderate as possible," but designed to prevent supplies from falling into rebel hands. New regulations were necessary as new parts of the Confederacy came under Union control, although no amount of authority could guarantee effective enforcement in the field.[88]

Problems were especially evident in New Orleans. Under Union control since April 1862, the city was commanded first by General Benjamin F. Butler and later by General Nathaniel P. Banks. Under Butler an illegal trade with parts of the Confederacy was permitted, especially in cotton and sugar. George S. Denison, the collector of the revenue there, reported to Chase about a trade he could not prevent. With cotton so much more valuable outside the Confederacy than in, Denison substantiated the widely held rumor that Butler's brother, Colonel Andrew J. Butler, was benefiting most from the illicit trade. The removal of General Butler in late 1862 was welcomed by many but it did not eliminate the problem. Chase soon recognized that General Banks, in attempting to suppress the trade, "took upon himself a task to which even his resources are inadequate." Penalties for anyone receiving goods brought from the Confederacy except by Treasury agents helped some, as did Lincoln's order transferring regulation of all trade from military authorities to the Treasury Department. The Treasury proceeded to divide the entire South and border areas into separate agencies, each with its own agents, but temptation for profits was too great to prevent abuses. Letters from Denison continued to tell of improper speculation: "the only good accruing therefrom, except to the enemy, is to the benefit of dishonest speculators."[89]

Treasury licenses and permits were invitations to fraud, a problem Chase recognized but could not control: "It is impossible for me to look after all the acts of all the agents of the department," but those found to be dishonest were dismissed. Typical was his removal of a Treasury agent on the Mississippi River for accepting a bribe in "the performance of official duties." There was little guarantee, however, that a successor would be any better. Chase noted that his appointments were designed "to secure the honest execution of the Acts of Congress," and he tried diligently to regulate the trade in an equitable way. Yet General Daniel E. Sickles was unfortunately accurate when he wrote of the whole South in 1864 that "direct trade with the enemy" abounded. The law was strengthened on July 2, 1864 with a provision granting the secretary control over all trade in rebel states and the exclusive power to purchase their products for resale. It also prohibited military personnel from participating in the trade for personal profit, but no law could eliminate the abuses entirely.[90]

Cotton was the most difficult part of trade within the Confederacy to control. The shortage of supplies in northern textile mills was extreme, but, because of restrictions, southern cotton planters often had difficulty finding a market. By 1864, cotton that was available for $.20 a pound in the South could be sold for as much as $1.90 in Boston. The possibilities for smuggling and corruption were, as a result, almost unlimited, and the Treasury Department faced an un-controllable situation. Generals Sherman and Grant opposed any purchase of cotton from Confederates, arguing that the goods should simply be seized, "for all in the South are enemies of all in the North." Although Chase understood the "importance of keeping from the rebels the proceeds of this crop," he believed that limiting purchases to the Treasury could solve the problem. General Grant argued convincingly that no system of permits would suffice because "there is too much corruption in the country for it." A steady stream of petitions flooded the Treasury from merchants and others in the Mississippi Valley protesting Grant's prohibition of trade.[91] No satisfactory solution was found, for even with purchases suppos-edly limited to government officials, Treasury permits to private citizens were still necessary to meet the need, and favoritism and smuggling abounded.

Cotton seized by Treasury agents was sometimes sold for private gain, and Grant charged that speculators added further discredit to the government. Predictably, Secretary Welles was quick to point out the "malconduct" of Treasury agents. Control of the cotton trade, he charged, was more than Chase's department could handle, but the secretary "is very ambitious and very fond of power," and believes that "the patronage of office, or bestowment of public favors is a source of popularity." More serious were the charges brought against the northern shipper, Harris Hoyt, which implicated Chase's future son-in-law, Senator William Sprague of Rhode Island. Hoyt had promised to work with loyal Union men in Texas who would supply cotton, but he was refused a permit by Stanton and Welles to bring cotton through the blockade. Chase also turned down the re-quest despite Sprague's urging. As a result, in December 1862, Hoyt began his illegal operation of shipping arms into the Confederacy from New York in return for Texas cotton. In July 1863, one of his ships was stopped by the Union navy and the operation was foiled. Although no evidence was produced directly implicating Sprague, critics remained suspicious that he had financed the project and influenced Chase to have his agents look the other way.[92] No conclu-sive evidence was ever produced to prove Chase was guilty of using his office for anything other than political advantage. Welles, one of Chase's sharpest critics, believed the Treasury secretary did not "re-ceive any pecuniary benefit himself."[93] It would have been far out of character for the highly moral Chase to tolerate knowingly the fraud his critics claimed.

How well Chase managed the nation's economy during these crisis years is, however, a matter for dispute. Hard money advocates believed his policies to be dangerously unsound. Welles contended that Chase did not have "the sagacity, knowledge, taste or ability of a financier.... Nor does he know now the elementary principles of finance and currency." But the navy secretary and other critics then and since have typically failed to appreciate the enormity of the problems Chase faced.[94] Almost everyone believed at the outset that the war would be over in less than a year. Chase held onto this conviction long after evidence was abundant that no quick conclusion could be produced on the battlefield. As a result, many of the early financial policies were makeshift and regarded as temporary. Not until 1863 did Chase act with an awareness of the likely duration of the war. Yet as early as December 1861 he recognized the need for banking reform to facilitate the placing of loans, a plan which Congress did not enact until 1863. In fact Congress failed to give the system sufficient authority until after Chase had left office. His decision to accept legal tender was made reluctantly and against his better judgment. But it was made with the political and financial courage required by the crisis.

The country had been without significant national taxation except for tariffs, and Chase had to overcome his own political reluctance and that of Congress to urge enactment of income and other taxes to meet the expenses of war. Taxes were never sufficient despite his pleas, and the government was instead forced to rely on huge bond issues—an experiment in deficit financing without precedent. The war thus forced Chase to alter his economic philosophy dramatically, and in so doing he demonstrated his flexibility and practicality in meeting the emergency. Espousing the traditional Democratic position of a limited role for the federal government in 1861, he moved forcefully in a period of crisis toward centralization of authority at the expense of the states in the vital areas of currency, banking, and taxation.

As Chase's economic philosophy evolved, he had the support of the president, although it was sometimes unspoken. For Lincoln, with his Whig background, the change in philosophy was not as dramatic. For the most part, Lincoln gave Chase a free hand in directing his department, explaining to John Hay how he "generally delegated to Mr. C. exclusive control" of Treasury matters. He rarely interfered with policy decisions, maintaining his concept of a limited role for the president. He preferred to leave economic questions to Congress and to his Treasury secretary, recognizing the historical link of that department with Congress. Burdened with the responsibility of directing the entire war effort, Lincoln resisted Chase's efforts to involve him more directly. To one such plea for an opinion on a financial issue, he responded: "You understand these things. I do not."[95] His efforts to influence Congress were usually limited to his annual messages with the major exception of banking reform and a minor role in the currency controversy. The president did understand financial issues, but clearly believed that his secretary of the Treasury was capable of dealing competently with them without his advice or interference.

Chase made many mistakes as Treasury secretary. He relied too heavily on private banker Jay Cooke to sell bonds, but for the most part the loans were wisely managed and Cooke produced the desired results. The Union debt, although huge, was not exorbitant when compared with debts incurred in later wars. Inflation was also kept as much under control as the chaotic conditions permitted. Paper money issued during the war totaled less than one-third that of the Confederacy. In all economic areas, the Union record compared favorably with that of the southern government. Chase was less successful in controlling trade within the South and border areas. His department was faced with an impossible task with which it had neither the resources nor the ability to cope. Political favoritism, while never admitted, was evident to all, although it was no more excessive than that practiced by most politicians. Despite Chase's concerted efforts and honesty of purpose, corruption among speculators and some Treasury agents was common. Nor was the secretary ready to accept criticism and admit errors. Late in his administration, Chase claimed to "have made few mistakes." Indeed, had he to do it over again, he would not do "materially otherwise than I have."[96] Yet despite his overbearing egotism, Chase's adherence to principle and devotion to the Union cause produced a record of which he could be justifiably proud.

The duties of the Treasury began to take their toll on Chase physically and emotionally before the war was a year old. Soon accustomed to workdays that averaged ten to twelve hours at his desk in the Treasury, Chase would frequently "retire to his library and work two or three additional hours" after dinner. Early in his tenure he wrote to a friend that he had "never worked nearly so hard before." The demands on the Treasury were such that he was "almost overwhelmed by the labor and anxiety of this Department." He complained throughout the war that the government lacked the organization and the economy necessary and that "neither the President, his counsellors nor his commanding general seem to care." Instead, "they rush on from expense to expense and from defeat to defeat, heedless of the abyss of bankruptcy and ruin which yawns before us." The secretary resolved self-righteously to do his best to overcome the problems created by others, for "the only remedy I can see is in patience and perseverance."[97] Despite his many setbacks and mistakes, Chase's flexibility allowed him to adapt to the constantly changing situation; his policies accomplished as much as the desperate and chaotic period permitted. Throughout the difficult times, he kept the full confidence of President Lincoln on financial matters. Had Chase confined his activities during the war to the Treasury, his government service might be considered a great success, but his political aspirations led him into other areas as well.

7

The Blue, the Gray, and the Black

It never occurred to Chase that he should confine his administrative activities to finances. From the time of his Treasury appointment, he assumed that the cabinet would not only play an important role in formulating military and racial policy, but that he would enjoy a special relationship with the president. He expected his advice would be sought especially on military matters. Although Lincoln never encouraged those feelings directly, every indication in the first months of the administration was that Chase's military opinions would be valued. There was a widely shared belief that Secretary of War Simon Cameron lacked the drive and ability to handle the crushing burden of directing the war effort. From the start, Lincoln had little confidence in him, having appointed him primarily for political reasons, and as early as May 1861, the president turned to Chase to frame the orders which organized the volunteer and regular troops.[1]

Lincoln assigned Chase special military responsibility in western border areas, including Kentucky, Tennessee, and Missouri. Specifically, Chase was asked to "frame the orders" under which Andrew Johnson would raise regiments in Tennessee. The secretary took this role seriously, corresponding with Union supporters in the West and urging their vigorous action to keep their areas loyal and to raise troops to protect against Confederate inroads.[2] Because "the loyalty of Kentucky is a great point gained," Chase personally planned the sending of arms and told General Sherman: "I shall exert myself to have more sent." Through 1861, he conferred regularly with Cameron, who willingly accepted Chase's help, although Chase explained later, "I never undertook to do anything in his department except when asked to give my help."[3]

In the absence of Cameron's leadership, Chase felt it his duty to help organize the entire northern war effort. Shortly after the fall of Fort Sumter, when rumors spread of potential unrest in New York City, possibly directed against the customhouse and subtreasury, Chase sent orders to be given to Police Commissioner John A. Kennedy on how to keep matters under control. He advised Lincoln to take strong steps in Maryland to prevent a Confederate attack on Fort McHenry and to stop a secession ordinance under consideration there. In September, he intervened in behalf of a volunteer in a Vermont regiment who had been condemned to death for sleeping on his post. Throughout the war, Chase attempted to influence military appointments; an early example was his important role in securing the appointment of Irvin McDowell as commander of the Army of the Potomac in 1861.[4]

Because Chase enjoyed the influence he had in military decisions and sympathized with Cameron's administrative problems, he was slow to join the growing clamor for the war secretary's removal. Cameron had lost control of the raising of troops to a number of more aggressive state governors. More seriously, his department permitted extensive graft and corruption especially in awarding contracts for military supplies. In response to attacks by Murat Halstead's *Cincinnati Commercial,* Chase argued that Cameron administered his department "vigorously, patriotically and honestly." Gradually, however, Chase came to recognize that a change was necessary, and by September he complained of the "defective organization" of the War Department.[5] Originally assuming that support of Cameron would strengthen his influence with the president, Chase finally concluded that in light of the growing party pressure, the war secretary's ineptness made him a liability.

By the end of the year, Cameron had become such an embarrassment to the president that a change was necessary. To avoid a party rift and to ease him out gently, Chase assisted Lincoln in persuading Cameron to accept an appointment as minister to Russia. Chase's loyalty to Cameron even after his departure was due to friendship and to a desire not to alienate a highly influential politician from a key Republican state. Chase thus attempted unsuccessfully to prevent the House of Representatives from condemning Cameron's conduct of the War Department as "highly injurious to the public service."[6]

Chase was also instrumental in the choice of Edwin M. Stanton as Cameron's successor in the War Department. The two men had known each other since the 1840s when Stanton had practiced law in Ohio. When Stanton moved to Pittsburgh in 1847, Chase had tried to persuade him to join the Free-Soil party. Although Stanton remained a Democrat, he sent Chase congratulations on his controversial election to the Senate in 1849.[7]

Stanton was an ideal selection for Lincoln because his Democratic background as Buchanan's attorney general plus his Pennsylvania residence would bring political balance to Lincoln's cabinet. Once in the War Department, Stanton did prove closer to Chase ideologically in military and antislavery issues than Cameron had been, but he was also much less pliable than Cameron. Stanton was fiercely independent and an efficient administrator who intended to direct his department without interference. Chase found that his opinions were welcome, but military decisions were made by Stanton and Lincoln without Chase's knowledge. Chase soon was explaining to friends, "I know too little to have any confident opinion about any military matter." Except in Treasury matters, he noted, "my advice is seldom followed."[8]

Through much of 1862, Chase nevertheless continued to try to influence military decisions and when success did not come on the battlefield he became increasingly critical of the president and several of his generals. Chase was optimistic in early 1862 following the capture of Roanoke Island and Forts Henry and Donelson in Tennessee and noted that these triumphs "dispel all doubt" about ultimate victory. But because the "finish must yet be given," he urged Lincoln and Generals McDowell and McClellan to initiate a vigorous move of Union forces toward Richmond. Having helped to secure McDowell's appointment to head the Army of the Potomac, Chase had retained his faith in him even after the defeat at Bull Run and his demotion to lead a smaller force defending Washington. Chase complained by late March that the lack of movement was causing the country to lose trust. McDowell must "inspire vigor and energy" and avoid all "which savors of show rather than action."[9]

Throughout 1862, Lincoln gave little indication of his reaction to Chase's many military suggestions, although he clearly valued Stanton's views more. In early May he asked Chase to accompany him and the war secretary to Fort Monroe at the mouth of the James River to try to inspire the army and navy into more forceful action. There they witnessed the fall of Norfolk, and Chase could write enthusiastically to his daughter Nettie that had it not been for their encouragement the city would still have been in enemy hands. Visiting Norfolk before returning to Washington, Chase noted proudly that "my campaign too is over." He wrote to McDowell urging him to move his army toward Richmond to join that of General McClellan moving up the peninsula.[10]

Chase's attitude toward McClellan, the most controversial of all Union military leaders, altered as the Ohio general's fortunes rose and fell during 1861 and 1862. Chase took credit for "the change of your commission from Ohio into a commission of major-general of the army of the Union" in the early months of the war. Following successes in western Virginia and McDowell's failure at Bull Run, Lincoln appointed McClellan commander of the Army of the Potomac in July 1861. The president's decision had Chase's support as did McClellan's elevation to general-in-chief in November following the retirement of Winfield Scott. To the secretary it was a decision for which northerners should "thank God and take courage." He expected McClellan to move his army quickly toward Richmond, and he had used McClellan's promise of victory to sell bonds in New York. But instead of taking decisive action the general delayed for a seemingly interminable period, defending his inaction by claims of insufficient troops and preparation.[11]

As the delay stretched into the spring of 1862, a frustrated Chase wrote to Greeley, "McClellan is a dear luxury—fifty days—fifty miles—fifty millions of dollars—easy arithmetic, but not satisfactory." McClellan, said Chase, "surrounded by a staff of letter-writers," successfully makes excuses for his failure to move decisively and "then he lags." Because of the general's overly cautious movement, the armies of Robert E. Lee and Thomas J. "Stonewall" Jackson were able to join forces. Seven days of bloody fighting in late June ended indecisively, but with the Confederates still in control of their capital.[12] McClellan had not taken Richmond.

The outcome in Virginia plunged the entire North into despair;

the president, deeply disappointed, faced increasing criticism from Chase and others who demanded McClellan's removal. Chase admitted there had been "an error of my judgment" in his early support of McClellan because the Peninsular campaign had convinced him that "my confidence had not been warranted." He now realized that the general's "immense and magnificently appointed army had been held in check for months by a force not one-third" its size. The secretary angrily wrote to his daughter Kate that McClellan's failure before Richmond was "shameful and attributable only to gross neglect and incompetency for which he should have been dismissed from the service in disgrace."[13]

Seeking new commanders with a greater willingness to engage the enemy, Lincoln bowed to the pressure of Chase and others by bringing John Pope from the West and placing him in charge of three armies in central Virginia. Henry W. Halleck was appointed general-in-chief and McClellan was reduced to a subordinate position and ordered to move his army to Aquia Creek on the Potomac to support Pope. The decision, said Chase after a cabinet discussion, was because of McClellan's "incompetency and indisposition to active movements." But McClellan was soon to become prominent again, for following the disastrous defeat of Pope's army at the second battle of Bull Run in August, Lincoln gave him command of those forces defending Washington. Lee's bold move to invade Maryland forced McClellan to meet him head on. The bloody battle of Antietam followed on September 17. McClellan's forces, far outnumbering Lee's, stopped the Confederate offense but failed to pursue their advantage and let Lee's army recross the Potomac into Virginia. Again Chase led the cries for McClellan's removal.[14]

Even before Antietam, Chase had begun the drive in the cabinet to oust McClellan because of his failure to send reinforcements to Pope at the second Bull Run. Chase's earlier admiration of the general for the training and discipline he had instilled in the rebellious troops who had fled from the first Bull Run had long since given way to impatience, a feeling reinforced by his opposition to the general's political views. Much of the criticism by Chase and other Republicans involved what they regarded as McClellan's meddling as much as it did his military record, especially in light of his Democratic inclinations. They viewed his "Harrison's Landing letter" of July 7, 1862 as unjustified interference in political matters, for among other recommendations to the president, McClellan had opposed "the forcible abolition of slavery." The president, said Chase, was at fault for rationalizing the general's blunders "instead of dismissing" McClellan immediately and finding leaders "of better qualifications."[15]

After the defeat of Pope's armies at the second battle of Bull Run and the subsequent charges against McClellan, Stanton and Chase drew up a petition which sought the support of other cabinet members in demanding McClellan's removal. The petition concluded that it was "not safe to entrust Major General McClellan, the command of any army of the United States" and was signed by Bates and Smith in addition to Chase and Stanton. It in effect charged McClellan with treason, with the petitioners implying a threat to resign if Lincoln refused their demand. Blair was not shown the petition due to his support of McClellan, and Seward was out of town at the time, but Welles was urged to support it and refused. The navy secretary agreed that the general should be removed, but preferred an open cabinet discussion on the issue rather than the "intrigue of Stanton's and Chase's."[16]

Lincoln's decision to place McClellan in charge of the armies defending Washington "after the second disaster at Bull Run" was thought by Welles "a severe mortification and disappointment" for both Stanton and Chase. In order to meet Welles's objections, Bates wrote a more moderate petition which merely protested against "continuing him in command," but Welles still did not sign. When the issue was discussed at a cabinet meeting on September 2, Lincoln refused to give in to complaints and concluded that "he could not see who could do the work wanted as well as McClellan."[17] It was only after the general's failure to follow up his advantage at Antietam that the president finally relieved him of his command, a decision delayed until November 1.

An important factor in Chase's drive to remove McClellan was that the general had, since his appointment, made public his disagreement with those Republicans who wanted the war goals expanded to include abolition. Much of Chase's assessment of prominent generals was based on political rather than military criteria. One of the reasons he admired McDowell was that for him, "whenever slavery stands in the way of successful prosecution, slavery must get out of the way," whereas McClellan had the support of "secession, semi-secession [and] anti-administration" papers. Two other antislavery military figures that Chase took into his confidence on political and military matters were Halleck and James A. Garfield, both of whom were in Washington during the event-filled fall of 1862.[18] In late September, Chase invited Garfield, who was awaiting reassignment, to live in his home; the two shared a belief in Lincoln's incompetence, and Garfield reinforced Chase's belief in McClellan's proslavery views. Chase concluded that McClellan had the support of "all the enemies of the administration," whereas the president, despite his "honest intentions," had "yielded to Border State and negrophobic counsels" and had "separated himself from the great body of the party which elected him."[19]

Chase's motives in trying to influence military and political affairs during the first eighteen months of the war are not easily evaluated. He had had no prior experience in military strategy, unlike many politicians, and he had no personal military career in mind. Until his efforts to replace McClellan during the summer and fall of 1862, he had sought more to bring greater vigor to the battlefield and reinforce Lincoln's efforts to defeat the Confederacy than to reverse or undermine the president's strategy. Part of Chase's concern over military events related to his leadership of the Treasury because every delay and every setback only compounded his financial tasks. He had reminded McClellan that "the army and Treasury must stand or fall together." After the general's appointment in 1861, Chase had promised New York bankers that "we were to have no going into winter quarters."[20]

Lincoln, recognizing Chase's intelligence, at least at first respected his opinions. Despite his lack of expertise, Chase had sound military instincts. After Antietam, he convinced Stanton and interested Lincoln in a combined army and navy expedition against Charleston from Port Royal, for with an immediate attack, the city "would be sure to fall." In cabinet discussions, Welles dampened Chase's enthusiasm by pointing out that the necessary ships could not be ready for a month. Although plans to take Charleston failed to materialize, Lincoln had shown interest and Chase had left the cabinet meeting "with more hope than I have felt for months."[21]

By this time Chase's motives had become more complex and involved political and antislavery considerations as well as military and financial concerns. After almost eighteen months of seemingly unending Union defeats in the field, Republicans knew that their chances in the elections that fall were seriously threatened. Chase was especially concerned about Democratic victories in New York, but he thought that throwing blame at Democrat McClellan might strengthen Republican chances. It might also strengthen Chase for he considered himself a worthy presidential candidate in 1864.[22] Chase was also increasingly eager to remove McClellan from authority as a man opposed to using the war as a means to end slavery. Although Lincoln had by this time issued the preliminary proclamation of emancipation, Chase's continued pressure on him to remove the general was part of a deepening split between the two men and Chase's always present political aspirations. Lincoln was fully aware of Chase's political ambitions and had during 1862 shown increasing reluctance to accept his advice.

Until late 1862, Chase had a significant influence on the administration's policies toward slavery. He helped to persuade Lincoln of the wisdom of emancipation despite the president's misgivings. Over the nineteen months that it took to reach that momentous decision, Lincoln and Chase disagreed frequently, but eventually reached a common position. Chase had not entered the administration with any immediate plans for emancipation because of the constitutional issues involved. Shortly after the election of 1860, he had emphasized that the Republican victory guaranteed "the denationalization of slavery," suggesting a continuation of his long-standing belief that the federal government should divorce itself from any responsibility for slavery but should not interfere with it where it existed.[23] Through much of the first year of the war, Chase showed little inclination toward a stronger stance.

Early in the war Chase was urged by many of his antislavery supporters to endorse abolition as a war aim, and Congress on occasion appeared inclined the same way. Chase's friend Congressman James M. Ashley urged him to do what he could to *"bring about the emancipation of every slave,"* but Chase played no part in formulating the Confiscation Act of August 6, 1861, which provided that when slaves were used in battle by the Confederacy, their owners' rights to their labor were forfeited. He seemed more inclined to endorse the Crittenden-Johnson resolution, passed by Congress the previous month, which stated that abolition of slavery was not the purpose of the war. Chase later explained that for a short period after Sumter he held to his idea "of non interference with slavery within State limits" because, even though he felt that the government had the power during war to "destroy slavery," he "doubted the expediency of its exercise."[24] He cautioned against precipitous action and defended Lincoln against those who called for immediate abolition. At that point he felt that to push too quickly toward total abolition might alienate the president and force him to endorse the views of more conservative advisers.

Chase began to adopt a more advanced position in the later summer of 1861 when General John C. Frémont forced the issue by proclaiming free those slaves of persons resisting the Union within his command in Missouri. Although the secretary endorsed Lincoln's action rescinding Frémont's order, he did so with some misgivings. Letters to Chase revealed how divided northern and border state opinion was over Frémont's order and Lincoln's quick revocation. His Cincinnati friend George Hoadly indicated that public opinion was "entirely with General Frémont" and warned that Lincoln's countermanding of the order to placate border areas failed to keep in mind that "the Free States may want a little reconciliation" also. Conversely, a border state observer noted that Frémont's order shocked him with "the effect of a bombshell" and was especially "inopportune for the Union party" because it played into the hands of the secessionists.[25]

Chase privately urged Lincoln not to revoke Frémont's action, although publicly he loyally explained that the president had no desire "to convert his war for the Union and for national existence . . . into a war upon any State institution." Chase recognized the constraints of northern politics under which Lincoln as president had to operate; moreover, he reasoned that Lincoln had no right to go beyond the Crittenden-Johnson resolution Congress had passed in July. Yet despite Chase's belief that slavery must be left "to the disposition of the States," he could not imagine the war continuing much longer "without harm to slavery." Frémont's further defiance of Lincoln and the revelation of widespread corruption and military incompetence within his Missouri command led finally to the general's removal on November 2, a decision which Chase supported.[26]

The subsequent actions of two other Union generals, who ordered the emancipation of slaves in occupied parts of the Confederacy, and actions in Congress led Chase to take a more forthright position. The first incident involved the directive of General David Hunter who had been placed in command of the Department of the South in late March 1862. On April 13, he declared that those slaves on the Sea Islands then under Union occupation were to be considered confiscated property and thus free. A month later he extended his order to the rest of his department, which included all of Georgia, Florida, and South Carolina. In May, General Benjamin F. Butler, in charge of Union occupying forces in New Orleans, ruled that all slaves coming within his lines were "contraband of war" and thus free. The previous month, Congress had abolished slavery in the District of Columbia with compensation for the owners and in June it would do the same in federal territories without compensation. Congress as well as Hunter and Butler appeared to be moving faster than the administration, and Chase, always attune to his political relationship with the more radical Republicans, was prepared to support and even encourage such actions.[27]

The Treasury had been given direct responsibility for confiscated and abandoned property in the Port Royal–Sea Island area experiment and thus was deeply concerned and affected by Hunter's action. General Hunter had been motivated by military need and intended to enlist those slaves emancipated, a policy that Chase understood and accepted. The secretary tried to convince Lincoln that concurrence in Hunter's order was good politics and was "of the highest importance" for both domestic and foreign relations. Noting that it was a military measure designed to meet the need for troops, Chase argued that the action should be allowed "to stand upon the responsibility of the commanding general who made it." He estimated that nine-tenths of the Republican electorate supported the general's action and would be alienated if it were revoked. Lincoln's response to Chase was curt, to the point, and, given his response to Frémont's action in Missouri, predictable: "No commanding general shall do such a thing upon my responsibility without consulting me." He would not permit his generals to force his hand on emancipation, for those were questions which "I reserve to myself." Lincoln's reaction reflected his desire to move cautiously against slavery as well as his concern for maintaining border state loyalty. In addition, he disagreed with Chase's assessment that northern public opinion demanded emancipation and believed instead that the majority would not sustain him if he took stronger action. Chase was clearly upset by Lincoln's action, indicating to Greeley that nothing had "so sorely tried" him as "the nullifying of Hunter's proclamation." Although unwilling to say that the general should have acted without consulting Lincoln, Chase thought that once made, the proclamation "should have been allowed to stand." Hunter had moved emancipation one step closer, Chase believed, and rejoiced that some progress had been made.[28]

In his correspondence with Butler, Chase encouraged the general's efforts to free the slaves of Louisiana and enlist them in his army. Chase explained that he had become convinced that "to abstain from military interference with slavery" was to contribute to "the continued subjugation of nearly four million loyal people." After Congress passed a second Confiscation Act in mid-July 1862, declaring free all slaves of anyone "engaged in rebellion," Chase told Butler, "We must give freedom to every slave" in the Gulf states. The act also authorized the use of these slaves for military and naval service as the president felt proper, thus setting the stage for the introduction of black troops into Union armies. Because he knew from cabinet discussions that a proclamation against slavery was virtually certain, he suggested to Butler at the end of July that annulling Hunter's order had been a mistake which "will not be repeated." He told New Orleans Treasury Agent George S. Denison in early September that Lincoln was "rapidly approaching" this position and that if Butler now took the action that Hunter had in May, he "would be in no danger of censure." His suggestions to Butler and Denison were a safe way of making political capital out of a presidential proclamation sure to come. His advice was a blend of idealism and sound politics, although he did not want to be on record as publicly advising such a step.[29]

In late August, Butler had moved to enroll free blacks in his regiments and made no effort to check whether those enlisting were in fact fugitives. On August 25, the War Department, also anticipating a presidential proclamation, authorized General Rufus Saxton of the Department of the South to accept "volunteers of African descent" into his armies.[30] The complex issues of black troops and emancipation had already been faced at the Port Royal experiment within the Department of the South, with Chase and his Treasury agents playing a major role in the steps taken; these actions would be factors in Lincoln's decision to issue his preliminary proclamation on September 22.

The Sea Islands of South Carolina fell under Union control early in the war when Samuel F. DuPont's South Atlantic Squadron took the area in November 1861. The Treasury Department, with its responsibility for confiscated and abandoned property, was given the task of administering the region. Because the planters had left behind many of their slaves as they fled inland, Chase had an opportunity to direct the first significant experiment in working with freedmen. In his eyes, those who had been abandoned could never be "reduced again to slavery" by the government "without great inhumanity." He therefore quickly appointed his abolitionist friend Edward L. Pierce of Boston to direct the effort to prepare them "for self-support by their own industry." [31]

Chase received little encouragement in this effort from the rest of the cabinet or the president. At the secretary's request, Pierce visited Lincoln to discuss what might be done for the freedmen. Impatiently, the president asked, "What's all this itching to get niggers into our lines?" He nonetheless reluctantly authorized Chase to give Pierce "such instructions in regard to Port Royal contrabands as may seem judicious." Chase realized that despite Lincoln's many reasons for hesitancy he was considering a general emancipation policy and might thus allow it in the limited confines of Port Royal before applying it elsewhere. Chase assumed that military emancipation had begun and that the government would take full responsibility for the freedmen. [32] He therefore expected to play a major role in the Port Royal experiment despite Lincoln's lack of enthusiasm.

Not all of those involved at Port Royal were as sympathetic to the plight of the area's blacks as Chase and Pierce. At the urging of Rhode Island governor, and Chase's future son-in-law, William Sprague, the secretary had appointed Lieutenant Colonel William H. Reynolds to supervise the collection of abandoned cotton in the region, and by mid-December Reynolds was in Beaufort as the Treasury agent. With Pierce in charge of organizing, employing, and providing for the blacks and Reynolds the collection and shipment of the cotton, Chase wrote to both men urging their mutual cooperation toward a common goal. He exhorted Reynolds to welcome Pierce's aid "in your arduous undertaking, and enter heartily into his views as he will doubtless into yours." [33]

Because the two men looked at the situation from different perspectives, Reynolds interested in efficiency of cotton production and

Pierce concerned for the freedmen, a clash quickly developed. Reynolds wanted the cotton shipped to New York for ginning, whereas Pierce felt this task could keep blacks employed "at the work which they have been accustomed to do." Pierce's plans included not only the economic well-being of his charges but also their "religious instruction, ordinary education and medical care." With recruitment aid from supporters in New York and Boston, missionaries and educators began to arrive at Port Royal.[34] When Chase ordered Reynolds to stop circulating disparaging accounts of missionary activities, the colonel responded that most of the missionaries were "totally unfit" for their work. Pierce and his people complained that Reynolds's agents did not have the freedmen's "moral interest" at heart and were "sadly prejudiced against them." In vain, Chase attempted to mediate from Washington.[35]

By April 1862, Chase agreed to transfer much of the work of the Treasury to the War Department. General Rufus Saxton, serving under the command of General Hunter's Department of the South, received orders to take control of the Port Royal area. The Treasury continued to play a role in the collection of cotton, so Chase was able to maintain contact with the missionary efforts. He endorsed Saxton's appointment as military commander as a "thorough-going Abolitionist" who fully sympathized with the efforts being extended to aid the freedmen. Even before his appointment, Saxton had urged the division of "the fertile lands of those islands" among the black families "in lots large enough for their subsistence."[36] Saxton's appointment made the transfer of authority to the War Department acceptable to Chase, and during the next months small plots were assigned, much of the land cultivated, and schools and churches established under missionary direction with Saxton's full approval.

Many difficulties remained, however. Further conflict between Chase and Colonel Reynolds led to the officer's dismissal amidst reports of extensive fraud committed by him and his agents. Chase and the president remained at odds over the racial implications of the Port Royal experiment. Of major importance was Lincoln's decision in May to revoke General Hunter's order freeing the slaves in South Carolina, Georgia, and Florida. Although the revocation had no immediate ramifications for the Port Royal blacks, whom the president apparently regarded as freedmen, it did for the overall issues of emancipation, land distribution, and the use of black troops. When Pierce complained of the lack of encouragement for his "social experiment" at Port Royal, Chase reminded him that his own efforts in its behalf were made "without suggestion or sympathy" from Lincoln; moreover, he had had to endure "the sneers of some of the members of the Cabinet." Chase believed that Lincoln was conservative on emancipation and the role of blacks in the war because "the colonization delusion and the negrophobia dread are too potent yet." Still, the Port Royal experiment proceeded with some success through the remainder of 1862.[37]

As Lincoln moved gradually toward an emancipation policy, Chase urged that it be accomplished by military orders from the commanding generals in the field rather than by presidential proclamation. Because military use had to be made of freed blacks, Chase thought emancipation should be declared by those who would direct the new soldiers. As the war lengthened with no immediate victory in sight, the Union continued to make little use "of the only loyal men" within the Confederacy. Yet for the Confederacy "they dig, they build, they construct, they shoot for the rebels as the rebels require." Therefore, Chase concluded, we must "declare free all Slaves of those States and invite them to organize for the suppression of rebellion." If he were a general he would announce "that no man loyal to the Union can be a slave." He noted with dismay that some generals were proslavery and asked John Sherman if "the proslavery views of West Point" had affected his brother as well as General Don Carlos Buell.[38]

At this time Chase's drive to remove McClellan emphasized that general's endorsement of slavery. In July 1862, Congress authorized black enlistments, a step Chase fully approved; he also endorsed the War Department's sanctioning of black recruitment in late August. He reasoned that only with a willingness to attack slavery on military grounds as a source of strength for the Confederacy could the war be won. He was so convinced "of the indispensable necessity" of abolition that he finally became "indifferent as to the mode," and he gave support to Lincoln's decision to issue a presidential order.[39]

Until the summer of 1862, the president remained adamant that emancipation come by state action and include compensation for the owners and a colonization plan for those freed. He worked vigorously to persuade the Union border states of the wisdom of that approach and feared any step that might antagonize those who had thus far remained loyal. Similarly, he worried that public opinion in the North might not sustain him and his party, especially in the approaching congressional elections. Deeply disappointed over the unwillingness of the border states to accept his approach, Lincoln informed his cabinet on July 22 of his intention to issue an order "proclaiming the emancipation of all slaves within States remaining in insurrection on the first of January, 1863." Included would be endorsements of both colonization and compensation. Several factors had changed his mind in addition to the border state recalcitrance. The growing foreign antislavery sentiment and the effect that a proclamation would have on assuring the neutrality of Great Britain and others, and the presence of thousands of slaves of uncertain status in Union army camps helped persuade the president that he must act. Finally, increasing pressure from many Republicans in Congress and in the cabinet, especially Chase, made Lincoln realize that if he tried too much to keep moderates content he might lose the support of the antislavery wing of his party in the process.[40]

Chase's reaction to the president's cabinet announcement was one of support but not enthusiasm. He noted in his diary that he would give the measure "my cordial support," but he would have preferred a policy which made no reference to compensation. Again he indicated his belief that emancipation could be accomplished better "by allowing Generals to organize and arm the slaves . . . and by directing the Commanders of Departments to proclaim emancipation within their Districts as soon as practicable." Nonetheless, he regarded the step as "so much better than inaction" and vowed to "give it my entire support." Several other factors tempered the secretary's enthusiasm. He believed the delay until January 1863 unfortunate, and he opposed any linking of the plan to Lincoln's colonization proposals. "How much better," thought Chase, "would be a manly protest against prejudice, against color! and a wise effort to give freedmen homes in America!"[41]

Lincoln and the cabinet agreed in late July that announcement of the preliminary proclamation should wait until after a significant victory on the battlefield to avoid the impression of acting out of desperation. Such a victory came when Lee's forces were held at Antietam on September 17. Even though McClellan permitted the southern army to escape back into Virginia, Lincoln determined to announce the new policy. Chase gave his support, but because of the call for colonization and compensation, he noted that the proclamation did not "mark out exactly the course I should myself prefer." Also, he wrote to General Butler urging him not to wait, but to "anticipate a little the operation of the Proclamation" in his command. At the urging of Seward and Chase, the passage relating to colonization was worded to indicate that emancipation would be attempted "only with the consent of the colonists." Thus, despite the opposition of many Union supporters, including Postmaster General Montgomery Blair, emancipation became a war aim.[42] Through skillful timing Lincoln retained the support of most northerners while adding a significant new dimension to the war.

When, as expected, the Confederate states rejected reentry into the Union and instead described Lincoln as a "fiend" who would destroy "four thousand millions of our property," the president convened the cabinet to consider the wording of the final proclamation. He also proposed an amendment to the Constitution which endorsed his compensated and gradual emancipation plan and which would delay complete freedom until 1900. Chase opposed such an amendment not only because of the gradual and compensation features, but also because he felt it could not be ratified and would thus weaken rather than strengthen the administration. In cabinet discussion, Chase proposed that instead of excepting parts of Virginia and Louisiana, such as the area under Butler's jurisdiction, the proclamation should apply to all parts of the seceded states.[43] Despite Secretary Welles's agreement with Chase, his suggestion was rejected. The president did accept Chase's wording for the final paragraph of the proclamation describing it as "an act of justice, warrantable by the Constitution upon military necessity" and invoking "the considerate judgment of mankind, and the gracious favor of Almighty God."[44]

The proclamation did urge the recruitment of freedmen into Union armies, thus expanding upon the policy already approved by the War Department the previous August for parts of the Confederacy. Little had been accomplished toward this goal since then by either Generals Saxton or Butler, but with Lincoln's official endorsement, the recruiting efforts would soon be systematized with much more positive results. Chase was in full agreement with this effort and rejoiced that blacks would "be called into the conflict, not as cattle, not now even as contrabands, but as men." He also urged that they be used in all varieties of military effort, for in this way, "from a burden they will become a support." In the ensuing months he kept constant watch over the use of black troops and endeavored to assure that they were treated fairly.[45] On the issues of emancipation and black conscription, the secretary and the president had reached an accommodation satisfactory to both. Without question, Chase's constant pressure on Lincoln had helped push the reluctant president in a direction which he had not at first wanted to go. Surely there were other critical factors in Lincoln's decision, but without Chase's urging, the emancipation policy would probably have evolved more slowly and emerged in a more modified form. Still, there were differences. To Chase the war had become a means to his long sought goal of emancipation, whereas to Lincoln emancipation was the means to a successful war and restoration of the Union. In other respects, their relationship had long since begun to deteriorate.

Chase's differences with Lincoln had been building since early 1862 and were intensified by growing disagreement over military strategy, appointments, and frustration over the lack of success on the battlefield. As the military situation worsened, Chase felt increasingly alienated by the president's unwillingness to take the cabinet into his confidence and by fear that Seward had influence Chase believed he alone deserved. Differences between Chase and Seward over patronage in New York, especially involving the customhouse, had intensified, adding to the tension. Initially, Chase and Seward had joined during the summer of 1862 in urging the removal of General McClellan, but by September Seward was conveniently absent as Chase and Stanton circulated their petition to remove the general. This Chase attributed to Seward's desire to stay on the right side of the president.[46] With Lincoln still unwilling to remove McClellan, even as the cabinet agreed on the preliminary proclamation of emancipation, Chase, in conversations and letters to friends, increased his criticism of the president over his disregard for the cabinet.

Chase's unhappiness with the president for ignoring his counsel and for misusing the cabinet predated by several months the climax of the McClellan situation. On July 15, 1862, Chase wrote to his friend James Hamilton complaining that his views were of so little value to Lincoln that "what I think ought to be done is so generally left undone, and what I think ought not to be done [is] so generally done." By the end of the summer, there seemed little left for him to do except to direct the Treasury "as well as I may under existing circumstances." Unfortunately, he told Greeley, Lincoln saw no collective role for the cabinet, preferring to have each secretary "turn his own machine, with almost no comparison of views or consultation of any kind." The war was totally in Lincoln's hands; Chase knew "so little of military matters that I could not possibly tell what our true position and prospect are." When Senator Sherman observed that the president and General McClellan were "the worst enemies of this country," Chase was prepared to agree.[47]

Gideon Welles shared Chase's views on the cabinet and noted how infrequently meetings were held and how useless they were in formulating policy. Seward, observed Welles, was frequently absent, although he spent considerable time with Lincoln "patronizing and instructing him" as well as "inculcating his political party notions." Chase felt his political influence waning and briefly considered resigning, noting that if things did not change he would "no longer expect to be useful here." Always mindful of using his cabinet post to position himself for another try for the presidency, Chase sensed he was being outmaneuvered by Seward. The more affable secretary of state was clearly closer to the president personally and seemed to Chase increasingly influential on policy matters as well. Chase resented the intimacy between Lincoln and Seward and believed that Seward's malignant influence was the cause of much of the administration's bungling. The staid, humorless Treasury secretary could not understand their jokes or boisterous laughter and increasingly feared that their closeness meant he was being frozen out of a role in critical decisions. Chase lamented that there was "no Cabinet except in name." He concluded in despair that it was painful "to hear complaints of remissness, delays, discords, dangers . . . and to know that one has no power to remedy the evils and yet is thought to have."[48]

Events during the fall and early winter of 1862 added to Chase's gloom and led to his fateful confrontation with Lincoln just before Christmas. In October, the congressional elections turned many Republicans out of office and especially in Ohio left the party in a gravely weakened position. The Republican or Union majority in the House was seriously eroded with the Ohio delegation now dominated by Democrats. In New York, the loss of the governorship to Democrat Horatio Seymour was equally harmful and concerned both Lincoln and Chase.[49] Both setbacks could be attributed in Chase's eyes to the president's bungled military strategy because Lincoln had "committed the management of the war almost exclusively to his political opponents." In the future, dissatisfaction would not be limited "to a mere rebuke of the Administration at a quiet election"; rather, the voters would "bury it beneath the storm!"[50]

Chase was naturally relieved when Lincoln finally removed McClellan in early November after the general's further procrastination. But his replacement, General Ambrose E. Burnside, led the army into one of the worst Union disasters of the war at Fredericksburg on December 13, when Lee's heavily outnumbered troops inflicted a shattering defeat. As northerners were plunged into even greater despair, cabinet and congressional leaders furiously sought a scapegoat. Chase and many others blamed Seward for having advocated a less forceful military policy than they deemed necessary. Furthermore, Chase recognized that if the president could be persuaded to dismiss Seward, his own political stature would rise accordingly.

Chase was the obvious leader of the radical faction of the Republican party which had for so long pressed for a more vigorous prosecution of the war and in recent months had urged the dismissal of McClellan and the adoption of an emancipation policy. Sentiment had been building among leading radical senators to force Lincoln to accept their views and to use the issue of Seward's removal as the means of asserting their authority over the president. They would avoid direct criticism of Lincoln by their attacks on Seward because they knew the president represented the moderate position on race and politics that so many voters shared. Many of the senators supported such an approach not only to enhance their faction's power but also to forward Chase's candidacy in 1864.

In November, Sumner told Chase he was willing to return to Washington several weeks before Congress convened "in order to help those influences which we want to prevail with the President." The disaster at Fredericksburg precipitated a caucus of Republican senators on December 16. Although some sought a resolution expressing no confidence in Seward, the majority agreed instead to call for "a change in and partial reconstruction of the cabinet." Using evidence against Seward supplied by Chase, the senators agreed that Seward had opposed a vigorous prosecution of the war. A committee was chosen to present their position to the president and demand his action. It was headed by the highly respected, seventy-one-year-old senator from Vermont, Jacob Collamer, and included Sumner, Wade, and Fessenden. In the words of one, their purpose was "to drive all the cabinet out—then force . . . the recall of Mr. Chase as Premier, and form a cabinet of ultra men around him."[51]

Before the committee could meet with Lincoln, Seward's New York colleague, Senator Preston King, told the secretary what to expect. Seward in turn wrote his resignation for King to give to Lincoln and then discussed the situation with the president. Lincoln was thus well prepared when he met with the Senate committee on December 18. At the three-hour meeting, the senators noted the widely held belief that the president did not consult the cabinet sufficiently on critical questions and made decisions without its approval. They saved their severest complaints for Seward, charging him "with indifference, with want of earnestness in the War," and noted that all but one of the thirty-two Republican senators (King being the exception) agreed that he should be removed. Clearly aware that their demands represented a challenge to his control of his administration, Lincoln said little other than to invite them back the next evening for further discussion. By then he had concluded that Chase "was at the bottom of this mischief" and that he must force his exposure to maintain control. Before the senators returned, the president called an emergency cabinet meeting with all but Seward present and told his secretaries that all of them, including Seward, were essential to him. Lincoln insisted that on fundamental questions of policy the cabinet had been consulted and that there had been unity. All nodded their agreement, although Welles noted later that Chase protested the presidential command that they all be present at the meeting with the senators that evening. Chase claimed to have "no knowledge whatsoever of the movement or the resignation" of Seward.[52]

The president could now adroitly expose Chase's efforts to function as both cabinet member and adviser to the Senate critics. At the meeting of senators and cabinet members, Lincoln defended Seward against his accusers and argued that the cabinet was in basic agreement on war policies. He had assembled his cabinet, he explained, to prove to the senators that his cabinet was united and had made basic decisions as a body. He then dramatically forced Chase's hand by asking each secretary his view. Bates, Welles, and Blair came to Seward's defense; Welles suggested that a "Senatorial combination to dictate to the President . . . cannot be permitted."[53]

Put on the spot, Chase hesitated and then stammered a weak endorsement of Lincoln's interpretation. He even admitted that Seward had faithfully supported the war effort, including the emancipation policy. Chase had been trapped in his own scheme and could only squirm in embarrassment. Humiliated in the presence of his supporters, Chase complained that he would not have come "had he known that he was to be arraigned before a committee of the Senate." Trying to retrieve lost ground he voiced regret "that there was not a more full and thorough consideration and canvass of every important measure in open Cabinet," but he agreed that key issues were usually debated. To endorse the senators more openly would make him appear disloyal to Lincoln and expose him as the promoter of the protest. Brilliantly outmaneuvered by the president, the senators could no longer realistically demand Seward's removal. When Senator Orville H. Browning later asked Collamer how Chase could have so changed his earlier view that "Seward exercised a back stairs and malign influence upon the President and thwarted all measures of the cabinet," Collamer responded, "He lied." In Fessenden's view, "He will never be forgiven by many for deliberately sacrificing his friends to the fear of offending his and their enemies."[54]

Having thus lost face with the president and the senators, the mortified Chase met with Lincoln the following day. Again claiming total unawareness of the senators' intentions, he explained that he had brought his resignation letter. In the presence of Welles, Lincoln said eagerly, "Let me have it," and Chase reluctantly surrendered the paper. To Welles, the president announced with great satisfaction: "This cuts the Gordian knot." Elatedly he added, "I can dispose of this subject now without difficulty." In his efforts to prevent either Seward or Chase from dominating the cabinet, Lincoln could not permit one and not the other to resign.[55] But he did not want to lose either man or the support of their factions, and with both letters in hand he could now refuse their resignations because "the public interest" would not permit it. In Welles's view, both men were essential: "Seward comforts him; Chase he deems a necessity." The confrontation reaffirmed Lincoln as the dominant figure and put him in a much stronger position politically, leaving Chase and Seward no choice but to withdraw their resignations.[56] Having won at least the grudging respect of the senators, he had adroitly cut the ground from under Chase's efforts to dominate the cabinet and to use the position to challenge Lincoln for the presidency. Lacking Lincoln's political vision and skill, Chase and his cohorts had not thought through what Lincoln might do to maintain control over internal Republican party politics. The ensuing months would see a much embittered and weakened Chase struggle to regain lost prestige.

During 1862, Chase began to consider returning to the Senate. Benjamin Wade's term was to expire in 1863, but Chase at first rejected suggestions from friends that he go after the seat Wade had held for two terms, commenting instead that the incumbent was "eminently worthy" of reelection. Despite past grievances with the senator for his role in the 1860 nomination struggle, Chase preferred "to forget all that" because Wade's actions in the Senate had been "bold, manly, and in judgement, wise."[57] Chase admitted, however, that he would prefer a Republican of Democratic rather than Whig background, such as Judge Rufus P. Spalding of the Ohio Supreme Court—someone whom he could "always confidently and freely consult."[58] Chase probably did not actually prefer a Spalding nomination, but hoped instead that by suggesting the judge's name he might undermine Wade's chances and thus enhance his own.

As his influence with the president waned, Chase suggested to friends that he might accept a Senate election after all. In October, he told James Monroe that he had decided not to decline a nomination because he felt he could be more useful in the Senate than as Treasury secretary. He presented himself as "the only one who could probably unite a majority." He was willing to be a candidate against Wade only if it became clear that Wade could not be reelected. To Wade, he explained somewhat insincerely his desire for the senator's reelection and his wish to forget all past differences. Wade responded with relief that "all is right now between us." Throughout November and December, as Chase's relations with Lincoln deteriorated and the Ohio election approached, Chase held to his announced position, explaining his desire to "let bygones be bygones" and urging Wade's reelection.[59]

Wade's decisive role in urging the ouster of General McClellan and the firing of Secretary Seward made it difficult for Chase to oppose him openly. Some critics, such as the *Portage County Democrat,* were unconvinced by Chase's support for Wade and labelled his pose as "political jugglery," a calculated effort "to produce the very conjuncture which it points." Said the paper, "he is plotting and counterplotting to succeed Mr. Lincoln in the Presidential chair," an ambition he could best forward by leaving the Treasury for the Senate. When the legislature decided to retain Wade in January 1863, Chase had to reconcile himself to his cabinet post despite his recent loss of face.[60]

Chase continued to discharge his duties faithfully in the Treasury and exert what influence he could over the president. The issue of immediate concern following the December cabinet crisis was the status of western Virginia, and here Chase was instrumental in persuading Lincoln to his point of view. With the secession of Virginia, a Unionist group centered at Wheeling quickly established its own legislature, elected a governor, and applied to Congress for admission as the state of West Virginia. In December 1862 both houses of Congress approved the request and Lincoln asked his cabinet for individual written opinions on the bill's constitutionality and expediency. The constitutional question involved whether the new state government was the only legal representative for the area—an issue complicated by the requirement that a new state could not be created from within the boundaries of an existing state without that state's concurrence.[61]

The cabinet was evenly divided on the issue with Chase, Stanton, and Seward in favor of admission and Welles, Blair, and Bates opposed. In Chase's eyes the bill was both constitutional and expedient. He took the highly debatable position that the Wheeling government spoke for the entire state, for in a case of insurrection "where a large body of the people remain faithful," they "must be taken to constitute the State." Moreover, he thought admission was expedient because it was "of vital importance" to the welfare of those Union loyalists who had desired separation for many years. Clearly, the fact that the proposed state had agreed to the gradual abolition of slavery was critical in his argument that admission was expedient; it expanded the emancipation process to areas not included in the Emancipation Proclamation. Bowing to party pressure, Lincoln gave his reluctant consent to the bill on December 31, and later declared the state admitted effective June 20, 1863.[62]

Chase was not as successful in winning acceptance of his views on emancipation in those areas of the Confederacy where Lincoln's order had not originally applied. In cabinet discussions he had urged that emancipation be extended to those parts of Louisiana and Virginia then occupied by Union forces. Eager to see the Port Royal experiment applied to other parts of the South, he believed that "no one of the Rebel States must be permitted to tolerate slavery for an instant."[63] Not only should all blacks be freed, but those emancipated should then help to complete the process as part of Union armies while the rest should be given work on former plantation lands owned by blacks themselves. Chase also urged that freedmen be given the right to vote in reconstructed areas as a means of justice and to protect their newly won freedom. During the remaining year and a half of his tenure in the Treasury, and even after his resignation, Chase worked diligently toward these goals. He was met at each step along this controversial path with determined resistance—a resistance supported and frequently led by the president.

Emancipation had begun on a limited scale both at Port Royal and New Orleans even before the announcement of Lincoln's proclamation. But Chase believed that the process could not be forwarded unless the excepted areas were included. He thus exhorted his supporters to urge Lincoln to revoke "the exceptions." The proclamation was the necessary first step, but "the hearts of the people must supply the omission." He even prepared a draft of a policy statement revoking the exceptions which the president told him he would consider. Any hope for a revised policy appeared doomed, however, when in September 1863 Lincoln reaffirmed his belief that "the exemptions were made because the military necessity did not apply" to areas already controlled by Union armies. Equally disturbing to the president, Chase's proposal would "drive friends in the border states against us" and be more in advance of northern public opinion than he dared move. Still, Chase would accept no other approach, and he refused to endorse a proposal that North Carolina might consider reentering the Union if allowed to follow a gradual emancipation plan which might take until 1875 to complete. Said the secretary, neither there "nor in any other State must there be any more slavery."[64] Chase thus faced an uphill struggle to convince Lincoln of the advisability of total emancipation. He had more success in winning support for the right of blacks to serve in Union armies.

The gradual movement toward Lincoln's limited emancipation policy in 1862 had given impetus to the organization of black troops even though the president had revoked General Hunter's order to begin efforts to arm those freed in his area. When in July the second Confiscation Act gave the chief executive authority to employ blacks in Union forces, Lincoln made it clear that although he would use blacks as laborers in the army, he was not ready to make them soldiers. Several days later Hunter was forced to disband his black regiment. Despite this, by the end of August, Secretary Stanton authorized General Rufus Saxton to enlist black troops in the same part of the South, a step which Lincoln accepted because it fit into his forthcoming emancipation policy. Stanton's order was an important turning point in the efforts to organize black regiments in 1863 and one that had Chase's full backing.[65]

A similar evolution of events occurred in New Orleans, again with Chase's enthusiastic urging. Initially, General Butler had resisted the use of black troops, and was soon at odds with his subordinate, General John W. Phelps, who welcomed Louisiana fugitives into his army. Chase helped to persuade Butler to arm black troops by telling the general of the approaching emancipation decision during the summer of 1862. Late in August, Butler invited free black militiamen in Louisiana to enroll in Union armies, thus avoiding the controversial step of arming slaves, but showing his willingness to move in that direction. Yet as Chase's Treasury Agent George S. Denison told him, in enlisting troops, "nobody inquires whether the recruit is (or has been) a slave." As a result, "the boldest and finest fugitives have enlisted" in the Free Colored Brigade. Throughout the summer and fall, Chase urged the president to increase his commitment to the use of black troops. In August, Chase expressed his "conviction for the tenth or twentieth time" in cabinet discussions that emancipated blacks ought to be organized "in companies and regiments, etc."[66]

In January 1863, Lincoln was at last ready to endorse black enlistment. Shortly after the announcement of that principle in the Emancipation Proclamation, he urged Stanton to take the necessary steps in the Mississippi Valley. The war secretary then directed Adjutant General Lorenzo Thomas to go West to coordinate the recruitment of blacks "to furnish useful service" as both soldiers and workers. The general in turn began enlisting blacks, while other freedmen were placed as workers on abandoned plantations. By the end of 1863, Thomas had organized twenty black regiments, traveling throughout the lower Mississippi Valley explaining his recruitment policy. Although Thomas's policies were not without controversy, Treasury Agent Mellen reported to Chase enthusiastically by May 1863 that there was widespread acceptance of black troops under both Generals Thomas and Grant. Chase in turn informed his friend Garfield that "the President is now thoroughly converted in this business." Organization of black troops was proceeding smoothly and would soon be "as effective as any in the service."[67]

In the New Orleans area much of the progress of late 1862 was slowed when General Butler was replaced by General Nathaniel P. Banks in December. In January 1863, Denison urged Chase to write to Banks encouraging him to continue Butler's policy, but by the end of February, the agent indicated he was discouraged by Banks's slow progress. When Banks finally began his efforts on May 1, 1863, with the organization of the Corps d'Afrique, he limited the regiments to 500 rather than the usual 1,000 men because, he argued, blacks were not accustomed to military service. Chase criticized his order for containing "an apology" for the use of "anything belonging to rebels for the suppression of rebellion," but rejoiced that he had finally begun the process of black recruitment. In August, Chase noted with satisfaction that Banks had expressed "confidence in the efficiency of these troops and clear opinions in favor of using them."[68]

The policy of black recruitment was being standardized throughout the South instead of being left to individual generals, some of whom, like Sherman, were not at all eager to include blacks in their armies. Chase believed correctly that he had played a significant role in the evolution from a limited, largely resisted policy to one which was more general and accepted, and he remained interested in the fair treatment of black troops throughout his tenure in the Treasury. In May 1864, Lincoln requested cabinet opinions on what retaliatory actions he should take against the Confederacy after the massacre of "a large number of our colored soldiers with their white officers" who had attempted to surrender at Fort Pillow near Memphis. Chase's recommendation, much in line with others in the cabinet, proposed "the execution of an equal . . . number of rebel officers and soldiers," a proposal never actually carried out. More significantly, the secretary urged that Union troops be placed "in all respects upon the same footing without regard to complexion."

Although never adhered to completely, Chase's recommendation received greater support as the war neared an end, especially in regard to pay for black troops.[69]

Chase's efforts to provide work for blacks as farm laborers and ultimately landowners met only limited success, in part because by the time a policy could be worked out his influence in the administration had declined dramatically and in part because of the radical nature of his proposals. Again his efforts were concentrated in areas under Union control: New Orleans, the lower Mississippi Valley, and the Sea Islands. The New Orleans situation was confined primarily to a plan of labor rather than land ownership and was complicated by General Banks's unwillingness to cooperate. A limited experiment begun by General Butler had disproved, claimed Denison, that "Sugar and Cotton can successfully be raised only by compulsory labor." In his view, freedmen worked with both "energy and industry," proving that emancipation "will increase and invigorate labor." The change to Banks's command, however, represented, in Denison's eyes, the reestablishment of slavery, for although the planters were happy with his methods, black workers felt themselves exploited. Many were cheated out of their wages, said Denison, and as a result had "no confidence" in "the old slave-holders" and "will not readily work for them" on the leased plantations. In response to Denison's misgivings Chase argued that the rights of freedmen must "be frankly recognized and fully protected," because it was vital "to make them feel that they have an interest in public order and in the cultivation of the soil."[70]

In the Mississippi Valley between Memphis and Vicksburg, General Thomas planned to place those blacks who could not serve in the army on abandoned plantations "to till the ground." He appointed commissioners to supervise the leasing of plantation lands, with labor to be provided by freedmen in the army contraband camps. The system was soon under attack by representatives of several freedmen's aid societies who charged the same kind of exploitation that Denison reported in the New Orleans area. James E. Yeatman of the Western Sanitary Commission called the system "a state of involuntary servitude worse than that from which they have escaped." He proposed to Chase a more humane labor program which would include some land redistribution.[71]

In March 1863, Congress had granted the Treasury Department control over abandoned lands in the Mississippi Valley, thus allowing Chase to challenge Thomas's leasing system. Following the outlines of Yeatman's proposals, he placed Treasury Agent Mellen in charge of the abandoned lands with instructions that the commissioners and lessees must not be the same people because no one "should have the least pecuniary interest." Instead, they must be "thoroughly honest, and capable and earnestly desirous to do justice and show kindness" to the freedmen, characteristics clearly not possessed by those appointed by Thomas. Workers should be paid at weekly or monthly intervals, "and their wages should be sufficiently liberal" to induce them to want to work. Going even further, Chase proposed sweeping land reform, stating that nothing would contribute more "to the improvement of the condition of the freedmen" than toil on their own land. In December 1863, Chase authorized Mellen to initiate plans to divide some plantations, with landlords encouraged to sell land to freedmen in amounts from forty to eighty acres.[72] If carried out, the proposal might have inaugurated in the Mississippi Valley the kind of black land ownership experiment already underway at Port Royal.

Between December and February, Chase and Mellen did their best to further their land reform plans as well as insure better treatment and pay for those freedmen employed on leased plantations. In February, Mellen urged Chase to seek authorization from Congress to expand this effort, "for thousands of the Freed people" will flock in "as they learn that they will be received, employed and protected." Noting the importance of employment both to their own morale and to the Union effort, Mellen predicted that hundreds of thousands of acres could be cultivated under his plan. He added that he had established three "Freedmen's Home Farms," one of them at Jefferson Davis's plantation, "as places of temporary labor for those who are not otherwise employed."[73] In Washington, Chase sought to implement Mellen's efforts.

The two men were resisted at each step by General Thomas who, according to the Treasury agent, emphasized "the profit of the planter" without reference to freedmen's needs. Thomas claimed the planters could not afford to pay the wages that Mellen had authorized and were abandoning their leases instead. In March, Thomas arrived at Vicksburg "full of fuss and feathers about the wages to be paid by lessees of abandoned plantations." The general brought with him new authorization from Lincoln "to take hold of and be master in the contraband and leading business." Said the president, Chase's system may have been "well-intended," but it was too complex to succeed.[74] There were other more basic reasons for Lincoln's reluctance. Chase had clearly moved too far in advance of public opinion for the president to continue sanctioning his land redistribution program. Few in the North endorsed the seizure of private property by the government for distribution to former slaves. Lincoln had to move slowly, whereas Chase as a cabinet officer could seek policy changes for which in the final analysis it was Lincoln whom the public held accountable. As Thomas took control away from Mellen, the Treasury's plans for land reform and better treatment of black workers received a major setback—a development which coincided with the failure of Chase's challenge to Lincoln for his party's presidential nomination.

Long before the Treasury lost jurisdiction in the Mississippi Valley, Chase helped initiate a similar program of land reform on the Sea Islands. Under laws passed in 1862 and 1863, Congress had authorized the Treasury to direct the confiscation of abandoned lands and to reserve some of them for "charitable purposes" for the freedmen; by early 1863, the commissioners at Port Royal had begun setting aside such lands. Treasury Agent Edward Pierce was authorized by Chase "to take charge of captured and abandoned property." Despite his efforts and those of Reverend Mansfield French and other northern abolitionists to protect the land for blacks, northern speculators began "privately contriving to secure these plantations." More than half the land was seized in this way. In French's view, "none need, none deserve these lands so much as the Negroes themselves." In September, at Chase's urging Lincoln authorized the sale of a small portion of the land in twenty-acre plots for $1.25 per acre with both French and General Saxton working to enlarge the amount available. Saxton also proposed that blacks be permitted to preempt land before it was opened for sale, a proposal that raised new controversy. French convinced Chase of the value of preemption, and on December 31, 1863, Chase authorized it.[75]

Almost immediately, many of the commissioners and northern speculators protested, claiming that preemption created chaos and confused the freedmen, who needed more order and direction. Bow-

ing to pressure, Chase agreed to withdraw the preemption authorization, despite French's plea against "the cruel effects of your late
suspending order." Instead, much of the land was again to be sold in
large blocks, thus curbing the opportunity of the freedmen to be
purchasers. Without the support of the commissioners Chase apparently felt his land reform effort would have to be more modest.
Perhaps he had begun to doubt the legality, wisdom, or practicality
of land redistribution and its challenge to the sanctity of private
property. Already in a discouraged frame of mind because of the
collapse of his presidential plans, he could find little to rejoice in
General William Birney's assessment in April 1864 of the deplor-
able condition of Sea Island blacks. Soldiers had "robbed them of
their vegetables, pigs, and poultry," Treasury agents had taken away
their personal property, while "the Tax Commissioners sold away
their lands" to speculators. Such was the result of not giving the
freedmen "an opportunity of taking the lease."[76] Birney's description may have exaggerated conditions but nonetheless reflected the
difficulties of bringing meaningful change.

Even with this setback in land reform at Port Royal, Chase and his
Treasury agents worked in early 1864 for passage of a Freedmen's
Bureau bill which they hoped would provide for land distribution
under Treasury jurisdiction throughout the South. After much congressional maneuvering, Senator Sumner produced a bill which included a provision for leasing abandoned and confiscated lands to
northern whites and, where possible, to freedmen. Sumner's bill
placed the bureau under Treasury jurisdiction. At Chase's direction,
Agent Mellen spent considerable time in Washington during the
spring of 1864 lobbying for that bill and other land proposals for
leasing plantations. Passage of Sumner's bill did not come in the
Senate until June, the month of Chase's resignation, and was delayed
in the House until March 1865. In its final form, the Freedmen's
Bureau was removed from Treasury jurisdiction, although the bill did
include the implied promise that confiscated land would be sold or
given to former slaves.[77] That this promise failed to materialize after
the war was due largely to the policies of President Andrew Johnson.
Chase's successors, William P. Fessenden and Hugh McCulloch, although in support of the concept, were not as committed to it as
he had been. Given the lack of enthusiasm for property confiscation among northerners, Chase would have had difficulty persuad-

ing either Johnson or Congress to his point of view had he remained secretary.

Along with his commitment to land redistribution, Chase became convinced of the value and justice of extending suffrage to the freedmen. As the reconstruction process began, even as the war continued, he argued not only that the exceptions to the emancipation policy must be dropped and statewide emancipation made a prerequisite for readmission to the Union, but also that black suffrage be required. He first expressed such views in 1863; earlier in the war he had agreed with Denison that the proposal to extend suffrage to blacks serving in Union armies was "too much in advance of the times." But with parts of Louisiana occupied and preparing to form a loyal government in 1863, Chase believed that to protect the freedmen from reenslavement they must be permitted to vote for members of a proposed constitutional convention. They comprised, said Chase, "a vast majority of the loyal people" of Louisiana and deserved suffrage. A necessary first step, he told Lincoln, was to make the Emancipation Proclamation "complete with the states in which it operates by revoking the exceptions" in Louisiana and Virginia.[78] An unspoken motive of political expediency may also have shaped Chase's thinking. He recognized that black voters would strengthen the Republican party in the South in general and his support in particular.

In December 1863, Lincoln announced a tentative plan of reconstruction, whereby as soon as 10 percent of the qualified voters in the 1860 election in a Confederate state took an oath of loyalty they could "reestablish a State government." The readmittance of Louisiana was foremost in his mind, and in February 1864, he urged General Banks to arrange for elections of state officials without mentioning, either in his proclamation or instructions to Banks, Chase's goals of completing emancipation and suffrage for freedmen. Chase, never willing to recognize the pressures the president faced from a society opposed to rights for blacks, noted his disappointment over Lincoln's failure to revoke the exceptions but was glad that Reconstruction could now commence. The plan did not include what he felt necessary, a firm statement that no state could reenter the Union without abolishing slavery and providing for at least limited black suffrage, but Chase concluded he would be "thankful for skim milk when cream is not to be had."[79]

Those two goals soon merged in Chase's mind as the necessary steps in the reconstruction process. He urged Louisiana Unionist leader Thomas J. Durant to insist on "universal suffrage of all men" who were literate at the upcoming constitutional convention. He explained to Greeley his belief that most Louisiana Unionists agreed with him that "ballots in their hands are as useful as bullets" to the black population.[80]

Chase concluded that a constitutional amendment abolishing slavery was necessary to complete the process of emancipation, reversing his earlier opposition to the idea. Since the Emancipation Proclamation, Lincoln had consistently refused to remove the exceptions to his policy because he could not justify it militarily. The president's December 1863 order again failed to recognize the need. Therefore, the states, Chase argued, should be reconstituted "with constitutions prohibiting slavery," while "a national prohibition" should be added to the federal Constitution. He knew that without Lincoln's support Louisiana might not abolish slavery or extend voting rights to freedmen. He objected to Lincoln's plan to limit the vote "to those who take the oath and *are otherwise qualified* according to the State laws in force before rebellion" because he feared it would be interpreted to exclude black voters. Since blacks were bearing arms, Chase asked: "Why should not *all* soldiers who fight for their country vote in it?"[81] As the Louisiana election approached, it was clear, however, that such was not the prevailing view among Unionists there.

Chase found himself deeply immersed in Louisiana politics. His supporters there, led by Denison and gubernatorial candidate Benjamin Flanders, another Treasury official, promoted his position on emancipation and suffrage. General Banks's candidate, Michael Hahn, represented a more cautious view, which was closer to that of the president. It was clear to all that more was at stake than the choice of a governor; a Flanders victory would enhance Chase's chances for a presidential nomination in 1864. Hahn's sweeping victory in February 1864 thus represented a personal defeat for Chase. As he explained to Greeley, "our truest men are set aside" because of their advocacy of black suffrage. With a state constitutional convention called for April, Chase continued to urge that the right to vote be determined "not by nativity or complexion, but by intelligence, character, and patriotism." That convention did abolish slavery but did not require black suffrage. Although Chase was disappointed, he was not surprised; in his eyes, "the President by his opposition to colored suffrage has done great harm."[82] Long before the Louisiana situation had been resolved, however, Chase's presidential aspirations had been defeated and Lincoln had accepted his Treasury secretary's resignation.

Lincoln was not as adamant in his opposition to black suffrage as Chase believed him to be any more than he was insistent that his reconstruction policy was the only possible approach. In fact, he had urged Hahn to consider giving the vote to a small number of blacks, "the very intelligent, and especially those who have fought gallantly in our ranks." The constitution did give the legislature the discretionary power to enfranchise blacks in the future and it did authorize a public school system for both blacks and whites. Even though Lincoln's policy alienated many Republicans including Chase in part because it failed to insist on black suffrage, it was a realistic one for Louisiana given the political climate.[83]

Throughout the politically stormy year of 1864, Congress refused admission to the Hahn-backed senators and representatives chosen in Louisiana. The action of Congress, achieved through an unlikely coalition of many Democrats and radical Republicans led by Sumner, represented a challenge to reconstruction by presidential order and a statement of belief that it should be done through the legislative process. Congressional action also reflected a desire by some that more stringent terms be imposed on the Confederacy, including a requirement for black suffrage. The Wade-Davis bill, which passed on July 2, 1864, required that a majority of white male citizens take an oath of loyalty (as opposed to Lincoln's 10 percent plan) for a state to be readmitted. It also insisted that a state abolish slavery, which Lincoln had not, but it did not include a black suffrage provision due to conservative opposition. In explaining his pocket veto of the bill, the president indicated that he was not committed to any single plan but would not consent to set aside the Hahn government in Louisiana. In this power struggle between Congress and the president, Chase, now a private citizen, agreed with Congress. In his eyes, had the president acted wisely "reconstruction might already have been accomplished in Louisiana." He also feared that through the veto, the president had not fully abandoned "the idea of the possible reconstruction with Slavery."[84]

Chase's fear was unfounded; he failed again to appreciate the president's commitment to emancipation by 1864 and the great political difficulties he faced. Although in April 1864 the Senate had passed the Thirteenth Amendment abolishing slavery, northern Democrats and border state conservatives had combined to block it in the House in June just as they had blocked black suffrage in the Wade-Davis bill.[85] Lincoln thus knew that he had to move slowly. He recognized how much more difficult even limited black suffrage would prove than emancipation. His opposition was not so much a resistance to racial equality as it was his recognition of political reality. Chase, on the other hand, was willing to take political risks ahead of public opinion and indeed in the face of overt political racism. He revealed a fuller commitment than the president but a poorer understanding of political possibilities.[86]

Despite the many setbacks, Chase believed that his efforts in behalf of blacks in Louisiana and elsewhere had achieved a great deal. He had helped bring the goals of emancipation, military service, and economic opportunity for blacks closer to reality. A more complete equality in terms of land ownership and suffrage, however, would require further efforts. At the same time, his involvement in the many controversies over military strategy and the status of blacks had jeopardized both his standing in the administration and his hopes for a presidential nomination.

8

Chase and Lincoln

C hase's diligent concern for his official duties and political goals normally left him little time for his family or a social life. Usually committing ten to twelve hours daily to Treasury concerns, only rarely did he take time to relax. His private life was not, however, altogether lonely, and he devoted what time he could to his family and friends. Although his aloof and forbidding personality did not usually allow him close friendships on more than a temporary basis, Charles Sumner was an exception. He and Chase dined frequently and corresponded on a regular basis when both were not in Washington. The crisis of the war years drew the two men even closer. For a period in the fall of 1862, Chase also enjoyed the company of Major General James Garfield who lived with him while he was in Washington awaiting reassignment. The two spent many evenings playing chess and discussing the latest military news. Chase treated Garfield like the son he never had, and his reaction to the young man clearly indicated a craving for warm and personal friendships. According to Garfield, Chase could even display a "playful and child-like spirit."[1] Most of all, what kept Chase's private life from becoming dull during the dark days of the war was the lively and expensive social life and impending marriage of his ambitious daughter Kate.

Kate Chase spent five rather confining years of her childhood at the fashionable New York school of Miss Henrietta Haines where she went first in 1849 when Chase moved the rest of his family to

Washington. Weekly letters from her father revealed Chase's love and concern for her welfare even if there were few opportunities for them to be together. In 1856, after one year at another school near Philadelphia, at the age of sixteen, Kate returned to Ohio to live with her father during his governorship, employing her beauty and beguiling nature to become the first lady of the governor's residence. Despite the restraints of Miss Haines's school, Kate had developed expensive tastes and habits. In December 1859, Chase estimated his net worth at $90,000, most of it in real estate investments, but his meager annual salary of $1,800 as governor left him little ready cash to pay Kate's bills. In Washington, they rented a three-story brick home at Sixth and E Streets, NW for $1,800 a year at a time when Chase's salary as Treasury secretary was only $8,000. Expenses mounted dramatically with the cost of daughter Nettie's education and Kate's extravagant taste in clothes adding to the price of servants and other "necessities" of maintaining a large and fashionable home. Even with income from property he owned in Brooklyn and Cincinnati, as well as interest and dividends on other investments equaling his official salary, Chase complained of constant and increasing debt. In late 1861, he cautioned Kate "to avoid extravagance" when she selected a closed carriage to be used in Washington that winter, for "it is going to be hard to make both ends meet here."[2]

Kate's aspirations to be a leader in Washington society, even to rival Mrs. Lincoln, led her to expensive entertaining that went far beyond Chase's modest means. Throughout the war Jay Cooke and New York bankers Augustus Brown and Charles Heckscher, along with New York Collector of Customs Hiram Barney, loaned him small amounts which together amounted to a substantial sum. Cooke at first confined himself to such gifts as furnishings for Chase's Washington home, although later in the war he advised Chase on investments and extended him loans. The secretary was careful to avoid any appearance of favoritism to his creditors and often reminded them that his public and private duties were to remain entirely separate: "How much and so much I may wish to oblige personal friends I cannot do so at the expense of any public interest."[3] This was not mere rhetoric as all evidence supports the sincerity of Chase's claim.

Partial relief from his financial burdens eventually came with the marriage of Kate to wealthy Rhode Island cotton manufacturer and prominent Republican William Sprague. Sprague, who was governor of the New England state early in the war, became a United States senator in 1863. At thirty-two, he was ten years older than Kate and lacked her drive and ambition. Any deficiencies were made up in Kate's eyes by his great wealth and social standing. Gideon Welles summed up the feelings in Washington political circles: "Few young men have such advantages as he, and Miss Kate has talents and ambition sufficient for both." Knowing that his own life would change following the wedding and that his close relationship with Kate might be jeopardized, Chase approached the nuptials with trepidation. "It makes me almost shudder to think of it," he told Garfield when the engagement was announced. Yet he bravely assured his future son-in-law that he wanted "to have Katie honor and love you with an honor and love far exceeding any due to me and I shall feel happiest when she makes your happiness most complete."[4]

After the November 1863 wedding, the couple planned to live with Chase at his Washington home. At first Chase had thought it best to seek another residence for himself, but by summer Kate had persuaded him not to move. He explained to Sprague that he and Kate had agreed on a division of the spacious home into two living areas, with a third part reserved to entertain "the friends of either or both as may happen." He also proposed paying the rent and servants' wages while Sprague took care of other household expenses. Chase's expenses were soon reduced when Sprague arranged to purchase the home for $32,000. Realizing that he would still have to pay his daughter's bills before the wedding, Chase cautioned her that "my resources are not great enough to admit of carelessness." As her extravagant purchases continued, he lamented that Kate would "never learn to be definite in money matters." He showed genuine concern for the happiness of the couple, urging neither to "expect perfection from the other." Trials could be faced by their "constant love" and "mutual respect." Shortly before the wedding, Chase assured Sprague of his faith that Kate would be "under a guardianship not less watchful and tender than my own." For his part, Sprague recognized "the delicate link which has so long united father and daughter," and pledged himself "to be worthy of the connection."[5]

The wedding was a highlight of the social season in war-weary Washington. At 8:30 in the evening of November 12, the tall, handsome, and by now slightly portly father of the bride proudly presented his beautiful and beguiling daughter in marriage. Kate was "tall and slender and exceedingly well formed," and her "vivacious hazel eyes shaded by dark lashes and arched over by proud eyebrows" were further highlighted by "waving gold-brown hair." According to Carl Schurz, "all her movements possessed an exquisite natural charm." Kate's wedding gown was an elaborate "white velvet dress with an extended train and a rice lace veil." Senator Sprague wore "a suit of rich black cloth, with the usual addition of a white satin vest." An Episcopal bishop from Rhode Island performed the ceremony before about fifty close friends and relatives in the parlor of the Chase home. A reception followed with five hundred guests dancing to the music of the Marine Band, which played the "Kate Chase Wedding March." As hundreds lined the streets to watch notables arrive, they saw the president, many foreign diplomats and military leaders, and all of the cabinet except Chase's bitter enemy Montgomery Blair. Chase did not record his feelings about the union of his pretentious and ambitious daughter to the wealthy Rhode Island senator, but he was surely pleased that she had apparently chosen so wisely and delighted that he could show the couple off to Washington society. Nor did he record the cost of the affair except to lament that he had borrowed heavily and had overdrawn his bank account. The wedding gifts, which were valued at between $60,000 and $100,000, included a diamond and pearl tiara and bracelet for Kate from the groom costing more than $6,000. There followed a wedding trip to New York and then to Sprague's home in Providence and finally to Ohio.[6] Thus began a stormy marriage whose publicity and political implications would enliven the last decade of Chase's life.

Kate was as possessive of her father after her marriage as before, and she remained jealous of his attention to other women as she planned for a Chase presidency. With his younger daughter Nettie, Chase was as protective and concerned a father as he had been with Kate. In explaining to the teenaged Nettie his frequent criticisms of her penmanship and study habits, he said that "there are plenty of things to admire and love in you," but his concern for her welfare made him speak "most of those things which most endanger it."[7] Kate no doubt resented the attention her father paid to her younger half-sister just as she resented several romantic interests he developed.

The thrice-widowed Chase was fifty-three when he entered the cabinet and, although it had been ten years since the death of his third wife, he may still have thought of marriage. Letters and diaries indicate at least mild interest in three women: Adele Cutts, the widow of his political nemesis Stephen A. Douglas; Susan Walker of Cincinnati, who served in an army hospital in Baltimore during the war and who, because of Kate's dislike of her, wrote directly to Chase at the Treasury instead of to his home; and Mrs. Carlotta Sewall Eastman, a widow of Beverly, Massachusetts.[8]

In late August 1862, Hiram Barney wrote to Chase that Kate, on a recent New York visit, was "very sad on account of the contemplated *marriage of her father*" to Mrs. Eastman. Chase corresponded frequently with her when she was not in Washington, occasionally writing in French, and, although the letters were flirtatious, there was no mention of marriage. Their friendship, he wrote, had "sweetened" many evenings. He thought of her "constantly," wished she were "here in our house—in this little library room—and that we could talk, instead of this writing by myself, while you are—where?" He frequently signed his letters to her, "Your amitor." Following his resignation from the cabinet, he spent several days during the summer of 1864 visiting her.[9] The decision to remain only friends was probably more the socially inclined widow's than it was Chase's, but it was one that most definitely pleased Kate Sprague.

Throughout the war, Chase tried to maintain close ties with other family members and friends. In October 1862, he was saddened to hear of the death of his last surviving brother Edward for whom he had helped secure an appointment as a deputy marshall in the Buffalo area. He continued to correspond with and help Edward's widow financially in the months ahead as he did with his niece Jane Auld. Chase showed not only a genuine humanitarian concern for others but on rare occasions even a hint of a sense of humor. When J. C. Rhodes expressed his desire to name his newborn son Salmon Portland Rhodes, he responded that although his uncle, after whom he had been named, "was an excellent man and Portland a very respectable city . . . if you have due regard to the feelings of your boy, fifteen years hence or twenty, I hardly think you will give it to him."[10]

Because of wartime pressures Chase could direct only limited time to family and personal matters. Devotion to career and commitment to official duties always seemed to take precedence. Although his

influence and stature in Lincoln's eyes did not revive following his
abortive effort to force Seward's removal in late 1862, Chase did not
let up his efforts to influence military and political events. Throughout 1863, he offered unsolicited advice to Lincoln on the movement
of armies and appointments of generals.[11]

This was especially true in his early unhappiness with Ulysses S.
Grant. When Grant's army appeared stalled at its base in Memphis
in early 1863, Chase was quick to report to Lincoln criticisms of the
general's drunken behavior. In early April, he forwarded the letter of
Murat Halstead of the *Cincinnati Commercial* describing Grant as "a
jackass in the original package" who was "a poor stick sober" and
was "most of the time more than half drunk and much of the time
idiotically drunk." In Chase's view, Sherman rather than Grant
should have been in command because "he is certainly an abler and
better and more reliable Commander." But after a string of victories
culminating in the successful siege of Vicksburg, Chase congratulated General Grant and told him of the many favorable reports of
his actions he had received from Treasury Agent William P. Mellen.[12]
Chase easily overcame his distaste for the general's personal habits
when he realized that in Grant the Union finally had a general who
was willing to challenge the enemy.

With all of his concern over military events, Chase never lost sight
of the need to keep Republicans and Unionists in Ohio satisfied with
his role in national politics. This became obvious as the gubernatorial election of 1863 approached, and Chase began to look to the
party's presidential nomination in 1864. He carefully avoided taking
sides publicly as Governor David Tod sought renomination. Although not happy with Tod because of his opposition to the Emancipation Proclamation, Chase urged his political supporters in Ohio
not to oppose him because, he noted, "We must be liberal to all who
are rowing our boat whether we like them, or are liked by them, or
not." Suggestions from several of his friends that John Brough would
more readily support a Chase presidential candidacy led him quickly
to congratulate Brough when he was nominated over Tod.[13] Chase
clearly understood that the governor's backing might be critical the
following year.

The October election in Ohio took on greater than normal importance following the Democratic nomination of Copperhead leader,
Congressman Clement L. Vallandigham, for governor. Vallandigham

was of national importance because of his leadership of the Peace Democrats, and thus his defeat in Ohio would be important to the national Republican party. He had been a source of major embarrassment to the Lincoln administration ever since his arrest in May 1863 for a speech at Mount Vernon, Ohio in which he accused the president of unnecessarily extending the war and converting it into one to free blacks and enslave whites rather than one to save the Union. Denied habeas corpus, Vallandigham was subjected to a quick military trial and jailed in Cincinnati.[14]

Belatedly recognizing the political ramifications of making Vallandigham a martyr, Lincoln commuted his sentence and banished him to the Confederacy. From there Vallandigham evaded the Union blockade, sought exile in Windsor, Ontario and accepted the unanimous Democratic nomination for governor of Ohio, a campaign he directed in absentia. Fearing that a Democratic victory would represent a repudiation of the administration and an endorsement of disunion, Chase, Wade, and other Ohio politicians made personal appearances to urge Brough's election. Union victories at Vicksburg and Gettysburg in July allowed them to argue that the defeat of the Confederacy was now in sight, and Vallandigham was defeated by more than one hundred thousand votes.[15] Throughout the North, Republican victories in 1863 represented a conditional endorsement of the administration's handling of the war effort.

Chase welcomed the opportunity to return to Ohio "to cast his vote on the side of the Union," knowing that the public exposure might help his own presidential candidacy. He expressed complete surprise over the warm "entirely spontaneous and popular" reception he received. The late-night rally at the Columbus depot "by an immense concourse of citizens," despite the lack of advance notice and planning, was followed the next day by an exuberant cheering response to his address at the Union League hall. As the *Ohio State Journal* noted: "he still possessed the hearts of his old neighbors and fellow citizens of Columbus." After speeches in Xenia and Cincinnati, he was "almost forced to Indianapolis where the people gave me another welcome such as I cannot forget." The friendly reception by Indiana Governor Oliver P. Morton provided further evidence that support was strong for a challenge to Lincoln the following year. The secretary noted with his usual false modesty that he had assumed until leaving Washington that his work in the Treasury "was too quiet to attract much attention from the masses."[16] After the election he spoke again in Columbus, where he recalled the history of the successes of his administration of the Treasury to the cheers of the crowd, which shouted their support of "greenback Chase." And he could only have rejoiced at the election outcome, for as former law partner Flamen Ball told him, Brough's victory over Vallandigham was regarded by many in Ohio as "a 'Chase Triumph.' "[17]

Chase's interest and activity in the Ohio election signified a general intensification of his political activity on all fronts. He had never totally reconciled himself to the loss of the presidential nomination in 1860, and his increasing alienation from Lincoln now propelled him into a fury of effort to win the nomination in 1864. His strategy was to keep himself and his position on war-related issues constantly before the people, while his supporters worked in his behalf. The Ohio results augured well for the future and led him to attempt to use his Treasury position in those parts of the country where it could be most effective. This included his patronage power and the significant role the Treasury would play in the soon-to-be-reconstructed areas of the South, especially Florida and Louisiana. To what degree Chase used his patronage in pursuit of the presidency is not easily assessed. Surely there were few active opponents of a Chase nomination among his key appointees and many of his strongest political proponents held Treasury positions, such as William Mellen, George Denison, Hiram Barney, Lyman D. Stickney and Richard Parsons.[18] It should be recognized, however, that Chase's use of patronage to advance his own cause, while clearly intended for that purpose, was nevertheless in line with accepted practice and not an act of disloyalty to the President.

The potential for using Treasury patronage to promote his candidacy was indeed great. Clerks in his Washington department numbered two thousand by the time Chase left office in 1864, whereas the number of special agents, internal revenue collectors, and customhouse officials multiplied throughout the war.[19] Chase vigorously denied using his power of appointment to promote his candidacy and in fact never admitted that he was even seeking a nomination. Throughout late 1863 and early 1864 he maintained: "I should despise myself if I felt capable of appointing or removing a man for the sake of the presidency." He explained to his son-in-law that personally he preferred Lincoln's reelection "to that of any man." On the other hand, he added that he doubted "the expediency of reelecting anybody." Moreover, he felt that "a man of different qualities from those the President has will be needed for the next four years." Still, he insisted that because Lincoln's "course toward me has always been so fair and kind," he would "consider as incompatible with perfect honor and good faith" any effort to replace him. His differences with the president were well-enough known for few to believe that such praise was genuine. Although he preferred to maintain the politically correct position, he was never able to hide his ambition for the presidency. To his friend Thomas Heaton of Cincinnati he said he would leave the nomination "wholly to the people." Those "who think that the public good will be promoted by adherence to the one term principle" were more competent than he "to bring the matter before the public generally." He would be content with whatever their decision was because "my time is wholly absorbed by my public duties."[20]

Many of Chase's friends and opponents remained unconvinced that he was a disinterested observer in the contest for the nomination or that he refrained from using his patronage to promote his own cause. Several of his cabinet antagonists were among his sharpest critics. In Bates's eyes, "Chase's head is turned by his eagerness in pursuit of the Presidency." According to the attorney general, Chase had long been "filling all the offices in his own vast patronage with extreme partisans." Although neither Bates nor Navy Secretary Welles was especially objective in his views of Chase, Welles accurately suggested that despite Chase's efforts to appear indifferent to the political maneuvering in his behalf, "no one of his partisans is so well posted as Chase himself."[21]

Few of his critics were willing to admit that Chase's appointees were in fact able men and that his appointments were no more partisan than those of other leading politicians. As defenders of the president they recognized that it made good sense to dismiss Chase's activities as motivated entirely by ambition. Yet the secretary's constant criticism of the president in letters to friends could not but convince supporters that he viewed himself as a worthy successor. To Joshua Leavitt, Chase complained that there had been no "administration in the true sense of the word" nor "a President conferring with his Cabinet and taking their united judgments." To another he observed, "The administration can not be continued as it is."[22] Virtually all who viewed the secretary's activities agreed that Chase believed he could provide the necessary leadership after 1864 that Lincoln had failed to provide in his first term. Most also recognized that the president's standing in his party was not strong and that Chase's efforts were justifiable. Long before the Ohio election Chase had begun to seek support in his drive for the nomination.

In early 1864, Chase had some reason to believe that he could successfully challenge Lincoln. The radical element of the Republican party had grown increasingly discontented under Lincoln's leadership, and many were eager to see him replaced by someone more closely aligned with their philosophy. Chase clearly fit that requirement, and with his obvious administrative and executive ability as well as his thinly disguised interest in a nomination, much of the anti-Lincoln sentiment naturally centered on him. His criticism of Lincoln's racial policy had sparked support among some Republicans as had his dislike of the president's support of Seward. In addition, many favored continuing the tradition of a one-term presidency. The rising importance of the antiwar movement and the concomitant rise of the Peace Democrats, despite Vallandigham's recent defeat, reflected on what many considered to be Lincoln's fumbling war policies. But the critics in Congress had been outmaneuvered by Lincoln in their December 1862 confrontation over Seward and had felt let down when Chase had failed to come to their defense. As a result, most of them would hesitate before openly supporting a Chase candidacy. Lincoln would have to provoke them further and his appeal among northern voters drop even more before members of Congress could become active in Chase's behalf.

As a result, during 1863, most of the interest in Chase for the presidency was expressed by those with little position or influence. The secretary received a series of flattering letters throughout the year, much as he had before the 1856 and 1860 nominations. Some of them came from people he had appointed to office, while others came from those seeking office. Thomas Heaton, a Treasury agent in Cincinnati, reported that support in Ohio was building for a Chase nomination. Some promised support in return for Chase's aid in securing an appointment, as when James Birney urged him to make him head of the Freedmen's Bureau should the bill to establish it pass Congress.[23] Some of his old friends from Liberty and Free-Soil days, including Joshua Giddings and Joshua Leavitt, urged Chase's candidacy. Neither man had any real influence in the Republican party and thus could do little in his behalf. Yet Giddings told Chase in early 1863 that he was "the only Republican candidate," while Leavitt indicated that he would like to see him either president or chief justice.[24]

The easily flattered secretary took all of the compliments and urgings seriously but, characteristically, never admitted that he was a candidate. He played his usual coy waiting game and as a result ignored Giddings's advice to urge his friends to adopt the necessary "principles of action" to organize a campaign. Instead, as he told Barney, he planned to let potential supporters "take their course" without encouraging or discouraging a Chase movement. Although he claimed to have little desire for a nomination, he did not "feel bound to object" when others showed support. Under the circumstances, Chase's technique was shrewd, and no alternate method on his part could have produced better results. He could not openly declare his candidacy and feared that any overt action by him or his supporters would jeopardize his position in the administration. Chase reacted the same way when reports reached him that his name was being mentioned as a possible candidate among Union Democrats.[25] When the idea failed to create much enthusiasm among Democrats, Chase wisely concentrated his efforts among Republicans.

There were conflicting reports as to how much Republican support he could expect. Conservative Union border state leaders in Kentucky and Missouri failed to show interest, and Joseph Medill's *Chicago Tribune* argued that efforts in behalf of Chase were "lost labor," because "Old Abe has the inside track so completely that he will be renominated by acclamation." Still, there were enough optimistic reports to keep Chase's hopes high throughout 1863. Reports from Indiana indicated that Governor Oliver P. Morton might back him. Such accounts were unconfirmed, however, and neither Chase nor his partisans made any concerted effort to organize supporters who might be influential in party circles.[26] Again, Chase preferred to let events take their course, banking on Lincoln's declining popularity to provide the impetus his candidacy needed.

Unwilling to move directly in his own behalf, Chase could benefit from Treasury Department activities in parts of the South. As Union armies expanded the areas of the Confederacy under northern control, the Treasury's immediate role was to administer the new direct tax law of 1862. Tax commissioners were to assess the property in occupied areas, impose the tax, and sell the property of delinquent owners at public auction. Chase recognized that the tax commissioners could also play a role in the reconstruction of a state thus forwarding the process of emancipation and enlistment of black troops. Such a reconstructed state might, with proper guidance and encouragement from the commissioners, support Chase for the Republican nomination out of gratitude for his assistance in winning their readmittance to the Union. He thus sought able appointees who could not only apply the tax regulations but who would also be loyal Chase partisans.

The example of Florida is one where the secretary sought the reconstruction of a state which might support his candidacy. There seemed to be a real chance by 1863 that enough of the state would be Union-occupied to expect reconstruction before the 1864 nominating convention and election. In appointing the three tax commissioners, Chase unfortunately included Lyman D. Stickney, a land-speculating lawyer and opportunist from Vermont, who convinced the secretary that he was a native Florida Unionist dedicated to the political reconstruction of his state.[27] With Stickney's optimistic reports of pro-Chase Union sentiments among Floridians, Chase unwisely believed that his campaign might receive a significant boost.

The project of reconstructing Florida and securing its commitment to Chase went badly from the start and reveals how misled the secretary could be in the pursuit of his political ambitions. Stickney stood to gain financially and perhaps even politically from his Treasury position, because a reconstructed Florida might readily turn to him for leadership. Chase accepted Stickney's argument that a federal army under General Quincy A. Gillmore should be sent to retake Jacksonville before reconstruction could begin. Stickney had informed Chase that Gillmore was dedicated to ending slavery and that he was "ready and able to redeem Florida from the rebels with Colored troops" if Stanton gave his approval. He added that it was "very important indeed for *you*" that Gillmore be given the task.[28]

Chase also appointed his private secretary, Homer C. Plantz, to the position of District Attorney at Key West to direct reconstruction and political activities in southern Florida. Plantz soon sent him a lengthy analysis of the political situation there. He explained that at least one-third of the people were Union men, more than enough to effect reconstruction. Although Plantz provided little evidence to prove such loyalty, Chase urged his supporters to begin the process of organizing a free state movement which would include suffrage for all freedmen "who have borne arms for the country or who can read and write, without any other distinction at present." Stickney and Plantz in turn reported on their successful efforts to organize Union meetings, at the same time urging immediate military pressure to bring more of the state under Union control.[29]

Attempting to picture the meetings organized in St. Augustine and Key West as in compliance with Lincoln's 10 percent plan of reconstruction, Stickney and Plantz in fact had made little effort to consult the people and enroll the numbers necessary. Yet Stickney optimistically told Chase that all was proceeding on schedule and voters would be organized quickly. Even better, he had "lately been occupied in organizing a free State league or if you please, a Chase league," which "will work to a charm." As Gillmore's forces occupied Jacksonville, accompanied by Stickney and Lincoln's private secretary John Hay, it became clear that not even 10 percent of the people would take an oath of loyalty. But Stickney persisted and informed Chase that he had Hay fooled in his efforts to make Florida a Chase state.[30]

Hay was not fooled and had kept Lincoln well informed of Stickney's machinations. Furthermore, a military reversal of Gillmore's forces at Olustee on February 20, 1864, meant that Florida could not be prepared for reentry into the Union before the presidential nomination. Nevertheless, Stickney and Plantz continued their efforts in Chase's behalf in the next months hoping that the country would still "call for your services."[31] In this sorry Florida episode Chase was the victim of overly optimistic encouragement by his Florida agents who had expected to profit through his candidacy. In his eagerness to believe the positive reports that he could be nominated, Chase had unwisely accepted the views of the unscrupulous Stickney and Plantz. Fortunately for Chase, the Florida events were largely overshadowed by developments elsewhere in which he was more wary of encouragement by subordinates.

In Louisiana, where Union occupation developed more quickly and in a more critical and heavily populated area, Chase was much better served by more able and honest appointees, although conflicts among factions complicated matters and led to further disappointments for the secretary. His best source of political intelligence there was the highly competent George S. Denison, whom he appointed acting customs collector in New Orleans shortly after the city was taken in the spring of 1862. In addition to the active role Denison played in suppressing trade with the enemy, Chase urged him to write weekly "of all that relates to persons and things not proper for the subject of official communications." Denison faithfully communicated all political and military developments over the next two years, giving the secretary an accurate and up-to-date view of Treasury and non-Treasury matters. On Denison's recommendation, Chase appointed Benjamin F. Flanders, a transplanted New England Republican, to head all Treasury affairs in the area; he would also rest much of his political hope on Flanders as Louisiana moved toward statehood. In addition, Chase worked closely with Benjamin F. Butler until his replacement by the less-cooperative General Nathaniel P. Banks in late 1862.[32]

As hopes for the readmission of a reconstructed Louisiana developed during 1863, Chase urged Flanders to work toward a convention which would initiate the process among those who were loyal. Other Treasury agents told the secretary that the restoration of the state and other neighboring parts of the Confederacy would yield twenty delegates pledged to him at the Republican convention of 1864. Predictably, the rival Union faction in the state was soon claiming that Treasury officers were "a swarm of electioneering spies and agents," a charge Chase of course denied. He responded self-righteously that the only zeal of his appointees was "for the restoration of the Union and for the Principles of the Proclamation," while "as to their personal preferences, I have never inquired and never shall." The issues began to clear following Lincoln's reconstruction proclamation of December 1863 and his direction to General Banks to arrange for state elections. Chase knew that Flanders, his candidate for governor, would be opposed by Banks's candidate, Michael Hahn, who was more closely aligned in policy to the president.[33] Lincoln and Chase thus indirectly confronted each other in the Louisiana election as the candidates of each vied for the governorship and for control of the state Republican party.

Chase believed that Banks used his influence to assure Hahn's victory and charged that the general had been unwilling to cooperate with Flanders and others not in full agreement with his policies as was "necessary to secure harmony." As Chase feared, Hahn was an easy winner over Flanders because, in the words of the losing candidate, "Every employee of the city government and of the state and all the quartermasters' men and the Louisiana soldiers were made to vote for the General's candidate." The election was to be followed by a state meeting to choose delegates to the national Republican convention. With blacks excluded from participation in Louisiana politics and the new governor to appoint the United States senators, Chase's hopes for immediate black rights under a reconstructed government received a major setback. Chase told Flanders that such slurs as "Negro heads, Negro-equality Men" had been used to assure his defeat.[34]

Politically, it was clear that Louisiana delegates to be chosen would support Lincoln and not Chase for the presidential nomination. Denison tried to reassure Chase and noted bravely that "we are forming a Chase club" through which "we can control the election of delegates to the National Convention." But Chase recognized that "political and military power" was being used "with a view to the reelection of the President." When the state convention in March chose a Lincoln slate of delegates to the Baltimore nominating convention, Denison lamented that "the combination of patronage and influence was too strong to allow us any chance of success."[35] Representing a more moderate position on racial issues, which appealed to Louisiana voters, Lincoln and his partisans dealt a major blow to the Treasury secretary's challenge to the president's control of the party.

Before events in Florida and Louisiana had strengthened Lincoln's renomination efforts, a small committee had formed in Washington to plan for Chase's challenge. The immediate catalyst was Lincoln's "Proclamation of Amnesty and Reconstruction," of December 8, 1863. It proposed leniency in granting pardons and relatively easy terms for reconstruction, thus threatening to take the issue out of congressional hands and angering many of the more radical Republicans because of its philosophy. An informal yet spontaneous group called the "Organization to make S. P. Chase President" met the next day, including several Ohioans—Congressmen Robert C. Schenck and Rufus P. Spalding and *Cincinnati Gazette* correspondent Whitelaw Reid—along with Senator Henry Wilson of Massachusetts.[36] State committees were established to coordinate the effort in Chase's behalf, and by early January the Washington committee was expanded under the name "the Republican National Executive Committee" to include Congressmen James Garfield and James Ashley and Senators John Sherman and Samuel C. Pomeroy of Kansas.[37]

Exactly when Chase was informed of the organization is not known, but in mid-January he wrote that a number of "the clearest headed and most judicious men here . . . have determined to submit my name to the people in connection with the next Presidency." Moreover, he "consented to their wishes." Several of the members had personal grievances against Lincoln in addition to political differences. Pomeroy, who became chairman of the committee, felt that he had not received his share of patronage from the president. In addition, Chase had rendered him a favorable ruling helping to make the Hannibal and St. Joseph Railroad, in which Pomeroy had a financial interest, a part of the transcontinental system. Sherman had been angered over the president's treatment of his brother William T. Sherman.[38]

Efforts in Chase's behalf were not limited to the Pomeroy committee. Chase agreed to provide material to author John T. Trowbridge of Boston so he could write a fictionalized biography which could serve as a popular story for boys as well as an unofficial Chase campaign biography. The Treasury secretary labored through the winter of 1863–64 to produce a series of long biographical letters for Trowbridge recounting the details of his life from birth to his appointment to the cabinet. Chase also placed his own picture on the new one dollar bank notes, explaining, "I had put the President's head on the higher priced notes and my own as was becoming, on the smaller ones." He was thus not above giving himself some added campaign exposure.[39] Reid wrote a number of favorable editorials. Financial assistance to the Pomeroy committee was provided by the firm of Jay Cooke and Company; Henry Cooke explained to his brother Jay, "As his personal friend I feel bound to do all that can honorably be done to advance his interests." Son-in-law William Sprague also provided significant financial support.[40]

The Pomeroy committee produced two important campaign documents in February, which, although designed to promote Chase's candidacy, had unexpected consequences. The first, called "The Next Presidential Election," was printed in many northern newspapers. Its author may have been James M. Winchell of New York, who had been a member of the Chase committee since its inception in December. The pamphlet, a propaganda blast against the president, never mentioned Chase by name but insisted that because the people had "lost all confidence" in Lincoln's ability to suppress the rebellion, the party needed in his place "a statesman profoundly versed in political and economic science, one who fully comprehends the spirit of the age in which we live." It described Lincoln in the most scurrilous terms as having badly bungled the war effort. Having thus prepared the ground, the committee followed on February 20 with the publication of the Pomeroy Circular, which specifically proposed Chase for the nomination because his record was "clear and unimpeachable, showing him to be a statesman of rare ability and an administrator of the highest order."[41] Although Chase was aware of the committee's existence, he played no role in the writing of either appeal, again preferring that others manage his campaign. He firmly believed his chances would improve if he remained in the background.

Reaction to the two documents was immediate and intense and had negative consequences for Chase's candidacy. The committee had badly miscalculated public opinion in its expectations of tapping a reservoir of anti-Lincoln sentiment. The bitter attacks on the president in the pamphlet, which had been somewhat modified in the Pomeroy Circular, revealed that Lincoln's moderate course on race and reconstruction issues was much preferred to Chase's more liberal position. Lincoln's military strategy, although not yet successful in early 1864 and still characterized by repeated frustration, nevertheless shows signs of movement toward eventual victory. The president had skillfully used his own patronage to build up his support and retain the backing of most party leaders. The ill-timed, intemperate appeal of the Chase committee thus precipitated a rush of politicians to join the Lincoln bandwagon and urge his renomination.

Reaction was perhaps most intense in Ohio where Senator Sherman was the first to feel the wrath of his constituents. A few endorsed his position, but the great majority attacked him for joining the anti-Lincoln group. He was especially criticized because "The Next Presidential Election" had been distributed in Ohio under his frank. Fortunately for Sherman his Senate term had two years remaining because, as one Republican noted, "If you were to resign tomorrow you could not get ten votes in the legislature."[42]

More seriously for Chase was the immediate endorsement of Lincoln by the caucus of the Republican party—renamed the Union party during the war—in the Ohio legislature. Chase had made it clear in his approval of the formation of the Pomeroy committee that the support of "a majority of our friends of Ohio" was essential before he could become a candidate. His hopes collapsed with the release of the Pomeroy Circular on February 20. With Governor David Tod firmly behind the president, the caucus met in Columbus five days later; no amount of parliamentary maneuvering by Chase partisans could prevent an endorsement of Lincoln's renomination.[43]

As Parsons told Chase, the Pomeroy Circular "produced a perfect convulsion in the party," causing the legislature "to move in concert at once." Just prior to the Ohio action, Indiana Republicans had endorsed Lincoln by a vote of 120 to 22; earlier indications of Governor Morton's interest in Chase had proven unfounded. Even before the Ohio decision was known, Representative James Garfield advised Chase to withdraw and avoid a split in the party, for "the people desire the reelection of Mr. Lincoln." According to the congressman, Chase had "no hope of success, and could only distract the party."[44] Before considering that advice, the embarrassed secretary was forced to explain his role in the affair to the president.

Although rarely an objective observer, Gideon Welles was accurate when he stated in his diary two days after the release of the circular that "it will be more dangerous in its recoil than its projectile. That is, it will damage Chase more than Lincoln." That Chase was fully aware of this danger was evident in his immediate effort to explain his role to the president and deny any prior knowledge of the circular. He admitted that he had known of the committee in late January and had agreed, against his better judgment, that their "use of my name as proposed would not affect my usefulness in my present position." He had told them, however, that he would give them no help; he first became aware of the circular when he saw it printed in the *Constitutional Union* on February 20. The embarrassed secretary concluded by indicating his "sincere respect and esteem" for the president and offering to resign: "I do not wish to administer the Treasury Department one day without your entire confidence."[45]

Chase's contriteness revealed him to be a rather inept politician. Desirous of the nomination, he appeared to be too cautious to do what was necessary to gain it. His indecisiveness showed him to be no match politically for the incumbent. To Carlotta Eastman Chase lamented his unhappiness over the release of the circular: "I see no very convincing signs that the people want me, and it would be more agreeable to have had nobody want me, than to be wanted by some but not enough." [46]

Lincoln's measured response a week later expressed no concern over an issue which he suggested had little to do with Chase's work as secretary of the Treasury. Although his advisors had informed him of the circular's existence before its publication, Lincoln claimed not to have read it and said he did not intend to; he knew "just a little of these things as my friends have allowed me to know." His only concern was Chase's service in the Treasury, and in that respect the president did "not perceive occasion for a change." To another, he said he was determined "to shut my eyes" to the affair and keep Chase in the cabinet. [47] Apparently Lincoln chose to tolerate Chase's methods and those of his backers, believing him to be less dangerous to him politically in the cabinet than outside. Needing support from all Republican factions to assure his renomination, Lincoln would not needlessly alienate the more liberal by allowing Chase to resign. Moreover, he considered Chase too effective a Treasury secretary to permit his removal at this time.

Chase now had to decide whether or not to withdraw himself from consideration as a presidential candidate, and on this he received conflicting advice. All of his supporters agreed that he had been seriously hurt by the affair, especially as Republican-Union coalitions throughout the North were beginning to endorse Lincoln. Most disappointing outside Ohio was the action in the president's favor in Rhode Island where Chase had hoped that Senator Sprague might have used personal influence in his father-in-law's behalf. Few of Chase's supporters urged an immediate withdrawal, however. James Winchell of the original Pomeroy committee suggested that such action would be premature. Horace Greeley told Chase that there was no need to make any announcement unless the Treasury were to suffer by his continuation as a candidate. But, as William Mellen indicated, there was little reason for optimism, and many of his friends felt that "the popular feeling in favor of Mr. L. is overwhelming."[48]

Chase was realistic enough to share their discouragement. He lamented that had he had his way his name would never have been mentioned in relation to the nomination until it was "absolutely necessary." But the damage had been done, and he told Mellen that there was no choice but to withdraw. Accordingly, he asked James C. Hall of Toledo, a supporter in the legislature, to release a letter he had written announcing his withdrawal. His letter, written on March 5, indicated that because of the caucus action he wished "no further consideration be given to my name."[49] Viewed within the context of the events of the war and especially considering Lincoln's weak standing in the party in late 1863 and early 1864, there had been justification for Chase's bid to win the nomination, but the secretary clearly miscalculated his organizational ability and underrated Lincoln's skill in using patronage to build party support.

Chase's withdrawal sparked mixed reactions. The *New York Times* and Greeley's *New York Tribune* greeted the decision as wise and statesmanlike; at the same time, James Gordon Bennett's *New York Herald* believed that Chase was still seeking a draft. The *Herald* warned its readers that "the Salmon is a queer fish; very shy and very wary, often appearing to avoid the bait just before gulping it down." Attorney General Bates believed that Chase's word on his withdrawal was "not worth much," and "it proves only that the *present* prospects of Mr. Lincoln are too good to be openly resisted." After the Pomeroy fiasco, Bates felt that Chase's partisans would act "more guardedly" but no less determinedly. Certainly Senator Pomeroy hoped that Chase would change his mind and planned for his committee to continue its efforts in his behalf.[50] Clearly not all were convinced that Chase's withdrawal was final and absolute.

Publicly, the secretary refused to endorse Lincoln's nomination, and in private he continued to question the president and his policies. To Greeley he indicated his disappointment that the president had not responded in kind to Chase's voiced esteem for him. But, said the long-suffering Chase, "This is not remarkable. Whatever appreciation he may feel for public service he never expresses any. So I have worked on." To others, Chase suggested that he might not labor on much longer. He told Mrs. Eastman that he would "devote myself wholly to my work," hoping that in two or three months he could turn the Treasury over to somebody else. Taking the negative reaction to the Pomeroy Circular personally, he complained that "if the people don't want my work, I am very well content that they should not have it." Against the continued turmoil of public life, "leisure for books, and friends, and private duties" looked appealing.[51] Before any such retirement or revival of his candidacy could occur, however, Chase would have to withstand a bitter and brutal attack from his long-time nemesis, the Blair family.

As postmaster general, Montgomery Blair had consistently opposed Chase's influence in the cabinet; as a border state representative, his conservative views were frequently at odds with most Republicans. He had resisted the Chase-Stanton drive to remove McClellan and had viewed the effort to remove Seward in December 1862 as a Chase device to increase his influence and that of more radical Republicans. When Lincoln announced his Reconstruction and Amnesty plan in December 1863, Chase and most of his faction attacked it, while Blair defended it.[52] His brother Francis P. Blair, Jr. of Missouri had come to Congress in 1861 where he defended Lincoln's policies after having helped secure the loyalty of his state for the Union. He had then returned home, serving under General Sherman as a brigadier general. Their well-known father, Francis P. Blair, a long-time Jacksonian Democrat, frequently advised the president from his home in Silver Spring, Maryland.

Brothers Frank and Montgomery had not only opposed Chase's philosophies and ambitions but they were also at odds with him over patronage. Each felt it his right to control appointments in his state; Chase instead had rewarded Treasury patronage to their rival Republican factions, led by Henry Winter Davis in Maryland and B. Gratz Brown and Charles D. Drake in Missouri. Feelings were especially intense in Maryland when Chase refused to appoint a Blair man to a Treasury job in Baltimore and removed another pro-Blair appointee as collector of internal revenue in favor of a Chase favorite. During the 1863 political campaign in Missouri, Frank accused Chase of creating a corrupt political machine and of using his patronage and control of trade regulations to further his own candidacy against Lincoln. In a Saint Louis address, he referred to Chase as "no whit better than Jefferson Davis," a speech which led Chase to suggest to Lincoln that "General Blair's unprovoked attack on me will injure its author more than its object."[53] Thus the Blair family was more than eager to pursue its attack on Chase when the Pomeroy Circular increased his vulnerability.

In early 1864, Frank Blair returned to Congress where he charged Chase with corrupt abuse of power in the granting of trade permits in Confederate territory. According to the general, only Chase's friends received the lucrative permits; supporters of the president were usually denied. Claiming that Chase awarded permits so as to strengthen his political machine and candidacy against Lincoln, Blair demanded a congressional investigation. His February 27 speech in the House, entitled "The Jacobins of Missouri," delivered without the president's prior knowledge, charged that as a result of corrupt Treasury practices, the Mississippi Valley was "rank and fetid with the frauds and corruptions of its agents" and that permits to buy cotton were "just as much a marketable commodity as the cotton itself." Postmaster General Blair accelerated the distribution of his brother's speech throughout the country and even accused Chase of having written the Pomeroy Circular.[54]

Throughout it all Chase, aware that any response on his part would only call more attention to the charges, took no part in the public debate. He did complain in private of the "most bitter and malignant attacks by those who take upon themselves to represent the President's general views of policy." To Greeley he lamented that he was the victim of "the most unscrupulous attacks of the Postmaster General and his brother," only because of his challenge to Lincoln for the nomination. With his decision to withdraw from the race, he told Mellen that his supporters could now "come forward earnestly" in defense of his leadership and "rebuke . . . the efforts of the Blairs to discredit it."[55]

Chase's announcement in early March that he would not seek a nomination brought an increase in the charges and countercharges. On March 11, Senator Thomas A. Hendricks, Democrat of Indiana, added to the controversy with a speech in the Senate attacking Jay Cooke and Company, which, he said, "had been made rich by the drippings from the Treasury," estimating its gain at "perhaps a million dollars" because of its special relationship. Senator Sherman came quickly to the defense by arguing that because there had been no machinery within the Treasury to raise the immediate revenue necessary to finance the war, the "active, efficient, able and expert"

Cooke had been employed. Although the available evidence suggests that Cooke's profits were only one-quarter of what Hendricks charged and that Sherman was correct in his assessment of the banker's role, political pressure soon forced Chase to curtail his special relationship with the Treasury to prevent further charges of favoritism.[56]

Chase's partisans fought back against the Blairs and their allies, thus intensifying the bitterness. Both sides added to the mudslinging and raised further unsubstantiated charges. The secretary's Missouri supporters accused Frank Blair of entering into fraudulent government contracts and engaging in illegal whiskey trade. The evidence, a requisition of General Blair, was soon revealed to be a forgery, and a House investigating committee cleared Blair of any wrongdoing. He used this opening to seize the offensive and in a speech before the House accused Chase of having engineered the forgery. He added that Chase was using the proceeds from the sale of abandoned lands to finance the Pomeroy committee. Furthermore, he claimed that Cooke's excessive profits from his privileged position as federal loan agent had been used to finance the Chase presidential campaign. He also charged that special cotton trade permits given to William Sprague could net the senator millions of dollars. Based on information provided by brother Montgomery of an early cabinet meeting, Blair accused Chase of seeking to appease the Confederacy during the secession crisis in April 1861. During his speech, the House was in an uproar, and Speaker Colfax tried unsuccessfully to rule Blair out of order as the Missourian further charged Chase with using Treasury patronage to unseat Lincoln.[57] The furor ended when Frank Blair left immediately for the White House to seek a military commission to rejoin General Sherman, a request which Lincoln quickly granted.

The repercussions of these events were immediate. Receiving the news of the speech and of Lincoln's renewal of Blair's commission that evening, April 23, 1864, as he was boarding a train for Baltimore, Chase exploded in a rare display of temper. In no mood to be consoled, he could not be restrained and his face flushed with fury. As angry at Lincoln as he was with Blair, the irate secretary shouted bitterly to his friend Albert G. Riddle: "All this has been done with the cordial approval of the President." To Chase it appeared as if Lincoln had endorsed the charges by his action. Several of Chase's

Ohio friends in Congress, including James M. Ashley, Riddle, and Rufus Spalding, confronted Lincoln and demanded a repudiation of the Blair speech, but the president explained that he had issued the commission before he knew anything of the speech; moreover, he would let the appointment stand and would make no public disavowal of Blair's actions even though he disapproved of them, nor would he issue any expression of confidence in Chase.[58] Having endured Chase's disloyalty for so long, Lincoln no doubt felt little remorse as he watched the secretary suffer under Blair's abuse. Furthermore, to repudiate Blair might anger moderates in the party. For the president, it was an ongoing struggle to try to satisfy all Republican factions.

Chase's friends in Congress maneuvered to prevent or delay the probe of Treasury activities that Blair demanded. The House eventually agreed to a special committee to investigate, but Speaker of the House Schuyler Colfax appointed James A. Garfield as its chairman and packed it with Chase supporters. The committee did little real investigating and the matter drifted inconclusively. The committee heard charges that "the Treasury Department has been converted into a house of orgies and baechanole [sic]." Superintendent of the Printing Bureau Clark allegedly led "a sort of carrousel in the Treasury building" late in the evening "where liquors were used freely and some of the female employees participated in the frolic." The Treasury allegedly was "a kind of Government house of ill fame, where pretty women toiled until morning over ale and oyster suppers." These unsubstantiated accusations suggested that Chase should be censured for keeping Clark in office despite the evidence that he was "corrupt and unworthy of trust or confidence." Garfield noted during the hearings, "Chase is coming out splendidly," and, in fact, his opponents were never able to substantiate their charges; nor did they seriously consider a censure motion. Instead, the hearings ended inconclusively. On the other hand, the Chase men in Congress made no satisfactory denial of charges made by Blair and others. Welles concluded that although Chase was not directly implicated in the corruption, "he has probably not discouraged, or discountenanced it."[59] Even that cannot be proven, however, and nothing in Chase's actions or character lends credibility to Welles's view, much less Blair's.

Whether or not Chase's partisans in the Mississippi Valley were guilty of corruption was never proven, for the evidence was incomplete. The Blairs were surely correct, however, in their charges that the secretary used his patronage to strengthen himself politically, although not necessarily any more blatantly than many other politicians. Realizing that Chase was likely to offer to resign again, his friends rushed to his defense and urged him to stay on even though they admitted he had just cause for leaving the administration. On reading of Blair's speech, Jay Cooke sympathized, "I don't wonder that somebody was a little wrathy" in Baltimore. Cooke and others felt that Chase should "demand of Lincoln an open reprimand of Blair and a disavowal of all sympathy for such base charges."[60] But Chase claimed to be satisfied that Lincoln had denied all connection with "Blair's assault and expressed his decided disapproval of it," even if only in private to the Ohio congressmen. Chase explained that he had "suppressed my inclination to resign my office and denounce the conspiracy." He agreed with Parsons that "the Blairs have tried their best to get you out of the Cabinet," and he would not let them force such an action. Moreover, he clearly believed that he could still accomplish much in the Treasury, both in economic and racial policy.[61]

With a temporary armistice in his ongoing battles with Lincoln, Chase thus stayed on in the cabinet, and some of his supporters began suggesting that his candidacy for the Republican or Union nomination be revived. Some hoped to get the early June convention postponed to give them more time to develop a new Chase movement. As Parsons told Chase, "Lincoln would not be the Union candidate for President" if the convention could be delayed until late summer. Chase appeared to be responding to the suggestion when he complained to Governor Brough of Ohio that an early convention "will not be regarded as a Union Convention but simply as a Blair-Lincoln Convention."[62]

In early May, Trowbridge's biography of Chase was published and, through a $2,000 gift from Jay Cooke, distributed to newspapers throughout the nation; one of its most laudatory chapters was published in *Atlantic Monthly*. The biography, called *The Ferry Boy and the Financier*, depicted the necessary humble origins for a presidential candidate. Delighted with the finished product, Chase told the author: "You have certainly thrown a great deal of attraction about what I remember as very dry facts."[63]

More than a campaign biography would be necessary to stop Lincoln's renomination. On May 25, the Ohio Union party convention endorsed the president and awarded him the four at-large delegates. The platform praised the "ability, fidelity and patriotism shown by Ohio in the field, cabinet and in the councils," but it failed to mention Chase by name; through the efforts of Chase's opponents, a resolution praising his work in the Treasury was omitted in the final draft. Endorsements of the president in other northern states made his nomination a foregone conclusion, and at Baltimore he received the votes of every state except one.[64] Chase's initial response to the decision was to urge his followers to do all they could to "ensure the success of the ticket," because "the loyal men of the country evidently demanded it."[65] Chase's chances of unseating Lincoln had never been good. The president had skillfully used all of his advantages as the incumbent to insure his renomination; moreover, a combination of poor organization and overly zealous and badly timed partisan activities by Chase's supporters, as well as the assaults by the Blairs, had finished the issue long before the Union party chose its candidate.

Chase's troubles compounded in the weeks after Lincoln's nomination until patronage conflicts in New York led him again to offer his resignation. The secretary had been engaged in an ongoing feud with the Seward-Weed faction over Treasury patronage since 1861. Especially at stake were the positions of collector of customs for the Port of New York and the assistant treasurer at New York, the first because of its substantial patronage influence and the second because of its importance in Treasury policy making as well as its patronage. Hiram Barney, a New York attorney, had received the collector position in 1861 in recognition of his efforts as a loyal Chase partisan at the Chicago convention of 1860 and his support of Lincoln when the Ohioan's chances faded. John J. Cisco was retained in the Treasury post, a position he had held since the Pierce administration; during those years he had won the confidence of many New York bankers. Neither choice had pleased the Seward-Weed faction, which saw only the loss of further patronage and the corresponding increase of Chase's influence in their state and especially in the nation's most important city. The secretary had had to fight to retain

Cisco in office in 1861; throughout the war, Chase's opponents worked to gain the control they felt belonged to them, seeking to discredit Barney and Cisco and force their removals.[66]

Barney's role as collector was a source of controversy from the start. In May 1861, he awarded a labor contract to his own firm of Barney, Parsons, and Butler, admitting later that the government could have done the work more cheaply itself. The Seward-Weed group was disgusted with Barney's use of patronage to help elect Chase partisan George C. Opdyke mayor of the city in 1861 and also to secure the nomination of the anti-Seward Republican James S. Wadsworth for governor the following year.[67] They constantly complained that Barney's lack of forceful leadership and his ineffective use of patronage were hurting the party and strengthening the Democrats. In early 1864, they saw their opening when one of Barney's secretaries, A. N. Palmer, was arrested and charged with aiding those engaged in contraband trade at a time when Barney was considering promoting him to deputy collector. Even Chase's friends were critical of Barney for refusing to move quickly to remove Palmer. As the controversy intensified, the Seward-Weed group demanded Barney's removal; some of Chase's own friends recommended that it would be in his best interest to appoint a new collector.[68]

Finally, Lincoln suggested that Barney "has ceased to be master of his position" and proposed appointing him minister to Portugal "as evidence of my continued confidence in him."[69] Having earlier expressed complete support for Barney, Chase argued that the Seward people had grossly misrepresented the customhouse situation; he continued to support Barney, "in whose integrity I have undiminished confidence." Chase felt that the Seward people were attempting to use the crisis to maneuver one of their own into office. For the time being, the secretary prevailed and Barney was retained, although his control over the customhouse was in greater jeopardy than ever.[70] Chase's opponents maintained their pressure on Lincoln to remove the collector in the next months, especially as the Pomeroy controversy made the secretary more vulnerable.

Following Chase's withdrawal of his candidacy in early March and the confrontation over the Blair charges, the Seward faction used its influence to insure Lincoln's renomination and prevent any possible resurgence by the Treasury secretary. Their success is evident in the selection of one of their members, *New York Times* editor Henry J.

Raymond, as chairman of the party's national Executive Committee which planned and directed the Union nominating convention. The group kept up its offensive with attacks on Horace Greeley and Mayor Opdyke. When the Seward-backed *Albany Evening Journal* accused Chase just prior to the convention of continuing his candidacy and using customhouse patronage to enhance his chances, the secretary responded that since his March withdrawal he had remained totally uninvolved in the contest and that Treasury patronage "is not and never has been used with reference to that nomination." As the verbal abuse increased in both directions, Lincoln again called on the embattled secretary to remove Hiram Barney from his post.[71]

The most serious crisis came when Assistant Secretary Cisco informed Chase in May of his desire to resign because of ill health. Knowing the furor that would rage over the appointment of a successor, Chase urged him instead merely to take a leave of absence "long enough to regain your health." Unable to persuade Cisco to remain on any longer, Chase informed Lincoln that a vacancy was impending and that he would soon recommend a successor. After several prominent New Yorkers rejected the post, he proposed Maunsell B. Field who was then an assistant secretary in the Treasury. The choice immediately met with opposition from the Seward-Weed faction and especially from powerful New York Senator Edwin D. Morgan. Lincoln, eager to keep the factions from further feuding, had urged Chase to get Morgan's approval on any appointment because of the senator's influence in New York commercial circles. Morgan, in fact, had suggested three names, all of whom Chase found unacceptable. Despite his awareness that Lincoln was eager to keep Morgan happy, Chase submitted Field's nomination "on grounds of integrity and capacity." Said Chase, "I fear Senator Morgan desires to make a political engine of the office." The president again urged Morgan and Chase to agree on a nominee whom he could appoint, but Chase insisted instead on a personal conference with him. This Lincoln refused, leading Chase to the conclusion that his right of Treasury appointment was being undermined.[72] Their relationship, once friendly and cordial, had by this time been reduced to an exchange of icy letters.

On June 28, in a final effort to avoid a confrontation, Chase wired Cisco, urging him to reconsider and to "give the country the benefit of your services at least another quarter longer." At the same time he informed Lincoln that if Cisco declined, he would insist on Field's appointment because "my duty to you and to the country" prevented him from accepting any of Morgan's choices. Both the secretary and the president were holding firm, but that evening Cisco agreed to withdraw his resignation, thus relieving Chase "from a very painful embarrassment."[73]

That same evening Chase received Lincoln's refusal to meet with the secretary. The president stated that their differences did not "lie within the range of a conversation between you and me." Furthermore, he argued, he had borne a great burden by retaining Barney in office when so many New Yorkers had demanded his removal, and the choice of Field would provoke an "open revolt" among those same Republicans. With relations already so strained and his right to control Treasury patronage thus challenged, Chase again submitted his resignation. He explained to Lincoln that although Cisco's action "relieved the present difficulty," he could not help but feel that "my position here is not altogether agreeable to you; and it is certainly too full of embarrassment and difficulty and painful responsibility to allow in me the least desire to retain it."[74]

Every indication suggests that Chase expected the president to reject his offer to resign as he had in the past. Nothing in Chase's correspondence or diary implies a real desire to step down, despite his statement to Lincoln that he "should feel really relieved" if his resignation were accepted. His writings reveal instead that he was preoccupied with financial and military questions, although in his diary the day before his resignation he noted, after reading St. Paul's letter to the Ephesians, "How stable is the City of God! How disordered is the City of Man!" He placed primary emphasis on taxes, trade, gold, and appointments, indicating a business-as-usual attitude.[75] Despite the hint of weariness with Washington politics, the egotistical Chase probably still thought that the administration could not do without him and that Lincoln would ask him to stay on and allow him to retain control over Treasury patronage.

Instead, Lincoln accepted Chase's resignation, because, he said, "You and I have reached a point of mutual embarrassment in our official relation which it seems can not be overcome, or longer sustained." The president had decided that, with his own nomination secure and Chase under fire from so many quarters, he could afford to let the secretary go. He explained to Ohio Governor John Brough that he was tired of Chase's many resignations and no longer felt himself obliged to "continue to beg him to take it back, especially when the country would not go to destruction in consequence." In the approaching presidential election the enthusiastic support of the Seward-Morgan group and other moderate Republicans was what mattered because he assumed that the radical faction would have no choice but to support him even with Chase out of the cabinet. He thus seized the opportunity and "did not long reflect."[76]

On learning that his resignation had been accepted, the surprised Chase reacted bitterly, still refusing to take responsibility for his differences with the president: "I had found a good deal of embarrassment from him but what he found from me I could not imagine." Self-righteously, he suggested that his only crime had been his "unwillingness to have offices distributed as spoils or benefits with more regard to the claims of divisions, factions, cliques and individuals than to fitness of selection." He went on to complain that Lincoln had never given him the support he needed on financial matters, failing even then to urge Congress to provide the revenue to match its "lavish" appropriations. Unwilling to acknowledge that he had become a liability to the president, Chase suggested that part of the problem was a difference in "temperament," for "I have never been able to make a joke out of this war."[77] The solemn Chase had never understood Lincoln's humor. In the next week he continued to rationalize his own position and in doing so defended himself on some of the real differences he had with the president. On the issue of abolition, he contended: "I am too earnest, too antislavery." Moreover, "I was too much for going ahead; he was . . . too much for drifting."[78] Blind to his own faults, Chase could not believe that his services were no longer regarded as indispensable.

Reactions to the resignation from Chase's friends were predictable. Jay Cooke was "deeply pained," and Greeley's *New York Tribune* regretted the loss of "one of the few great men left." Chase immodestly reflected on his financial success on meeting "the vast demands of the war," but he regretted not being able to "finish what I began." He explained to Cooke that he could no longer tolerate not being allowed to control his own department, although he hated to leave, "especially at a moment of peril." He told Cisco that the attacks of the Blairs, indirectly sustained by the president, had added to his discomfort.[79]

Cabinet members Welles and Bates expressed surprise on learning of the resignation but noted that the reaction in Washington was relief and "a hope of better things" rather than shock. A month later Welles said, "Chase's retirement has offended nobody and has gratified almost everybody." Most elated were the Blairs and the Seward-Weed group. The elder Blair rejoiced that Chase, after having "hung on as long as possible," had "dropped off at last like a rotten pear." His efforts to "bully Lincoln by threatening to resign" had received the contempt they deserved. Weed's reaction was to ask that "Heaven be praised for this gleam of sunshine." Of the cabinet members, only Stanton expressed regret to Chase personally and showed the courtesy of calling on him before he left Washington.[80]

In his letter of resignation Chase had pledged that he would "most cheerfully render to my successor any aid he may find useful in entering upon his duties," a promise he willingly honored. Lincoln's first choice for a new Treasury secretary was former Ohio governor David Tod, a hard money advocate clearly opposed to many of Chase's policies. Feeling that the position should go to an Ohioan, the president appeared less concerned about the financial philosophy of the nominee than most cabinet members were, especially Stanton and Welles. When Tod informed the president that ill health would prevent his acceptance, Lincoln dropped the Ohio consideration and nominated William P. Fessenden of Maine, chairman of the Senate Finance Committee. Fessenden, who had worked closely with Chase on many financial questions, was by 1864 a supporter of his policies. The recommendation of two men of such opposing persuasions as Tod and Fessenden was proof to Welles of Lincoln's "want of knowledge on the subject," for "his attention never has been given to the finances."[81]

Although aligned with the more radical, Fessenden's views toward the South and slavery were more moderate than those of his predecessor. His appointment might thus satisfy Republicans of all persuasions. Chase's reaction to the news was positive, for the new secretary "has the confidence of the country and many who have become inimical to me will give their confidence to him and their support." When Fessenden considered declining the offer, Chase urged him to accept, immodestly pointing out that "all the great work of the Department was now fairly blocked out and in progress" so that his major task would be only to administer those programs. In the next several days, Chase willingly explained the workings and procedures of the Treasury office to Fessenden. He noted later that his successor "fully appreciates the work I have done in the Department and now I believe, concurs in all my views."[82]

For all his good will and cooperation as he prepared to leave Washington, Chase could not help but express both bitterness and regret. He told his daughter Nettie that although he was glad to be free of the administration, he was "sorry to miss the opportunity of doing the great work I felt confident I could with God's help accomplish." His feelings, he told Simon Cameron, were mixed: "regret that I leave great works half done—satisfaction in relief from cares and manifold annoyances." When Congress completed work on the bill giving the secretary of the Treasury effective control over trade in Confederate territory and the right to lease abandoned property and provide care for the freedmen, Chase lamented: "How much good I expected to accomplish under this bill!" He feared that Fessenden would not pursue his goals in that area with sufficient vigor, because "he had not the same heart for this measure that I had." On July 13, Chase left the capital for Philadelphia and New York, aware that "half of my fifty-seventh year is ended," but still unable to understand why more Republicans seemed not to appreciate his accomplishments.[83]

Chase spent much of July and August traveling in the East enjoying visits with Jay Cooke and other bankers as well as Carlotta Eastman and New Hampshire relatives and an extended stay with Kate and her husband in Rhode Island. During his New Hampshire stop, he had reunions with a niece and an elderly aunt and made a trip to his mother's grave, recording in his diary the inscription on her gravestone.[84] It was his first return to his boyhood home in more than thirty years, an indication of his preoccupation with his own career since moving to Washington in 1826. But the trip, coming during one of the few lulls in his busy life, permitted him to reflect on those who had once been the center of his life.

During this period his interest in politics never abated. Shortly before he left Washington he had received an inquiry as to whether he would consider running for the House of Representatives from the Cincinnati district. In early August, William Mellen indicated that the nomination could be his only through "active exertion" to overcome the opposition of Benjamin Eggleston, a long-time political foe. Chase's response was a telegram to Mellen: "Unanimous nomination would command acceptance but cannot compete and must not be regarded as competitor." At the nominating meeting in Cincinnati, supporters read a letter from Chase that he would accept a nomination "if spontaneously and unanimously demanded." Chase soon learned from Mellen, however, that his partisans had badly mismanaged his candidacy, for "your name was not withdrawn, nor was a fight made for you." The humiliating result was that he was beaten by Eggleston "in your own home by two to one!" No amount of rationalization by his friends that Eggleston had packed the convention with his supporters who had defeated "the wishes of their constituents" could change the fact that Chase's rather amateurish partisans had been outmaneuvered and that Chase, who had refused to compete for the nomination, possessed definite political limitations. In typical understatement, Chase suggested that the situation had subjected him to "some unnecessary misapprehension."[85]

Discontent with Lincoln's nomination did not focus entirely on Chase, although his name was again mentioned as a possible presidential candidate. Before the Union party chose the Lincoln–Andrew Johnson ticket in early June, an unusual group of dissidents met in Cleveland on May 31 and nominated John C. Frémont on a third-party ticket. Calling themselves the Radical Democrats, they included such abolitionists as Wendell Phillips, such border state Republicans as B. Gratz Brown of Missouri, and various discontented Democrats. The platform combined the interests of the several factions by calling for equality of the races and the distribution of confiscated lands "among soldiers and settlers" along with a Democratic-inspired attack on Lincoln's civil liberties record. Although no prominent Republicans endorsed Frémont, dissatisfaction with the president remained intense, especially after his pocket veto of the congressional plan of Reconstruction embodied in the Wade-Davis bill. With Union armies still unable to force a Confederate surrender, a group of the most alienated northerners, including David Dudley Field, George C. Opdyke, and Horace Greeley, began urging another Republican convention to seek a replacement for Lincoln. As the situation deteriorated and reports reached Washington of terrible Union casualties in Virginia, even Lincoln concluded gloomily that "it seems exceedingly probable that this administration will not be reelected."[86]

Chase's reaction to these events of late summer are not fully recorded and can only be surmised. Predictably, many of his opponents were suspicious and assumed that as long as a nomination remained at stake Chase would seek it. Before leaving Washington in early July, he indicated he was "not willing now to decide what duty may demand next fall." When Senator Pomeroy suggested that some Democrats were mentioning him as a candidate, Chase admitted an interest if they would "cut loose from Slavery and go for freedom." Revealingly, Chase visited many prominent Republicans during his travels in the East including some in the stop-Lincoln movement. He conferred with one of the leading Republican dissidents, William C. Noyes, a prominent New York attorney and member of the anti-Seward faction, even giving him a letter to bring to a New York meeting of the insurgents. Noyes promised to write him of the results, although Chase indicated he had "little or no faith in it."[87] Chase wisely kept his interest in either a Democratic or dissident Republican nomination private, for events suddenly began to turn in Lincoln's favor, assuring him the reelection he so recently had despaired of achieving.

Prominent Democrats had never considered Chase a viable candidate because they were unwilling to support emancipation; some even wanted to negotiate a settlement with the Confederacy. At their Chicago convention at the end of August, they chose General George B. McClellan, who had been a critical bystander ever since Lincoln had relieved him of his command in late 1862. McClellan's nomination served to bring feuding Republicans together in opposition, aware suddenly that there could be something worse than a second Lincoln administration. Victories by General Philip H. Sheridan in the Shenandoah Valley and Admiral David G. Farragut at Mobile, and especially Sherman's entrance into Atlanta, suggested that the defeat of the Confederacy might be in sight. Plans for an insurgent Republican convention were quietly abandoned, and on September 22, Frémont announced his withdrawal as a third-party candidate. On the following day, Lincoln accepted the resignation of Postmaster General Montgomery Blair. Although the two events were not directly related, Blair's removal made radical Republicans more willing to support the president's reelection. Chase could take some solace in the fact that the man who had abused him so violently had fallen victim to political attack as well. Although Chase could take no direct credit for Blair's removal, the pressure of his supporters had been a major factor. The party appeared suddenly united, and even Chase recognized the need to support the Lincoln-Johnson ticket. Believing that "the great public interest will be best promoted by their success," he nonetheless lamented, "We can't have everything as we would wish."[88]

In the interest of party harmony, Lincoln also agreed to the Sewardites' demand for the removal of Collector Hiram Barney. The New York faction convinced the president that a more forceful leader than Barney was needed to control the state's patronage during the campaign. With Chase gone from the cabinet and Fessenden not committed to Barney's retention, Lincoln was free to make a change. As Barney explained to Chase, the president requested his resignation "as a personal and political favor of great value and importance to *him*." A Seward man, Simeon Draper, was named in his place and other Chase partisans were also replaced. Although Chase's friends in the Senate managed to prevent confirmation of Draper until the last day of the congressional session in March 1865, the delay could not hide the fact that the last vestige of Chase's influence in New York was disappearing.[89]

Such developments did not prevent Chase from joining in the campaign efforts for Lincoln's reelection, because he now clearly realized that success in the war effort as well as his own future public career might depend on it. By late September, he was on the stump, beginning his efforts at a mass meeting in Cincinnati. Honestly convinced that Lincoln's reelection would "turn every hope of rebellion to despair," he nevertheless admitted to daughter Kate after meeting with Lincoln that "I feel I do not know him." Although he could never forget the supposed wrongs done to him by the president, he nonetheless felt that "the general interests of the country will be best promoted by his reelection." Thus Chase threw himself wholeheartedly into the effort, speaking throughout the Ohio Valley and the Old Northwest, including rallies at Louisville, Saint Louis, Cleveland, Detroit, and Chicago. Following a Lexington address to more than a thousand listeners, he wrote Stanton enthusiastically: "I gave them one of my old fashioned speeches such as you have heard in old times." Chase could thus share the Republican joy in the president's substantial victory on November 8 and noted enthusiastically, "I really felt more satisfaction on the stump pleading our case and our candidates than I ever did in any office."[90] Long before the election, the death of Chief Justice Roger Taney had given him new incentive. Considering his bleak future up to this point, the availability of such an important office opened new horizons and offered new incentives.

Chase's interest in a Supreme Court appointment had been apparent ever since his resignation from the cabinet, and with the eighty-seven-year-old Taney in failing health for some time, a vacancy appeared imminent. Despite Chase's lack of judicial experience, leadership of the highest court appealed to him, especially when Lincoln's renomination in early June apparently precluded the presidency for another four years. Early in Lincoln's first term Chase had let the president know that he "preferred judicial to administrative office" and that he would rather be "Chief Justice of the United States than hold any other position that could be given me." Later, Justices Stephen J. Field and Samuel F. Miller indicated their preference for Chase because he "was familiar with all the questions out of which had grown the Civil War and . . . all the legislation of Congress during its progress." Lincoln told several Republicans at the time of Chase's resignation from the cabinet that he would have named Chase to the Supreme Court then if a vacancy had existed. To those who suggested to the president that he punish Chase for past disloyalty by denying him the appointment, Lincoln responded compassionately, "I'm not in favor of crushing anybody out! If there is anything that a man can do and do it well I say let him do it." Lincoln clearly hoped that if appointed Chase would uphold such critical administration policies as emancipation and legal tender that as Treasury secretary he had helped to formulate. The president noted: "We cannot ask a man what he will do. . . . Therefore we must take a man whose opinions are known."[91] Lincoln also knew that a Chase appointment would help to pacify many discontented Republicans.

Much of Chase's willingness to campaign for Lincoln during the fall of 1864 may have resulted from the obvious conclusion that loyalty to the president would be a prerequisite for a nomination to the bench. Chase already had active supporters among the more radical, and on news of Taney's death on October 12, Sumner immediately urged Lincoln to appoint him. In the senator's words, Taney's death was "a victory for Liberty and the Constitution." Now the fundamental law would "be interpreted for Liberty" rather than slavery. Senator Sherman also lobbied in Chase's behalf, writing the president while on a campaign trip in Iowa that virtually all he talked to preferred Chase. He explained that the former secretary would "reflect higher honor" on the position and his appointment "could be justified by obvious political reasons."[92] With his usual indirection and belief in protocol, Chase would not seek the appointment openly, but admitted privately that he would be "disappointed" if he were not chosen. He told Sumner that he could "do more for our cause and the country in that place than in any other."[93]

By waiting until after the election to announce his decision, Lincoln assured himself the support of each of the Republican factions. Both Fessenden and Sumner told Chase in late October that the president was ready to appoint him but, because he wanted to let each faction make its case, was in no hurry to announce his decision. Thus while the various hopefuls were kept in suspense, the maneuvering by Chase and the others continued. Eager to avoid giving his enemies "the occasion to say that I solicit or even ask such an appointment as a favor or as a reward for political service," Chase stayed away from Washington and instead awaited the decision in Cincinnati. But he did not hesitate to urge others to solicit for him. To Richard Parsons he wrote: "Talk as you always do cordially and friendly with the President and those who are near him in places of confidence."[94]

Chase's friends followed his advice; in late November, Sumner told Chase he had just written Lincoln a third letter in his behalf. A group of Ohio legislators petitioned the president in Chase's behalf, claiming to represent "the almost unanimous wish of the Union men" in their state. Although he claimed to have supported Lincoln's reelection "without reference to any personal advantage to myself," Chase nonetheless found ways to remind the president of his interest. When told by a secretary that a friendly letter had arrived from Chase, the president knowingly responded without reading it: "File it with his other recommendations."[95]

There were numerous other contenders for the appointment, the most prominent of whom were Justice Noah H. Swayne, William M. Evarts, Montgomery Blair, and Stanton. Yet with such strong sentiment for Chase, his many enemies were never able to concentrate on a single candidate and thus may have helped assure Chase the appointment. Especially vocal in their efforts to dissuade Lincoln from choosing Chase were his long-time Ohio foes. Former Whig politician Thomas Ewing, Sr. informed Lincoln that Chase was not acceptable to the Ohio bar: "He is a politician rather than a lawyer and unless he changes his nature always will be even if made Chief Justice." Former Governor Dennison, now postmaster general in Blair's place, told an agreeing Welles that Chase and Lincoln "could not assimilate," for the former "never forgets or forgives those who have once thwarted him." Chase's ambition for the position blinded him to the fact that his friend Stanton was also an aspirant; he insensitively wrote the war secretary in October asking Stanton whether he should accept the position if offered. When Stanton understood Chase's feelings and that General Grant wanted him to remain in the War Department because of his able leadership there, he gracefully withdrew his candidacy and supported Chase.[96]

More serious were the challenges of Swayne, Evarts, and Blair. Lincoln's close friend, Justice David Davis led the efforts to elevate Swayne to chief justice. Davis claimed to speak for the majority of his colleagues on the Court in preferring Swayne to Chase, but the other justices were clearly divided on the matter. Evarts, an able New York lawyer, was Weed's favorite and, like Swayne, was also rumored to be the choice of several members of the Court. Chase admitted that Evarts was "a much greater lawyer than I ever pretended to be" but still felt that when "tried by the Marshall standard [I] should make a better judge." Having been forced out of the cabinet in September, Blair had strong spokesmen including Seward and Welles. Predictably, the Blair family did all it could to thwart a Chase appointment, seeing Montgomery as a more appropriate alternative. The fear of losing the spot to a Blair horrified Chase and his supporters, although Lincoln apparently never seriously considered any of the several alternatives.[97]

Despite his differences with Chase, Lincoln had determined that the advantages of his appointment far outweighed the disadvantages. He noted that of "Mr. C's ability and of his soundness on the general issues of the war there is of course, no question." He told Republican Congressman Augustus Frank of New York: "We have stood together in the time of trial, and I should despise myself if I allowed personal differences to affect my judgment of his fitness for the office of Chief-Justice." But, said Lincoln, he did have one major reservation: "He is a man of unbounded ambition, and has been working all his life to become President." Fearing that he would continue these efforts as Chief Justice, he concluded: "If I were sure that he would go on the bench and give up his aspirations and do nothing but make himself a great judge, I would not hesitate a moment." To this qualification, Speaker of the House Schuyler Colfax assured him that Chase "would dedicate the remainder of his life to the Bench."[98] Finally, on December 6, almost two months after Taney's death, Lincoln overcame his misgivings and sent Chase's name to the Senate for confirmation. Several factors had combined to lead Lincoln to his decision. Among the most important were faith in Chase's ability as well as the president's compassion for him, his hope for judicial approval of Civil War legislation, and his desire to make peace with the radicals and thus bind together the Republican factions.

Chase was elated at the news, immediately informing Lincoln of his acceptance, thanking him warmly "for this mark of your confidence," and assuring him that he valued his "good-will more than nomination to office." Rather than referring the nomination to committee, the Senate unanimously confirmed his appointment and Chase was sworn in as the sixth chief justice one week later. His friends were quick to extend congratulations. Joseph Medill, editor of the *Chicago Tribune,* expressed confidence that Chase would defend the Constitution "in accordance with the principles of Freedom and Human Rights." Abolitionist supporters Lydia Maria Child and Lewis Tappan were overjoyed that the proslavery days of the Court under Taney had given way "to the cause of Freedom." Of his many supporters, only Kate Sprague, with her mind still very much on the presidency for her father, expressed displeasure at his appointment. When Sumner rushed in exuberantly to tell Chase of the Senate's confirmation, she raged at her father's friend: "You too, in this business of shelving papa?"[99]

Chase's enemies were also unhappy but for other reasons. Welles, fearing Chase's continuing ambitions, argued that he would always be a candidate for president: "his restless and ambitious mind is already at work." Frank Blair told his brother Montgomery that "Chase's appointment *shakes my confidence in the President's integrity,*" because "he must know that Chase is dishonest as well as an enemy to him and the Government." Chase's long-time Ohio antagonist Ben Wade commented sarcastically on hearing of his selection: "Chase is a good man, but his theology is unsound. He thinks there is a fourth person in the Trinity." Unknowingly, Wade had raised a real issue for the days ahead. Could a man with Chase's ego and political ambition be content to hold the less conspicuous position of chief justice and give up the political prominence to which he was accustomed? The newest member of the Supreme Court himself concluded: "I have been so long an active leader that I fear that I may find judicial administration somewhat irksome, but I will do my best." [100]

9

Chase, Johnson, and the Republicans

S almon Chase's appointment as chief justice brought a temporary end to the active political role he had played since the early 1840s. He had not practiced law for fifteen years. Nor had he had any judicial experience; since 1849, he had been totally immersed in politics and Treasury matters. It was to be expected, therefore, that the transition from an active political and financial role during the war to a less conspicuous and politically inactive position as Supreme Court justice would be a difficult one. Adjusting to the court routine in early 1865, Chase found himself out of place. His tasks were equally demanding on his time, although "far less anxious than those of the Treasury Department." He did not find the work especially pleasing or the results rewarding: "Working from morning till midnight and no result, except that John Smith owned this parcel or land or other property instead of Jacob Robinson; I caring nothing, and nobody caring much more, about the matter."[1]

During the 1864–65 term, the Court faced few important cases. Many were reviews of circuit court decisions which involved no federal law; rather, they were disputes between citizens of two different states. With little of significance or precedence to be decided in these cases, Chase became increasingly bored. By the end of March, he told General McDowell that perhaps he should not have accepted the appointment because he found "the task of adjudicating cases however important as somewhat irksome."[2] But Chase did not confine himself to the specific business of the Supreme Court. Critical

Reconstruction issues raised by the ending of the war as well as his continuing interest in politics combined to make Chase a very political chief justice.

Chase's interest in nonjudicial matters made him a frequent visitor at the White House and in Congress. On Inauguration Day, March 4, 1865, he briefly attended a cabinet meeting; when Congress was in session he was frequently seen in the Senate. Unable to remain aloof from the pressing political questions facing the president and Congress, he rarely kept his view to himself. Some of his concern dealt with financial issues, and in early March he wrote to Senator Sherman at length offering his opinion on a currency bill pending in Congress.[3]

Much more significant was the chief justice's continued interest in the issues of Reconstruction, and especially black suffrage. Early in the year, he encouraged William Lloyd Garrison and Wendell Phillips as well as political friends, such as Sumner, in their calls for universal manhood suffrage. He also sought to persuade those not already in agreement, especially the president. He wrote two strong letters to Lincoln renewing his argument that justice required "the enrollment of the loyal citizens without regard to complexion." He argued that it would be "a crime and a folly if the colored loyalists of the rebel states are left to the control of restored rebels." Turning to the continuing controversy in Louisiana, Chase suggested to Lincoln that he remind the recently elected Governor Michael Hahn of "the importance" of freedmen voting. He even implied his own willingness to support Lincoln's 10 percent plan of Reconstruction if the president accepted black suffrage.[4]

Chase knew that in February Lincoln had urged Governor Hahn to consider suffrage for some blacks, that is the "very intelligent and especially those who have fought gallantly in our ranks." In his last public speech on April 11, the president endorsed the proposed Louisiana constitution which omitted a black suffrage requirement, saying that it was the best possible one under the circumstances. He conceded, however, that the state legislature could still add such a requirement. The president concluded by noting that he was planning "some new announcement" on Reconstruction "to the people of the South." Chase's letter of April 12 congratulated Lincoln for advocating limited black suffrage and hoped that the president might soon agree to complete political equality. Accounts of Lincoln's last cabinet meeting on April 14 led Chase to agree with Attorney General James Speed that Lincoln had "never seemed so near our views."[5]

On Good Friday, April 14, Chase took a carriage ride with his daughter Nettie, intending to stop at the White House to talk with the president "about universal suffrage in reorganization." But feeling he "might annoy him and do harm rather than good," Chase postponed his visit. That evening after retiring, he was awakened with word from Treasury Agent William Mellen that the president had been shot while attending the theater. Thoroughly alarmed by the news, Chase got little sleep that night as he imagined the turmoil to come should Lincoln not survive. He was soon aware that a guard had been posted around his home; "their heavy tramp-tramp was heard under my window all night. . . . It was a night of horrors." At dawn a heavy rain was falling, and Chase hurried with Mellen to the house opposite Ford's Theatre, only to learn that "the President was already dead." He went immediately to see Andrew Johnson at Kirkwood House on Pennsylvania Avenue and found him "calm . . . but very grave." In consultation with Secretary of the Treasury Hugh McCulloch and Attorney General Speed, Chase planned the swearing in of the new president for ten that morning. With Speed, he checked the precedents set by Vice Presidents Tyler and Fillmore concerning the assumption of the presidency. Chase later recorded that "every countenance was sad" as he administered the oath.[6] The turbulent Lincoln-Chase relationship had ended with feelings between the two more positive and differences less obvious than at any time since Chase's resignation from the Treasury. The chief justice at first believed that he could establish a similar relationship with Andrew Johnson.

Chase sought to commit the new president to his views on Reconstruction, and at first he had reason to be optimistic. As the military governor of Tennessee, Johnson had endorsed Lincoln's emancipation policy and had called for punishment for the leaders of the Confederacy. Johnson's name was on the list of state representatives in the "Original Chase Organization Meeting" of late 1863 which had proposed Chase as an alternative candidate to Lincoln. Yet Chase and other Republicans realized Johnson's firm support for states rights and his belief that emancipation did not necessarily mean full equality for blacks. In the confusion of the first few weeks following the assassination, the new president's indecision and lack of experience led Chase to believe that Johnson could be won over. In the first tumultuous hours after Lincoln's death, at his own initiative, Chase had written a short address for the new president to deliver to those assembled for his swearing in, expressing his shock and grief at Lincoln's death as well as his determination to carry out his new duties. Johnson did not use Chase's remarks, but three days later, following a lengthy visit, Chase concluded hopefully: "He seems thoroughly in earnest and much of the same mind with myself."[7]

Before that meeting on April 18, Johnson had requested the chief justice's counsel in preparing a speech to announce his Reconstruction policy. Chase's draft advocated a simple process in which a state would call a constitutional convention and choose a legislature which would then provide for the election of members of Congress. The critical feature of the proposal was that loyal citizens, black and white, would be granted suffrage. Johnson conferred with other Republicans, including Secretary Stanton, who offered similar advice. Chase objected to the president's plan to invite North Carolina to reorganize for readmission first, by suggesting that it would be "far better to make Florida and Louisiana really free states with universal suffrage and then let other states follow."[8] The long occupation of those states by Union forces and the existence of loyal Union governments there made them more logical places to begin the Reconstruction process, he said. The meeting on the eighteenth apparently resolved their differences, and they conversed several more times before the end of the month.

On April 29 Chase brought another draft of a Reconstruction policy, again including "a distinct recognition of a loyal colored man as citizen, entitled to the right of suffrage." Johnson hesitated, however, explaining that he could not "issue such a document now. I am new and untried and cannot venture what I please." Chase persisted in his argument and later recorded his hope that "the President's reluctance was conquered." About to visit parts of the Confederacy, Chase believed that he could provide further evidence which would lead the president to issue "the new crowning proclamation . . . securing equal and universal suffrage in reorganization."[9]

Chase had been planning a trip into the South for some time, perhaps even before Johnson's assumption of the presidency. Given the rapport Chase had developed with the new president, Johnson may even have requested that he make the trip to assess conditions there. Surely Chase had Johnson's support if not his active encouragement. Sumner concluded that Chase had been authorized by the president "to do everything he can to promote organization without distinction of color." Although it is unlikely that Chase was given such a mandate, he clearly intended to use the trip to support black suffrage. The trip would be made on the revenue cutter *Wayanda* with orders from Johnson and Stanton to civil and military officers in the area to extend to Chase every possible courtesy and assistance. Before leaving, the chief justice reminded the president of the importance of suffrage to stop the unrest and "outrages" being committed against southern blacks. A Johnson statement endorsing equal voting rights, he said, would "excite the admiration of all men" and give the president "a name and fame equal to that acquired by the Proclamation of Emancipation." Chase told Sprague before he left, however, that he feared Johnson might not accept the suggestion because he lacked the necessary confidence for bold leadership: "He distrusts himself . . . too much."[10] Although aware that it would be difficult to convince the president, Chase remained outwardly optimistic that the trip would help convert him.

Chase left Washington on May 1, 1865, with his eighteen-year-old daughter Nettie and a small group of friends, including Whitelaw Reid of the *Cincinnati Gazette* and William Mellen. From Norfolk the *Wayanda* sailed to Beaufort, North Carolina where the party visited New Berne and Morehead City before continuing to Wilmington. In South Carolina, they observed conditions in Charleston and Hilton Head and in Florida in Jacksonville and Fernandena before reaching Key West on May 23.[11] During the trip Chase wrote seven letters to Andrew Johnson describing conditions and making recommendations. The South he described had just begun to accept the defeat of the Confederacy and the need for terms of reentry into the Union. He especially emphasized the need for racial harmony. His extended discussions with military leaders, politicians, freedmen, and southern whites, including many former slaveowners, led him to two basic recommendations: the means to a permanent and successful Reconstruction process was black suffrage and it could best be brought about by firm presidential leadership. With Congress not to convene until December, both Chase and the president knew that Johnson had an opportunity to seize the initiative.

Reinforced by first-hand observation, Chase informed Johnson of the need for equal justice and the right of blacks to vote to protect the freedom just achieved. He admitted that any move toward suffrage could succeed only over vehement white opposition. At each of his stops he found the thought of blacks voting "distasteful" to most whites, and a conservative element even wanted slavery restored. The majority everywhere wanted a permanent peace and were willing to "take any course the Government may desire" to secure it. A third group of "progressives" felt that those made free "must be citizens and being citizens must be allowed to vote." It was the majority, "the acquiescents," who would insure the success of any policy which Johnson chose to recommend. To Chase there was no other option "if we wish to promote . . . the interests of all classes except to give suffrage to all." Such leadership from the president would not be regarded by southern whites as interference; rather, they would "welcome some simple recommendation from yourself and would adopt readily any plan which you would suggest." Without such leadership, he feared a restoration of the old order. Conversations in Jacksonville and Fernandena led Chase to conclude that those refusing to recognize the results of the war were waiting for the opportunity to seize power.[12]

Chase proposed to the president that until the enrollment of loyal black and white voters could be accomplished, military supervision would be necessary. Generals chosen for the task must be "ready to maintain the rights and promote the welfare of black as of white citizens."[13] In Florida, he learned that General Alexander D. McCook was granting paroles on the condition that the parolee must conform to the laws in force before February 1861, which appeared to Chase to sanction a return to slavery. It was important, therefore, that "no *even* apparent support should be given to slavery by generals in command." Once enrolled, citizens would elect delegates to a constitutional convention to amend or rewrite the existing fundamental state law. After it was ratified by the voters, the commander would arrange for elections for a state government and military functions "would be confined to the repression of disorder."[14] Military rule should thus be firm but as brief as possible, ending entirely with the state's readmission into the Union.

One general whose influence in the Reconstruction process Chase especially feared was William Tecumseh Sherman. Even before his trip, Chase had scolded Sherman for his negative views of blacks and had urged him to reconsider his opposition to their voting. Chase feared that the general's views might win over the president. Noting that Sherman had called for ridding his camp "of the surplus Negroes, mules, etc.," Chase reminded him that "classing men with cattle" could only accentuate racial tensions. Sherman responded that military considerations had to take precedence over "Negro equality" and that he believed that suffrage "should be rather abridged than enlarged." While at Beaufort, Chase found Sherman's ship also in port and sent him copies of the letters he had written to Lincoln on Reconstruction just before the assassination. He implied that his views also represented those of President Johnson, who would "be gratified to have all loyal citizens participate in this work without reference to complexion." Sherman's response suggested that blacks were not prepared to vote; to force black suffrage on the South would "produce new war" which would "be more bloody and destructive than the last." Chase persisted and wrote Sherman again in behalf of extending suffrage "to all loyal citizens." As a result of this exchange, Chase complained to Johnson of the general's apparent unwillingness to cooperate in the process of Reconstruction or to recognize "the great changes produced by the conversion of slaves into free citizens." [15]

One of Chase's most telling arguments in behalf of suffrage was the earnest desire of blacks themselves. Throughout his tour, he found them organizing in "Union Leagues." According to the chief justice, "They attach very great importance to the right of voting—more perhaps than any other except that of personal liberty." The Union Leagues, led by the most educated, would exercise a tremendous influence over other blacks and all of southern politics. Said Chase pointedly: "They form a power which no wise Statesman will disregard." In Fernandena, he recorded his pleasure at swearing in a new mayor elected by an integrated electorate. Such an event he believed to be inevitable throughout the South, and Johnson would clearly be well advised to lead rather than resist the trend. [16] Chase encouraged blacks to believe the vote would soon be theirs, although he did remind them that although he "would give it at once," the decision was the president's. Johnson, he believed, would decide according to his "own judgment, with the best policy towards all men of all classes." Chase's message was thus clear: Johnson could serve his own and the South's best interests by taking the lead in the drive for equal rights, for "nothing will more exalt your character in the estimation of mankind."[17]

Chase delivered only one major address on his tour, speaking to a large gathering of blacks at a Charleston church. There, after immodestly reviewing his own record in behalf of emancipation, arming blacks, and urging land distribution, he concluded that the ballot was "the freeman's weapon in peace" as the bayonet had been "his weapon in war." He also lectured paternalistically on the need for blacks to be industrious and respectful, showing themselves fit for suffrage. If it were granted immediately, "they must not abuse it," but if not "they must be patient." He recorded that his audience was pleased with his message, but he resisted further demands that he speak, "fearing I might be taken for a politician or preacher rather than a Chief Justice."[18]

Chase's many critics had long since concluded that politics was the ulterior motive of his southern tour. Two of his old cabinet antagonists were especially suspicious, with Welles suggesting that, besides equality, Chase had "other schemes for Presidential preferment in hand in this voyage." Bates, no longer a part of the cabinet, remained just as hostile with his charge that some Republicans planned to promote Chase's candidacy by "making *negro suffrage* their war cry." The Democratic *New York Herald* and *New York World* made similar charges. Chase and his supporters could not convince the critics that his belief in racial equality and a desire to learn "the true condition of the country" were the real reasons for his southern tour.[19]

Throughout his tour, Chase had urged Johnson to keep him informed of his Reconstruction decisions. At Charleston on May 12, he urged the president to write him at New Orleans where he would be at the end of the month. Johnson's answer came not in a letter to the chief justice but rather in two presidential proclamations issued on May 29. The first established terms of amnesty for southern whites seeking to regain political rights, and the second established a provisional government in North Carolina with the appointed governor authorized to call a constitutional convention. Only white men who had taken an oath of loyalty and had received amnesty could be elected as delegates to that convention. Several procedural points followed Chase's proposals, but nowhere was there any suggestion that black men should vote. Based on a draft Secretary Stanton had introduced at a cabinet meeting, it omitted the key element that both Stanton and Chase had sought when it left suffrage requirements up to the states. With the cabinet divided on black suffrage, Johnson had settled the issue according to his belief that the federal government had no authority on voting qualifications.[20] In the following weeks the president issued similar orders for six other southern states. Never an advocate of black equality, Johnson, having established his self-confidence as president, determined to assert his leadership by promoting his own Reconstruction policies. Equal suffrage was not to be a part of that policy.[21]

Chase had optimistically believed since mid-April that Johnson could be persuaded to his position. In New Orleans he had advised a committee of freedmen that because they were citizens, they were "entitled to the rights of citizens," implying that the right to vote would soon be theirs. Chase was therefore bitterly disappointed with Johnson's proclamations. The president, he said, had made "a moral, political and practical mistake," because "the vanquished rebels were ready to accept, though of course reluctantly, universal suffrage." He urged Sumner not to give up hope; Congress would surely refuse to admit southern governments "with lily-white electorates." Ultimately, he suggested, a constitutional amendment might be necessary to assure "the instincts of humanity and the voice of justice."[22]

Sumner responded that many Republicans wanted to work with the president, but he concluded that Reconstruction policies could not be promulgated by presidential proclamation. On his return to Washington in late summer, Chase was inclined to agree with Sumner. When he called on the president, he found him "less cordial than before I went South," and anxious to shorten the interview. Johnson was not interested in arguments for black suffrage and talked instead of the dangers of black legislators and congressmen, "maybe black Governors and possibly . . . a black President." Chase's reaction was typical of an increasing number of Republicans: "Are we all to go under," he asked, "or will Congress save the country?"[23]

Andrew Johnson made it clear during the remainder of 1865 that he intended to carry out his own Reconstruction program without consulting Congress. The provisional governors he appointed were men who had opposed secession in 1861 but had shown little concern for equal rights. The constitutional conventions they were to call had merely to ratify the Thirteenth Amendment abolishing slavery, nullify secession, and repudiate state debts incurred during the period of the Confederacy and the state would qualify for readmission. Johnson's suggestions to Mississippi Governor William L. Sharkey revealed how far from Chase's program the president had moved. He urged Sharkey to give the vote only to those blacks who owned $250 worth of property or were literate; he would thus "completely disarm the adversary." This concession would not jeopardize white supremacy, he said, because only about one in ten blacks would qualify and "the radicals who are wild upon negro franchise will be completely foiled."[24] As Johnson became more secure in the presidency, his willingness to defy the Republicans increased. At the same time, Chase's early optimism gave way to the realization that the president could not be persuaded from his desire to maintain southern society with little change.

Johnson also showed no interest in land confiscation and redistribution. His amnesty proclamation restored the land belonging to those pardoned, and the Freedmen's Bureau controlled insufficient land to make major inroads into the problem through grants. On August 16, 1865, Johnson ordered all lands restored; any hope for significant suffrage and land distribution now rested with Congress. Chase told Parsons: "I am afraid of the executive policy of reorganization." Justice, he said, demanded that all be given the right to vote; he still hoped "that Congress will insist on this and that the President will reconsider his programme."[25] Chase and many other Republicans were becoming aware that Johnson's policy was not reconstruction but restoration. Under restoration Johnson could count on Democratic support in the North and the aid of pragmatic southern whites; and perhaps he could further divide Republicans.

Johnson's actions encouraged the southern governments to resist meaningful change, thus intensifying the anger of Republicans as Congress convened in December. None of the legislatures or conventions accepted or even seriously considered the limited suffrage proposed by the president, and two, Mississippi and Texas, refused even to ratify the Thirteenth Amendment abolishing slavery. The legislatures began instead to enact black codes denying freedmen civil rights and restricting their economic opportunities. To the outside observer, the South appeared headed toward a full restoration of its prewar society. Republicans in Congress, despite major differences among themselves, agreed that vast changes were necessary in the South and that Congress should determine whether newly elected representatives should be readmitted. They decided instead of accepting the elected southern delegates, to create a joint committee of nine representatives and six senators to consider more deliberately the entire Reconstruction process. At this point the majority, which constituted the moderate-conservative wing of the Republican party, was still eager to reach an accommodation with the president but was equally determined to have a major voice in the process. Most hoped with Chase "that all will come out well if Congress stands firm, and we also, while earnest, are conciliatory."[26]

As the scene shifted to Congress and the confrontation between Johnson and the Congress intensified, Chase found himself an observer only, although far from a passive one. Congress passed two bills in early 1866 which were immediately vetoed by the president, indicating that the possibility of compromise was remote. The first renewed the life of the Freedmen's Bureau and expanded its jurisdiction and authority. Johnson vetoed it on February 19, with Congress unable to override despite strong Republican support. When the president publicly denounced those Republicans as traitors in an intemperate speech, Congress responded with a modified Freedmen's Bureau proposal which was again vetoed but this time overridden.[27] Despite the endorsement of every cabinet member save Welles, Johnson also vetoed a moderate civil rights bill granting blacks citizenship but stopping short of enfranchisement. This veto was also overridden, and it was clear to Chase that there was little chance of compromise.[28]

The Joint Committee on Reconstruction drafted a proposed amendment to the Constitution which it reported to Congress as a possible basis for the readmission of the seceded states. For six weeks Congress debated, before passing on June 13, the complex proposal which defined blacks as citizens and prohibited the states from abridging "the privileges or immunities" of citizens or denying "any person of life, liberty or property without due process of law." The amendment only indirectly required suffrage by proportionally reducing congressional representation in those states which refused to grant it; thus, the ultimate decision on suffrage was left to the states. The amendment also disqualified from office former federal officials who had served in the Confederacy, although Congress could "remove such disability" by a two-thirds vote of each house.[29] The amendment was a victory for moderate Republicans. As such it accurately reflected northern thinking in June 1866. Many Republicans hoped the measure might even please Andrew Johnson and many in the North who opposed black voting rights.

Chase's reaction to the debate in Congress was to endorse the amendment in principle, all the time wishing he could be a part of the discussion so that he might work to strengthen it. Although arguing that Congress might have to accept some modification, he said the proposal was "on the whole fair and just." Most important, it would "facilitate . . . equal suffrage for all." Chase was willing to accept the amendment's indirect endorsement of black suffrage even though it fell far short of the full approval he sought. Perhaps he realized that the mood in Congress and in northern states would not support a more stringent requirement. Throughout the congressional debates and ensuing ratification struggle, Chase felt frustration and regret that he could not "throw off the judicial robes" and assist those who were "upholding the right."[30]

Ratification of the Fourteenth Amendment in the rest of the South was not so easily achieved, especially after the president openly urged its rejection. The proposed amendment quickly became pivotal in the 1866 congressional elections. A racial disturbance in Memphis which cost forty-six lives and an attack in New Orleans by a white mob on a black suffrage convention, with the loss of forty lives, added to the tensions. While on a preelection speaking tour, Johnson further provoked northern voters by blaming "traitorous" Republicans for the racial unrest and defending the "loyal" South. In retaining their three to one majority in Congress, the Republicans apparently won an endorsement of the Fourteenth Amendment and their Reconstruction policies. In Chase's eyes, the people "vindicated Congress" and made "every scheme of usurpation impossible." Ratification, however, would still require the support of at least four former Confederate states, an unlikely prospect in light of Johnson's position.[31]

Chase took no public part in the ratification campaign, but he made his position abundantly clear in correspondence. Johnson, he wrote, should have left the issue to the states, because his opposition separated him from those "who were really attached to him" and gave new "strength to men who are no friends of his." Originally hopeful that ratification was possible, Chase became less optimistic with the president's hardening stand.[32] He even attempted to reconcile Johnson's differences with Republicans by proposing to substitute a clause in the amendment which combined "universal suffrage with universal amnesty" in place of the reduction in representation and the clause disqualifying Confederate leaders from holding office. He urged this compromise in two personal interviews with Johnson to no avail. Chase thus concentrated his efforts on persuading friends in the South to push for ratification. Chase urged quick action in Alabama, but he was told by a supporter there that the president's opposition produced the cry, "We can't desert our President," and the legislature soon rejected the amendment. As other southern states followed suit, it became apparent that Congress would have to determine the next step.[33]

Throughout the struggle, Chase emphasized the importance of universal suffrage, although he came to accept a general amnesty policy as a means to achieve it. He had called for suffrage for "every male citizen" in a bill applying to the District of Columbia which he had suggested to Republican congressmen in late 1865.[34] In answer to critics who suggested that his activist role in behalf of blacks would "lower the dignity of the bench and damage my own," he responded that he hoped he would always "have courage enough" to serve "the cause of humanity." To Chase, the position "that all freemen are entitled to suffrage upon equal terms" was "an axiom of free government." He advised federal judges in the South that the courts had a role to perform in removing prejudice against black suffrage.[35] He supported blacks who organized in behalf of their own suffrage, advising John M. Langston of the National Equal Rights League of the advantages of united action. And he accepted an honorary presidency of a committee of freedmen seeking equal rights in Baltimore. But as Reconstruction policy remained unresolved in Washington, he began to see a way out of the stalemate through a combination of amnesty and suffrage. Governments, he argued, should work toward "conciliation and restoration, and exert the prerogative of mercy rather than that of justice."[36]

Chase was no longer in complete accord with the more radical Republicans. Many were unwilling to consider his amnesty proposal.

The issue of military occupation of the South especially concerned him as Congress enacted the first Reconstruction act on March 2 over Johnson's veto. The bill, drafted by John Sherman, divided the ten unreconstructed states into five military districts. This was too moderate for many Republicans. The already existing governments were to be considered provisional only, subject to the authority of the occupation forces. Initially, Chase agreed that military rule was necessary, and he had implied as much in his letters to Johnson during his southern tour of May 1865. He explained to Gerrit Smith in May 1866 that until the states were restored on the basis of "full recognition of the freedom" of blacks, they "must remain subject to such military control as is necessary to maintain freedom and order." So he did not oppose the act of March 2, 1867 or its amending act on March 23. The plan after all provided that military occupation would end when a state ratified the Fourteenth Amendment and adopted a constitution providing for black suffrage, and those were his major goals in any plan of restoration.[37]

Chase did fear, however, that Congress was attempting "to supercede the President as the Commander of the army" by giving General Grant sole power of review over the conduct of district commanders. The Command of the Army Act of March 2, 1867 required that all orders by the president to the army be issued by the general of the army. Chase thought the act of July 19, 1867 also went too far in giving the military commanders power to remove state and local officials and in making the state governments completely subordinate to military rule.[38]

Chase's growing reservations about military government in the South were based on a number of factors which had been accumulating since the end of the war. Especially critical in his view was what a military presence would do to the independence of the federal judiciary. The immediate issue at war's end was the holding of circuit court in those areas of the South occupied by federal troops. Chase and Justice James M. Wayne were most directly affected; the Chief Justice's circuit included the occupied states of Virginia, North Carolina, and South Carolina, and Wayne's much of the rest of the South. When asked by the president in the fall of 1865 when he planned to attend a term of the court in Virginia, Chase said he wanted to wait until "the complete restoration" of the southern states "and the supersedure of the military by the civil administration." He believed that a civil court in an area under martial law could only act "by the sanction and under the supervision of military power." It would not be appropriate for "the justices of the Supreme Court to exercise jurisdiction." In this opinion he indicated he had the full support of Justice Wayne. Chase advised the various district judges that they could organize and even hold their courts without a Supreme Court justice in attendance, but he encouraged them to avoid conflict with the military.[39]

Chase hoped that the president would revoke martial law and the suspension of habeas corpus, thus removing any "claim that the judicial is subordinate to the military power." There could be no question, he told Greeley, that the Court "cannot with propriety or decency be subordinated to any military authority." The opposition of Chase and his Supreme Court colleagues to a military role in judicial matters was revealed even more forcefully in the Court's decision in 1866 in *Ex Parte Milligan*. In that case the Court ruled that a military court could not function in an area where martial law was not in force.[40]

On August 20, 1866, Johnson proclaimed that "peace, order, tranquility and civil authority now exist" in the South. A month earlier, Congress had passed a judiciary act that reduced the number of Supreme Court justices to seven but failed to assign the justices to the realigned circuits. The lawmakers did not remedy this omission until March 1867, and Chase thus avoided going to his circuit until the summer session of that year.[41] By that time the Reconstruction act of July 19, 1867, was about to become law, and that led the chief justice to his first open show of unhappiness with the congressional plan of Reconstruction.

Despite his initial willingness to support military governments in the South, Chase had never been comfortable with such control over civilians during peacetime. In June 1867, he addressed the members of the bar in Raleigh, North Carolina as he prepared to open the first circuit court to be held in the southern states since secession. He noted with relief that because military control over the civil tribunals had been revoked and habeas corpus restored, he could now carry out his circuit court duties. He explained that "military authority in civil matters" had been abrogated and no longer extended to the federal courts. Later in 1867, the chief justice showed his determination to maintain the supremacy of the courts over the military by sharply rebuking General Daniel E. Sickles for challenging the federal court's jurisdiction over some of his soldiers in North Carolina. Said Chase: "The Reconstruction Acts, in my judgment, authorized no such interference."[42]

Chase's concern over the role of the military intensified when the Reconstruction bill under consideration in July gave military officials the power to remove civil officials and appoint their successors. Chase could agree with the power to remove state officials who "put themselves in the way of reconstruction," but their successors must be "elected by *universal suffrage*," not appointed by military officials. He believed that the best solution was for the southern governments to comply promptly with the congressional terms for Reconstruction by ratifying the Fourteenth Amendment and adopting a state constitution granting black suffrage. With all states thus readmitted, "real harmony founded on real justice and general good will" could be reestablished. Although still trusted by radical Republicans, Chase had come to doubt the wisdom of the congressional approach by the time of the Reconstruction act of July 1867. Genuinely desirous of less harsh terms for the restoration of the South than Congress intended, he feared the consequences of the program now emerging. His goal was still "the earliest possible reorganization under the Constitution securing to all equal rights," whereas too many members of Congress appeared to him more interested in "whatever seems most harsh on the rebels."[43] This difference combined with his opposition to military rule and the challenge it presented to the independence of the judiciary were early manifestations of Chase's eventual break with the Republicans. Political differences had not yet become obvious, but the chief justice had begun to feel by 1867 that his personal power was being challenged by the congressional plan of Reconstruction.

Despite his increasing unhappiness with the congressional program, Chase found himself caught in the middle in the accelerating hostility between the president and Congress. In March 1867, Congress passed the Tenure of Office Act, requiring Senate consent for dismissal of cabinet members as well as other officials whose appointment had necessitated Senate approval. The act was designed to protect Secretary Stanton from dismissal by Johnson because of his support of and efforts to enforce congressional Reconstruction. Johnson waited until Congress adjourned and in August suspended Stanton and appointed General Grant as interim secretary. Chase advised Johnson against the move, because "the restoration of the rebel States" and universal suffrage were being forgotten in the struggle. In early August, just prior to suspending Stanton, Johnson had sought Chase's opinion on the removal of General Philip H. Sheridan, commander of the Louisiana-Texas district. Lines of communication between the president and chief justice had not yet been totally severed. Chase, anticipating congressional anger, had warned against removing Sheridan for Johnson's "own sake and for that of the country," but the president proceeded anyway.[44] Johnson's vetoes and removal of federal officials opposed to his policies combined with the military domination insisted on by Congress set the executive and legislative branches on a collision course. Talk of impeachment of the president intensified, and Chase found himself in an increasingly uncomfortable position.

Other issues dividing the president and Congress also involved Chase and made his position difficult. Long before the conflict reached its climax, Chase played a critical role in the dispute over whether to try Jefferson Davis for treason. The chief justice was faced with balancing the concerns for a fair trial with the competing demands of many northerners for Davis's execution as Confederate president. Because of the commonly held belief that Davis was implicated in the Lincoln assassination plot, Johnson offered a $100,000 reward for his capture. Davis was arrested on May 10, 1865, and Chase, who was on his southern tour at Hilton Head, South Carolina, observed the steamer carrying the Confederate president to prison. He explained to Johnson that he did not let any of his party see Davis, not wishing to "make a show of a fallen enemy." But he also congratulated the president that "the arch leader of the rebellion is now in your hands."[45]

Public opinion in the North demanded a quick trial, a feeling reflected in a number of resolutions introduced in Congress as well as in the president's position. The cabinet agreed that treason should be the charge and that the trial should be held in the Virginia district court under Chase's jurisdiction—a location chosen because of the Confederacy's capital in Richmond. Whether a conviction would be possible from a Richmond jury was uncertain. Sumner noted his "regret that Jeff Davis was not shot at the time of his capture." At first, the president saw no need to hesitate, and on Chase's return to

Washington in August 1865, immediately planned a conference with him to consider "the time, place, and manner of trial." Technically, the district judge, John C. Underwood, could have heard the case, but all assumed that in a trial of this magnitude the presence of the chief justice would be necessary to give the proceedings the fullest judicial authority. The fact that Underwood, an undisguised partisan Republican, implied he might attempt to pack the jury to insure a conviction made Chase's participation almost mandatory. As Greeley told Chase, Underwood would "be out of his depth on such an occasion."[46]

Chase was reluctant at first to be a part of the trial because it was to be held in an area where martial law was still in effect. He told his friend Jacob Schuckers that although the lower courts might function, "members of the Supreme Court could not properly hold any court" in an area subject "in any degree, to military control." When Greeley urged him to preside anyway, Chase responded that he would only after "a proper proclamation of the President" ending martial law. During the delay, Judge Underwood added to the pressure by securing a grand jury indictment of Davis for treason which accused him of "falsely, wickedly, maliciously and traitorously" commanding his subordinates "to make and carry on war" against the United States. As with other cases in the circuit, Chase used the failure of the judicial act of July 1866 to set new circuit boundaries to delay the trial further despite the president's proclamation in August ending martial law. In doing so, he faced additional pressure from the president, who on his campaign tour in the fall of 1866, responded to hecklers' cries of "Hang Jeff Davis" with "Why don't Judge Chase. . . . Why don't he try him?" Chase's hesitancy stemmed from several sources. He feared that a Richmond jury would never convict a fellow southerner; Greeley predicted: "We all know that he *isn't to be* convicted."[47] Even with a conviction for treason, Davis could have received as light a sentence as a fine of $10,000 and imprisonment of ten years or less. The trial might easily be an embarrassment to Chase, whether or not a guilty verdict was returned.

Until Congress passed the necessary legislation in March 1867, assigning Supreme Court justices to specific circuits, Chase was quite willing to delay the proceedings. After that it was the administration which was less than eager to hurry, apparently fearing a not guilty verdict which might hurt the president politically. Judge Underwood set May 13, 1867 for the trial, but when it became evident that the prosecution would not be ready, the judge agreed to a postponement. He also agreed to a habeas corpus writ, releasing Davis from military custody and setting bail at $100,000.[48]

Sentiment changed dramatically in the two years following Davis's arrest, and although many including the president still hoped for a conviction, it was now clear that Davis had known nothing of the assassination plot. Many still sought revenge on the South through a Davis trial, but others, including Chase, were no longer so concerned with punishment as they were for a restoration of full peace between North and South. The chief justice continued to advocate amnesty for Confederate leaders in return for universal suffrage; his desire was to put the hatred of the war years in the past.

In the succeeding efforts to bring Davis to trial in 1867 and 1868 Chase pleaded on several occasions that the crush of Supreme Court business in Washington prevented his appearance in Richmond. In the fall of 1867, Chase told Underwood to plan for a November trial, but when it was finally scheduled for late that month, he explained that the December term of the Supreme Court would prevent his presence for "more than four or five days."[49] Since Davis's attorneys had refused an earlier date when Chase could be present, administration lawyers, William M. Evarts and Richard Henry Dana, moved for a postponement until the next term of the court in March 1868. Almost three years after his arrest, a trial for Jefferson Davis was finally a real possibility. But Chase was unavailable in late March because he had to preside at the president's impeachment trial, so Underwood delayed the Davis proceedings until May 2. This date also proved unworkable when the Senate trial dragged on. Attorney Evarts, himself exhausted by the impeachment proceedings, then asked the court for a delay of the Davis case until the fall.

By the time that Chase was finally ready to preside in June 1868, interest in a trial had declined dramatically. Perhaps this is exactly what Chase had hoped for, because with the ratification of the Fourteenth Amendment completed in July 1868, dropping the case seemed more logical than ever. The third section of the amendment disqualified Confederate leaders from officeholding, and Chase now argued that this precluded any other punishment for Davis's acts. When the case came before the circuit court again in November 1868, Chase and Underwood disagreed on the defense motion that the case be dismissed because the Fourteenth Amendment barred any further legal action. President Johnson then issued a complete amnesty proclamation on Christmas Day 1868, and in February 1869, the government dismissed the case.[50] A proceeding that Chase had been reluctant to pursue originally was finally dropped after four tortuous years without ever coming to trial. To Chase, Johnson, and an increasing number of northerners, punishing Jefferson Davis no longer seemed as important as it had in 1865.

Chase's role in the Davis case drew attention to his position as chief justice and to that of the Supreme Court in the intensifying Reconstruction disputes. The Court did not seek confrontation during the Johnson presidency, but it did play an active role and under Chase's leadership maintained its independence against the threat of congressional intimidation. At the time of Chase's appointment, he was asked to preside over a court which had remained in the background during the war years, but whose members had sharply differing views on the issues separating North and South.

Four justices, appointed before Lincoln's election, came from Democratic, states' rights backgrounds. They included James M. Wayne of Georgia, appointed by Andrew Jackson in 1835; Samuel Nelson of New York, appointed by John Tyler in 1845; Robert C. Grier of Pennsylvania, appointed by James K. Polk in 1846; and Nathan Clifford of Maine, appointed by James Buchanan in 1857. Chase's appointment in December 1864 following the death of Roger B. Taney was Lincoln's fifth opportunity to name a Supreme Court justice. Of those he appointed, two could be counted as strong supporters of congressional Reconstruction, Noah H. Swayne of Ohio and Samuel F. Miller of Iowa. David Davis, a personal friend of Lincoln, political ally, and manager of his 1860 nomination, was assumed to stand against many Republican proposals, as was Stephen J. Field of California, a War Democrat with a narrow view of national government power. Chase was believed to be a supporter of congressional Reconstruction because of his advocacy of black suffrage. Many assumed, too, that he would endorse a more limited role for the national government on economic questions because of his own Democratic antecedents; these people failed to reckon with the changes his philosophy underwent while Chase was secretary of the Treasury.[51]

The diverse group over which Chase presided got along better with each other than might have been expected, the result in part of the chief justice's firm but conciliatory leadership. The members sat as a unit only from December until April each year and attended to their own circuit court responsibilities for the remainder of the year. During the months they worked together Chase sought to keep on good terms with them both individually and collectively and especially to overcome the suspicions of several justices concerning his political ambitions and their fear that he would attempt to dominate their proceedings. Apparently he succeeded even with Justice Davis who had been the most critical and suspicious of Chase at the time of his appointment. After a difference of interpretation in 1867 on a technical question in which Chase admitted his error, Davis's response indicated how attitudes had changed in two years. "I have learned to like and esteem you, and if I were allowed to speak for my brethren, I think I could say you have been growing in their confidence and attachment, ever since your accession to the bench. You certainly have in mine."[52]

Part of the reason Chase's stature improved in the eyes of a potentially hostile group of justices was his commitment to hard work through hours of preparation. Because of his fifteen-year absence from the practice of law he had some catching up to do, and he impressed his colleagues with his willingness to immerse himself in even the most pedestrian litigation. He told Senator Sprague in 1866 that he planned to spend two and a half months "hard at work on my cases," to prepare for the December term. His close attention to oral arguments in court and his forceful written opinions, based on a careful and objective study of the evidence, impressed his fellow justices and helped create a more unified court than most would have predicted.[53]

During the 1864–65 session, few important cases were pending, a situation which permitted Chase to adjust more easily to his new role. A review of circuit court judgments with little federal law involved characterized most of the Court's work. Although not especially interested in much of the unspectacular work in cases involving real property, contracts, trusts, and commercial transactions, Chase nevertheless exerted strong leadership throughout his years on the Court, and before 1871 he had written more opinions than any other justice in any court term except one. For the most part he tried to confine his leadership to cases growing out of the war. During his first two years on the bench, he was especially active in prize and confiscation cases involving ships taken in areas of southern waters where federal authority had been restored. Here he had significant background, having been responsible for such trade as secretary of the Treasury. He was quick to master admiralty law, and his decisions on prize cases were regarded by most as fair and conciliatory.[54] He also used his Treasury experience to take a leading role in tax and banking cases. Thus, despite any discontent he might have felt from being out of the political spotlight, he did his job well and offered the judicial leadership expected of a chief justice.

There were in fact many obstacles to effective leadership. The Supreme Court had enjoyed little prestige since the Dred Scott decision of 1857. And following the war, differences among the justices could be expected to resurface; finding a common position on the controversial issues of Reconstruction would be especially difficult as the conflicts over military occupation of the South reached the Court.

During Chase's tenure as chief justice, the Supreme Court, although frequently divided, tended to see the Reconstruction process as a political one to be left to the legislative and executive branches. In most cases the Court's belief in judicial self-restraint on political questions meant that it felt judicial intervention was inappropriate. In maintaining its basically neutral position, the Court in effect allowed Congress to have its way on most issues, more because the justices agreed with the legislators for constitutional reasons than because of intimidation as some have claimed.[55] Three early decisions alarmed radical Republicans, however, because they could be construed as a challenge to congressional Reconstruction in the South. In all three instances, the Court divided five to four, with Chase taking the more moderate minority position which was less willing to challenge congressional authority.

The first significant case with implications for Reconstruction policy involved an Indiana Copperhead, Lambdin P. Milligan, who had been found guilty by a military commission of conspiracy to overthrow the government by setting free Confederate prisoners and plotting to take over the state governments of Ohio, Indiana, and Illinois. Shortly before the war ended, a military court in Indiana sentenced Milligan to death by hanging; he then sought release by habeas corpus, arguing that the military had no right to try him in an area where martial law did not exist. The decision of the Court in *Ex parte Milligan* was handed down in April 1866, although the opinions were not issued until December. The Court agreed unanimously that the military commission's authority to try such a case had not been specifically granted by Congress because the offense had not occurred in an area of military operation. Chase, Wayne, Miller, and Swayne argued that Congress "in a time of public danger . . . had the power under the Constitution to provide for the organization of a military commission" even if the federal courts continued to operate, although because it had not issued such permission in this instance, Milligan's court martial had been illegal.[56]

The majority, in an opinion written by Justice Davis and endorsed by four Democratic justices, went further in arguing that neither Congress nor the President could authorize military trials of civilians under any circumstances when civil courts were operating. This opinion had clear ramifications for the future, for in setting aside military authority outside of a war zone, it might jeopardize plans of some Republicans for military rule during Reconstruction; the South after 1865 could no longer be considered a war zone.[57]

In two other decisions handed down in January 1867, the Court, by five to four votes, appeared ready to challenge congressional plans for the South. In both cases involving test oaths of loyal conduct during the war, Chase was in the minority with Republicans Swayne, Miller, and Davis, voting to sustain the oaths, whereas the five Democrats on the bench, led by Field, determined them to be unconstitutional. In the more controversial of the two, *Cummings* v. *Missouri,* the Court struck down an oath prescribed by the Missouri constitution of 1865 requiring officeholders, voters, attorneys, and clergymen to swear they had never in any way supported the Confederate cause. John A. Cummings was a Roman Catholic priest who had performed the rites of his church without taking the test oath. The oath had become an issue in the state election of 1866 with Republicans arguing for its validation and Democrats demanding it be declared unconstitutional. The decision was finally announced after the Missouri Republicans had won the state election. Chase agreed with the dissenting opinion of Justice Miller that no punishment was being inflicted in requiring such an oath. Although he felt the oath was "detestable," he argued that the state must nevertheless be permitted to regulate suffrage and professions of public significance.[58]

Chase did not address the implications of his opinion for the issue of state regulation of suffrage, but he must have known that with such authority the states might effectively nullify any black voting.

The other case, *Ex parte Garland,* was concluded on the same day and involved the Federal Test Act of 1865, which required attorneys to take an oath similar to that in Missouri before practicing in federal courts. As with the Missouri oath, the majority declared it unconstitutional, for neither Congress nor the states could pass a bill of attainder or ex post facto law. The Court argued that the oath provided punishment for acts of disloyalty committed before the law was enacted. Again Chase joined with Miller's dissent which argued that Congress could impose what qualifications it felt necessary because the practice of law was a privilege and not an absolute right. In both instances Chase and the three dissenting justices believed that the Court should not interfere with the political aspects of Reconstruction. After the decision there was much protest in the press and in Congress over what appeared to some as the Court's efforts to challenge congressional Reconstruction. The protest went to the extent of the House passing a bill requiring two-thirds of the justices to declare an act of Congress unconstitutional. Although the Senate took no action on the issue, the minority on the Court would soon find additional support for its belief that the justices should avoid further confrontations with Congress.[59]

The case that revealed that the Court was not prepared to challenge Congress more directly than it had in the Milligan and test oath suits was concluded in April 1867. It is clear, however, that rather than having been intimidated by Congress, the Court in *Mississippi* v. *Johnson* wisely determined not to use a highly dubious opportunity to declare the Reconstruction acts unconstitutional. The suit was brought by attorneys for the state of Mississippi, which was about to be displaced by a military district headed by army officers. The state sought to prevent the president from enforcing the Reconstruction acts of March 1867 establishing military government, alleging them to be unconstitutional. Chase spoke for a unanimous Court and refused to accept jurisdiction or to rule on the acts' constitutionality. The president, who opposed the legislation which had become law only over his veto, argued through Attorney General Henry Stanbery, that it was his duty to carry out the law and that there was no precedent for the Court restraining him.[60]

The chief justice and his colleagues agreed that they had no authority to prevent the president from performing an "executive and political" duty. Far from evading the issue as critics charged, the Court merely recognized that the president had a duty to carry out the legislation. In recognition of the separation of powers principle, Chase argued the impracticality of issuing an injunction against the president: "If the President refuse obedience, it is needless to observe that the Court is without power to enforce its process." If, on the other hand, the president complied with the Court and refused "to execute the acts of Congress, is it not clear that a collision may occur between the executive and legislative departments of the government? May not the House of Representatives impeach the President for such refusal?" Chase concluded elegantly with a rhetorical question: "And in that case could this Court interfere in behalf of the President, thus endangered by compliance with its mandate, and restrain by injunction the Senate of the United States from sitting as a court of impeachment?" The justices reaffirmed this position by rejecting a subsequent effort of Georgia to restrain Secretary of War Stanton from putting the same acts into effect.[61] Again the unanimous Court prudently refrained from challenging the Reconstruction legislation. To act differently would have needlessly angered a Congress still unhappy over the test oath decisions and placed the Court on questionable grounds.

The other significant litigation involving the congressional Reconstruction program during Chase's tenure as chief justice occurred during and shortly after the impeachment controversy. The circumstances surrounding the first of these cases, *Ex parte McCardle*, revealed that Congress would tolerate no interference with its Reconstruction program. William H. McCardle was a Mississippi editor who had questioned the authority of Congress to establish military tribunals. He had been tried for writing "libelous and incendiary" articles about Reconstruction which the tribunal concluded were incitements to insurrection and disorder. McCardle, in petitioning for a writ of habeas corpus, argued that the court which convicted him existed by an unconstitutional act of Congress. His appeal was taken to the Supreme Court from the circuit court under a law of February 1867 which broadened the Supreme Court's jurisdiction to include habeas corpus suits. Chase, in speaking for the court, concluded in February 1868 that it could properly hear Mc-

Cardle's appeal.[62] It was clear that the Court would have to determine the validity of at least part of the Reconstruction legislation in hearing the appeal.

Recognizing this threat to its program, Congress acted to remove Supreme Court jurisdiction, and on March 27, 1868 overrode Johnson's veto of the bill repealing that part of the 1867 law which gave McCardle the right to appeal the circuit court decision to the Supreme Court.[63] The new law affected only one case immediately— that of McCardle. The Court waited while Congress overrode the veto, for as Chase noted: "It would not become the Supreme Court to hasten their decision of an appeal for the purpose of getting ahead of the legislation of Congress." The justices then agreed over the objection of Field and Grier to postpone further consideration of the suit. Finally, a year later, the Court unanimously dismissed the McCardle case on the grounds that the new act of Congress had removed its jurisdiction in the case. Although Congress legislated to prevent the Court from interfering, the Court did not capitulate. As Chase explained: "The Constitution gives to the Supreme Court jurisdiction of appeals only with such exception and under such regulations as the Congress shall make." Congress acted legally, albeit harshly, in removing Supreme Court jurisdiction and, said Chase, "We are not at liberty to inquire into the motives of the legislature." Chase and his colleagues had no choice but to back away from confrontation, but in so doing, they retained their stature with unimpaired authority to deal with future Reconstruction legislation.[64]

During the following year, Chase and the Court had the opportunity to reaffirm their position that the terms of Reconstruction were basically a political rather than judicial matter, although the question of military commissions operating within the occupied South was of judicial concern. In *Texas* v. *White*, the chief justice and his colleagues endorsed the congressional Reconstruction process as well as the Republican view of secession and the status of the states that had left the Union. The case involved an effort by the Johnson government in Texas to recover title to United States bonds that had been sold by the Confederate state government during the war for the purchase of rebel supplies. In ruling five to three (Grier, Swayne, and Miller dissenting), the majority held that the actions of the Confederate government of Texas were invalid and that Texas had never ceased to be a state in the Union. "The Constitution," said Chase, "was ordained 'to form a more perfect Union.' " The fundamental law, he continued, "in all its provisions looks to an indestructible Union, composed of indestructible States." Texas, in joining the Union, had "entered into an indissoluble relation," as much so "as the union between the original States." After secession occurred, Congress had the constitutional duty to reorganize the states, recognizing that the nature of the population had changed from before the war. Said Chase: "The new freedmen necessarily became a part of the people," and a state could not be restored until the whole population was granted suffrage. Although not commenting on the constitutionality of the specific Reconstruction acts, the Court nonetheless recognized the right of Congress to set the terms for reestablishing the states in the Union and its duty to guarantee to each state a republican form of government.[65] The majority thus took the opportunity to endorse Chase's major beliefs on secession, Reconstruction, and suffrage. It also continued the tradition of judicial self-restraint on political questions.

A ruling later in 1869 gave the Court one more opportunity to deal with the constitutionality of the military governments in the South, and although it accepted jurisdiction of the case, a means of compromise short of confrontation was again found. The case, *Ex parte Yerger,* involved Mississippian, Edward M. Yerger, who had been found guilty by a military commission of killing an army officer and who now sought release on a writ of habeas corpus. By the time his case reached the Supreme Court, the peak of emotionalism over Reconstruction had passed and Congress was about to readmit Mississippi to the Union. Chase ruled for the Court that it had jurisdiction under the Federal Judiciary Act of 1789.[66] The case proceeded no further, however, because Yerger's counsel and Attorney General Ebenezer R. Hoar agreed to turn the plaintiff over to state authorities after Mississippi was recognized by Congress in early 1870. With each of the remaining southern states on the verge of readmittance, it appeared likely that there would be no state to which a court decision on the constitutionality of Reconstruction would apply. Since the Court might rule against the federal government, the Grant administration was quite willing to turn jurisdiction back to state officials. And the Supreme Court seemed equally willing to avoid an unnecessary confrontation with Congress. Little could be accomplished by directly challenging Congress, and the Court thus felt it had not compromised itself by allowing Mississippi to deal with Yerger.[67]

Although Reconstruction issues were far from settled in 1869, the Court's role concerning the status of military government had declined in significance. From the Milligan case of 1866 to that of Yerger in 1869, the Supreme Court, in large part through Chase's skillful leadership, had maintained its prestige and authority yet had avoided needlessly antagonizing the Republican dominated Congress which, if pushed too far, might have threatened the Court's independence. The willingness of the Court under Chase's leadership to validate so much of the congressional Reconstruction program thus indicated a prudent realism rather than any basic support for the policies of Congress.

With the Reconstruction controversies at their peak during the Johnson presidency, Chase had also to attend to many other judicial duties not directly related to the struggles between Johnson and Congress. Among his most important functions was that of presiding judge of the Fourth United States Circuit Court. He may have exaggerated when he told a friend: "It is only as a circuit judge that the Chief Justice or any Justice of the Supreme Court has, individually, any considerable power." The importance of Chase's role was nevertheless great.[68] The fourth circuit included Maryland, Virginia, West Virginia, North Carolina, and South Carolina, with courts in Baltimore; Richmond; Charleston, West Virginia; Raleigh; and Charleston, South Carolina. After the controversy over the military occupation of the three former Confederate states in his circuit ended, Chase regularly attended circuit court to the extent that his Supreme Court duties and health permitted. He kept in close touch with the judges of his circuit, guiding them through correspondence when other duties prevented his attendance in their courts.

There were occasional judicial and political problems in his circuit. His most difficult relationship was with Judge John C. Underwood of the United States District Court in Virginia, who proved an embarrassment because of his lack of discretion and excessive support of the Republican goals and methods. In late 1868, Underwood tried to void the judgments of several Virginia judges who became ineligible to hold office under the terms of the Fourteenth Amendment barring former Confederate officials. Underwood was prepared to release several prisoners sentenced earlier by these judges when

Chase intervened and forced him to change his mind. Chase then made a point of being in Richmond for the circuit court sessions as much as possible rather than letting the judge hear cases by himself. With Justice Wayne in precarious health, Chase assumed some duties in his circuit as well. Chase also tried to intervene but without success in Alabama, where Judge Richard Busteed caused problems similar to those of Underwood by "acting like a madman."[69]

Chase faced controversy in judicial patronage as well. Within his own circuit he clashed in 1867 with Judge William Giles who preferred to fill vacancies in his court with fellow Democrats rather than with the loyal Republicans Chase and his party wanted. A compromise was reached when both Giles and Chase gave up their favorites to a third candidate for commissioner of the court. Friendly relations between the two were then restored with Chase noting that his "profound and sincere" esteem for Giles was based on "my confidence in your rectitude, your learnings and your ability."[70]

Chase's most difficult patronage problem followed the passage of the Bankruptcy Act on March 2, 1867, which provided that the chief justice nominate the registrars of bankruptcy to assist the district courts. Senator Sherman and others argued that this additional responsibility would prevent Chase "from performing the ordinary functions of his office," but efforts to amend the bill failed. Chase soon complained bitterly about the time involved, describing to daughter Nettie the constant coming and going of candidates in his office "to press their applications in person." Requests were "exceedingly numerous," with "four or five clerks constantly employed" for the purpose, and the machinery looking like "that of a regular bureau." Chase might complain, but he had apparently done little to prevent the provisions from becoming law. Justice David Davis noted unsympathetically: "The Chief Justice has drawn an 'elephant' and has so found out." Davis felt Chase could have stopped the bill before it passed, "for he was advised in relation to it." Instead, he had accepted the patronage power and complained only when he discovered too late what a burden it imposed.[71]

Chase also used his position to try to persuade Congress to reduce the size of the Court and increase the pay of the justices accordingly. He was only partially successful. An act of Congress of July 1866 reduced the court's size to seven by providing that the next two vacancies not be filled. Members of the Court, led by Chase, actively supported the bill, which included a realignment of the circuits and a reduction of the circuit duties of the Supreme Court justices. Chase made it clear in his correspondence with other Court members that the major purpose in reducing the size of the Court was to use the revenue saved to increase the pay of those on the Court. He felt that their pay "ought not to be less than those of the highest Military Officers." Accordingly, he proposed that the $6,000 salary for associate justices and $6,500 for the chief justice be raised to $10,000 and $12,000, respectively. As he explained to Senator Sprague: "No Judge can now live and pay his travelling expenses on his salary." The bill that Andrew Johnson signed, however, contained no salary increases. In the rush of Reconstruction legislation, Congress had not been sufficiently moved by the plea of Chase and his brethren. In subsequent years, the chief justice would try again, although in the meantime, he lost much of the personal support of the Republicans in Congress over his handling of the impeachment trial of Andrew Johnson.[72]

Johnson's impeachment trial during the spring of 1868 was the culmination of the deterioration of relations between the more radical and the chief justice and finally led to Chase's decision to break with his fellow Republicans. Many Republicans had begun to realize in early 1867 that Chase could not be relied on to back up their plans for the South when he questioned the legitimacy of the military government there. Even before that he had displeased many Republicans with his refusal to sit with the circuit court wherever military government existed. By the summer of 1867, he openly advocated less harsh terms of Reconstruction and a faster restoration of the southern states as well as the pardoning of former Confederate leaders. Although the Supreme Court under his leadership avoided direct confrontation with Congress, it became clear during 1867 that the differences in philosophy could not be kept submerged indefinitely. Chase's opinion for the Court in February 1868 that it would hear the appeal of William H. McCardle challenging the military government in Mississippi indicated that the constitutionality of the Reconstruction legislation in 1867 was in jeopardy. It was toward the end of February that the House of Representatives voted to impeach the president. Chase as chief justice, would now be the presiding officer at the trial in the Senate. Short of giving in completely to the demands of radical senators, Chase had no way to avoid the confrontation.

By the time the trial opened, many Republicans suspected that Chase could not be counted on to put party ahead of adherence to strict legal procedure. When the president attended the weekly Wednesday reception at Chase's home on March 4, mistrust of the chief justice increased. According to rumor, Chase sympathized with Johnson and did not believe there was enough evidence to convict him. Republican senators knew that the previous year Chase had urged the president to abandon his own policy "in favor of restoration and universal suffrage" in order to avoid impeachment. Chase, in fact, admitted to a friend that his sympathies were with Johnson, for "I remembered his loyalty at the outset of the war and his patriotism all through it." But he claimed complete objectivity in the trial: "as a judge I can recognize no party obligation whatever." He explained further that ever since Johnson had established a provisional government in North Carolina in May 1865 without providing for black suffrage, he had opposed his plans. Instead, Chase endorsed the Congressional policy "so far as it contemplated equal rights for all," although he did not "believe in military domination any more than . . . in slaveholding oligarchy." Civil government "regulated by Congress" could have accomplished everything that military occupation had achieved. He concluded that although opposed to Johnson's "attempt to impose on the colored population of the South the rule of the ex-rebel population . . . I have not thought it necessary to revile him." [73]

When Andrew Johnson removed Secretary Stanton from the War Department for the second time in February, the House drew up eleven articles of impeachment which charged him with violating the Tenure of Office Act as well as attempting to "bring into disgrace, ridicule, hatred, contempt, and reproach the Congress of the United States." [74] Senate leaders planned to conduct the trial as if it were a political proceeding and thus to consider allegations against the president not necessarily confined to specific legal offenses. Rather than a court of law, which would bind them to the rules of legal evidence, they were prepared to consider testimony having little to do with offenses defined by federal law. In contrast, Chase made his position clear at a meeting with Senate leaders on February 26, when he argued that for the trial, the Senate was a court which must follow the rules of a judicial proceeding. As the presiding judge, he intended to have his powers respected as he would in any court; additionally, his powers would include those of the vice president as presiding officer of the Senate. Thus he must be permitted to rule on points of evidence, including the power to vote in case of ties. He argued forcefully in a letter on March 4 that the Senate must "sit as a court" made up of the senators, "with the Chief Justice presiding." When the Senate adopted its procedural rules for the trial without further consultation with him, Chase indicated that no such rules could be formulated until the Senate formally organized itself as a court. Thus when the trial opened on March 5 and the Senate officially adopted its rules again, the differences became public and were even more difficult to resolve.[75]

Following an elaborate swearing-in ceremony in which Chase administered the oath to each senator and Justice Samuel Nelson did the same for Chase, the prosecution made it clear that Republican leaders intended to run the trial themselves and over the chief justice's objections if necessary. Officially they acquiesced in Chase's interpretation of the rules of procedure, thus giving the impression that they recognized impeachment as a judicial rather than political procedure. It was soon obvious, however, that they were humoring Chase rather than accepting his leadership. House manager Benjamin Butler opened for the prosecution by claiming the political rather than judicial nature of the proceedings, reminding the senators that they were "bound by no law." Rather, he said, "You are a law unto yourselves, bound only by the natural principles of equality and justice." As Chase explained to Gerrit Smith: "I feel and am felt as a sort of foreign element" in the Senate. He looked to the Constitution "for my powers and duties," but the senators had their own interpretation of those powers.[76]

The chief justice and the senators frequently clashed over rules of procedure. When Chase cast a tie-breaking vote on a minor point, Senator Charles Sumner moved that such a vote was illegal, arguing that because Chase was not a member of the Senate he "has no authority to vote on any question during the trial." Sumner's motion failed to carry, but Chase found the situation alarming. What would his duty be if the Senate had denied him "the casting vote which belongs to the President of the Senate . . . so refusing, in effect, to recognize my right to preside?" Although not forced to answer the question, Chase was surely disturbed that long-time friends like Sumner had turned against him. The Senate sustained his right to make rulings, although his interpretations were subject to appeal by a single senator's request. With a close vote on conviction expected and many senators still undecided, many Republicans continued to view Chase as a threat to their drive to remove the president. Chase's rulings established his position that during the trial the Senate was a court and as such "a distinct body from the Senate sitting in its legislative capacity." [77] The trial would thus be conducted according to the rules of judicial procedure and the chief justice would have the authority of a presiding officer.

The issue for which Chase's rulings were more critical involved the president's violation of the Tenure of Office Act. Especially important was any evidence that might explain Johnson's motives for removing Stanton, because the defense maintained that Johnson had been trying to protect the powers of the presidency against infringement by Congress and thus had acted only to bring a test case to the courts. On this issue the Senate overruled Chase's opinion that the testimony of Generals Lorenzo Thomas and William T. Sherman was relevant. Excluding such evidence over the ruling of the chief justice did little to win additional support for conviction and may instead have served to improve Johnson's chances for acquittal. Perhaps even more damage to the prosecution occurred when the Senate overturned Chase's ruling on the testimony of Secretary of Navy Gideon Welles. If allowed to testify, Welles would have argued that the cabinet as a whole felt the Tenure of Office Act unconstitutional and had agreed with Johnson that a test case should be pursued. Stanton himself had helped prepare the bill's veto message. Yet by a vote of 20 to 29 the Senate rejected the chief justice's argument that Welles should be allowed to testify because he could clarify the issue of the president's intent in removing Stanton. Chase agreed privately that in this instance it was "the clear duty of the President to disregard the law" to force a test of the law's constitutionality. Republican leaders had won their point but had not added to their strength. [78]

Chase won much sympathy and support by his unsuccessful efforts to defy the Senate. Even the *New York Tribune* believed Chase should have power to rule and indicated its lack of "sympathy with the men who have been denouncing him." Former Chase antagonist

Gideon Welles now praised him for his firm leadership and called it "ridiculous to see such . . . small lights sit in their seats and overrule the Chief Justice on law points." Prominent Democrats, such as John Dash Van Buren of New York, were less than objective themselves and began talking of Chase as their own candidate in the fall presidential election; they noted that only the chief justice had gained reputation during the trial: "You have gained it by simply refusing to turn either to the right hand or the left." The *New York Herald* concluded: "Chief Justice Chase stands prominently before the country today as the people's candidate for the Presidency."[79]

As the trial came to a close and the outcome remained in doubt, Chase privately noted that "my own judgment and feeling favors acquittal." He decried the efforts of outside groups, including "legislatures, political conventions, even religious bodies," to tell senators how to vote. He felt it was "of the utmost consequence" that senators be left alone to vote their consciences. Pressure on undecided senators increased dramatically as the day of the vote neared. When the lawmakers finally voted on May 16, all of Washington waited anxiously for the verdict. During the roll call, tensions mounted as the result remained in doubt to all, including the dignified Chief Justice, until the very end. As the drama unfolded seven moderate Republicans joined with the twelve Democrats to give Johnson the bare minimum number of votes to prevent conviction.[80]

Many factors had combined to bring a verdict of not guilty. The trial had dragged on for eleven weeks so that the emotional atmosphere demanding conviction in March could not be sustained through May. Some opposed conviction because the charges were based more on political than judicial reasons; they thus endorsed the position that Chase had maintained from the start. Others feared that the precedent of removing a president for political reasons might threaten the balance of power between legislative and executive branches. Chase wondered "what possible harm" could result if Johnson remained president a few more months, "compared with that which must arise if impeachment becomes a mere mode of getting rid of an obnoxious President?" Johnson had moderated his actions during the last months, strengthening his chances for acquittal. The Republican nomination of Ulysses S. Grant before the final Senate vote on May 26 may also have dampened the spirit of those seeking Johnson's removal, for there seemed no reason to exacerbate an issue that might hurt the party in the fall.[81]

Among the factors which influenced Chase's actions was his dislike and distrust of the president pro tem. of the Senate, Benjamin Wade, who would become president if Johnson were convicted. The chief justice had earlier asked Gerrit Smith to raise the question publicly of whether his long-time rival Wade would be considered merely acting president while retaining his position in the Senate. Chase had even prepared an oath of office for Wade in which he would agree to act "as President of the United States until a President shall have been elected." While never a friend of Wade, Chase regretted that ill-feelings had developed with some Republican associates. Relations with Charles Sumner resumed their former closeness after the fall election but were not restored with Stanton. At the time of the secretary of war's death the following year, Chase lamented that "the alienation was always painful to me," and he had always hoped that "it might be healed." But Chase made few overtures to his Republican colleagues. After the Senate vote on May 16, Chase claimed that the important thing was not acquittal or conviction, but that the senators "should render an honest and impartial judgment according to the Constitution and the laws." He defended his own role in the trial and claimed to have been "perfectly unbiased."[82] Many Republicans disagreed.

Some chose Chase as a scapegoat for their failure to convict the president. Some professed to believe that he had been part of a conspiracy to influence the outcome and had "neglected no opportunity to stab the prosecution by his rulings." They claimed he had contrived to influence the votes of the seven moderate Republicans who supported acquittal. Horace Greeley's *New York Tribune* charged that Chase had influenced Senators Peter G. Van Winkle of West Virginia and John B. Henderson of Missouri and had tried unsuccessfully to persuade his son-in-law William Sprague in the same direction. He had thus "done more than all others . . . to secure the result." Chase's response to such charges was that "I have not exerted myself to influence anybody one way or the other." To stories of dinners with Henderson and rides in the country with Van Winkle, Chase denied all "except that there is a grain of fact sunk in gallons of falsehood." He denied having predicted the outcome and claimed that there was "no man in the country who had less personal interest in the result than myself."[83] Although Chase exaggerated his impartiality, his conduct of the trial had been clearly that of an objective chief justice of the Supreme Court rather than a partisan. He had courageously maintained his judicial independence in the face of heavy Republican pressure.

Not all were convinced that Chase had been so disinterested as he claimed. Many assumed that he still wanted badly to be president. The probability of Grant's receiving the Republican nomination was increasing daily, and all other aspirants were virtually eliminated even before the trial began. In all likelihood, the trial itself was the final factor convincing Chase that any presidential future he had was as a Democrat. He had been visibly upset by the Senate's reversal of his rulings and the Republican desire to convert the trial into a largely political event. The slowly evolving differences with Republicans in both the House and the Senate and the role of the Court in regard to military government in the South also climaxed in the spring of 1868. Having broken with Andrew Johnson over Reconstruction policies, Chase had concluded that the Republican approach to the South was equally unacceptable. To such Republican critics as James Garfield, who had once been Chase's close friend, the chief justice had not only used his influence to convince wavering senators but he was "trying to break the Republican party and make himself President by the aid of the Democracy." Although Chase denied any interest in a nomination and argued: "The subject of the Presidency has become distasteful to me," few in either party believed his disclaimers.[84]

10

Chief Justice as Presidential Candidate

S almon Chase had never been content to confine his years as chief justice to judicial matters, and he therefore surprised few when his interest in politics accelerated as the presidential election of 1868 neared. Long before his role in the impeachment trial had completed his break with Republican colleagues, he had been considering a return to a more active political life. He had found the life of a Supreme Court justice "rather irksome," surmising that had he been appointed before becoming "so largely identified with political measures," he would have been more content. To his critics, his every action on the Court had a political motive. His southern tour of May 1865, they said, was designed to seek support for the 1868 Republican nomination. Especially with his close friend Cincinnati journalist Whitelaw Reid describing the trip in detail for northern readers, it could be viewed as a campaign tour. Although such an interpretation depreciated his genuine concern for southern conditions and black suffrage, the tour did afford Chase some opportunity to assess his chances for a nomination.[1] And for his first three years as chief justice there were good reasons to believe that some Republicans still viewed him as a possible candidate for the presidency.

Until mid 1867, Chase remained in basic support of congressional Reconstruction. When President Johnson turned his back on Chase's proposals and alienated many of his northern supporters, Chase agreed that the only chance for an equitable policy was with the Republican members of Congress. Never happy with the military occupation of the South or Republican desire for harsh treatment of Confederate leaders, he nevertheless accepted much of their program. Through mid 1867, he avoided any public criticism of congressional Reconstruction and helped steer the Court away from a confrontation. And throughout the period he privately entertained ambitions for the presidency. In late 1866, he told Schuckers that he was "not indifferent" to the talk of his candidacy; to another supporter he stressed the need for Ohio to be united behind him before he considered actively seeking the nomination. As had happened so often in the past, his friends consistently told him that his chances were improving and that they were working strenuously in his behalf. As in the past, unfortunately, they were making few concrete organizational efforts. Unlike in earlier campaigns, Chase's position as chief justice made any open efforts in his behalf more difficult.[2] Also by 1866 Ulysses S. Grant had already emerged as a formidable rival whose popularity almost assured his nomination.

Grant's reputation as the general who defeated the Confederacy made him a war hero with unparalleled status. His early identification with Johnson's approach to Reconstruction had worried many Republicans, but by 1867 he endorsed the congressional program. Chase had been preferred by some party leaders until many state elections in 1867 went against the Republicans and pointed to the need for someone with more popular appeal. In 1867, the Democrats improved their showing substantially, in part by a blatant appeal to antiblack sentiment in the North. As a result, Republicans not only wanted a candidate with public appeal, but also one who could blunt the potency of Democratic racism. That candidate might be one with no public record on the racial issue or one whose personal popularity made racism secondary. In either case, Chase's chances declined, and Grant, who had said little about the suffrage issue, found his position even stronger.[3]

Chase was probably correct when he told daughter Nettie before the state elections that "if there were no military names before the public, the choice of the people might fall upon me." But, he concluded, the nomination of Grant or some other general by the Republicans "is a predestined event." By 1867 Chase openly questioned military rule in the South and was increasingly unhappy with Republican policies. In early 1868, Chase admitted that Grant would get the nomination if he wanted it, a belief which no doubt made it easier for him to challenge the Republican efforts to make the impeachment trial a political event. Nonetheless, the primary reason for his break was one of principle rather than politics. After the first vote in the Senate at the impeachment trial on May 16, 1868, Republican leaders won a ten-day recess over Chase's opposition. During the interim, they hoped to find the additional vote necessary for conviction; they also increased their attacks on Chase for his handling of the trial. Before the Senate reconvened, the Republican party met in convention and nominated Grant for president. Chase would now have to look for support elsewhere if he intended to pursue the presidency.[4]

As soon as Grant's nomination appeared assured and Chase's differences with the party became public, the chief justice considered again his political future as a Democrat. Despite his leading role in Republican politics since the party's formation in 1854, a switch in parties would not be inconsistent with his political philosophy. Since joining the Liberty party in 1841, Chase had been primarily concerned with stopping the spread of slavery. As a Liberty and Free-Soil leader, he had worked strenuously to bring the Democratic party to a position on slavery which would permit its merger with an antislavery party. Although unable to move the Democrats because of the dominance of southerners, Chase never fully gave up his efforts. Instrumental in changing the name of the Free-Soil party to Free Democratic, he had supported Democrats over third-party candidates in Ohio in 1851 in the hopes of forging a coalition. On such economic issues as the tariff and banking he supported the Democratic position. But the passage of the Kansas-Nebraska Act in 1854 dashed any chance of the Democrats embracing anti-extensionism, and he assumed a leadership role in the new Republican party. There he had remained through the Civil War despite three disappointments in his search for the presidency. Now with Grant's nomination and his differences with party leaders deepening, it was quite natural for him to reconsider the Democrats.

The first sign of such a move came in early 1868. Chase's response to early inquiries was that he was "neither candidate nor aspirant for any political place or distinction," noting that his judicial position eliminated him from any consideration for a nomination. He was "not a suitable candidate for either party." As chief justice he was asked to rule on numerous issues of political import, and he could not maintain the impartiality required of his position and also please party leaders. He concluded: "I can not be a party judge." Nevertheless, as his differences with Republicans at the impeachment trial became obvious, some Democrats began to talk enthusiastically of his candidacy. Especially in the New York and Cincinnati press, discussion began in earnest by late March. Even though a backer of Grant, *New York Sun* editor Charles Dana proposed the Democrats nominate Chase and allow the country to choose between the country's two most prominent men. Murat Halstead's *Cincinnati Commercial* as well as the *Cincinnati Gazette* urged his nomination. Others were more skeptical that Chase could be nominated even if he agreed to run. William Cullen Bryant's *New York Evening Post* found him to be an excellent choice but feared that Democrats would not "be sufficiently wise or superior to their prejudices" to select him. Greeley's *New York Tribune* viewed such talk as Democratic bribery of the chief justice; moreover, the paper predicted that nothing would "deter him from his duty."[5]

Among prominent northern Democrats urging Chase to consider joining their party were John Dash Van Buren, Samuel J. Tilden, and Alexander Long. Van Buren, a young New York reporter and protégé of Tilden, wrote a series of laudatory letters urging Chase to become a candidate, while Tilden, an influential Democrat and longtime Chase friend since Barnburner days, worked behind the scenes on his behalf. Long, a Cincinnati lawyer and Peace Democrat who had been Chase's longtime foe in Ohio politics, was also a rival of Cincinnatian George H. Pendleton, a major contender for the nomination. Long thus hoped to deny Pendleton with Chase's nomination. Chase's first response was that he would not be a candidate, but Long urged him to reconsider if the platform conformed to his position. To Chase, such a platform meant "suffrage for all; amnesty for all," and if the Democrats accepted his position, Chase said: "I should not be at liberty to refuse the use of my name." Long therefore accelerated his efforts for Chase, working especially with Chase's secretary Jacob W. Schuckers in the ensuing weeks to win supporters. By early May, other Democrats were joining the movement and the *New York Herald* was urging the party to nominate Chase to "rally the masses of the country."[6]

Much in Chase's position appealed to Democrats in both North and South. Because he was against military occupation and in favor of general amnesty, many Democrats responded to him enthusiastically. There were serious flaws in his candidacy, too, most notably his advocacy of universal manhood suffrage. Far fewer Democrats than Republicans shared his enthusiasm for blacks voting. Those who did had been long-standing supporters and were working to convince other Democrats of their point of view. As Schuckers told Long, southern whites had little to fear from black suffrage, a "small price for relief from their own political liabilities." Most Democrats agreed instead with the *New York World* that party members "may be unable to revoke what has been done; but they certainly are not going to endorse" black suffrage as Chase would have them do. New York Democratic leader Sanford Church spoke for many when he rejected the nomination of Chase on an equal suffrage platform and insisted that "we can win with a Democrat."[7]

The solution for many was to leave suffrage to the individual states rather than prescribing it by the central government. The Republican platform inconsistently defended the action of Congress insisting on black suffrage in the South, although "in all the loyal States" it "properly belongs to the people of those States." To many Democrats, on the other hand, southern as well as northern states should make their own decision. Chase thought that the readmission of the seceded states must be on the basis of universal suffrage. At this time he did not indicate whether this should be achieved through a constitutional amendment binding the North as well, although he implied that Congress should simply require it of the South. Moreover, he would "refuse the throne of the world if it were offered me at the price of abandoning the cause of equal rights and exact justice to all men."[8]

During the month before the convention Chase rethought and finally modified his position on suffrage, and interest in his candidacy began to grow. There had been limited talk during May among conservative Republicans who were unhappy with the Grant nomination that a third party with Chase as its candidate appeared promising. The most prominent advocate was James Gordon Bennett's *New York Herald,* which called for a "fusion of all the anti-radical elements" combining dissident Republicans and northern Democrats. Chase remained noncommittal, however, and the idea died. Chase and his supporters felt instead that the Democratic party was a much more promising vehicle for his presidential nomination. On

June 10, in Philadelphia a committee formed to seek support for a Chase nomination. It included Long, Van Buren, Schuckers, Hiram Barney, John Cisco, and Chase's daughter Kate Sprague. It arranged for a Chase headquarters at the Chamber House on Fourteenth Street directly opposite Tammany Hall, site of the convention.[9] But beyond editorial support in New York and Cincinnati, the Chase campaign lacked effective organization and direction.

As in previous campaigns, Chase confined his activities to letters to supporters and other influential Democrats, arguing that his position as chief justice required him to remain in the background. But he indicated his willingness to run if the platform were acceptable. To Manton Marble, editor of the *New York World,* he outlined his political views and explained his Republican past. Only the slavery issue had forced him to remain separate from the Democrats despite his election to the Senate in 1849 by a Democratic-Free-Soil coalition. He felt that "upon questions of finance, commerce and administration generally, the old Democratic principles afford the best guidance." On Reconstruction issues, he attacked radical Republicans for "the establishment of despotic, military government" and the authorization of "military commissions for the trial of civilians in time of peace." He sought to heal differences between North and South "by acts of genuine kindness and sincere good will." Still claiming that he did not seek a nomination, he insisted that the opinions he expressed must "not be published as my views and that my name . . . not be connected with them if printed." He was mortified to find his instructions immediately violated, and he feared it would "be taken as evidence that I seek the Democratic nomination and also to dictate the platform."[10]

Reaction to his candidacy varied according to party and philosophy. For the most part, Republican friends were shocked and disappointed that he would consider a Democratic nomination. Although publicly silent, Jay Cooke expressed regret to his brother that "Chase's overweening desire . . . for the Presidency" led him to union with "Copperheads." Despite his friendship, Cooke indicated that he and his friends would "stick by Grant." Many Democrats failed to respond as well. The Blairs were vocal in their opposition, with Montgomery unable to imagine that any Democrat could seriously consider Chase. Other longtime Democrats, such as Arphaxed Loomis of New York, claimed Chase's candidacy had "great defects" and argued that his name would have "no strength with Democrats." The *New York Leader,* organ for Tammany Hall and strong advocate of the nomination of Horatio Seymour, claimed confidently by mid-June that the Chase movement was dying.[11]

Chase's supporters felt otherwise and labored to convince their candidate and fellow Democrats that only Chase could defeat Grant. Bennett's *Herald* remained among his strongest advocates, suggesting that "all other Democrats have too many liabilities." Seymour, who had earlier announced he was not a candidate himself, expressed interest in Chase especially after persuasive arguments by Tilden and Van Buren. Other New York leaders, such as William Cullen Bryant and Samuel L. M. Barlow, joined in the effort and all sought to convince Chase that his candidacy could be successful. Chase expressed surprise at the extent of his New York backing. Barlow explained that many Democrats supported Chase out of necessity "to show that there is no practical barrier between the races." John L. Trowbridge, the author of Chase's 1864 biography, suggested a new edition "at this time when your very prominent position" might otherwise be misunderstood. Long, Van Buren, Cisco, and Barney, all wrote optimistically that the party was moving in his direction. Chase alone was more realistic, having been disappointed so often in the past. With the suffrage issue in mind, he wrote pessimistically to Schuckers that "the talk about me will come to nothing. The Democracy is not democratic enough yet."[12]

Chase recognized that a Democratic nomination could be achieved only by modifying his stand on suffrage, a change he finally determined to accept. Schuckers told him in early June of the "tenacity" with which Democrats "cling to the theory that the States must regulate suffrage," and that leaves "little hope . . . for any results to the discussion of your name." By June 18, with the Democratic convention less than three weeks away, Chase told a southern editor of the "wisdom and expediency" of leaving suffrage to the States, although he was not yet prepared to agree that Congress had no power over the issue. At the same time, he asked his old abolitionist friend Gerrit Smith whether it would "not be my duty to accept" a Democratic nomination on a platform endorsing universal suffrage "to be applied in the states by the states." He claimed that while in Richmond recently for the circuit court, he observed the "great progress made in the South" toward acceptance of the principle and a desire to do "justice to the black citizens." On the eve of the convention he could argue that although "all disfranchisements and disabilities" should be removed in the South, suffrage "is for the people of the States themselves" to decide, "not for outsiders."[13]

Chase's new position was made public on July 1 in a fifteen point platform drawn up with Van Buren's assistance. Chase described the statement as one on which "all democrats may consistently and harmoniously stand together." Few could argue realistically that if suffrage were left to the states that blacks would be granted the vote in the foreseeable future. Chase was seeking approval when he suggested that Smith and others like him recognized that "nothing in what I have done or declared" was inconsistent with his "faith in Human Rights."[14]

Chase's new stance on suffrage was consistent with congressional sponsorship of the Fourteenth Amendment, which implied that states had this power. In that sense, Chase agreed with the majority of Republicans and did not abandon black rights. Moreover, the Republican platform on black suffrage in 1868 also suggested that voting regulations were a state matter. In essence, Republicans had somewhat evasively accepted suffrage as a state concern—both in a major constitutional amendment and in their platform. On that basis, Chase could move to the Democrats and try to get them to come to terms with an issue that was both complex and significant. Chase's candidacy for the Democratic nomination was based on a firm reading of that political reality. Thus it was not simply expediency on Chase's part to suggest state suffrage, nor an abandonment of blacks, although he altered his position to better his chance for the nomination. The key to his hopes rested on Democratic acceptance of the compromise that the Fourteenth Amendment suggested—state suffrage. If Democrats would officially end the racial politics which had been so potent an issue in the state elections of 1867, both his interests and those of black Americans would be served.

Another question of contention which Chase addressed in his platform was the proposal to pay off the debt with paper money. At issue especially was whether payment of the 5–20 bonds negotiated by Chase during the war should be in gold or paper. Former Congressman Pendleton endorsed the greenback proposal, but it was resisted in many Democratic circles, particularly among easterners led by

Horatio Seymour and national party chairman August Belmont. Despite his acceptance of paper currency to finance the war, Chase's basic philosophy and past record advocated the hard money position. Since the end of the war the Supreme Court had not faced the issue, but it was known that Chase opposed the Pendleton plan and supported "an early return to specie payments." Pendleton was also a serious contender for the Democratic nomination, and his proposal won him significant support in Ohio and among other western Democrats. Long reminded Chase that the Pendleton men were capitalizing on the controversy by claiming "that you cannot support the Greenback issue and that you are the candidate of the Eastern bondholders." As a result Chase modified his opposition somewhat. He endorsed "the honest payment of the public debt" but suggested that creditors were not "entitled to special favor." With this carefully phrased statement, Chase again appeared eager to please both sides.[15]

Several days before the convention opened Long encouraged Chase to pledge to support whomever the Democrats nominated. Long felt that such a position might improve his chances for a nomination, and Chase indicated his qualified agreement. He immediately regretted having done so, telling Van Buren: "I have never in my life bound myself to the support of unknown candidates before an unknown platform, nor have I ever asked such promises from anybody." He requested that Van Buren prevent Long from publicizing his agreement, but newspapers in Cincinnati and New York soon contained the story. It did Chase's chances little good, for it could be interpreted as an indication of his willingness to withdraw from the race; it also served to embarrass the chief justice in his efforts to appear above the political struggle.[16]

Lacking the optimism of many of his advocates, Chase was better prepared to accept the disappointing results of the convention. Because of Pendleton's following in Ohio, the chief justice was not surprised to learn before the convention opened that Ohio's delegation was seriously divided. A lack of united support from his own state was all too familiar to Chase. With the convention scheduled to open on July 4, the Chase committee met on the third. Since the delegates were expected to be divided among several candidates with none having the necessary strength for an early nomination, the committee agreed that Chase not be placed in nomination immediately; instead, his name would be presented as a compromise choice only after the expected deadlock developed among Pendleton, Senator Thomas A. Hendricks of Indiana, General Winfield S. Hancock, Francis P. Blair, Jr., and Andrew Johnson. Frederick A. Aiken, a member of the Chase committee, told Chase that Horatio Seymour would nominate him "at the proper time." At that point Bennett's *Herald* agreed that Seymour was "an active worker for Chase" and "out of the fight as a candidate." Chase remained in Washington during the proceedings, thanking his many supporters and agreeing to "acquiesce cheerfully" if the convention chose someone else.[17]

Kate Sprague shared his realism but continued to hope for a change from past misfortunes. Still highly ambitious for herself and her father, she envisioned herself as "the presiding lady at the White House." Critics even suggested that Chase's desire to be president was "less due to his own ambition than to his elder daughter's." Her residence on Fifth Avenue was a center of activity before and during the convention as she met numerous Chase partisans, most notably New York leaders August Belmont and Samuel Tilden. Despite her eagerness, she adopted Chase's official line that he was in no sense "seeking the Democratic nomination." When consulting with trusted followers, she was much more direct. On several occasions, Chase cautioned her against too active a role in his behalf. In 1864 he had urged "that she should keep entirely aloof from everything connected with politics." Regarding more recent proceedings at Tammany Hall he admonished: "you are acting too much the politician." Having been a part of his past disappointments, she knew that success was unlikely, and on the eve of the convention she wrote to her father that she was relieved he would not be disappointed if not chosen: "I would like to see this bright jewel added to your *brow* of earthly distinctions and I *believe* it *will* be, but we can live and be happy and just as proud of you without it. Will the country do as well?"[18]

The adoption of the platform gave both Chase and his daughter every reason to be pessimistic because it reflected the influence of Pendleton and Blair. It endorsed the greenback proposal of the Pendleton men, which he opposed, and the platform's vehement attack on Republican Reconstruction was too strong to please the chief justice, despite his own differences with Congress. Although he might agree with its criticism of the military occupation and tribu-

Kate Chase after the war. From Alice Hunt Sokoloff, *Kate Chase for the Defense* (New York: Dodd, Mead, 1971).

nals established in the South, its argument that the Reconstruction legislation was "unconstitutional, revolutionary, and void" would, said Chase, force many to support Grant and the Republicans. Voters would reject a declaration that seemed to say, "Let us have war." He could not have agreed that the congressional program had subjected the South to "negro supremacy." Most serious was the platform's lack of commitment even to the general concept of universal suffrage. Although he had backed away from his earlier stance by suggesting that the states should be encouraged to enact black suffrage, the platform insisted instead that suffrage had always been the exclusive right of the states and any attempt of the federal government to prescribe conditions for voting would be "unqualified despotism." Chase nevertheless maintained a brave front when he wrote to Van Buren that the platform was "in the main, very good." To Kate he explained he could accept it, "but I can't say that I like it."[19] He must have known that it did not auger well for his chances for a nomination.

The balloting went as expected with the two-thirds rule preventing any of the many candidates from approaching the number necessary for nomination. Through the first fifteen ballots Pendleton led, with Hendricks, Hancock, and Johnson showing some strength. Hancock led on ballots sixteen through twenty-one and Hendricks on the twenty-second. Because Chase's supporters held his name in reserve, the position of the New York and Ohio delegations became critical. John Van Buren, who acted as Chase's unofficial campaign manager, sought to persuade the New York delegates to support Chase. Instead, the delegation, at Seymour's urging, agreed to turn to Chase only if Hendricks's support began to decline. As the balloting continued through three days, Chase's strongest newspaper support, the *New York Herald,* called on Pendleton to withdraw gracefully and "accept an honorable position in Chase's Cabinet." It called on the Ohio delegation to take the lead in urging Chase, the people's choice, to lead the "opposition against the military dictators and Jacobins of Congress." Chase's name was mentioned by one California delegate on the sixteenth ballot and "was received with a burst of enthusiasm spontaneous and universal." But when Kate called on Van Buren to have her father's name placed in nomination, he could not find the necessary support in the New York delegation.[20]

In the confusion which followed on the last day of the balloting, Clement L. Vallandigham of the Ohio delegation, a supporter of Chase, withdrew Pendleton's name. Fearing the rise of Hendricks, Vallandigham urged Tilden to swing New York to Chase, a request Tilden refused because New York was committed to Hendricks as long as he remained a possibility. Vallandigham then determined that the only way to stop Hendricks was to nominate Seymour, a step another Ohio delegate took as the twenty-second ballot closed. Immediately, the states began abandoning their earlier commitments to rush to the Seymour bandwagon and he was quickly chosen by acclamation. Tempers were short and the delegates appeared more eager to go home and escape the heat of the city than to prolong the balloting any longer.[21]

That Seymour's name rather than Chase's was placed in nomination suggests that the chief justice and his supporters were out of touch with the mood of the convention and that his nomination had never been realistic. After an hour's recess, the delegates quickly nominated Chase's longtime foe, Francis P. Blair, Jr. for vice president. There was small consolation for Chase when the convention adopted a resolution before adjourning thanking him "for the justice, dignity, and impartiality with which he presided" over the impeachment trial.[22] The convention had its ticket, but politicians would spend the next several weeks debating how it had come about and how Chase had again been denied a presidential nomination.

Among the factors most important in the convention decision to turn to Seymour rather than Chase were the lack of support for the chief justice in the Ohio delegation, an awareness that he could not wholeheartedly endorse the platform, confusion among his own supporters as to the best strategy to follow, and the course pursued by New Yorkers Van Buren, Tilden, and Seymour himself. Of the Ohio delegation, Vallandigham supported the chief justice, but few others did. Hence the decision to propose Seymour when Hendricks appeared close to victory. Chase believed that this decision was a key factor in the outcome. He felt that Seymour sincerely sought Chase's nomination and "would have declared it had not the action of the Ohio delegation prevented it."[23]

Not all agreed that Seymour was such a disinterested bystander. Chase wondered later if his actions were "entirely candid." Kate

Sprague was critical of Van Buren as well as Seymour and Tilden. It was Van Buren, she claimed, who refused to take advantage of the atmosphere in Chase's favor created by the mention of his name by the California delegate, and thus in effect allowed the Seymour movement to develop. In her view, "Mr. Tilden and Mr. Seymour have done their work and Mr. Van Buren has been *their tool*." As a result, she told her father, he had been "cruelly deceived and shamefully used by the man whom you trusted implicitly." Chase clearly had trusted Van Buren and had urged Kate to put her full confidence in him.[24] Whether or not Chase believed his daughter and others of the same persuasion, he maintained his friendship and told Van Buren after the event: "I know you would not deceive."[25]

Part of the reason for Kate's anger was Van Buren's refusal to indicate to the New York delegation and others that Chase would accept the platform. Van Buren, she said, had advised her father "to answer no questions in regard to the platform." Chase in fact had deferred to his judgment on "all enquiries" about it, and according to Kate, this "was the block put in the way of your nomination." Hiram Barney agreed that had he been willing "to stand upon the same platform" he might have been chosen. Chase thus never publicly endorsed a platform he privately loathed but had told both Kate and Van Buren he could live with. He later told Gerrit Smith, he could have written "an interpretation of it acceptable to other members of the party and not inconsistent with my own views."[26] Whether he could have done so in good conscience or could have convinced enough delegates of his sincerity in doing so is problematic. Significantly, Chase never blamed Van Buren for a decision he may privately have agreed with.

Perhaps more serious than Van Buren's action on the platform was the lack of unity and cohesion among Chase's own supporters. Two key strategists, Alexander Long and Van Buren, never met before the convention, an indication of a lack of planning. Long later admitted that "we were so completely outwitted and outgeneraled," and he willingly accepted much of the blame himself. During the proceedings, Chase complained to Kate that there was little cohesion among his supporters and wished that "a few of my most discreet friends could and would consult together." There was little agreement on exactly when to put Chase's name forward, a question, said Van Buren, which "gave rise to much speech making which continued so long that I gave up in despair of action."[27] How important this confusion was to the outcome is debatable, but surely it did Chase's chances little good. As in 1856 and 1860, mismanagement of his candidacy by his supporters contributed to his failure.

Chase's leadership of the Democratic ticket in 1868 would have placed tremendous strains on a party which clearly did not wish to go in the direction he felt best. He had hoped that his nomination would provide a chance "of giving peace to the country and to its sections and its races." Those urging his nomination, he said, had hoped to unite "the opponents of certain obnoxious measures and tendencies of the Democratic party." His nomination was sought, he said, by those "who desired new and better issues," but the party "chose old issues which I couldn't accept."[28]

Chase's position, particularly on suffrage, was indeed one that the party could not accept. Few Democrats in North or South could support Chase's general endorsement of suffrage, even as modified before the convention. Success in the state elections in 1867 had shown that opposition to blacks voting was a potent issue. Thus, even though many Democrats recognized that a Chase nomination might give the party great respectability and undercut Republican charges of disunionism, more found the idea of his nomination unacceptable. Said one Democrat, "As I can perceive no other reason for the selection of the founder of the republican party than his supposed availability, I should deeply regret such a nomination by the Democracy." Many who had opposed him for a generation or more could not trust his leadership in 1868. As Chase explained to Elizur Wright, there was "too large a number of those with whom I have had to contend in times past and could not put off their old hostility." He professed to believe that the voters "outside of the convention" had wanted him but that the delegates had been chosen before this popular groundswell developed. Evidence is lacking that any such movement existed. Instead, the factors which denied Chase the nomination were that his old reputation still haunted him, his supporters were disunited, and his position on suffrage was unacceptable to most Democrats. Although he would be a factor in the ensuing campaign, he told Wright that he was "now separated from all political aspiration." Whatever chance he had had to use the presidency for realizing his goals was gone. "It shall hereafter be the limit of my ambition to do all the good I can" as chief justice.[29]

Taking no part in the campaign was made easier for Chase by the platform, which he found undesirable, and by a letter written by vice presidential candidate, Francis P. Blair, Jr. On June 30, Blair had written to Missouri lawyer James Brodhead that the only way to end Republican interference in the South was for the new president to declare the Reconstruction acts "null and void . . . , disperse the carpetbag State governments," and "allow the white people to reorganize their own governments." The Brodhead letter, which appeared before the convention opened, had major significance because the Blair supporters got their plank attacking the Reconstruction laws included in the platform and their candidate nominated for vice president. Few were surprised, therefore, when Chase planned no role in the campaign. Only Tammany Hall could unrealistically predict that Chase would endorse the platform and declare the nominations "eminently judicious and worthy of popular ratification." Noting that it was "plainly improper" for a Supreme Court justice to participate in the campaign, Chase pointed out that Blair's position and nomination "would deprive me of all power to be useful politically" anyway. He was sure that had Seymour had his choice, he "would have made a very different platform."[30]

Chase made it clear to close friends throughout the summer that Seymour was his personal choice over Grant but that he would probably not make the long trip to Ohio to vote. To Barney he confided that Seymour "is much better than the platform as Blair is worse." But, said Chase "we differ on some questions and I cannot vote for him." If unencumbered by the platform and the Brodhead letter, he would prefer Seymour to Grant.[31]

When Gerrit Smith and other friends urged him to support Grant, he responded that he saw no evidence that the general favored rights for blacks. Although acknowledging Grant's fine war record, he was "reluctant to give even an implied [approval] to the policy of military Governments for States and military Commissions for civilians" which the general's party endorsed. As a result he did not think it "worth while to travel five or six hundred miles" to vote in Cincinnati even if judicial duties did not already make the trip impossible. Rejecting proposals of Susan B. Anthony that he lead a third-party ticket, he concluded: "I mean to limit myself to the duties of a quieter sphere of usefulness."[32]

Seymour's chances were further jeopardized during the fall campaign. With the failure of the Democrats to make hoped-for gains in state elections in September and early October, a movement developed to force Seymour and Blair to step down as candidates and be replaced by a ticket headed by Chase. Democratic defeats in Maine, Pennsylvania, Ohio, and Indiana created enough panic among some Democrats to lead Manton Marble of the *New York World* to spearhead a drive to change the ticket at the last minute. There had been some talk immediately after the nominations that Seymour might refuse to accept. Long had told Seymour there was no chance of victory because of Blair's role; Long and others implied that he should still defer to Chase.[33] But Seymour persisted and was soon complaining that Chase's men were attacking him. Recognizing that Chase was not behind these efforts, he nevertheless asked Van Buren to urge Chase "to call off his Dogs" and show his "disapproval of their falsehoods." Chase was quick to grant his request and told his supporters: "Justice to Gov. Seymour is duty from us." Yet Chase reminded Van Buren that the platform and Blair's candidacy would "drive these dissatisfied Republicans" who had hoped for a Chase nomination "back to their party."[34]

Chase and his partisans did not instigate the movement to change the Democratic ticket, although some of the chief justice's more zealous followers did try to capitalize on it. New York Democrat Samuel L. M. Barlow and Manton Marble were the prime movers, and Barlow indicated on October 14 that "if Governor Seymour would now come out boldly for Chase, call a Convention here for next Monday . . . , in three weeks we can elect our President, carry a majority of Congress, [and] put an end to Radical rule." The *World* followed suit and Marble called on Democratic leaders to act. Although urging both Seymour and Blair to resign from the ticket, the paper emphasized more the need to remove Blair because he was a "much harder man" for many to vote for than Seymour. Tilden, because of his prominence in New York politics and his position on the Democratic national committee, received numerous requests asking that Chase replace Seymour. Said Vallandigham, "The new movement [will] almost certainly save us. Nothing else can."[35]

Chase wisely showed no interest in a movement which he felt could bring him only further embarrassment. He was advised by Van

Buren that Seymour might be persuaded to step down, but that "a change now would demoralize our own party" and would expose "the new candidates to certain defeat." The chief justice thus authorized Van Buren to release a letter from him saying that "under no circumstances would such a substitution be acceptable." Even so, Alexander Long was still enthusiastic for a Chase candidacy, noting that the demand for it was universal.[36]

Few others agreed, realizing a change at this late date could only expose the party to ridicule. Tammany's *New York Leader* called the *World* move a "blunder," whereas the *Herald* argued that "no more suicidal policy could be suggested by the worst enemy of the Democracy." With other Democratic papers agreeing, party leaders met at Tammany Hall on the nineteenth and reaffirmed their support of the Seymour-Blair ticket. Said the committee, the idea of a change "is regarded as absurd and is received by our masses with astonishment, derision and indignation." On election day, New Yorkers supported their former governor by a narrow margin; but Grant won the election by an electoral majority of 214 to 80 and a popular majority of more than 300,000 votes of close to six million cast. Chase concluded that the result was "best for the country, though I could not bring myself to make a choice. Anything certainly is better than Blair and revolution."[37]

Chase's disappointment in 1868 was somewhat eased by the movement which developed shortly after the election to extend blacks the right to vote by a constitutional amendment. He had retreated from universal suffrage during the 1868 campaign, conceding that the vote should be provided by state rather than federal action. He would thus have some difficulty moving back to his original position when the proposed Fifteenth Amendment was debated in Congress and state legislatures. The Republicans would also have to alter their platform position, which had advocated leaving suffrage to the states in areas outside of the South. Both parties knew that the majority of white voters North and South opposed extending voting rights to blacks. Not wanting to jeopardize Grant's election, the Republicans had refrained from urging federal action. But in the Reconstruction legislation of 1867 they had required that southern states include suffrage for blacks before being readmitted.

As late as 1868, the right to vote was still denied to blacks in eleven of twenty-one northern states and in all five border states, thus laying the Republicans open to charges of inconsistency and hypocrisy. But the party also recognized the tremendous political potential if all were given the vote, for one-sixth of the nation's blacks lived in the North and border states. While political expediency was a factor, many Republicans who supported suffrage in 1869 had also called for civil and political rights for blacks before, during, and after the war. Endorsing the amendment did involve some political risk—in some cases outweighing the political benefits that might be gained.[38] At the same time, Republicans knew that the overwhelming majority of northern and southern blacks would prefer them to the Democrats who had made their opposition very explicit.

Several northern states had turned down referendums on the issue since the war.[39] Chase had been especially embarrassed by the sizeable Ohio rejection in 1867 when the Democrats won control of both houses of the legislature and almost won the governorship.[40] Thus the Republicans had good political reasons not to press the issue during the presidential campaign of 1868. But they did control more than three-quarters of the state legislatures necessary to ratify a constitutional amendment; they thus might avoid the frequent rejection of the issue by referendums. Therefore, with Thaddeus Stevens leading the way, they devoted much of the third session of the Fortieth Congress opening in December 1868, to drafting the Fifteenth Amendment. The proposal they finally agreed to stated simply that the rights of citizens to vote "shall not be denied or abridged by the United States or any state, on account of race, color, or previous condition of servitude," with Congress given the power to enforce it by "appropriate legislation." Many congressmen realized that southern states might use literacy and property requirements to get around the intent of the amendment but feared ratification would be blocked if stronger terms were included.[41]

The ratification process involved the chief justice. Within four months of approval by Congress, all seventeen Republican-controlled legislatures which met in 1869 had ratified, whereas the four under Democratic control, including Ohio, had rejected it. Chase was eager that his state be included among those ratifying, especially with national approval not yet assured. But because of his position in 1868, his endorsement of the amendment was somewhat reluctant. He noted that although he still believed suffrage should be left to the states because "centralization and consolidation have gone far enough," he nonetheless favored the proposal as "the only way of settling this question, permanently and satisfactorily." Although unhappy that Congress retained the power to enforce the amendment, he felt that "this power will hardly be exercised to any extent if at all; . . . and the main principle of the amendment is right—equality of political rights for all citizens."[42]

While not initially enthusiastic about the amendment, Chase nevertheless worked behind the scenes to secure Ohio's ratification. He corresponded with several Ohio lawmakers, urging them to endorse the amendment. In particular, he asked Thomas H. Yeatman of Cincinnati to remind legislators that their support of the repeal of Ohio's black laws in 1849 had "secured" the state for years, and similar action now could have the same positive effect. He cautioned Yeatman that his letters to him were private, and, although Yeatman might share his views with others, the letters should not "get into print." His position as chief justice, he argued, prevented any open political activity. By January, it appeared that ratification by the required number of legislatures was assured, but with New York rescinding its earlier approval, a possibility still remained that Ohio's support would be necessary. Thus, said Chase, "if Ohio ratifies there can be no question."[43]

He was not to be disappointed, for a group of independent Cincinnati legislators joined with Republicans in January to push approval through over unanimous Democratic opposition. Ratification was achieved by the slenderist of margins, 19 to 18 in the Senate and 57 to 55 in the House. Chase wired Yeatman: "I congratulate you and the country."[44] He exuberantly told a group of Cincinnati blacks that equal suffrage had at last been "made part of the supreme law of the land."[45] Although some Republicans may have sought suffrage more for the sake of political expediency, not all had been so motivated, and Chase could be proud that he acted out of a belief in the principle of political equality which he had advocated since before the war's end.

Late in 1869, the Supreme Court finally faced another issue which had been pending ever since the war's end, that of currency. At stake was the constitutionality of the Legal Tender Act of 1862 which Chase had so reluctantly accepted while secretary of the Treasury. He had supported greenbacks as a necessary expedient to finance the escalating costs of the war. Toward the end of his tenure in the

Treasury he indicated his hope that greenbacks would be withdrawn as soon as the war ended and the country could return to the gold standard. "Inflated paper currency" was in his opinion a "great evil, and should be reformed as soon as possible." He argued that however unwise, Congress nevertheless had the constitutional authority to issue legal tender notes. But he had never looked on them as anything more than a temporary means for financing the war to be redeemed when the emergency ended. As Chase explained: "My whole plan has been that of a bullionist and not that of a mere paper-money man." Although forced "to substitute paper for specie for a time," he "never lost sight of the necessity of resumption."[46] His return to the hard money philosophy which he had advocated before the Civil War was thus one of principle rather than opportunism, for his policy as secretary of the Treasury had been followed reluctantly and only because of the emergency conditions created by war.

Resumption of specie payments was also the hope of Secretary of Treasury Hugh McCulloch after the war, and Congress soon began a policy of gradual reduction of the greenbacks in circulation. Chase supported the plan and argued that resumption should begin immediately.[47] The Contraction Act of 1866, which had authorized the removal of greenbacks from circulation, was soon under fire, however, because it made debts harder to pay. Some blamed the worsening economic conditions of early 1867 on the plan and demanded its reversal. Congress bowed to the pressure and ended the greenback retirement provision of the act. Debate continued, but as political and economic factors clashed, stalemate followed. The closely related issue of why federal bonds were redeemed in gold when greenbacks were accepted as legal tender for other exchanges became a factor in the 1868 presidential election. Ohio Democrat George H. Pendleton became a leading candidate with his proposal for redeeming the national debt in greenbacks, whereas Chase's somewhat hedging hard money stand cost him considerable support among midwestern Democrats. With Grant's election, the controversy remained largely unresolved; it would be up to the Supreme Court to face the issue which Chase himself had helped to create during the war.

Several cases were pending on the constitutionality of the Legal Tender Act as early as the December term of 1867, but it was not until late 1869 that the fundamental issue was dealt with.[48] The case that the Court ruled on at that time, *Hepburn* v. *Griswold,* involved an appeal from the Kentucky courts with the case argued in the 1867–68 term; it was not finally discussed by the justices in conferences until late November 1869. The Court was divided sharply into Republican and Democratic factions; Chase spoke for the hard money Democrats in ruling the act unconstitutional as it applied to contracts made before the statute creating paper money became law in 1862. After early uncertainty, the chief justice concluded that the legal tender laws violated the Constitution, but in order to get a majority to agree with him he had to delete that portion of his opinion which applied to contracts made after the passage of the law. The Court divided five to three, with Nelson, Clifford, Field, and Grier joining Chase, while Miller wrote the dissenting opinion concurred in by Swayne and Davis.[49]

Chase used the highly controversial argument that the legal tender acts were not included in the implied powers of Congress; thus they violated the spirit of the Constitution rather than a specific article. Legal tender notes, argued Chase, were not an appropriate means of putting into effect a specific power of Congress. Nonetheless, the real division on the Court was more on the merits of conflicting financial policies than it was on the broader constitutional question. Miller and Chase, representing the opposing factions, disagreed fundamentally on the financial need and wisdom of legal tender notes. Although the decision applied only to preexisting contracts, given Chase's desire to see all paper money eliminated, it appeared possible that the Court might soon extend its ruling to contracts made subsequent to the 1862 law. The decision, which was thus grounded more in economic philosophy than constitutional law, was as controversial for politicians and the public as it had been for the justices. Said one critic of the chief justice, the opinion would cause "distress and ruin among a class of people already in debt." Republicans in general bitterly criticized Chase for the reversal of his Civil War position, whereas Democrats applauded.[50]

The decision was made all the more controversial with the retirement of Justice Grier and the recently passed legislation increasing the Court to nine members. Thus President Grant had two appointments to make, and on the same day that the Court announced its decision in the Hepburn case, he nominated two candidates assumed to oppose the decision, William Strong of Pennsylvania and

Joseph P. Bradley of New Jersey. Following Senate confirmation, Attorney General Ebenezer R. Hoar moved for a reconsideration of the Hepburn decision. The motion created a bitter dispute among the justices with Chase, eager to prevent a reversal, accusing Grant of making the appointments primarily for that purpose. Critics accused Grant of having prior knowledge of the Hepburn decision before making his appointments and thus choosing Bradley and Strong with a reversal of the opinion his goal. In fact, Chase had informed Secretary of the Treasury George Boutwell "about two weeks in advance of the delivery of the opinion" of how the Court would rule because he wanted him to be prepared in case a financial disturbance resulted. Whether Boutwell informed the president is not known.[51]

Following the appointments, Chase made every effort to prevent the case from being argued again. He contended that it would be reopened only if "a member of the Court who concurred in the judgement desires it." During the prolonged debate Chase delayed a decision as long as possible. Justice Miller led the fight to overturn the Hepburn decision and charged that Chase had "resorted to all the stratagems of the lowest political trickery" to prevent it. Chase's ruling did block a rehearing of the Hepburn case, but on the last day of the session the Court voted five to four to hear another similar case at its next session. The two new justices joined the three Hepburn dissenters to form the majority.[52] There was thus little doubt that the legal tender decision would be reversed as soon as the new majority had the opportunity. Chase's efforts to defend his hard money philosophy were destined to fail in the face of growing Republican sentiment in defense of paper currency and the lack of sound constitutional arguments to prevent it.

The Court was forced to postpone further consideration of legal tender until the spring of 1871 primarily because of Chase's illness. Then, it reversed the Hepburn decision in *Knox* v. *Lee* by a five to four vote, with the same justices making up the majority who had agreed to reopen the issue at the previous court session.[53] The Court now held that legal tender notes were valid in relation to both prior and subsequent debts. Justice Strong wrote the opinion for the majority and argued that issuing paper money was a constitutional means of carrying out other specific powers of Congress. The dissenters included Chase, Field, Clifford, and Nelson, with all but

Nelson writing long opinions. Field stressed that the greenbacks had not assisted the government's financial efforts during the war, while Chase reviewed the familiar ground he had taken a year earlier in his effort "to leave my settled judgment on this great question upon the public records." A policy he had so reluctantly accepted as a wartime expedient had been reaffirmed in time of peace much to his dissatisfaction.[54]

Chase had one final opportunity as a member of the Court to reaffirm his belief in equal rights for blacks when he dissented in the *Slaughterhouse Cases* just three weeks before his death in the spring of 1873. The previous year he had been the lone dissenter in a decision which upheld a contract for the purchase of a slave made before the war. He had argued then that the Thirteenth Amendment forbade enforcement of such an agreement.[55] Earlier, in a circuit case, *In re Turner* (1867), Chase had upheld the Civil Rights Act of 1866 using the Thirteenth Amendment to strike down an apprenticeship system for blacks in Maryland, claiming that it reestablished a form of slavery.

In the Slaughterhouse situation, he found the reasoning of Justice Miller limiting the scope of the Fourteenth Amendment equally detrimental to black interests. The case involved a Louisiana law passed in 1869 which had granted a monopoly to a New Orleans firm to slaughter cattle. Competitors of the Crescent City Company had argued that the law violated the Fourteenth Amendment by denying them equal protection of the law. The case involved white butchers, but Chase and three colleagues said in dissent that the Court must act to protect individual rights of blacks or whites if state laws were unjust. The majority, in an opinion written by Miller, distinguished between United States and state citizenship. The Fourteenth Amendment was designed to protect blacks, Miller said, but only in those rights arising from an individual's direct relationship with the federal government, such as the right to petition or engage in interstate commerce. Other rights were aspects of state citizenship and thus were not covered by the amendment. Otherwise, he argued, the federal government would be interfering in state matters, and that had not been the intent of the framers of the amendment. The dual citizenship doctrine thus greatly restricted the degree to which the federal government could protect citizens against the states. The minority, with Field writing the dissenting opinion, contended that effective protection could only be achieved by applying the amendment to such situations as that in New Orleans.[56] The case had significant implications for the future of economic and civil rights and would be followed by a century of reinterpretation. In light of subsequent limitations on the Fourteenth Amendment's ability to defend civil rights against state action, the case would have great importance in the years ahead as blacks lost the constitutional protection that they had been granted during Reconstruction.

Chase's role in this initial decision was minor. In failing health, he offered no separate opinion, merely concurring in Field's dissent. But the case provided a fitting conclusion to Chase's public life. A career which had begun in the 1830s with Chase as the "attorney general for runaway Negroes" now ended with Chase still defending the civil rights of blacks.

11

Chase in Decline

S almon Chase was not able to live out his last years peacefully. In the midst of his political and judicial concerns he had also to contend with an ongoing family crisis involving the stormy marriage of his daughter Kate and William Sprague. The beautiful Kate was so thoroughly ambitious and demanding for herself and her father that Sprague found it difficult to meet her expectations. The couple's relationship had always been unstable also because of the senator's moody and noncommunicative nature. Both were highly sensitive and proud and easily offended by even the most minor transgression of the other, a situation compounded by Sprague's drinking habits and feelings of insecurity. Both were given to frequent outbursts of temper which made Chase's situation uncomfortable as he continued to live with them in Washington at Sixth and E Streets. Domestic relations were further complicated for Chase because of the political situation. As Chase's differences with Republicans evolved during 1867 and 1868, Sprague's position as a member of the party added to the tensions. This was particularly true during the impeachment trial and as Kate began her personal efforts to secure the Democratic nomination for her father.

Following the wedding in November 1863, there had been a degree of harmony in the Sprague–Chase household. While Chase was on his southern tour during the spring of 1865 Kate gave birth to a son whom she wanted to name after her father. Chase convinced her, however, to name him after Sprague, because he must "take the name of the one to whom *your first duties* belong." It was during the next winter that Kate's relations with her husband began to deteriorate. She complained constantly of not feeling well and directed much of her ill feelings against Sprague. The senator in turn resumed his old drinking habits, frequently humiliating her at public functions. The couple remained separated much of the time, with Kate in Rhode Island at the Sprague family home and the senator in Washington.[1]

In the spring of 1866, as rumors spread of Sprague's affairs with other women, Kate took her young son and her sister Nettie and sailed for Europe. During her absence several newspapers reported that she would soon file for divorce. The stories hurt Chase deeply because he had grown fond of Sprague; he made every effort to defer to Sprague's wishes on household questions, and told him "to do just as you think best." He added that his greatest wish was for "the assurance of reciprocal love and mutual trust between you and Katie." Following reports of further unhappiness between the two, Chase lectured his daughter that it was her wifely duty "to acquiesce cheerfully and affectionately" in her husband's wishes. He also asked his secretary Jacob W. Schuckers to issue a tactful public denial to dispel the "scandalous libel" which "touches the domestic relations of Governor and Mrs. Sprague." Her return to Washington brought only increased tensions. Chase, concerned again by Kate's "society whirl," urged her to spend more time "in making home attractive to husband and child."[2]

The political turmoil of 1868 put further pressure on the household, especially as rumors spread that Chase and his daughter were trying to persuade the senator to vote for Andrew Johnson's acquittal. New York and Philadelphia papers reported that Kate had left for Narragansett after threatening divorce if Sprague voted against the president. Again Chase tried to intervene, telling her that Sprague was "almost unmanned—near to tears" when she left, so upset was he by their differences. She *"must love away all his reserve"* and reflect on "how generous, self-sacrificing and indulgent a husband he has been to you."[3]

Kate's reaction to Sprague's vote for the conviction of the president was not recorded, nor was his to Kate's efforts to secure for her father the Democratic nomination in July. But the couple remained apart, although Chase reminded Kate that "there can be but one head to a family." In the spring of 1869, divorce was rumored more widely, and Chase urged Kate to take the initial step toward reconciliation. Although he acknowledged that both were at fault, he nonetheless urged her to "humble your pride. Yield even when you know you have the right on your side." Instead of remaining apart, she should be with her husband in Washington "bearing all things, believing all things, hoping all things, a real helpmate." Chase's efforts to persuade Sprague to relent in his hostility failed completely. As he explained to his daughter, Sprague refused to be "controlled by you."[4]

Whether or not they were influenced by Chase's intervention, the couple temporarily put aside their differences, and during the summer of 1869 he visited the reunited family in Rhode Island after a vacation trip with daughter Nettie in Minnesota. The contrast of the Great Lakes wilderness country with the Sprague's sixty-three room Victorian mansion, called "Canonchet," at Narragansett Bay was indeed striking. Kate had completely remodeled the home until it included balconies and turrets and rivaled the most fashionable homes of Newport. More important to Chase than the extravagance of the overindulged Kate was his "great delight to see the restoration of the old affection between you and your husband." Although he complained of not being informed earlier that his second grandchild was due in October, he was genuinely happy over the reconciliation.[5]

Perhaps because the Sprague family was enlarging or perhaps because the reunion was only surface-deep and the continuing tensions were too much for him to endure, Chase decided that fall to move with Nettie to a house on Vermont and I Streets. Chase grieved that he seemed unable to win Sprague's love and trust. "If he could only feel towards me as a son how glad I should be." Without a son of his own he had genuinely sought such a relationship with Kate's husband. In explaining his decision to Kate to live with Nettie, he noted, "You presided over my home some five years and did it admirably. I rather shall like to have her try her hand." Chase's explanation that "the street cars abridge distance" was no doubt small consolation to the ever-jealous Kate.[6] Despite Kate's personal problems and excessive ambition, his concern for his daughters was as great at this point as when they had been young girls.

Perhaps part of the reason for Chase's decision to move away from Kate and her husband was his desire to end his financial dependence on Sprague, especially after the problems in the senator's marriage led to increasingly strained relations between the two men. Although they had shared household expenses since 1863, Sprague's ample fortune and Chase's relatively meager resources had meant that Sprague assumed a greater share. The chief justice thus sought to end any further dependence on his son-in-law. Sprague may have resented that financial dependence or may have become jealous of the closeness of Chase and Kate. Whatever led to the change, Chase was particularly preoccupied with his own financial situation in the years after the Civil War. His $6,500 salary as chief justice was not enough to maintain his lifestyle, so he augmented his income with several rental properties and with United States bonds and investments managed by the Jay Cooke banking firm. Having settled many of his earlier debts, owed to such friends as Hiram Barney and Charles H. Marshall during the war years, he remained obligated to the Cooke firm which handled his investments and allowed him to overdraw his account when necessary.[7]

Chase's relationship with Jay Cooke remained a close one throughout the Reconstruction years, even though the banker never understood Chase's foray into Democratic politics. In late 1865, the chief justice proposed selling his government bonds and investing in the Cooke firm, because the idea of being "a sleeping partner of yours now that I am no longer Secretary" appealed to him. Cooke apparently did not take the offer seriously.[8] By late 1866, with his financial situation unimproved, Chase suggested to another business friend that he would consider becoming president of the Union Pacific Railroad if offered the post, because he would "greatly prefer active business life to the monotonous labors and dull dignity of my judicial position." Three years later he proposed that Jay Cooke appoint him president of the Cooke-controlled Northern Pacific Railroad, noting "my antecedents and reputation would justify a good salary." According to Chase, his judicial position paid only "in slander and misrepresentation."[9] Again, Cooke rejected the offer, but he continued to invest for him, with Chase ever sensitive to any suggestion of favoritism being shown him. Cooke's advice on investments, as well as his willingness to let Chase fall far behind on his account, helped the chief justice cope with his inadequate salary.[10]

It was a Cooke loan of $22,000 which permitted Chase in late 1869 to purchase a home of his own, his first since he lived in Cincinnati in the 1840s. Aware that his living arrangements with daughter Nettie would be temporary because of her pending engagement to William Sprague Hoyt, he purchased a large old home with more than thirty acres of property three miles north of his Supreme Court chambers.[11] Although the home, which Chase soon named Edgewood, was "sadly dilapidated" and would require extensive renovation to make it liveable, Chase viewed it as the perfect place to live his remaining years. He tried unsuccessfully to sell his rental property in Cincinnati to raise the necessary cash, but instead was forced to borrow more heavily from Cooke. Despite his financial plight he gloried in the remodeling, and commissioned Supreme Court marshal and close friend, Richard C. Parsons, to oversee the operation during his absence from Washington. For one wing he planned a tower which would "certainly make the place much more elegant." Complete with servants' quarters, two parlors and a library, it would be a truly fitting home for a chief justice, although his lack of the $10,000 necessary to finance remodeling plus the extensive work done would delay completion of Edgewood for almost two years. He placed P. E. Jones in charge of farming his land and corresponded regularly with his overseer on such everyday problems as the growing of crops, purchase of farm equipment, and the proper kind of manure. He soon found himself purchasing more lots, until his Edgewood estate included fifty acres. His financial situation worsened; he explained to Henry Cooke in early 1871 that "in consequence of Nettie's wedding and of repairs to my house," he would have to overdraw his account "considerably beyond my wont."[12]

Although the Cooke brothers remained tolerant of Chase's financial plight, it clearly bothered the chief justice; even though his economic situation soon stabilized, he labored hard to secure a much-needed salary increase. In late 1870 and early 1871 Congress finally took up the matter, having left salaries unchanged in 1866 when it reduced the size of the Court. Various proposals were introduced, and Chase hoped that the chief justice's salary would be increased to $12,500, which would almost double the existing scale. The Senate found the proposals excessive, but did give serious consideration to raising the chief justice's salary to $10,500 and that of associate justices to $10,000. Even this proposal was rejected in the Senate appropriation committee—but only by one vote, that of William Sprague! Parsons asked the obvious question: "Why would he not help us in this emergency? Had he left the Senate or *not* voted, we should have won the day." Chase could offer no explanation; instead, the justices had to be content with increases to $8,500 and $8,000. Sprague's vote on the salary bill may have been his way of retaliating. Resentful of Kate's devotion to her father, Sprague may have expressed his feelings against both by securing the defeat of a bill so important to the chief justice. Sprague did not record his motivation, but it is also possible that he voted against the bill because he did not want to appear partisan in favor of his father-in-law.[13]

To what degree problems such as these contributed to Chase's declining health can only be guessed, but from 1868 on, when he reached his sixtieth birthday, Chase realized that he was "growing old." The strain of Court work plus the tensions of the presidential campaign took their toll, and he found he did not recover as quickly from minor illnesses. In late 1869, he suffered from "a general nervous disorder with irregular action of the heart," and the next spring he told Nettie he was "not well enough to write a note worth reading." To his longtime Cincinnati associate Flamen Ball he admitted, "We have both lived to be old men. I cannot expect the vigor of youth."[14]

To get his mind off his work Nettie took him again to Minnesota early in the summer of 1870, hoping that the change would reinvigorate him. But on their way home, after a stop at Niagara Falls, Chase suffered a serious stroke. His right side was paralyzed and he experienced a partial loss of his speech. He was brought to New York City, and because he showed rapid improvement his doctors permitted him to be moved to Narragansett where he remained under the care of daughter Kate. Two more minor strokes during the fall set back his recovery considerably. Long in vigorous health, Chase was slow to realize that it would take "a good while for restoration." He told Parsons not to expect him in Washington for the adjourned term of the Court that fall. Nor did he expect to be able to take his place at the regular term beginning in December. He asked Henry Cooke to look over a new will he had just written; although he expected to recover fully and was "much better," he took the precaution of arranging his estate "because life is uncertain and I have been admonished pretty seriously of its uncertainty."[15]

Chase was determined that his illness would not force him to a premature retirement from the bench. He thus followed his doctor's

Chase as chief justice, about 1870. National Archives, 111-B-3131.

orders and gave him regular and detailed accounts of his progress. He enjoyed partial recovery from his paralysis and gradually increased his daily walk to two miles. Watching his diet faithfully, he received advice from friends and strangers on how best to accelerate his recuperation. General Joseph Hooker told him that visits to the magnetic springs in Saint Louis, Michigan had helped him following a stroke; a man in Cleveland advised him that a diet of "oatmeal mush and milk" had sped his recovery from a similar affliction.[16]

After a brief stay in New York for additional medical treatment, Chase returned to Washington in March 1871 in time for Nettie's wedding. Friends found him frail and aging, and a few even failed to recognize him. Nevertheless, he stayed for the remainder of the Court's term, but only because the legal tender case of a year earlier had been reopened, "and I did not feel at liberty to be absent from my post . . . when questions of such moment were to be argued." He still could do little writing, and it required two painstaking hours for him to pen a short letter.[17]

His stay in Washington was brief; when the Court adjourned in June, he took General Hooker's advice and sought out the healing qualities of the magnetic springs. After a three-week stay in Michigan, he traveled to the resort at the Bethesda Springs of Waukesha, Wisconsin. There, after two months, he reported enthusiastically that he had gained back some weight and that the spring waters had worked such "wonders" that he hoped soon to "make quite a respectable appearance." He regarded himself as "substantially better" than he had been a year earlier before his stroke. Before his return, Kate urged him to "devote all his energies for awhile to getting quite well, that he may yet live a long while to gladden the hearts of his children," adding significantly, "and if need be . . . his country." On his return to Washington, Chase moved into the recently completed Edgewood and frequently walked the three miles to the Supreme Court from his home.[18]

Chase renewed an active pace on the Court in late 1871 and throughout the next year, although by no means keeping the schedule of a fully healthy person. Immediately following his stroke, there had been speculation that he might have to resign. Two of his fellow justices, Miller and Davis, wondered on the other hand if Chase, urged on by Kate, still considered himself a presidential candidate for 1872 despite his illness. According to Miller, Kate "will never consent to his retiring to private life," whereas Davis suggested that "his family are contriving to keep his exact condition concealed from the public." Davis wondered if knowledge of his true condition might "hurt his political prospect," for Chase was in his eyes "the most ambitious man . . . that I ever knew personally."[19] Kate did in fact still dream of the presidency for her father, although Chase was realistic enough to know that his health precluded it. Characteristically, he did little to discourage those who felt otherwise.

Had Chase's health remained strong after 1868, there is reason to believe that significant demand for his candidacy for the presidency would again have developed in 1872. Under the circumstances, the chief justice seemed genuinely sincere when he indicated a lack of interest in another try at the elusive goal. He told Alexander Long even before his stroke, "I prefer the place I hold to any other—even a higher one." Still, friends like Cincinnati editor Murat Halstead told him to expect a Chase movement to develop. In the fall of 1871, the chief justice reaffirmed that although he considered himself a Democrat, he paid "no attention to politics, except to form my own opinions and give my own votes."[20]

As the 1872 conventions approached, and with his health markedly improved, Chase could not resist the temptation at least to offer his advice. During the latter part of Grant's first term, dissension had developed within Republican ranks to the point where many influential leaders, calling themselves Liberal Republicans, were prepared to bolt the party. Among the most prominent were Senator Carl Schurz of Missouri, Horace Greeley, and Charles Francis Adams. Upset with the party's Reconstruction policies, some also demanded civil service reform, a reduction in the protective tariff, and an end to what they regarded as government subservience to business. With the idea of a separate nomination developing, Chase urged Liberal Republicans and Democrats to unite on a common candidate.[21]

As the Liberal Republican convention approached in the spring of 1872 and an alliance with the Democrats appeared likely, Chase's friends again began to present him as a logical candidate. Chase had a hard time convincing them that he was not interested, and before the convention he seemed on the verge of succumbing to just one more try. In March, Judge M. C. Church informed him that Washington supporters were circulating a call for his nomination. He responded that he did not desire the nomination as he had in the past; still, "If those who agree with me in principle think my nomination will promote the interests of the country, I shall not refuse the use of my name." He responded to Flamen Ball and Alexander Long in the same way, and the latter interpreted Chase's explanation as an invitation to organize a movement in his behalf. He informed Chase just ten days before the convention that he planned to secure the attendance of as many of his friends as possible from "any place where they can be induced to come and advocate your nomination."[22]

Kate Sprague decided that this was the opportune time to show the country how healthy and physically and mentally qualified her father was for a nomination. Accordingly, on the eve of the convention she held an elaborate party in his honor in Washington. New York papers which had supported him in 1868 devoted much attention to the evening; the *World* noted that he looked "so much his old self," and the *Herald* observed that Chase "seems to have discovered the fountain of youth for he appeared as robust in health and alert in intellect as ten years ago." Carl Schurz, one of the leaders behind the Liberal Republican effort, had long been suspicious of Chase's motives, and he observed that Chase's "futile efforts to appear youthfully vigorous and agile were pathetically evident." Chase probably allowed the event only to please Kate, knowing that his still precarious health would lead the party to preclude him from consideration no matter how logical his nomination might be otherwise.[23]

The Liberal Republicans met in Cincinnati on May 1 and adopted a platform which Chase found much to his liking; it called for complete amnesty and the protection of suffrage as provided in the Fifteenth Amendment, as well as civil service reform and "a speedy return to specie payment." Adams led on the first ballot, but Horace Greeley emerged the nominee on the sixth, with Chase receiving only a scattering of votes. The relatively unknown Governor B. Gratz Brown of Missouri was chosen for vice president. Long's efforts in Chase's behalf had been largely futile. John Van Buren told Chase that only his health prevented him from being the most desirable candidate.[24]

In no way disappointed, Chase showed great enthusiasm for the ticket, and he told Church and Halstead that Democrats should unite behind Greeley. When the party agreed to accept Greeley and the Liberal Republican platform in July, Chase rejoiced in what he called "a rejuvenated democracy." He indicated to friends that the ticket and platform were totally to his liking. A Greeley administration would "thoroughly harmonize" with his views on "currency, amnesty and reform."[25] He noted sadly that politics had become "a show in which I have no part to act." This he regretted deeply for he believed that "I would have been useful to my country." Chase at last appeared ready to accept, albeit reluctantly, the inevitable conclusion that the presidency could never be his. As the election approached, he retained his enthusiasm for Greeley but concluded that his health would not permit the trip to Cincinnati to vote. He expressed disappointment but not surprise in Grant's relatively easy victory over Greeley. Grant won 56 percent of the votes; Greeley won only six states, all of them in the South or border areas.[26] Greeley's death three weeks later left Chase in a state of "numbing shock."[27] He could only reflect with foreboding at the passing of a long time friend and contemporary.

Following his stroke in August 1870, Chase returned to the Court only briefly during the spring of 1871 before resuming his position on a more full-time basis that fall. From that time through the spring of 1872 he attended to his duties faithfully, as he did during the next term of the Court extending into the spring of 1873. But his role as chief justice was more limited after the stroke. Although his condition improved, he was never able to write effectively, and his speech remained partially slurred; he now dictated even his personal letters to secretaries. Unlike the period up to 1870 when Reconstruction issues dominated the Court's proceedings, after his stroke Chase rarely spoke for his fellow justices and usually only when a short opinion was necessary. His waning interest in the presidency in 1872 was a further indication of his declining health; he admitted that "politicians do not want me and I don't want them."[28]

In December 1872, he arranged for the writing of his biography, perhaps recognizing that his condition was worsening. He chose Robert Bruce Warden, a Cincinnati lawyer and friend of long-standing as the writer and invited him to live at Edgewood with him as his private secretary while the project went on. There he gave Warden all of his personal letters and diaries, seeking in him a biographer who would be objective but nonetheless appreciative of his role in history. He urged that nothing be suppressed because "the truth was very seldom really injurious to any interest."[29] Chase was willing to bare his private correspondence and allow Warden to write openly of both his public and private life. He had finally attained the wisdom to accept his accomplishments as highly significant in themselves even without having attained that elusive goal of the presidency. He wrote on May 5, 1873, just two days before his death, that he was "too much of an invalid to be more than a cipher. Sometimes," he continued, "I feel as if I were dead, though alive." He expected little improvement in his health, despite plans for further treatment in Boston, for "the lapse of sixty-five years is hard to cure."[30]

Those close to Chase in Washington were increasingly concerned about his failing health; he had lost considerable weight and had aged visibly in the last several months. His face appeared haggard and thin and, with his recently grown beard, some of his friends failed even to recognize him. Chase nonetheless planned a busy spring and summer. At the end of the spring term of the Supreme Court he expected to spend a few days with Nettie and her husband in New York, followed by a visit in Rhode Island with Kate and Sprague, and then a summer trip to Colorado. Before leaving Washington he visited briefly with his closest friend, Senator Charles Sumner, himself very ill, and the two "discussed public affairs," Chase "with his accustomed clearness and ability." He also called on Henry Cooke at his Washington bank where he paid "an installment upon his note and interest to date." To the optimistic Cooke, Chase had "not looked so well for a year past as he did then." In New York at Nettie's Chase suffered another stroke on May 6. A servant discovered early that morning that he had been "seized with a spasm" while sleeping. Nettie was immediately summoned and then a doctor, whose efforts to bring relief failed. He lingered in unconsciousness for more than twenty-four hours. "His two daughters remained by his bedside till 10:30 this morning when he breathed his last."[31]

Funeral services for Chase followed on May 9 at St. George's Episcopal Church in New York where he had lain in state since his death. Several thousand mourners visited the church before the service. In attendance at the funeral were Vice President Henry Wilson, several Supreme Court associates, and numerous other dignitaries. Pallbearers included friends and such sometime-antagonists as Gideon Welles, Gerrit Smith, William Tecumseh Sherman, Hiram Barney, and John J. Cisco. The body was then taken to Washington where "it was placed within the bar of the Supreme Court room." A final service held in the Senate chamber was attended by President Grant and his cabinet, members of Congress and the Supreme Court, and others who heard the Rev. O. H. Tiffany observe: "The life of a great man is a great lesson; the death of a great man is a great loss; the dying of a great man is a mysterious lesson of woe." As the funeral procession of a hundred carriages moved to Oak Hill

Cemetery in Georgetown, mourners lined the streets of Washington to pay their last respects.[32]

Reaction to Chase's death concentrated on the role he had played during his last eight years as chief justice, but as contemporaries evaluated his role as the leader of the Supreme Court, they in effect offered a judgment on his whole life. His colleagues on the Court were for the most part positive in their assessment, including those with whom he had frequently clashed. Coming to the Court with no judicial experience, he had won the respect even of those who were originally opposed to his appointment. As Justice Davis pointed out after serving close to three years with him: "No one ever questioned your ability." Although they frequently disagreed, Davis concluded that "you have a good heart," and "consideration of hatred, malice or revenge would never influence you on any question." Chase had been able to work effectively even with those with whom he had differences, whether it be Seward or Welles in the cabinet or Miller or Davis on the Court. Justice Strong, who knew Chase as a judge only after his stroke, believed "he was greater as a statesman than as a judge," for "he was not a thoroughly trained and learned lawyer," but "he was always 'thoroughly persuaded' before he acted, and always followed his convictions." Field, who frequently concurred with Chase's opinions but was never close to him personally, expressed "admiration for his abilities and respect for his character," a view shared by many of his contemporaries.[33]

The most frequent criticism of the chief justice was for his political ambition, especially as it was manifested in his presidential candidacy in 1868. His frequent antagonist during his last years on the Court, Justice Samuel Miller, found his positive traits "warped, perverted, shrivelled by the selfishness generated by ambition." Chase, said Miller, judged every important man he met with the question, "how can I utilize him for my presidential aspirations?" His Ohio colleague Rutherford B. Hayes summed up the prevailing view of Chase when he charged that "political intrigue, love of power and boundless ambition were striking features of his life and character." But even Miller concluded that "he was a great man, and a better man than public life generally leaves one, after forty years of service." Many agreed with Strong that Chase "never allowed his political aspirations to warp his judicial conduct."[34] The feeling persisted, however, that he would have been a more effective chief justice if his political aspirations had been kept better in check.

Several of his fellow justices also criticized Chase for his domineering ways. Strong suggested that he may not have been conscious of his "imperious manner," but it was obvious to others. Miller noted that although Chase expected to dominate the Court, his brethren made him realize that he was "the Moderator and presiding officer . . . and not possessed of any more authority than the rest of the Bench chose to give him." [35]

Until his stroke, Chase clearly exerted the kind of leadership over the Court that most expected of a chief justice. He was the dominant figure on Reconstruction issues and successfully steered the Court toward a moderate position which prevented a confrontation with Congress. In legislation affecting judicial matters, Chase was usually the intermediary with Congress, both because of his position and as a result of his acquaintance with many members; however, as seen in the salary disputes, he did not always get his way. His leadership of the Court failed most obviously in the legal tender cases. Unable to convince his deeply divided associates of his point of view and hampered by failing health, he let his financial and political views take precedence over constitutional concerns. Chase by no means dominated the Court's decisions in all areas as several chief justices before and after him did; he was a strong leader, nonetheless, especially in areas where his expertise was greatest. Writing more than his share of opinions, he dissented only thirty-three times during his eight-year tenure. Usually preferring not to call attention to his disagreement with the majority, he wrote opinions in only nine of those dissents. [36] He represented the Court with dignity and integrity, perhaps best seen in the manner in which he presided over Johnson's impeachment trial.

During Chase's tenure, the Court struck down a surprising number of federal laws. Only two acts of Congress had been ruled unconstitutional before 1865, whereas ten were voided by the Court between the end of the war and Chase's death. Most of the rulings affected legislation which was not overly significant, but it is evident that the Court was asserting itself and making it clear to Congress where possible that it did not intend to be a subordinate branch of government. [37] The Court surely did not share the power and influence of Congress during Chase's tenure, but it did regain some of the prestige it had lost in the sectional struggles prior to the Civil War. Chase was in large part responsible for that resurgence.

Chase's life must be evaluated in light of his whole career rather than simply in relation to his last eight years as chief justice. In his more than forty years of public service he functioned in every part of government: legislative, administrative, and judicial; and his part was played on local, state, and national levels. He displayed both the strengths and weaknesses which one might expect from a public official who held a variety of positions from city councilman to chief justice and who advocated a variety of causes from emancipation and black suffrage to banking and tax reform. His greatest cause was racial equality, but his was a career which contemporaries remembered equally as one motivated by ambition. Chase constantly worked for political position and during his last twenty years primarily sought the presidency. Largely because of his ambition, Chase made many enemies among public leaders and unfortunately had few lasting friendships. Most contemporaries and historians have thus been overly critical of the role he played and have emphasized too much his undeniable ambition at the expense of his lasting achievements.

An important factor in the negative evaluation so often accorded to Chase were some personality traits which were less than admirable and which made him difficult at times to know and to get along with. Often rather cold and aloof, he found it difficult to relate to his fellow politicians or to the voters to whom he appealed for support. Surely it was his reputation as a self-seeking public figure which hurt him most. His desire for personal advancement at the expense of others—critics would charge at the expense of the causes he defended—first revealed itself in a dramatic way in his election to the Senate by the Ohio legislature in 1849, and his many political maneuverings continued until close to death. Although guilty of excessive ambition, Chase never mastered the political skills needed to form the organization which could effectively advocate his candidacy. Thus his major goal of the presidency continually eluded him.

If Chase found it difficult to relate well to many politicians and voters, he nevertheless showed a genuine concern for others. Throughout his sixty-five years, he maintained the closest ties with his immediate family. Beginning with his boyhood in New Hampshire and Ohio—and especially through the loss of three wives and four children—Chase faced more than his share of grief and loneliness. A deep religious faith maintained since boyhood helped him bear that grief with strength and resolution. His devotion to Kate and Nettie was constant. Throughout his life he helped his struggling brothers and sisters financially whenever possible, and his generosity occasionally got him into serious economic difficulty. As a young adult in Cincinnati, he acquired the lifelong habit of contributing his time and support to a variety of reform interests. He gave generously to his own Episcopal church as well as to other religious groups. Schuckers accurately described him as "a quiet, unobtrusive worker in religious and benevolent enterprises." But in lending his name to a mission project, he explained with a characteristic sense of self-importance: "It is not much that I can do financially, but God has given me a certain position and influence." His concern for others, especially blacks, led him to reaffirm his support for the Colored Orphan Asylum of Cincinnati. Having helped in its establishment in the 1840s, he bequeathed an additional gift in 1873.[38] Even his lifetime nemesis Montgomery Blair, in recalling past battles, concluded that Chase "was too great and good a man to harbor such feeling" toward him or his family.[39]

Chase could engender both loyalty and distrust. He received the greatest loyalty from a group of rising young men—those who worked in his law office in Cincinnati—showing here, as he did with his daughters, a sincere concern for teaching and guiding those younger than he. On the other hand, his vanity and absorption with his own advancement made close personal friendships difficult. He sat frequently for photographers, encouraged campaign and other biographies of himself, and even arranged for a sculptor to do his bust. His Supreme Court colleagues agreed that "pride of opinion" was the characteristic which described him best.[40]

But Chase should be remembered for his achievements. An intelligent, diligent, and efficient administrator committed to hard work, he effectively guided the Union through the financial difficulties of the war years and skillfully led the Supreme Court through the equally trying years of Reconstruction. He maintained a reputation for honesty and fought consistently for a program of reform. "The real glory of his life" lay in his "persevering agitation against slavery" and all forms of racial injustice.[41]

Notes

Preface

1. Chase to Jacob W. Schuckers, June 6, 1868, Chase Papers, Library of Congress.

2. Carl Schurz, *The Reminiscences of Carl Schurz, 1852–1863,* 3 vols. (New York: Doubleday, Page and Co., 1917), 2:172.

3. Albert Bushnell Hart, *Salmon P. Chase* (Boston: Houghton Mifflin Co., 1899).

4. Thomas G. Belden and Marva R. Belden, *So Fell the Angels* (Boston: Little Brown and Co., 1956); Lincoln quoted in Hart, *Chase,* p. 435.

5. Although recognizing the enormity of the financial crisis and Chase's valiant efforts to cope with it, two recent studies nonetheless give the secretary an overall negative evaluation for his Treasury policies: Robert P. Sharkey, *Money, Class and Party: An Economic Study of the Civil War and Reconstruction* (Baltimore: Johns Hopkins Univ. Press, 1959); Bray Hammond, *Sovereignty and an Empty Purse: Banks and Politics in the Civil War* (Princeton: Princeton Univ. Press, 1970). The traditional view of Chase's tenure as chief justice has been largely discredited, and in the 1960s "revisionist" historians began to produce more appreciative accounts of congressional Reconstruction. The old school is best represented by Claude Bowers, *The Tragic Era: The Revolution After Lincoln* (Boston: Houghton Mifflin, 1929).

6. Eric Foner, *Free Soil, Free Labor, Free Men: The Ideology of the Republican Party Before the Civil War* (New York: Oxford Univ. Press, 1970); William E. Gienapp, "Salmon P. Chase, Nativism and the Formation of the Republican Party in Ohio," *Ohio History* 93 (1984): 5–39, and "Nativism and the Creation of a Republican Majority in the North Before the Civil War," *Journal of American History* 72 (1985): 529–59. David Donald, ed., *Inside Lincoln's Cabinet: The Civil War Diaries of Salmon P. Chase* (New York: Longmans Green and Co., 1954); David Hughes, "Salmon P. Chase: Chief Justice," *Vanderbilt Law Review* 18 (1965): 569–614 (hereafter cited as

"Chase, Chief Justice"); Stanley I. Kutler, *Judicial Power and Reconstruction Politics* (Chicago: Univ. of Chicago Press, 1968).

Chapter One

1. Trowbridge used his material to write an idealized life of Chase for young readers entitled *The Ferry Boy and the Financier* (Boston: Walker, Wise and Co., 1864).

2. The best known of Ithamar's brothers included Philander, a bishop in the Episcopal church and founder of Kenyon College, and Dudley, a United States senator from Vermont. Salmon was named after another of Ithamar's brothers, a Dartmouth graduate who died in Portland, Maine. See Hart, *Chase,* pp. 2–3; Jacob W. Schuckers, *The Life and Public Services of Salmon Portland Chase* (New York: D. Appleton and Co., 1874), pp. 1–4; Robert B. Warden, *An Account of the Private Life and Public Services of Salmon Portland Chase* (Cincinnati: Wilstach, Baldwin and Co., 1874), p. 24.

3. Chase to Trowbridge, Jan. 19, 1864, Dec. 27, 1863, Chase to John H. Prentiss, n.d., in Warden, *Chase,* pp. 22, 25, 34–35.

4. Chase to John H. Prentiss, n.d., p. 22; Chase, Autobiographical Sketch, July 10, 1853, Chase Papers, Library of Congress (hereafter cited as LC); Schuckers, *Chase,* p. 8. For a revealing picture of the early nineteenth century New England childhood experience, see Joseph Kett, "Growing up in Rural New England, 1800–1840," in Tamara K. Hareven, ed., *Anonymous Americans: Explorations in Nineteenth Century Social History* (Englewood Cliffs, N.J.: Prentice Hall, 1971), pp. 1–16. Kett notes the frequent disruption of New England family life by the death of one or both parents and suggests that most fathers died before the youngest child reached maturity.

5. Chase to Trowbridge, Dec. 27, 1863, in Warden, *Chase,* pp. 55–56.

6. Chase, Autobiographical Sketch, Chase Papers, LC; Chase to Prentiss, n.d.; Chase to Trowbridge, Dec. 27, 1863, Jan. 19, 1864, in Warden, *Chase,* pp. 22, 40, 59–60; Chase, Diary, Jan. 27, 1836, in ibid., p. 280.

7. Chase, Autobiographical Sketch, Chase Papers, LC.

8. Trowbridge took the title for his biography from Chase's ferrying experience on the Cuyahoga; Schuckers, *Chase,* p. 11n.; Chase, Autobiographical Sketch, Chase Papers, LC; Chase to Trowbridge, Jan. 21, 1864, in Warden, *Chase,* p. 65.

9. Chase to Trowbridge, Jan. 25, 29, 1864, in Warden, *Chase,* p. 83, 89.

10. Chase to Trowbridge, Jan. 25, 29, 1864, in Warden, *Chase,* pp. 70–71, 88–89.

11. Chase to Trowbridge, Jan. 29, 1864, in Warden, *Chase,* pp. 90–91; Richard C. Wade, *The Urban Frontier: Pioneer Life in Early Pittsburgh, Cincinnati, Lexington, Louisville and St. Louis* (Chicago: Univ. of Chicago Press, 1959), pp. 190, 195.

12. Chase to Trowbridge, Jan. 31, 1864, in Warden, *Chase,* pp. 93–95; Chase, Autobiographical Sketch, Chase Papers, LC.

13. Chase to Trowbridge, Jan. 21, 1864, in Warden, *Chase,* pp. 105–7; Chase, Autobiographical sketch, Chase Papers, LC.

14. Chase to Trowbridge, Feb. 1, 1864, in Warden, *Chase,* pp. 107–8; Chase, Autobiographical Sketch, Chase Papers, LC.

15. Frederick Chase, *A History of Dartmouth College and the Town of Hanover, New Hampshire* (Cambridge, Mass.: J. Wilson and Sons, 1913), pp. 199–200; Russel B. Nye, *The Cultural Life of the New Nation, 1776–1830* (New York: Harper and Row, 1960), pp. 184–88; Chase to Trowbridge, Feb. 7, 1864, in Warden, *Chase,* pp. 109–13; Chase, Autobiographical Sketch, Chase Papers, LC.

16. Chase to Thomas Sparhawk, July 8, 1827, Jan. 2, Sept. 3, 1828, in Arthur M. Schlesinger, ed., "Salmon Portland Chase, Undergraduate and Pedagogue," *Ohio State Archaeological and Historical Quarterly* 28 (April 1919): 136–39, 141–44, 146–48; Chase, Autobiographical Sketch, Chase Papers, LC.

17. Chase to Sparhawk, Mar. 16, 1826, in Schlesinger, "Chase," pp. 129–30; Chase to Adaline Hitchcock, Apr. 29, 1826, Chase Papers, Historical Society of Pennsylvania (hereafter cited as HSP); Chase to Sparhawk, May 15, 1826, in Schlesinger, "Chase," pp. 131–32.

18. Alexander R. Chase to Chase, Nov. 4, 1825, Chase Papers, LC; Chase, Autobiographical Sketch, Chase Papers, LC.

19. Chase to Trowbridge, Feb. 13, 1864, in Warden, *Chase,* p. 129; Advertisement in *National Intelligencer,* Dec. 23, 1826, in Schlesinger, "Chase," pp. 132–33; Constance McLaughlin Green, *Washington: Village and Capital, 1800–1878* (Princeton: Princeton Univ. Press, 1962), pp. 92–93.

20. Chase to Trowbridge, Feb. 8, 1864, in Warden, *Chase,* pp. 119–21. Chase went on in this letter to express relief that his uncle denied his request: "Had I become a clerk it is almost certain I would have remained a clerk or should have been at least disqualified by clerk habits for the work I have actually done."

21. Chase to Trowbridge, Feb. 8, 1864, in Warden, *Chase,* pp. 122–23.

22. Chase to Gen. Bernard, July 10, 1829, Chase Papers, HSP; Chase to Trowbridge, Feb. 8, 1864, in Warden, *Chase,* pp. 119–21; Peter Walker, *Moral Choices: Memory, Desire and Imagination in Nineteenth Century Abolition* (Baton Rouge, Louisiana State Univ. Press, 1978), p. 317.

23. Chase to Sparhawk, Jan. 2, 1828, Sept. 30, 1829, Jan. 15, 1830, in Schlesinger, "Chase," pp. 143–44, 154–55, 156–58.

24. Chase to Charles Cleveland, June 3, 1828, Chase Papers, LC; Chase to Trowbridge, Feb. 8, 1864, in Warden, *Chase,* pp. 122–23; Chase to Sparhawk, Sept. 30, 1829, in Schlesinger, "Chase," pp. 154–55.

25. Chase, Autobiographical Sketch, Chase Papers, LC; Chase to Joseph Denison, Nov. 10, 1827, Chase Papers, LC; Chase, Diary, Jan. 31, 1829, Chase Papers, LC.

26. Chase to Sparhawk, Sept. 18, 1827, Sept. 3, 1828, Apr. 20, 1829, in Schlesinger, "Chase," pp. 139–41, 146–48, 152–54; Chase, Personal Memoranda, June 30, 1853, Chase Papers, LC.

27. Chase, Personal Memoranda, June 30, 1853, and Autobiographical Sketch, Chase Papers, LC.

28. Chase to Trowbridge, Feb. 8, 1864, in Warden, *Chase,* p. 125; Chase, Diary, Jan. 31, 1829, Chase Papers, LC; Chase to Abigail Colby, Dec. 15, 1827, Chase Papers, HSP; Chase to Sparhawk, Apr. 20, 1829, in Schlesinger, "Chase," pp. 152–54.

29. Schuckers, *Chase,* pp. 25–26n.; Chase, Diary, Apr. 8, July 31, 1829, Chase Papers, LC; William Wirt to Chase, Dec. 21, 1829, Nov. 11, 1831, Wirt Papers, Maryland Historical Society.

30. Chase to Sparhawk, Jan. 2, Nov. 10, 1828, in Schlesinger, "Chase," p. 142; Chase to Cleveland, June 3, 1828, Chase Papers, LC; Chase to Lauretta Hitchcock, Apr. 1828, in Schuckers, *Chase,* pp. 27–28; Chase, Diary, Mar. 4, 1829, Chase Papers, LC.

31. Chase, Diary, Jan. 7, 1830, in Warden, *Chase,* p. 149; Chase, Diary, Jan. 10, Apr. 14, 1829, Chase Papers, LC; Chase to Sparhawk, Jan. 15, 1830, in Schlesinger, "Chase," pp. 156–58.

32. Chase, Diary, Feb. 14, 1829, in Warden, *Chase,* pp. 165–66; Chase, Diary, Jan. 31, 1829, Chase Papers, LC; Chase to Sparhawk, Apr. 20, 1829, in Schlesinger, "Chase," pp. 152–54.

33. Chase to Sparhawk, Nov. 10, 1828, in Schlesinger, "Chase," pp. 151–52; Chase, *History of Dartmouth College,* p. 208; Green, *Washington,* p. 99; Chase, Autobiographical Sketch, Chase Papers, LC. See also Robert H. Gruber, "Salmon P. Chase and the Politics of Reform" (Ph.D. diss., University of Maryland, 1969), pp. 21–31.

34. Chase to Sparhawk, Nov. 10, 1828, in Schlesinger, "Chase," pp. 151–52.

35. Chase, Diary, Dec. 31, 1829, in Warden, *Chase,* p. 165; Chase to Joseph Denison, Nov. 14, 1828, Chase Papers, LC.

Chapter Two

1. Chase to Cleveland, Nov. 23, 1829, Chase Papers, LC; Chase to William Wirt, June 6, 1829, Chase Papers, HSP.

2. Chase, Diary, Feb. 23, 1830, Chase Papers, LC; Chase, Diary, Mar. 1, 1830, in Warden, *Chase,* pp. 182–84; Chase to Cleveland, Feb. 9, 1830, Chase Papers, LC.

3. Chase, Diary, Feb. 23, 1830, Chase to Cleveland, Mar. 18, 1830, Chase Papers, LC.

4. Chase to Cleveland, Dec. 21, 1831, Chase Papers, HSP; Chase to Cleveland, Mar. 18, 1830, Chase Papers, LC; Alexis de Tocqueville, *Journey to America,* ed. J. P. Mayer (Garden City, N.Y.: Doubleday and Co., 1971), pp. 84–85.

5. Edward L. Pierce, Manuscript Biography of Chase, Chase Papers, LC; Chase Letter in *Cincinnati American,* in Warden, *Chase,* pp. 198–200; Chase to Cleveland, Jan. 4, 1831, Chase Papers, HSP.

6. *North American Review* 34 (January 1832): 220–46, 33 (July 1831): 227–61; Chase, Diary, Mar. 2, 1831, Chase Papers, LC; Pierce, Manuscript Biography of Chase, Chase Papers, LC; Chase to Brougham, Nov. 15, 1831, Chase Papers, HSP.

7. Chase to Corresponding Secretary of the American Temperance Society, June 27, 1831, Chase Papers, HSP; Chase, Diary, Jan. 6, 1841, Chase Papers, LC; Chase, Diary, Mar. 13, 1841, in Warden, *Chase,* pp. 294–95.

8. Robert Wharton to Chase, Oct. 2, 1843, Chase Diary, Feb. 21, 1836, Jan. 9, 1833, Chase Papers, LC.

9. Chase, Diary, Feb. 8, 1834, in Warden, *Chase,* pp. 228–29.

10. Chase, Diary, May 5, 1833, Chase Papers, LC; Chase, Diary, Jan. 18, 1833, in Warden, *Chase,* p. 220.

11. Chase, Autobiographical Sketch, Chase Papers, LC; Chase, Dairy, June, Sept. 30, 1830, in Warden, *Chase,* pp. 192, 193.

12. Chase, Autobiographical Sketch, Chase Papers, LC; Chase to Edward Chase, Sept. 17, 1830, in Schuckers, *Chase,* pp. 32–33n.

13. Chase, Autobiographical Sketch, Chase Papers, LC; Chase, Diary, Apr. 10, 1832, May 22, 1830, in Warden, *Chase,* pp. 210, 192.

14. Chase, Diary, Nov. 1, 1832, in Warden, *Chase,* p. 211; Chase, Autobiographical Sketch, Daniel Caswell to Chase, July 7, 1834, Chase, Memorandum to Caswell, Jan. 25, 1834, Chase Papers, LC.

15. Chase, Diary, June 26, 1840, Chase Papers, LC; Chase, Diary, Apr. 29, 1831, in Warden, *Chase,* p. 208; Chase to Cleveland, Feb. 9, 1830, Chase Papers, LC.

16. Chase, ed., *The Statutes of Ohio and of the Northwestern Territory Adopted or Enacted from 1788 to 1833 Inclusive Including a Preliminary Sketch of the History of Ohio* 3 vols. (Cincinnati: Corey and Fairbank, 1833–1835); Chancellor James Kent to Chase, July 1, 1835, Joseph Story to Chase, Mar. 1, 1834, in Schuckers, *Chase,* pp. 35–37; Chase, Autobiographical Sketch, Chase Papers, LC.

17. D. W. Fairbank to Chase, Dec. 19, 1832, Chase Papers, LC; Schuckers, *Chase,* p. 37.

18. Chase, Autobiographical Sketch, Chase Papers, LC; Chase, *Statutes of Ohio,* 1:11, 21, 39–40; Chase to Kent, Nov. 25, 1833, Chase Papers, HSP.

19. Chase, *Statutes of Ohio,* 1:48; Tocqueville, *Journey to America,* pp. 84–85.

20. Chase, Autobiographical Sketch, Chase, Law Partnership Accounts, Chase Papers, LC. See, for example, Chase to Flamen Ball, July 5, 1839, Chase Papers, LC.

21. Among those who worked briefly for the Chase firm were Stanley Matthews, Chase's close collaborator in the legislature during his controversial election to the Senate in 1849, Edward L. Pierce of Massachusetts, later a Treasury official in South Carolina during the Civil War, and George Hoadly, who would become governor of Ohio in 1884. For a time Hoadly was a partner in the firm of Chase, Ball, and Hoadly. At least one future opponent, George Pugh, also served as a student under Chase. Pugh was chosen by the Democrats in the legislature to replace Chase in the United States Senate in 1855 because of his more moderate stand on slave-related issues. See Hart, *Chase,* pp. 24–25.

22. Ball to Chase, July 19, 1845, Chase Papers, HSP.

23. Chase to Nicholas Longworth, June 3, 1835, in Warden, *Chase,* pp. 244–45. For two estimates of Chase as a lawyer, see Gruber, "Chase and the Politics of Reform," pp. 41–42, and Hart, *Chase,* pp. 22–26.

24. Chase to Cleveland, June 2, 1830, Chase Papers, LC; Chase, Diary, n.d., in Warden, *Chase,* p. 238; William Baringer, "The Politics of Abolition: Salmon P. Chase in Cincinnati," *Cincinnati Historical Society Bulletin* 29 (1971): 84.

25. Chase, Diary, n.d., in Warden, *Chase,* pp. 238–41; Catherine Garniss, quoted in ibid., pp. 241–42.

26. Chase, Diary, Nov., 1835, in Warden, *Chase,* pp. 238–41.

27. Ibid., pp. 257, 261–63.

28. Ibid., p. 262, and Dec. 30, 1835, p. 269.

29. Chase, Diary, Jan. 2, 1836, in Warden, *Chase,* p. 271; Chase, Diary, Feb. 17, 1836, Chase Papers, LC; Chase to Cleveland, Apr. 6, 1836, Chase Papers, HSP.

30. Chase, Diary, Dec. 27, 1835, in Warden, *Chase,* p. 267.

31. Ibid., Jan. 18, 1836, pp. 277–78; Chase to Helen Chase, Apr. 24, 1836, Chase Papers, HSP; Baringer, "Politics of Abolition," p. 84; Alice Hunt Sokoloff, *Kate Chase for the Defense* (New York: Dodd, Mead and Co., 1971), pp. 21–22.

32. Abigail Chase to Chase, Apr. 10, 1832, Chase papers, HSP; Chase, Diary, Jan. 27, 1836, in Warden, *Chase,* p. 280.

33. Chase, Diary, Aug. 12, 1840, in Warden, *Chase,* p. 290; Chase to Cleveland, Aug. 29, 1840, Chase Papers, HSP.

34. Chase to Cleveland, Feb. 7, 1840, Chase Papers, HSP; Chase, Diary, Jan. 1, 1841, May 2, 1840, Chase Papers, LC.

35. Eliza Smith Chase to Chase, June 22, 1844, Chase Papers, LC; Chase, Diary, Nov. 24, Dec. 2, 1845, in Warden, *Chase,* p. 302; Chase to Cleveland, Feb. 3, Oct. 1, 1845, Chase Papers, HSP.

36. Chase to Kate Chase, Dec. 5, 1851, Chase Papers, HSP.

37. William Bond to Chase, June 21, 1834, July 3, 1835, Chase Papers, LC.

38. Henry Paine to Chase, Sept. 10, 1832, William Chase to Chase, Mar. 24, 1833, Apr. 27, 1835, A. W. Corey to Chase, Aug. 16, 1837, Lewis F. Thomas to Chase, Jan. 17, 1840, Chase to William Chase, Sept. 12, 1836, William G. Eliot to Chase, Feb. 15, June 9, 1840, Chase, Diary, Dec. 10, 1852, Chase Papers, LC.

39. Richard C. Wade, "The Negro in Cincinnati, 1800–1830," *Journal of Negro History* 39 (1954): 43–57; Wade, *The Urban Frontier,* pp. 224–29.

40. Edward Mansfield et al. to Chase, Nov. 26, 1834, Chase Papers, HSP; *Cincinnati Gazette,* Dec. 19, 1834.

41. Betty Fladeland, *James Gillespie Birney: Slaveholder to Abolitionist* (Ithaca: Cornell Univ. Press, 1955), p. 129.

42. *Cincinnati Gazette,* in *Frankfort Commonwealth,* Aug. 10, 1836; *Philanthropist,* July 24, 1836; Fladeland, *Birney,* pp. 138–39, 141–42. For a careful analysis of the makeup of the mob, see Leonard L. Richards, *Gentlemen of Property and Standing: Anti-Abolition Mobs in Jacksonian America* (New York: Oxford Univ. Press, 1970), pp. 92–100, 134–50.

43. Chase, Autobiographical Sketch, Chase Papers, LC.

44. Ibid.

45. Chase to *Cincinnati Gazette,* Aug. 4, 1836, Chase, Autobiographical Sketch, Chase Papers, LC.

46. Chase, Autobiographical Sketch, Chase Papers, LC, Chase to Cleveland, Feb. 17, 1837, Chase Papers, HSP; Fladeland, *Birney,* p. 146.

47. Chase to Trowbridge, Mar. 16, 1864, in Warden, *Chase,* pp. 282–84; Chase, Autobiographical Sketch, Chase Papers, LC; Fladeland, *Birney,* pp. 149–54. The roles of Chase and other attorneys in challenging intersectional comity are developed in three recent studies: Paul Finkelman, *An Imperfect Union: Slavery, Federalism and Comity* (Chapel Hill: Univ. of North Carolina Press, 1981), William M. Wiecek, *The Sources of Antislavery Constitutionalism in America, 1760–1848* (Ithaca: Cornell Univ. Press, 1977), and Robert M. Cover, *Justice Accused: Antislavery and Judicial Process* (New Haven: Yale Univ. Press, 1975). For a thorough and revealing analysis of Chases's position on the constitutional responsibility of the federal government for slavery, see Foner, *Free Soil, Free Labor, Free Men,* pp. 73–102.

48. Chase to Trowbridge, Mar. 16, 1864, in Warden, *Chase,* pp. 282–84; Chase, Autobiographical Sketch, Chase Papers, LC; Chase, *Speech of Salmon P. Chase in the Case of the Colored Woman, Matilda, Who Was Brought Before the Court of Common Pleas of Hamilton County, Ohio by Wirt of Habeas Corpus, March 11, 1837* (Cincinnati: Pugh and Dodd, 1837); Wiecek, *The Sources of Antislavery Constitutionalism,* pp. 191–93; Fladeland, *Birney,* pp. 152–53; Finkelman, *An Imperfect Union,* pp. 160–62. See also Cover, *Justice Accused,* pp. 164–65.

49. Chase, *Speech in the Case of the Colored Woman Matilda.* For a thorough description of *Somerset v. Stewart,* see Wiecek, *The Sources of Antislavery Constitutionalism,* pp. 24–39, and Cover, *Justice Accused,* p. 98.

50. *Birney v. The State of Ohio,* 8 Ohio, 230–39 (1837).

51. Chase to Trowbridge, Mar. 16, 1864, in Warden, *Chase,* pp. 282–84; *Philanthropist,* Dec. 20, 1837, Jan. 2, 1838; Baringer, "Politics of Abolition," pp. 86–87; Finkelman, *An Imperfect Union,* pp. 162–64.

52. Chase to Trowbridge, Mar. 16, 1864, in Warden, *Chase,* pp. 282–84; *Philanthropist,* Jan. 30, 1838; Fladeland, *Birney,* pp. 153–54.

53. Chase, Autobiographical Sketch, Chase Papers, LC.

54. The early careers of Seward and Sumner are best described by their most recent biographers. See Glyndon G. Van Deusen, *William Henry Seward* (New York: Oxford Univ. Press, 1967), and David Donald, *Charles Sumner and the Coming of the Civil War* (New York: Alfred Knopf, 1960).

55. Foner, *Free Soil, Free Labor, Free Men,* pp. 83–87.

56. *Cincinnati Gazette,* May 21, June 1, 1841; Finkelman, *An Imperfect Union,* p. 166.

57. Chase to Trowbridge, Mar. 18, 1864, in Warden, *Chase,* pp. 296–98.

58. Ibid.; Finkelman, *An Imperfect Union,* pp. 246–48; Cover, *Justice Accused,* pp. 246–47.

59. *Prigg v. Pennsylvania,* 16 Peters 539 (1842). Chase's argument is in Schuckers, *Chase,* pp. 56–63.

60. Chase to Trowbridge, Mar. 18, 1864, in Warden, *Chase,* pp. 296–98; Chase to Lewis Tappan, Mar. 18, 1847, in Schuckers, *Chase,* pp. 65–66; Chase, *Reclamation of Fugitives from Service* (Cincinnati: R. P. Donogh and Co., 1847), pp. 84–86.

61. Chase to John P. Hale, May 12, 1847, in Warden, *Chase,* pp. 312–15; Chase to Charles Sumner, Apr. 24, 1847, in Edward G. Bourne et al., eds., "Diary and Correspondence of Salmon P. Chase," *Annual Report of the American Historical Association, 1902* 2 (Washington, D.C., 1903), 113–16.

62. Francis D. Parish to Chase, Oct. 15, 1845, June 17, 1847, Chase Papers, HSP; Chase to Trowbridge, Mar. 19, 1864, in Warden, *Chase*, pp. 310–11.

63. *State* v. *Hoppess*, 2 Western L. J. (Ohio), 279–92 (1845); Chase to Trowbridge, Mar. 19, 1864, in Warden, *Chase*, pp. 309–10; Schuckers, *Chase*, pp. 74–79; Fladeland, *Birney*, p. 154; Finkelman, *An Imperfect Union*, pp. 167–72.

64. Chase, "The Address and Reply on the Presentation of a Testimonial to S. P. Chase by the Colored People of Cincinnati," (Cincinnati: Henry Derby and Co., 1845); *Cincinnati Gazette*, May 8, 23, 24, 1845. Chase's advocacy of civil rights for blacks was later used against him in his race for governor of Ohio in 1855. See Chase to Trowbridge, Mar. 19, 1864, in Warden, *Chase*, pp. 309–10; Schuckers, *Chase*, pp. 79–80.

65. Chase to Trowbridge, Mar. 21, 1864, Chase Papers, Cincinnati Historical Society (hereafter cited as CHS).

66. Chase to Flamen Ball, Dec. 27, 1844, Ball to Chase, memorandum, 1872, Chase Papers, LC; Wendell P. Dabney, *Cincinnati's Colored Citizens: Historical, Sociological and Biographical* (Cincinnati: Dabney Publishing Co., 1926), pp. 357, 72–73. Longworth was quite willing to assist the black community as long as it remained totally separate from whites and as long as there was no challenge to slavery itself. S. P. Brux, "An Appeal to the Citizens of Ohio," in *Cincinnati Gazette*, Dec. 4, 1844. See also *Cincinnati Gazette*, Aug. 14, 1844.

Chapter Three

1. Chase to Trowbridge, Mar. 18, 1864, Chase Papers, CHS; Chase to Cleveland, Dec. 21, 1831, Aug. 13, 1832, Chase Papers, HSP. For a revealing explanation of why Wirt agreed to head the third-party ticket see Wirt to Chase, Nov. 11, 1831, Wirt Papers, Maryland Historical Society.

2. Chase to Trowbridge, Mar. 18, 1864, Chase Papers, CHS. See James Stegemoeller, "That Contemptible Bauble: The Birth of the Cincinnati Whig Party, 1834–1836," *Cincinnati Historical Society Bulletin* 39 (1981); 209–12.

3. Birney to Chase, June 5, 1837, Chase Papers, LC.

4. *Cincinnati Gazette*, Mar. 19, Apr. 6, 8, 23, 1840; Chase, Diary, May 29, 1840, Chase Papers, LC.

5. *Philanthropist*, Feb. 4, June 30, 1840; Chase, Diary, July 1, 1840, Chase Papers, LC. In 1837, Birney moved to New York to assume the post of secretary of the American Anti-Slavery Society. Bailey had already become editor of the *Philanthropist* by that time. See Fladeland, *Birney*, p. 155.

6. Chase to Cleveland, Aug. 29, 1840, Chase Papers, HSP.

7. Chase to Harrison, Feb. 13, 1841, Harrison Papers, LC.

8. Chase to Sumner, Mar. 9, 1849, Chase to [?], 1868, in Hart, *Chase*, pp. 88–89; Ball to Chase, Sept. 4, 1841, Chase Papers, HSP; Richards, *Gentlemen of Property and Standing*, pp. 122–29.

9. Bailey's *Philanthropist* opposed a third-party nomination through the spring of 1840 and reversed itself only during the summer. *Philanthropist*, Apr.–July 1840, Jan. 6, 1841.

10. Chase to Trowbridge, Mar. 18, 1864, Chase Papers, CHS. The early stages of Liberty party formation in the Old Northwest in the months preceding Chase's decision to participate have been described by several historians. See Stanley Harrold, "Forging an Antislavery Instrument: Gamaliel Bailey and the Formation of the Ohio Liberty Party," *Old Northwest* 2 (1976): 371–87, Fladeland, *Birney,* and Richard Sewell, *Ballots for Freedom: Antislavery Politics in the United States, 1837–1860* (New York: Oxford Univ. Press, 1976). These works expand on the still useful study of Theodore C. Smith, *The Liberty and Free Soil Parties in the Northwest* (New York: Longmans Green and Co., 1897). For further explanations of these complex maneuverings see Stanley Harrold, *Gamaliel Bailey and Antislavery Union* (Kent, Ohio: Kent State Univ. Press, 1986), and Vernon Volpe, "Forlorn Hope of Freedom: The Liberty Party in the Old Northwest, 1838–1848" (Ph.D. diss., University of Nebraska, 1984).

11. *Philanthropist,* Jan. 27, Feb. 3, 1841; *Cincinnati Gazette,* Apr. 5, 13, 1841; Chase to Cleveland, May 18, 1841, Chase Papers, HSP.

12. *Philanthropist,* Aug. 20, 23, Sept. 1, 1841; George Hoadly, "Memorial Address," in Hart, *Chase,* p. 88; Harrold, *Bailey,* pp. 50, 58.

13. Chase to Cleveland, Oct. 22, 1841, Chase Papers, LC.

14. Ibid.; Chase to Trowbridge, Mar. 18, 1864, Chase Papers, CHS; *Cincinnati Gazette,* Nov. 1841; Warden, *Chase,* pp. 295–96.

15. *Philanthropist,* Jan. 13, 1842; Harrold, "Forging an Antislavery Instrument," pp. 382–83; Chase to Cleveland, Oct. 22, 1841, Chase Papers, LC.

16. Chase to Giddings, Dec. 30, 1841, Jan. 21, 1842, Giddings Papers, Ohio Historical Society (hereafter cited as OHS).

17. Chase to Giddings, Jan. 21, 1842, Giddings Papers, OHS; Chase to Birney, Jan. 21, 1842, in Dwight L. Dumond, ed., *Letters of James Gillespie Birney, 1831–1857,* 2 vols. (New York: D. Appleton Century Co., 1938), 2:661–62; Smith, *Liberty and Free Soil Parties,* p. 56; *Whig Almanac,* 1843.

18. *Emancipator,* May 27, 1841; Sewell, *Ballots for Freedom,* pp. 121–22.

19. Leavitt to Chase, Dec. 6, 1841, Chase Papers, HSP; "Address of the Liberty Convention to the People of Ohio" (Columbus, 1841); Chase to Birney, Jan. 21, 1842, in Dumond, *Letters of Birney,* 2:661–62; *Philanthropist,* Jan. 13, 1842.

20. Birney to Committee of National Convention, Jan. 10, 1842, in *Signal of Liberty* [Ann Arbor], Mar. 16, 1842; Birney to Chase, Feb. 2, 1842, in Bourne, ed., "Chase Correspondence," pp. 459–62.

21. Chase to Giddings, Jan. 21, 1842, Giddings–Julian Papers, LC; Chase to Tappan, Sept. 15, May 26, 1842, Chase Papers, LC; Chase to Thaddeus Stevens, Apr. 8, 1842, Stevens Papers, LC; Chase to Giddings, May 19, 1842, Giddings Papers, OHS.

22. Chase to J. Q. Adams, Sept. 24, 1842, Chase Papers, HSP; Chase to Tappan, Sept. 24, 1842, Feb. 15, 1843, Chase Papers, LC; William Birney to James Birney, Apr. 29, 1843, Leavitt to Birney, Feb. 28, 1843, in Dumond, *Letters of Birney,* 2:736–38, 719–20; Leavitt to Chase, Feb. 16, 1843, Tappan to Chase, Mar. 20, 1843, Chase Papers, HSP; Harrold, *Bailey,* pp. 64–66.

23. Kirk Porter and Donald Johnson, eds., *National Party Platforms, 1840–1972,*

5th ed. (Urbana: Univ. of Illinois Press, 1973), pp. 4–8; Schuckers, *Chase*, p. 69; Warden, *Chase*, p. 300; Chase to Trowbridge, Mar. 18, 1864, Chase Papers, LC.

24. Porter and Johnson, *National Party Platforms*, pp. 4–8; Tappan to Chase, Sept. 20, 1843, Chase Papers, HSP; William Birney to James Birney, Feb. 26, 1844, in Dumond, *Letters of Birney*, 2:794–95; Sewell, *Ballots for Freedom*, p. 100.

25. Chase to Tappan, Sept. 12, 1843, Chase Papers, LC. See also William Birney to James Birney, Jan. 26, 1844, in Dumond, *Letters of Birney*, 2:776.

26. Smith, *Liberty and Free Soil Parties*, p. 80; *Cincinnati Herald*, Dec. 25, 1844.

27. "Call for a Southern and Western Liberty Convention," in Dumond, *Letters of Birney*, 2:934–35 n.; Seward to Chase, May 28, 1845, Chase Papers, LC. See also Tappan to Chase, Apr. 28, 1845, Chase Papers, HSP.

28. Leavitt to Birney, Jan. 25, 1845, Birney Papers, LC; Chase to Birney, Apr. 21, 1845, in Dumond, *Letters of Birney*, 2:934–35; Fladeland, *Birney*, p. 254.

29. Chase, "The Address of the Southern and Western Liberty Convention Held at Cincinnati," in Charles D. Cleveland, ed., *Antislavery Addresses of 1844 and 1845* (London, 1867).

30. Smith, *Liberty and Free Soil Parties*, pp. 88–89; William Birney, *James G. Birney and His Times* (New York, 1890), pp. 364–65; Chase, "Address of the Southern and Western Liberty Convention"; Chase to Q. F. Atkins, July 21, 1845, Atkins Papers, Hayes Memorial Library.

31. Chase to Cleveland, Oct. 20, 1845, Chase Papers, HSP; Chase, "Address of the Southern and Western Liberty Convention"; Stanley Harrold, "Southern Strategy of the Liberty Party," *Ohio History* 87 (1978): 28–30; Harrold, *Bailey*, pp. 73–74, 86.

32. Fladeland, *Birney*, pp. 255–60; Birney to Liberty Party, Sept. 1, 1846, in *Signal of Liberty* [Ann Arbor], Sept. 12, 1846.

33. Schuckers, *Chase*, p. 74; Chase to Cleveland, Feb. 3, 1845, Chase Papers, HSP; Chase, "Address of the Southern and Western Liberty Convention."

34. Chase to James H. Smith, May 8, 1849, Chase to W. G. Kephart, June 19, 1849, in Bourne, "Chase Correspondence," pp. 171–77; Chase to Smith, Sept. 8, 1846, Smith Papers, Syracuse University.

35. *Congressional Globe*, 29th Cong., 2d Sess., Appendix, Feb. 8, 1847, pp. 317–18; ibid., 33d Cong., 1st Sess., July 14, 1854, p. 1744, July 21, 1854, p. 1844, Appendix, July 20, 1854, pp. 1121–22; *National Era*, July 20, 1848.

36. Chase to Hale, May 12, 1847, in Warden, *Chase*, pp. 312–15; Chase to Giddings, Oct. 20, 1846, in Bourne, "Chase Correspondence," pp. 108–11; Harrold, *Bailey*, pp. 83–87. See Fladeland, *Birney*, p. 261 for Birney's opposition to Bailey as editor. He preferred his friend Leavitt.

37. Chase to Preston King, July 15, 1847, in Bourne, "Chase Correspondence," pp. 120–22.

38. *Congressional Globe*, 29th Cong., 2d Sess., Appendix, Feb. 11, 1847, pp. 211–18; Chase to Sumner, Sept. 22, 1847, in Bourne, "Chase Correspondence," p. 122; Sumner to Giddings, Nov. 1, 1847, Giddings Papers, OHS. See also Hal W. Bochin, "Tom Corwin's Speech Against the Mexican War: Courageous But Misunderstood," *Ohio History* 90 (1981): 33–54.

39. Chase to McLean, Jan. 22, 1847, McLean Papers, LC; Chase to Sumner, Apr. 24, 1847, in Bourne, "Chase Correspondence," pp. 113–16; "Marcellus" [Chase] to Bailey, Nov. 11, 1847, in *National Era,* Nov. 18, 1847; Seward to Chase, Nov. 27, 1844, Chase to Tappan, Mar. 18, 1847, Chase Papers, LC.

40. Sewell, *Ballots for Freedom,* pp. 127–30; Chase to Hale, Jan. 30, 1846, Hale Papers, New Hampshire Historical Society (hereafter cited as NHHS); Richard Sewell, *John P. Hale and the Politics of Abolition* (Cambridge: Harvard Univ. Press, 1965), pp. 88–89; Stanton to Chase, Aug. 6, 1847, Chase Papers, LC; Sumner to Giddings, July 28, 1847, Giddings Papers, OHS.

41. Chase to Hale, Sept. 23, 1847, Chase Papers, NHHS; Chase to Sumner, Sept. 22, 1847, Chase to Leavitt, June 16, 1847, in Bourne, "Chase Correspondence," pp. 116–17, 122–24; *National Era,* Apr. 15, 22, May 6, 1847; Smith, *Liberty and Free Soil Parties,* p. 118. The poll of the committee was conducted by Corresponding Secretary Joshua Leavitt with the results reported in the *Emancipator* on June 23, 30, 1847.

42. Stanton to Chase, Aug. 6, 1847, Chase Papers, LC; Bailey to Chase, Sept. 16, 1847, Ball to Chase, Sept. 1, 1847, Chase Papers, HSP; Chase to Sumner, Dec. 2, Sept. 22, 1847, Chase to John Thomas, June 24, 1847, in Bourne, "Chase Correspondence," pp. 118–20, 122–27.

43. Fladeland, *Birney,* p. 265; Ralph Harlow, *Gerrit Smith: Philanthropist and Reformer* (New York: Henry Holt & Co., 1939), pp. 178–79; Aileen S. Kraditor, *Means and Ends in American Abolitionism: Garrison and His Critics on Strategy and Tactics, 1834–1850* (New York: Random House, 1967), pp. 153–57; William Goodell, *Slavery and Anti-Slavery* (New York, 1853), pp. 475, 477; *National Era,* Nov. 4, 11, 1847.

44. *Cincinnati Herald,* Nov. 3, 1847; Joseph G. Rayback, "The Liberty Party Leaders of Ohio: Exponents of Antislavery Coalition," *Ohio State Archaeological and Historical Quarterly* 67 (1948): 177; *National Era,* Nov. 11, 1847.

45. Chase to Sumner, Dec. 2, 1847, in Bourne, "Chase Correspondence," pp. 124–27; *National Era,* Jan. 27, 1848, printed Hale's letter of acceptance.

46. Chaplain W. Morrison, *Democratic Politics and Sectionalism: The Wilmot Proviso Controversy* (Chapel Hill: Univ. of North Carolina Press, 1967), pp. 81–84; O. C. Gardiner, *The Great Issue, or the Three Presidential Candidates* (New York: William C. Bryant and Co., 1848), pp. 50–72; *Albany Evening Atlas,* Oct. 27, 1847; Arthur B. Darling, *Political Changes in Massachusetts, 1824–1848: A Study of Liberal Movements in Politics* (New Haven: Yale Historical Publications, 1925), pp. 342–45; William G. Bean, "Party Transformations in Massachusetts with Special Reference to the Antecedents of Republicanism, 1848–1860" (Ph.D. diss., Harvard University, 1922), pp. 27–28.

47. Kinley J. Brauer, *Cotton Versus Conscience: Massachusetts Politics and Southwestern Expansion, 1843–1848* (Lexington: Univ. of Kentucky Press, 1967), pp. 207–8; Sumner to Chase, Oct. 1, 1847, Chase Papers, LC; Adams, Diary, Sept. 25, 28, 29, 1847, Adams Papers, Massachusetts Historical Society (hereafter cited as MHS); Chase to Sumner, Dec. 2, 1847, in Bourne, "Chase Correspondence," pp. 124–27.

48. Chase to Belle Chase, Jan. 2, 1848, Chase Papers, LC; Chase to Giddings, Feb. 29, 1848, Giddings Papers, OHS.

49. Chase to Sumner, Feb. 19, Mar. 25, 1848, in Bourne, "Chase Correspondence," pp. 128–32; McLean to Chase, Dec. 22, 1847, Chase Papers, HSP; Chase to McLean, Jan. 10, Feb. 12, 1848, McLean Papers, LC; *Emancipator,* Nov. 17, 1847; *National Era,* Dec. 2, 1847.

50. Giddings to Chase, Mar. 16, 1848, Chase Papers, HSP; Smith, *Liberty and Free Soil Parties,* pp. 129–34.

51. *National Era,* June 29, July 6, 13, 1848; "Addresses and Proceedings of the State Independent Free Territory Convention of the People of Ohio Held at Columbus, June 20, 21, 1848" (Cincinnati, 1848); Harrold, *Bailey,* pp. 117–18.

52. Chase to Sumner, June 20, 1848, in Bourne, "Chase Correspondence," pp. 137–38; Sewell, *Ballots for Freedom,* p. 150n.

Chapter Four

1. Frederick J. Blue, *The Free Soilers: Third-Party Politics, 1848–54* (Urbana: Univ. of Illinois Press, 1973), p. 57; A. Willey to Chase, July 10, 1848, Chase Papers, LC; Samuel J. Tilden to Chase, July 29, 1848, in Bourne, "Chase Correspondence," pp. 468–70.

2. Chase to Hale, June 15, 24, 1848, Chase Papers, NHHS; Hale to Chase, June 14, 1848, Chase Papers, HSP; *National Era,* July 6, 13, 1848; L. Tappan to Hale, July 8, 1848, Hale Papers, NHHS; L. Tappan to Chase, June 14, 1848, Chase Papers, HSP.

3. Chase to McLean, May 20, 1848, McLean Papers, LC; Sumner to Chase, June 12, 1848, Chase Papers, LC; Chase to Sumner, June 20, 1848, in Bourne, "Chase Correspondence," pp. 137–38; Giddings to Joseph Giddings, Mar. 12, June 23, 1848, Giddings Papers, OHS; Sumner to Chase, July 7, 1848, Chase Papers, LC; Stanton to Chase, July 28, 1848, McLean Papers, LC.

4. Chase to McLean, Aug. 2, 4, 1848, McLean Papers, LC; McLean to Chase, Aug. 2, 4, 1848, Chase Papers, HSP; Chase to Sumner, June 20, 1848, in Bourne, "Chase Correspondence," pp. 137–38; Chase to Belle Chase, July 26, 1848, Chase Papers, LC.

5. Gardiner, *The Great Issue,* pp. 137–41; "Official Proceedings of the National Free Soil Convention Assembled at Buffalo, N.Y., August 9th and 10th, 1848"; (*Buffalo Republic,* Extra); Oliver Dyer, *Phonographic Report of the Proceedings of the National Free Soil Convention at Buffalo, N.Y., August 9th and 10th, 1848* (Buffalo, 1848); Charles Francis Adams, Jr., *Charles Francis Adams* (Boston, 1890), p. 90. In addition to the numerous contemporary descriptions, several historians have put great emphasis on the Free Soil party's origins at the Buffalo convention and Chase's role there. The accounts include Sewell, *Ballots for Freedom,* John Mayfield, *Rehearsal for Republicanism: Free Soil and and the Politics of Antislavery* (Port Washington: Kennikat Press, 1980), Joseph G. Rayback, *Free Soil: The Election of 1848* (Lexington: Univ. Press of Kentucky, 1970), and Blue, *The Free Soilers.*

6. Chase to Trowbridge, Mar. 21, 1864, in Warden, *Chase,* pp. 318–19; Chase to James W. Taylor, Aug. 15, 1848, Chase Papers, HSP; Dyer, *Phonographic Report,* p. 5; Morrison, *Democratic Politics,* pp. 152–53.

7. Smith, *Liberty and Free Soil Parties,* p. 139; Oliver Dyer, *Great Senators of the United States Forty Years Ago (1848–1849)* (New York, 1889).

8. Porter and Johnson, *National Party Platforms,* pp. 13–14; Chase to Trowbridge, Mar. 21, 1864, in Warden, *Chase,* pp. 318–19.

9. Gardiner, *The Great Issue,* pp. 138–40; Smith, *Liberty and Free Soil Parties,* p. 140; Porter and Johnson, *National Party Platforms,* pp. 13–14; Dyer, *Phonographic Report,* p. 5.

10. McLean to Chase, Aug. 4, 1848, Chase Papers, HSP; Chase to McLean, Aug. 12, 1848, Aug. 13, 1852, E. S. Hamlin to McLean, Aug. 17, 1848, McLean Papers, LC.

11. Charles Francis Adams, Diary, Aug. 10, 1848, Adams Papers, MHS; Stanton to Hale, Aug. 20, 1848, Leavitt to Hale, Aug. 22, 1848, Hale Papers, NHHS; Bertram Wyatt-Brown, *Lewis Tappan and the Evangelical War Against Slavery* (Cleveland: Case Western Reserve Univ. Press, 1969), p. 280; Gardiner, *The Great Issue,* pp. 140–41.

12. Chase to J. W. Taylor, Aug. 15, 1848, Chase to Adams, Aug. 16, 1848, Chase Papers, HSP.

13. Dyer, *Phonographic Report;* "Official Proceedings," pp. 3–4.

14. Chase to Martin Van Buren, Aug. 21, 1848, Van Buren to Butler, White, and Chase, Aug. 22, 1848, Van Buren to Louis Lapham, Oct. 16, 1848, Chase to John Van Buren, Sept. 30, 1848, Van Buren Papers, LC; *National Era,* Aug. 24, 31, 1848.

15. Hale to Lewis, Aug. 28, 1848, in *National Era,* Sept. 7, 1848.

16. *National Era,* Aug. 31, 1848; Adams, Diary, Aug. 11, 1848, Adams Papers, MHS; Edward Stanwood, *A History of the Presidency from 1788 to 1897* (Boston and New York: Houghton Mifflin Co., 1898), p. 243; Chase to Sumner, Nov. 27, 1848, in Bourne, "Chase Correspondence," pp. 142–45.

17. Blue, *Free Soilers,* p. 191; Chase to Ford, July 11, 1848, in Bourne, "Chase Correspondence," pp. 138–39; James Briggs to Chase, Sept. 28, 1848, Chase Papers, LC; Smith, *Liberty and Free Soil Parties,* pp. 152–53; Chase to Matthews, Jan. 29, 1849, in Annie A. Nunns, ed., "Some Letters of Salmon P. Chase," *American Historical Review* 34 (1929): 546–48. A Free Soil meeting in Columbus had suggested that the third party endorse Chase for governor, but he had rejected the idea. See *Ohio Standard,* Sept. 1848, clipping in Chase Papers, LC.

18. In the Ohio House there were thirty-two Democrats, thirty Whigs and eight Free Soilers. There were seventeen Democratic senators, fourteen Whigs, and three Free Soilers. Smith, *Liberty and Free Soil Parties,* pp. 162–63.

19. Hale to Chase, Mar. 2, 1849, Chase Papers, LC; Edgar A. Holt, "Party Politics in Ohio, 1840–1850," *Ohio State Archaeological and Historical Quarterly* 38 (1929): 320–24; Francis P. Weisenburger, *The Passing of the Frontier,* vol. 3 of *The History of the State of Ohio,* Carl Wittke, ed. (Columbus: Ohio State Archaeological and Historical Society, 1941), pp. 470–71; Smith, *Liberty and Free Soil Parties,* p. 163. On the passage of the apportionment bill in February 1848 see Senate Journal, 46th General Assembly, 1st sess., Feb. 18, 1848, pp. 566–69; Stephen E. Maizlish, *The Triumph of Sectionalism: The Transformation of Ohio Politics, 1844–1856*

(Kent, Ohio: Kent State Univ. Press, 1983), p. 122.

20. Chase to Matthews, Dec. 23, 1848, in "Some Letters of Chase," pp. 536–37; Matthews to Chase, Jan. 11, 1849, Chase Papers, LC; E. S. Hamlin to Chase, Jan. 18, 25, 1849, Chase Papers, HSP.

21. Chase to Eli Nichols, Nov. 9, 1848, in Bourne, "Chase Correspondence," pp. 139–41; Chase to Matthews, Jan. 18, 1849, in "Some Letters of Chase," pp. 539–41; Riddle to Giddings, Jan. 15, Feb. 21, 1849, Chase to Giddings, Apr. 4, 23, 1849, Giddings Papers, OHS; Chase to Belle Chase, Dec. 30, 1848, Stanley Matthews to Chase, Jan. 11, 20, 1849, Chase Papers, LC; *Cleveland True Democrat,* Jan. 4, 1849.

22. Giddings to Riddle, Nov. 11, 1848, Riddle to Giddings, Nov. 18, Dec. 22, 1848, Giddings Papers, OHS. See also Giddings's diary for his reactions to the senatorial election, Jan. 23, 1849, ibid.; James B. Stewart, *Joshua Giddings and the Tactics of Radical Politics* (Cleveland: Press of Case Western Reserve Univ., 1970), pp. 173–76.

23. Chase to Giddings, Jan. 20, 1849, Chase Papers, HSP; Chase to E. S. Hamlin, Jan. 27, 1849, in Bourne, "Chase Correspondence," pp. 160–61.

24. Chase to Morse, Jan. 19, 1849, Matthews to Chase, Jan. 20, 1849, T. Noble to Chase, Feb. 24, 1849, Chase, Diary, Jan. 7, 1849, Chase Papers, LC; John Teesdale to McLean, Feb. 22, 1849, McLean Papers, LC.

25. Chase to Belle Chase, Feb. 19, 1849, Chase Papers, LC; *Ohio State Journal* [Columbus], Feb. 22, 1849; Giddings, Diary, Feb. 23, 1849, Giddings Papers, OHS; Giddings to Chase, Mar. 14, 1849, Chase Papers, HSP.

26. Senate Journal, 47th General Assembly, 1st sess., Feb. 22, 1849, p. 403; Matthews to Chase, Feb. 23, 1849, Chase Papers, LC; Hamlin to Chase, Feb. 23, 1849, Chase Papers, HSP; Maizlish, *The Triumph of Sectionalism,* pp. 142–43.

27. *Laws of Ohio* 5 (1807): 53–54, 46 (1848): 81–82; Frank U. Quillin, *The Color Line in Ohio: A History of Race Prejudice in a Typical Northern State* (Ann Arbor: Univ of Michigan Press, 1913), pp. 21–24; *Ohio Statesman,* Dec. 30, 1848.

28. Matthews to Chase, Jan. 26, 1849, Chase Papers, LC; Morse to Chase, Jan. 24, 1849, Chase Papers, HSP; *Laws of Ohio* 47 (1849): 17–18.

29. Chase, Diary, Jan. 7, 1849, Chase Papers, LC; Chase to Hamlin, Jan. 20, 1849, in Bourne, "Chase Correspondence," pp. 153–55; Hamlin to Chase, Jan. 30, 1849, Chase Papers, HSP.

30. Chase to Hamlin, Jan. 16, 20, 24, 1849, in Bourne, "Chase Correspondence," pp. 145–48, 153–55, 156–60; *Cleveland True Democrat,* Mar. 26, 1850. See also *National Era,* Feb. 22, 1849.

31. *Ohio State Journal,* Apr. 19, 1849; A. G. Riddle to Giddings, Feb. 21, 1849, Giddings Papers, OHS; Chase to George Reber, June 19, 1849, in Bourne, "Chase Correspondence," pp. 178–79; Chase to Belle Chase, Feb. 11, 1849, Chase Papers, LC.

32. Sumner to Chase, Feb. 27, 1849, H. B. Stanton to Chase, Feb. 24, 1849, J. P. Hale to Chase, Mar. 2, 1849, Chase Papers, LC; Chase to Giddings, Jan. 20, 1849, Chase Papers, HSP; Chase to George Reber, June 19, 1849, in Bourne, "Chase Correspondence," pp. 178–79. See also Schuckers, *Chase,* pp. 103–4.

33. Chase to John F. Morse, Aug. 15, 1849, in Warden, *Chase,* p. 321; *National Era,* May 17, 1849; Smith, *Liberty and Free Soil Parties,* pp. 177–78; Stewart, *Giddings,* pp. 177–78.

34. Chase to John G. Breslin, July 30, 1849, in Schuckers, *Chase,* pp. 101–3.

35. Chase to Townshend, July 4, 1849, Chase Papers, HSP; *Cleveland Plain Dealer,* Oct. 24, 1849; *Ohio State Journal,* Oct. 16, 1849; Giddings to Sumner, Oct. 29, 1849, Sumner Papers, Harvard University.

36. Belle Chase was the niece of Justice John McLean's wife, a relationship which made Chase's role in the 1848 Free-Soil convention all the more difficult.

37. Chase to Belle Chase, July 28, 1850, Mar. 15, 1849, Chase Papers, LC; Chase to E. S. Hamlin, Dec. 21, 1849, in Bourne, "Chase Correspondence," pp. 192–93.

38. Chase to Belle Chase, Jan. 6, July 28, 1850, Dec. 14, 1851, Chase Papers, LC; Chase to Sumner, Jan. 28, 1850, in Bourne, "Chase Correspondence," p. 200.

39. Chase to Kate Chase, July 22, Aug. 13, 1850, Mar. 2, 1851, Chase Papers, HSP.

40. Chase to Kate Chase, Feb. 21, 1852, Feb. 6, Sept. 6, 1853, July 5, 1854, Chase Papers, HSP.

41. Chase to William Chase, Apr. 11, May 23, 1849, Chase, Diary, Dec. 10, 1852, Chase Papers, LC.

42. Chase to Edward Chase, 1849, Chase to James Skinner, Jan. 8, 1850, Chase Papers, LC; Chase to E. S. Hamlin, Aug. 27, 1852, in Bourne, "Chase Correspondence," pp. 245–46; Chase to Belle Chase, July 28, 1850, Chase Papers, LC.

43. Chase to Hamlin, Dec. 17, 1849, Jan. 2, 1850, Chase to Sumner, Dec. 14, 1849, in Bourne, "Chase Correspondence," pp. 188–95; *Congressional Globe,* 31st Cong., 1st sess., Dec. 18, 1849, p. 40; Hart, *Chase,* p. 114.

44. *Congressional Globe,* 31st Cong., 1st sess., Appendix, Jan. 24, 1850, pp. 80–81, 83.

45. *Congressional Globe,* 31st Cong., 1st sess., Dec. 11–12, 1849, pp. 16–22, 63–66; Blue, *Free Soilers,* pp. 191–96; Chase to Sumner, Apr. 13, Dec. 14, 1850, in Bourne, "Chase Correspondence," pp. 206–9, 224; Chase to [?], 1850, in Hart, *Chase,* p. 113.

46. Chase to Sumner, Sept. 8, 1850, Apr. 28, 1851, in Bourne, "Chase Correspondence," pp. 219–20, 235–36.

47. Chase to Kate Chase, Aug. 27, 1852, Chase Papers, HSP; Chase boarded in Bailey's spacious home for the first two years of his Senate term. Chase to Belle Chase, Mar. 6, 1849, Chase Papers, LC; Chase to Giddings, Mar. 6, 1849, Giddings Papers, OHS; Grace Julian Clarke, *George W. Julian* (Indianapolis, 1923), pp. 89–90; Stewart, *Giddings,* p. 181; Harrold, *Bailey,* pp. 132–33.

48. *Congressional Globe,* 31st Cong., 1st sess., Jan. 10, 29, Feb. 4, 1850, pp. 133, 244–77; Chase to Hamlin, Feb. 2, 1850, in Bourne, "Chase Correspondence," pp. 200–201; Hart, *Chase,* pp. 123–24.

49. James D. Richardson, ed., *A Compilation of the Messages and Papers of the Presidents,* 20 vols. (New York: Bureau of National Literature, 1897–1916), 5:27–30; Chase to Sumner, Jan. 28, Apr. 13, 1850, in Bourne, "Chase Correspondence," pp. 200, 206–9; Holman Hamilton, *Prologue to Conflict: The Crisis and Compromise of*

1850 (Lexington: Univ. Press of Kentucky, 1964), pp. 46–48; Michael F. Holt, *The Political Crisis of the 1850's* (New York: John Wiley and Sons, 1978), pp. 76–78.

50. Chase to Sumner, March 24, 1850, in Bourne, "Chase Correspondence," pp. 205–6.

51. *Congressional Globe,* 31st Cong., 1st sess., Appendix, Mar. 26–27, 1850, pp. 468–80; Schurz, *Reminiscences,* 2:34; *National Era,* May 16, 1850. Chase received numerous letters from supporters endorsing his stand. See Chase Papers, LC, Mar.– May 1850 for examples. Chase to Belle Chase, Mar. 27, 1850, Chase Papers, LC; Chase to Sumner, Apr. 4, 13, 1850, in Bourne, "Chase Correspondence," pp. 206– 9.

52. *Congressional Globe,* 31st Cong., 1st sess., Apr. 11, May 28, 30, June 5, 6, 7, 1850, pp. 711, 1083–84, 1134, 1145–46; *National Era,* July 18, 1850; Chase to Belle Chase, July 12, 1850, Chase Papers, LC; Hamilton, *Prologue to Conflict,* pp. 106–7.

53. Chase to E. S. Hamlin, Feb. 18, Aug. 14, 22, 1850, Adam Klippel to Chase, Sept. 14, 1849, in Bourne, "Chase Correspondence," pp. 201–3, 216–19, 470–76; *Congressional Globe,* 31st Cong., 1st sess., Appendix, Aug. 14, 1850, pp. 1557–60. On the defeat of the Omnibus proposal, see Hamilton, *Prologue to Conflict,* pp. 109– 11.

54. *Congressional Globe,* 31st Cong., 1st sess., Appendix, Aug. 23, 1850, pp. 1587, 1619–23; Schuckers, *Chase,* p. 125.

55. *Congressional Globe,* 31st Cong., 2d sess., Appendix, Feb. 22, 1851, pp. 309– 10, Feb. 24, 1851, p. 671.

56. *Congressional Globe,* 31st Cong., 1st sess., Sept. 23, 1850, p. 1945; 2d sess., Dec. 9, 1850, p. 19, Feb. 4, 1851, p. 401; 32d Cong., 1st sess., Apr. 14, 1852, pp. 1065–66, 1083; Chase, Manuscript Biography, Chase Papers, LC; Hart, *Chase,* pp. 116–17.

57. *Congressional Globe,* 33d Cong., 1st sess., July 12, 1854, p. 1702, July 13, 1854, pp. 1717, 1740.

58. Ibid., 33d Cong., 1st sess., July 14, 1854, p. 1744, July 21, 1854, p. 1844, Appendix, July 20, 1854, pp. 1121–22.

59. Chase to Douglass, May 4, 1850, Chase Papers, HSP; *Congressional Globe,* 32d Cong., 2d sess., Mar. 3, 1853, p. 1064; Douglass to Chase, May 30, 1850, Chase to J. M. Langston, Nov. 11, 1850, Chase Papers, LC.

60. Chase was consistent in his defense of individual blacks whom he believed were the victims of injustice. For example, he defended the Africans of the *Amistad* when he objected in the Senate to a bill to compensate their Spanish captors on the grounds that the Supreme Court had earlier ruled the blacks to be free. *Congressional Globe,* 31st Cong., 2d, sess., Feb. 4, 1851, pp. 401, 402.

61. Ibid., 32d Cong., 2d sess., Mar. 3, 1853, p. 1094. The bill was vetoed by President Pierce on the grounds that such aid was a function of the states, not the central government. Alice Felt Tyler, *Freedom's Ferment: Phases of American Social History from the Colonial Period to the Outbreak of the Civil War* (New York: Harper and Row, 1964), pp. 305–7.

62. *Congressional Globe,* 32d Cong., 1st sess., Feb. 5, 1852, pp. 449, 450.

63. Chase to [?], June 15, 1850, Chase Papers, LC.

64. Chase to Butler, July 26, 1849, in Bourne, "Chase Correspondence," pp. 180–82; Butler to Chase, July 30, 1849, Chase Papers, HSP.

65. Chase to Sumner, Sept. 15, 19, 1849, in Bourne, "Chase Correspondence," pp. 183–88; Sumner to Chase, Sept. 25, 1849, Chase Papers, LC.

·66. Chase to Belle Chase, Jan. 15, 1850, Chase to Hamlin, Jan. 22, 1850, Chase Papers, LC; Chase to Hamlin, Jan. 17, Feb. 2, 18, Mar. 16, 1850, in Bourne, "Chase Correspondence," pp. 197–99, 200–205.

67. Chase to Hamlin, Apr. 16, 1850, Hamlin to Chase, July 1, 1850, Chase Papers, LC; Adams, Diary, Sept. 8, 1849, Adams Papers, MHS; Smith, *Liberty and Free Soil Parties,* pp. 185–87; Maizlish, *The Triumph of Sectionalism,* pp. 156–58.

68. Chase to Giddings, Oct. 22, Nov. 1, 1850, Giddings Papers, OHS; Chase to Sumner, Dec. 14, 1850, in Bourne, "Chase Correspondence," p. 224.

69. Chase to Sutliff, Jan. 16, 1851, in Bourne, "Chase Correspondence," pp. 230–32; *Ohio State Journal,* Mar. 17, 1851; Hans L. Trefousse, *Benjamin Franklin Wade: Radical Republican From Ohio* (New York: Twayne Publishers, 1963), p. 67.

70. Chase to Sumner, June 28, 1851, in Bourne, "Chase Correspondence," pp. 237–38; Chase to Giddings, Mar. 24, 1851, Giddings Papers, OHS.

71. Chase to Sumner, June 28, 1851, in Bourne, "Chase Correspondence," pp. 237–38; Chase to Giddings, Aug. 9, 1851, Chase Papers, LC; *National Era,* Sept. 11, 1851; *Cleveland True Democrat,* Sept. 8, 11, 1851; Maizlish, *The Triumph of Sectionalism,* pp. 170–71.

72. Smith, *Liberty and Free Soil Parties,* p. 240; Birney, Diary, Oct. 4, 1851, in Fladeland, *Birney,* p. 217n; Lewis Tappan Journal, Sept. 25, 1851, Tappan Papers, LC; *National Era,* Sept. 11, 1851; Chase to D. W. A. Brisbane, Sept. 15, 1851, Chase Papers, HSP; Chase to Giddings, Sept. 9, 1851, Chase Papers, LC.

73. Chase to Hamlin, Dec. 5, 1851, in Bourne, "Chase Correspondence," pp. 238–40; Chase to Trowbridge, Mar. 21, 1864, in Warden, *Chase,* pp. 336–38.

74. Chase to Hamlin, Mar. 10, 1852, in Bourne, "Chase Correspondence," pp. 240–41; Chase to Hamlin, Aug. 3, 1852, Chase Papers, LC; Chase to Townshend, June 21, 1852, Chase Papers, HSP.

75. Porter and Johnson, *National Party Platforms,* pp. 16–18; Chase to Martin Van Buren, June 27, 1852, Van Buren Papers, LC; Chase to Butler, July 15, 1852, R. McBratney to Chase, June 20, 1851, Chase Papers, LC; Chase to Hamlin, June 28, 1852, in Bourne, "Chase Correspondence," pp. 242–43.

76. Adams, Diary, Aug. 6, 10, 1852, Adams Papers, MHS; Blue, *The Free Soilers,* p. 240; Chase to Hale, Aug. 5, 1852, Hale Papers, NHHS; Chase to Hamlin, July 19, 1852, in Bourne, "Chase Correspondence," pp. 243–44. Among those interested in a Chase candidacy was Gamaliel Bailey. See Harrold, *Bailey,* p. 152.

77. Chase to Hale, Aug. 7, 1852, Hale Papers, NHHS; Adams, Diary, Aug. 12, 1852, Adams Papers, MHS; Lewis to Julian, Aug. 19, 1852, Giddings-Julian Papers, LC; Porter and Johnson, *National Party Platforms,* pp. 18–20.

78. Chase to E. S. Hamlin, Aug. 13, 27, 1852, Chase to Sumner, Sept. 9, 1852, in Bourne, "Chase Correspondence," pp. 244–48. Giddings won reelection for an eighth term in the House, while Hale received 9 percent of the Ohio vote; outside the Western Reserve the third-party showing was disappointing. Stanwood, *A History of the Presidency,* p. 32; Smith, *Liberty and Free Soil Parties,* pp. 252–53.

79. Chase to Hamlin, Feb. 4, 1853, in Bourne, "Chase Correspondence," pp. 248–50; Chase to Hamlin, Feb. 8, 1853, Chase Papers, LC.

80. *Cleveland True Democrat,* Nov. 17, 1852, Jan. 12, 19, 26, 1853; *National Era,* Jan. 20, 27, 1853. The 1852 Free Democratic platform had omitted any call for black rights. See *National Era,* Aug. 19, 1852; Blue, *The Free Soilers,* p. 247.

81. Smith, *Liberty and Free Soil Parties,* pp. 268–74; R. W. P. Muse to Chase, July 12, 1853, Chase Papers, LC; Eugene H. Roseboom, *The Civil War Era,* vol. 4 of *The History of the State of Ohio,* Carl Wittke, ed. (Columbus: Ohio State Archaeological and Historical Society, 1944), pp. 220–25; Maizlish, *The Triumph of Sectionalism,* pp. 182–83.

82. Chase to Hamlin, July 21, 1853, Chase Papers, LC.

83. Chase to Giddings, July 4, 1853, Chase to Gerrit Smith, Oct. 19, 1853, Chase to Hamlin, June 6, Oct. 17, 1853, Chase Papers, LC; Chase to Edward Pierce, Jan. 17, Mar. 17, 1854, Chase to Hamlin, Jan. 22, 1854, in Bourne, "Chase Correspondence," pp. 252–56; Maizlish, *The Triumph of Sectionalism,* pp. 195–96.

84. Chase to George Pugh, Mar. 8, 1854, Chase to James Briggs, Apr. 26, 1854, Chase Papers, LC.

Chapter Five

1. Chase to Sumner, Sept. 13, 1854, Sumner Papers, Harvard University; Holt, *The Political Crisis of the 1850's,* pp. 144–45. A thorough description and analysis of the Douglas bill and the motives of its sponsor may be found in Robert W. Johannsen, *Stephen A. Douglas* (New York: Oxford Univ. Press, 1973), pp. 390–434.

2. Chase to Hamlin, Jan. 22, 23, 1854, in Bourne, "Chase Correspondence," pp. 254–57.

3. *Congressional Globe,* 33d Cong., 1st sess., Jan. 24, 1854, p. 239, Jan. 30, 1854, p. 276; *National Era,* Jan. 24, 1854. The text of the "Appeal" is in the *Congressional Globe,* 33d Cong., 1st sess., Jan. 30, 1854, pp. 281–82. Sumner, Representatives Edward Wade of Ohio, Gerrit Smith of New York, and Alexander DeWitt of Massachusetts also signed it. Originally it was endorsed by Senators Benjamin Wade and Seward and Representative Lewis Campbell of Ohio, but these three Whigs asked that their names be removed shortly before publication. See also Dick Johnson, "Along the Twisted Road to Civil War: Historians and the 'Appeal of the Independent Democrats,' " *The Old Northwest* 4 (1978): 136–37.

4. *Congressional Globe,* 33d Cong., 1st sess., Jan. 30, 1854, pp. 281–82; Foner, *Free Soil, Free Labor, Free Men,* pp. 94–95; David Potter, *The Impending Crisis, 1848–1861* (New York: Harper and Row, 1976), pp. 163–64.

5. *Congressional Globe,* 33d Cong., 1st sess., Jan. 30, 1854, pp. 275-81, Appendix, Feb. 3, 1854, pp. 133–40; Schurz, *Reminiscences,* 2:34; Johannsen, *Douglas,* pp. 418–20; William E. Gienapp, "The Origins of the Republican Party, 1852–1856" (Ph.D. diss., University of California, Berkeley, 1980), p. 287.

6. Chase to Hamlin, Feb. 10, 1854, Chase to E. L. Pierce, Mar. 12, 1854, in Bourne, "Chase Correspondence," pp. 257–60; James Taylor to Chase, Feb. 19,

1854, Chase Papers, LC; *Ohio State Journal,* Feb. 14, 1854; Holt, *The Political Crisis of the 1850's,* pp. 152–53.

7. *Congressional Globe,* 33d Cong., 1st sess., Feb. 15, 1854, p. 421, Mar. 2, 1854, p. 520, Appendix, Mar. 2, 1854, pp. 280–96, 298–301; Johannsen, *Douglas,* pp. 425–28. The House later removed the ban on immigrant voting and the Senate accepted this change.

8. *Congressional Globe,* 33d Cong., 1st sess., Appendix, Mar. 3, 1854, pp. 335–36, Appendix, May 25, 1854, p. 780; Chase to E. L. Pierce, Aug. 8, 1854, in Bourne, "Chase Correspondence," p. 263.

9. Chase to Hamlin, Apr. 25, 1854, Jan. 23, 1854, in Bourne, "Chase Correspondence," pp. 260, 256–57.

10. Chase to James Grimes, Apr. 29, 1854, Chase Papers, HSP; Sewell, *Ballots for Freedom,* p. 261; Gienapp, "The Origins of the Republican Party," pp. 326–28, 410; Henry Wilson, *History of the Rise and Fall of the Slave Power in America,* 2 vols. (Boston: J. R. Osgood and Co., 1873–77), 2:410–11.

11. The Ohio meetings had been preceded by a meeting at the end of February 1854 in Ripon, Wisconsin, which was the first to call for a new antislavery party. A meeting of Michigan citizens at Jackson on July 6 had officially adopted the name Republican. Roseboom, *The Civil War Era,* p. 282; Chase to William Schouler, May 28, 1854, Schouler Papers, MHS, in Reinhard H. Luthin, "Salmon P. Chase's Political Career Before the Civil War," *Mississippi Valley Historical Review* 29 (1943): 524; *Ohio State Journal,* July 13, 14, 15, 1855; Chase to E. S. Hamlin, July 21, 1854, in Bourne, "Chase Correspondence," pp. 262–63; Chase to "My Dear Friend," May 30, 1854, Chase to Hamlin, July 21, 1854, Chase to Townshend, July 7, 1854, Chase Papers, HSP; *National Era,* June 15, 1854; Gienapp, "The Origins of the Republican Party," pp. 411–17; *Ohio State Journal,* May 25, June 5, 26, July 14, 1854; Chase to John Jay, July 16, 1854, Jay Papers, Columbia University.

12. Fusionists also won the few state offices at stake. See *Ohio State Journal,* Nov. 25, 1854; Roseboom, *The Civil War Era,* pp. 293–96; Potter, *The Impending Crisis,* pp. 247–48. The origins of the Republican party present a complex historiographical issue complicated by the nativist movement which competed with it to replace the Whigs in the two-party system. Among those historians who stress the antislavery origins of the Republican party are Sewell, *Ballots for Freedom* and Foner, *Free Soil, Free Labor, Free Men.* James Rawley's study of the conflict in Kansas and its ramifications on northern politics, *Race and Slavery: "Bleeding Kansas" and the Coming of the Civil War* (Philadelphia: L. B. Lippincott, 1969), also emphasizes the sectional interpretation. The view which gives priority to the ethnic and religious aspects of party realignment is effectively argued by Holt, *The Political Crisis of the 1850's,* Joel Silbey, *The Partisan Imperative: The Dynamics of American Politics Before the Civil War* (New York: Oxford Univ. Press, 1985), and Gienapp, "Nativism and the Creation of a Republican Majority." For an interpretation which stresses socio-economic rather than ethnocultural factors as most responsible for the political changes in Chase's Ohio in the three decades before the 1850s see Donald J. Ratcliffe, "Politics in Jacksonian Ohio: Reflections on the Ethnocultural Interpretation," *Ohio History* 88 (1979): 5–36. The best study of Ohio politics in the 1840s and 1850s is Maizlish, *The Triumph of Sectionalism.* Despite the differences in interpretation, virtu-

ally all historians recognize the central role of Salmon P. Chase in the political upheaval of the 1850s.

13. Roseboom, *The Civil War Era,* pp. 287–92; Andrew W. Crandall, *The Early History of the Republican Party, 1854–1856* (Boston: Gorham Press, 1930), 207–8; Eugene H. Roseboom, "Salmon P. Chase and the Know Nothings," *Mississippi Valley Historical Review* 25 (1938): 338–40; Gienapp, "The Origins of the Republican Party," pp. 338, 353–54. For the Cleveland movement see Thomas W. Kremm, "The Rise of the Republican Party in Cleveland, 1848–1860," (Ph.D. diss., Kent State University, 1974), p. 115. See also Maizlish, *The Triumph of Sectionalism,* pp. 204–5, 211; Holt, *The Political Crisis of the 1850's,* pp. 156–70; Thomas W. Kremm, "The Old Order Trembles: The Formation of the Republican Party in Ohio," *Cincinnati Historical Society Bulletin* 26 (1978): 206–11; Gienapp, "Salmon P. Chase, Nativism and the Formation of the Republican Party in Ohio."

14. Chase to [?], Jan. 12, 1855, Chase Papers, LC; Chase to Follett, Jan. 1, 1855, in L. Belle Hamlin, ed., "Selections from the Follett Papers," *Quarterly Publication of the Historical and Philosophical Society of Ohio* 13 (1918): 61, 64–65; Chase to E. S. Hamlin, Jan. 22, 1855, in Bourne, "Chase Correspondence," pp. 267–68. Election as governor did mean the end of Chase's Cincinnati law partnership with Flamen Ball, for Chase could no longer devote sufficient time to his practice. While a senator, Chase had contributed extensive business to the firm both in Washington and Cincinnati and received half of the income it earned. The two men quarrelled over the terms of the dissolution of the partnership and over Chase's later suggestion that there was only one remedy for Ball's "habit of intemperance," that being "total abstinence." These differences were later resolved, and during the Civil War Chase secured Ball a federal appointment, while the intemperate partner resumed handling much of Chase's Cincinnati business. See Chase to Ball, May 10, 1858, Ball to Chase, Nov. 9, 1859, Chase Papers, HSP; Hart, *Chase,* p. 219.

15. Joseph Medill to Follett, Dec. 20, 1854, Jacob Brinkerhoff to Follett, May 21, 1855, "Follett Papers," 13 (1918): 77–78, 75–76.

16. Chase to John Paul, Dec. 28, 1854, in Schuckers, *Chase,* pp. 156–58; Chase to Follett, Feb. 14, 1855, "Follett Papers," 13 (1918): 64.

17. Chase to Paul, Dec. 28, 1854, in Schuckers, *Chase,* pp. 156–58; Chase to A. M. Gangewer, Feb. 15, 1855, in Bourne, "Chase Correspondence," pp. 271–72; Chase to J. S. Pike, Mar. 22, 1855, in J. S. Pike, *First Blows of the Civil War* (New York: American News Co., 1879), p. 294; Chase to Follett, Feb. 14, May 4, 1855, "Follett Papers," 13 (1918): 64–65, 73–74; Follett to Chase, May 2, 1855, Chase Papers, LC; Maizlish, *The Triumph of Sectionalism,* pp. 212–14; Gienapp, "Chase, Nativism," pp. 9–10.

18. Chase to Follett, Feb. 14, 1855, "Follett Papers," 13 (1918): 64–65; Chase to Hamlin, Feb. 9, 1855, in Bourne, "Chase Correspondence," pp. 169–70.

19. J. H. Coulter to Chase, May 27, 1855, Chase Papers, LC; A faction of Know-Nothings, nicknaming themselves the "Know Somethings," had evolved with the purpose of making the order more aggressively antislavery. The Know Somethings won control of the separate convention which met in Cleveland. The faction turned down a separate state ticket and instead proposed cooperation with the Chase people. Ohio Know-Nothings also led the walkout of northern nativists from

the parent movement at the national convention meeting in Philadelphia in June when a plank that Congress had no power over slavery in the territories had been adopted. All of this made the Chase people more confident and willing to insist on their position. See Roseboom, *The Civil War Era,* pp. 301–2; William E. Van Horne, "Lewis D. Campbell and the Know Nothing Party in Ohio," *Ohio History* 76 (1967): 207–9; Gienapp, "The Origins of the Republican Party," pp. 666–69.

20. Chase to Campbell, May 29, 1855, Chase Papers, LC; Chase to Campbell, May 25, 1855, in Bourne, "Chase Correspondence," pp. 273–74; Chase to Campbell, June 2, 1855, Campbell Papers, OHS.

21. Ashley to Chase, May 29, June 16, 1855, Chase Papers, LC; Chase to Pike, June 20, 1855, in Pike, *First Blows,* pp. 295–96; Chase to Grimes, June 27, 1855, Chase Papers, HSP; Gienapp, "Chase, Nativism," pp. 19–20.

22. *Ohio State Journal,* July 13, 1855. Chase received 225 votes to 102 for Judge Joseph Swan and 42 for Hiram Griswold. *Ohio State Journal,* July 14, 1855; Roseboom, *The Civil War Era,* pp. 303–4; Maizlish, *The Triumph of Sectionalism,* pp. 215–16; Gienapp, "Nativism and the Creation of a Republican Majority," pp. 538–39.

23. Chase to James Grimes, June 27, 1855, Chase Papers, HSP; *Ohio Statesman,* July 28, Aug. 7, Oct. 3, 5, 1855.

24. *National Era,* July 19, 1855; *Ohio Columbian,* Aug. 29, 1855; *Cincinnati Gazette,* July 14, Aug. 30, Sept. 27, 1855; *Ohio State Journal,* Aug. 18, Sept. 25, 1855; Harrold, *Bailey,* pp. 170–72.

25. *Gallipolis Journal,* Aug. 30, 1855; *Ohio State Journal,* Aug. 9, 10, 1855; Roseboom, *The Civil War Era,* pp. 306–8; Gienapp, "Chase, Nativism," pp. 28–29.

26. Campbell to Chase, Aug. 6, 1855, Chase Papers, LC; Roseboom, "Chase and the Know Nothings," p. 347; *Cincinnati Gazette,* Aug. 22, 1855; *Ohio State Journal,* Aug. 14, 1855.

27. Schurz, *Reminiscences,* 2:34; C. R. M. in *Brooklyn Daily Times,* Sept. 27, 1871, in Schuckers, *Chase,* pp. 167–68n, 613; Hayes, Diary, Aug. 14, 1851, in Charles R. Williams, ed., *Diary and Letters of Rutherford Birchard Hayes* 5 vols. (Columbus: Ohio State Archaeological and Historical Society, 1922–26), 1:384.

28. The vote was Chase: 146,659; Medill: 130,789; Trimble: 24,209. *Ohio State Journal,* Nov. 27, 1855; *Cincinnati Gazette,* Oct. 11, 12, 1855; Roseboom, *The Civil War Era,* p. 312; Gienapp, "The Origins of the Republican Party," pp. 682–88.

29. Ashley to Chase, Oct. 21, 1855, Chase Papers, LC; Chase to Edward L. Pierce, Oct. 20, 1855, Pierce Papers, Houghton Library, Harvard University; Maizlish, *The Triumph of Sectionalism,* p. 223; Chase to Pike, Oct. 18, 1855, in Pike, *First Blows,* pp. 298–300. Campbell was perhaps not quite so disinterested as Chase suggested, for he soon asked Chase's help in his own efforts to be elected Speaker of the House in Washington. When critics charged that a deal had been made, Chase responded that Campbell had never "directly or indirectly sought my support for any office whatsoever." See Chase to David Heaton, John Martin and George Jacobs, Oct. 23, 1855, Chase Papers, LC. In the speakership race, Chase favored Joshua Giddings, but indicated he would consider Campbell if Giddings could not be elected. When, after a long deadlock Nathaniel Banks of Massachusetts was chosen, Campbell was bitter over what he imagined was the treachery of some Republicans. Chase to Campbell, Nov. 8, 1855, Campbell Papers, OHS; Campbell

to Chase, Jan. 14, Feb. 9, 1856, Chase Papers, LC; Van Horne, "Campbell and the Know Nothings," pp. 212–15.

30. E. L. Pierce to Chase, Nov. 9, 1855, Chase Papers, LC; George Bunce to Chase, Oct. 22, 1855, Chase to Gideon Welles, Oct. 26, 1855, Welles Papers, LC; Crandall, *Republican Party*, pp. 48–49; Giddings to Chase, Aug. 26, Sept. 7, 1855, Chase Papers, HSP; Bingham to Chase, Nov. 16, 1855, Chase Papers, LC; Grimes to Chase, Apr. 8, 1855, in William Salter, *The Life of James W. Grimes* (New York: D. Appleton and Co., 1876), p. 68.

31. Crandall, *The Early History,* p. 49; *Ohio Statesman,* Oct. 10, 1855; Chase to Welles, Oct. 26, 1855, Welles Papers, LC; Chase to Bingham, Oct. 19, 1855, Chase Papers, HSP.

32. Chase, "Inaugural Address of Salmon P. Chase, Governor of the State of Ohio Delivered Before the Senate and House of Representatives, January 14, 1856" (Columbus, 1856), pp. 12–15.

33. *New York Tribune,* Jan., 1856, in Pike, *First Blows,* pp. 302–3; *National Era,* Jan. 24, 1856; Ohio Laws, *Acts,* 52 (1856): 61–63, 237–38.

34. The Garner case and that of another fugitive slave, Peyton Polly, are covered in Roseboom, *The Civil War Era,* pp. 343–45, and Schuckers, *Chase,* pp. 171–76. Chase's exchange with Governor Morehead concerning the Garners is found in Chase to Morehead, Mar. 4, 1856, and Morehead to Chase, Mar. 7, 1856, Chase Papers, OHS. Chase's efforts in behalf of the Polly family, a case which stretched over the administrations of five governors, can be seen in numerous letters in the Chase Papers, OHS.

35. Parker to Chase, July 25, 1856, Smith to Chase, Mar. 21, 1856, Chase Papers, HSP; *National Era,* Mar. 20, 1856; Chase to Trowbridge, Mar. 13, 1864, in Schuckers, *Chase,* pp. 174–75. Late in the Civil War Chase was again criticized, this time by Wendell Phillips, for having permitted the Garners to be removed from Ohio. See chap. 8.

36. Chase's other fugitive slave cases are described in Schuckers, *Chase,* pp. 177–79; Hart, *Chase,* pp. 163–71; Gruber, "Chase and the Politics of Reform," pp. 178–90.

37. *Ohio Statesman,* May 28, 1859; Hart, *Chase,* pp. 168–69; Roseboom, *The Civil War Era,* pp. 345–49. The cases are covered in *Ex parte Simeon Bushnell* and *Ex parte Charles Langston, Ohio State Reports,* n.s., 9 (1859): 62–260.

38. Charles Robinson to Chase, Feb. 22, 1856, in Bourne, "Chase Correspondence," pp. 475–76; Kansas Council for Public Safety to Northern Governors, May 22, 1856, Ohio Citizens to Chase, Nov. 4, 1856, Samuel Wood to Chase, Nov. 1, 1856, Chase Papers, OHS; Chase to James Grimes, Aug. 23, 1856, Chase Papers, LC.

39. Chase to Geary, Dec. 3, 1856, Chase Papers, OHS; *Ohio State Journal,* Sept. 13, 1856, Sept. 14, 1857; Chase to H. J. Adams, May 11, 1857, in Warden, *Chase,* pp. 341–42; Robinson to Chase, Feb. 22, 1856, in Bourne, "Chase Correspondence," pp. 475–76.

40. Chase to Sumner, May 23, 1856, Sumner Papers, Harvard University; Chase to Sumner, Dec. 13, 1856, in Bourne, "Chase Correspondence," pp. 274–75; Chase to Theodore Parker, June 23, 1856, Chase Papers, HSP.

41. Chase, "Preliminary Sketch," p. 35; Schuckers, *Chase,* p. 595; Chase, "Inaugural Address," pp. 2–5.

42. Gruber, "Chase and the Politics of Reform," pp. 254–55.

43. *Ohio State Journal,* Jan. 15, 1856; *Ohio Statesman,* Jan. 6, 1857, Jan. 3, 1860.

44. *Ohio Statesman,* Jan. 6, 1857, Jan. 3, 1860; H. A. Converse to Chase, Oct. 21, 1859, L. D. Griswold to Chase, May 17, July 6, 1858, Chase Papers, OHS; Gruber, "Chase and the Politics of Reform," pp. 257–58.

45. *Ohio Statesman,* Jan. 6, 1857; Roseboom, *The Civil War Era,* p. 236. Largely through Chase's efforts the legislature adopted a much-needed reorganization of the state militia in 1857. See Schuckers, *Chase,* p. 183; Hart, *Chase,* p. 158.

46. William G. Shade, *Banks or No Banks: The Money Issue in Western Politics, 1832–1865* (Detroit: Wayne State Univ. Press, 1972), pp. 178, 182–83, 187–89; Roseboom, *The Civil War Era,* pp. 124–38; Maizlish, *The Triumph of Sectionalism,* pp. 163–64.

47. Hoadly to Chase, Dec. 8, 1857, Hiram Barney to Chase, Nov. 24, 1857, Chase to Hoadly, May 21, 1856, Chase Papers, OHS; Chase to James Elliot, Mar. 3, 1858, Chase Papers, LC. John McCormick wrote to Chase, "At every fall election for twenty-seven years I have been one of the county stumpers as a Whig or Republican and up to the present time have not asked for a slice from the State Loaf or a nubbin from the public crib. I now say to you that I am willing to accept any appointment that you may think proper to confer." McCormick to Chase, Nov. 27, 1857, Chase Papers, OHS.

48. Molitor to Chase, Feb. 25, Mar. 27, 1856, Chase Papers, LC; Chase to Hassaurek, Apr. 7, 1857, Chase Papers, HSP; *Ohio State Journal,* Apr. 17, May 6, 1857; *Ohio Laws,* 1857, 54:110–12, 136–38; Maizlish, *The Triumph of Sectionalism,* p. 227; Roseboom, *The Civil War Era,* pp. 225–26; Gruber, "Chase," pp. 259–60.

49. Kremm, "The Old Order Trembles," pp. 197–205.

50. Ashley to Chase, May 29, Oct. 21, 1855, Chase Papers, LC; Bailey to Chase, Nov. 27, 1855, Chase Papers, HSP; Bailey to Chase, Feb. 21, 1856, T. M. Tweed to Chase, Oct. 25, 1855, Chase Papers, LC; Harrold, *Bailey,* p. 172.

51. Spooner to Chase, Feb. 5, 1856, Chase Papers, LC; Ford to McLean, Nov. 27, 1855, McLean Papers, LC; Wilson to Chase, Jan. 15, 1856, Chase Papers, HSP; Crandall, *The Early History,* pp. 38–39.

52. Crandall, *The Early History,* pp. 50–52; Bailey to Chase, Jan. 20, 1856, Ashley to Chase, Jan. 18, 1856, Spooner to Chase, Feb. 5, 1856, Chase Papers, LC; John Niven, *Gideon Welles: Lincoln's Secretary of the Navy* (New York: Oxford Univ. Press, 1973), pp. 265–66; Robert F. Horowitz, *The Great Impeacher: A Political Biography of James M. Ashley* (New York: Brooklyn College Press, 1979), pp. 31–32; Bailey to Chase, Nov. 27, 1855, Chase Papers, HSP; Bailey to Adams, Jan. 14, 20, 1856, Adams Papers, MHS; Gienapp, "The Origins of the Republican Party," pp. 830–35; Harrold, *Bailey,* pp. 172–77.

53. William B. Hesseltine and Rex G. Fisher, eds., *Trimmers, Trucklers and Temporizers: Notes of Murat Halstead from the Political Conventions of 1856* (Madison: State Historical Society of Wisconsin, 1961), pp. 12–15; George H. Mayer, *The Republican Party,* 2d ed. (New York: Oxford Univ. Press, 1967), pp. 35–37; Crandall, *The Early History,* pp. 52, 60–61; Michael F. Holt, *Forging a Majority: The Formation of the*

Republican Party in Pittsburgh, 1848–1860 (New Haven: Yale Univ. Press, 1969), pp. 176–77; Gienapp, "The Origins of the Republican Party," pp. 837–49; Thomas Bolton to Chase, Feb. 25, 1856, Chase to Cleveland, Mar. 21, 1856, Chase Papers, HSP; *National Era*, Feb. 28, 1856.

54. Jacob Heaton to Chase, Feb. 25, 1856, Bailey to Chase, Jan. 20, Feb. 21, 1856, Ashley to Chase, Oct. 21, 1855, Chase Papers, LC; *National Era*, June 12, 1856; Giddings to Bailey, Nov. 11, 1855, Giddings-Julian Papers, LC.

55. Ashley to Chase, Feb. 26, 1856, Chase Papers, OHS; Grimes to Chase, Mar. 28, 1856, in Salter, *Grimes*, pp. 79–80; Chase to Cleveland, Mar. 21, 1856, Chase Papers, HSP; Chase to Sumner, May 3, 1856, Sumner Papers, Harvard University.

56. Hesseltine and Fisher, *Trimmers, Trucklers and Temporizers*, p. 82; Bailey to Chase, Apr. 18, 1856, Chase Papers, HSP; Sumner to Chase, May 15, 1856, Chase Papers, LC.

57. Gienapp, "The Origins of the Republican Party," pp. 861–64, 949–69.

58. Bingham to Chase, June 7, 1856, D. McBride to Chase, June 7, 1856, Chase Papers, LC; Chase to George Hoadly, Mar. 16, 1856, Chase Papers, HSP; Chase to Hamlin, June 2, 12, 1856, Chase Papers, LC; Roseboom, *The Civil War Era*, p. 317.

59. Chase, Manuscript Diary, June 1856, Chase to George Hoadly, June 12, 1856, Chase Papers, LC; Chase to Philadelphia Convention, June 1856, in Hesseltine and Fisher, *Trimmers, Trucklers and Temporizers*, p. 94. The vote on the informal ballot was Frémont: 359, McLean: 196. Roseboom, *The Civil War Era*, p. 318; Crandall, *The Early History*, p. 184.

60. Porter and Johnson, *National Party Platforms*, pp. 27–28; Chase to George Julian, July 17, 1856, Giddings-Julian Papers, LC; Chase to Frémont, June 27, 1856, Chase Papers, LC; *Ohio State Journal*, Sept. 23, 1856; Chase to Sumner, May 1, 1857, Sumner Papers, Harvard University; Chase to Sumner, Jan. 18, 1858, in Bourne, "Chase Correspondence," pp. 176–77. For a detailed account of the Frémont campaign see Gienapp, "The Origins of the Republican Party," pp. 1040ff.

61. Hesseltine and Fisher, *Trimmers, Trucklers and Temporizers*, p. 97; Gienapp, "The Origins of the Republican Party," pp. 992–98; Potter, *The Impending Crisis*, pp. 257–58; Gienapp, "Nativism and the Creation of a Republican Majority," pp. 545–47.

62. Chase to Hamlin, June 2, 1856, Chase Papers, LC; Barney to Chase, June 21, 1856, Chase Papers, HSP.

63. Ashley to Chase, Nov. 27, 1856, Chase Papers, LC; Chase to Giddings, Jan. 7, 1857, Giddings Papers, OHS; Chase to Sherman, July 30, 1857, Sherman Papers, LC.

64. Chase to Henry Reed, June 25, 1857, Chase to J. M. Wright, June 22, 1857, Chase Papers, LC; Chase to John Trowbridge, Mar. 1864, in Warden, *Chase*, pp. 351–52. Chase carried on a lengthy effort to force the extradition of Breslin from Canada but received minimum help from Democratic Secretary of State Lewis Cass, who claimed that existing treaties between the United States and Great Britain did not include embezzlement as a condition for extradition. Cass to Chase, Aug. 4, 27, 1857, Apr. 16, 1859, Chase to Cass, Mar. 30, 1859, Chase Papers, OHS; Roseboom, *The Civil War Era*, pp. 325–26.

65. Another issue which caused Chase and the Republicans difficulty involved irregularities in canal repair contracts. Both Republicans and Democrats had benefited from these contracts, and the governor was unable to resolve the differences sufficiently to avoid divisiveness during the campaign. Hamlin to Chase, Feb. 18, 1858, Chase to Hamlin, Feb. 20, 25, 1858, Chase Papers, LC. During his second term Chase recommended the sale of the canal system to relieve the state of the responsibility. Instead, the legislature agreed to lease the canals; but when no bidders could be found, leasing was delayed until 1861. Roseboom, *The Civil War Era*, pp. 104–5, 324.

66. E. B. Andrews to Chase, Aug. 20, 1857, Chase Papers, LC; *Ohio Statesman*, Aug. 11, 1857; *Ohio State Journal*, Mar. 11, 1857; W. J. Bascom to Richard Howe, Aug. 8, 1857, Howe Papers, OHS.

67. B. W. Collins, "Economic Issues in Ohio's Politics During the Recession of 1857–1858" *Ohio History* 89 (1980): 52–54; Roseboom, *The Civil War Era*, pp. 139, 328; Shade, *Banks or No Banks*, p. 190.

68. *Ohio State Journal*, Aug. 13, 1857; John B. Weaver, "The Decline of the Ohio Know Nothings, 1856–60," *Cincinnati Historical Society Bulletin* 40 (1982): 235–46.

69. Chase to Giddings, Oct. 27, 1857, Giddings Papers, OHS; Chase to Elihu Washburne, Nov. 3, 1857, Washburne Papers, LC; Chase, Manuscript Diary, 1857, Chase Papers, LC. The election results were Chase: 160,568; Payne: 159,065; Van Trump: 9,263. *Ohio State Journal*, Nov. 4, 5, 11, 1857.

70. *Ohio State Journal*, Oct. 27, 1857; Chase to Cleveland, Nov. 3, 1857, Chase Papers, HSP.

71. *Ohio State Journal*, Feb. 6, Aug. 18, 1859; Roseboom, *The Civil War Era*, pp. 341–42.

72. "Message of the Governor of Ohio to the Fifty-third General Assembly at the Regular Session Commencing January 4, 1858." Although the legislature did protest against the Lecompton Constitution, it included an endorsement of Buchanan which Republicans naturally rejected. *Ohio State Journal*, Jan. 12, 14, 1858.

73. Giddings to Chase, Mar. 18, 1858, Chase Papers, HSP.

74. Sumner to Chase, Jan. 18, 1858, Chase Papers, LC; Chase to Sumner, Jan. 18, 1858, in Bourne, "Chase Correspondence," pp. 275–77; Chase to Seward, Mar. 11, 1858, in Warden, *Chase*, pp. 342–43; Chase to "My Dear Friend," Mar. 30, 1858, Chase Papers, HSP; Chase to James S. Pike, May 12, 1858, in Pike, *First Blows*, pp. 418–20.

75. Lincoln to Chase, June 9, 20, 1859, Chase to Lincoln, June 13, 1859, Lincoln Papers, LC.

76. Chase to Charles Robinson, Sept. 14, 1856, in Franklin B. Sanborn, *The Life and Letters of John Brown: Liberator of Kansas and Martyr of Virginia* (Boston: Roberts Brothers, 1891), pp. 330–31, 363. Chase's words were appended to Robinson's letter. See Stephen Oates, *To Purge This Land With Blood: A Biography of John Brown* (New York: Harper and Row, 1970), p. 177.

77. Brown to Chase, Sept. 10, 1857, in Hart, *Chase*, pp. 174–75; Oates, *To Purge This Land*, p. 206; Chase to H. H. Barrett, Oct. 29, 1859, in Oates, *To Purge This Land*, p. 311; *National Era*, Jan. 19, 1860; Chase, "Message to the Legislature, Jan.

1, 1860," in Schuckers, *Chase,* pp. 192–93; Wise to Chase, Nov. 1859, in Hart, *Chase,* p. 175; Chase to Wise, Dec. 1, 1859, in Schuckers, *Chase,* p. 192.

78. Chase to Cleveland, Nov. 3, 1857, Chase Papers, HSP.

79. Giddings to Chase, Feb. 1, 1858, Barney to Chase, Nov. 10, 1859, Chase Papers, HSP; Patterson to Chase, Nov. 15, 1859, Briggs to Chase, Nov. 9, 1858, Ashley to Chase, Feb. 17, 1858, Chase Papers, LC.

80. Julian to Chase, Apr. 25, 1859, Robinson to A. M. Gangewer, May 6, 1859, Chase Papers, OHS; Thomas P. Winthrow to Chase, Mar. 26, 1858, Cleveland to Chase, May 21, 1859, Chase Papers, LC.

81. Chase to Barney, Feb. 28, 1858, Chase to Briggs, Apr. 7, 1859, Chase Papers, HSP; Chase to Barney, Jan. 19, 1858, Chase Papers, LC.

82. Ashley to Chase, Feb. 17, 1858, Chase to Barney, Feb. 9, 1858, Ashley to Chase, July 29, Aug. 26, 1859. Chase Papers, LC; Ashley to Chase, Mar. 28, 1859, Chase Papers, OHS; Horowitz, *The Great Impeacher,* p. 51.

83. Joshua Hanna to Chase, May 18, 1859, Israel Green to Chase, Jan. 26, 1859, William Wilkeson to Chase, Feb. 13, 1859, Chase Papers, LC; J. D. Halbert to A. M. Gangewer, May 30, 1859, Chase Papers, OHS.

84. Chase to Israel Green, Mar. 16, 1859, Chase Papers, HSP; Chase to Briggs, Apr. 16, Nov. 13, 1859, Chase Papers, LC; Chase to T. R. Stanley, Oct. 25, 1859, in Bourne, "Chase Correspondence," pp. 281–82.

85. William Brisbane to Chase, Mar. 14, 28, 1859, Chase Papers, OHS; Schurz, *Reminiscences,* 2:172; Schurz to Chase, July 7, 1859, Bailey to Chase, Jan. 16, Mar. 28, 1859, Chase Papers, HSP; L. Clephane to A. M. Gangewer, June 8, 1859, Chase Papers, OHS. The loans, in the form of fifty dollar shares, were to be covered by the sale of Bailey's Chicago property. Despite the efforts of his widow to keep the *Era* going, she was forced to suspend publication in 1860 when a suitable purchaser could not be found. Chase continued his financial efforts in Mrs. Bailey's behalf during the Civil War years. See Bailey to Chase, Feb. 13, 1858, Chase to Gerrit Smith, Dec. 11, 1860, Chase Papers, HSP; Donn Piatt to Chase, June 29, 1859, Mrs. M. L. Bailey to Chase, Mar. 11, 1860; Chase to Pike, Apr. 2, 1860, in Pike, *First Blows,* pp. 504–6; Harrold, *Bailey,* pp. 191–92, 207–9.

86. Chase to Sumner, June 20, 1859, in Bourne, "Chase Correspondence," pp. 280–81; James A. Briggs to Chase, Oct. 19, 1859, Ashley to Chase, Dec. 19, 1859, William Patterson to Chase, Nov. 15, 1859, John Bingham to Chase, Nov. 1859, Chase Papers, LC; Chase to Briggs, Nov. 21, 1859, Chase Papers, HSP; *Ohio Statesman,* Feb. 2, 3, 1860; Roseboom, *The Civil War Era,* p. 361; Chase to Sumner, Jan. 20, 1860, in Bourne, "Chase Correspondence," pp. 284–85.

87. *Ohio State Journal,* Mar. 2, 1860; Earl W. Wiley, " 'Governor' John Greiner and Chase's Bid for the Presidency in 1860," *Ohio State Archaeological and Historical Quarterly* 58 (1949): 259–73; Joseph P. Smith, *History of the Republican Party in Ohio,* 2 vols. (Chicago: Lewis Publishing Co., 1898), 1:101–4; Chase to Wade, Mar. 4, 1860, Wade Papers, LC.

88. J. H. Barrett to Chase, Mar. 3, 1860, Ashley to Chase, Dec. 19, 1859, Chase Papers, LC; McLean to John Teasdale, Sept. 3, 1859, McLean Papers, OHS; Horowitz, *The Great Impeacher,* pp. 51–52.

89. Giddings to Chase, Mar. 26, 1860, Barney to Chase, Apr. 3, 1860, Cleveland to Chase, Apr. 13, 1860, Chase Papers, HSP; J. H. Baker to Chase, Feb. 24, 1860, Chase Papers, LC; Chase to Pike, Apr. 2, Mar. 19, 1860, in Pike, *First Blows,* pp. 502–6.

90. Lincoln to Samuel Galloway, July 28, 1859, Mar. 24, 1860, in Roy P. Basler, ed., *The Collected Works of Abraham Lincoln,* 8 vols. (New Brunswick: Rutgers Univ. Press, 1953), 3:395; 4:33–34. Seward's nomination might be jeopardized by the lingering perception of many Republicans that his opposition to slavery was too strong. In addition, with nativists making up an important element in the Republican party, his record of opposition to the Know-Nothing movement was also a liability. See Holt, *The Political Crisis of the 1850's,* p. 215; Gienapp, "Nativism and the Creation of a Republican Majority," p. 553.

91. Chase to Parsons, Apr. 5, 10, 1860, Chase to Briggs, Apr. 27, 1860, Chase Papers, HSP; Chase to Briggs, Apr. 29, 1860, Chase Papers, LC; Chase to Pike, Mar. 9, 1860, in Pike, *First Blows,* pp. 502–3; Chase to B. R. Cowen, Apr. 23, 1860, Chase Papers, CHS; Chase to Giddings, May 10, 1860, Giddings Papers, OHS.

92. Briggs to Wade, Feb. 22, 1860, Paine to Wade, Mar. 22, 1860, Chase to Wade, Mar. 4, 1860, Wade Papers, LC; Wade to Chase, Mar. 5, 1860, Chase Papers, HSP; Chase to Giddings, May 10, 1860, Giddings Papers, OHS.

93. Chase to Giddings, May 10, 1860, Giddings Papers, OHS; James Elliott to Chase, May 21, 1860, Chase Papers, LC.

94. Roseboom, *The Civil War Era,* pp. 362–63; William Hesseltine, ed., *Three Against Lincoln: Murat Halstead Reports the Caucuses of 1860* (Baton Rouge: Louisiana State Univ. Press, 1960), pp. 168–71; D. Taylor to Chase, May 22, 1860, Chase Papers, LC; Chase to Parsons, May 30, 1860, Chase Papers, HSP; Potter, *The Impending Crisis,* pp. 428–29.

95. Chase to Homer Plantz, May 30, 1860, Chase Papers, CHS; Chase to Parsons, May 30, 1860, Chase Papers, HSP; Chase to Lincoln, May 17, 1860, in Warden, *Chase,* pp. 363–64; Edward Chase to Chase, May 21, 1860, William Green to Chase, May 19, 1860, Chase Papers, LC; Chase to William G. Hosea, June 5, 1860, in Donnal V. Smith, *Chase and Civil War Politics* (Columbus: F. J. Heer Printing Co., 1931), p. 21; Chase to Briggs, July 14, 1860, Chase to Wade, Dec. 20, 1860, Wade to Chase, Dec. 29, 1860, Chase Papers, HSP.

96. Chase to Briggs, May 8, 1860, Erastus Hopkins to Chase, May 17, 1860, Edward Chase to Chase, May 21, 1860, Chase Papers, LC.

97. Chase to Sherman, May 6, 1858, R. Brinkerhoff to Chase, June 19, 1860, Chase Papers, LC.

98. J. M. Ashley, "Reminiscences of the Great Rebellion. Calhoun, Seward and Lincoln. Address of Hon. J. M. Ashley at Memorial Hall, Toledo, Ohio, June 2, 1890" (Toledo, 1890), p. 33.

99. Chase to Briggs, July 14, 1860, Chase Papers, HSP; *Ohio State Journal,* June 18, Nov. 5, 1860; Joseph Brand to Chase, Nov. 3, 1860, John Bingham to Chase, Nov. 7, 1860, Chase Papers, LC; Chase to Lincoln, Nov. 7, 1860, in Warden, *Chase,* p. 364.

Chapter Six

1. Giddings to Chase, Dec. 7, 1860, Chase Papers, HSP; H. B. Stanton to Chase, Nov. 30, 1860, in Bourne, "Chase Correspondence," pp. 485–87; George Opdyke to Chase, Dec. 26, 1860, Chase Papers, LC; Lincoln to Chase, Apr. 30, 1859, in Basler, *Collected Works of Lincoln,* 3:378.

2. Chase to Charles Dana, Nov. 10, 1860, Chase to George C. Fogg, Nov. 10, 1860, in Bourne, "Chase Correspondence," pp. 290–92; Chase to Lyman Trumbull, Nov. 12, 1860, Trumbull Papers, LC; Chase to B. R. Cowen, Nov. 26, 1860, Chase Papers, CHS.

3. Fogg to Chase, Nov. 7, 1860, Opdyke to Chase, Dec. 26, 1860, Chase Papers, LC; Leavitt to Chase, Nov. 7, 1860, in Bourne, "Chase Correspondence," pp. 483–84; *New York Tribune,* Jan. 5, 1861; Burton Hendrick, *Lincoln's War Cabinet* (Boston: Little Brown and Co., 1946), p. 111; Chase to Trowbridge, Mar. 19, 1864, in Warden, *Chase,* pp. 364–65.

4. H. B. Stanton to Chase, Jan. 7, 1861, in Bourne, "Chase Correspondence," pp. 489–91; Harry Carman and Reinhard H. Luthin, *Lincoln and the Patronage* (New York: Columbia Univ. Press, 1943), pp. 36–37; Chase to Opdyke, Jan. 9, 1861, Chase Papers, HSP; Chase to Trowbridge, Mar. 19, 1864, in Warden, *Chase,* pp. 364–65; Willard L. King, *Lincoln's Manager, David Davis* (Cambridge: Harvard Univ. Press, 1960), pp. 162–66; Stephen B. Oates, *With Malice Toward None: The Life of Abraham Lincoln* (New York: Harper and Row, 1977), pp. 202–3.

5. Carman and Luthin, *Lincoln and the Patronage,* p. 35; Chase to Lincoln, Jan. 11, 1861, in David C. Mearns, ed., *The Lincoln Papers: The Story of the Collection with Selections to July 4, 1861,* 2 vols. (New York: Doubleday, 1948), 2:400–401; Chase to George Opdyke, Jan. 9, 1861, Chase Papers, HSP.

6. Lincoln to Trumbull, Jan. 7, 1861, in Basler, *Collected Works of Lincoln,* 4:171; E. B. Washburne to Chase, Jan. 10, 1861, in Bourne, "Chase Correspondence," p. 491; J. F. Farnsworth to Chase, Jan. 10, 1861, Sumner to Chase, Jan. 19, 1861, Chase Papers, LC; Chase to Washburne, Jan. 14, 1861, Washburne Papers, LC; Chase to Giddings, Feb. 1, 1861, Giddings Papers, OHS.

7. Hendrick, *Lincoln's War Cabinet,* pp. 114–19; Carman and Luthin, *Lincoln and the Patronage,* pp. 46–48; Hart, *Chase,* pp. 205–6; *New York Tribune,* Feb. 26, 1861. The Morrill bill became law on Mar. 2, 1861, before Chase took office. Gabor S. Boritt, *Lincoln and the Economics of the American Dream* (Memphis: Memphis State Univ. Press, 1978), pp. 197–99.

8. Chase to Trowbridge, Mar. 19, 1864, in Schuckers, *Chase,* p. 207; Chase to Lincoln, Mar. 6, 1861, in Mearns, *The Lincoln Papers,* 2:466. An account of Chase's resignation of his Senate seat is in Chase to William Dennison, Mar. 6, 1861, in Schuckers, *Chase,* pp. 207–8. Before Chase's acceptance of the Treasury post was known, the *Cincinnati Enquirer,* Mar. 9, 1861, reflecting Democratic suspicions, commented sarcastically that Chase would probably refuse the appointment because he could not "play second fiddle to Mr. Seward."

9. For a thorough description of the background of each cabinet member, see Hendrick, *Lincoln's War Cabinet,* pp. 36–92 passim. Recent biographies of each of

the more important cabinet members are available. Among the best are Van Deusen, *Seward,* Harold Hyman and Benjamin Thomas, *Stanton: The Life and Times of Lincoln's Secretary of War* (New York: Alfred Knopf, 1962), and Niven, *Gideon Welles.*

10. Mrs. Randall Hunt to Chase, Nov. 23, 1860, Chase Papers, LC; Chase to Mrs. Hunt, Nov. 30, 1860, in Schuckers, *Chase,* pp. 199–201; Chase to Henry Wilson, Dec. 13, 1860, in Bourne, "Chase Correspondence," pp. 293–95.

11. Chase to Seward, Jan. 11, 1861, in Schuckers, *Chase,* p. 202; Chase to Lincoln, Jan. 28, 1861, in Mearns, *The Lincoln Papers,* 2:424–25; Sumner to Chase, Jan. 19, 1861, Chase Papers, LC; Stevens to Chase, Feb. 3, 1861, Chase Papers, HSP; Kenneth Stampp, *And the War Came: The North and the Secession Crisis, 1860–1861* (Chicago: Univ. of Chicago Press, 1950), p. 185.

12. *Congressional Globe,* 36th Cong., 2d sess., Dec. 18, 1860, p. 114; Chase to Giddings, Jan. 31, Feb. 1, 1861, Giddings Papers, OHS. For an anti-Chase view of his presence at the peace conference, see *Cincinnati Enquirer,* Feb. 1, 1861. The paper attacked his appointment because "he has declared himself in advance as opposed to all and any compromise." See also Chase to Sumner, Jan. 26, 1861, Sumner Papers, Harvard University; Chase to Lincoln, Jan. 28, 1861, Lincoln Papers, LC.

13. The northern states not attending were Michigan, Wisconsin, Minnesota, California, and Oregon. Arkansas and all of the lower southern states were not represented. The most complete secondary account of the peace conference is Robert Gunderson, *Old Gentlemen's Convention: The Washington Peace Conference of 1861* (Madison: Univ. of Wisconsin Press, 1961).

14. Chase, Speech at Peace Conference, Feb. 1861, in Warden, *Chase,* pp. 378–80; Lucius E. Chittenden, *A Report of the Debates and Proceedings in the Secret Sessions of the Conference Convention for Proposing Amendments to the Constitution* (New York: D. Appleton and Co., 1864), pp. 427–33; Chase to Trowbridge, Mar. 19, 1864, in Warden, *Chase,* p. 365; *New York Tribune,* Feb. 27, 1861, Schuckers, *Chase,* pp. 204–6; Gunderson, *Old Gentlemen's Convention,* pp. 59, 64, 86–87.

15. *Congressional Globe,* 36th Cong., 2d sess., Feb. 27, Mar. 2, 1861, pp. 1254–55, 1402; Chittenden, *Report of the Debates,* pp. 427–33; Gunderson, *Old Gentlemen's Convention,* pp. 94–96.

16. Richardson, ed., *Compilation,* 7:3206–13; Hendrick, *Lincoln's War Cabinet,* p. 160; Chase to Lincoln, Mar. 16, 1861, in Warden, *Chase,* pp. 370–71.

17. Chase, "Notes," Mar. 29, 1861, in John G. Nicolay and John Hay, *Abraham Lincoln: A History,* 10 vols. (New York: Century Co., 1866), 3:430; T. J. Young to Chase, Mar. 12, 1861, Chase Papers, LC. For the hardening of northern resolve on Sumter, see Stampp, *And the War Came,* pp. 266–70.

18. Chase to Alphonso Taft, Apr. 28, 1861, Chase Papers, HSP; Hart, *Chase,* pp. 209–10; Chase's southern correspondence was collected by Hart, ed., "Letters to Secretary Chase from the South," *American Historical Review* 4 (1899): 331–47. See especially Richard Ela to Chase, Apr. 12, 1861, and Mrs. Randall Hunt to Chase, May 20, 1861, pp. 333–39.

19. Schuckers, *Chase,* p. 211; Donald, *Inside Lincoln's Cabinet,* pp. 27–28.

20. Chase to Lincoln, July 3, 1862, National Archives, Treasury Department, Press Copies of Letters to the President, R. G. 56, no. 473 (hereafter cited as NA); *New York Tribune,* Mar. 8, 1862; McCulloch to Chase, Apr. 11, 1863, McCulloch Papers, LC; Chase to McCulloch, Apr. 18, 1863, Chase Papers, HSP; Chase to Lincoln, May 9, 1863, Lincoln Papers, LC; Lincoln to Chase, May 10, 1861, in Basler, *Collected Works of Lincoln,* 4:363–64.

21. Lincoln to Chase, May 10, 1861, in Basler, *Collected Works of Lincoln,* 6:269; Donald, *Inside Lincoln's Cabinet,* pp. 28–31; Hart, *Chase,* pp. 216–20.

22. Chase to [?], Apr. 16, 1861, Chase to John Roberts, May 21, 1861, in Schuckers, *Chase,* pp. 274–75; Chase to Lincoln, Nov. 25, 1861, NA, Treasury Dept. Press Copies of Letters to the President, R. G. 56, no. 463; Chase to Thomas Spooner, Aug. 25, 1862, Chase Papers, LC; Chase to C. C. Lathrop, July 1, 1861, Chase Papers, CHS.

23. Chase to Horace E. Dresser, Aug. 12, 1863, NA, R. G. 56, Series K, Misc. Letters Sent, p. 233; Chase, Diary, Aug. 7, 18, 1862, in Donald, *Inside Lincoln's Cabinet,* pp. 110–11, 114.

24. Joseph G. Brand to Chase, Nov. 13, 1860, H. B. Stanton to Chase, Apr. 1, 1861, Chase Papers, LC. See also Thomas Heaton to Chase, Apr. 9, May 11, 1861, Chase Papers, LC.

25. Swayne to Chase, Apr. 4, 1861, Chase Papers, LC; Clay to Chase, Jan. 16, 1861, in Bourne, "Chase Correspondence," p. 492; Cleveland to Chase, Mar. 24, 1861, Chase Papers, HSP; Chase to James Monroe, Mar. 3, 1862, Chase Papers, CHS; Chase, Diary, Sept. 10, 1862, in Donald, *Inside Lincoln's Cabinet,* pp. 129–30; Charles Elliott to Chase, n.d., NA, R. G. 56, Series K, Misc. Letter Recd. Chase's decision not to aid Chivington is significant considering the soldier's later notoriety in the massacre of Cheyenne and Arapaho tribesmen at their Sand Creek Camp in Colorado in November 1864.

26. Chase to Seward, Mar. 20, 1861, Chase Papers, LC; Chase to Parsons, Apr. 10, 1861, Chase Papers, HSP; Carman and Luthin, *Lincoln and the Patronage,* pp. 105–6.

27. Chase to Seward, Mar. 27, 1861, Chase Papers, LC; Chase to Lincoln, Mar. 28, 1861, Lincoln Papers, LC; Chase to Seward, Mar. 27, 1861, in Frederic Bancroft, *Life of W. H. Seward,* 2 vols. (New York: Harper and Bros., 1900), 2:356–57n; Chase to John Sherman, n.d., Sherman Papers, LC.

28. Chase to Lincoln, Apr. 18, 1861, Lincoln Papers, LC; Seward to Lincoln, Mar. 1861, in Mearns, *The Lincoln Papers,* 2:502–3; Barney to Chase, June 19, 1861, Chase to Seward, Sept. 26, 1862, Chase to James Monroe, Oct. 2, 1862, Chase Papers, HSP.

29. Wade to Chase, July 22, 1862, Chase to Wade, July 30, 1862, Chase Papers, HSP. See chap. 7 for Chase's role in Wade's reelection.

30. Chase to Lincoln, Feb. 27, 1863, Lincoln to Chase, Mar. 2, 1863, in Schuckers, *Chase,* pp. 491–92; Chase to Lincoln, Mar. 2, 1863, in Warden, *Chase,* p. 525.

31. Among contemporary critics, Gideon Welles was perhaps the most outspoken when he charged that Chase "intends to press his pretensions as a candidate and much of the Treasury machinery and the special agencies have that end in

view." Among twentieth-century historians Burton Hendrick vigorously indicts Chase for disloyalty to Lincoln and agrees with the secretary's nineteenth-century critics "that all the customs houses in the nation had been organized into a Chase machine." Most recently James McPherson has concluded that "Chase built up a cadre of political lieutenants in the Treasury Department who worked for his presidential nomination." In contrast, Harry Carman and Reinhard Luthin argue that the Treasury was administered with less partisanship than any other department in the Lincoln administration. Gideon Welles, *Diary of Gideon Welles, Secretary of the Navy Under Lincoln and Johnson,* ed. Howard K. Beale, 3 vols. (Boston: Houghton, Mifflin Co., 1911), Feb. 13, 1864, 1:525; Hendrick, *Lincoln's War Cabinet,* p. 407; James M. McPherson, *Ordeal by Fire: The Civil War and Reconstruction* (New York: Alfred A. Knopf, 1982), p. 262; Carman and Luthin, *Lincoln and the Patronage,* p. 105.

32. Ira Rankin to Chase, May 30, 1862, Victor Smith to Chase, July 20, 1863, Chase Papers, LC; Lincoln to Chase, May 8, 11, 13, 1863, Chase to Lincoln, May 11, 1863, in Warden, *Chase,* pp. 527–28; Carman and Luthin, *Lincoln and the Patronage,* p. 230; Donald, *Inside Lincoln's Cabinet,* p. 30.

33. Sharkey, *Money, Class and Party,* pp. 17–18.

34. Robert T. Patterson, "Government Finance on the Eve of the Civil War," *Journal of Economic History* 7 (1952): 35–44.

35. Chase to [?], Dec., 1862, in Hart, *Chase,* p. 237. Chase's requests to Congress are recorded in a message received on July 5, 1861, *Congressional Globe,* 37th Cong., 1st sess., pp. 11, 13; *U.S. Statutes at Large* (Washington, D.C.: Government Printing Office, 1861), 12:309.

36. Sharkey, *Money, Class and Party,* pp. 18–20; Hammond, *Sovereignty and an Empty Purse,* pp. 40–41; Hart, *Chase,* p. 221; Ellis P. Oberholtzer, *Jay Cooke: Financier of the Civil War,* 2 vols. (Philadelphia: George W. Jacobs and Co., 1908), 1:286–87. The Sharkey and Hammond studies are the most thorough and reliable accounts of Civil War finances and Chase's role in the Treasury. Both are highly critical of Chase's efforts.

37. Barney to Chase, May 9, 1861, Chase Papers, HSP; Sharkey, *Money, Class and Party,* p. 21; Donald, *Inside Lincoln's Cabinet,* p. 38.

38. Simeon Nash to Chase, July 18, 1861, Chase Papers, LC; *Congressional Globe,* 37th Cong., 1st sess., Aug. 1, 1863, p. 383; Chase to Fessenden, July 26, 1861, NA, Treasury Records, Correspondence with Committees, vol. 5, 1860–64.

39. Chase to Trowbridge, n.d., in Warden, *Chase,* pp. 386–88; Hammond, *Sovereignty and an Empty Purse,* pp. 73–84; Sharkey, *Money, Class and Party,* pp. 21–23.

40. Chase, *Report of the Secretary of the Treasury on the State of the Finances for the Year Ending, June 30, 1861* (Washington: Government Printing Office, 1861); John Sherman, *Recollections of Forty Years in the House, Senate and Cabinet: An Autobiography,* 2 vols. (Chicago: Werner, 1895), 1:269; Boritt, *Lincoln and the Economics of the American Dream,* pp. 42–50, 203–4.

41. Chase, *Report, 1861,* pp. 9, 15–16, 17–20; James G. Blaine, *Twenty Years of Congress from Lincoln to Garfield,* 2 vols. (Norwich, Conn.: Henry Bill Publishing Co., 1884), 1:407; *Appleton's Annual Cyclopaedia* (1861), p. 66; Alphonso Taft to Chase,

Dec. 11, 1861, Chase Papers, LC; Hammond, *Sovereignty and an Empty Purse,* pp. 133–36; Sharkey, *Money, Class and Party,* pp. 17–20.

42. Chase to Belmont, June 19, July 1, 1861, Chase Papers, LC; Belmont to Chase, July 3, 1861, Chase Papers, HSP; Irving Katz, *August Belmont: A Political Biography* (New York: Columbia Univ. Press, 1968), pp. 100–101; Belmont to Chase, Aug. 15, 1861, Chase to Belmont, Oct. 31, 1861, Belmont Papers, LC; Belmont to Chase, Oct. 31, 1861, Chase Papers, HSP.

43. Chase, Diary, Dec. 25, 1861, in Donald, *Inside Lincoln's Cabinet,* pp. 53–55; Belmont to Chase, Dec. 8, 1861, Belmont Papers, LC; William Aspinwall to Chase, Apr. 16, May 5, June 5, 1863, Chase to Aspinwall and John Forbes, Mar. 16, May 14, 1863, Chase Papers, HSP; Chase to Walker, Mar. 30, 1863, Chase Papers, LC.

44. Cisco to Chase, Dec. 16, 1861, Cisco Papers, LC; Chase, Diary, Dec. 9, 1861, in Donald, *Inside Lincoln's Cabinet,* p. 48; Hart, *Chase,* p. 232; Sharkey, *Money, Class and Party,* pp. 24–26; Hammond, *Sovereignty and an Empty Purse,* pp. 131–33.

45. *Congressional Globe,* 37th Cong., 2d sess., Jan. 8, 1862, p. 218; Chase, *Report, 1861,* pp. 17–20; *New York Tribune,* Jan. 13, 1862.

46. Elbridge Spaulding, *A Resource of War—The Credit of the Government Made Immediately Available. History of the Legal Tender: Money Issued During the Great Rebellion,* 2d ed. (Buffalo, 1869), p. 13; *Congressional Globe,* 37th Cong., 2d sess., Dec. 31, 1861, p. 181; Sharkey, *Money, Class and Party,* pp. 28–30.

47. Chase, "Inaugural Address," Jan. 14, 1856; Chase, *Report, 1861,* in Oberholtzer, *Cooke,* 1:169–70.

48. Trist to Chase, Jan. 31, 1862, Chase Papers, LC; *New York Tribune,* Jan. 14, 1862; Chase to Trowbridge, n.d., in Warden, *Chase,* pp. 386–88; Sharkey, *Money, Class and Party,* p. 30; Spaulding, *A Resource of War,* p. 16; Stevens to Chase, Jan. 21, 1862, Chase Papers, HSP; Opdyke to Chase, Jan. 28, Feb. 8, 1862, Chase Papers, LC; Jeannette P. Nichols, "John Sherman," in Kenneth W. Wheeler, ed., *For the Union: Ohio Leaders in the Civil War* (Columbus: Ohio State Univ. Press, 1968), pp. 394–95.

49. *Congressional Globe,* 37th Cong., 2d sess., Jan. 28, 1862, p. 523; *New York Tribune,* Jan. 19–29, 1862. See especially the issue of Jan. 29, 1862.

50. Chase to Spaulding, Jan. 29, 1862, in Blaine, *Twenty Years of Congress,* 1:413–14; Chase to Spaulding, Feb. 3, 1862, Chase to Stevens, Jan. 29, 1862, in Schuckers, *Chase,* pp. 243–45; Spaulding, *A Resource of War,* p. 27; *Congressional Globe,* 37th Cong., 2d sess., Feb. 4, 1862, p. 695.

51. Sherman, *Recollections,* 1:274; Chase to Fessenden, Feb. 8, 1862, U.S. Senate, Finance Comm. Records, 37th Cong., NA, R. G. 46; *Congressional Globe,* 37th Cong., 2d sess., Feb. 13, 1862, p. 790; *New York Tribune,* Feb. 10, 11, 14, 26, 1862; John J. Patrick, "John Sherman: The Early Years, 1823–1865" (Ph.D. diss., Kent State University, 1982), p. 152.

52. *Congressional Globe,* 37th Cong., 2d sess., June 7, 1862, p. 2768, June 17, 1862, pp. 1766–68, July 2, 1862, pp. 2903, 3079; Chase, *Report of the Secretary of the Treasury, Dec. 4, 1862* pp. 12, 24; *Congressional Globe,* 37th Cong., 3d sess., Jan. 12, 1863, pp. 283–84, Jan. 15, 1863, p. 334; *New York Tribune,* June 13, 14, 1862. For the circumstantial evidence of Lincoln's influence on Chase see Boritt, *Lincoln*

and the Economics of the American Dream, p. 206. See also, Chase, Interview with Schuckers, Schuckers Papers, LC. Chase received advice from some unusual and unsolicited sources. Spiritualist Amanda Haight informed him in Mar. 1863 of her vision in which a "folio opened and out of it fell all manner of Green Notes from one dollar up," proof, she claimed, that the Lord had sanctioned his efforts. Haight to Chase, Mar. 2, 1863, Chase Papers, LC.

53. Opdyke to Chase, Feb. 8, 1862, Chase Papers, LC; *New York Tribune,* May 20, June 14, 1862; Pike to Chase, Dec. 31, 1862, in Robert Durden, *James Shepherd Pike, Republicanism and the American Negro, 1850–1882* (Durham: Duke Univ. Press, 1957), pp. 118–19.

54. The new bonds carried the stipulation that the interest was to be paid in gold. The question of the principal was not specified and this issue would be a major problem after the war.

55. Chase to William Cullen Bryant, Feb. 4, 1862, in Warden, *Chase,* p. 409. The tax bill passed the House 125 to 14 and the Senate 37 to 1. See *Congressional Globe,* 37th Cong., 2d sess., Apr. 8, 1862, p. 1576, June 6, 1862, pp. 2607, 2611; *New York Tribune,* Mar. 8, 22, 1862; Sharkey, *Money, Class and Party,* pp. 269–80.

56. *Ohio State Journal,* Apr. 10, 27, 1860; Oberholtzer, *Cooke,* 1:92–94, 128–31; Chase to Jay Cooke, Apr. 29, 1861, NA, R. G. 56, Series K. Misc. Letters Sent; Chase to Cooke, Apr. 20, 1861, Jay Cooke to Chase, May 15, 1861, Jay Cooke to Henry Cooke, May 15, 1861, in Oberholtzer, *Cooke,* 1:136–39.

57. Cooke to Chase, July 12, 1861, Sept. 7, 1861, Chase to Cooke, Sept. 4, 1861, in Oberholtzer, *Cooke,* pp. 143–44, 158–59. See also pp. 147–51.

58. Henry Cooke to Jay Cooke, Sept. 5, 1862, in Oberholtzer, *Cooke,* 1:207–8. See also pp. 187–88; Chase, Diary, Sept. 8, 1862, in Donald, *Inside Lincoln's Cabinet,* p. 124; Chase to Jay Cooke, Nov. 8, 1862, NA, R. G. 56, Series K, Misc. Letters Sent; Chase to Joshua Hanna, Nov. 8, 1862, Chase Papers, HSP.

59. Jay Cooke to Chase, Nov. 17, 1863, Chase, *Report to Congress,* Dec. 1863, in Oberholtzer, *Cooke,* 1:289, 285; Henrietta Larson, *Jay Cooke, Private Banker* (Cambridge: Harvard Univ. Press, 1936), pp. 148–50.

60. Chase to Cooke, Nov. 13, 1862, June 1, 1863, in Oberholtzer, *Cooke,* 1:221–22, 258; Larson, *Cooke,* pp. 148–50.

61. Henry Cooke to Jay Cooke, Sept. 20, 1862, Jay Cooke to Chase, Jan. 16, 1864, in Oberholtzer, *Cooke,* 1:208, 300–308, 259, 261; *New York World,* May 21, 1863.

62. Chase to Cisco, July 13, 1863, Jan. 4, 1863, Chase Papers, HSP; Chase to Colfax, Apr. 1, 1864, in Oberholtzer, *Cooke,* 1:319–24; Chase to Lincoln, Jan. 13, 1864, in Warden, *Chase,* pp. 556–57; Jay Cooke to Chase, Jan. 16, 1864, Henry Cooke to Jay Cooke, Mar. 25, 1863, Chase, *Report to Congress,* Dec. 1863, in Oberholtzer, *Cooke,* 1:300–308, 230, 285, 388–89. See chap. 8.

63. Chase to Jay Cooke, Dec. 16, Nov. 21, 1861, Feb. 7, 1862, Oberholtzer, *Cooke,* 1:182–84, 210.

64. Chase to Jay Cooke, June 17, 1862, Chase Papers, HSP; Chase even briefly considered resigning from his Treasury position to become president of the company which Congress had authorized to build Washington's first street railroad. Instead, he decided "to hold out where I am, till I see my whole scheme of finance

realized, if it is to be realized at all." Chase to Jay Cooke, May 31, 1862, in Oberholtzer, *Cooke,* 1:188n.

65. Chase to Jay Cooke, Apr. 29, 1862, Chase Papers, HSP; Chase to Jay Cooke, Aug. 8, 1862, in Jessie E. Young, "Some Unpublished Letters of Salmon P. Chase" (M.A. thesis, Columbia University, 1922), pp. 43–44; Chase to Jay Cooke, Oct. 24, 1862, June 2, 3, 1863, in Oberholtzer, *Cooke,* 1:210–11, 274–75.

66. Chase, *Report to Congress,* Dec., 1863, p. 19; Donald, *Inside Lincoln's Cabinet,* pp. 40–41.

67. Oberholtzer, *Cooke,* 1:331–32.

68. Henry Cooke to Jay Cooke, Nov. 26, 1862, in Oberholtzer, *Cooke,* 1:329–30; Richardson, *A Compilation,* 7:3331; Hammond, *Sovereignty and an Empty Purse,* pp. 290–91. For Lincoln's earlier position on a national bank see Boritt, *Lincoln and the Economics of the American Dream,* pp. 64–78.

69. Chase to Stevens, Dec. 23, 1862, in Andrew M. Davis, *The Origins of the National Banking System* (Washington: Government Printing Office, 1910), p. 71; Chase to Greeley, Jan. 28, 1863, Chase to Medill, Dec. 18, 1862, in Schuckers, *Chase,* pp. 382–83, 386–87; *New York Tribune,* Dec. 27, 1862; Hammond, *Sovereignty and an Empty Purse,* pp. 293–94; *Congressional Globe,* 37th Cong., 3d sess., Jan. 19, 1863, pp. 383, 384–87, 392–93.

70. Henry Cooke to Jay Cooke, Jan. 23, 1863, in Oberholtzer, *Cooke,* 1:332–33; *Congressional Globe,* 37th Cong., 3d sess., Jan. 26, 1863, p. 505, Feb. 12, 1863, pp. 896–97; *New York World,* Jan. 27, 1863; Hammond, *Sovereignty and an Empty Purse,* p. 324; Patrick, "John Sherman," pp. 158–59. Cooke and Sherman were close friends, a relationship dating back at least ten years to when Cooke was the editor of a newspaper in Sandusky and a resident of Sherman's congressional district.

71. *New York Times,* Jan. 28, 31, Feb. 2, 3, 1863; Henry Cooke to Jay Cooke, Feb. 12, 1863, in Oberholtzer, *Cooke,* 1:333; Larson, *Cooke,* pp. 138–39; Patrick, "John Sherman," pp. 159–60; *Congressional Globe,* 37th Cong., 3d sess., Feb. 10, 1863, pp. 840–46, Feb. 12, 1863, pp. 896–97; Chase to Jay Cooke, Feb. 3, 1863, Chase Papers, HSP. The Senators whom Stoddard influenced were Timothy O. Howe of Wisconsin and probably Jacob M. Howard of Michigan. William O. Stoddard, *Inside the White House in War Times* (New York, 1890), pp. 181–84; Boritt, *Lincoln and the Economics of the American Dream,* pp. 201–2, 344n. Fessenden's explanation of his vote is found in Fessenden to Thomas S. Pike, Mar. 6, 1864, Taney Papers, LC.

72. *Congressional Globe,* 37th Cong., 3d sess., Feb. 19, 1863, pp. 1113–16; Chase to Lincoln, Feb. 19, 20, 1863, Lincoln Papers, LC; Chase to Sherman, Feb. 26, 27, 1863, Sherman Papers, LC; *Congressional Globe,* 37th Cong., 3d sess., Feb. 20, 1863, p. 1148; Blaine, *Twenty Years of Congress,* 1:478.

73. McCulloch, memorandum, n.d., McCulloch to Morris Ketchum, May 11, 1863, McCulloch Papers, LC; Greeley to Chase, July 31, 1863, Chase to Andrew Curtin, Dec. 22, 1863, Chase Papers, HSP; Hart, *Chase,* pp. 279–80.

74. Chase to George Harrington, Nov. 19, 1863, Chase Papers, HSP; Chase, *Report to Congress,* Dec. 1863; Hammond, *Sovereignty and an Empty Purse,* pp. 345–46.

75. Nichols, "John Sherman," pp. 424–26; Hart, *Chase,* pp. 281–82; Oberholtzer, *Cooke,* 1:358–59; Chase to Lincoln, Apr. 15, 1864, in Warden, *Chase,* pp. 578–

79; Chase to Lincoln, Apr. 14, 25, 1864, Chase to Fessenden, Apr. 11, 1864, Lincoln Papers, LC; Chase to Joseph Medill, Jan. 30, 1864, Chase Papers, HSP; Chase to McCulloch, Apr. 16, 1864, Sherman Papers, LC; Welles, *Diary,* Apr. 12, 1864, 2:11; Boritt, *Lincoln and the Economics of the American Dream,* p. 203.

76. Chase to William Dodge, Mar. 31, 1864, Chase to Leavitt, Mar. 31, 1864, Chase to Stevens, Apr. 11, 1864, in Schuckers, *Chase,* pp. 400–402; Chase to Greeley, Apr. 6, 1864, Chase Papers, HSP; Sharkey, *Money, Class and Party,* p. 229.

77. Chase to Stevens, Feb. 19, 1864, Chase Papers, HSP; Chase to Cisco, Apr. 1, 1864, Chase to Jay Cooke, Apr. 10, 1864, in Young, "Some Unpublished Letters of Chase," pp. 59, 64–65; Chase, Diary, June 24, 1864, in Donald, *Inside Lincoln's Cabinet,* pp. 212–13; Chase to Sherman, Apr. 14, 1864, Sherman Papers, LC; Hart, *Chase,* pp. 283–86; J. G. Randall and David Donald, *Civil War and Reconstruction,* 2d ed., rev. (Boston: D.C. Heath and Co., 1969), pp. 348–50.

78. Chase to Cyrus Field, Feb. 17, 1864, Chase Papers, HSP; Chase to Edward Haight, July 24, 1862, Chase Papers, CHS. For earlier examples of Chase's efforts to keep troop requests within reason see Chase to Cameron, Nov. 26, 1861, Chase Papers, LC; Chase to Cameron, Nov. 27, 1861, in Schuckers, *Chase,* pp. 279–81.

79. Chase to Fessenden, June 20, 1864, Lincoln Papers, LC; *U.S. Statutes,* 8:223, 281.

80. Chase to Thomas Hornbrook, Jan. 7, 1862, Mar. 17, 1863, Chase to J. K. Pullen, Feb. 6, 1864, Chase Papers, LC; James Guthrie to Chase, June 17, 1861, Chase Papers, HSP; Chase to William Mellen, Aug. 29, 1861, Chase to James Hawes and others, Oct. 9, 1861, NA, R. G. 56, Series K, Misc. Letters Sent; Chase to William Mellen, June 8, Sept. 10, 1861, NA, R. G. 366, Civil War Special Agencies.

81. Thomas Heaton to Chase, Jan. 22, 1864, Chase Papers, HSP; St. Louis Merchants to Chase, Sept. 1, 1863, Chase to St. Louis Merchants, Sept. 3, 1863, Lincoln Papers, LC; Chase, Diary, Sept. 1, 4, 1863, in Donald, *Inside Lincoln's Cabinet,* pp. 184, 187; David Barnitz to Mellen, Sept. 29, 1862, NA, R. G. 366, BE Series, Civil War Special Agencies.

82. Stanton to Chase, Jan. 23, 1864, Stanton Papers, LC; W. D. Gallagher to Chase, Mar. 25, 1864, Lucien Anderson to Chase, Jan. 29, 1864, Willian Mellen to Chase, May 24, 1864, Lincoln Papers, LC; Mellen to David Barnitz, Apr. 14, 1864, NA, R. G. 366, BE Series, Civil War Special Agencies.

83. Chase to Halleck, Mar. 9, 1862, in Warden, *Chase,* pp. 418–19; Chase to Grant, July 4, 1863, Grant Papers, LC; Chase to Maj. Gen. John Pope, July 31, 1862, NA, R. G. 56, Series K, Misc. Letters Sent. See also, Ludwell H. Johnson, "Contraband Trade During the Last Year of the Civil War," *Mississippi Valley Historical Review* 49 (1963): 635–36.

84. Welles, *Diary,* Oct. 10, 24, 1862, 1:165–66, 177; John A. Dix to Chase, Nov. 4, 1862, Lincoln Papers, LC; Welles to Chase, Oct. 24, 1862, Welles Papers, LC.

85. Boritt, *Lincoln and the Economics of the American Dream,* p. 243; Welles to Chase, Jan. 8, 16, 1863, Welles Papers, LC; Welles, *Diary,* Oct. 24, 1862, May 30, 1863, 1:177, 318.

86. Welles to Chase, Feb. 12, 18, 1864, Chase to Welles, Feb. 17, 1864, Welles Papers, LC.

87. Welles to Chase, Feb. 18, 1864, Chase to Welles, Mar. 5, 1864, Welles Papers, LC; Welles, *Diary,* Feb. 17, Mar. 7, 17, 22, 29, 1864, 1:527, 537, 543–45, 548, July 5, 1864, 2:66–67; Niven, *Gideon Welles,* pp. 461–63.

88. Chase to Washburne, Apr. 22, 1862, Washburne Papers, LC; Chase to Stevens, July 1, 1862, Sherman Papers, LC; Chase to George Denison, Aug. 26, 1863, Chase Papers, HSP; Chase to Hiram Barney, May 16, 1862, NA, R. G. 366, BE Series, Civil War Special Agencies; Young, "Some Unpublished Letters of Chase," pp. 77–79; Johnson, "Contraband Trade," pp. 635–36.

89. Denison to Chase, Dec. 17, 1862, Jan. 8, Feb. 27, 1863, in Bourne, "Chase Correspondence," pp. 339–40, 346, 363; Chase to Denison, Mar. 3, Aug. 26, 1863, Denison Papers, LC. Some evidence suggests that Denison used his influence to force bribes from those trading in the New Orleans area. See Ludwell H. Johnson, *Red River Campaign: Politics and Cotton in the Civil War* (Baltimore: Johns Hopkins Univ. Press, 1958), p. 53.

90. Chase to Gen. James G. Blunt, May 4, 1864, in Warden, *Chase,* p. 582; Chase to Denison, Aug. 26, 1863, Chase Papers, HSP; Chase to [?], May 24, 1864, in Schuckers, *Chase,* p. 329; Hart, *Chase,* pp. 227–29; Young, "Some Unpublished Letters of Chase," pp. 77–79; Chase, Diary, July 2, 1864, in Donald, *Inside Lincoln's Cabinet,* pp. 228–29; Harrington to Mellen, July 11, 1864, NA, R. G. 366, BE Series, Civil War Special Agencies.

91. Randall and Donald, *Civil War and Reconstruction,* p. 486; William T. Sherman to Chase, Aug. 11, 1862, Chase Papers, HSP; Chase to William T. Sherman, Aug. 2, 1862, NA, R. G. 56, Series K, Misc. Letters Sent; Chase, Diary, Sept. 22, 30, 1862, in Donald, *Inside Lincoln's Cabinet,* pp. 152–53, 165; Johnson, *Red River Campaign,* p. 13; Johnson, "Contraband Trade," pp. 635–36; Grant to Chase, July 21, Sept. 26, 1863, Grant Papers, LC; "Petition to the President from Boston and New York Merchants," Feb. 20, 1863, NA, R. G. 366, BE Series, Civil War Special Agencies.

92. Harrington to Mellen, July 11, 1864, NA, R. G. 366, BE Series, Civil War Special Agencies; Welles, *Diary,* May 16, 17, 1864, 2:33–34; Grant to Chase, Feb. 23, 1863, Grant Papers, LC; U.S. Cong., 41st Cong., 3d sess., Senate Executive Document #10, pt. 3, p. 26; Sprague to Chase, Oct. 14, 1862, William H. Reynolds to Chase, Oct. 17, 1862, Sprague to Chase, June 23, 1863, Chase Papers, LC; Johnson, *Red River Campaign,* p. 25. In the spring of 1864, after the collapse of Chase's presidential bid, Rep. Frank Blair charged that Chase was aware that cotton trading permits were sold to the highest bidder, that bribery was commonplace, and that investigations were stiffled. See chap. 8. The Hoyt case is discussed in Belden and Belden, *So Fell the Angels,* pp. 100–121, 142–62. Based on insufficient and circumstantial evidence and speculation, that study concludes that Chase's Treasury administration was characterized by "improper bonding, bribery and favoritism" (p. 143). The Beldens suggest further that Chase's friends in the administration, including Secretary Stanton, conspired to prevent Hoyt's trial from leading to Sprague and Chase.

93. Welles, *Diary,* Oct. 10, 1862, 1:165–66.

94. Welles, *Diary,* June 25, 1864, 2:58–59; Welles to Chase, Nov. 14, 1863, Welles Papers, LC. Typical of late nineteenth and early twentieth century criticisms is the conclusion of Albert S. Bolles: "Unskilled in finance, unwilling to learn, and when going astray, persisting in his course, Mr. Chase's failure was inevitable." *The Financial History of the United States from 1861 to 1885* (New York: D. Appleton and Co., 1886), p. 116.

95. Hay, Diary, Dec. 25, 1863, in Tyler Dennett, ed., *Lincoln and the Civil War Diaries and Letters of John Hay* (New York: Dodd, Mead and Co., 1939), pp. 144–45; Chase, Diary, Sept. 11, 1863, in Donald, *Inside Lincoln's Cabinet,* p. 192; Boritt, *Lincoln and the Economics of the American Dream,* pp. 199–205.

96. Chase to J. W. Hartwell, Feb. 25, 1864, in Warden, *Chase,* p. 570. The turbulent economic conditions in the Confederacy are summarized in Randall and Donald, *Civil War and Reconstruction,* pp. 256–66.

97. Schuckers, *Chase,* pp. 601–2; Schuckers to Mrs. Schuckers, May 7, 1873, Chase Papers, HSP; Hart, *Chase,* pp. 215–16; Chase to John Sherman, Oct. 1, 1861, Sherman Papers, LC; Chase to Brig. Gen. Robert Anderson, Sept. 28, 1861, Anderson Papers, LC; Chase, Diary, Sept. 12, 1862, in Donald, *Inside Lincoln's Cabinet,* pp. 135–36; Chase to George Blunt, Apr. 9, 1862, Chase Papers, CHS.

Chapter Seven

1. Hart, *Chase,* pp. 211–12.

2. Chase to Trowbridge, Mar. 31, 1864, Chase to James Guthrie, June 13, 1861, in Schuckers, *Chase,* pp. 418–20, 426; Chase to M. Sutliff, May 1, 1861, Garrett Davis to Chase, Aug. 21, 1861, B. Rush Plumly, Aug. 29, 1861, in Bourne, "Chase Correspondence," pp. 295–96, 498–502.

3. Chase to W. T. Sherman, Sept. 17, 1861, Chase to Trowbridge, Mar. 31, 1864, in Schuckers, *Chase,* pp. 429, 418–20.

4. Chase to Barney, Apr. 20, 1860, Chase Papers, LC; Chase to Lincoln, Apr. 25, 1861, in Schuckers, *Chase,* p. 424; Chase to Lincoln, Sept. 8, 1861, Chase Papers, HSP; John Jay to Chase, Apr. 1, 1861, John A. Kennedy to Hiram Barney, Apr. 16, 1861, Reverdy Johnson to Chase, May 8, 1861, in Bourne, "Chase Correspondence," pp. 493–94, 497–98; Donald, *Inside Lincoln's Cabinet,* pp. 12–13.

5. Hendrick, *Lincoln's War Cabinet,* pp. 220–24; Chase to D. Potter, July 8, 1861, Chase to Cameron, July 8, Aug. 31, 1861, Cameron to Chase, Jan. 1862, Cameron Papers, LC; Chase to William Gray, Sept. 18, 1861, in Schuckers, *Chase,* p. 430.

6. Chase to Cameron, Nov. 21, 26, 1861, Cabinet Letters, vol. 15, NA, R. G. 56, pp. 261–62; Chase, Diary, Jan. 12, 1862, in Donald, *Inside Lincoln's Cabinet,* pp. 60–62; Hendrick, *Lincoln's War Cabinet,* pp. 234–35, 262; Chase to Cameron, May 5, 1862, Cameron Papers, LC; Chase to [?], May 21, 1862, Chase Papers, LC;

Congressional Globe, 37th Cong., 2d sess., Apr. 30, 1862, p. 1888. No sooner was Cameron in Russia than he sought a leave from his post to come home and campaign for a return to the Senate, seeking the seat held by David Wilmot. Chase at first gave him little encouragement but later agreed to try to secure for Wilmot an influential appointment which might permit Cameron to win the Senate seat without a fight. Chase was unsuccessful, and Lincoln refused to intervene in Cameron's behalf. The question became moot when the Democrats gained control of the legislature and elected one of their own. Cameron returned to the Senate in 1867. See Chase to Cameron, July 23, Sept. 12, 1862, June 9, 1863, Cameron Papers, LC; Chase to C. A. Herkscher, Nov. 19, 1862, Chase Papers, HSP.

7. Stanton to Chase, Feb. 24, 1849, Chase Papers, LC; Thomas and Hyman, *Stanton*, pp. 42–43, 135–37; Chase, Diary, Jan. 12, 1862, in Donald, *Inside Lincoln's Cabinet*, pp. 60–62.

8. Welles, *Diary*, n.d., Sept. 25, 1862, 1:61,149; Hendrick, *Lincoln's War Cabinet*, pp. 263–64; Donald, *Inside Lincoln's Cabinet*, p. 15; Warden, *Chase*, p. 462; Chase to Philip B. Swing, Oct. 1862, Chase Papers, HSP.

9. Chase to Charles P. McIlvaine, Feb. 17, 1862, Chase to M. D. Potter, Feb. 17, 1862, Chase Papers, CHS; Chase to Lincoln, Mar. 8, 1862, Lincoln Papers, LC; Chase to McDowell, Mar. 26, May 14, 1862, in Warden *Chase*, pp. 422, 433.

10. Chase to Nettie Chase, May 7, 11, 1862, in Donald, *Inside Lincoln's Cabinet*, pp. 75–78, 79–86; Chase to McDowell, May 14, 1862, in Warden, *Chase*, p. 433.

11. Chase to McClellan, July 7, 1861, Chase, "Notes on the Union of the Armies of the Potomac and the Army of Virginia," Sept. 2, 1862, in Schuckers, *Chase*, pp. 427–28, 445–50; Chase to Col. T. M. Key, Nov. 1, 1861, McClellan Papers, LC; Donald, *Inside Lincoln's Cabinet*, p. 13.

12. Chase to Greeley, May 21, 1862, in Hart, *Chase*, p. 296; Chase to McDowell, May 14, 1862, in Warden, *Chase*, p. 433; Chase, Diary, June 26, 1862, in Donald, *Inside Lincoln's Cabinet*, pp. 87–92.

13. Chase, "Notes on the Union of the Armies," Sept. 2, 1862, in Schuckers, *Chase*, pp. 445–50; Chase, Diary, Sept. 11, 1862, in Donald, *Inside Lincoln's Cabinet*, pp. 132–33; Chase to Kate Chase, June 29, July 1, 1862, Chase to Parsons, July 20, 1862, Chase Papers, HSP.

14. Chase, Diary, July 21, 1862, in Donald, *Inside Lincoln's Cabinet*, p. 97.

15. Chase to Kate Chase, July 1, 1862, Chase Papers, HSP; Harris Fahnestock to Jay Cooke, July 7, 1862, in Oberholtzer, *Cooke*, 1:197–98; Chase to [?], Aug. 5, 1862, Chase Papers, CHS; McClellan to Lincoln, July 7, 1862, Lincoln Papers, LC.

16. Memo to Lincoln, Aug. 1862, Stanton Papers, LC; Chase, Diary, Sept. 15, 1862, in Donald, *Inside Lincoln's Cabinet*, p. 144; Welles, *Diary*, Sept. 1, 3, 1862, 1:100–105.

17. Welles, *Diary*, Aug. 31, Sept. 7, 1862, 1:93–95, 108–9, 112–14; Chase to William Cullen Bryant, Sept. 4, 1862, in Schuckers, *Chase*, pp. 450–51; Chase, Diary, Aug. 30, Sept. 1, 2, 1862, in Donald, *Inside Lincoln's Cabinet*, pp. 116–17, 119–20; Hendrick, *Lincoln's War Cabinet*, pp. 308–12.

18. Chase to [?], Sept. 4, 1862, in Warden, *Chase*, pp. 460–61; Chase, Diary, Sept. 25, 1862, in Donald, *Inside Lincoln's Cabinet*, pp. 158–59.

19. Garfield to J. H. Rhodes, Sept. 26, 1862, Garfield Papers, LC; Allan Peskin, *Garfield* (Kent, Ohio: Kent State Univ. Press, 1978), p. 152; Chase to [?], Sept. 4, 1862, in Warden, *Chase,* pp. 460–61; Chase, Diary, Sept. 12, 1862, in Donald, *Inside Lincoln's Cabinet,* p. 136.

20. Donald, *Inside Lincoln's Cabinet,* p. 13; Chase, "Notes on the Union of the Armies," Sept. 2, 1862, in Schuckers, *Chase,* pp. 445–50.

21. Chase, Diary, Sept. 27, 28, Oct. 7, 1862, in Donald, *Inside Lincoln's Cabinet,* pp. 161–62, 169–70; Garfield to Mrs. Garfield, Sept. 27, 1862, Garfield Papers, LC; Peskin, *Garfield,* p. 157.

22. Chase to Barney, Oct. 28, 1862, Chase Papers, HSP.

23. Chase to Charles Dana, Nov. 10, 1860, Chase Papers, LC.

24. Ashley to Chase, May 5, 1861, Chase Papers, LC; Chase to Butler, June 24, 1862, in Schuckers, *Chase,* pp. 375–76.

25. George Hoadley to Chase, Sept. 18, 1861, in Bourne, "Chase Correspondence," pp. 502–5; Green Adams to Chase, Sept. 7, 1861, Chase Papers, HSP.

26. Chase to Simeon Nash, Sept. 26, 1861, Chase to Green Adams, Sept. 5, 1861, in Schuckers, *Chase,* pp. 277–78, 428–29; Howard K. Beale, ed., "The Diary of Edward Bates, 1859–1866," in *Annual Report of the American Historical Association, 1930* 4 (Washington: U.S. Government Printing Office, 1933), Oct. 22, 1861, p. 198. Elihu B. Washburne told Chase that his House committee had concluded that "such robbery, fraud,.extravagance, peculation as have been developed in Frémont's Department can hardly be conceived of." In Washburne's eyes, a government "failing to strike at Frémont and his hordes of pirates acknowledges itself a failure." See Oran Follett to Chase, Nov. 6, 1861, Chase Papers, LC; Richard Smith to Chase, Nov. 7, 1861, Washburne to Chase, Oct. 31, 1861, in Bourne, "Chase Correspondence," pp. 506–9.

27. *The War of the Rebellion: Official Records of the Union and Confederate Armies* (Washington, 1880–1902), 1st ser., Vol. 14, 333; Hart, *Chase,* pp. 256–57, 262–63; Dudley T. Cornish, *The Sable Arm: Negro Troops in the Union Army, 1861–1865* (New York: Longmans, Green and Co., 1956), pp. 35–36. In light of the continuing controversy among historians concerning an acceptable definition of the radical or liberal faction of the Republican party both during and after the war, I have chosen to follow Michael Les Benedict's logical approach of using the term *radical* to apply only to those Republicans who urged a more advanced antislavery position than Lincoln was willing to take prior to the Emancipation Proclamation and "a more vigorous prosecution of the war" after 1862. On Reconstruction issues during and after the war, *radicalism* implies the granting of a "meaningful role" in politics to blacks. Benedict has shown beyond question the division of the Republican party in both periods into radical or liberal, moderate or centrist, and conservative factions. At least during the war Chase logically allied himself with the radical group on issues relating to slavery and political rights for blacks. See Benedict, *A Compromise of Principle: Congressional Republicans and Reconstruction, 1863–1869* (New York: W. W. Norton, 1974), pp. 22-26.

28. Chase to Greeley, May 21, 1862, Chase Papers, HSP; Chase to Lincoln, May 16, 1862, in Warden, *Chase,* pp. 433–34; Lincoln to Chase, May 17, 1862, Lin-

coln, "Proclamation Revoking General Hunter's Order of Military Proclamation of May 9, 1862," May 19, 1862, in Basler, *Collected Works of Lincoln,* 5:219, 222–23.

29. Chase to Butler, June 24, 1862, in Schuckers, *Chase,* pp. 375–76; Chase to Denison, Sept. 8, 1862, Chase Papers, HSP; Chase to Butler, July 31, 1862, in Jesse A. Marshall, ed., *Private and Official Correspondence of General Benjamin F. Butler During the Period of the Civil War,* 5 vols. (Norwood, Mass: Plimpton Press, 1917), 2:133–34.

30. Cornish, *The Sable Arm,* pp. 59, 66, 78.

31. Chase to Pierce, Dec. 20, 1861, Chase Papers, LC; Chase to Pierce, Jan. 4, 1862, in Warden, *Chase,* pp. 395–96; Willie Lee Rose, *Rehearsal for Reconstruction: The Port Royal Experiment* (Indianapolis: Bobbs Merrill, 1964), p. 21. Pierce had already had some experience in working with blacks in Union-controlled areas of Virginia.

32. Lincoln to Chase, n.d., in Hart, *Chase,* p. 259; Lincoln to Chase, Feb. 15, 1862, Lincoln Papers, LC; Chase to Pierce, Feb. 18, 1862, Chase Papers, LC; Rose, *Rehearsal for Reconstruction,* pp. 17–18, 34.

33. Chase to Reynolds, Jan. 4, 1862, Chase to Pierce, Jan. 4, 1862, in Warden, *Chase,* pp. 396n., 395–96; Rose, *Rehearsal for Reconstruction,* pp. 17–19.

34. Pierce to Chase, Jan. 19, 1862, item 36, Port Royal Correspondence, NA; Chase to H. W. Pierson, Feb. 1, 1862, in Warden, *Chase,* p. 397n.; Chase to Pierce, Feb. 24, 27, 28, 1862, Chase Papers, LC; Rose, *Rehearsal for Reconstruction,* pp. 21–25, 30.

35. Chase to Reynolds, Mar. 10, 1862, Chase Papers, CHS; Mansfield French to Chase, Mar. 1862, Chase Papers, LC; Rose, *Rehearsal for Reconstruction,* pp. 68–69, 142.

36. Chase to Pierce, Apr. 11, 17, 23, 1862, Chase Papers, LC; Chase to Charles C. Leigh, Apr. 23, 1862, in Warden, *Chase,* pp. 424–25; Chase to Pierce, Apr. 23, 1862, Restricted Commercial Intercourse Records, Treasury Department, p. 130, NA; Saxton to Mansfield French, Feb. 10, 1862, in *New York Times,* Mar. 2, 1862; Rose, *Rehearsal for Reconstruction,* pp. 152–54, 211.

37. Chase to Saxton, May 21, 1862, Chase Papers, LC; Rose, *Rehearsal for Reconstruction,* p. 143; Pierce to Chase, Apr. 2, 1863, Chase Papers, HSP; Chase, Diary, July 21, 1862, in Donald, *Inside Lincoln's Cabinet,* p. 96; Chase to Pierce, Aug. 2, 1862, in Rose, *Rehearsal for Reconstruction,* p. 183.

38. Chase to John Bigelow, Aug. 9, 1862, Thomas Heaton to Chase, Oct. 12, 1862, Chase Papers, LC; Chase to John Pope, Aug. 1, 1862, in Schuckers, *Chase,* pp. 378–79; Chase to John Sherman, Sept. 20, 1862, Sherman Papers, LC.

39. Chase to Robert Dale Owen, Sept. 20, 1862, in Schuckers, *Chase,* p. 379.

40. Chase, Diary, July 21, 1862, in Donald, *Inside Lincoln's Cabinet,* p. 99; Richardson, *A Compilation,* 7:3297–99. Lincoln's proclamation was a conservative measure deliberately designed to convince the public that it was a necessary war measure. Slaves in states still in rebellion on January 1, 1863 would then be free. The proclamation also endorsed the voluntary colonization of those freed and included a plea for gradual emancipation in border states.

41. Chase, Diary, July 22, 24, Aug. 15, 1862, in Donald, *Inside Lincoln's Cabinet,*

pp. 99–100, 112, 156. Rumors spread later that the reservations Chase expressed
at the cabinet meeting on July 22 had delayed the process. Stanton even suggested
that Chase felt the proclamation was "a measure of great danger and would lead to
universal emancipation." In Thomas and Hyman, *Stanton,* pp. 239–40. There is
little evidence to prove, however, that Chase delayed cabinet approval or that his
reservations were based on reasons other than his preference for military action, his
opposition to compensation and colonization, and his desire to see emancipation
go into effect before January 1, 1863.

42. Chase, Diary, Sept. 22, 1862, in Donald, *Inside Lincoln's Cabinet,* pp. 150–
52; Richardson, *A Compilation,* 7:3297–99; Lincoln to the Senate and House of
Representatives, July 14, 1862, in Basler, *Collected Works of Lincoln,* 5:324–25; Chase
to Butler, Sept. 23, 1862, in Marshall, *Butler Correspondence,* 2:324; Blair to Lincoln,
July 23, 1862, Chase Papers, LC.

43. *Richmond Whig,* Oct. 1, 1862, in Randall and Donald, *Civil War and Reconstruction,* p. 387; see also, p. 384; Basler, *Collected Works of Lincoln,* 5:537; Chase to
Lincoln, Nov. 28, 1862, Lincoln Papers, LC. The only exception should be "the
forty-eight counties of West Virginia," the area then being considered for admission
to the Union as a separate state. Chase to Lincoln, Dec. 31, 1862, in Schuckers,
Chase, pp. 461–63.

44. Chase to Lincoln, Dec. 31, 1862, in Schuckers, *Chase,* pp. 461–63; Welles,
Diary, Dec. 29, 1862, 1:209; Richardson, *A Compilation,* 7:3358–60; Hart, *Chase,*
p. 270.

45. Chase to Loyal National League, Apr. 9, 1863, Lincoln Papers, LC; Hart,
Chase, p. 292.

46. Chase, Diary, Sept. 15, 1862, in Donald, *Inside Lincoln's Cabinet,* p. 144;
Welles, *Diary,* Sept. 1, 1862, 1:100–105.

47. Chase to Hamilton, July 15, 1862, Chase to William Dickson, Aug. 29,
1862, Chase Papers, CHS; Chase to Greeley, Sept. 7, 1862, Chase Papers, LC;
Chase, Diary, Sept. 11, 1862, in Donald, *Inside Lincoln's Cabinet,* pp. 132–33; John
Sherman to Chase, Sept. 9, 1862, Chase Papers, HSP.

48. Welles, *Diary,* Sept. 12, 16, 1862, 1:124, 131–32, 136; Chase to S. G.
Arnold, Sept. 16, 1862, Chase to Zachariah Chandler, Sept. 20, 1862, Chase
Papers, CHS; Oran Follett to Chase, Sept. 16, 1862, Chase Papers, LC; Chase to
John Sherman, Sept. 20, 1862, in Warden, *Chase,* pp. 484–85.

49. See Chase to Barney, Oct. 28, 1862, Chase Papers, HSP. By late 1861,
Republicans in several states were joining with some Democrats who supported the
war effort in coalitions called the Union party. The new organization emerged in
Ohio, although Chase and others who were more radical showed little enthusiasm
for it. In the 1861 Ohio election, David Tod, a War Democrat, received the Union
party nomination for governor and won an easy victory. The situation in 1862
varied greatly in northern states with the coalition maintaining only a slender
majority in the House of Representatives. In 1864, the Republican National Committee made the name change official and in the presidential election it was called
the Union party. See Mayer, *The Republican Party,* p. 99; Randall and Donald, *Civil
War and Reconstruction,* pp. 457–59.

50. Chase to John Young, Oct. 27, 1862, in Schuckers, *Chase,* pp. 458–59; R. C. Parsons to Chase, Oct. 21, 1862, S. G. Arnold to Chase, Oct. 20, 1862, Chase Papers, LC.

51. Sumner to Chase, Nov. 7, 1862, Chase Papers, LC; Hendrick, *Lincoln's War Cabinet,* p. 333; Orville H. Browning, *The Diary of Orville Hickman Browning,* Theodore C. Pease and J. G. Randall, eds., *Collections of the Illinois State Historical Library* (Springfield, Ill., 1925), 20:604.

52. Browning, *Diary,* 602–4; Welles, *Diary,* Dec. 19, 1862, 1:194–95; Hendrick, *Lincoln's War Cabinet,* p. 334.

53. Welles, *Diary,* Dec. 20, 1862, 1:198–99; Chase, Diary, Sept. 11, 1862, in Donald, *Inside Lincoln's Cabinet,* pp. 132–33; Hendrick, *Lincoln's War Cabinet,* pp. 339–42.

54. William Pitt Fessenden, Dec. 19, 1862, in Francis Fessenden, *Life and Public Services of William Pitt Fessenden,* 2 vols. (Boston, 1907), 1:243–46; Welles, *Diary,* Dec. 20, 1862, 1:196–97; Browning, *Diary,* p. 603; Fessenden to James S. Pike, Apr. 5, 1863, Taney Papers, LC; Oates, *With Malice Toward None,* pp. 328–30.

55. Welles, *Diary,* Dec. 20, 1862, 1:201–3; Fessenden, *Fessenden,* Dec. 20, 1862, 1:249; Chase to Lincoln, Dec. 20, 1862, Lincoln to Chase, Dec. 20, 1862, Lincoln to Seward and Chase, Dec. 20, 1862, in Schuckers, *Chase,* pp. 489–91. After the meeting of senators and cabinet secretaries, Stanton also offered his resignation, but the president exclaimed: "I dont want yours." Pointing to Chase's letter, he continued: "This is all I want. This relieves me, my way is clear; the trouble is ended." Welles, *Diary,* Dec. 20, 1862, 1:201–3; Thomas and Hyman, *Stanton,* p. 255.

56. Lincoln to Seward and Chase, Dec. 20, 1862, Chase to Seward, Dec. 21, 1862, Chase to Lincoln, Dec. 22, 1862, in Schuckers, *Chase,* pp. 489–90; Welles, *Diary,* Dec. 23, 1862, 1:205; Nicolay and Hay, *Lincoln,* 6:270–71.

57. Chase to Rush R. Sloan, Jan. 27, 1862, in Warden, *Chase,* p. 408; A. P. Stone to Chase, Feb. 5, 1862, Chase Papers, LC. For a thorough discussion of Wade's reelection and Chase's role see Kenneth B. Shover, "Maverick at Bay: Ben Wade's Reelection Campaign, 1862–1863," *Civil War History* 12 (1966): 23–42.

58. Chase to James Monroe, Mar. 3, 1862, Chase Papers, CHS; Chase to M. D. Potter, Feb. 17, 1862, in Warden, *Chase,* p. 415; James Monroe to Chase, Mar. 7, 1862, Chase Papers, LC.

59. Chase to Homer Plantz, July 14, 1862, Chase to James Monroe, Oct. 2, 1862, Chase Papers, CHS; Chase to Parsons, Oct. 21, 1862, Chase to Wade, Nov. 2, 1862, Wade to Chase, Nov. 7, 1862, Chase to Parsons, Dec. 8, 1862, Chase to William Miner, Nov. 24, 1862, Chase to W. K. Upham, Dec. 1, 1862, Chase Papers, HSP.

60. *Portage County Democrat,* Dec. 1862, clipping in Chase Papers, LC; J. K. Herbert to Wade, Nov. 18, 1861, Wade Papers, LC; *Ohio State Journal,* Jan. 22, 1863; Trefousse, *Wade,* p. 192; Shover, "Maverick at Bay," pp. 39–40.

61. U.S. Constitution, article 4, sec. 3; E. M. Norton to Chase, Feb. 18, 1862, Chase Papers, LC.

62. Lincoln to Cabinet members, Dec. 23, 1862, in Basler, *Collected Works of Lincoln,* 5:17, 17n.; Chase to Lincoln, Dec. 29, 1862, in Schuckers, *Chase,* pp. 459–

61; Welles, *Diary,* Dec. 23, 1862, 1:205; Richardson, *A Compilation,* 7:3368.

63. Welles, *Diary,* Aug. 13, 1863, 1:402–3.

64. Chase to Rev. G. B. Cheever, July 16, 1863, Chase Papers, HSP; Chase to Benjamin F. Flanders, Aug. 20, 1863, Chase Papers, CHS; Chase to Giddings, July 17, 1863, Giddings Papers, OHS; Chase, Diary, Aug. 29, 1863, in Donald, *Inside Lincoln's Cabinet,* pp. 178–79; Lincoln to Chase, Sept. 2, 1863, in Basler, *Collected Works of Lincoln,* 6:428–29; Welles, *Diary,* Aug. 13, 1863, 1:402–3; Chase, Diary, Sept. 6, 1863, in Donald, *Inside Lincoln's Cabinet,* pp. 189–90.

65. *New York Times,* Aug. 6, 1862; Cornish, *The Sable Arm,* pp. 46–51, 53, 80–81.

66. Chase to Butler, June 24, July 31, 1862, in Schuckers, *Chase,* pp. 375–78; Butler to Chase, July 10, 1862, Chase Papers, HSP; Denison to Chase, Sept. 9, 24, Oct. 8, Nov. 14, 1862, in Bourne, "Chase Correspondence," pp. 312–13, 315–16, 319, 330.

67. Chase, Diary, Aug. 3, 1862, in Donald, *Inside Lincoln's Cabinet,* pp. 105–6; see also Chase to Lincoln, Nov. 28, 1862, Lincoln Papers, LC; Stanton to Thomas, Mar. 25, 1863, Letters of the Secretary of War, Military Affairs, Records of the Secretary of War, R. G. 107, NA; Thomas to Sherman, Apr. 1, 1863, Records of the Adjutant Generals Office, R. G. 95, NA; Louis S. Gerteis, "Salmon P. Chase, Radicalism and the Politics of Emancipation," *Journal of American History* 60 (1973): 54; Mellen to Chase, May 7, 1863, Chase Papers, HSP; Chase to Garfield, May 31, 1863, Garfield Papers, LC; Cornish, *The Sable Arm,* pp. 112–13, 116–118.

68. Denison to Chase, Jan. 8, Feb. 26, 1863, in Bourne, "Chase Correspondence," pp. 345–47, 360–62; Chase to Banks, May 19, 1863, Banks Papers, LC; Chase, Diary, Aug. 29, 1863, in Donald, *Inside Lincoln's Cabinet,* pp. 178–79; Cornish, *The Sable Arm,* pp. 126–27.

69. Lincoln to Cabinet members, May 3, 1864, in Basler, *Collected Works of Lincoln,* 7:328–29; Chase to Lincoln, May 6, 1864, Lincoln Papers, LC; Nicolay and Hay, *Lincoln,* 6:481; Cornish, *The Sable Arm,* pp. 184, 192, 195.

70. Denison to Chase, Nov. 14, 1862, Mar. 14, 31, Sept. 21, 1863, in Bourne, "Chase Correspondence," pp. 329, 366–67, 376–79, 408–10; Cuthbert Bullett to Chase, Mar. 14, 1863, Chase Papers, LC; Chase to Mellen, Nov. 20, 1863, Chase Papers, HSP.

71. Thomas to Stanton, Apr. 1, 1863, General's Papers, Records of the Adjutant General's Office R. G. 94, NA; James E. Yeatman, *A Report on the Conditions of the Freedmen of the Mississippi Presented to the Western Sanitary Commission, Dec. 17, 1863* (St. Louis, 1864), pp. 6, 13; Louis S. Gerteis, *From Contraband to Freedman: Federal Policy Toward Southern Blacks, 1861–1865* (Westport, Conn.: Greenwood Press, 1973), pp. 135–38.

72. Chase to Mellen, Nov. 20, Dec. 27, 1863, Chase Papers, HSP; Chase to Mellen, Dec. 17, 1863, Civil War Special Agencies, R. G. 366, NA; Gerteis, "Chase," pp. 56–57; Gerteis, *From Contraband to Freedman,* pp. 138–39.

73. Mellen to Chase, Feb. 11, 1864, Civil War Special Agencies, R. G. 366, NA.

74. Mellen to A. M. McFarland, Mar. 8, 1864, Mellen to David Barnitz, Mar. 10, 1864, Civil War Special Agencies, R.G. 366, NA; *War of the Rebellion,* 3d ser.,

vol. 4, 143, 139; Gerteis, *From Contraband to Freedman,* pp. 147–48; Herman Belz, *Emancipation and Equal Rights: Politics and Constitutionalism in the Civil War Era* (New York: W. W. Norton Co., 1978), pp. 52–55.

75. Chase to Pierce, May 1, 1863, Fifth Special Agency, Treasury Department, NA; French to Chase, Jan. 6, 1863, Lincoln Papers, LC; French to Chase, Aug. 22, 1863, Chase Papers, LC; Rose, *Rehearsal for Reconstruction,* pp. 237, 277–85.

76. French to Chase, Feb. 15, 1864, Chase Papers, LC; Birney to Chase, Apr. 25, 1864, Chase Papers, HSP. Birney was the son of Liberty party leader James G. Birney. Rose, *Rehearsal for Reconstruction,* pp. 290–93; William L. Barney, *Flawed Victory: A New Perspective of the Civil War* (New York: Praeger Publishers, 1975), p. 179.

77. Mellen to Barnitz, Apr. 10, 13, 22, 1864, Civil War Special Agencies, R. G. 366, NA; *Congressional Globe,* 38th Cong., 2d sess., Mar. 3, 1865, p. 1402; *United States Statutes at Large* 13 (1863–1865): 507–9; LaWanda Cox, "The Promise of Land for the Freedmen," *Mississippi Valley Historical Review* 45 (1958): 413–40.

78. Denison to Chase, Nov. 29, 1862, in Bourne, "Chase Correspondence," pp. 335–36; Chase to Stanton, June 12, 1863, Chase Papers, HSP; Chase to Lincoln, Nov. 25, 1863, Lincoln Papers, LC.

79. Lincoln, Proclamation, Dec. 8, 1863, in Richardson, *A Compilation,* 7:3414–16; Welles, *Diary,* Aug. 22, 1863, 1:410; Chase to Benjamin F. Flanders, Aug. 20, 1863, Chase Papers, CHS; Chase to Henry Ward Beecher, Dec. 26, 1863, Chase Papers, HSP. Earlier in the war, Chase's view of the reconstruction process was far different from his position in 1864. Late in 1861, he had supported the conquered province theory of many Republicans, believing that when a state seceded, its "organization was forfeited and it lapsed into the condition of a territory with which we could do what we pleased." It could only be readmitted under conditions "Congress should provide." At the same time he was not willing to change the boundaries of the old states: "South Carolina should ever be South Carolina, but reformed I hope." Rather than the military governments proposed by the president, Chase preferred "civil provisional government authorized by Congress." See Chase, Diary, Dec. 11, 1861, in Donald, *Inside Lincoln's Cabinet,* pp. 50–51; Chase to Mellen, Mar. 26, 1862, Chase Papers, CHS.

80. Chase to Durant, Dec. 28, 1863, Chase to Horace Greeley, Dec. 29, 1863, Greeley to Chase, Dec. 31, 1863, Chase Papers, HSP.

81. Lincoln to Chase, Sept. 2, 1863, Lincoln Papers, LC; Chase to Gerrit Smith, Mar. 2, 1864, in Schuckers, *Chase,* pp. 399–400.

82. Chase to Greeley, Mar. 4, 1864, Chase Papers, HSP; Chase to Banks, Apr. 13, 1864, in Warden, *Chase,* p. 577; Chase to Denison, Aug. 15, Nov. 11, 1864, Denison Papers, LC; Fred Harvey Harrington, *Fighting Politician: Major General N. P. Banks* (Philadelphia: Univ. of Pennsylvania Press, 1948), pp. 144–46.

83. Lincoln to Hahn, Mar. 13, 1864, in Basler, *Collected Works of Lincoln,* 7:243. The convention and the resulting constitution are best covered in Peyton McCrary, *Abraham Lincoln and Reconstruction: The Louisiana Experiment* (Princeton: Princeton Univ. Press, 1978), pp. 244–65. Politics and reconstruction in Louisiana have been of significant interest among historians. In addition to McCrary's fine study of the

war years, a more recent account looks at the entire period of Reconstruction: Ted Tunnel, *Crucible of Reconstruction: War, Radicalism and Race in Louisiana, 1862–1877* (Baton Rouge: Louisiana State Univ. Press, 1984). A focal point of any study of reconstruction in Louisiana is the status of blacks and the issue of suffrage for them. The most thorough study of this topic is provided in La Wanda Cox, *Lincoln and Black Freedom: A Study in Presidential Leadership* (Columbia: Univ. of South Carolina Press, 1981). McCrary, Tunnel, and Cox suggest that Lincoln was more advanced on racial issues than most earlier writers give him credit for.

84. *Congressional Globe,* 38th Cong., 1st sess., July 2, 1864, pp. 3491, 3581; Chase to Denison, Aug. 15, 1864, Denison Papers, LC; Chase, Diary, July 4, 1864, in Donald, *Inside Lincoln's Cabinet,* p. 230.

85. The House fell thirteen votes short of the necessary two-thirds when it voted 93 to 65 for the amendment on June 15, 1864. *Congressional Globe,* 38th Cong., 1st sess., pp. 1490, 2995. With the help of extensive administration lobbying among Democrats, the House finally approved the amendment 119 to 56 on January 31, 1865. Ibid., 2d sess., p. 531.

86. See Cox, *Lincoln and Black Freedom,* pp. 3–43.

Chapter Eight

1. Garfield to Schuckers, Apr. 20, 1874, Garfield to J.H. Rhodes, Sept. 26, Oct. 5, 1862, Garfield Papers, LC; Peskin, *Garfield,* pp. 151–53.

2. Chase, Will, Dec. 1, 1859, Chase Papers, LC; Chase to J. B. Varnum, Feb. 1863, Chase Papers, HSP; Belden and Belden, *So Fell the Angels,* pp. 17–18; Chase, Financial Records, 1863, Chase Papers, LC; Chase to Kate Chase, Oct. 25, 1861, Chase Papers, HSP.

3. Chase to Brown, June 9, Aug. 1, 1862, Feb. 9, 1863, Chase to Barney, Feb. 10, 1863, Barney to Chase, Mar. 25, 1861, Chase Papers, HSP; Barney to Chase, June 2, 1862, Chase to Barney, Apr. 25, 1864, Chase Papers, LC; Chase to Heckscher, Oct. 18, 1861, Chase to Barney, May 27, 1861, in Young, "Some Unpublished Letters of Chase," pp. 1, 7–8.

4. Welles, *Diary,* May 19, 1863, 1:306; Chase to Garfield, May 31, 1863, Garfield Papers, LC; Chase to Sprague, June 6, 1863, Chase Papers, HSP.

5. Chase to Sprague, June 6, July 14, 1863, Chase to Kate Chase, Aug. 12, Oct. 3, 1863, Chase to Sprague, Oct. 31, 1863, Chase Papers, HSP; Sprague to Chase, Nov. 4, 1863, Chase Papers, LC; Sokoloff, *Kate Chase,* p. 86.

6. Chase to George Harrington, Nov. 19, 1863, Chase Papers, HSP; Alice Skinner to Chase, Nov. 22, 1863, Sprague to Chase, Nov. 21, 1863, Chase Papers, LC; *New York Times,* Nov. 12, 13, 15, 1863; *Cincinnati Gazette,* Nov. 12, 1863; Belden and Belden, *So Fell the Angels,* pp. 94–97; Schurz, *Reminiscences,* 2:169; Sokoloff, *Kate Chase,* p. 84.

7. Chase to Nettie Chase, Aug. 19, Nov. 28, 1863, Chase Papers, HSP.

8. Mrs. Douglas to Chase, Aug. 28, 1862, Chase Papers, LC; Hendrick, *Lincoln's War Cabinet,* pp. 379–80.

9. Barney to Chase, Aug. 25, 1862, Chase Papers, HSP; Chase to Mrs. Eastman, n.d., Chase Papers, LC; Chase to Mrs. Eastman, Feb. 1, 1864, in Warden, *Chase,* pp. 567–68; Chase to Mrs. Eastman, June 8, 1863, Chase Papers, HSP; Donald, *Inside Lincoln's Cabinet,* p. 236.

10. A. G. Stewart to Chase, Oct. 24, 1862, Jane Auld to Chase, May 6, 1863, Chase to Jane Auld, Aug. 20, 1864, Chase Papers, LC; Chase to J. C. Rhodes, Dec. 29, 1863, Chase Papers, HSP.

11. See for example, Chase to Lincoln, Oct. 31, 1863, Lincoln Papers, LC.

12. Halstead to Chase, Apr. 1, 1863, Lincoln Papers, LC; Halstead to Chase, Apr. 4, 1863, Chase to Lincoln, Apr. 4, 22, 1863, Hay Papers, LC; Chase to Elihu Washburne, Apr. 13, 1863, Washburne Papers, LC.

13. Chase to Parsons, June 15, 1863, Tod to Chase, July 5, 1863, Chase Papers, HSP; Joseph Geiger to Chase, June 18, 1863, Chase to Brough, June 20, 1863, Ashley to Chase, June 23, 1863, Chase Papers, LC.

14. Chase to Parsons, June 15, 1863, in Schuckers, *Chase,* pp. 391–92; Lincoln to Ambrose Burnside, May 29, 1863, in Basler, *Collected Works of Lincoln,* 6:237.

15. *New York Tribune,* Oct. 10, 1863; Chase to Lincoln, Oct. 17, 1863, Lincoln Papers, LC.

16. *Ohio State Journal,* Oct. 12, 13, 1863, *Cincinnati Gazette,* Oct. 12, 13, 1863; Chase to E. D. Mansfield, Oct. 18, 1863, Chase to John Conness, Oct. 18, 1863, Chase Papers, HSP.

17. *Ohio State Journal,* Oct. 16, 1863; Briggs to Chase, Oct. 17, 1863, Ball to Chase, Oct. 21, 1863, Henry Carrington to Chase, Dec. 16, 1863, Chase Papers, LC.

18. Mellen was special agent of the Treasury at Cincinnati; Denison, acting surveyor of customs at New Orleans; Barney, collector of customs for the port of New York; Stickney, commissioner and special agent of the Treasury in Florida; and Parsons, consul to Rio de Janiero in 1861 and collector of internal revenue in Cleveland from 1862 to 1866.

19. Donald, *Inside Lincoln's Cabinet,* p. 28. Schuckers estimated that there were 15,000 Treasury employees by 1865. *Chase,* p. 481.

20. Hart, *Chase,* p. 311; Chase to Sprague, Nov. 26, 1863, in Schuckers, *Chase,* pp. 494–95; Chase to Heaton, Jan. 28, 1864 in Warden, *Chase,* pp. 565–66.

21. Bates, *Diary,* Oct. 17, 1863, pp. 310–11; Welles, *Diary,* Feb. 22, 1864, 1:529.

22. Chase to Leavitt, Jan. 24, 1864, Chase to William M. Dickson, Jan. 27, 1864, in Warden, *Chase,* pp. 561–62, 564.

23. James Birney was the eldest son of Liberty leader James Gillespie Birney. During the Civil War the younger Birney was judge of the eighteenth judicial circuit in Michigan. See Birney to Chase, Jan. 25, 1864, Heaton to Chase, Sept. 2, 1863, Chase Papers, LC.

24. Joshua Leavitt to Chase, Sept. 30, 1863, Chase Papers, LC; Giddings to Chase, Jan. 13, 1863, Chase Papers, HSP.

25. Giddings to Chase, Jan. 13, 1863, Chase to Barney, Nov. 7, 1863, Chase Papers, HSP; Chase to Spencer, Dec. 4, 1863, Chase to Daniel S. Dickinson, Nov.

18, 1863, in Schuckers, *Chase,* pp. 495, 494; Edward Gilbert to Chase, Feb. 20, 1864, Chase Papers, LC.

26. *Chicago Tribune,* Dec. 17, 1863, in Nicolay and Hay, *Lincoln,* 8:323; Thomas Heaton to Chase, Aug. 17, 1863, Thomas Brown to Chase, Jan. 4, 1864, Joseph H. Geiger to Chase, Aug. 28, 1863, Henry B. Carrington to Chase, Dec. 16, 1863, Chase Papers, LC. Occasionally, Chase faced opposition to his nomination from an unlikely source, as when Boston abolitionist Wendell Phillips dredged up an old charge that when he was governor of Ohio, Chase had not acted vigorously enough to secure the release of fugitive slave Margaret Garner. *New York Tribune,* Dec. 23, 24, 1864. See chap. 5 herein for details of the Garner case. Dismissing the charge as the rantings of a Garrisonian abolitionist, Chase found it ironic that he "should require any vindication against the charge of *remissness* in antislavery work or spirit." Nonetheless, he felt it necessary to defend his role lest the charges might damage his presidential hopes. Later in 1864, Phillips endorsed the third-party candidacy of John C. Frémont against Lincoln. Chase to Rev. Henry Ward Beecher, Dec. 26, 1863, Chase to William Dennison, Dec. 30, 1863, Chase Papers, HSP; George Hoadly to Chase, Jan. 6, 1864, Chase Papers, LC; Chase to Hoadly, Jan. 20, 1864, Chase Papers, CHS.

27. For a full account of Chase's agents in Florida see Ovid L. Futch, "Salmon P. Chase and Civil War Politics in Florida," *Florida Historical Quarterly* 32 (1954): 163–88, esp. 163–65.

28. Stickney to Chase, Dec. 11, 1863, Chase Papers, LC.

29. Plantz to Chase, Dec. 17, 1863, Jan. 12, 1864, Stickney to Chase, Jan. 7, 1864, Chase Papers, LC; Chase to Stickney, Dec. 29, 1863, Chase Papers, HSP.

30. Stickney to Chase, Feb. 5, 16, 1864, Chase Papers, LC.

31. Plantz to Chase, Mar. 28, 1864, Chase Papers, LC; Futch, "Chase and Politics in Florida," pp. 179–84.

32. Chase to Denison, July 23, 1862, Denison to James Denison, Mar. 14, 1863, Denison Papers, LC; Denison to Chase, June 28, 1862, in Bourne, "Chase Correspondence," pp. 306–9; Chase to Stanton, May 28, 1863, Banks Papers, LC; Chase to Butler, Dec. 14, 1862, Feb. 24, Apr. 10, 1863, in Marshall, *Butler Correspondence,* 2:541–42, 3:15, 57.

33. Chase to Flanders, May 24, 1863, Chase Papers, HSP; B. R. Plumly to Chase, Jan. 2, 1863, Frank Howe to Chase, Jan. 14, 1864, Chase Papers, LC; Chase to Denison, Aug. 26, 1863, Denison Papers, LC; Chase to Flanders, Aug. 20, 1863, Chase Papers, CHS; Flanders to Chase, Jan. 31, 1864, Chase Papers, HSP; Denison to Chase, Feb. 5, 1864, in Bourne, "Chase Correspondence," p. 430; Johnson, *Red River Campaign,* pp. 60–63.

34. Banks to [?], Feb. 3, 1864, Chase to Frank E. Howe, Feb. 20, 1864, Chase to John F. Morse, Feb. 22, 1864, Flanders to Chase, Feb. 26, 1864, Chase Papers, HSP; Thomas I. Durant to Chase, Feb. 21, 1864, John Hutchins to Chase, Feb. 24, 1864, Chase Papers, LC; Chase to Flanders, Mar. 7, 1864, Chase Papers, HSP.

35. Denison to Chase, Mar. 5, Apr. 1, May 1, 1864, in Bourne, "Chase Correspondence," pp. 432–37; Chase to Denison, Mar. 16, 1864, Denison Papers, LC.

36. Reid had recently published a collection of Chase's speeches, "Going Home to Vote," portraying Chase's popular reception during the October 1863

campaign. Wilson, *History of the Slave Power,* pp. 63, 69; Hendrick, *Lincoln's War Cabinet,* p. 402.

37. The *Cincinnati Enquirer,* Feb. 21, 1864, estimated that twenty-seven senators had secretly expressed an interest in the movement. Patrick, "John Sherman," p. 176.

38. Chase to William M. Dickson, Jan. 16, 1864, Chase to P. Odlin, Jan. 18, 1864, Chase to Pomeroy, Nov. 17, 1863, Chase Papers, HSP; Chase to James C. Hall, Jan. 18, 1864, in Schuckers, *Chase,* p. 497; Nicolay and Hay, *Lincoln,* 8:319–20; Nichols, "John Sherman," pp. 413–15; Patrick, "John Sherman," pp. 173–75.

39. Chase to David Chase, Dec. 17, 1863, Chase Papers, HSP; Nicolay and Hay, *Lincoln,* 9:395. Today, Chase's picture is on the $10,000 Federal Reserve note and thus remains largely unknown to most twentieth-century Americans.

40. Hendrick, *Lincoln's War Cabinet,* p. 402; Henry Cooke to Jay Cooke, Jan. 14, 1864, in Oberholtzer, *Cooke,* 1:361–62. No exact figures are known, but Jay Cooke's biographer suggests that the firm's contribution was $20,000 and Sprague's twice that amount. Oberholtzer, 1:364–65. The Beldens inflate the Cooke contribution to $90,000. Belden and Belden, *So Fell the Angels,* p. 106.

41. Charles R. Wilson, "The Original Chase Organization Meeting and *The Next Presidential Election," Mississippi Valley Historical Review* 23 (1936): 71–76; *Cincinnati Enquirer,* Feb. 10, 1864; Hendrick, *Lincoln's War Cabinet,* p. 413; "The Pomeroy Circular," in Schuckers, *Chase,* pp. 499–500; *New York Tribune,* Feb. 23, 26, 1864; Smith, *Chase and Civil War Politics,* pp. 115–22.

42. G. W. Gordon to Sherman, Feb. 26, 1864, Sherman Papers, LC; Sherman, in *Cincinnati Gazette,* Mar. 3, 1864; Wilson, "Original Chase Organization Meeting," pp. 65–68; William F. Zornow, "Lincoln, Chase and the Ohio Radicals in 1864," *Bulletin of the Historical and Philosophical Society of Ohio* 9 (1951): 3–32; Patrick, "John Sherman," pp. 177–78.

43. Chase to James Hall, Jan. 18, 1864, in Schuckers, *Chase,* p. 497; Chase to P. Odlin, Jan. 18, 1864, Chase Papers, HSP; Chase to Flamen Ball, Feb. 2, 1864, in Warden, *Chase,* pp. 569–70; Tod to Lincoln, Feb. 24, 1864, in Nicolay and Hay, *Lincoln,* 8:324; Elizabeth Yager, "The Presidential Campaign of 1864 in Ohio," *Ohio State Archaeological and Historical Quarterly* 34 (1925): 548–89; Zornow, "Lincoln, Chase and the Ohio Radicals in 1864," pp. 23–25.

44. Parsons to Chase, Mar. 2, 1864, Chase Papers, LC; James Hamilton to Chase, Feb. 25, 1864, Chase Papers, HSP; Garfield to Chase, Feb. 25, 1864, in Theodore C. Smith, *The Life and Letters of James Abram Garfield,* 2 vols. (New Haven: Yale Univ. Press, 1925), 1:375–76; Garfield to Harmon Austin, Mar. 4, 1864, Garfield Papers, LC.

45. Welles, *Diary,* Feb. 22, 1864, 1:529; Chase to Lincoln, Feb. 22, 1864, in Warden, *Chase,* pp. 573–74.

46. Chase to Mrs. Eastman, Feb. 23, 1864, Chase Papers, HSP.

47. Lincoln to Chase, Feb. 29, 1864, in Basler, *Collected Works of Lincoln,* 7:212–13; Nicolay and Hay, *Lincoln,* 8:316–17.

48. Nicolay and Hay, *Lincoln,* 8:324; J. M. Winchell to Chase, Mar. 4, 1864, Chase Papers, LC; Greeley to Chase, Mar. 7, 1864, Mellen to Chase, Mar. 1, 2, 1864, Chase Papers, HSP.

49. Chase to Gerrit Smith, Mar. 2, 1864, Chase Papers, LC; Chase to Hall, Mar. 5, 1864, in Schuckers, *Chase*, pp. 502–3; Chase to Mellen, Mar. 5, 1864, Chase to Hall, Mar. 6, 1864, Chase Papers, HSP; *New York Tribune*, Mar. 5, 7, 1864; *Ohio State Journal*, Mar. 11, 1864.

50. *New York Times*, Mar. 11, 12, 1864; *New York Tribune*, Mar. 11, 12, 1864; *New York Herald*, Mar. 12, 1864; Bates, *Diary*, Mar. 13, 1864, p. 345; *Congressional Globe*, 38th Cong., 1st sess., Mar. 10, 1864, pp. 1025–47.

51. Chase to Greeley, Mar. 4, 1864, Chase Papers, LC; Chase to Mrs. Eastman, Feb. 23, 1864, Chase to Joshua Hanna, Apr. 5, 1864, Chase Papers, HSP; Chase to A. G. Riddle, Mar. 7, 1864, in Warden, *Chase*, p. 576.

52. Elbert B. Smith, *Francis Preston Blair* (New York: Free Press, 1980), p. 331.

53. Montgomery Blair to Lincoln, 1864, Blair Papers, LC; Francis Cockran to Chase, Dec. 31, 1863, Apr. 21, 1864, Joseph Stewart to Chase, Feb. 3, 1864, Chase Papers, LC; Carman and Luthin, *Lincoln and the Patronage*, pp. 209–11; Chase to Lincoln, Oct. 5, 1863, Lincoln Papers, LC; Bates, *Diary*, Oct. 20, 1863, p. 311.

54. *Congressional Globe*, 38th Cong., 1st sess., Feb. 27, 1864, Appendix, 46–51; Parsons to Chase, Mar. 7, 1864, Chase Papers, LC; Zornow, "Lincoln, Chase and the Ohio Radicals in 1864," p. 26; Smith, *Blair*, pp. 336–37; Hendrick, *Lincoln's War Cabinet*, p. 426; Smith, *Chase and Civil War Politics*, pp. 136–37.

55. Chase to Thomas Brown, Feb. 26, 1864, Chase to Greeley, Feb. 29, 1864, Chase to Mellen, Mar. 5, 1864, Chase Papers, HSP.

56. *Congressional Globe*, 38th Cong., 1st sess., Mar. 11, 1864, p. 1046; Oberholtzer, *Cooke*, 1:309–19; see chap. 6 herein.

57. *Congressional Globe*, 38th Cong., 1st sess., Mar. 9, 1864, pp. 1013–17, Apr. 23, 1864, pp. 1827–32; Smith, *Chase and Civil War Politics*, pp. 137–38; Hart, *Chase*, p. 313; Hendrick, *Lincoln's War Cabinet*, pp. 427–28.

58. Albert G. Riddle, *Recollections of War Times: Reminiscences of Men and Events in Washington, 1860–1865* (New York: G. Putnam's Sons, 1895), pp. 267, 270; Warden, *Chase*, p. 584.

59. Garfield to J. H. Rhodes, Apr. 28, May 9, 1864, Garfield Papers, LC; Welles, *Diary*, Apr. 22, 1864, 2:20. For the charges of Treasury orgies see "Hamilton" to [?], June 1, 1864, Chase Papers, LC. The Clark in question may have been S. Morton Clark, chief of the first division of the National Currency Bureau. See also Margaret Leech, *Reveille in Washington, 1860–1865* (New York: Harper and Brothers, 1941), p. 317.

60. Jay Cooke to Chase, May 4, 1864, in Oberholtzer, *Cooke*, 1:416; Thomas Heaton to Chase, Apr. 29, 1864, Chase Papers, HSP; John Wilson to Chase, May 2, 1864, Chase Papers, LC.

61. Chase to Jay Cooke, May 5, 1864, in Schuckers, *Chase*, p. 503; Parsons to Chase, May 16, 1864, Chase Papers, LC.

62. Parsons to Chase, May 16, 1864, Chase Papers, LC; Chase to Brough, May 19, 1864, in Warden, *Chase*, p. 593.

63. Daniel W. Wise to Cooke, Apr. 25, 1864, in Oberholtzer, *Cooke*, 1:364; Trowbridge, "The First Visit to Washington," *Atlantic Monthly* 13 (April 1864): 448–57; Chase to Trowbridge, May 12, 1864, in Warden, *Chase*, p. 589. The

reference to "ferry boy" in the biography's title recalls Chase's efforts while on his way to live with his uncle in Ohio in 1821 to ferry passengers across the Cuyahoga River at Cleveland. See chap. 1 herein.

64. *Cincinnati Gazette,* May 26, 1864; *Cincinnati Commercial,* May 27, 1864. Missouri gave its twenty-two votes to Grant on the first ballot. Carman and Luthin, *Lincoln and the Patronage,* pp. 249–52; Zornow, "Lincoln, Chase and the Ohio Radicals in 1864," p. 31; Yager, "The Presidential Campaign of 1864 in Ohio," pp. 556–59.

65. Chase to J. M. Tomery, June 10, 1864, Chase Papers, HSP.

66. Chase to Lincoln, Apr. 18, 1861, Lincoln Papers, LC; Hart, *Chase,* pp. 217–18, 222.

67. Donald, *Inside Lincoln's Cabinet,* p. 297n.; Rufus Andrews to Chase, Dec. 15, 1863, Chase Papers, LC. Wadsworth was beaten by Democrat Horatio Seymour in the general election. Some evidence suggests that Seward and Weed withheld enough support from Wadsworth to assure Seymour's election. Carman and Luthin, *Lincoln and the Patronage,* pp. 243–44.

68. Chase to Barney, Dec. 12, 1863, John Austin to Chase, Jan. 8, 1864, S. Dewitt Bloodgood to Chase, Jan. 11, 1864, Chase Papers, HSP; *New York Herald,* Jan. 9, 1864; Rufus Andrews to Chase, Dec. 15, 1863, William A. Butler to Chase, Dec. 24, 1863, Opdyke to Chase, Jan. 4, 1864, Chase Papers, LC.

69. Lincoln to Chase, Feb. 12, 1864, in Schuckers, *Chase,* pp. 498–99; Chase to Barney, Jan. 19, 1864, Chase Papers, HSP; Chase to Lincoln, Jan. 1864, Lincoln Papers, LC; Chase to Lincoln, Jan. 13, 1864, in Warden, *Chase,* pp. 556–57.

70. Chase to Lincoln, Jan. 12, 1864, Lincoln Papers, LC; Lincoln to Chase, Feb. 12, 1864, in Schuckers, *Chase,* p. 499; J. F. Bailey to Chase, Jan. 13, 1864, Opdyke to Chase, Jan. 15, 1864, Chase Papers, LC; Barney to Chase, Feb. 11, 1864, Chase Papers, HSP; Carman and Luthin, *Lincoln and the Patronage,* pp. 245–46.

71. *New York Tribune,* June 20, 1864, Carman and Luthin, *Lincoln and the Patronage,* pp. 262–65; *Albany Evening Journal,* May 24, 1864; Chase to Seward, May 30, 1864, in Schuckers, *Chase,* p. 505.

72. Chase to Cisco, May 24, 1864, in Young, "Some Unpublished Letters of Chase," pp. 68–69; Chase to John Stewart, June 25, 1864, in Warden, *Chase,* p. 608; Nicolay and Hay, *Lincoln,* 9:90–92; Chase, Diary, June 27, 28, 29, 1864, in Donald, *Inside Lincoln's Cabinet,* pp. 215–20; Carman and Luthin, *Lincoln and the Patronage,* pp. 446–47; Hart, *Chase,* p. 316.

73. Chase to Cisco, June 28, 29, 1864, Chase to Lincoln, June 28, 1864, in Schuckers, *Chase,* pp. 506, 508; Cisco to Lincoln, June, 1864, Chase Papers, HSP; Chase, Diary, June 28, 29, 1864, in Donald, *Inside Lincoln's Cabinet,* pp. 217–21.

74. Lincoln to Chase, June 28, 1864, in Basler, *Collected Works of Lincoln,* 7:412–14; Chase to Lincoln, June 29, 1864, in Schuckers, *Chase,* p. 508.

75. Chase to Lincoln, June 29, 1864, in Schuckers, *Chase,* p. 508; Chase, Diary, June 28, 29, 1864, in Donald, *Inside Lincoln's Cabinet,* pp. 217–21.

76. Lincoln to Chase, June 30, 1864, in Basler, *Collected Works of Lincoln,* 7:419; Brough's version of Lincoln's reaction to Chase's resignation is found in "Private

Memoranda—War Times,'' William Henry Smith Papers, OHS. See also Maunsell B. Field, _Memoirs of Many Men and Some Women_ (New York: Harper and Bros., 1874), p. 296; Hendrick, _Lincoln's War Cabinet_, pp. 446–48.

77. Chase, Diary, June 30, 1864, in Donald, _Inside Lincoln's Cabinet_, pp. 223–24; Chase to Whitelaw Reid, n.d., in Hart, _Chase_, p. 318.

78. Chase, Diary, July 4, 1864, in Donald, _Inside Lincoln's Cabinet_, p. 231; Chase to Frank Howe, July 8, 1864, Chase to Parsons, July 8, 1864, Chase Papers, HSP.

79. Jay Cooke to Chase, June 29, 1864, Chase to Jay Cooke, July 1, 1864, in Oberholtzer, _Cooke_, 1:419, 421–22; _New York Tribune_, July 1, 1864; Chase to Cisco, July 1, 1864, Chase Papers, LC; Chase to Kate Sprague, July 2, 1864, Chase Papers, HSP; Chase to Stanton, June 30, 1864, Chase to William Cullen Bryant, June 30, 1864, in Schuckers, _Chase_, pp. 509, 405.

80. Bates, _Diary_, June 30, 1864, p. 381; Welles, _Diary_, June 29, Aug. 5, 1864, 2:62, 93–94; _Albany Evening Journal_, June 30, 1864; Chase, Diary, July 13, 1864, in Donald, _Inside Lincoln's Cabinet_, p. 240.

81. Chase to Lincoln, June 29, 1864, in Schuckers, _Chase_, p. 508; Welles, _Diary_, July 1, 1864, 2:64–65; Nicolay and Hay, _Lincoln_, 9:99; Thomas and Hyman, _Stanton_, pp. 314–15.

82. Chase, Diary, July 1, 5, 1864, in Donald, _Inside Lincoln's Cabinet_, pp. 226–28, 232; Chase to Kate Sprague, July 9, 1864, Chase to Parsons, Sept. 14, 1864, Chase Papers, HSP.

83. Chase to Nettie Chase, July 5, 1864, Chase Papers, LC; Chase to Cameron, July 11, 1864, in Warden, _Chase_, p. 628; Chase, Diary, July 2, 13, 1864, in Donald, _Inside Lincoln's Cabinet_, pp. 228–29, 240.

84. Chase, Diary, Aug. 29, 1864, in Donald, _Inside Lincoln's Cabinet_, pp. 249–50; see also, p. 236.

85. William Stanton to Chase, July 9, 1864, Chase Papers, LC; Chase, Diary, Aug. 3, 1864, in Donald, _Inside Lincoln's Cabinet_, p. 244; Chase to Charles S. May, Aug. 31, 1864, in Warden, _Chase_, pp. 628–29; Mellen to Chase, Aug. 10, 1864, Chase Papers, HSP.

86. _New York Tribune_, June 1, Aug. 31, 1864; McPherson, _Ordeal by Fire_, p. 407; Lincoln, ''Memorandum Concerning His Probable Failure of Reelection,'' Aug. 23, 1864, in Basler, _Collected Works of Lincoln_, 7:514.

87. Chase, Diary, July 6, Aug. 13, 16, 19, 1864, in Donald, _Inside Lincoln's Cabinet_, pp. 233, 245–47.

88. Chase to Parsons, Sept. 14, 1864, Chase Papers, HSP. Blair was replaced by former Governor William Dennison of Ohio, thus restoring the cabinet seat that Lincoln felt Ohio should have. See Welles, _Diary_, Sept. 23, 1864, 2:158n.; Smith, _Blair_, pp. 346–48. On the relationship of Blair's removal to Frémont's withdrawal see Randall and Donald, _Civil War and Reconstruction_, p. 475n., and McPherson, _Ordeal by Fire_, pp. 441–42.

89. Barney to Chase, Sept. 5, 1864, Chase Papers, HSP; Welles, _Diary_, Sept. 5, 1864, 2:137–38; U.S. Senate, _Executive Journal_, vol. 14, pt. 1 (1864–1866): 89, 96, 162, 215, 220; _New York Herald_, Mar. 3, 1865; Carman and Luthin, _Lincoln and the Patronage_, pp. 279–80, 314.

90. Chase to John Sherman, Oct. 2, 1864, Sherman Papers, LC; Chase to Kate Sprague, Sept. 17, 1864, Chase Papers, LC; Chase, Diary, Sept. 17, Sept. 21–Nov. 8, 1864, in Donald, *Inside's Lincoln's Cabinet,* pp. 254–55, 256–59; Chase to Stanton, Oct. 24, 1864, Stanton Papers, LC; Chase to McCulloch, Oct. 25, Nov. 10, 1864, McCulloch Papers, LC.

91. Chase, Diary, June 30, 1864, in Donald, *Inside Lincoln's Cabinet,* p. 224; Field, in Donn Piatt, *Memories of Men Who Saved the Union* (New York: Bedford, Clark and Co., 1887), pp. 120–23; Pease and Randall, *Browning Diary,* 20:686; Lincoln, in Belden and Belden, *So Fell the Angels,* pp. 137–39; Hendrick, *Lincoln's War Cabinet,* pp. 462–63.

92. Sumner to Chase, Oct. 14, 1864, in Schuckers, *Chase,* p. 512; Sumner to Lincoln, Oct. 12, 1864, Sherman to Lincoln, Oct. 22, 1864, Lincoln Papers, LC.

93. Chase to Stanton, Oct. 13, 1864, Stanton Papers, LC; Chase to McCulloch; Oct. 25, 1864, McCulloch Papers, LC; Chase to Sumner, Oct. 19, 1864, in Schuckers, *Chase,* p. 512.

94. Sumner to Chase, Oct. 24, 1864, Chase Papers, LC; Fessenden to Chase, Oct. 20, 1864, Chase to Parsons, Nov. 19, 1864, Chase Papers, HSP; Chase to Sherman, Nov. 12, 1864, Sherman Papers, LC; Chase to George Denison, Nov. 11, 1864, Denison Papers, LC.

95. Sumner to Chase, Nov. 20, 1864, Chase Papers, HSP; Ohio Union Legislators to Lincoln, Dec. 5, 1864, Sherman Papers, LC; Chase to McCulloch, Nov. 27, 1864, McCulloch Papers, LC; Nicolay and Hay, *Lincoln,* 9:391–92.

96. Nicolay and Hay, *Lincoln,* 9:392; Ewing to Lincoln, Dec. 3, 1864, Ewing to Orville Browning, Oct. 24, 1864, Ewing Papers, LC; Chase to Stanton, Oct. 13, 1864, Stanton Papers, LC; Fessenden to Chase, Oct. 20, 1864, Chase Papers, HSP; *Cincinnati Gazette,* Nov. 18, Dec. 12, 1864; Thomas and Hyman, *Stanton,* pp. 336–39.

97. Welles, *Diary,* Nov. 26, 1864, 2:181–83; Whitelaw Reid to Chase, Nov. 24, 1864, Chase Papers, HSP; Davis to Lincoln, Oct. 4, 1864, Lincoln Papers, LC; King, *Davis,* pp. 222–24; Carman and Luthin, *Lincoln and the Patronage,* p. 317; Chase, in Hart, *Chase,* pp. 320–21; Hendrick, *Lincoln's War Cabinet,* p. 461; William E. Smith, *The Francis Preston Blair Family in Politics,* 2 vols. (New York: Macmillan Co., 1933), 2:299.

98. Congressman Frank, in David F. Hughes, "Salmon P. Chase: Chief Justice" (Ph.D. diss., Princeton University, 1963), pp. 53–54, hereafter cited as "Chase"; Nicolay and Hay, *Lincoln,* 9:394; George S. Boutwell, *Reminiscences of Sixty Years in Public Life* 2 vols. (New York: McClure Phillips and Co., 1902), 2:29; Carman and Luthin, *Lincoln and the Patronage,* pp. 319–20; Colfax to Chase, Dec. 5, 1864, Chase Papers, HSP.

99. Chase to Lincoln, Dec. 6, 1864, in Schuckers, *Chase,* p. 513; Donald, *Inside Lincoln's Cabinet,* p. 260; Henry Cooke to Jay Cooke, Dec. 6, 1864, in Oberholtzer, *Cooke,* 1:463; Medill to Chase, Dec. 9, 1864, Chase Papers, HSP; Child to Chase, Dec. 13, 1864, Chase Papers, LC; Tappan to Chase, Dec. 21, 1864, Tappan Papers, LC; Kate Sprague, in Warden, *Chase,* p. 630. Greeley also gave the appointment his full editorial support. See *New York Tribune,* Dec. 7, 9, 1864.

100. Welles, *Diary,* Dec. 6, 15, 1864, 2:192–93, 196; Frank Blair to Montgom-

ery Blair, Jan. 17, 1865, Blair Papers, LC; Wade, in Dennett, *Lincoln and John Hay,* p. 53; Trefousse, *Wade,* p. 235; Chase to Stanley Matthews, Dec. 17, 1864, in Young, "Some Unpublished Letters of Chase," pp. 81–82.

Chapter Nine

1. Chase to Mrs. Gamaliel Bailey, Jan. 6, 1865, in Young, "Some Unpublished Letters of Chase," pp. 91–92; Donald, *Inside Lincoln's Cabinet,* p. 261.

2. Charles Fairman, *History of the Supreme Court of the United States,* vol. 6, *Reconstruction and Reunion, 1864–88,* pt. 1 (New York: Macmillan Co., 1971), p. 32; Chase to McDowell, Mar. 30, 1865, Chase Papers, HSP.

3. Welles, *Diary,* Mar. 4, 1865, 2:251; Chase to Sherman, Mar. 1, 1865, Sherman Papers, LC.

4. Chase to Garrison, Jan. 22, 1865, Chase to Phillips, Feb. 7, 1865, Chase to Sumner, Apr. 12, 1865, Chase Papers, HSP; Chase to Lincoln, Apr. 11, 1865, in Schuckers, *Chase,* pp. 514–15; Chase to Lincoln, Apr. 12, 1865, in Basler, *Complete Works of Lincoln,* 8:399–401n.

5. Lincoln, Apr. 11, 1865, in Basler, *Complete Works of Lincoln,* 8:399–405; Chase, Diary, Apr. 12, 15, 1865, in Donald, *Inside Lincoln's Cabinet,* pp. 265–66, 268.

6. Chase, Diary, Apr. 14, 1865, in Donald, *Inside Lincoln's Cabinet,* pp. 266–67. After the ceremony, Chase greeted Montgomery Blair with the hope "that from this day there will cease all anger and bitterness between us." Smith, *Blair,* p. 371; Chase, Diary, Apr. 15, 1865, in Donald, *Inside Lincoln's Cabinet,* pp. 267–69.

7. Wilson, "Original Chase Organization Meeting," pp. 69–70; Chase, speech for Andrew Johnson, Apr. 15, 1865, in Warden, *Chase,* p. 641; Chase, Diary, Apr. 18, 1865, in Donald, *Inside Lincoln's Cabinet,* p. 269.

8. Andrew Johnson, "An Address to the People of the United States," Apr. 16, 1865, Johnson Papers, LC; Chase to Johnson, Apr. 18, 1865, Chase Papers, HSP; James E. Sefton, *Andrew Johnson and the Uses of Constitutional Power* (Boston: Little Brown and Co., 1980), p. 110; Howard K. Beale, *The Critical Year: A Study of Andrew Johnson and Reconstruction* (New York: Frederick Ungar, 1958), p. 62.

9. Chase, Diary, Apr. 29, 1865, in Donald, *Inside Lincoln's Cabinet,* pp. 271–72.

10. Sumner to Francis Lieber, May 2, 1865, in Edward L. Pierce, *Memoir and Letters of Charles Sumner,* 4 vols. (Boston: Roberts Bros., 1877–93), 4:243; Chase to Stanton, Apr. 29, 1865, Stanton to Department Commanders, Apr. 29, 1865, Stanton Papers, LC; Andrew Johnson, Apr. 29, 1865, in Warden, *Chase,* p. 642; Benedict, *A Compromise of Principle,* p. 105; Chase to Johnson, Apr. 30, 1865, Chase to Sprague, Apr. 30, 1865, Chase Papers, HSP; Chase, Diary, Apr. 29, 1865, in Donald, *Inside Lincoln's Cabinet,* pp. 271–72.

11. After a brief stay in Havana, they stopped at New Orleans before moving up the Mississippi and Ohio Rivers to Cincinnati. The trip is described in James E. Sefton, ed., "Chief Justice Chase as an Advisor on Presidential Reconstruction," *Civil War History* 12 (1967): 242–64. Reid provided a contemporary interpretation of the trip in *After the War: A Southern Tour* (Cincinnati, 1866).

12. Chase to Johnson, May 4, 7, 12, 21, 1865, in Sefton, "Chase as Advisor on Reconstruction," pp. 244–48, 249–53, 260–61. All of the Chase letters to Johnson are also found in Chase Papers, CHS, and in the Johnson Papers, LC.

13. Chase even recommended those generals he felt best suited for the task, including John M. Schofield, Quincy Adams Gillmore, Rufus Saxton, and John P. Hatch. Chase to Johnson, May 17, 1865, in ibid., pp. 253–60.

14. Chase to Johnson, May 23, 7, 17, 1865, in Sefton, "Chase as Advisor on Reconstruction," pp. 261–63, 246–48, 253–60.

15. Chase to Sherman, Jan. 2, 1865, Sherman Papers; Sherman to Chase, Jan. 11, 1865, Chase Papers, HSP; Chase to Sherman, May 5, 1865, Sherman Papers, LC; Sherman to Chase, May 6, 1865, in *The War of the Rebellion,* ser. 1, vol. 47, pt. 3, 410–12; Chase to Sherman, May 6, 1865, in Schuckers, *Chase,* pp. 520–21; Chase to Johnson, May 7, 1865, in Sefton, "Chase as Advisor on Reconstruction," pp. 246–48.

16. Chase to Johnson, May 17, 21, 1865, in Sefton, "Chase as Advisor on Reconstruction," pp. 253–61; Chase to Sumner, May 20, 1865, in Schuckers, *Chase,* pp. 523–24.

17. Chase to Johnson, May 12, 17, 1865, in Sefton, "Chase as Advisor on Reconstruction," pp. 249–60.

18. Chase, Speech, May, 1865, in Warden, *Chase,* pp. 643–44; Chase to Johnson, May 12, 17, 1865, in Sefton, "Chase as Advisor on Reconstruction," pp. 249–60.

19. Bates, *Diary,* June 21, 1865, p. 489; Welles, *Diary,* May 10, 1865, 2:304; *New York Herald,* June 1, 1865; *New York World,* May 22, 1865; Reid to Blair, June 26, 1865, in Carman and Luthin, *Lincoln and the Patronage,* p. 320; Schuckers, *Chase,* p. 519. Historians in the early twentieth century were as critical of Chase and his motives as some of his contemporary opponents. Among the most extreme, Claude Bowers thought Chase advocated black suffrage primarily because former slaves might help him win the presidency and suggested that Chase "found potential voters entitled to the ballot" among blacks who were "unwilling to work, but eager for the ballot." Bowers, *The Tragic Era,* pp. 57, 58. Howard K. Beale wrote a more balanced and scholarly account but one which was highly critical of the radicals and Chase. Said Beale: "The South swarmed with Radical trouble-makers and nascent carpetbaggers who aroused resentment and then interpreted it as perverse ill feeling. . . . Chase and his lieutenants organized the Florida blacks and non-resident whites to demand negro suffrage." Beale, *The Critical Year,* p. 155.

20. Chase to Johnson, May 12, 1865, in Sefton, "Chase as Advisor on Reconstruction," pp. 249–53, 263; Johnson, Proclamation, May 29, 1865, in Richardson, *A Compilation,* 8:3508–12; McPherson, *Ordeal by Fire,* pp. 498–99; Sefton, *Johnson,* pp. 109–11.

21. The six states were Mississippi, Georgia, Texas, Alabama, South Carolina, and Florida. Richardson, *A Compilation,* 8:3512–29. In Louisiana, Tennessee, and Arkansas, Johnson recognized the governments which had been authorized by Lincoln as well as the loyalist government in Virginia which had functioned during the war. See Sefton, *Johnson,* p. 114.

22. Chase to New Orleans Blacks, June 6, 1865, Chase to Pike, July 8, 1865, in

Durden, *Pike,* p. 163; Chase to Sumner, June 25, 1865, Chase to Schuckers, July 7, 1865, Chase Papers, LC; Sumner to Carl Schurz, June 29, 1865, Schurz Papers, LC.

23. Sumner to Chase, June 28, 1865, Chase to Sumner, Aug. 20, 1865, Chase to Sprague, Sept. 6, 7, 1865, Chase Papers, LC; Sumner to Chase, July 1, 1865, Chase Papers, HSP.

24. Johnson to Sharkey, Aug. 15, 1865, Johnson Papers, LC.

25. Chase to Parsons, Sept. 18, 1865, Chase Papers, HSP.

26. McPherson, *Ordeal by Fire,* pp. 503–5; Chase to Sumner, Oct. 20, 1865, in Warden, *Chase,* p. 646. Exactly how "radical" Republican Reconstruction policies were is an issue of rapidly changing historical interpretation. In the 1960s historians, in rejecting the "tragic era" concept, placed much of the blame for Reconstruction failures on the stubborn racism of Andrew Johnson and viewed Republican leaders as idealists and reformers. See, for example, Eric L. McKitrick, *Andrew Johnson and Reconstruction* (Chicago: Univ. of Chicago Press, 1960). More recently, however, a number of Reconstruction scholars have questioned the degree to which Republicans were committed to racial progress and brought meaningful change. See William Gillette, *Retreat from Reconstruction, 1869–1879* (Baton Rouge: Louisiana State Univ. Press, 1979), and Michael Perman, *The Road to Redemption: Southern Politics, 1869–1879* (Chapel Hill: Univ. of North Carolina Press, 1984). Equally significant, some questioned the degree to which the radical faction dominated Congress. Michael Les Benedict's *A Compromise of Principle* shows the influence of more moderate Republicans in preserving continuity and minimizing change. See also Benedict, "Preserving the Constitution: The Conservative Basis of Radical Reconstruction," *Journal of American History* 61 (1974): 65–90. Eric Foner's *Nothing But Freedom: Emancipation and Its Legacy* (Baton Rouge: Louisiana State Univ. Press, 1983), represents a step back toward the revisionist views of the 1960s by suggesting that abolition and Reconstruction did bring meaningful and lasting changes in race relations for North and South. See also Foner, "Reconstruction Revisited," *Reviews in American History* 10 (1982): 82–100. Throughout the debate, Chase's roles as chief justice and politician remain important.

27. The Senate failed to override the first veto by a vote of 30 to 18 on Feb. 20, 1866. Johnson's second veto was on July 16, 1866. The House overrode it on the same day, 104 to 33, as did the Senate, 33 to 12. *Congressional Globe,* 39th Cong., 1st sess., pp. 943, 3850–51, 3842; Richardson, *A Compilation,* 8:3596–3603, 3620–24.

28. Johnson's veto on Mar. 27, 1866, is in Richardson, *A Compilation,* 8:3603–11. The Senate overrode this veto 33 to 15 and the House, 122 to 41. *Congressional Globe,* 39th Cong., 1st sess., Apr. 6, 1866, p. 1809, Apr. 9, 1866, p. 1861.

29. The Senate approved the amendment 33 to 11 on June 8, 1866, the House, 120 to 32, on June 13. *Congressional Globe,* 39th Cong., 1st sess., pp. 3042, 3149; Benedict, *A Compromise of Principle,* p. 160. See also William Gillette, *The Right to Vote: Politics and the Passage of the Fifteenth Amendment* (Baltimore: Johns Hopkins Univ. Press, 1965), p. 71.

30. Chase to Field, Apr. 30, 1866, in Schuckers, *Chase,* pp. 526–27; Chase to Schuckers, May 1866, Chase to Nettie Chase, May 19, 20, 1866, Chase Papers,

LC; Chase to Cole, June 9, 1866, Chase Papers, HSP; Chase to A. J. Hamilton, June 1866, Chase Papers, LC.

31. McPherson, *Ordeal by Fire,* pp. 519–20; Chase to B. R. Corwin, Nov. 8, 1866, Chase Papers, HSP.

32. Chase to Heaton, June 28, 1866, Chase to Barney, Nov. 21, 1866, Chase Papers, HSP; Chase to Nettie Chase, Oct. 15, 1866, Chase Papers, LC.

33. Chase to L. D. Stickney, Nov. 6, 1866, Chase to Wager Swayne, Dec. 4, 1866, Chase Papers, HSP; Chase to Robert A. Hill, Mar. 2, 1867, in Warden, *Chase,* p. 651; Chase to R. M. Patton, Mar. 11, 1867, Swayne to Chase, Dec. 10, 1866, Chase Papers, LC; McPherson, *Ordeal by Fire,* pp. 518–21.

34. The bill, passed in late 1866, was vetoed in January 1867 and then immediately repassed over the veto, in the Senate, 29 to 10, and in the House, 113 to 38. *Congressional Globe,* 39th Cong., 2d sess., Jan. 7, 8, 1867, pp. 313–14, 344; Richardson, *A Compilation,* Jan. 5, 1867, 8:3670–81; Benedict, *A Compromise of Principle,* p. 212.

35. Chase to Ball, Apr. 10, 1866, Chase to Robert A. Hill, July 10, 1866, Chase Papers, HSP; Chase to Phillips, May 1, 1866, in Warden, *Chase,* p. 649.

36. Langston to Chase, Nov. 26, 1866, Thomas Conway to Chase, Apr. 23, 1867, Chase Papers, LC; Chase to Langston, Nov. 30, 1866, Chase to J. M. McKim, Oct. 16, 1866, Chase Papers, HSP; Chase Opinion in *Shortridge and Co.* v. *Macon,* June, 1867, in Bradley T. Johnson, *Reports of Cases Decided by Chief Justice Chase in the Circuit Court of the United States Fourth Circuit, 1865–1869,* ed., Ferne Hyman and Harold Hyman (New York: DeCapo Press, 1972), pp. 141–42.

37. Chase to Smith, May 31, 1866, Chase Papers, HSP. The Reconstruction act of Mar. 2, 1867 was passed over Johnson's veto in the House 126 to 46, and in the Senate 38 to 10. *Congressional Globe,* 39th Cong., 2d sess., pp. 1733, 1976. The veto message is in Richardson, *A Compilation,* 8:3696–3709. The act of Mar. 23, 1867 was passed over Johnson's veto in the House 114 to 25 and in the Senate 40 to 7. *Congressional Globe,* 40th Cong., 1st sess., pp. 314–15, 303. The veto message is in Richardson, *A Compilation,* 8:3729–33.

38. Chase to Theodore Tilton, July 9, 1867, Chase Papers, LC. The Command of the Army provision was attached to an army appropriation bill and thus not vetoed by Johnson. See McPherson, *Ordeal by Fire,* p. 523. The Act of July 19, 1867 was passed over Johnson's veto 32 to 4 in the Senate and 108 to 25 in the House. *Congressional Globe,* 40th Cong., 1st sess., pp. 732, 747. The veto message is in Richardson, *A Compilation,* 8:3734–43.

39. Johnson to Chase, Oct. 12, 1865, Chase to Johnson, Oct. 12, 1865, in Johnson, *Reports,* pp. 9–10; Chase to Kate Sprague, n.d., 1865, Chase Papers, LC; Chase to John Sherman, Mar. 3, 1866, Sherman Papers, LC. A district judge could hold circuit court by himself without a Supreme Court justice being present, although he joined with the latter to constitute an appellate court. Fairman, *Reconstruction and Reunion,* pp. 85–86; Chase to G. W. Brooks, Mar. 20, 1866, Chase Papers, HSP; Hughes, "Chase," pp. 274–78.

40. Chase to Schuckers, May 15, 1866, in Schuckers, *Chase,* pp. 536–37; Chase to Gerrit Smith, May 31, 1866, Chase to Greeley, June 1, 1866, Chase Papers, HSP; Chase to Greeley, June 5, 1866, Chase Papers, LC.

41. Johnson, Proclamation, Aug. 20, 1866, in Richardson, *A Compilation*, 8:3632–36; Hughes, "Chase, Chief Justice," pp. 584–85. See note 72 for a discussion of why Congress changed the size of the Court.

42. Chase, Speech to Members of the Bar, Raleigh, June 6, 1867, in Johnson, *Reports*, p. 135; Chase to Sickles, Sept. 19, 1867, Chase Papers, LC. Sickles was shortly removed from his command by Johnson because of his close affinity to the radical position. See McPherson, *Ordeal by Fire*, p. 529.

43. Chase to John R. Young, June 29, 1867, in Warden, *Chase*, pp. 667–68; Chase to David Davis, June 24, 1867, Chase to Nettie Chase, July 11, 1867, Chase Papers, LC; Chase to Greeley, Jan. 17, 1868, Greeley Papers, New York Public Library.

44. *Congressional Globe*, 39th Cong., 2nd sess., Mar. 2, 1867; Johnson veto of Mar. 2, 1867, in Richardson, *A Compilation*, 8:3690–96; James C. Kennedy to Johnson, Feb. 22, 1868, in Charles H. Coleman, *The Election of 1868: The Democratic Effort to Regain Control* (New York: Columbia Univ. Press, 1933), p. 80; Chase to Greeley, Aug. 5, 1867, in Warden, *Chase*, pp. 669–70; Chase to Garfield, Aug. 7, 1867, Garfield Papers, LC; McKitrick, *Andrew Johnson*, pp. 498–99n. Johnson's Attorney General Henry Stanbery ruled that commanders could not remove political officials after Sheridan had removed several such people in his district. When Sheridan responded that Stanbery's ruling opened "a broad macadamized road for perjury and fraud to travel on," Johnson replaced him with a more conservative general. See McPherson, *Ordeal by Fire*, pp. 527–28.

45. Chase to Johnson, May 17, 1865, in Sefton, "Chase as Advisor on Reconstruction," pp. 253–60. The best account of the Davis proceedings is Roy F. Nichols, "United States vs. Jefferson Davis, 1865–1869," *American Historical Review* 31(1926): 266–84.

46. Sumner to Chase, June 25, 1865, Chase Papers, LC; Johnson to Chase, Aug. 11, 1865, in Warden, *Chase*, p. 645; Chase to Sumner, Aug. 20, 1865, Chase Papers, LC; Hughes, "Chase," p. 178; Greeley to Chase, May 31, 1866, Chase Papers, LC.

47. Chase to Kate Sprague, n.d., 1865, Chase to Greeley, June 5, 1866, Chase Papers, LC; Chase to Schuckers, n.d., in Schuckers, *Chase*, pp. 536, 540–42; Greeley to Chase, May 31, 1866, in Bourne, "Chase Correspondence," p. 514; Chase to Sprague, Sept. 24, 1866, Chase Papers, HSP; Indictment, in Johnson, *Reports*, p. 71; Johnson to Stanbery, Oct. 6, 1866, in ibid., pp. 32–33; Greeley to Chase, May 4, 1866, Chase Papers, HSP; Fairman, *Reconstruction and Reunion*, pp. 175–77.

48. Johnson, *Reports*, p. 38. Greeley, Gerrit Smith, and Cornelius Vanderbilt were among those who agreed to act as sureties on the bail bond.

49. Chase to Underwood, Oct. 22, 1867, Chase Papers, LC; Chase to Underwood, Nov. 23, 1867, Underwood Papers, LC.

50. Nichols, "United States vs. Jefferson Davis," pp. 283–84.

51. Field's appointment in 1863 had increased the size of the Court to ten, a change justified by the creation of the new judicial circuit for the Pacific coast. The death of John Catron of Tennessee in May 1865, returned the Court to nine members, and the vacancy was left unfilled during the struggle between Johnson and

Congress. Fairman, *Reconstruction and Reunion*, pp. 1–4; Hughes, "Chase, Chief Justice," pp. 581–84; Carl B. Swisher, *Stephen J. Field: Craftsman of the Law* (Washington: Brookings Inst., 1930), pp. 116–19.

52. Davis to Chase, Aug. 12, 1867, Chase Papers, LC.

53. Chase to Sprague, July 25, 1866, Chase Papers, HSP; Hughes, "Chase, Chief Justice," pp. 602–5.

54. Hughes, "Chase, Chief Justice," pp. 603–4. For a discussion of the specific prize cases, see Fairman, *Reconstruction and Reunion*, pp. 36–43.

55. For a historiographical discussion of the Chase Court, see Hyman and Hyman, Introduction, in Johnson, *Reports*, i–xiv. For a spirited defense of the Court against charges that it was controlled and intimidated by Congress see Kutler, *Judicial Power*. The most thorough accounts of Chase's judicial role are found in Hughes, "Chase, Chief Justice," and Fairman, *Reconstruction and Reunion*.

56. 4 Wallace, 2 (1866). Milligan's defense was ably presented by Attorney Jeremiah S. Black, a Democrat, and his young Republican partner, James A. Garfield, Chase's friend and former protégé. Peskin, *Garfield*, pp. 272–73; Fairman, *Reconstruction and Reunion*, pp. 204–7.

57. Hughes, "Chase, Chief Justice," p. 585; Charles Fairman, *Mr. Justice Miller and the Supreme Court* (Cambridge: Harvard Univ. Press, 1939), pp. 90–96; King, *Davis*, pp. 254–55.

58. 4 Wallace, 277 (1867); Chase to Miller, June 5, 9, July 1866, Chase to C. D. Drake, Apr. 24, 1866, Chase Papers, HSP; Chase to Alexander Long, Feb. 10, 1870, Chase Papers, LC; Hughes, "Chase, Chief Justice," pp. 587–88; Fairman, *Reconstruction and Reunion*, pp. 156–60.

59. 4 Wallace, 333(1867); Hughes, "Chase, Chief Justice," p. 588; Swisher, *Stephen J. Field*, pp. 150–51. Augustus H. Garland, the attorney in question, had been admitted to federal practice in December 1860 but had served in the Confederate Congress before being pardoned in July 1865.

60. 4 Wallace, 475(1867).

61. Ibid.; Fairman, *Reconstruction and Reunion*, pp. 378–83; *Georgia* v. *Stanton*, 6 Wallace, 50(1867); Kutler, *Judicial Power*, pp. 96–98.

62. 6 Wallace, 318(1868); *Congressional Globe*, 39th Cong., 2d sess., pp. 730, 790; Hughes, "Chase," p. 251; Stanley I. Kutler, "Ex parte McCardle: Judicial Impotency? The Supreme Court and Reconstruction Reconsidered," *American Historical Review* 72 (1967): 840.

63. The Senate overrode the veto 33 to 9, the House, 114 to 34. *Congressional Globe*, 40th Cong., 2d sess., Mar. 26, 27, 1868, pp. 2128, 2170. The veto message of Mar. 25, 1868 is in Richardson, *A Compilation*, 9:3844–46.

64. 7 Wallace, 506(1869); Chase to John Van Buren, Apr. 5, 1868, Chase Papers, HSP; Hughes, "Chase, Chief Justice," pp. 591–93; Fairman, *Reconstruction and Reunion*, pp. 433–70; Kutler, "Ex parte McCardle," p. 844.

65. 7 Wallace 700(1869); Warden, *Chase*, pp. 663–64; Hughes, "Chase," pp. 194–95; Draft of Chase to *Cincinnati Commercial*, 1865, Chase Papers, HSP; Kutler, *Judicial Power*, pp. 110–11.

66. 8 Wallace 85(1869). Kutler argues convincingly that the Court's acceptance of the case and Chase's subsequent opinion proved that the justices had not backed

down in the McCardle case, but in fact remained ready to challenge Congress on the question of military rule and Supreme Court jurisdiction. See Kutler, *Judicial Power,* pp. 104–7.

67. Robert J. Walker to Chase, June 21, 1869, Chase Papers, HSP; Fairman, *Reconstruction and Reunion,* p. 584; Hughes, "Chase, Chief Justice," pp. 594–95.

68. Chase to John D. Van Buren, Mar. 20, 1868, Chase Papers, LC.

69. Chase to Underwood, Nov. 23, 1867, Nov. 19, 1868, Feb. 14, 1869, Underwood Papers, LC; Chase to William Giles, Oct. 20, 1866, Chase Papers, HSP; Chase to George W. Brooks, Nov. 6, 1866, Chase to Underwood, Jan. 14, 1869, Wager Swayne to Chase, June 3, 1867, Chase Papers, LC; Nichols, "United States vs. Jefferson Davis," p. 276; Hughes, "Chase," pp. 279–80, 282–83.

70. Chase to Giles, Mar. 16, Apr. 1, 1867, Chase Papers, LC.

71. Chase to Miller, Mar. 11, 1867, in Warden, *Chase,* p. 653; *Congressional Globe,* 39th Cong., 2d sess., Feb. 12, 22, 1867, pp. 1192, 1708; 40th Cong., 1st sess., Mar. 22, 1867, pp. 277–81; Chase to Nettie Chase, Mar. 23, 1867, Chase Papers, LC; Chase to Parsons, Nov. 8, 1866, Chase Papers, HSP; Davis to Judge Rockwell, Apr. 2, 1867, in Fairman, *Reconstruction and Reunion,* pp. 358–59, also pp. 355–65; Hughes, "Chase," pp. 287–89.

72. *Congressional Globe,* 39th Cong., 1st sess., July 19, 1866, pp. 3909, 3922, 3933; Chase to Miller, June 15, July 3, 1866, Chase to Sprague, July 25, 1866, Chase, Draft Proposal for Judiciary Act, July 1866, Chase Papers, HSP; Miller to Chase, June 27, 1866, Chase Papers, LC; Fairman, *Reconstruction and Reunion,* pp. 170–71. Scholars have claimed that the reduction of the Court's size to seven was a vindictive congressional effort to deprive Andrew Johnson of his power of appointment, but Reconstruction issues had little to do with it. In 1866, differences between the president and Congress were only beginning to surface. Johnson signed the bill without hesitation, even though it nullified his recent appointment of Henry Stanbery to a Court vacancy. The reasons for the bill were almost entirely judicial and financial. See Stanley I. Kutler, "Reconstruction and the Supreme Court: The Numbers Game Reconsidered," *Journal of Southern History* 32(1966): 42–58: Fairman, *Reconstruction and Reunion,* pp. 1–4; Hughes, "Chase, Chief Justice," pp. 581–84.

73. Chase to Garfield, Aug. 7, 1867, Garfield Papers, LC; Chase to Heaton, Mar. 23, 1868, in Warden, *Chase,* p. 682; Chase to J. E. Snodgrass, Mar. 16, 1868, in Schuckers, *Chase,* pp. 575–76; Bowers, *The Tragic Era,* p. 179.

74. The House voted 126 to 47 to impeach Johnson on February 24, 1868. *Congressional Globe,* 40th Cong., 2d sess., pp. 1400ff. Impeachment efforts had been developing for more than a year. In January 1867, the House passed a resolution offered by Chase's friend James M. Ashley to begin proceedings. Ibid., 39th Cong., 2d sess., Jan. 7, 1867, pp. 320–21. These efforts climaxed in December with the House rejecting its Judiciary Committee's resolution to impeach by a vote of 108 to 57. Ibid., 40th Cong., 2d sess., Dec. 7, 1867, p. 68.

75. *Congressional Globe,* 40th Cong., 2d sess., Mar. 2, 1868, pp. 1591–94, 1601–3; Chase to Jacob M. Howard, Feb. 27, 1868, Chase Papers, HSP; Schuckers, *Chase,* pp. 550–51; Chase to U.S. Senate, Mar. 4, 1868, in *Congressional Globe,* 40th Cong., 2d sess., p. 1644; Chase to Pomeroy, Mar. 5, 1868, Chase Papers, HSP; M.

Kathleen Perdue, "Salmon P. Chase and the Impeachment Trial of Andrew Johnson," *Historian* 27(1964): 76–79; Hughes, "Chase," pp. 123–25; Greeley's *New York Tribune*, a strong advocate of conviction, argued on Mar. 5, 1868 that Chase was mistaken in claiming a right to participate in the framing of the rules of procedure: "He acts not in the capacity of a judge sitting with a jury. . . . He is a presiding officer . . . and is subject to the rules which may be adopted for the trial by the Senate." Michael L. Benedict, *The Impeachment and Trial of Andrew Johnson* (New York: W. W. Norton, 1973), pp. 116–18.

76. U.S. Congress, Senate, *Trial of Andrew Johnson, President of the United States, Before the Senate of the United States, on Impeachment By the House of Representatives for High Crimes and Misdemeanors.* 40th Cong., 2d sess. (Washington, 1868), 1:90; Chase to Smith, Apr. 2, 1868, in Schuckers, *Chase,* pp. 576–77; Benedict, *The Impeachment and Trial of Andrew Johnson,* pp. 115–22; Hans L. Trefousse, *Impeachment of a President: Andrew Johnson, the Blacks and Reconstruction* (Knoxville: Univ. of Tennessee Press, 1975), p. 152.

77. *Trial of Johnson,* 1:12, 187; Sumner, in Schuckers, *Chase,* p. 556; Chase to Smith, Apr. 2, 1868, in Schuckers, *Chase,* pp. 576–77; Fairman, *Reconstruction and Reunion,* p. 523; Welles, *Diary,* Mar. 31, Apr. 1, 1868, 3:327–28; Perdue, "Chase and the Impeachment Trial," pp. 80–83. For a thorough description of Chase's clash with the radicals over these procedural points as well as a balanced account of the entire trial, see Benedict, *The Impeachment and Trial of Andrew Johnson,* esp. pp. 118–22.

78. *Trial of Johnson,* 1:415–508, 517–30, 701; Chase to Gerrit Smith, Apr. 19, 1868, in Schuckers, *Chase,* pp. 577–78; Perdue, "Chase and the Impeachment Trial," pp. 84–88; Hughes, "Chase," pp. 123–24.

79. *New York Tribune,* Apr. 1, 1868; Welles, *Diary,* Apr. 21, 1868, 3:336; Van Buren to Chase, May 9, 1868, Chase Papers, LC; *New York Herald,* May 7, 1868. John Dash Van Buren was not the son of the former president. The president's son John had died in 1866. For an indication of the Democratic party's changing opinion of Chase see Jerome Mushkat, "The Impeachment of Andrew Johnson: A Contemporary View," *New York History* 48(1967): 275–86, which includes the diary of conservative New York Congressman John V. L. Pruyn.

80. Chase to Kate Sprague, May 11, 1868, Chase Papers, LC; Chase to Barney, May 13, 1868, in Warden, *Chase,* pp. 693–94. The vote was on the all-inclusive Article 11. Two subsequent votes were held on May 26, with the same 35 to 19 results on Articles 2 and 3 dealing with the removal of Stanton and the appointment of Thomas in his place. The prosecution then called off the proceedings. *Congressional Globe,* 40th Cong., 2d sess., Supplement, May 16, 26, 1868, pp. 412, 414, 415.

81. Chase to Clark Williams, May 16, 1868, in Warden, *Chase,* pp. 694–95; Fairman, *Reconstruction and Reunion,* pp. 525–26; Benedict, *The Impeachment and Trial of Andrew Johnson,* pp. 137–39.

82. Chase to Smith, Apr. 19, 1868, in Schuckers, *Chase,* pp. 577–78; Chase to Parsons, Dec. 30, 1869, Chase, Memorandum, May 27, 1868, Chase Papers, HSP; Trefousse, *Impeachment of a President,* pp. 149–50, 178, 228n.

83. Chase, Memorandum, May 18, 1868, Chase Papers, LC; *New York Tribune,*

May 18, 1868; Trefousse, *Impeachment of a President,* pp. 177–78. As a "near neighbor" of the chief justice, Henderson had dined twice with Chase during the trial. Chase to Greeley, May 19, 1868, in Schuckers, *Chase,* pp. 581–82; Chase to H. S. Bundy, May 21, 1868, Chase to Murat Halstead, May 22, 1868, in Warden, *Chase,* pp. 697–99; Van Winkle to Chase, May 26, 1868, Chase Papers, LC.

84. Harold M. Hollingsworth, "The Confirmation of Judicial Review Under Taney and Chase" (Ph.D. diss. University of Tennessee, 1966), pp. 154–55. Garfield wrote: "It is the hardest thing I ever had to do . . . to withdraw confidence and love from a man to whom I have once given them but the conduct of Mr. Chase during the trial has . . . been outrageous." Garfield to J. H. Rhodes, May 18, 20, 1868, Garfield Papers, LC; Chase to Gerrit Smith, Apr. 2, 1868, in Schuckers, *Chase,* p. 576.

Chapter Ten

1. Donnal V. Smith, "Salmon P. Chase and the Nomination of 1868," in Avery Craven, ed., *Essays in Honor of William E. Dodd* (Chicago: Univ. of Chicago Press, 1935), p. 293; Coleman, *The Election of 1868,* p. 69.

2. Chase to Schuckers, Nov. 29, 1866, Chase Papers, LC; Chase to R. M. Corwine, Aug. 3, 1867, Chase Papers, HSP; Dwight Bannister to Chase, May 17, 1867, Mellen to Chase, June 27, 1867, Chase Papers, LC.

3. Chase to Schuckers, Nov. 29, 1866, Chase Papers, LC; Coleman, *The Election of 1868,* pp. 74–75; Benedict, *A Compromise of Principle,* pp. 270–76; Joel H. Silbey, *A Respectable Minority: The Democratic Party in the Civil War Era, 1860–1868* (New York: W. W. Norton and Co., 1977), pp. 215–16; William S. McFeely, *Grant: A Biography* (New York: W. W. Norton and Co., 1981), p. 279; Gillette, *The Right to Vote,* p. 36.

4. Chase to Nettie Chase, July 11, 1867, Chase to General N. Buford, Oct. 17, 1867, Chase Papers, LC; Chase to Garfield, Aug. 7, 1867, Garfield Papers, LC; Chase to Underwood, Feb. 19, 1868, in Warden, *Chase,* p. 677; *Congressional Globe,* 40th Cong., 2d sess., Supplement, May 16, 1868, p. 412; McFeely, *Grant,* pp. 276–77; Benedict, *A Compromise of Principle,* pp. 280–81.

5. Chase to John D. Van Buren, Mar. 25, 1868, Chase Papers, LC; Chase to William B. Thomas, Mar. 10, 1868, in Warden, *Chase,* pp. 680–81; *New York Sun,* Mar. 21, 1868; *Cincinnati Commercial,* Mar. 23, 1868; *Cincinnati Gazette,* Mar. 23, 1868; *New York Evening Post,* Mar. 23, 1868; *New York World,* Mar. 26, 1868; *New York Tribune,* Mar. 31, 1868.

6. Van Buren to Manton Marble, Apr. 1, 1868, Marble Papers, LC; Van Buren to Tilden, Apr. 25, 1868, Tilden Papers, New York Public Library (hereafter cited as NYPL); Chase to Van Buren, Mar. 25, 1868, Chase Papers, HSP; Long to Chase, Apr. 6, 1868, Long Papers, CHS; Chase to Long, Apr. 8, 1868, in Warden, *Chase,* p. 684; Chase to Long, Apr. 19, 1868, in Schuckers, *Chase,* pp. 578–79; Edward S. Perzel, "Alexander Long, Salmon P. Chase and the Election of 1868," *Bulletin of the Cincinnati Historical Society* 23(1965): 6–8; Jerome Mushkat, *The Reconstruction of the*

New York Democracy, 1861–1874 (Rutherford, N.J.: Fairleigh Dickinson Univ. Press, 1981), pp. 129–33; *New York Herald,* May 5, 6, 1868.

7. Hollingsworth, "Confirmation of Judicial Review," pp. 155–56; Schuckers to Long, May 9, 1868, Long Papers, CHS; Van Buren to Seymour, May 20, 1868, Seymour Papers, New-York Historical Society; Church to William Cassidy, June 8, 1868, Seymour Papers, New York State Library; Mushkat, *The Reconstruction of the New York Democracy,* pp. 134–35.

8. Porter and Johnson, *National Party Platforms,* p. 39; Thomas Hawley to Tilden, May 22, 1868, Tilden Papers, NYPL; *New York Herald,* June 17, 21, 25, July 2, 1868; Gillette, *The Right to Vote,* pp. 37–38; Chase to August Belmont, May 30, 1868, Chase to Barney, May 29, 1868, in Schuckers, *Chase,* pp. 563, 583–86; Barney to Chase, May 28, 1868, Chase Papers, LC.

9. *New York Herald,* May 27, 29, 1868; Coleman, *The Election of 1868,* pp. 112–16; George F. Gordon to Chase, June 10, 1868, F. A. Aiken to Chase, June 26, 1868, Chase Papers, LC; Smith, "Chase and the Nomination of 1868," p. 311.

10. Chase to Marble, May 30, 1868, Marble Papers, LC; Chase to I. F. Pourley, June 17, 1868, Chase to Cisco, June 25, 1868, Chase Papers, LC; Chase to Van Buren, June 25, 1868, Chase Papers, HSP.

11. Jay Cooke to Henry Cooke, May 30, 1868, Henry Cooke to Jay Cooke, June 2, 1868, in Oberholtzer, *Cooke,* 2:68; Montgomery Blair to Francis P. Blair, Jr., June 4, 1868, Blair Family Papers, LC; Montgomery Blair to Samuel L. M. Barlow, June 10, 1868, Barlow Papers, Henry E. Huntington Library; Loomis to Tilden, June 8, 1868, Tilden Papers, NYPL; *New York Leader,* June 13, 1868.

12. *New York Herald,* May 21, June 2, 3, 19, 1868; Van Buren to Seymour, June 9, 1868, Seymour Papers, New York State Library; Long to Chase, Apr. 6, 1868, Chase Papers, CHS; Coleman, *The Election of 1868,* pp. 178–80; Chase to Halstead, June 1, 1868, Chase Papers, LC; Bryant to Chase, June 23, 1868, in Bourne, "Chase Correspondence," pp. 519–20; Barlow to Tilden, June 21, 1868, Tilden Papers, NYPL; Trowbridge to Chase, June 19, 1868, Van Buren to Chase, June 19, 1868, Barney to Chase, June 26, 1868, Chase to Schuckers, June 6, 1868, Chase Papers, LC; Long to Chase, June 17, 1868, Chase Papers, CHS; Cisco to Chase, June 23, 1868, Chase Papers, HSP; Perzel, "Long, Chase and the Election of 1868," p. 6.

13. Schuckers to Chase, June 3, 1868, James Lyons to Chase, June 16, 1868, Chase Papers, LC; Chase to Lyons, June 18, 1868, in Schuckers, *Chase,* pp. 586–88; Chase to Gerrit Smith, June 17, 1868, Chase Papers, LC; Chase to [?], July 1, 1868, in *New York Herald,* July 6, 1868; Chase to Van Buren, July 2, 1868, Chase Papers, HSP; Coleman, *The Election of 1868,* p. 137.

14. Chase Platform, in Schuckers, *Chase,* pp. 567–70; Chase to Smith, June 17, 1868, Chase Papers, LC; Coleman, *The Election of 1868,* pp. 121–22; Phyllis F. Field, *The Politics of Race in New York: The Struggle for Black Suffrage in the Civil War Era* (Ithaca: Cornell Univ. Press, 1982), pp. 180–81; Mushkat, *The Reconstruction of the New York Democracy,* pp. 134–35.

15. Coleman, *The Election of 1868,* pp. 28–35, 139; *New York Herald,* June 3, 1868; Long to Chase, June 17, 1868, Chase Papers, CHS; Chase Platform, in Schuckers, *Chase,* p. 569.

16. Chase to Long, July 1, 1868, Long Papers, CHS; Chase to Long, July 4, 1868, Chase Papers, CHS; Long to Chase, July 3, 1868, Chase to Van Buren, July 1, 1868, Chase Papers, HSP; *Cincinnati Enquirer,* July 2, 1868, Chase to Cisco, in *New York Leader,* July 4, 1868; Perzel, "Long, Chase and the Election of 1868," p. 10.

17. S. Ward to Chase, June 26, 1868, Chase Papers, LC; Aiken to Chase, July 3, 1868, Chase Papers, HSP; *New York Herald,* July 3, 1868; Chase to Aiken, July 4, 1868, Chase Papers, HSP; Chase to Schuckers, July 6, 1868, in Schuckers, *Chase,* pp. 589–90.

18. *Louisville Courier-Journal,* n.d., in Warden, *Chase,* p. 705; *New York Herald,* July 7, 1868; Kate Sprague to Samuel Barlow, June 23, 1868, Barlow Papers, Huntington Library; Chase to Mrs. M. L. Bailey, Apr. 26, 1864, in Warden, *Chase,* pp. 581–82; Chase to Kate Sprague, July 7, 1868, Kate Sprague to Chase, July 2, 1868, Chase Papers, HSP.

19. Porter and Johnson, *National Party Platforms,* pp. 37–39; Chase to Kate Sprague, July 7, 1868, Chase Papers, HSP; Chase to Van Buren, July 8, 1868, in Schuckers, *Chase,* p. 590; Gillette, *The Right to Vote,* pp. 38–39.

20. Coleman, *The Election of 1868,* pp. 382, 224–25; Silbey, *A Respectable Minority,* pp. 204–5; *New York Herald,* July 8, 9, 10, 1868; Schuckers, *Chase,* p. 565; Van Buren to Chase, July 24, 1868, Chase Papers, LC; Fairman, *Reconstruction and Reunion,* p. 546.

21. Seymour later suggested that one reason that the delegates joined the movement for his nomination so quickly was that they "were impatient to return to their homes. . . . Impatience to close the work of the convention had much to do with its final unconsidered action." Seymour to Schuckers, Sept. 12, 1873, in Schuckers, *Chase,* pp. 570–73; Coleman, *The Election of 1868,* pp. 240–42; Mushkat, *The Reconstruction of the New York Democracy,* pp. 136–37. Seymour also insisted "that he had only accepted it because he was physically and morally broken down." Maunsell Field to Chase, Oct. 26, 1870, Chase Papers, HSP.

22. Porter and Johnson, *National Party Platforms,* p. 39; Coleman, *The Election of 1868,* p. 214.

23. Chase to Jay Cooke, July 11, 1868, Chase to William N. Thomas, July 17, 1868, Chase Papers, LC; Seymour to Schuckers, Sept. 12, 1873, in Schuckers, *Chase,* pp. 570–72.

24. Chase to Kate Sprague, July 10, 1868, Chase Papers, HSP; Kate Sprague to Chase, July 10, 1868, Chase Papers, LC. On hearing the news of Seymour's nomination, Chase reportedly asked: "How does Kate take it?" Bowers, *The Tragic Era,* p. 229.

25. Chase to Van Buren, July 10, 1868, Chase Papers, LC. For his part, Van Buren denied having any influence over Seymour and did not "carry any advice to him of which I heard at Mrs. Sprague's." Instead he worked where he could for Chase and assumed Seymour would do the same. On the other hand, Van Buren implied that Tilden had supported Seymour. Van Buren to Long, July 24, 1868, Long Papers, CHS.

26. Chase to Kate Sprague, July 10, 1868, Barney to Chase, July 10, 1868,

Chase Papers, HSP; Kate Sprague to Chase, July 10, 1868, Chase to Smith, July 28, 1868, Chase Papers, LC.

27. Long to Chase, Sept. 10, 1868, Chase to Kate Sprague, July 7, 1868, Chase Papers, HSP; Van Buren to Chase, July 24, 1868, Chase Papers, LC.

28. Chase to Cisco, July 10, 1868, Chase to James Gordon Bennett, July 10, 1868, Chase Papers, LC; Chase to Long, Sept. 30, 1868, Long Papers, CHS.

29. James A. Bayard to Samuel Barlow, May 31, 1868, Barlow Papers, Huntington Library; Chase to Wright, July 9, 1868, Wright Papers, LC; Chase to Gerrit Smith, July 28, 1868, Chase Papers, LC; Silbey, *A Respectable Minority*, pp. 201–3.

30. Francis P. Blair, Jr. to James O. Brodhead, June 30, 1868, in Smith, *The Francis Preston Blair Family in Politics*, 2:406–7; *New York World*, July 3, 1868; *New York Leader*, July 18, 1868; Chase to I. G. Jones, July 11, 1868, Chase Papers, LC; Chase to Whitelaw Reid, Aug. 23, 1868, Reid, Memorandum, 1868, Reid Papers, LC.

31. Chase to Schuckers, July 20, 1868, in Schuckers, *Chase*, p. 590; Chase to Barney, Aug. 9, 1868, Chase Papers, HSP; Chase to Dr. John Paul, Oct. 1, 1868, Chase to Charles A. Dana, Oct. 1, 1868, Chase Papers, LC; Mushkat, *The Reconstruction of the New York Democracy*, p. 138.

32. *New York Evening Post*, Aug. 15, Oct. 17, 1868; C. W. Walker to Chase, Aug. 30, 1868, Chase to Smith, Sept. 30, 1868, Chase to Charles A. Dana, Oct. 1, 1868, Chase to Gerrit Smith, Sept. 30, 1868, Chase Papers, LC; Chase to A. J. H. Duganne, Sept. 21, 1868, Chase to John Colyer, Aug. 25, 1868, in Schuckers, *Chase*, pp. 592, 591; Chase to Anthony, July 14, 1868, in Warden, *Chase*, pp. 710–11.

33. Schuckers to Long, July 14, 17, 1868, Long Papers, CHS; Long to Seymour, July 14, 1868, Seymour Papers, New York State Library; Fairman, *Reconstruction and Reunion*, p. 550; Silbey, *A Respectable Minority*, pp. 235–36.

34. Barney to Seymour, Sept. 10, 1868, Seymour to Van Buren, Sept. 24, 1868, Van Buren to Seymour, Sept. 24, 1868, Fairchild Collection, New-York Historical Society; Chase to Long, Sept. 30, 1868, Long Papers, CHS. See also Chase to Van Buren, Oct., 1868, Chase Papers, LC.

35. Barlow to Kernan, Oct. 14, 1868, Francis Kernan Papers, Cornell University; Barlow to Tilden, Oct. 14, 15, 1868, Vallandigham to Tilden, Oct. 17, 1868, Tilden Papers, NYPL; *New York World*, Oct. 16, 19, 20, 1868.

36. Van Buren to Chase, Oct. 17, 1868, Chase Papers, HSP; Chase to Van Buren, Oct. [?], 17, 1868, Chase Papers, LC. Long's efforts to force Chase's candidacy included the publication of a letter he claimed to have received from Chase: "Should our friends urge my acceptance in the event of Mr. Seymour's withdrawal, I should stand as the candidate for the Presidency in his stead." Chase to Long, Oct. 17, 1868, in *New York Times*, Oct. 26, 1868. Chase denied ever having written such a letter, and no copy in Chase's writing was ever found. See Chase to Long, Oct. 27, 1868, Long Papers, CHS. It was apparently a fabrication and a last-ditch effort by Long to force a change in the ticket. Perzel, "Long, Chase and the Election of 1868," pp. 16–17; Coleman, *The Election of 1868*, pp. 344–52.

37. *New York Leader*, Oct. 17, 1868; *New York Herald*, Oct. 17, 1868; *Albany Argus*, Oct. 18, 1868; *Buffalo Courier*, Oct. 19, 20, 1868; A. Schell to Jonah Hoover,

Oct. 18, 1868, Tilden Papers, NYPL; Mushkat, *The Reconstruction of the New York Democracy*, p. 141; Coleman, *The Election of 1868*, p. 384; Chase to Gerrit Smith, Nov. 6, 1868, Chase Papers, LC.

38. For the more appreciative view of Republican motives, see LaWanda Cox and John H. Cox, "Negro Suffrage and Republican Politics: The Problem of Motivation in Reconstruction Historiography," *Journal of Southern History* 33 (1967): 303–30; Glenn M. Linden, "A Note on Negro Suffrage and Republican Politics," *Journal of Southern History* 36 (1970): 411–20; Benedict, *A Compromise of Principle*, pp. 325–27, 446–47n.

39. In 1865, voters in Connecticut, Wisconsin, and Minnesota rejected black suffrage with the small Republican majorities in support offset by Democrats solidly opposed. In 1867, suffrage proposals lost in New York, Connecticut, Minnesota, as well as in Ohio, whereas voters did approve in Iowa and Minnesota the following year. For a full discussion of the issue see Leslie Fishel, "Negro Prejudice and Negro Suffrage, 1865–1870," *Journal of Negro History* 39 (1954):8–26. For an analysis of the suffrage issue in New York, see Field, *The Politics of Race in New York*, pp. 183, 187–219.

40. Republican candidate Rutherford B. Hayes had campaigned on a suffrage platform and won by less than 3,000 votes. David A. Gerber, *Black Ohio and the Color Line, 1860–1915* (Urbana: Univ. of Illinois Press, 1976), p. 38.

41. *Congressional Globe*, 40th Cong., 3d sess., Feb. 26, 1869, p. 1641; Gillette, *The Right to Vote*, pp. 71–78; Benedict, *A Compromise of Principle*, pp. 332–35.

42. Chase to William Byrd, Apr. 3, 1869, Chase to Van Buren, Nov. 20, 1869, Chase Papers, LC.

43. Chase to Yeatman, Oct. 19, 1869, Jan. 12, 1870, Chase Papers, CHS; Chase to Hill, Jan. 7, 1870, Chase Papers, LC; Field, *The Politics of Race in New York*, p. 218.

44. *Ohio State Journal*, Jan. 14, 15, 19, 20, 21, 1870; Chase to Yeatman, Jan. 22, 1870, Chase Papers, CHS; Gerber, *Black Ohio and the Color Line*, p. 40; Gillette, *The Right to Vote*, pp. 140–41. The required number of legislatures ratified by the end of March.

45. Chase to Yeatman, Feb. 12, 1870, Chase to Ball, Dec. 5, 1870, CHS; Chase to Peter Clark, et al., Mar. 2, 1870, in Schuckers, *Chase*, pp. 531–32. Chase was quick to point out to the Cincinnati blacks that he had "neither abandoned or compromised" the principle which he had so long supported. He also argued that the regulation of the issue was left "to the whole people of each state."

46. Chase to Jesse Baldwin, May 18, 1864, in Warden, *Chase*, pp. 409–10; Chase to S. DeWitt Bloodgood, May 9, 1864, in Schuckers, *Chase*, pp. 402–3.

47. Chase to Van Buren, Apr. 10, 1866, Chase Papers, HSP; Walter T. K. Nugent, *The Money Question During Reconstruction* (New York: W. W. Norton and Co., 1967), pp. 11, 67.

48. In *Veazie Bank* v. *Fenno* (8 Wallace 533 [1869]) Chase spoke for the Court in upholding the federal bank notes he had worked to establish under his national banking plan. In this decision, Chase argued in support of the act of Congress of March 1865 imposing a 10 percent tax on state bank notes, in effect destroying their use. Fairman, *Reconstruction and Reunion*, p. 711.

49. 8 Wallace 603 (1870); Chase to Parsons, Dec. 17, 1870, Chase Papers, LC. Great controversy arose over the vote of Justice Grier, who in conference on November 27, 1869, voted with those upholding the law, only to change his vote a few days later. Extremely ill at the time, Grier was felt by some of the justices to be senile. Accordingly, a committee representing the Court asked him to resign. Grier agreed, although his resignation took effect a week before the opinion was officially delivered on February 7, 1870, casting doubt on whether his vote should be included. The case is dealt with in detail in Fairman, *Reconstruction and Reunion,* pp. 713–19; Swisher, *Stephen J. Field,* pp. 173–77; see also Hughes, "Chase," pp. 335–36n.

50. T. C. Minturn to Chase, Feb. 12, 1870, Chase Papers, LC. Criticism among historians is based more on the constitutional reasoning of the opinion. See Fairman, *Mr. Justice Miller,* p. 162; Swisher, *Stephen J. Field,* pp. 177–78; Hollingsworth, "Confirmation of Judicial Review," pp. 180–84; Kutler, *Judicial Power,* pp. 120–24.

51. Chase, "Some Facts," Schuckers Papers, LC; Boutwell, *Reminiscences of Sixty Years in Public Life,* 2:209; Swisher, *Stephen J. Field,* pp. 182–83; McFeeley, *Grant,* p. 387; Sidney Ratner, "Was the Supreme Court Packed by President Grant?" *Political Science Quarterly* 50(1935): 350–52.

52. Chase, "Some Facts," Schuckers Papers, LC; Hart, *Chase,* pp. 399–401; Miller to Judge Rockwell, Apr. 21, 1870, in Fairman, *Reconstruction and Reunion,* pp. 744–45, 751–52; Ratner, "Was the Supreme Court Packed?" pp. 353–56.

53. It was combined with another case, *Parker* v. *Davis,* to be known as the *Legal Tender Cases,* 12 Wallace 457 (1871).

54. Chase to J. R. Tucker, May 1, 1871, Chase Papers, LC; Swisher, *Stephen J. Field,* pp. 189–93; Hollingsworth, "Confirmation of Judicial Review," p. 190; Ratner, "Was the Supreme Court Packed," pp. 357–58.

55. 16 Wallace 36 (1873); Kutler, *Judicial Power,* pp. 165–67; *Osborn* v. *Nicholson,* 13 Wallace, 654 (1872); Fairman, *Reconstruction and Reunion,* p. 1321.

56. Fairman, *Reconstruction and Reunion,* pp. 1324–63.

Chapter Eleven

1. Chase to Kate Sprague, June 25, 1865, Chase Papers, LC; Chase to Kate Sprague, Oct. 14, 1865, Chase Papers, CHS; Belden and Belden, *So Fell the Angels,* pp. 163–64.

2. *New York World,* Sept. 14, 1866; Chase to Sprague, July 25, 1866, Chase to Kate Sprague, Aug. 9, 1866, Jan. 4, 1867, Chase Papers, HSP; Chase to Schuckers, Oct. 16, 1866, Chase Papers, LC; Belden and Belden, *So Fell the Angels,* p. 165; Sokoloff, *Kate Chase,* pp. 117–29.

3. *Philadelphia Evening Star,* May 15, 1868; *New York World,* May 4, 1868; Chase to Kate Sprague, May 10, 1868, Chase Papers, LC.

4. Chase to Kate Sprague, Nov. 14, 1868, Apr. 15, 17, 1869, Chase Papers, HSP; Chase to Kate Sprague, May 4, 1869, Chase Papers, LC.

5. Chase to Kate Sprague, Aug. 1, Sept. 15, 1869, Chase Papers, HSP; Belden and Belden, *So Fell the Angels,* pp. 219–21.

6. Chase to Kate Sprague, Oct. 1, 1869, Chase Papers, HSP.

7. Chase to Henry Cooke, Jan. 31, 1871, Chase Papers, LC; Schuckers, *Chase,* pp. 615–16. Chase's income tax returns for 1866, 1867, and 1868 showed a total annual income ranging between $14,000 and $15,800. Chase Papers, LC.

8. Chase to Jay Cooke, Dec. 26, 28, 1865, in Oberholtzer, *Cooke,* 2:60. Cooke half-jokingly suggested that Chase go to England to establish a London branch of the firm.

9. Chase to Thomas Brown, Oct. 18, 31, 1866, Chase to Barney, Jan. 2, 1867, Chase Papers, HSP; Chase to Jay Cooke, Aug. 24, 1869, in Oberholtzer, *Cooke,* 2:130.

10. As during the Civil War, Chase refused to allow Cooke to make any purchase of stock for him which was to be sold immediately for profit unless he actually paid cash for the stock. To the chief justice, such a transaction "wears too much the appearance of a present from yourself." Chase to Jay Cooke, Nov. 17, 1868, in Oberholtzer, *Cooke,* 2:72–73. Cooke's investments for Chase did not always bring the expected profit, as when he purchased $50,000 of Northern Pacific Railroad bonds in late 1869. See Hart, *Chase,* p. 418. Although usually tolerant of Chase's debts, Cooke reminded Chase on at least one occasion that "we do not like to carry overdrawn accounts on our ledgers." Cooke to Chase, Mar. 28, 1870, Mar. 5, 1872, Chase Papers, LC.

11. Hoyt was a second cousin of William Sprague. Chase always appeared well-pleased with Nettie's decision to marry Hoyt.

12. Chase to Ball, Aug. 26, Oct. 4, 1869, Feb. 16, 1870, Chase Papers, CHS; Parsons to Chase, Dec. 12, 1870, Chase Papers, LC. During Chase's prolonged absence from Washington in late 1870 and 1871, there was a constant stream of letters from Parsons on the renovation work and from Jones on farm problems. See Chase Papers, LC. W. W. Cox to Chase, Nov. 14, 1870, Chase to Henry Cooke, Jan. 31, 1871, ibid.

13. Parsons to Chase, Jan. 20, Feb. 14, 16, 1871, Chase to Parsons, Feb. 8, 17, 1871, Chase Papers, LC. At the time Sprague was also under extreme pressure from a Senate investigation of his alleged involvement in illegal trade with the Confederacy during the war. The year before he had leveled a series of intemperate attacks on his fellow senators, leading some to question his mental stability. The Senate later found Sprague innocent of any wrongdoing in relation to Confederate trade. This sorry episode in the life of Kate and William Sprague and its effect on Chase are detailed in Belden and Belden, *So Fell the Angels,* pp. 221–40, 247–58.

14. Chase to Nettie Chase, Mar. 8, 1867, June 17, 1870, Chase Papers, LC; Chase to Barney, Aug. 9, 1868, Chase Papers, HSP; Chase to Ball, Mar. 7, 1870, Chase Papers, CHS.

15. Chase to Parsons, Sept. 26, 1870, Chase Papers, HSP; Chase to Henry Cooke, Oct. 22, 1870, Chase to Thomas Yeatman, Nov. 29, 1870, Chase Papers, LC; Schuckers, *Chase,* pp. 619–20.

16. Hooker to Chase, Sept. 27, 1870, Thomas Yeatman to Chase, Nov. 3, 1870, John A. Foote to Chase, Nov. 18, 1870, Chase Papers, LC.

17. Chase to Ball, Mar. 22, 1871, Chase Papers, CHS; Chase to H. C. Cabill,

Dec. 6, 1870, Chase to E. D. Mansfield, Apr. 24, 1871, Chase to Nettie Hoyt, June 23, 1871, Chase Papers, LC; Belden and Belden, *So Fell the Angels,* pp. 259–60.

18. Chase to Ball, May 17, 1871, Chase Papers, CHS; Chase to Schuckers, June 7, 1871, Kate Sprague to Chase, Aug. 29, 1871, Chase Papers, LC; Chase to Parsons, Aug. 9, 1871, in Warden, *Chase,* p. 725; Chase to Whitelaw Reid, Sept. 1, 1871, Reid Papers, LC; Schuckers, *Chase,* pp. 621–22.

19. Miller to Judge Rockwell, Nov. 6, 1870, in Fairman, *Mr. Justice Miller,* p. 251; Davis to Judge Rockwell, Nov. 30, 1870, in Fairman, *Reconstruction and Reunion,* p. 1465.

20. Chase to Long, Dec. 14, 1869, Chase Papers, LC; Halstead to Chase, Oct. 20, 1869, in Bourne, "Chase Correspondence," pp. 521–22; Chase to Ashley, Sept. 5, 1871, in Warden, *Chase,* p. 727.

21. Chase to M. W. Olin, Mar. 13, 1872, Charles Grady to Chase, Mar. 29, 1872, William B. Thomas to Chase, Apr. 12, 1872, Chase Papers, LC. Richard A. Gerber, "The Liberal Republicans of 1872 in Historical Perspective," *Journal of American History* 62 (1975): 40–73, traces the historiography of the often-ignored movement.

22. Church, Mar. 1872, in Fairman, *Reconstruction and Reunion,* pp. 1468–69; Chase to Church, Mar. 26, 1872, in Warden, *Chase,* p. 728; Ball to Chase, Apr. 5, 1872, Chase Papers, LC; Chase to Ball, Apr. 8, 1872, in Warden, *Chase,* p. 729; Chase to Long, Apr. 15, 1872, Long Papers, CHS; Long to Chase, Apr. 22, 1872, Chase Papers, HSP.

23. *New York World,* Apr. 28, 1872; *New York Herald,* Apr. 28, 1872; Schurz, *Reminiscences,* 2:187; Fairman, *Reconstruction and Reunion,* pp. 1466–67; Belden and Belden, *So Fell the Angels,* pp. 264–65.

24. Porter and Johnson, *National Party Platforms,* pp. 44–45. One of Chase's associates on the Court, David Davis, had also emerged as a contender for the nomination. Greeley managed to secure the votes of many Davis delegates on the final ballot. Davis had been nominated by the Labor Reform party in February but declined the offer after the Liberal Republican decision. Chase noted his unwillingness "to be put in the attitude of rivaling Judge Davis." Chase to Judge M. C. Church, Mar. 26, 1872, in Warden, *Chase,* p. 728; Van Buren to Chase, June 16, 1872, Chase Papers, HSP. Matthew T. Downey's "Horace Greeley and the Politicians: The Liberal Republican Convention in 1872," *Journal of American History* 53 (1967): 727–50, esp. p. 727, effectively challenges the thesis that Greeley was nominated by "a crass bargain manipulated by politicians" despite the high idealism of the reform movement.

25. Chase to Barney, July 12, 1872, Chase Papers, HSP; Chase to Church, May 10, 1872, Chase to Halstead, May 20, 1872, in Warden, *Chase,* pp. 733–34; Chase to Demarest Lloyd, Aug. 14, Sept. 15, 1872, in Schuckers, *Chase,* p. 593; Chase to Reid, July 5, 1872, Reid Papers, LC; Downey, "Greeley and the Politicians," p. 744.

26. Chase to Schuckers, June 24, 1872, Chase Papers, LC; Chase to Ball, Oct. 17, Nov. 4, 1872, Chase Papers, CHS; Chase to Barney, Nov. 9, 1872, Chase Papers, HSP; McFeely, *Grant,* pp. 383–85. The difficulty many abolitionists had in deciding for whom to vote is discussed by James McPherson in "Grant or Greeley?

The Abolitionist Dilemma in the Election of 1872," *American Historical Review* 71 (1965): 43–61. See also Gerber, "The Liberal Republicans," pp. 55–58.

27. Reid to Chase, Nov. 30, 1872, Chase to Reid, Dec. 2, 1872, Reid Papers, LC.

28. Chase to Schuckers, June 24, 1872, Chase Papers, LC; Fairman, *Reconstruction and Reunion,* p. 1466.

29. Warden, *Chase,* p. 772. At the same time, Kate was making plans to have a much more sympathetic biography of her father written by Jacob W. Schuckers, who had held a minor post in the Treasury Department and had been one of Chase's several secretaries. For an account of Kate's efforts to thwart the writing and publication of Warden's biography after Chase's death and to speed that of Schuckers see Frederick J. Blue, "Kate's Paper Chase: The Race to Publish the First Biography of Salmon P. Chase," *The Old Northwest* 8 (1982–83), 353–63.

30. Chase to Parsons, May 5, 1873, in Schuckers, *Chase,* p. 623.

31. *New York World,* May, 1873, in Warden, *Chase,* pp. 737–38; Henry Cooke to Jay Cooke, May 7, 1873, in Oberholtzer, *Cooke,* 2:415; Warden, *Chase,* p. 838.

32. Schuckers, *Chase,* pp. 623–25. Chase's remains were moved to Spring Grove Cemetery in Cincinnati at the urging of daughter Kate in October 1886. A modest monument in his memory was dedicated there on the fiftieth anniversary of his death in May 1923, with Chief Justice William Howard Taft delivering the address. See George Hoadly, "Address at Music Hall, Cincinnati, Ohio, on the Occasion of the Removal of the Remains of Salmon P. Chase to Spring Grove Cemetery, Oct. 14, 1886" (Cincinnati, 1887); "Addresses at the Unveiling of a Monument by the American Bar Association to Chief Justice Salmon P. Chase at Spring Grove Cemetery, Cincinnati, Ohio, May 30, 1923" (Pamphlet in Cincinnati Public Library). See also Belden and Belden, *So Fell the Angels,* pp. 333–35; *Cincinnati Enquirer,* Oct. 13, 1886. The remainder of Kate's life was filled with tragedy. After a celebrated affair with Senator Roscoe Conkling, her marriage with Sprague ended in divorce in 1882. She spent some time in Europe before returning to Edgewood where she lived with her retarded daughter. Following the suicide of her son, Willie, in 1890, she withdrew from society. Faced with mounting debts, she sold much of her land and finally much of her furniture. Unable to raise money to restore the home, she allowed it to fall into disrepair as her own health deteriorated. A recluse, living in the ruins of what had been Chase's pride, she died in July 1899 at fifty-eight. In contrast, Nettie's life was happier, as she lived with her husband, William Hoyt, and children and gained some reputation as a writer of children's books. Belden and Belden, *So Fell the Angels,* pp. 327, 334, 348; Sokoloff, *Kate Chase,* pp. 213–92. In 1979, while doing research in Washington, I searched in vain for what might be left of Edgewood on the hill adjacent to Catholic University. The wooded land was about to fall to the bulldozer and the building of condominiums, but the beautiful view of the Capitol which Chase had enjoyed in his last years was still a striking one.

33. Davis to Chase, Aug. 12, 1867, Chase Papers, LC; Strong to William Evarts, Sept. 10, 1874, Personal Papers, Miscellaneous, LC; Field, in Hughes, "Chase, Chief Justice," p. 608.

34. Miller, May 14, 16, 1873, in Fairman, *Mr. Justice Miller,* pp. 251–52; Charles R. Williams, ed., *Diary and Letters of Rutherford Birchard Hayes,* 5 vols. (Columbus: Ohio State Archaeological and Historical Society, 1922–26), 3:242–43; Strong to William Evarts, Sept. 10, 1874, Personal Papers, Miscellaneous, LC.

35. Strong to William Evarts, Sept. 10, 1874, Personal Papers, Miscellaneous, LC; Miller, Interview in 1878, in Fairman, *Reconstruction and Reunion,* pp. 26–27.

36. Hughes, "Chase, Chief Justice," p. 614.

37. Hughes, "Chase, Chief Justice," pp. 596–97. Two important laws were affected. *Ex parte Garland,* involved the Reconstruction question of loyalty oaths. Part of the Legal Tender Act was struck down in *Hepburn* v. *Griswold.* One of the laws partially affected was that establishing the income tax. In *Collector* v. *Day,* 11 Wallace 113 (1871), the Court ruled that the income tax could not be levied on a state officer. But by not extending its ruling to others, the Court in effect found the income tax laws, which Chase had argued for as secretary of the Treasury, to be constitutional. Chase was not present for this case, due to his illness. Fairman, *Reconstruction and Reunion,* pp. 1419–21, 1435–36. See also Kutler, *Judicial Power,* pp. 116–20, 142.

38. Schuckers, *Chase,* pp. 594–95. In addition to bequests of $10,000 each to Wilberforce and Dartmouth, the remainder of his estate, estimated at $150,000 before the settlement of debts, was divided in equal parts between Nettie and Kate with "the interest of $6,000 at seven percent going to his niece, Jane Auld." Newspaper clipping, n.d., Chase Papers, CHS.

39. Blair to Warden, May 12, 1873, Blair Papers, LC.

40. Mary E. Sherwood to Chase, Nov. 20, 1868, Miscellaneous Papers, NYPL; Hughes, "Chase, Chief Justice," p. 579.

41. Warden, *Chase,* p. 816. In 1877, John Thompson and his son Samuel founded the Chase National Bank, naming it in honor of a public figure whom they very much admired. The elder Thompson's First National Bank had been in 1863 one of the first New York City banks to receive a charter in Chase's newly created national banking system. A friend of Chase, Thompson chose the name for his new bank in full awareness that it would provide instant name recognition; the Chase name remains prominent today partly as a result of his action.

Bibliographical Essay

PRIMARY SOURCES

Manuscripts

The most important manuscript collections for a biography of Salmon P. Chase are those of the subject himself, especially the two large holdings at the Library of Congress and the Historical Society of Pennsylvania. Included here are vast amounts of incoming correspondence as well as numerous letters written by Chase, many of them found in letterbooks. Also included are financial and legal material, newspaper clippings, and speeches. The National Archives contains a great bulk of material related to Chase's direction of the Treasury Department. Among the hundreds of routine letters in the record groups of the Treasury Department and Civil War Special Agencies are occasional revealing Chase letters. Also important is the Port Royal Correspondence. The Ohio Historical Society includes a large collection relating to Chase's gubernatorial years. Smaller Chase collections are found at the Cincinnati Historical Society and the New Hampshire Historical Society. A major problem in each of these collections is Chase's abominable handwriting which worsened with time.

Other important Library of Congress collections include those of Abraham Lincoln, Andrew Johnson, John McLean, John Sherman, Martin Van Buren, Benjamin Wade, Jacob Schuckers, and Gideon Welles. Two significant Ohio collections are those of Joshua R. Giddings at the Ohio Historical Society and Alexander H. Long at the Cincinnati Historical Society.

Newspapers

Newspapers provide an invaluable aid in dealing with party politics, for each journal was extremely partisan. Especially important are New York and Ohio papers. The *Cincinnati Gazette,* the *Cincinnati Enquirer,* and the *Ohio State Journal* (Columbus) are the most useful for Ohio events, especially those surrounding the Free-Soil campaigns, the formation of the Republican party, and Chase's governorship. Horace Greeley's *New York Tribune,* the *New York Evening Post,* and Manton Marble's *New York World* are significant for New York and national politics, especially for the period of Chase's abortive 1868 quest for the Democratic presidential nomination. Antislavery newspapers of value are the *Philanthropist* (Cincinnati) and the *Cleveland True Democrat.* Most important for Chase's role in the formation of the Free-Soil and Republican parties and his efforts to win the 1856 presidential nomination is Gamaliel Bailey's *National Era* (Washington).

Other Primary Sources

Chase's writings are among the most significant published primary sources available. Particularly revealing is his compilation of Ohio laws, which includes a brief survey of Ohio history until 1833, *The Statutes of Ohio and of the Northwestern Territory Adopted or Enacted from 1788 to 1833 Inclusive, Including a Preliminary Sketch of the History of Ohio,* 3 vols. (Cincinnati, 1833–35). Important for an understanding of Chase's financial philosophy and plans as secretary of the Treasury is his *Report of the Secretary of the Treasury on the State of the Finances* (Washington, 1861–64), issued annually; most significant is his initial report for 1861. Revealing for Chase's years in Cincinnati are his two essays, "The Effects of Machinery," and "The Life and Character of Henry Brougham," both published in the *North American Review* 34 (Jan. 1832): 220–46, and 33 (July 1831): 227–61.

There are several invaluable twentieth-century collections of Chase letters and diaries. Most important are Edward G. Bourne et al., eds., "Diary and Correspondence of Salmon P. Chase," in the *Annual Report of the American Historical Association,* 1902, vol. 2 (Washington, 1903), and David Donald, ed., *Inside Lincoln's Cabinet: The Civil War Diaries of Salmon P. Chase* (New York, 1954). Bourne provides several hundred Chase letters encompassing his entire career, and Donald edits the revealing diary which Chase kept sporadically until the time of Lincoln's death. Two biographies published shortly after Chase's death in 1873 are useful more for the Chase letters they include than for the authors' interpretations. They are Robert B. Warden, *An Account of the*

Private Life and Public Services of Salmon Portland Chase (Cincinnati, 1874), and Jacob W. Schuckers, *The Life and Public Services of Salmon Portland Chase* (New York, 1874). Arthur M. Schlesinger's "Salmon Portland Chase, Undergraduate and Pedagogue," *Ohio State Archaeological and Historical Quarterly* 28 (April 1919): 119–61, is a collection of letters written by Chase to Dartmouth classmate Thomas Sparhawk in the 1820s. It is highly revealing of the evolution of Chase's thinking on political, religious, and social issues. Chase's letters to Andrew Johnson, written during his tour of parts of the defeated Confederacy during the spring of 1865, are reprinted in James E. Sefton, ed., "Chief Justice Chase as an Advisor on Presidential Reconstruction," *Civil War History* 12 (1967): 242–64. The letters to Chase from his close friend and political ally Charles Sumner are found in Beverly Wilson Palmer, ed., "From Small Minority to Great Cause: Letters of Charles Sumner to Salmon P. Chase," *Ohio History* 93 (1984): 164–83.

Other important collections of letters include *The Collected Works of Abraham Lincoln,* edited by Roy P. Basler, 8 vols. (New Brunswick, 1953), and *Private and Official Correspondence of General Benjamin F. Butler During the Period of the Civil War,* edited by Jesse A. Marshall, 5 vols. (Norwood, Mass., 1917). Diaries of two key cabinet members during the Civil War, Gideon Welles and Edward Bates, provide insight into Chase's official and political policies. Welles and Bates usually evaluated Chase negatively and were always highly suspicious of his political motives: *Diary of Gideon Welles, Secretary of the Navy Under Lincoln and Johnson,* edited by Howard K. Beale, 3 vols. (New York, 1960), and *The Diary of Edward Bates, 1859–1866,* also edited by Beale, in *Annual Report of the American Historical Association for the Year 1930,* vol. 4, 1933. Reminiscences of two of Chase's wartime colleagues, Carl Schurz and John Sherman, are also useful to an understanding of Chase and the period: Carl Schurz, *The Reminiscences of Carl Schurz, 1852–1863,* 3 vols. (New York, 1909), and John Sherman, *Recollections of Forty Years in the House, Senate and Cabinet: An Autobiography,* 2 vols. (Chicago, 1895). Other more official but equally significant information is found in the debates of Congress, *The Congressional Globe,* the 29th through the 41st Congresses (1845–71), and *A Compilation of the Messages and Papers of the Presidents,* 20 vols. (New York, 1897), edited by James D. Richardson. The former is especially important for Chase's term in the Senate (1849–55) and the latter for Andrew Johnson's many veto messages.

SECONDARY SOURCES

Books Other Than Biographies

Several secondary accounts of the politics of the 1830s and 1840s deal with

Chase's early role in antislavery issues. An essay by Peter Walker in *Moral Choices: Memory, Desire and Imagination in Nineteenth Century American Abolition* (Baton Rouge, 1978), analyzes Chase's conservative upbringing as a background to his interest in the plight of the fugitive slave. The best study of Chase's advocacy of the divorce of the federal government from slavery is in Eric Foner's *Free Soil, Free Labor, Free Men: The Ideology of the Republican Party Before the Civil War* (New York, 1970). Chase's legal strategy in defense of alleged fugitives and those accused of defending them is expertly analyzed by Paul Finkelman in *An Imperfect Union: Slavery, Federalism, and Comity* (Chapel Hill, 1981). Also useful on the issue of the Constitution, the courts, and slavery are Robert J. Cover's *Justice Accused: Antislavery and the Judicial Process* (New Haven, 1975), and William M. Wiecek, *The Sources of Antislavery Constitutionalism in America, 1760–1840* (Ithaca, 1977).

Several studies of antislavery political parties deal extensively with Chase's role. They are Theodore C. Smith's *The Liberty and Free Soil Parties in the Northwest* (New York, 1897), which covers the Great Lakes states only; Richard H. Sewell's *Ballots for Freedom: Antislavery Politics in the United States, 1837–1860* (New York, 1976), which is an overview of the Liberty, Free-Soil, and Republican parties; and Frederick J. Blue's *The Free Soilers: Third-Party Politics, 1848–54* (Urbana, 1973), which emphasizes Chase's vital role in the third-party's formation. Chase's complex role in Ohio politics in the 1840s and early 1850s, especially his maneuvering to win election to the United States Senate, is described by Stephen E. Maizlish in *The Triumph of Sectionalism: The Transformation of Ohio Politics, 1844–1856* (Kent, Ohio, 1983). Holman Hamilton's *Prologue to Conflict: The Crisis and Compromise of 1850* (Lexington, Ky., 1964) is the best account of the strategy used by all participants, including Chase and the Free-Soilers, to secure or prevent passage of the major congressional settlement at mid-century. Michael P. Holt's *The Political Crisis of the 1850s* (New York, 1978) effectively analyzes the transition to the third-party system, emphasizing the role of the nativistic Know-Nothing party and Chase's connection with it. A detailed although dated study of the formation of the Republican party including Chase's role is provided in Andrew W. Crandall's *The Early History of the Republican Party, 1854–1856* (Boston, 1930).

Two volumes in the *History of the State of Ohio*, edited by Carl Wittke, are important in providing a detailed account of Ohio politics and society during Chase's lifetime. Francis P. Weisenburger's *The Passing of the Frontier*, vol. 3 (Columbus, 1941), competently describes the development of the antislavery movement in Ohio in the 1830s and 1840s, while Eugene Roseboom's *The Civil War Era, 1850–1873*, vol. 4 (Columbus, 1944), includes a thorough description of Chase's governorship. For an account of early Cincinnati, including the racial tensions in the city at the time of Chase's arrival in 1830, see Richard C. Wade's *The Urban Frontier: Pioneer Life in Early Pittsburgh, Cincinnati,*

Lexington, Louisville and St. Louis (Chicago, 1959).

Chase's role in the financing of the Union Civil War effort, including banking, taxes, and currency, is dealt with in detail in two highly competent studies. They are Bray Hammond's *Sovereignty and an Empty Purse: Banks and Politics in the Civil War* (Princeton, 1970), and Robert P. Sharkey, *Money, Class and Party: An Economic Study of the Civil War and Reconstruction* (Baltimore, 1959). Both are highly critical of Chase's policies as Treasury secretary. Gabor S. Boritt's *Lincoln and the Economics of the American Dream* (Memphis, 1978), emphasizes Lincoln's concept of the presidency and his economic philosophy and reveals an important aspect of Chase's relationship with the president. The background for Civil War financial issues as well as Chase's earlier position is provided by William G. Shade's *Banks or No Banks: The Money Issue in Western Politics, 1832–1865* (Detroit, 1972).

The best overall studies of the Civil War and Reconstruction years are J. G. Randall and David Donald, *The Civil War and Reconstruction,* 2d ed., rev. (Boston, 1969), and James M. McPherson, *Ordeal By Fire: The Civil War and Reconstruction* (New York, 1982). The latter includes the most recent historiography, while both provide a thorough background for Chase's critical role in the complex issues. Chase's role in cabinet patronage conflicts and especially his differences with the president are outlined in Harry J. Carman and Reinhard H. Luthin, *Lincoln and the Patronage* (New York, 1943). The overall cabinet problems and relationships are thoroughly developed by Burton Hendrick in *Lincoln's War Cabinet* (Boston, 1946). The Washington Peace Conference of February 1861 and the reluctant part played by Chase is described by Robert G. Gunderson in *Old Gentlemen's Convention: The Washington Peace Conference of 1861* (Madison, 1961).

Chase's role in the changing racial policies as the Lincoln administration moved toward emancipation, the use of black troops, and black land ownership are covered in several important studies. Willie Lee Rose's *Rehearsal for Reconstruction: The Port Royal Experiment* (Indianapolis, 1964) looks at the Treasury Department's role and many conflicts as the Sea Island blacks were given freedom and land beginning in 1862. Dudley T. Cornish, *The Sable Arm: Negro Troops in the Union Army, 1861–1865* (New York, 1956), deals competently with the evolution of Lincoln's policy toward the employment of black troops and the role Chase played in urging their greater use. Louis S. Gerteis, *From Contraband to Freedman: Federal Policy Toward Southern Blacks, 1861–1865* (Westport, 1973), looks at the issues of black troops in Union armies as well as land and suffrage policies for the freedmen. The Louisiana experiment in Reconstruction, begun before the fighting ended, is covered from different angles in two recent studies. Peyton McCrary's *Abraham Lincoln and Reconstruction: The Louisiana Experiment* (Princeton, 1978) looks in detail at the complex maneuvering of the various factions including Chase's Treasury agents in New Orleans. La-

Wanda Cox's *Lincoln and Black Freedom: A Study in Presidential Leadership* (Columbia, S.C., 1981) is a refreshing appreciation of the pressures Lincoln labored under and his realistic policy of moderation despite efforts by Chase and other Republicans to move more quickly on racial issues.

Chase's role as chief justice of the Supreme Court and the critical cases faced by the Court during the Chase years are covered in detail by Charles Fairman, *History of the Supreme Court of the United States,* vol. 6, *Reconstruction and Reunion, 1864–1888,* pt. 1 (New York, 1971). Stanley I. Kutler argues convincingly in *Judicial Power and Reconstruction Politics* (Chicago, 1968) that far from being intimidated by the Republican-dominated Congress, the Chase-led Supreme Court maintained its independence and initiative and actually enhanced its judicial authority. Thomas G. Belden and Marva R. Belden's *So Fell the Angels* (Boston, 1956) is a study of the Chase-Sprague families during the Civil War and Reconstruction years. Highly critical of Chase, Kate, and William Sprague, the Belden's well-written account claims, with circumstantial evidence only, that Sprague was involved in corrupt trade practices with the Confederacy, which Chase knew of and did little to stop. Throughout, Kate is revealed accurately as both overly ambitious and coniving as she attempted to place her father in the White House.

Several important studies deal with the complex Reconstruction years and add insight into Chase's role. The best study of the election of 1868, with much emphasis on Chase's abortive effort to win the Democratic nomination, is provided by Charles H. Coleman, *The Election of 1868: The Democratic Effort to Regain Control* (New York, 1933). Democratic politics are described in two recent studies. Joel Silbey looks at the party on the national level in *A Respectable Minority: The Democratic Party in the Civil War Era* (New York, 1977), while Jerome Mushkat does the same for New York where the Chase boom in 1868 had its origins: *The Reconstruction of the New York Democracy, 1861–1874* (Rutherford, N.J., 1981). The Republican party during Reconstruction is competently analyzed by Michael L. Benedict in *A Compromise of Principle: Congressional Republicans and Reconstruction, 1863–1869* (New York, 1974). Benedict has also written an important study of the Johnson impeachment controversy, *The Impeachment and Trial of Andrew Johnson* (New York, 1973), as has Hans L. Trefousse in *Impeachment of a President: Andrew Johnson, the Blacks and Reconstruction* (Knoxville, 1975). Each deals briefly with Chase's role in the Senate proceedings. The issue of black suffrage and the Fifteenth Amendment has been skillfully analyzed on the national level by William Gillette in *The Right to Vote: Politics and the Passage of the Fifteenth Amendment* (Baltimore, 1965) and in the key state of New York by Phyllis F. Field, *The Politics of Race in New York: The Struggle for Black Suffrage in the Civil War Era* (Ithaca, 1982). David A. Gerber's *Black Ohio and the Color Line, 1860–1915* (Urbana, 1976) looks briefly at the same issue in Chase's home state.

Biographies

There has been no twentieth-century biography of Salmon P. Chase. Albert B. Hart's *Salmon P. Chase* (Boston, 1899) is an excellent study but lacks the benefit of recent research and a modern perspective. Biographies of Chase written at the time of his death by Jacob W. Schuckers and Robert B. Warden are valuable for the great number of Chase letters which each includes. Both Schuckers and Warden were personal friends and associates of Chase and neither could be objective in his evaluation of his subject. A popularized, although useful, account of Chase's ambitious daughter Kate is provided by Alice H. Sokoloff, *Kate Chase for the Defense* (New York, 1971).

Chase's contemporaries for the most part have fared better than he in the attention given them by modern historians. Among his antislavery colleagues in the 1840s and 1850s, James G. Birney is the subject of a perceptive biography by Betty Fladeland, *James Gillespie Birney: Slaveholder to Abolitionist* (Ithaca, 1955). Two other excellent studies of Free-Soil colleagues are James B. Stewart, *Joshua R. Giddings and the Tactics of Radical Politics* (Cleveland, 1970), and Richard Sewell, *John P. Hale and the Politics of Abolition* (Cambridge, 1965). Birney, Giddings, and Hale worked closely with Chase during much of the antebellum period. One of Chase's closest antislavery associates during the 1840s and 1850s, Gamaliel Bailey, is the subject of a thorough and balanced biography by Stanley Harrold, *Gamaliel Bailey and Antislavery Union* (Kent, Ohio, 1986). Harrold shows both the cooperation and the occasional disputes between the two men.

Biographies of most of the important Civil War associates and antagonists of Chase have been written in the last three decades. Chase's Ohio colleague and sometime political manager James M. Ashley is the subject of a recent study by Robert F. Horowitz, *The Great Impeacher: A Political Biography of James M. Ashley* (New York, 1979). An excellent interpretation of James A. Garfield is provided by Allan Peskin, *Garfield* (Kent, Ohio, 1978). Modern biographies of key senators, including Charles Sumner, Benjamin Wade, and Stephen A. Douglas are available. David Donald's *Charles Sumner and the Coming of the Civil War* (New York, 1960), studies Sumner's pre–Civil War career, and *Charles Sumner and the Rights of Man* (New York, 1970) deals with the war and Reconstruction years. Chase's Ohio antagonist Wade is the subject of Hans L. Trefousse's biography: *Benjamin Franklin Wade, Radical Republican from Ohio* (New York, 1963). Douglas, one of Chase's chief Senate opponents during the 1850s, is thoroughly described in a perceptive evaluation by Robert Johannsen, *Stephen A. Douglas* (New York, 1973). Jay Cooke is treated in an early twentieth-century biography by Ellis P. Oberholtzer which includes many Chase letters: *Jay Cooke: Financier of the Civil War,* 2 vols. (Philadelphia, 1907). James E. Sefton has written a short biography of Andrew Johnson, *Andrew Johnson and the Uses of Constitutional Power* (Boston, 1980), in which he has perceptively analyzed his subject, as has William S. McFeely for Grant in *Grant: A Biography* (New York, 1981).

Lincoln and his key cabinet members other than Chase have received extensive biographical treatment in recent years. The president has been the subject of a vast number of studies, the best of which is Stephen B. Oates's *With Malice Toward None: The Life of Abraham Lincoln* (New York, 1977). Seward, Stanton, and Welles have found insightful biographers who deal in depth with their subjects' relationship with the Treasury Secretary. They are Glyndon G. Van Deusen, *William Henry Seward* (New York, 1967), Benjamin P. Thomas and Harold M. Hyman, *Stanton: The Life and Times of Lincoln's Secretary of War* (New York, 1962), and John Niven, *Gideon Welles: Lincoln's Secretary of the Navy* (New York, 1973). Several members of Chase's Supreme Court are the subject of twentieth-century biographies of high quality, including David Davis, Stephen J. Field, and Samuel F. Miller. Their biographies are Willard L. King, *Lincoln's Manager, David Davis* (Cambridge, 1960), Carl B. Swisher, *Stephen J. Field: Craftsman of the Law* (Washington, 1930), and Charles Fairman, *Mr. Justice Miller and the Supreme Court* (Cambridge, 1939).

Secondary Articles

There are a surprising number of articles on various phases of Chase's career. His role in the formation and strategy of the Ohio Liberty party is discussed by Stanley G. Harrold in "Forging an Antislavery Instrument: Gamaliel Bailey and the Formation of the Ohio Liberty Party," *The Old Northwest* 2 (1976): 371–87, and "The Southern Strategy of the Liberty Party," *Ohio History* 87 (1978): 21–36. Dick Johnson has written two articles which cover aspects of Chase's role in the early history of the Republican party: "Along the Twisted Road to Civil War: Historians and the Appeal of the Independent Democrats," *The Old Northwest* 4 (1978): 119–41, and "The Role of Salmon P. Chase in the Formation of the Republican Party," *The Old Northwest* 3 (1977), 23–38. Chase's relationship with the Ohio Know-Nothing movement as he sought the governorship is dealt with by William E. Gienapp in "Salmon P. Chase, Nativism and the Formation of the Republican Party in Ohio," *Ohio History* 93 (1984): 5–39. Equally important is Gienapp's study of the impact of nativism on the national Republican party: "Nativism and the Creation of a Republican Majority in the North Before the Civil War," *Journal of American History* 72 (1985): 529–59. Frederick J. Blue studies Chase's use of the governorship as a means to the presidency in "Chase and the Governorship: A Stepping Stone to the Presidency," *Ohio History* 90 (1981): 197–220.

Chase's racial policy and strategy during the Civil War, his efforts to convince Lincoln of the wisdom of emancipation and black land ownership and to use these policies to forward his own political career are dealt with in two articles: Louis Gerteis, "Salmon P. Chase, Radicalism and the Politics of Emancipation, 1861–1864," *Journal of American History* 60 (1973), 42–62, and Ovid Futch, "Salmon P. Chase and Civil War Politics in Florida," *Florida Historical Quarterly* 32 (1954): 163–88. LaWanda Cox looks at the larger land issue in "The Promise of Land for Freedmen," *Mississippi Valley Historical Review* 45 (1958): 413–40. Chase's political challenge to Lincoln for the 1864 Republican nomination is dealt with in Charles R. Wilson, "The Original Chase Organization Meeting and The Next Presidential Election," *Mississippi Valley Historical Review* 23 (1936): 61–79, and William F. Zornow, "Lincoln, Chase and the Ohio Radicals in 1864," *Bulletin of the Historical and Philosophical Society of Ohio* 9 (1951), 3–32.

Chase's career as chief justice is the subject of a highly perceptive article by David Hughes, "Salmon P. Chase: Chief Justice," *Vanderbilt Law Review* 18 (1965): 569–614. Hughes covers Chase's role on the Court on the most critical issues of Reconstruction in an evenhanded and competent manner. Roy F. Nichols, "United States vs. Jefferson Davis, 1865–1869," *American Historical Review* 31 (1926): 266–84, looks at Chase's skillful strategy to prevent the Davis case from ever coming to trial. M. Kathleen Perdue studies Chase's role as presiding officer at the Johnson impeachment trial and the chief justice's confrontation with radical leaders in "Salmon P. Chase and the Impeachment Trial of Andrew Johnson," *Historian* 27 (1964): 75–92. Chase's drive for the 1868 Democratic nomination and the strategy of Alexander H. Long of Ohio to obtain it for him are the subject of Edward S. Perzel's "Alexander Long, Salmon P. Chase and the Election of 1868," *Bulletin of the Cincinnati Historical Society* 23 (1965): 3–18. The effort to publish the first biography at the time of his death in 1873 is the subject of Frederick J. Blue's "Kate's Paper Chase: The Race to Publish the First Biography of Salmon P. Chase," *The Old Northwest* 8 (1982–83): 353–63.

Unpublished Dissertations

Several dissertations deal with Chase's career and should be consulted for a full picture. Robert H. Gruber, "Salmon P. Chase and the Politics of Reform" (University of Maryland, 1969), competently and thoroughly surveys Chase's career before the outbreak of the Civil War, while David F. Hughes, "Salmon P. Chase, Chief Justice" (Princeton University, 1963), does the same for his years on the Court. William G. Gienapp's "The Origins of the Republican Party, 1852–1856" (University of California, Berkeley, 1980) is a superb and detailed account of the period of transition from the decline of the Whig party through the Frémont campaign with great emphasis on the Know-Nothing movement. Gienapp effectively shows the central role played by Chase in the many critical events of these years. (*Salmon P. Chase: A Life in Politics* went to press before Gienapp's book on the Republican party was available.) John J. Patrick's "John Sherman: The Early Years, 1823–1865" (Kent State University, 1982) studies one of Chase's important contemporaries and especially their relationship on the key economic questions of the Civil War. Finally, Vernon Volpe emphasizes the Liberty party's history and Chase's role in it in Ohio in "Forlorn Hope of Freedom: The Liberty Party in the Old Northwest, 1838–1848" (University of Nebraska, 1984).

Index

87; interest in Chase 1852 nomination, 340 n.76; and Know-Nothing movement, 110–11; and 1856 Republican nomination, 112–13; and 1860 nomination, 122; Chase financial aid to 122; 349 n.85; mentioned, 43, 56, 101, 105. *See also National Era*

Ball, Flamen: Chase law partner, 21, 328 n.21, 343 n.14; Chase admits aging to, 313; mentioned, 214, 316

Baltimore, 229, 259, 274

Baltimore Union convention: Lincoln 1864 nomination, 232

Banking Reform, 108–9, 116, 322, 323. *See also* National Banking Act

Bankruptcy Act, 275

Banks, Nathaniel: elected Speaker, 344 n.29; supports Frémont in 1856, 113–14; trade in New Orleans, 167–68; and freedmen, 198, 199; and Louisiana politics, 204, 220

Barlow, Samuel L. M., 289

Barnburners: insist on Wilmot Proviso, 57–58; Utica convention, 59–60; insist on Van Buren nomination, 61; at Free-Soil convention, 63; unite with Hunkers, 73, reject Free Democrats in 1852, 88

Barney, Hiram: at 1860 Republican convention, 120–21; goes to Springfield for Chase, 131; mediates between Seward and Chase, 140; suggests meeting with New York bankers, 145; loans to Chase, 208, 311; patronage feuds; 232–34; removal from office, 241; mentioned, 115, 214, 296, 298, 319, 369 n.18

Bates, Edward: appointed to Lincoln cabinet, 133; and Fort Sumter, 136; and McClellan removal, 178; defends Seward, 192–93; on Chase desire for presidency, 215, 254; reaction to Chase resignation, 237; mentioned, 195, 226

Beale, Howard K., 377 n.19

Beaufort, South Carolina, 184, 251, 253

Beaumont, Gustave, 15, 20

Bedini, Gaetano, 97

Beecher, Lyman, 23

Belden, Thomas G. and Marva R., x–xi, 359 n.92

Belmont, August, 148, 291, 292

Benedict, Michael Les, 362 n.27

Bennett, James Gordon, 226, 287, 292. *See also New York Herald*

Bethesda Springs, 315

Bingham, John A., 122–23

Bingham, Kinsley, 103

Birney, James, 216

Birney, James G.: editor of *Philanthropist*, 29; defended by Chase, 30, 33, 34; in 1840 campaign, 44; Chase opposes as Liberty candidate, 48, 49; attends Southern and Western Liberty convention, 50–51; has stroke, 52; accepts post with American Anti-Slavery Society, 331 n.5; attacks Chase, 87

Birney, William, 202

Black, Jeremiah S., 381 n.56

Black Codes, 256

Black suffrage: issue in Louisiana, 203–6, 221; blocked in Wade-Davis bill, 206; Chase in favor of, 248–53, 258, 259, 266; Johnson on, 250–56; W. T. Sherman on, 253; Chase and 1868 nomination, 287, 290, 297; Democratic 1868 platform, 294; Fifteenth Amendment, 300–302; in Ohio, 301–2; in northern states, 388 n.39

Black troops, 196–201

Blacks, free: Chase view of, 20, 49; in Cincinnati, 27–28, 39; not mentioned at Southern and Western Liberty convention, 51; not mentioned in Free-Soil platform, 64; and public lands, 83; discrimination against in Ohio, 117. *See also* Black suffrage

Frederick J. Blue is Professor of History at Youngstown State University, Youngstown, Ohio, and the author of *The Free Soilers: Third Party Politics, 1848–54.*